Lecture Notes in Computer Science 2072

Edited by G. Goos, J. Hartmanis and J. van Leeuwen

T0216255

Springer

Berlin
Heidelberg
New York
Barcelona
Hong Kong
London
Milan
Paris
Singapore
Tokyo

Jørgen Lindskov Knudsen (Ed.)

ECOOP 2001 – Object-Oriented Programming

15th European Conference
Budapest, Hungary, June 18-22, 2001
Proceedings

Springer

Series Editors

Gerhard Goos, Karlsruhe University, Germany
Juris Hartmanis, Cornell University, NY, USA
Jan van Leeuwen, Utrecht University, The Netherlands

Volume Editor

Jørgen Lindskov Knudsen
University of Aarhus, Department of Computer Science
Åbogade 34, 8200 Århus N, Denmark
E-mail: jlk@daimi.au.dk

Cataloging-in-Publication Data applied for

Die Deutsche Bibliothek - CIP-Einheitsaufnahme

Object oriented programming : 15th European conference ; proceedings /
ECOOP 2001, Budapest, Hungary, June 18 - 22, 2001. Jørgen Lindskov
Knudsen (ed.). - Berlin ; Heidelberg ; New York ; Barcelona ; Hong
Kong ; London ; Milan ; Paris ; Singapore ; Tokyo : Springer, 2001
   (Lecture notes in computer science ; Vol. 2072)
   ISBN 3-540-42206-4

CR Subject Classification (1998): D.1-3, H.2, F.3, C.2, K.4, J.1

ISSN 0302-9743
ISBN 3-540-42206-4 Springer-Verlag Berlin Heidelberg New York

Springer-Verlag Berlin Heidelberg New York
a member of BertelsmannSpringer Science+Business Media GmbH

http://www.springer.de

© Springer-Verlag Berlin Heidelberg 2001
Printed in Germany

Typesetting: Camera-ready by author, data conversion by Boller Mediendesign
Printed on acid-free paper   SPIN: 10781755   06/3142   5 4 3 2 1 0

Preface

The field of Object Technology has conquered the IT world, including the education system, the commercial world, and the many diverse research communities. The ECOOP community can be proud of this evolution, if not revolution, since the research results that have been published by this community over the past 17 years (also counting two European workshops preceding the official ECOOP conference series) have had a great impact on the development of Object Technology.

This legacy sets great expectations for any new ECOOP conference. The conference must present important new research results and developments within new applications of Object Technology. At the same time, the conference must strengthen Object Technology itself by advancing the richness in structure and expressiveness. Furthermore, the conference should aim at questioning the commonly accepted truths in order to look for new insights even to the extent of tearing down some of the generally accepted research results in the quest to find new directions of research. That is, the conference may possibly find ways to the technologies that might follow Object Technology.

It was with great honor that I worked as Program Chair of this 15th European Conference on Object-Oriented Programming, ECOOP 2001, held in Budapest, Hungary, June 18-22, 2001. The Program Committee, consisting of 30 excellent fellow Object Technology researchers, did an outstanding job in selecting 18 technical papers out of a total of 108 submitted papers. Besides these technical papers, the conference presented three invited speakers: Charles Simonyi, Erik Meijer, and Alistair Cockburn. Erik Meijer accepted to write an invited paper, which is included in these proceedings. In addition to the technical program, the conference program included 22 workshops and 21 tutorials.

It is impossible to organize an event like the ECOOP conference without the tireless efforts of everybody involved. Instead of mentioning them individually, I would like to express my thanks to everyone, not only those mentioned explicitly elsewhere in these proceedings, but also the many volunteers that worked hard at making ECOOP 2001 a success. Last but not least, I would like to thank the authors for writing the many interesting papers, the reviewers for the hard work they put into evaluating the submissions, the Program Committee for making the selection process run smoothly, the conference attendees for making ECOOP 2001 an inspiring and interactive event, and finally you, the reader of these proceedings, for putting the research results presented here into use in education, enterprise, and future research. Only through the use of these results, will the work become truly worthwhile.

April 2001   Jørgen Lindskov Knudsen

Organization

ECOOP 2001 was organized by the Department of General Computer Science of Eötvös Loránd University, Budapest, under the auspices of AITO (Association Internationale pour les Technologies Objets).

Executive Committee

Conference Chairs: Gerti Kappel (University of Linz)
    László Varga (Eötvös Loránd University)
Program Chair: Jørgen Lindskov Knudsen (University of Aarhus)
Organizing Chairs: László Kozma (Eötvös Loránd University)
    Zoltán Horváth (Eötvös Loránd University)

Organizing Committee

Tutorial Chairs: Judit Nyéky-Gaizler (Eötvös Loránd University)
    Giuseppe Castagna (École Normale Supérieure)
    Katalin Pásztor-Varga (Eötvös Loránd University)
Workshop Chairs: Ákos Frohner (Eötvös Loránd University)
    Jacques Malenfant (Université de Bretagne sud)
    Erzsébet Angster (Dennis Gabor College)
Panel Chair: Tamás Kozsik (Eötvös Loránd University)
Poster Chairs: Viktória Zsók (Eötvös Loránd University)
    István Juhász (University of Debrecen)
Demonstration Chairs: János Vida (Eötvös Loránd University)
    Károly Kondorosi (Technical University of Budapest)
Exhibit Chairs: Zoltán Csörnyei (Eötvös Loránd University)
    László Blum (University of Veszprém)
Social Events: Rozália Szabó-Nacsa (Eötvös Loránd University)
Advertizing, Website: Zoltán Istenes (Eötvös Loránd University)
    Attila Kovács (Eötvös Loránd University)
Industrial Relations: Bálint Dömölki (IQSOFT Rt.)
    Albert Fazekas (Classys of Informatics Co.)
    Miklós Havass (SZÁMALK Rt.)
Operational Support: Zoltán Porkoláb (Eötvös Loránd University)
    Ferenc Steingart (Eötvös Loránd University)
Submission Site: Richard van de Stadt (Borbala Online Conf. Services)

Program Committee

Mehmet Akşit	University of Twente, The Netherlands
Suad Alagić	Wichita State University, USA
Elisa Bertino	University of Milan, Italy
Gilad Bracha	Sun Microsystems, USA
Jean-Pierre Briot	Paris 6 University, France
Frank Buschmann	Siemens AG, Corporate Technology, Germany
Giuseppe Castagna	École Normale Supérieure de Paris, France
Pierre Cointe	École des Mines de Nantes, France
Serge Demeyer	University of Antwerp, Belgium
Peter Dickman	University of Glasgow, UK
Bjørn N. Freeman-Benson	QuickSilver Technology, Inc, USA
Carlo Ghezzi	Politecnico di Milano, Italy
Yossi Gil	Technion, Haifa, Israel
Rachid Guerraoui	EPFL, Lausanne, Switzerland
Görel Hedin	Lund University, Sweden
Urs Hölzle	UCSB, USA
Eric Jul	University of Copenhagen, Denmark
Gerti Kappel	University of Linz, Austria
Karl Lieberherr	Northeastern University, USA
Cristina Videiro Lopes	Xerox Palo Alto Research Center, USA
Satoshi Matsuoka	Tokyo Institute of Technology, Japan
Mira Mezini	Technical University of Darmstadt, Germany
Ana Moreira	Universidade Nova de Lisboa, Portugal
James Noble	Victoria University of Wellington, New Zealand
Rui Oliveira	Universidade de Minho, Portugal
Jens Palsberg	Purdue University, USA
Markku Sakkinen	University of Jyväskylä, Finland
Dag Sjøberg	University of Oslo, Norway
Jan Vitek	Purdue University, USA
John Vlissides	IBM T.J. Watson Research Center, USA

Kasper Østerbye	Patrick Sallé
Marc Pantel	Andreas Schrader
Martti Penttonen	Peter Sewell
Jean-François Perrot	Mark Skipper
Frédéric Peschanski	Bjarne Steensgaard
Gian Pietro Picco	Tarja Systä
Sara Porat	John Tang Boyland
Tony Printezis	Val Tannen
Reza Razavi	Bedir Tekinerdoğan
Sigi Reich	Ewan Tempero
Arend Rensink	Pascale Thévenod
Werner Retschitzegger	Frank Tip
Nicolas Revault	Julien Vayssiere
Ran Rinat	Mitchell Wand
Tobias Ritzau	Akinori Yonezawa
Per Runeson	Olivier Zendra
Kenneth Russell	Matthias Zenger
Mario Südholt	Mikal Ziane
Paulo Sérgio Almeida	Yoav Zibin

Conference Sponsors

Referees

Ole Agesen
Davide Ancona
Bente Anda
João Araújo
Joco Arazjo
Yariv Aridor
Erik Arisholm
Isabelle Attali
Jean Bézivin
Godmar Back
Carlos Baquero
Wolfgang Beer
Eran Belinsky
Véronique Benzaken
Klaas van den Berg
Lodewijk Bergmans
Paul Bergstein
Marina Biberstein
Dietrich Birngruber
Anders Blomdell
Jeff Bogda
Noury Bouraqadi-Saâdani
Lars Bratthall
Pim van den Broek
Kim Bruce
Ciaran Bryce
Michele Bugliesi
Luís Caires
Denis Caromel
Craig Chambers
Robert G. Clark
Tal Cohen
Uriel Cohen
Adriana Compagnoni
Patrick Cousot
Gianpaolo Cugola
Uri Dekel
Dave Detlefs
Anne Doucet
Rémi Douence
Karel Driesen
Sophia Drossopoulou
Niels Elgaard Larsen
Patrick Eugster

Paulo Ferreira
Alex Garthwaite
Maurice Glandrup
Miguel Goulão
Giovanna Guerrini
Roger Henriksson
Stephan Herrmann
David Hill
Erik Hilsdale
David Holmes
Wade Holst
Marieke Huissman
Magne Jørgensen
Elisabeth Kapsammer
Amela Karahasanovic
Murat Karaorman
Pertti Kellomäki
Kai Koskimies
Svetlana Kouznetsova
Gerhard Kramler
Stein Krogdahl
Gary Leavens
Thomas Ledoux
Keunwoo Lee
Ole Lehrmann Madsen
José Luiz Fiadeiro
António Luís Sousa
Olav Lysne
Laurent Magnin
Mesiti Marco
Jean-Marc Menaud
Isabella Merlo
Thomas Meurisse
Hanspeter Mössenböck
Mattia Monga
Oscar Nierstrasz
Else Nordhagen
Jacques Noyé
Isabel Nunes
Martin Odersky
José Orlando Pereira
Alessandro Orso
Klaus Ostermann
Johan Ovlinger

Contents

Keynote Speech

Sharing and Encapsulation

Type Inference and Static Analysis

Language Design

Invited Talk

*Erik Meijer (Microsoft), Nigel Perry (Massey University), and
Arjan van Yzendoorn (Utrecht University)*

Implementation Techniques

Olivier Raynaud and Eric Thierry (Lirmm)

*Martin Hirzel, Amer Diwan (University of Colorado at Boulder),
and Antony Hosking (Purdue University)*

*David F. Bacon and V.T. Rajan
(IBM T.J. Watson Research Center)*

Reflection and Concurrency

*Michiaki Tatsubori, Toshiyuki Sasaki (University of Tsukuba),
Shigeru Chiba (University of Tsukuba, and PRESTO, Japan Science
and Technology Corporation), and
Kozo Itano (University of Tsukuba)*

*Denis Caromel and Julien Vayssière
(University of Nice - CNRS, I3S/INRIA Sophia Antipolis)*

*Robert Strom and Joshua Auerbach
(IBM T.J. Watson Research Center)*

Invited Talk

Alistair Cockburn (Humans and Technology)

Language Design

Testing and Design

Keynote Speech:

Language, Objects, and Intentionality

Charles Simonyi

Microsoft Corporation
One Microsoft Road
Redmond, WA 98052-6399

Abstract. The multiplicity of natural languages and the multiplicity of computer languages invite a false parallel. In fact computer languages have settled into an evolutionary rut that was carved by the needs of the earliest computers, while natural language evolves to even greater efficiencies. The talk will discuss "intentionality" as an important aspect of natural language, and the uses of intentionality in computer languages and in object oriented programming.

J. Lindskov Knudsen (Ed.): ECOOP 2001, LNCS 2072, pp. 1-1, 2001.

Capabilities for Sharing*
A Generalisation of Uniqueness and Read-Only

John Boyland[1], James Noble[2], and William Retert[1]

[1] University of Wisconsin-Milwaukee, USA,
{boyland,williamr}@cs.uwm.edu
[2] Victoria University of Wellington, New Zealand,
kjx@mcs.vuw.ac.nz

Abstract. Many languages and language extensions include annotations on pointer variables such as "read-only," "unique," and "borrowed"; many more annotations have been proposed but not implemented. Unfortunately, all these annotations are described individually and formalised independently – assuming they are formalised at all. In this paper, we show how these annotations can be subsumed into a general capability system for pointers. This system separates mechanism (defining the semantics of sharing and exclusion) from policy (defining the invariants that are intended to be preserved). The capability system has a well-defined semantics which can be used as a reference for the correctness of various extended type systems using annotations. Furthermore, it supports research in new less-restrictive type systems that permit a wider range of idioms to be statically checked.

1   Introduction

Pointers to objects in imperative languages provide a powerful programming tool but one that has the potential to create hard-to-spot errors [23]. Even ignoring issues such as object allocation and deallocation, *aliasing* – sharing mutable state – can lead to undesired situations where two parts of a program unintentionally communicate.

Problems of *representation exposure* are well known [27]. For example, manipulating reference fields of a link object supposedly encapsulated within a linked list can cause the linked list to return incorrect values or loop indefinitely. *Argument exposure* is a more subtle problem: if an element of a collection such as a binary search tree, sorted list, or hash table is modifiable from outside, changing the element can break the invariant of the collection structure

---

* Work supported in part by the National Science Foundation (CCR-9984681) and the Defense Advanced Research Projects Agency and Rome Laboratory, Air Force Materiel Command, USAF under contract F30602-99-2-0522. The views and conclusions contained herein are those of the authors and should not be interpreted as necessarily representing the official policies or endorsements, either expressed or implied, of the National Science Foundation, Defense Advanced Research Projects Agency, Rome Laboratory, or the U.S. Government.

J. Lindskov Knudsen (Ed.): ECOOP 2001, LNCS 2072, pp. 2–27, 2001.

Immutable	No change of state is visible through this reference. Also known as: Clean [35].
Borrowed [9]	This reference may not be stored into an object's field. Also known as: Limited [10]; Temporary [25]; Lent [4]; Unconsumable [30]; Unique [22].
Anonymous [8]	This reference neither may be stored into an object's field, nor may be compared via pointer equality.
Read-Only [27]	This reference may only be used to read an object; the object to which it refers may be changed via other reference. Also known as: Read [22]; Const [39]; Immutable [20].
Unique [1, 9, 22]	This is the only reference to the object to which it refers. Also known as: Linear [5]; Free [22, 35]; Unshareable [30].
Shared	This reference is unrestricted: this is the default meaning of most pointers.

Fig. 1. Reference annotations from the literature.

of which it is a part [35]. For a recent summary of these issues, with particular attention to object-oriented systems, see the summaries from the IWAOOS 1999 workshop [34].

1.1 Annotations for Controlling References

To enable programmers to manage aliasing in their programs, and to support optimisation, many programming language mechanisms have been provided (and many more proposed) that restrict the use of pointers and objects in programs. For instance, many languages now support a *read-only* annotation (such as C++'s const and Java's final) which prevents references from being changed. Many more flexible annotations have been proposed. If an object is declared to be completely *immutable*, that is, its state can never be changed via any reference, sharing that object always is benign [29]. Alternatively, if a reference to an object is *unique*, that is, it is the only reference to that object, then that object can always be mutated without affecting other parts of the program [22]. Figure 1 summarises a number of the most important annotations that have been developed to date.

The proliferation of annotations causes a number of problems. Each annotation is typically described independently, without reference to other annotations. Similarly, each annotation is formalised independently, in a formal system suited to that particular purpose. The names given to annotations are quite arbitrary – for example, we believe that Hogg's read [22], readonly in Modula-3 [32], JAC [24] and Universes [31], and some senses of C++'s const [39] all have the roughly the same semantics that we call *read-only*. Subtle differences remain because each annotation is defined within a different context. For instance, *read* (reference) variables in Hogg's Island system may not appear on either side of an assignment. Annotations' semantics can be as arbitrary as their names, of course, so a read-only annotation could protect a variable, a single object (as in the example above), or provide transitive protection (as in Flexible Alias Protection's clean or JAC's readonly). The same annotation may have different meanings in a single system depending where it is applied: "unique" in Hogg's islands means what we call "unique" when applied to a field declaration, but is closest to what we call "borrowed" when applied to a parameter.

This variability in semantics makes it difficult to compare annotations: it is hard to determine if, say, Islands [22] offer the same protection as Guava [4], because the semantics of their respective annotations are unclear. Combining annotations is difficult because annotations are usually phrased negatively, as *restrictions* on the source language: a `final` annotation forbids write operations upon the reference to which it is attached; a `free` annotation would forbid different operations. As a result, understanding any given annotation is difficult: understanding a language with several annotations, or determining how annotations from different proposals could be integrated, is next to impossible.

We believe one profound reason for the confusion is the lack of a low-level model (that is, a level below that of the annotations) of properties that the annotations are intended to preserve. It is difficult to prove the correctness of something when there is nothing to compare it to!

1.2   Capabilities for Sharing

This paper describes a system of *capabilities* for sharing: a capability consists of an address together with a set of primitive access rights that can be combined to model most of the reference annotations proposed for programming languages. The capabilities are given semantics in an untyped language that can serve as the reference for various type systems that define annotations in terms of access rights and give statically checkable rules that show execution does not get stuck.

The access rights give precise meanings to the properties that annotations are intended to preserve, and so provide a vocabulary for naming and discussing annotations. The precise semantics also support formal modelling directly, and as importantly, can clearly distinguish different annotations from each other. The semantics are expressed positively – each right grants its possessor the ability to perform a task otherwise beyond their power, making the semantics of combinations of annotations clear. The result is a comprehensive system that allows the extent of sharing to be precisely specified. This system can be supported by a static analysis so that the rights retain no run-time presence.

The remainder of this paper is as follows: Sect. 2 describes our system of capabilities and shows how it can be used to model the proposed annotations; Sect. 3 presents the semantics of our capabilities, and then Sect. 4 describes how we can model previous work; Sect. 5 discusses the consequences of this model; Sect. 6 places our capabilities into the context of related work, and Sect. 7 concludes the paper.

2   Access Rights

In our system, a (pointer) variable contains a *capability* which consists of two parts, an address of an object and a set of access rights. The full set of access rights is shown in Fig. 2. We have seven access rights, organised into three

R	Read	permits fields of the object to be read.
W	Write	permits fields of the object to be written.
I	Identity	permits comparisons between addresses.
R̄	Exclusive Read	means no other variable has a capability to the object with read access.
W̄	Exclusive Write	means no other variable has a capability to the object with write access.
Ī	Exclusive Identity	means no other variable has a capability to the object with identity access.
O	Ownership	Gives right to fully assert rights. Protects from assertion by "borrowed" capabilities.

Fig. 2. Access Rights for Sharing.

groups. The first three *base rights*, (read) **R**, (write) **W**, and (identity) **I**, describe the operations that may be performed via the capability. The next three *exclusive rights* indicate what operations (under certain circumstances) may not be permitted through other capabilities to the same object. The last one (the *ownership*) right affects how incompatibilities between capabilities are resolved.

Access rights define how a pointer to an object can be used; they say nothing about the objects themselves. For example, if some variable v pointing to an object o has has read and identity rights, but not the write right, then o's fields cannot be written via v: however this does not mean o's fields cannot be written: some other variable v' with a capability to o may have the write right, in which case o could be written via v'.

2.1   Base Rights

For example, to read a field f from an object y, as in

```
x := y.f;
```

the capability in variable y needs to have the read (**R**) right. Similarly, to write a field, as in

```
y.f := z;
```

the capability in the variable through which the write occurs (y) must have the write (**W**) right. To compare two capabilities (as in the test of the following "if" statement):

```
if (x == y) {
   System.out.println("x and y point to the same object");
}
```

the capabilities in both variables must have the identity (**I**) right.

In this paper, we model only the most low-level operations. In a user-level object-oriented language, we would want to combine these concepts with access protection (permitting accesses to the field only in methods of the class, for instance) and perhaps some additional base access rights permitting dynamic dispatch, or dynamic type testing. The semantics we give easily accomodates new rights.

2.2 Exclusive Rights

The second group of three rights (the three *exclusive* rights: exclusive read ($\bar{\mathbf{R}}$), exclusive write ($\bar{\mathbf{W}}$), and exclusive identity ($\bar{\mathbf{I}}$)) control the same operations as the corresponding base rights: field access, field assignment, and so on. The difference between base and exclusive rights is that while a base right *permits* an operation to be performed on an object via this variable, an exclusive right can be used to *prevent* those operations on that object via any other variable in the program.

An exclusive right is not a negative right: the possession of an exclusive right gives more power to the variable than it would have without the right. For example, if a variable has a capability with the $\bar{\mathbf{W}}$ right, then the object referred to by that variable can only be written via that variable. This is a good thing for the part of the program containing the variable with the $\bar{\mathbf{W}}$ right: for example, the object's fields can be cached safely since they can only be invalidated by writes through that variable.

A program must *assert* an exclusive right to enforce these restrictions. Asserting an exclusive right ensures that no other variables have capabilities with the right in question, if necessary by forcibly stripping those capabilities of incompatible rights. For example, when a program asserts the $\bar{\mathbf{W}}$ right for a variable, no other variables must be able to write to the object referred to by that variable. To ensure this, any $\mathbf{W}$ rights will be stripped from all other variables referring to that object. A system may use static analysis to ensure this denial of access rights does not cause other parts of the program to suddenly fail. Alternatively, a dynamic interpreter could locate other capabilities in the system and remove their rights.

An exclusive right and its associated base right are duals. Asserting an exclusive right denies other variables the base right, while asserting a base right denies other variables the exclusive right. We say that two capabilities to the same object are *compatible* if neither has a right which the other has in dual form.

More subtly, possession of an exclusive right does not imply possession of the base right. An important example is the concept of "immutable." Immutability is represented in our system by the lack of the write right (cannot modify the object) and the possession of the exclusive write right (no one else can modify it either). Asserting this right ensures no one can write the object.

The exclusive rights are a key aspect of our system, one that strongly distinguishes it from most previous work, such as ACE [25]. Exclusive rights also give somewhat the same flavor as a linear type system with some important differences. Most importantly they do not imply uniqueness unless asserted. Nothing prevents a capability laden with exclusive rights from being copied into multiple variables, such as a linked list. However, unless these variables are all in a single analysis unit, a static type system will be unable to ensure they do not interfere, and thus must assume that the aliases deny their fellow aliases any access rights that they have the ability to do.

2.3   The Ownership Right

The one access right that does not have an exclusive form is the ownership right which modifies the semantics of access right assertion. If a capability has this access right, we call it an *owned* capability; otherwise it is a *borrowed* capability. Asserting the access rights of a borrowed capability affects only other aliasing variables with incompatible borrowed capabilities but asserting the access rights of an owned variables affects all aliasing variables with incompatible capabilities. This access right can be used to express ownership or uniqueness according to the particular policy in use.

If two variables with incompatible owned capabilities refer to the same object, each has the ability to force the other to be compatible with it. The successful execution of the program may depend on which variable asserts its rights first, a race condition of sorts. Adding concurrency makes it a true race condition. Ensuring that race conditions do not happen is the job of a policy supported perhaps by static analysis. For instance, in the case that the two variables are in the same analysis unit (that is reflect the 'same' owner), it may be possible to ensure cooperative behavior. In other situations, in which only one of the two variables is available during a modular analysis, the analysis may simply assume the worst: that the other pointer acts first. Since, as we shall see, correct program execution never depends on the *lack* of an access right, this assumption is always sound.

One common component of policies is the following rule: the first time a program fragment reads a capability, it asserts all its (required) access rights. In this case, once you are given an owned capability, you force all aliases to be compatible, and never have to worry about losing an access right again, unless you give it out to someone else or voluntarily yield some access rights. In essense an owned capability means the variable storing it can hold onto its access rights indefinitely. On the other hand, a borrowed capability has no such guarantee. A policy defines the (basically temporal) extent of the borrowing and static analysis can ensure that the access rights are indeed preserved during this extent.

Given the connection the ownership right has with denying access rights, it is not clear that giving the ability to deny this access right is interesting or useful. Ownership by itself has no interesting effect; with a capability with just this access right, one does not even have the ability to compare the address, read or write through the capability, let alone deny other aliases their access rights.

2.4   Composing Access Rights

These access rights do not stand alone, rather they are designed to be combined to provide semantics for reference annotations that will be useful within

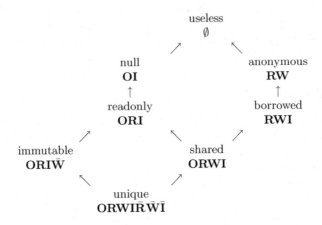

Fig. 3. Lattice ordering of reference annotations (compare Fig. 1).

programs. In particular, we expect that they will be combined to produce semantics similar to those provided by existing monolithic annotation systems. Figure 3 shows how the annotations from Fig. 1 can be situated in a sub-lattice of the subset lattice of access rights.

At the bottom, we have "unique" which means the object pointed to is unshared. The lattice also shows the relative position of "shared" capabilities which are unrestricted in their use but which provide no uniqueness guarantees. Elsewhere we see that read-only generalises both immutable and shared (since a read-only capability is limited in its use but has no guarantees concerning outside mutation). Borrowed capabilities are capabilities that are only temporarily available, and anonymous capabilities are those that additionally cannot be compared with other capabilities using address equality. Null capabilities (as well as having a special address) permit identity comparison but it is not permitted to read or write fields through a null capability. Capabilities at the top of the lattice ("useless") cannot be used for anything, and have no guarantees at all. All these concepts fall out naturally in our capability-based system.

3   Semantics of Capabilities

We define the semantics of our capabilities using a simple language of objects. The language includes simple variables and fields. An object is represented by its integer "address." The only values we have are capabilities, that is, pairs of an address and a set of access rights. We make the simplifying assumption that any object can have any field. Thus a store is represented by a (complete) function from variables (both simple variables, and (object,field) pairs for field variables) to capability. The initial store gives interesting values to two special

$$
\begin{aligned}
x, y \; &\in \; V = \mathit{Identifiers} \quad \text{(Simple Variables)} \\
f, g \; &\in \; F = \mathit{Identifiers} \quad \text{(Fields)} \\
o \; &\in \; O = \mathbb{N} \quad \text{(Objects)} \\
p, q \; &\in \; P = V \cup (O, F) \quad \text{(Pointer Variables)} \\
r \in \boldsymbol{r} \; &\subseteq \; R = \{\mathbf{O}, \mathbf{R}, \mathbf{W}, \mathbf{I}, \bar{\mathbf{R}}, \bar{\mathbf{W}}, \bar{\mathbf{I}}\} \quad \text{(Access rights)} \\
c \; &\in \; C = (O \times R) \quad \text{(Capabilities)} \\
\sigma \; &\in \; \Sigma = P \to C \quad \text{(Store)} \\
\sigma_0 \; &= \; [\texttt{null} \mapsto (0, \{\mathbf{O}, \mathbf{I}\}), \texttt{new} \mapsto (1, R), \text{all others} \mapsto (0, \{\})] \quad \text{(Initial Store)} \\
s \; &\in \; S \quad \text{(Statements)} \\
b \; &\in \; B \quad \text{(Boolean expressions)}
\end{aligned}
$$

$$
\begin{aligned}
S ::= \; & x\texttt{:=new} \mid x\texttt{:=}y \mid x\texttt{:=}y.f \mid x.f\texttt{:=}y \\
\mid \; & \texttt{limit}\, x\, r \mid \texttt{assert}\, x\, r \mid \texttt{assert}\, x.f\, r \\
\mid \; & \texttt{skip} \mid s\,;\,s' \mid \texttt{if}\, b\, \texttt{then}\, s\, \texttt{else}\, s' \mid \texttt{while}\, b\, \texttt{do}\, s \\
B ::= \; & x\texttt{==}y \mid x\texttt{!=}y \mid \texttt{true} \mid \texttt{false}
\end{aligned}
$$

Fig. 4. Basic domains and syntax

variables $\texttt{null}$ (predefined constant) and $\texttt{new}$ (a keyword).[1] The statements in the language include assignments, selection, iteration and special operations on access rights ($\texttt{limit}$ and $\texttt{assert}$). The only condition that can be tested directly is object identity. The domains and syntax are defined in Fig. 4.

The $\texttt{limit}$ statement and the two kinds of $\texttt{assert}$ statements are the key aspects of an otherwise conventional plain language. The $\texttt{limit}$ statement removes excess rights from a capability. The $\texttt{assert}$ statement has two effects. First, it stops execution unless the variable has a capability with the asserted access rights. Second, when asserting a set of access rights, it strips any rights of *other* variables that are incompatible with the asserted ones. Unless asserting the $\mathbf{O}$ right, only variables with borrowed capabilities are affected. We have two forms of $\texttt{assert}$ (for local values and for objects' fields respectively) because neither can be simulated using the other without using a write.

3.1 Evaluation

In this section, we give a "small-step" semantics of our language. In a "small-step" semantics, we show how a single program step can be accomplished through a program transformation. At each point, we have an input store and the result of evaluation will be an output store. We write

$$
\sigma \vdash s \to s' \mid \sigma'
$$

---

[1] The null variable may not be assigned and $\texttt{new}$ may only be used in the special allocation statement.

to indicate that if the store is σ, the program s will be transformed into program s' yielding resulting store σ'. (Although our language is imperative, our formalism is declarative.) We use a similar notation for boolean expressions:

$$\sigma \vdash b \rightarrow b'$$

A boolean expression has no effect on the store. The steps are a little bit bigger than one might expect since we treat each kind of assignment statement as an atomic unit. Conditions on the transformation are written above a line above the transformation.

We write updates on a store using the notation $\sigma[p \mapsto c]$ which has the following semantics:

$$\sigma[p \mapsto c](p') = \begin{cases} c & \text{if } p = p' \\ \sigma(p') & \text{if } p \neq p' \end{cases} .$$

Multiple updates are written as one compound update.

If you read from new, you get a new object not yet in the store, and get the full set of access rights. None of the fields are initialised (and so default to $(0, \emptyset)$, the useless pointer to the null object):

$$\frac{\sigma(\text{new}) = (o, R)}{\sigma \vdash [\![x\text{:=new}]\!] \rightarrow [\![\text{skip}]\!] \mid \sigma[x \mapsto (o, R), \text{new} \mapsto (o+1, R)]} .$$

When evaluating an assignment between two variables, we simply copy the address and access rights (reads aren't destructive). After the assignment the two pointers are aliases, possibly incompatible:

$$\sigma \vdash [\![x\text{:=}y]\!] \rightarrow [\![\text{skip}]\!] \mid \sigma[x \mapsto \sigma(y)]$$

Storing a value in a field requires the write right. Again, we simply copy the capability. A policy may wish to insert extra checks on a write to the heap but the basic semantics treats it much the same as a simple assignment between variables:

$$\frac{\sigma(x) = (o, r), \mathbf{W} \in r}{\sigma \vdash [\![x.f\text{:=}y]\!] \rightarrow [\![\text{skip}]\!] \mid \sigma[(o, f) \mapsto \sigma(y)]} .$$

Reading a value is similar, but requires the read right:

$$\frac{\sigma(y) = (o, r), \mathbf{R} \in r}{\sigma \vdash [\![x\text{:=}y.f]\!] \rightarrow [\![\text{skip}]\!] \mid \sigma[x \mapsto \sigma(o, f)]} .$$

One can limit the access rights of a variable to be no more than a given set:

$$\frac{\sigma(x) = (o, r)}{\sigma \vdash [\![\text{limit } x \ r']\!] \rightarrow [\![\text{skip}]\!] \mid \sigma[x \mapsto (o, r \cap r')]} .$$

More interestingly, one can assert some set of access rights for a simple variable which first requires that one have the access rights and then produces a new store:

$$\frac{\sigma(x) = (o, r), r \supseteq r'}{\sigma \vdash [\![\text{assert } x \ r']\!] \rightarrow [\![\text{skip}]\!] \mid Assert(x, o, r', \sigma)} .$$

And one can assert for a field of an object (if one has the read right for the object):

$$\frac{\sigma(x) = (o, \mathbf{r}), \mathbf{R} \in \mathbf{r} \qquad \sigma(o, f) = (o', \mathbf{r}'), \mathbf{r}' \supseteq \mathbf{r}''}{\sigma \vdash \llbracket \text{assert } x.f \ \mathbf{r}'' \rrbracket \rightarrow \llbracket \text{skip} \rrbracket \mid Assert\,((o, f), o', \mathbf{r}'', \sigma)} \ .$$

Asserting a set of access rights makes other aliases compatible:

$$Assert\,(p, o, \mathbf{r}, \sigma) = \sigma[p' \mapsto (o, MakeCompat\,(\mathbf{r}', \mathbf{r})) \mid \sigma(p') = (o, \mathbf{r}'), p \neq p'] \ .$$

The *MakeCompat* helper function takes two sets of access rights: the first for the alias being affected and the second being the set asserted. If the alias is an owned pointer variable, and one asserts without the ownership right, the alias is unaffected. If asserting with the ownership right, even owned pointer variables are affected. Borrowed pointer variables are affected in any case. Any access right of the alias whose dual is being asserted is stripped away:

$$MakeCompat\,(\mathbf{r}', \mathbf{r}) = \begin{cases} \mathbf{r}' & \text{if } \mathbf{O} \in \mathbf{r}', \mathbf{O} \notin \mathbf{r} \\ \mathbf{r}' - \{r \mid \bar{r} \in \mathbf{r}\} & \text{otherwise} \end{cases} \ .$$

(NB: $\bar{\bar{x}} = x$ for $x \in \{\mathbf{R}, \mathbf{W}, \mathbf{I}\}$.)

We evaluate the left hand-side of the sequence operator unless it is already skip:

$$\frac{\sigma \vdash s_1 \rightarrow s_1' \mid \sigma'}{\sigma \vdash \llbracket s_1; \ s_2 \rrbracket \rightarrow \llbracket s_1'; \ s_2 \rrbracket \mid \sigma'} \ ;$$

$$\sigma \vdash \llbracket \text{skip}; \ s \rrbracket \rightarrow s \mid \sigma \ .$$

Conditional statements first require the condition to be evaluated, and then select one of two results:

$$\frac{\sigma \vdash b \rightarrow b'}{\sigma \vdash \llbracket \text{if } b \text{ then } s_1 \text{ else } s_2 \rrbracket \rightarrow \llbracket \text{if } b' \text{ then } s_1 \text{ else } s_2 \rrbracket \mid \sigma} \ ;$$

$$\sigma \vdash \llbracket \text{if true then } s_1 \text{ else } s_2 \rrbracket \rightarrow s_1 \mid \sigma \ ;$$

$$\sigma \vdash \llbracket \text{if false then } s_1 \text{ else } s_2 \rrbracket \rightarrow s_2 \mid \sigma \ .$$

"While" loops are transformed into "if" statements:

$$\sigma \vdash \llbracket \text{while } b \text{ do } s \rrbracket \rightarrow \llbracket \text{if } b \text{ then } s; \text{ while } b \text{ do } s \text{ else skip} \rrbracket \mid \sigma \ .$$

The only conditions we have are equality and inequality (we need both for while). In either case, we need the identity capability for both pointers:

$$\frac{\sigma(x) = (o, \mathbf{r}), \mathbf{I} \in \mathbf{r}, \sigma(x') = (o', \mathbf{r}'), \mathbf{I} \in \mathbf{r}'}{\sigma \vdash \llbracket x \ R \ x' \rrbracket \rightarrow \begin{cases} \llbracket \text{true} \rrbracket & o \ R \ o' \\ \llbracket \text{false} \rrbracket & \text{otherwise} \end{cases}} \ .$$

We lift subset inclusion on access rights to a partial ordering on stores. (The lattice ordering is the reverse of subset ordering.) We only order those stores that have the same address for all variables:

$$\sigma \sqsubseteq \sigma' \equiv (\forall_{p \in P} \exists_{o \in O, \mathbf{r}' \subseteq \mathbf{r} \subseteq R} \ \sigma(p) = (o, \mathbf{r}) \wedge \sigma'(p) = (o, \mathbf{r}')) \ .$$

3.2   Execution Gets Stuck Only when Access Rights Missing

Execution is stuck only if a necessary access right is missing.

Theorem 1. *Let* $s \in S$ *where* $s \neq$ *skip be an unfinished program, and let* $\sigma \in \Sigma$ *be any store. Then there exists a store with the same addresses* $\sigma^* \sqsubseteq \sigma$ *under which this program can be evaluated one step:* $\sigma^* \vdash s \rightarrow s' \mid \sigma'$.

The read and write rights (**R** and **W**) are needed when reading and writing fields of records, respectively. The identity right (**I**) is needed when comparing capabilities. Access rights are also checked in assert statements.

Theorem 2. *The evaluation function is monotonic over the partial order of stores and does the same program steps (if evaluation is possible at all):*

$$
\begin{array}{c}
\sigma_1 \sqsubseteq \sigma_2 \wedge \\
\sigma_1 \vdash s \rightarrow s_1' \mid \sigma_1' \wedge \\
\sigma_2 \vdash s \rightarrow s_2' \mid \sigma_2'
\end{array}
\Rightarrow
\begin{array}{c}
s_1' = s_2' \wedge \\
\sigma_1' \sqsubseteq \sigma_2'
\end{array} \quad .
$$

If at the end of a program, we are only interested in the address part in variables, then if a program executes successfully it would have the same result if we ignored access rights entirely. This important property would be absent if it were possible to test for the presence of rights if an **if** statement.

As a result, in the context of a static checking system that guarantees the absence of capability errors, access rights incur no (direct) overhead in space or time.[2]

There are three reasons a pointer may not have a required access right:

1. The pointer may not have been initialised;
2. The pointer may have lost the access right through a **limit** statement;
3. The pointer may have lost the access right through an **assert** statement applied to an alias.

The first two situations can be addressed through standard analyses that track access rights through assignments. The third situation is peculiar to our way of expressing uniqueness and ownership; to statically check for such situations, one must track aliasing of pointers, which makes sense since uniqueness is an invariant concerning aliases.

4   Policy and Mechanism

An important advance over previous work is that the capability system separates sharing *policy* from the *mechanism* used to implement that policy. There are two ways in which policy can be separated from mechanism:

---

[2] There may be indirect costs involved in meeting the dictates of the static capability type system.

- In this paper, we separate the executable semantics of capabilities (mechanism) from the invariants that are intended to be preserved concerning annotated variables in a particular system (sharing policy).
- One may also separate the analysis mechanism used to check that execution will not get stuck from the coding policy concerning rules the programmer needs to know in order to satisfy the analysis.

While this paper does not directly address the second separation, it assists the definition of such an analysis mechanism by providing a semantics against which it can be checked.

Sharing policy is expressed in our framework by adding **assert** and **limit** (and perhaps other) statements wherever annotated variables are used. Where this choice of policy is really made manifest is in the meaning of exclusive rights. As seen in Sect. 3, the system does not prevent a "unique" pointer (more precisely, a pointer with all seven access rights) from being aliased in arbitrary ways. What the semantics does do, is provide a way to express (in an executable manner) the desired invariants. Thus if we wish certain variables (designated the "unique") variables to always have exclusive access to an object, we can assert the seven access rights upon every use of the capability. Exactly how that is done depends on the policy: one may have a more "linear" view of uniqueness, or one may use "null" as a legal value for non-unique "unique" variables. The system is flexible enough to admit different views of uniqueness; this section gives several examples.

Once one has the intended invariants encoded using **assert** and **limit** statements, one then needs some way to ensure that these invariants are maintained. The semantics we give permit a dynamic-checking approach, in which access rights are stored at run-time and lists of invisible back-pointers are maintained for each object, but this technique has a high price, both in the extra run-time overhead and in the fact that the program simply crashes when an invariant is not met. Instead, if a static analysis can prove execution at the capability level will never get stuck, we can ignore access rights completely in the implementation. A single policy could be supported by several analyses, that may differ in being local or global, flow-sensitive or flow-insensitive, etc. A particular analysis may require a particular sub-policy to be introduced: additional annotations and additional **assert** and **limit** statements.

4.1 Example: Uniqueness

To illustrate how sharing policy can be realised with capabilities, this section presents examples of several different techniques for maintaining uniqueness, roughly meaning that a variable has sole access to the referred object. We show how various policies for maintaining uniqueness can be realised in our system. In each of the examples below, u and v are unique variables (according to the flavor being described) and x and y are variables referring to temporary values. We show how reading or writing a unique variable is expressed, and handle the special case where we have a copying assignment between two unique variables.

Pure Linear References A linear reference may only be assigned/bound to something of linear type and may only be used once [17, 5]. Using the variable a second time is illegal.

Program	Expanded Program
$u := x$	$u := x$; assert u **ORWIR̄W̄Ī**
$y := v$	$y := v$; limit v $\emptyset$
$u := v$	$u := v$; limit v $\emptyset$; assert u **ORWIR̄W̄Ī**

This way of expressing linear reads does not quite match the semantics of linearity, because multiple reads are still permitted, but the later reads get a useless result. Another difference is that the capabilities do not force the variable to be read (as in true linearity.)

Checking linearity essentially becomes checking that the variable is only read once. With local variables, this is easy to do, but with fields of potentially shared objects, it becomes much harder. Thus we see versions of uniqueness that leave behind a useful value after a read.

Destructive Reads A destructive read is one that replaces the former contents of the read variable with null when it is read, and allows null as a valid value for an otherwise unique variable. Baker uses destructive reads for reading unique fields of possibly shared mutable objects [5]. Destructive reads have been used to avoid the need to synchronise on shared objects [3]. Islands [22] and Eiffel* [30] also use destructive reads.

Program	Expanded Program
$u := x$	$u := x$; if u != null then assert u **ORWIR̄W̄Ī** else skip
$y := v$	$y := v$; $v := $ null
$u := v$	$u := v$; $v := $ null; if u != null then assert u **ORWIR̄W̄Ī** else skip

The ease of checking destructive reads has a dual property, now the programmer must handle the fact that the 'unique' variable may not actually refer to an unshared object but instead is null.

Swapping If a unique variable can only be swapped with another unique variable, and never otherwise read or assigned after being initialised, (as in RESOLVE [21] for example) uniqueness can be assured:

Program	Expanded Program
$u.\texttt{init}(x)$	$u := x$
	assert u **ORWIR̄W̄Ī**
$u :=: v$	$\texttt{t} := u;$
	$u := v;$
	$v := \texttt{t};$
	assert u **ORWIR̄W̄Ī**;
	assert v **ORWIR̄W̄Ī**

If null is a legal value, the asserts must be made conditional.

Copying One of the rules for Balloons [2] is that balloon fields can only be initialised with/assigned to newly copied (or newly created) references. But once ensconced, the field can be read many times, always resulting in a value which cannot be saved in another field of balloon type. Assuming that a copy operations is expressed explicitly in the language, and that it should return a unique capability, we can express Balloon field writes and reads as follows:

Program	Expanded Program
$u := x$	$u := x;$
	assert u **ORWIR̄W̄Ī**
$y := v$	$y := v;$
	limit y **RWI**

The invariant that is maintained is the lack of *static aliases* (that is, field aliases). There may be many *dynamic aliases*. Balloons also have an "ownership" style invariant.

Alias Burying The basic invariant for alias-burying is that a field variable annotated "unique" must be unique only upon (that is, just before) reads. It may have aliases at this point, but all aliases must be *dead*, never to be used again. A close approximation is to have all aliases have at most the ownership right (**O**). Alias burying can be implemented in our system by having the uniqueness of these fields asserted just before a read (in this case, let u be a unique field):

Program	Expanded Program
$y := x.u$	assert $x.u$ **ORWIR̄W̄Ī**;
	$y := x.u$

Once again, we will need a conditional **assert** if null is legal as well.

4.2   Example: Borrowed Pointers

Every set of basic and exclusive rights has an owned version (with **O** added) and a borrowed version (without **O**). The semantics provides a mechanism for implementing various policies for what "borrowed" should mean. According to our semantics, a borrowed variable (that is, a variable with a borrowed capability) can only affect other borrowed variables in its assertions; it cannot strip access rights of the variable from which it was 'borrowed.' An owned variable can affect both borrowed and owned variables.

Borrowed Parameters Intuitively, a borrowed capability is one that is valid only for a limited extent of time, after which it is no longer valid. Typically, this extent is the dynamic lifetime of a parameter so marked. Borrowed parameters are also known as "limited" [10] or "lent" [4]. The source of the borrowing (for instance a unique variable) may be used to strip incompatible access rights from the borrowed variable when 'time is up.' Here we suppose our source language uses begin-end to delimit the dynamic extent of the borrowed parameter:

Program	Expanded Program
begin	$p := v;$
borrowed $p := v;$	limit p **RWI**
...	...
end	assert v **ORWI$\overline{\mathrm{R}}$$\overline{\mathrm{W}}$$\overline{\mathrm{I}}$**

Restricting Borrowed Values A policy will often have a rule that borrowed capabilities cannot be stored in the heap and some policies additionally require that borrowed capabilities cannot be returned from a procedure. For, for example, for a "shared" field/return value:

Program	Expanded Program
$y.f := x$	assert x **ORWI**;
	$y.f := x$
return x	assert x **ORWI**;
	return x

Typically these policies assert a field or return value's annotation (as a set of access rights) before the store/return.

Alternatively, it can be seen that in a typed system, a field will have a certain set of required access rights. Without the ownership right, it is impossible for a borrowed capability to ensure that it will not eventually lose these required access rights. Thus a borrowed capability is not a good candidate for being stored in a field. This intuition can be modeled by having every field type include the ownership right so that values without this access right cannot be stored into these fields.

However, these restrictions are questions of how the invariant can be maintained, not in defining the invariant so they are not built into the semantics of the store. It may be useful, for example, to permit temporary structures holding borrowed capabilities. We also do not wish to restrict the dynamic extent of a borrowed capability to be equal to the lifetime of some stack frame, as seen in our treatment of iterators (Sect. 4.2).

Read-Only Borrowed Islands [22] have a "read" mode that can be used for dynamic aliases to internal structures (including unique pointers). This mode can be realised using a "borrowed readonly" set of access rights (**RI**). The read-only'ness is transitive as well (see Sect. 4.3).

Anonymous Confined types [8] have a particular kind of method called an "anonymous method" in which the receiver cannot be compared to any other value using object-identity. We model that restriction by ensuring the this capability receiving the method has been limited to **RW** rights only.

Iterators An *iterator* [16] is a special object that refers to some position within a container object. Often, for efficiency, that position is indicated through the use of pointers to internal structures of the container. For example, an iterator to an extensible array object may have a direct pointer to the underlying array used to implement the container [33]. This situation (aliasing of a kind) may lead to difficulties when the container is mutated which may result in a change to the internal structures. For example, a new, larger, array may be allocated to hold the contents of the container. Some iterator systems simply state that it is an error to use an iterator after a mutation, but then never check for this eventuality. In Java's 1.2 collections framework, iterators are 'fail-fast': using an iterator after any mutation of the container results in an exception throw.

Previous systems for unique variables or ownership types had difficulties modeling such limited forms of aliasing (but see later work by Clarke [12]). The situation can be modeled with capabilities. First, we have the creation of an iterator (here simply a variable):

Program	Expanded Program
$i := u$	$i := u$;
	limit i **RWI**

Whenever the internal state is used in a non-modifying situations, the policy does not add any `assert` statements, but when it needs to be mutated, we first assert the uniqueness of the internal structure:

Program	Expanded Program
$x := u$	assert u **ORWIR̄W̄Ī**;
	$x := u$

and then use x for mutations.

Checking that an iterator is never used incorrectly can be difficult. To be able to prove that a given 'fail fast' technique does not use a variable whose access rights has been lost, an analysis will need some way to connect run-time values (for example version stamps) with access right status. Here we have simply shown how checking this property can be modeled as checking in a capability-based program; we don't say how to do the analysis.

4.3   Example: Read-Only

A read-only capability is one that lacks the write right. In these examples, c is a variable annotated read-only (or const), and x is any other value.

Const In C++, a const pointer (or reference) cannot be used for modification:

Program	Expanded Program
$c := x$	$c := x;$
	limit c **ORI**

If another pointer is loaded from a field of the object pointed to by a const pointer, the const'ness of the original pointer is irrelevant.

   C++ permits const'ness to be "cast away" which has undefined semantics in some situations (subsequent writes may fail if the variable was truly read-only). In our system, it is impossible to recover a lost capability. One could model C++ by either not actually removing the write right when something passed as const, or else extending the system with an `acquire` statement that adds access rights.

Transitive Read-Only The annotations "val" in Flexible Alias Protection [35] "read" in Islands [22], "deeply immutable" for Hakonen et al [20], "readonly" in JAC [24] and Universes [31] all represent *transitive* restrictions. Any references read through the read-only reference are read-only themselves. This restriction can be implemented when the system knows which variables may hold read-only capabilities:

Program	Expanded Program
$c' := c.f$	$c' := c.f;$
	limit c' **ORI**

This realisation technique is not as robust as the other techniques mentioned above because one section of code cannot be sure some other section of code is not "cheating." Section 5.4 discusses why we do not use transitivity by default.

   Flexible Alias Protection also includes a transitive immutable restriction, "arg." In the case of Universes, read-only'ness can be cast away (in certain checked situations) and thus should not be modeled by lack of an access right, but rather by lack of knowledge of the access right.

4.4   Procedures and Modular Static Checking

It is easier to prove invariants modularly if we have extra information on the interfaces of modules. As we mentioned above, under some policies, parameters may be annotated "borrowed" which means they lead to no lasting aliases. This is a particular instance of annotations on module interfaces. Both the caller and callee may perform additional `assert` and `limit` statements: before passing a capability to a procedure, the caller may limit its access rights to those of the parameter to ensure that the procedure "does not cheat." The callee may assert the declared access rights of its parameters to make sure it was not "cheated." Similarly, on procedure return, the callee may limit the return value and the caller assert that it has the promised access rights.

Modules, and more particularly procedures, communicate not only through parameters and return values, but also through the store. Assuming we have a type system that says what fields have valid values (capabilities) for each (live) object in the system, and what access rights the capabilities should have, we wish to ensure that whenever a capability is read from the store, it has the required access rights. A policy may move the check from the read to the last store, essentially putting an **assert** in place after every store. It will then also be necessary to trace every store variable read during a procedure and assert its capability's rights before the procedure returns, or when it calls a procedure that may read the variable.

4.5   Ownership

Ownership of objects has been proposed by Clarke et al [13], by Müller and Poetzsch-Heffter in Universes [31], or by Bacon et al for Guava [4]. In these systems, each owned object is owned respectively by one object, one universe or one monitor or value. This ownership is not necessarily realised through the use of a single reference variable; there may be multiple (owning) variables referencing the owned object, but they all are declared within a single context.

Our system does not define a notion of an owning context, leaving this up to a particular policy. Our system permits an object to have several owners, that is, several variables with owned capabilities. Each owner may have a capability with a different set of access rights. It is up to a policy and supporting analyses to ensure that these owners cooperate, using **assert** and **limit** statements as necessary to ensure that rights are controlled. We have seen above how various kinds of unique variables assert their rights after being read or written to maintain their uniqueness. To handle ownership, one needs to treat transfers into or out of the context differently than transfers within the context.

For example, a policy (with supporting analyses) could define a context for "exclusive write" ownership. When the first capability to an object is stored in an owning context, all access rights would be asserted, but a second or later store would assert only the non-ownership rights. When an owned field is read for read-only access, it would be limited:

Program	Expanded Program
$u := x$	$u := x$; assert u **ORWI$\bar{\text{W}}$**
$u := v$	assert v **RWI$\bar{\text{W}}$**; $u := v$
$y := v$	assert v **RWI$\bar{\text{W}}$**; $y := v$; limit y **RI**

Our system naturally models policies that permit *ownership transfer*, in which a capability with a full set of rights enters or leaves a context. In order for this action to be carried out safely, the variable must hold the only useful capability to the object at the time of transfer (no other owner is holding on to an alias). An `assert` statement at the point of transfer ensures this requirement is met (here we show what happens when ownership is transferred out of a context with exclusive write ownership):

Program	Expanded Program
y := v	y := v;
	`assert` y **ORWIW̄**

4.6   Type Systems

A type system is a means of expressing constraints that avoid certain run-time errors. In the capabilities system, a type system could be used as part of a policy to ensure execution does not get stuck because of lack of capabilities. Our system supports research in new more powerful type systems in that

- It gives a well-defined basis for checking properties;
- The mechanism is broad enough to cover a wide range of policies.

In particular, a uniqueness invariant need not be as strict as linearity; we don't need to refuse to store borrowed capabilities on the heap; we can support a variety of different kinds of assignment; we do not require strict transitivity of read-only'ness. We view this separation of mechanism from policy one of the most important contributions of this paper.

5   Discussion

In this section, we describe some possibilities for extensions and implementations.

5.1   Object Rights vs. Capability Rights

As we have described it, access rights are part of particular capabilities and are not part of the object. To determine all actions that can be performed upon an object, one must consider the union of the access rights of all capabilities to an object over the course of the program: an object can be written to, for example, if it is ever referred to by a capability with a **W** right; an object can be subjected to pointer comparison if it is ever referred to by a capability with a **I** right, and so on.

When a new object is allocated (using **new**), one receives a capability with all seven access rights. These rights can subsequently be given away via the `limit` statement. For example, giving away all the exclusive rights allows an object to be shared: once no capability for an object in the system exists with a certain right, the right no longer exists for that object in the system and can never be recovered. For instance, an object can be made immutable by giving away the write right **W** when one has the sole access to the object. Once gone, this right can never be recovered for that object in the system. When no variable has a capability with any rights, the object can be reclaimed, as described in the following section.

5.2   Memory Management

If no pointer variable has any of the base or exclusive rights to an object, that object can be safely reclaimed by the garbage collector, that is made available for subsequent **new** operations. (In this case, **new** would need to keep track of free objects explicitly rather than simply allocating linearly through the space of objects.) Such a garbage collector would need to work below the level of capabilities, since it needs to compare addresses not necessarily associated with **I** rights, and since it needs to manufacture a capability with all the access rights for the object.

The garbage collector must not collect an object for which there exists a variable holding a capability with any of the base rights. Otherwise, the reuse of memory could be detected by code with access to the variables. Neither can it collect an object with extant capabilities with exclusive rights, because these pointers could be used to strip access rights from unsuspecting users of **new**. However, it can ignore pointers that only have the ownership right **O** since (by itself) this access right provides no way to affect or be affected by other pointers.

Rather than assume automatic memory management, one can work within the system, and write manual allocation routines. An allocation routine can keep track of a list of free objects, using **new** when the list is empty. An object can be deallocated if and only if one has a capability to it with all seven access rights (as with Crary et al's unique regions [14]). Having all seven access rights is necessary in order to present them upon allocation, and they are sufficient because the deallocation routine accepting a pointer **p** can immediately assert all access rights:

assert p $\mathbf{ORWI\bar{R}\bar{W}\bar{I}}$

This ensures that **p** is now the only variable with a capability with any of the six base or exclusive rights.

5.3   Concurrency

Concurrency is not addressed in our semantics, but annotations such as we have discussed can be very useful when proving the correctness of concurrent code. The non-local nature of the **assert** statement demonstrates the importance of applying such operations only in critical sections or in objects already known to be unique. More specifically, fetching (and asserting) a unique references from a shared object required locking, but once one has a unique reference, one may access its fields without further synchronisation. We are interested in pursuing concurrency further.

5.4   Access Rights Are Single-Level

The access rights of a reference are relevant only to the object referenced and have no effect on capabilities fetched from the object. This definition is particularly relevant in the case of read-only annotations. In our system, a mutable capability can be fetched from a read-only capability and used for writing. This situation contrasts with the transitive definitions of *read* mode as defined in Islands [22], *arg* mode in flexible alias protection [35], and *readonly* in JAC [24] and Universes [31]. The reason why we do not use this rule is because it is not always the "right" thing. Objects that notionally are part of the object to which only read access is given should not be modified, but objects that are not considered sub-objects should have no additional restrictions. For example, if I have read-only access to a hash table, I should not be able to modify the table by adding or deleting items, but it makes sense to use the table to translate a key to a mutable data object, such as a stream. In C++ [39] the distinction for `const` is made between objects nested inside other objects and those accessed through pointers. As described below in Sect. 5.6, we intend our capability work to be combined with an effects system thus giving the proper control for transitivity.

Therefore since our system is intended for application to languages such as Java which use references to objects exclusively, and since the intended application for transitivity can be modelled better with an effects system, the less restrictive choice is taken. A policy can be more restrictive than the underlying semantics, but if the underlying semantics is too restrictive, then by definition a policy cannot safely make the rule looser.

5.5   Implementations

The semantics we give in this paper carefully ensures that the address in any capability cannot depend on the rights of any capability at all (as formalised in Theorems 1 and 2). This *phase separation* ensures that if static analysis can show that execution of a program with capabilities never gets stuck, the same program will have the same behavior if all access rights are completely ignored. Earlier, we mentioned that a policy is realised by adding `limit` and `assert` statements. If a program can be shown never to get stuck *with* these additions, then we can execute it *without* the additions!

If the program cannot be proved never to go wrong, one may either reject it, or run it with certain dynamic checks. The run-time system could keep track (using backpointers) of every variable that refers to an object, and use these backpointers to implement `assert` statements. Alternatively, asserts could be logged, and used to update variables lazily upon the next access. Either method seems overly expensive for practical use.

5.6   Access Rights for Parts of Objects

We would like to combine this work with work on object-oriented effects [19], permitting a capability to have rights for part of an object, not necessarily the whole thing. This extension would have the added advantage that the transitivity problem would be addressed because the effects annotations permit one to declare which sub-objects are considered part of the object. Currently sub-objects considered part of the object must be strictly unique. It remains to be investigated whether weaker sets of rights (such as "unique write" (**ORWIW̄**)) could be used to express a limited transitivity.

5.7 Other Rights

A common operation not directly captured by the three base rights is a type-safe downcast (a "dynamic cast" in C++ parlance). To ensure that a module taking an `Object` parameter is cleanly polymorphic, we might want to ensure that the code never uses type-tags to determine exactly what kind of object it has. If the system had a 'cast right,' this restriction could be modelled by passing a capability without this right. Alternatively, the type-tag could be seen as part of the object and thus a read right to this section of the object (using rights for parts of objects) could be used instead.

The system could easily be extended to permit new user-defined base rights. These would have effect only in `assert` and `limit` statements and would be used to specify user-defined invariants. A type system that permitted user-defined rights should permit some polymorphism so that the new rights would work well with library code.

6   Related Work

Capabilities originated [15] as a model unifying ad-hoc techniques developed to allow simultaneously executing processes to share system resources. Variations of this framework have since been used in a variety of systems, notably the Cambridge CAP system [41] and the Hydra/C.mmp [42].

Capabilities as used here provide an approximation of many other annotation-based approaches. These include various formulations of read-only [18, 20, 22, 24, 31, 32, 39], borrowed [4, 10], read-only borrowed [22], and anonymous [8] references, as discussed earlier. Some methods for determining or enforcing uniqueness, such as linear references [5, 17], free references [22, 35], destructive reads [5, 22, 30], swapping [21], forced copying (as in Balloons [2]), and alias burying [9], can be modelled using our capability system, as has been demonstrated. Virginity [26] cannot be modelled directly because when a "pivot field" is initialised, it asserts exclusive ownership without asserting exclusive read and write privileges. Essentially, all remaining aliases are forced to be borrowing. Systems like Almeida's Balloons [2], Universes [31], or Flexible Alias Protection [12, 13, 35] which require a notion of ownership of objects can partly be modelled using the **O** right.

There are several techniques available that resolve similar issues, but do not rely on attaching annotations to references. Reynolds [37] provides a means of reasoning about whether statements *interfere*; if so, they cannot be safely executed in parallel. This is extended [38] to apply to heap-allocated objects, using a logical conjunction & (sometimes written *) that requires on heap independence. Löhr [28] proposes several (apparently unchecked) concurrency annotations including one that indicates that a method can be run in parallel with all other methods. Typically such methods access immutable state.

Several optimisations (for example to remove unnecessary synchronisation) need to determine variables that "escape" some execution context. Escape analysis [6, 7, 11, 36, 40] is used to track aliases and depending on how precise the analysis is, may be able to determine that no new aliases are created in some execution context. A static analysis that checks "borrowed" capabilities is a form of escape analysis.

Capabilities and rights have been recently been suggested in several other incarnations. Crary et al [14] developed a Capability Calculus, which applies capabilities to a typed low-level language. A type system is introduced to track when capabilities are copied and revoked, to statically determine when a region's memory may be freed. The only rights division is between unique and general capabilities.

Kniesel created ACE [25] which uses *keys* (what we call capabilities). Lists of access rights are explicitly attached to all arguments and returns. Access rights are multivalued and inherently ordered: method write implies method read implies method execute. They are strictly transitive. The choice of rights gives greater precision in specifying which pieces of referred-to objects may be accessed, but fewer modes of access. There are also rights specific to the reference itself (duration). Kniesel presents both a dynamic approach using a runtime system to monitor execution, and a static approach which requires annotations of required rights on every variable declaration; a variable must demand up front all rights it might possibly need for all possible program executions. This can done in our system by assertion.

JAC [24], by Kniesel and Theisen, provides a simple hierarchy (*writeable* $\geq$ *readonly* $\geq$ *readimmutable* $\geq$ *readnothing*) of access rights and the keyword `mutable` to mitigate their effect on certain parameters or return values. This hierarchy is required for analysis as references cannot assert their rights. The differing orders between JAC's readonly and readimmutable and our read-only and immutable owe to our use of an exclusive write right. The JAC system also enforces strict transitivity.

7   Conclusion

We have described a system of capabilities in which every pointer variable stores a capability with an address and a set of access rights. In this capability system, aliasing is modelled easily – indeed aliasing is implicit and natural while uniqueness and ownership are explicit and special. Objects can be transferred or shared between different parts of the program naturally, modelling the way computers and pointers actually work, while capabilities can be asserted when necessary to control sharing and ensure program executions meet their specifications.

The capability system provides a mechanism for describing sharing in object-oriented programs. This mechanism can support many different policies, as we have shown by modelling diverse annotation-based systems using the capability system. The semantics of the capabilities are clearly and formally defined, giving a reference-point against which to check the correctness of an implementation or static analysis, facilitating comparisons between existing annotation-based systems, and supporting future research on type systems for managing sharing in object-oriented programs.

References

[1] Peter Achten, John van Groningen, and Rinus Plasmeijer. High level specification of I/O in functional languages. In John Launchbury and P. Samson, editors, *Workshop on Functional Programming, Glasgow 1992*, Ayr, UK, July 6–8, Workshops in Computer Science, pages 1–17. Springer, Berlin, Heidelberg, New York, 1993.

[2] Paulo Sergio Almeida. Balloon types: Controlling sharing of state in data types. In Mehmet Akşit and Satoshi Matsuoka, editors, *ECOOP'97 — Object-Oriented Programming, 11th European Conference*, Jyväskylä, Finland, June 9–13, volume 1241 of *Lecture Notes in Computer Science*, pages 32–59. Springer, Berlin, Heidelberg, New York, 1997.

[3] G. R. Andrews and J. R. McGraw. Language features for process interaction. In Davd B. Wortman, editor, *Proceedings of an ACM Conference on Language Design for Reliable Software*, ACM SIGPLAN Notices, 12(3):114–127, March 1977.

[4] David F. Bacon, Robert E. Strom, and Ashis Tarafdar. Guava: A dialect of Java without data races. In *OOPSLA'00 Conference Proceedings—Object-Oriented Programming Systems, Languages and Applications*, Minneapolis, Minnesota, USA, October 15–19, *ACM SIGPLAN Notices*, 35(10):382–400, October 2000.

[5] Henry G. Baker. 'Use-once' variables and linear objects—storage management, reflection and multi-threading. *ACM SIGPLAN Notices*, 30(1):45–52, January 1995.

[6] Bruno Blanchet. Escape analysis for object-oriented languages: application to Java. In *OOPSLA'99 Conference Proceedings—Object-Oriented Programming Systems, Languages and Applications*, Denver, Colorado, USA, November 1–5, *ACM SIGPLAN Notices*, 34(10):20–34, October 1999.

[7] Jeff Bogda and Urs Hölzle. Removing unnecessary synchronization in Java. In *OOPSLA'99 Conference Proceedings—Object-Oriented Programming Systems, Languages and Applications*, Denver, Colorado, USA, November 1–5, *ACM SIGPLAN Notices*, 34(10):35–46, October 1999.

[8] Boris Bokowski and Jan Vitek. Confined types. In *OOPSLA'99 Conference Proceedings—Object-Oriented Programming Systems, Languages and Applications*, Denver, Colorado, USA, November 1–5, *ACM SIGPLAN Notices*, 34(10):82–96, October 1999.

[9] John Boyland. Alias burying: Unique variables without destructive reads. *Software Practice and Experience*, 31(6):533–553, May 2001.

[10] Edwin C. Chan, John T. Boyland, and William L. Scherlis. Promises: Limited specifications for analysis and manipulation. In *Proceedings of the IEEE International Conference on Software Engineering (ICSE '98)*, Kyoto, Japan, April 19–25, pages 167–176. IEEE Computer Society, Los Alamitos, California, 1998.

[11] Jong-Deok Choi, Manish Gupta, Mauricio Serrano, Vugranam C. Sreedhar, and Sam Midkiff. Escape analysis for Java. In *OOPSLA'99 Conference Proceedings— Object-Oriented Programming Systems, Languages and Applications*, Denver, Colorado, USA, November 1–5, *ACM SIGPLAN Notices*, 34(10):1–19, October 1999.

[12] David Clarke. An object calculus with ownership and containment. In *The Eighth International Workshop on Foundations of Object-Oriented Languages (FOOL 8)*, London, England, January 20. 2001.

[13] David G. Clarke, John M. Potter, and James Noble. Ownership types for flexible alias protection. In *OOPSLA'98 Conference Proceedings—Object-Oriented Programming Systems, Languages and Applications*, Vancouver, Canada, October 18–22, *ACM SIGPLAN Notices*, 33(10):48–64, October 1998.

[14] Karl Crary, David Walker, and Greg Morrisett. Typed memory management in a calculus of capabilities. In *Conference Record of the Twenty-sixth Annual ACM SIGACT/SIGPLAN Symposium on Principles of Programming Languages*, San Antonio, Texas, USA, January 20–22, pages 262–275. ACM Press, New York, 1999.

[15] Jack B. Dennis and Earl C Van Horn. Programming semantics for multiprogrammed computations. In *Communications of the ACM*, pages 143–154. ACM Press, New York, March 1966.

[16] Erich Gamma, Richard Helm, Ralph Johnson, and John Vlissides. *Design Patterns: Elements of Reusable Object-Oriented Software*. Addison-Wesley, Reading, Massachussetts, USA, 1995.

[17] Jean-Yves Girard. Linear logic. *Theoretical Computer Science*, 50(1):1–102, 1987.

[18] James Gosling, Bill Joy, and Guy Steele. *The Java™ Language Specificaion*. The Java™ Series. Addison-Wesley, Reading, Massachussetts, USA, 1996.

[19] Aaron Greenhouse and John Boyland. An object-oriented effects system. In Rachid Guerraoui, editor, *ECOOP'99 — Object-Oriented Programming, 13th European Conference*, Lisbon, Portugal, June 14–18, volume 1628 of *Lecture Notes in Computer Science*, pages 205–229. Springer, Berlin, Heidelberg, New York, 1999.

[20] Harri Hakonen, Ville Leppänen, Timo Raita, Tapio Salakoski, and Jukka Teuhola. Improving object integrity and preventing side effects via deeply immutable references. In *Proceedings of the Sixth Fenno-Ugric Symposium on Software Technology, FUSST'99*, pages 139–150. 1999.

[21] Douglas E. Harms and Bruce W. Weide. Copying and swapping: Influences on the design of reusable software components. *IEEE Transactions on Software Engineering*, 17(5):424–435, May 1991.

[22] John Hogg. Islands: Aliasing protection in object-oriented languages. In *OOPSLA'91 Conference Proceedings—Object-Oriented Programming Systems, Languages and Applications*, Phoenix, Arizona, USA, October 6–11, *ACM SIGPLAN Notices*, 26(11):271–285, November 1991.

[23] John Hogg, Doug Lea, Alan Wills, Dennis deChampeaux, and Richard Holt. The Geneva convention on the treatment of object aliasing. *OOPS Messenger*, 3(2), April 1992.

[24] Günter Kniesel and Dirk Theisen. JAC – access right based encapsulation for Java. *Software Practice and Experience*, 31(6), May 2001.

[25] Günther Kniesel. Encapsulation = visibility + accessibility. Technical Report IAI-TR-96-12, Universität Bonn, November 1996. Revised March 1998.

[26] K. Rustan M. Leino and Raymie Stata. Virginity: A contribution to the specification of object-oriented software. *Information Processing Letters*, 70(2):99–105, April 1999.

[27] B. Liskov and J. Guttag. *Abstraction and Specification in Program Development.* The MIT Press, Cambridge, Massachussetts, USA and London, England, 1986.

[28] Klaus-Peter Löhr. Concurrency annotations. In *OOPSLA'92 Conference Proceedings—Object-Oriented Programming Systems, Languages and Applications*, Vancouver, British Columbia, October 18–22, *ACM SIGPLAN Notices*, 27(10):327–340, October 1992.

[29] B. Maclennan. Values and objects in programming languages. *ACM SIGPLAN Notices*, 17(2):70–80, 1982.

[30] Naftaly Minsky. Towards alias-free pointers. In Pierre Cointe, editor, *ECOOP'96 — Object-Oriented Programming, 10th European Conference*, Linz, Austria, July 8–12, volume 1098 of *Lecture Notes in Computer Science*, pages 189–209. Springer, Berlin, Heidelberg, New York, July 1996.

[31] Peter Müller and Arnd Poetzsch-Heffter. A type system for controlling representation exposure in Java. In Sophia Drossopolou, Susan Eisenbach, Bart Jacobs, Gary T. Leavens, Peter Müller, and Arnd Poetzsch-Heffter, editors, *2nd ECOOP Workshop on Formal Techniques for Java Programs*, Nice, France, June 12. 2000.

[32] Greg Nelson, editor. *Systems Programming with Modula-3*. Prentice Hall Series in Innovative Technology. Prentice-Hall, Englewood Cliffs, New Jersey, USA, 1991.

[33] James Noble. Iterators and encapsulation. In *TOOLS Europe 2000*, pages 431–442. IEEE Computer Society, Los Alamitos, California, 2000.

[34] James Noble, Jan Vitek, and Doug Lea. *Report of the Intercontinental Workshop on Aliasing in Object-Oriented Systems*, volume 1743 of *Lecture Notes in Computer Science*. Springer, Berlin, Heidelberg, New York, 2000.

[35] James Noble, Jan Vitek, and John Potter. Flexible alias protection. In Eric Jul, editor, *ECOOP'98 — Object-Oriented Programming, 12th European Conference*, Brussels, Belgium, July 20–24, volume 1445 of *Lecture Notes in Computer Science*. Springer, Berlin, Heidelberg, New York, 1998.

[36] Young Gil Park and Benjamin Goldberg. Reference escape analysis: Optimizing reference counting based on the lifetime of references. In *ACM SIGPLAN Workshop on Partial Evaluation and Semantics-Based Program Manipulation (PEPM'91)*, New Haven, Colorado, USA, June 17–19, *ACM SIGPLAN Notices*, 26(9):178–189, September 1991.

[37] John C. Reynolds. Syntactic control of interference. In *Conference Record of the Fifth ACM Symposium on Principles of Programming Languages*, Tucson, Arizona, USA, pages 39–46. ACM Press, New York, January 1978.

[38] John C. Reynolds. Intuitionistic reasoning about shared mutable data structure. In *Millenial Perspectives in Computer Science*. Palgrave, to appear. Draft dated July 28, 2000.

[39] Bjarne Stroustrup. *The C++ programming Language*. Addison-Wesley, Reading, Massachussetts, USA, third edition, 1997.

[40] John Whaley and Martin Rinard. Compositional pointer and escape analysis for Java programs. In *OOPSLA'99 Conference Proceedings—Object-Oriented Programming Systems, Languages and Applications*, Denver, Colorado, USA, November 1–5, *ACM SIGPLAN Notices*, 34(10):187–206, October 1999.

[41] M.V. Wilkes and R.M. Needham. *The Cambridge CAP Computer and its operating system*. Elsevier, London, 1978.

[42] William A. Wulf, Roy Levin, and Samuel P. Harbison. *HYDRA/C.mmp: An Experimental Computer System*. McGraw-Hill, New York, 1981.

Sealing, Encapsulation, and Mutability

Marina Biberstein[1], Joseph (Yossi) Gil[2*], and Sara Porat[1]

[1] IBM Research Lab in Haifa, Advanced Technology Center,
Haifa 31905, Israel
{biberstein, porat}@il.ibm.com
[2] Technion – Israel Institute of Technology,
Haifa 32000, Israel
yogi@cs.technion.ac.il

Abstract. Both encapsulation and immutability are important mechanisms, that support good software engineering practice. Encapsulation protects a variable against all kinds of access attempts from certain sections of the program. Immutability protects a variable only against write access attempts, irrespective of the program region from which these attempts are made. Taking mostly an empirical approach, we study these concepts and their interaction in JAVA. We propose code analysis techniques, which, using the new sealing information, can help to identify variables as encapsulated, immutable, or both.

1 Introduction

Encapsulation and immutability are two different, but related, aspects of the kind of protection required for large-scale, modular design. Encapsulated entities are protected against *all* kinds of access made by a *certain* set of modules—those modules that were not granted access rights. Immutable entities are protected against a *certain* sort of access, specifically modification, by *all* modules.

Both aspects of protection are complicated by the interaction with inheritance, and by compound objects whose state spans not only the values stored in their fields, but also objects referenced by these fields. The polymorphic nature of reference fields contributes yet another dimension to the complexity of the problem. It is even more difficult to define and enforce protection rules in view of the *aliasing problem*, i.e., when a reference to an object might be shared by several other variables, each of which defines a different protection scheme of its contents.

The similarity between encapsulation and immutability motivates us to study them together. The approach we choose is largely empirical, and relies on a current language (specifically JAVA [2]) and existing code base (specifically the run time library). Our objective is to *gauge* the extent to which encapsulation and immutability can be found in actual use, rather than *invent* new mechanisms to support them. When development of language features matures, and systems for visualizing samples of dynamic object graphs [22] arrive, the time will be ripe to introduce annotations into existing mammoth bodies of library code with the purpose of enhancing its reliability and reusability.

---

* Work done in part while with IBM Research Lab in Haifa.

J. Lindskov Knudsen (Ed.): ECOOP 2001, LNCS 2072, pp. 28–52, 2001.

Therefore, this work is an initial empirical step towards what is called[1] "ownership- and immutability- 'type' inference".

Our research involves the study of existing language features (such as **final** and access level) and imminent ones (sealing[2]), and the development and application of code analysis techniques. Principal concerns are problems of object oriented type analysis [18] and call graph construction, for which we contribute several new techniques. Naturally, aliasing issues will concern us as well.

Prior research on encapsulation and immutability has largely taken a language design approach. Common to much of this work is the struggle with the recalcitrant sharing problem—a problem that touches many other OO language design issues (see e.g., the work of Grogono and Sakkinen [19] on copying and comparing). Hakonen et al. [21] struggle with this problem in their work on *deep immutability* by attaching mutability annotations to references rather than to objects. Our work is different in that we attach the immutability property to the object, the main reason being that static dataflow analysis is applied at the byte code level.

There were several serious attempts to contain the sharing problem by restricting the ways in which aliases can be created. The work of Hogg on islands [23] uses lingual constructs and formalisms of policies to impose restrictions on the patterns of aliases that may be created. Minsky's unique pointers [28] are implemented by system rules, which essentially extend the syntax of the host language. Balloon types [1] address the sharing problem by an extension of the type system.

A significant line of research, related to both immutability and the sharing problem, is the restriction of access rights, and in particular, modification rights, to references, rather than restricting the creation of aliases. *Flexible alias protection* by Noble, Vitek, and Potter [29] is a conceptual framework at the language level (which was later formalized by an extension to the type system [10]) for defining different kinds of protection policies on references and statically checking them.

The above mentioned research concentrated on protection, i.e., the defense against accidents and non-modular programming. *Security*, i.e., defense against programming malice, also suffers from the aliasing problem and has also attracted a significant body of research. Techniques here include extensions to the programming language (e.g., confined types and anonymous methods [5]), runtime support [20], or a combination of both [6]. More akin to our research is a static analysis approach, either dataflow-based [12] or type-based [33], to security issues.

The difference in our approach is that we aim at what may be called the "common programming practice" [11] of encapsulation and immutability. There are two layers to this study. First, we strive to understand better the consequences of JAVA language features supporting immutability and encapsulation. JAVA is a particularly interesting subject, since other than being modern and widely used, it poses the challenge of coping with a lack of static binding and the possibility of dynamic class loading, making a whole program analysis next to impossible.

---

[1] John Potter, private communication, November 2000

[2] http://java.sun.com/products//jdk/1.2/docs/guide/extensions/-spec.html#sealing

Perhaps surprisingly, *sealing*, a JAVA language feature designed with security in mind, has interesting implications in terms of protection. From the language design perspective, we will see that sealing makes JAVA packages into more cohesive, modular structures. And, from the theoretical standpoint, sealing gives rise to two new interesting sorts of morphism: *oligomorphism* and *nilmorphism*.

The second layer is that of code analysis, which includes alias analysis, type analysis and call graph construction, with the attempt of *discovering* immutable entities. The bountiful `.class` format removes the need for tiresome parsing of the source code, thus making JAVA very suitable for code analysis.

The selection of `rt.jar`, the large JAVA run time library, as a code base is guided by a similar consideration. On one hand, it is a challenge to infer with, since it provides only a very partial picture of possible executions. On the other hand, any such inference is very meaningful with `rt.jar` being an ingredient of all JAVA applications. The techniques are however applicable to any library and any program, and are likely to produce more accurate results, when fed with more complete data.

Based on sealing information, we developed two sophisticated, but easy to implement, techniques: *marching forests* and *fencing* for OO type analysis in the difficult terrain of dynamic binding and incomplete program information so inherent to JAVA. Fencing and marching forests make it possible to significantly improve on the devirtualization results of Zaks, Feldman and Aizikowitz [40], which rely on plain sealing. The fact that these techniques are applicable and effective in the partial analysis context, sets them apart from classical call graph construction algorithms such as RTA and its extensions [36].

Our analysis provides concrete empirical data, which can be used by continuing theoretical work. The information elicited on particular variables is a valuable tool for program understanding and for the automatic detection of outliers (i.e., variables whose use appears to be in contradiction with what might be inferred from their declaration). At this stage, the analysis provides results on **static** variables (sometimes called class variables). To avoid the "immutable variable" oxymoron we refer to these variables as *class fields*. Currently, *instance fields* (i.e., fields defined for each instance of a class rather than for the whole class) are analyzed only to the extent required to elicite information on globals. The following reasons guide this choice:

1. *Software engineering considerations.* Global variables are generally perceived as an abomination, and even more so in OO programming. Yet, recognizing the importance of global variables in duties served by `System.out` (and its likes) and by the SINGLETON pattern [16], it is not surprising that most OO languages, including JAVA, do support them. Our findings indicate that class fields are abundant, at least in the run time library, which is used by all JAVA programs. We strive to find out how many of these are indeed global variables, or conversely, the extent of their encapsulation and immutability. Note that the encapsulation and mutability of class fields is more critical than that of instance fields. Even a **public** instance field can only be accessed using a class instance, which must be created, and a reference to it must be available. In contrast, class fields are immediately accessible once the class was loaded.

2. *Value for program understanding.* The lifetime of class fields spans from class loading, which tends to occur at an early stage during program execution, until program termination.[3] Effectively, any piece of code with access permissions to a certain class field can access it at any time, possibly causing the defining class to be loaded. Complementing the software engineering considerations, we argue that class fields, due to their longevity and potentially global access rights, can serve as key components in program understanding. One of the contributions of this paper is the discovery that most class fields in rt.jar are immutable. Conversely, the enumeration of potential violations of encapsulation and immutability of class fields makes a useful tool for pinpointing program faults.

3. *Security considerations.* The JAVA security model restricts applications from modifying global system state, as represented by class fields. For example, a famous security breach[4] was caused by exposure of a global variable, which had been believed to be encapsulated. This bug served as one of our prime motivations.

4. *Impact on performance.* Dispatch time and object size have already been recognized [14, 15] as performance penalties that OO brings along with its blessings. We note that there is an additional toll of initialization time: the loading of classes in the run time library and the execution of class fields initializers. In general, performance of JAVA is believed to be a critical issue. The fact that the JAVA Virtual Machine (JVM) has to be restarted for each execution and the abundance of small applications and applets place a greater importance on the initialization toll (see [7] for a related research).

An ongoing research at IBM [13] is the implementation of a reusable JVM, which has to be restarted only if the previous program run through it has mutated the global state. A primary hurdle to this implementation is that the huge size of the JAVA runtime library and the large number of class fields in it (see Section 4 for details) precludes manual inspection to ensure that all mutations of the global state are taken into account. The code analysis tools developed here were instrumental to this project, pinpointing the possible locations of modifications and leaks, reducing the set of suspect methods, and helping ensure that no such method is overlooked.

5. *Implementation and definitional issues.* It has long been observed [34] that the interaction of inheritance and encapsulation touches several delicate issues. When an instance field of a class C is said to be encapsulated (or immutable for that matter), then the questions of context arise: Is that variable encapsulated only within a specific instance of C, or within any its instance? Is that variable encapsulated only within C, or also within all subclasses of C? One may fathom a varying degree of refinement in the classification of possible contexts of a variable. In comparison, class fields are associated with exactly one context.

Since the instance fields were only of an auxiliary importance, our analysis did not make the possible distinctions between the different contexts in which an instance field could be initialized.

---

[3] More precisely, the life span might be terminated earlier by the rare operation of class unloading, which is even impossible for some classes.

[4] http://java.sun.com/security/getSigners.html

Our findings for class fields in rt.jar can be summarized as follows. Almost 64% of these fields are constants, about half of these being **public**. Another 1% of the class fields are globally modifiable variables. We consider such fields to be extremely problematic; we call them the "broth", since they might be spoiled by too many cooks that have access to them.

The remaining 35% consist of variables that may be immutable or not, depending on the actual runtime use. We find that 38% of these variables can be statically identified as immutable. Our study also identified that about 66% of encapsulated non-constant fields may leak, i.e., there may be external code that obtains references to parts of their internal state, therefore being able to modify them. Sealing proved to be an important factor in determining the run time immutability and leaking of class fields.

The discourse is organized as follows. Specific research questions are discussed in Section 2, in a form of taxonomy of class fields, based on their encapsulation and immutability properties. The first, lingual level of our research is presented in Section 3, where we study some of the implications of sealing at the language level, and introduce the notions of oligomorphism and nilmorphism.

The presentation of the second, empirical level of our work begins in Section 4, where we present the data set used, broken down by the criteria proposed in Section 3. Section 5 describes the novel, sealing-based, code analysis techniques and presents data on how they can be used to devirtualize polymorphic calls. In Section 6 we describe the use of these techniques for the purpose of mutability analysis.

Finally, Section 7 concludes the paper and offers a global perspective on our results. To our knowledge, this is the first empirical research of this scale on immutability and encapsulation of OO programs.

2   Taxonomy of Fields

We employ the following definition of immutability: A field is *immutable* if its state never changes after initialization. The initialization of an instance field is defined as the execution of the constructor of the containing object. A class field is considered initialized when the class initialization routine terminates. The *state* of a field is defined recursively as its value along with the state of the referenced object. The *state* of an object is the state of all of its instance fields. A class is immutable if all of its instances are immutable. The class String is thus immutable, and so (for example) is a class whose instance fields are **final** and of type String or **int**. Overall, we identified some 661 immutable classes of the run time library, which are 19% of all concrete classes.

Figure 1 depicts a taxonomy of class fields from the encapsulation/immutability point of view. Although geared towards JAVA, the taxonomy is not too specific to it. Also, the same hierarchy applies in principle to instance fields, with the added dimension of classifying these fields according to their context of instantiation as explained above.

The first distinction made in Figure 1 is between fields that are language constants and fields that are not. In JAVA, the constants are defined via the **final** keyword and are either primitives or Strings. These constants play a similar role to the constants defined in PASCAL [39] **CONST** section.

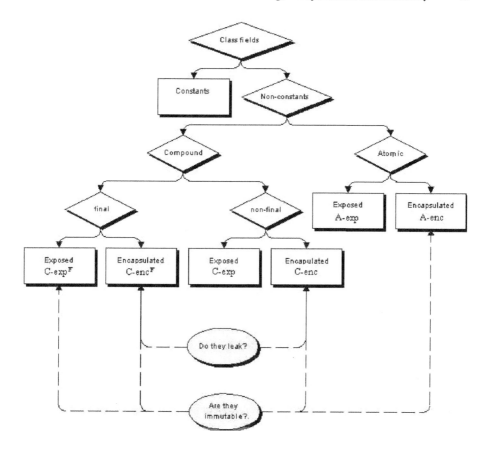

Fig. 1. Taxonomy of class fields

Next, the *non-constants* are divided into those that are *atomic*, for which the immutability of the variable is simply derived by the ability to change the value held in the variable itself, versus those *compound* variables of reference type, the state of which depends on the referenced object. As with constants in JAVA, the atomic non-constants ones are non-**final** primitives or Strings.

A field that can be accessed from outside its module (either the class or the package), is said to be *exposed*. Otherwise we say that the field is *encapsulated*. In JAVA, for example, all **private** fields are encapsulated. Section 3 shows that all the other fields are exposed unless package sealing is applied.

In what follows, we use shortcuts to denote the taxonomic categories of fields. The shortcuts are of the form $\{A|C\}\text{-}\{exp|enc\}^{\{F\}?}$, where A stands for atomic, C for compound, exp for exposed, enc for encapsulated, and the superscript F is added for **final** fields.

Non-**final** exposed fields, both atomic and compound, A-exp and C-exp, can be modified from outside the module that defines them. From a software engineering perspective, these "broth" fields are probably the worst case. All such fields are considered to be mutable, and may be indicative of bad programming style.

Atomic encapsulated fields, A-enc, serve as local variables to their respective modules. Such fields are expected and even desirable in large programs, where packages and classes serve as the unit of modularization. Their immutability is guaranteed if there is no code within the module that modifies them. For a field in the A-enc category, it is appealing to check whether it is an *outlier*, i.e., whether it is immutable and should have probably been declared as a *constant* of the module with the **final** keyword. (There is still a possibility, while arguably remote, that the field is intended to be mutable, but no changes are made to it by the current version of the code.)

Compound variables are more difficult to analyze since each of their components may have different immutability and encapsulation properties. In JAVA, just as in C++ [35], it is impossible to associate a deep immutability [21] property with a reference. The closest approximation in JAVA is a **final** declaration, which states that the reference itself cannot be modified; C++ is only slightly more expressive. A declaration of a compound variable as **final** may be interpreted as an expression of the programmer's wish to protect the reference *and its contents* from modifications.

Exposed compound **final** fields C-exp^F are immutable if they reference immutable classes. This has turned out to be a common pattern. Mutable C-exp^F and C-exp fields pose both a security and design flaw and should be avoided.

Even if a compound field is encapsulated, it still might be the case that some of its components *leak*, i.e., external code obtains references, and thereby access abilities, to some of its components. Even if leaking occurs, a C-enc or C-enc^F field could still be immutable, specifically, when the leaked component is of an immutable class type.

As a side comment we note the similarity of leaking to "escape" analysis [4, 9, 38]. The main difference is that the term "escape" pertains to a certain JAVA method or context of execution.

Escape analysis is carried out mostly for the purposes of garbage collection. It should be noted however that the application of sealing and the code analysis techniques we contribute are applicable in escape analysis, just as some of the escape analysis techniques are applicable for our purposes.

In summary, the main points observed in this section were:

- Good software engineering practice prescribes to avoid non-**final** exposed fields.
- Code analysis is required for testing encapsulated fields and **final** exposed fields for immutability.
- Code analysis is required for detecting breach of encapsulation, nicknamed "leaking", of encapsulated compound fields. Such leakage may be indicative of programming errors (and as observed in the previous section, may hinder optimization of a rebootable JVM).

3   Sealing and Encapsulation

To manage the rights of inheriting classes and the accessibility of fields and methods, JAVA provides an elaborate set of language rules involving access modifiers: **private**, **protected**, **public**, and default *package* access level. Closer examination reveals that access modifiers constitute only a basic, coarse, and limited encapsulation mechanism. It is coarse precisely because the dynamic nature of JAVA excludes any sort of whole program analysis. Other than **private**, access modifiers fail to draw an encapsulation boundary around an entity that is known to a human or an automatic analyzer. A **protected** entity may be accessed from unanalyzed classes that inherit it or from unanalyzed classes added to the defining package. A package level entity may always be accessed from unanalyzed classes added to the defining package.

Immunity from all changes, i.e., immutability, is one of the strongest forms of encapsulation. Again, support for immutability is limited in JAVA, since fields denoted as **final** are not immutable, unless very specific conditions are met. In particular, the object referenced by a **final** field does not receive any protection from external changes. In a similar fashion, a severe limitation of access modifiers is that an object referenced by (say) a **private** field is not generally guarded from external accesses. A **private** reference does not grant any protection to the referenced object, if the reference itself is leaked.

Pivotal to this research is the regard of *sealing*, a simple mechanism residing at the Java Archive (JAR) level and conceived with security purposes in mind, as a powerful lingual-level, encapsulation mechanism! A package contained in a JAR file may be marked as sealed, in which case it must be entirely contained in that JAR file. Any attempt to load a violating class will fail, throwing a java.lang.SecurityException exception.

A recent paper by Ghemawat et al. [17] exploits fields' access restrictions to derive useful properties; their optimizations rely on the assumption that the contents of the class path do not change between compilation time and run time. Zaks et al. [40] presented an interesting application of sealing for code optimization, specifically devirtualization of method calls. In contrast, our perspective raises sealing from the optimization and byte code level, and regards it as a legitimate *lingual construct*, drawing a crisp encapsulation boundary around packages. Sealed packages serve as closed modules that the programmer, or the analysis tool, can examine as a whole.

Even when regarded as a lingual construct, we see that there is no choice other than placing the seal mark in the JAR file. A JAVA package is defined as the set of all classes that declare themselves part of this package. There is no single file that defines the package, and if not compressed in a sealed archive, it may even spread across several directories.

Sealing turns a JAVA package into a cohesive unit of modularization, larger than a class. We assume that the language processor (a compiler, or other static analyzer), and likewise the programmer, have access to the entire code of the sealed package. Also, it is henceforth tacitly assumed that all packages are sealed unless specifically noted otherwise.

An important difference between classes and packages in their capacity as units of modularization is that classes can be extended by inheritance, whereas sealed packages cannot. There are multiple non-trivial consequences to the encapsulation interplay when an extensible class is embedded in a sealed, non-extensible package. We devote considerable attention to the study of these consequences with the expectation that sealed packages will quickly become standard in JAVA libraries and application code. This expectation is supported by the fact that in JDK 1.2., which spans diverse areas such as networking, GUI, databases, and audio, only two packages out of 127 are not sealed.

Due to the dynamic nature of JAVA, it is impossible in general to bound the set of heirs[5]. We say that these classes and interfaces are *polymorphic*, since a reference to them may assume an unbounded number of different dynamic types. *Monomorphic* classes are classes whose references can only take one dynamic type. For example, all **final** classes are monomorphic.

Sealing gives rise to yet a third sort of classes—the *oligomorphic* classes. A class (or an interface for that matter) is *oligomorphic* if a reference to it can assume dynamic types taken from a bounded set, which is known to the language processor. That is to say, the set of heirs to this class is known. Since the similarities between the different shapes are systematic rather than coincidental, oligomorphism is very different from ad-hoc polymorphism [8]. We think of oligomorphism as a restricted version of (inclusion) polymorphism, and of monomorphism as a restricted version of oligomorphism.

As an example, consider Figure 2 that depicts a sealed package P and three hierarchies in it.

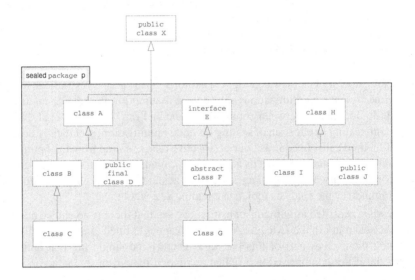

Fig. 2. An example of a sealed package with oligomorphic classes

We see that class J is non-oligomorphic because it is **public** and not **final**; classes outside P can extend it. Also, class X cannot be oligomorphic, because it has classes in P inheriting from it, even though it is not in that package. Class H is non-**public** and hence cannot be directly extended from outside P. However, H is poly-

---

[5] Since JAVA has three different kinds of "inheritance" we use the term heir. In accordance with EIFFEL terminology [27], we say that class or interface A is a proper heir of a class or interface B if A directly or indirectly **extends** or **implements** B; A is a heir of B, written $A \leq B$, if $A = B$ or A is a proper heir of B.

morphic since it has a polymorphic heir J. Classes C, D, F, G, I, and interface E are monomorphic (and hence also oligomorphic). Class D, because it is **final**, classes C, G, and I, because they have no heirs within the package and are not declared **public**. Interface E and abstract class F are monomorphic because they have only one concrete class, specifically G, implementing them. The non-**public** classes A and B are oligomorphic. B, because its only proper heir (C) is monomorphic, and A, because all its proper heirs are oligomorphic.

A bottom-up algorithm for identifying the morphism level of a class should be clear from the example. In fact, there is an easy class hierarchy analysis algorithm that outputs, for each class or interface, the sets of its concrete heirs, along with a raised flag if additional heirs may exist in other packages. (A similar algorithm can be found in [40]).

It is interesting to note that there is yet another degenerate morphism level. We say that a class or interface is *nilmorphic* if the set of its concrete heirs is empty. Thus, a non-**public** abstract class (or an interface) with no heirs in the package is nilmorphic. Nilmorphic classes give an extra tool in the hands of the OO programmer. They can be used for creating non-instantiable modules, e.g., for realizing constant pools, and other packaging of global functionality. Since in JAVA a class cannot be both **abstract** and **final** at the same time, the technique of defining **private** constructors was traditionally used for making nilmorphic classes. Sealing provides a more elegant solution, which also allows non-instantiable classes to be organized in a hierarchy.

Sealing can in many cases provide the assurance that an analysis has covered all methods that can possibly access an entity, even if that entity is not **private**, thus creating a statically bounded scope that is larger than a single class. The catch is, however, that access rights to entities within a sealed package can be obtained from outside the package by means of inheritance. Thus, sealing is not hermetic! Beyond the theoretical interest and the application in optimization, the importance of oligomorphism is that it helps to identify entities for which access rights do not leak to outside the sealing boundary.

We use the term *sealed class field* for an encapsulated **static** field declared in a sealed package. The following is an operational classification of sealed class fields:

1. All **private static** fields are sealed.
2. All package-scoped **static** fields are sealed.
3. **protected static** fields are sealed if they are declared in an oligomorphic class.
4. **public static** fields are sealed if they are declared in an oligomorphic class or interface that has no **public** heirs.

The last two clauses in the above definition guard against leaking by inheritance through the sealing boundary. Suppose for example that a **protected** static member s is defined in class H of Figure 2. Then, although s cannot be accessed as $H.s$ from outside p, it is not sealed since it can be accessed as $J.s$. Access rights to **static public** members may leak in a similar manner.

A similar leaking of access rights to instance fields may occur. The main difference is that such leaking affects the incarnations of the field within the *inheriting* class. In the last example, if s was an instance field, then the expression $J.s$ does not grant access to a field s in instances of H. We say that a field f is *weakly-sealed* in class X if sealing prevents access to f in all instances of X. It is *strongly-sealed* in case it is weakly-sealed in X and in all heirs of X.

If f is declared in Y, and X is an heir of Y ($X \leq Y$), then f is weakly sealed in X if it is **private, protected** or has package scope. If f is **public**, then it is weakly sealed if every class or interface Z, $Z \leq Y$ and $X \leq Y$, is sealed. Field f is strongly sealed if X is oligomorphic and it is weakly sealed in every $Z \leq X$.

The above definitions may be extended to class and instance methods. A class method is sealed under the same conditions as a class field being sealed; in such a case, it cannot be externally called. The definition of sealed instance methods is more intricate since such a method can be invoked from outside its package, even though it cannot be externally referenced. A case in point is a method defined in an oligomorphic class, which overrides a method in an ancestor polymorphic class. Such a method can be invoked from outside, provided that a reference to that object finds its way there.

In a similar fashion, we may define the notion of sealed classes and interfaces. A similar intricacy applies here, since even if a class or an interface is not **public**, code external to the package can gain access to instances of this class by ways of polymorphism. Note that sealed classes and interfaces are not necessarily oligomorphic.

At this stage, we did not employ the definitions of sealed classes, interfaces, instance fields and instance methods in the analysis. The benefits to the accuracy of the analysis in doing so is a matter for further research.

4   Data Set

Our data set consisted of the JAVA runtime library, which is included as part of the JAVA Development Kit (JDK) version 1.2 [6]. All .class files of this library are compressed together into a single file, rt.jar. Together, the data comprises 4,239 classes and interfaces grouped together in 127 packages, i.e., on average there are about 33 classes and interfaces in a package. With the exception of two packages (sun.io and java.text.resources), comprising 33 classes and no interfaces, all packages in the run time library are sealed.

As many as 3,516 (83%) of all classes are concrete (non-**abstract**). Of those, 699 classes are **final**; this forms 16% of all classes. Sealing reveals an additional number of 1110 classes (26%) as being monomorphic. (Recall that monomorphic class is not necessarily **final**, and may even have heirs.)

Figure 3 shows the distribution of morphism levels of classes in our data set.

The large fraction (42.1%) of monomorphic classes may be surprising. These are topped by the small fraction (1.3%) of truly oligomorphic classes. Only one class was identified as nilmorphic.[7] We were somewhat surprised by this finding since the architecture of the run time library includes a large number of classes and interfaces that appear to serve as constant pools.

---

[6] http://java.sun.com/products/jdk/1.2/

[7] Manual inspection revealed that it was an interface defined in a non-**public** class, intended for future code evolution.

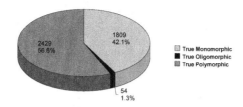

Fig. 3. Distribution of morphism types in the JDK

The run time library has 35,999 method declarations, including overriding methods, but only 31,490 method bodies. The remaining 4,509 methods are either **native** (1,109 methods) or **abstract** (3,400 methods).

Turning to our primary focus, we found that there are 6,650 **static** fields in the JDK. An indication for the popularity of **static** fields is the fact that the JDK has only 8,842 non-**static** fields. Thus, as many as 43% of all fields are **static**! In comparison, there are only 3,968 **static** methods, i.e., 11% of the total number of methods.

On average, each class has 1.6 **static** fields. However, 3197 (48%) classes do not define any statics at all. Figure 4 shows the distribution in the number of static fields defined by a class.

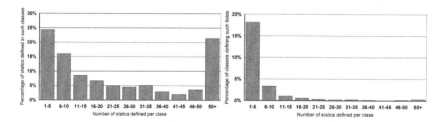

Fig. 4. Distribution of the number of class fields defined in a class

As can be seen in Figure 4, most classes define only a small number of class fields (if any). There are few classes with a large number of class fields. Such classes are probably made for the purpose of defining global constants such as character names. We call these classes *constant pools*. Interestingly, most of the class variables are defined either in classes each defining very few (less than five) class fields, or in classes each defining a large number (more than 50) of class fields.

Table 1 presents a breakdown of class fields by their access level, the morphism of their declared type, and their **final** characteristics. Strings are regarded here as atomic fields, and are not counted as variables that refer to an oligomorphic type. Thus, rows (and columns) of the table represent disjoint sets of fields.

It is interesting to note that most cells of the table have zero or very few fields. In other words, various language features are far from being orthogonal. The correlated use

	private	Default	protected		public		Total	
			sealed	unsealed	sealed	unsealed		
final primitive	728 (10%)	354 (5%)	125 (1%)	51 (0%)	70 (1%)	2,194 (32%)	3,522 (52%)	
Non-**final** primitive	114 (1%)	38 (0%)	0 (0%)	11 (0%)	1 (0%)	14 (0%)	178 (2%)	
final String	194 (2%)	69 (1%)	0 (0%)	11 (0%)	30 (0%)	416 (6%)	720 (10%)	
Non-**final** String	31 (0%)	11 (0%)	0 (0%)	3 (0%)	0 (0%)	3 (0%)	48 (0%)	
final oligomorphic	29 (0%)	16 (0%)	2 (0%)	0 (0%)	0 (0%)	417 (6%)	464 (6%)	
Non-**final** oligomorphic	55 (0%)	174 (2%)	0 (0%)	4 (0%)	0 (0%)	0 (0%)	233 (4%)	
final true polymorphic	313 (4%)	60 (0%)	0 (0%)	7 (0%)	1 (0%)	408 (6%)	789 (11%)	
Non-**final** true polymorphic	414 (6%)	249 (3%)	0 (0%)	28 (0%)	0 (0%)	5 (0%)	696 (10%)	
Total	1,878 (28%)	971 (14%)	137 (2%)	105 (1%)	102 (1%)	3,457 (51%)	6,650 (100%)	

Table 1. Signature analysis of class fields

of these suggests that programmers employ them together in specific patterns to express a deeper notion of abstraction. These findings give empirical support and motivation to the theoretical research on ownership, encapsulation and even more advanced lingual constructs.

In Table 1 we see that nearly 64% (4,242) of all class fields are JAVA *constants* (**final** primitive or **final** String) whose values cannot be modified at runtime. As might be expected, the majority (2,610) of these constants are **public**, i.e., true globals.

The number of global primitive variables (14), and global string variables (3) seems small; together they comprise less than 0.3% of all class fields. Nonetheless, good software engineering practice and the fact that their globality affects all JAVA programs dictates that there should be none.

We now examine the degree of exposure of the remaining fields. If no sealing analysis is applied, all fields with non **private** access level are exposed. Summing the corresponding columns in Table 1, with the exception of the language constant rows, we obtain that 1452 fields (22% of the total number) are exposed.

With sealing, only columns marked as *unsealed* correspond to exposed fields. This reduces the number of exposed non-constants by 39% to 890 fields.

We would have liked these 890 class fields (13% of the total) to be immutable. Table 1 shows that indeed 832 of these are **final**. However, this declaration does not protect against modifications of the referenced object. Without further analysis, it cannot be established whether such variables are indeed immutable.

A similar concern arises for the 1,518 class fields, in which access is limited to the analyzed library. It may occur that while the field itself can be accessed only from within the library, the object referenced by it is accessible from outside the library.

Returning to the issue of oligomorphism discussed in the previous section, we observe that besides the fields' accessibility, class oligomorphism also affects the structure of the objects referenced by the fields. Table 1 shows that more than half of all the fields of oligomorphic types are String fields. However, it is interesting to observe that non-String oligomorphic fields follow the pattern that is characteristic of String fields, to be **final** and accessible from outside the library. This is very different from the fields of polymorphic types, which tend to be encapsulated.

Figure 5 depicts a breakdown of class fields in the data set, according to the categories of Figure 1. The bars below the leaf nodes show how sealing affects the partitioning of a certain category of fields into two disjoint sets, exposed- vs. encapsulated fields.

Each leaf in the taxonomy tree (except for the JAVA constants), corresponds to a subset of some category of fields, and represents either the set of exposed fields or the set of encapsulated fields in this category. The bars below the leaf nodes show how sealing affects the distribution of fields between the two nodes corresponding to a certain category. Observe the strong effect that sealing has on classification of non-**final** fields. Such fields, if exposed, are externally modifiable and thus problematic from both the design and the security points of view. The diagram shows that while without sealing a sizable chunk of non-final fields is exposed, sealing reduces their number from 81 to 31 for atomic fields and from 460 to 37 for compounds.

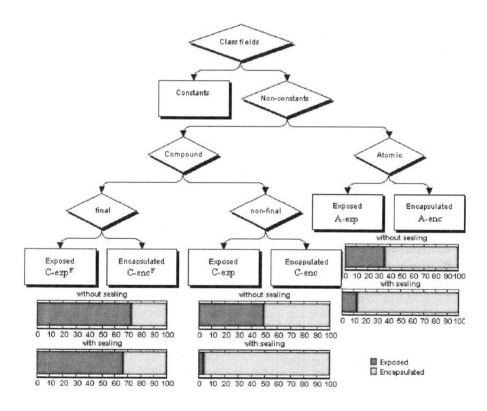

Fig. 5. Breakdown of class fields in JAVA

5   Sealing and the OO Type Analysis Problem

The object-oriented type-analysis (OOTA) problem is to determine, under the *all paths probable* assumption, the set of possible types of each variable at every program location. If the problem is constrained to the most interesting programming locations, i.e., virtual call sites, then it is commonly known as the *call graph construction* (CGC) problem, which is at the core of every OO code analysis. The complexity of a precise OOTA (or CGC) [18] is a result of the recursive nature of its definition: at a virtual call site, the probable paths are dependent on the possible types of the receiver.

CGC becomes even more challenging in a setting of partial program analysis. Every virtual call site has then the potential of invoking code on which the analyzer has absolutely no information. The worst case assumptions that must be made on this code carry an adverse effect on the results of the analysis. In the domain of whole program analysis, algorithms are measured by their ability to reduce the number of target implementations of a virtual call. In partial program analysis, the challenge is primarily in showing that a virtual call site may never lead to an external target. A reduction in the branching degree is a secondary objective.

Perhaps the most rudimentary algorithm for OOTA is *Class Hierarchy Analysis* (CHA), in which the possible types of a variable are the concrete heirs of its static type declaration. There is a minor difficulty in applying CHA to the JAVA bytecode language, in which locations in the stack frame have no global static type declaration. As an alternative, CHA uses the base method identification as it appears in the virtual call instruction, in order to determine the possible call targets, which are the set of overriding methods. CHA is of minimal value in partial program analysis because the whole inheritance hierarchy is not available to the analyzer. Thus, a simple minded CHA analysis of JAVA determines that a virtual call has *bounded branching* only if it refers to a **final** method, or to a non-**final** method in a **final** class.

Sealed calls analysis (SCA) [40] is the natural extension to CHA, where sealing is used to identify oligomorphic classes. This makes it possible to bound the branching of more call sites. In the remainder of this section, we present two new techniques: marching forests and fencing, which employ sealing even more effectively in the difficult setting of partial program analysis.

Our first technique, *marching forests*, is an intraprocedural dataflow analysis to determine the set of possible types that may be stored at each stack frame location. The process is similar in principle to the working of the .class file verifier, and specifically to the dataflow analysis it carries out in order to determine that no runtime type error occurs [26, Section 4.9.2]. The improvement is that instead of managing the most general type known for each slot s in the method frame and for each instruction ℓ, marching forests manages a set of trees

$$F(s, \ell) = \{\langle t_1, b_1\rangle, \ldots, \langle t_n, b_n\rangle\},$$

where for $i = 1, \ldots, n$, t_i is a class, an interface, or a primitive type, and b_i is a label drawn from the set $\{\mathsf{exact}, \mathsf{tree}\}$. The set $F(s, \ell)$ means that the analysis has so far discovered that the slot s at instruction ℓ may be of any of the types t_i, $i = 1, \ldots, n$ (provided of course they are concrete); in addition, its type may also be any concrete type that is an heir of t_i, in case $b_i = \mathsf{tree}$. If $b_i = \mathsf{exact}$, then the type of s in ℓ cannot be a proper heir of t_i; such exact type information is discovered at object creation. The complexity of the resulting dataflow algorithm is not much greater than that of the verifier.

The algorithm is most effective when it can use oligomorphism information. If all of t_i are oligomorphic, then regardless of the value of b_i, it is guaranteed that s has a bounded set of types in ℓ.

Moreover, it could be the case that the most general type of two oligomorphic types is non-oligomorphic. For example, consider Figure 6, which shows part of the implementation of Figure 2.

```
package P;
abstract class F implements E extends X {
  // ...
};
class A extends X {
  protected A a;
  public F f;
  void foo(int i) {
    X x = a;
    if (i % 2 == 0)
      x = f;
    x.bar(); // A virtual call site
  }
  // ...
};
```

Fig. 6. Part of the implementation of package p of Figure 2

The virtual call site to bar in method foo of class A is a merge point of the dataflow analysis. The verifier can only assert that at that point, the type of x is X, which is the least common ancestor of A and F. Since X is non-oligomorphic, the SCA analysis of [40] cannot conclude that it does not lead to an external code; in particular the call cannot be devirtualized regardless of which implementations of bar are known.

The marching forests technique records its conclusion for the type of x at this program location as the set $\{\langle A, \text{tree}\rangle, \langle F, \text{tree}\}$. It follows that at this point, x cannot be anything other than of type A, B, C, D, and G, and the call never leads to an external code. If, in addition, bar has an implementation only in class X, then the call can be devirtualized.

The *fencing* technique tries to globally determine the set of types that may be assigned to a certain field. The fence is an exhaustive global list of all instructions that make assignment into this field. The set of possible types of the field is the union of the sets of types that each of the instructions in the fence may assign to it.

The fence of a **private** field is built by simply examining all methods defined in the class. Sealing takes the technique much further by making it possible to build a fence around all sealed fields that are not necessarily **private**. The crucial observation is that if the field is sealed, then it is possible to examine *all* methods that may access it. Since access rights to a non-**private** sealed field are not limited to methods in its class, the fence, in general, transgresses the class boundary.

Fencing can rely on the results of various intraprocedural analyses, including the one made by the verifier, or the more sophisticated marching forests. Moreover, the information obtained by fencing may even be fed back into the intraprocedural analyzer. This suggests a new sort of dataflow analysis, which stands between intra- and inter-procedural analysis. For example, one can apply marching forests and fencing iteratively on all methods of a package until relaxation is reached.

CHA determines the set of possible call targets by identifying all overriding methods that are applicable for the concrete heirs of a certain base type. The marching forests technique improves CHA, since the types it records are always heirs of the base type used by CHA, thus reducing the branching degree of virtual calls. Both techniques coincide for those instructions that retrieve a field's value (e.g., `getstatic`), by simply using the field's static type. Fencing enhances the marching forest analysis at these instructions by taking into account only a subset of heirs of the field's declared type.

Table 2 presents the efficacy of the techniques presented here for devirtualization of call sites.

	Without Sealing	With Sealing
Class Hierarchy Analysis	54.0%	57.7%
Marching Forests	56.7%	61.1%
Fencing after Marching Forests	58.9%	63.9%

Table 2. Efficacy of the analysis techniques for devirtualization

In Table 2, we see that vanilla SCA [40] devirtualizes an additional 3.7% of all call sites beyond what is achieved by CHA. In comparison, marching forests adds 2.7% devirtualized calls to CHA, while fencing add another 2.2%, for a total of 4.9%.

Fencing and marching forests do not compete with sealing. In fact, together they work slightly better after sealing has been applied, devirtualizing an additional 5.0% of all call sites. In total, we can achieve an additional 9.9% of devirtualized calls, which we suspect is getting close to the actual number of monomorphic call sites.

In the case where no devirtualization is possible, the techniques may have been effective in reducing the out degree of the call graph. However, this effect has been observed only in a negligible (less than 0.5%) number of call sites.

6   Sealing and Mutability Analysis

After having discussed the application of sealing for OOTA, we turn to investigate its effect on the more difficult *mutability analysis* problem. The difficulty lies in the need of alias analysis for tracking down all the objects that a certain variable may refer to, and showing that these cannot be modified in the analysis scope, or leaked outside. The details of our algorithm can be found in [32]; here we provide the essential definitions required for understanding the various techniques and the results.

Let v be a variable, and let $R(v)$ be the set of objects reachable from v. In saying that v is *modified*, we mean that its value is changed after initialization. A modification of $R(v)$ is a change to the values stored in the objects of $R(v)$ after v is initialized.

Four conditions must be met in order for v to be immutable.

1. *shallow internal immutability* (SII): no internal code, i.e., code within the analysis scope modifies v.
2. *deep internal immutability* (DII): no internal code modifies $R(v)$.
3. *shallow external immutability* (SXI): v cannot be modified by external code.
4. *deep external immutability* (DXI): $R(v)$ cannot be modified by external code.

The conditions are recursive in nature since a leaking field can be identified as immutable if it references an immutable class. To show that a class is immutable, it is necessary to show that each of its instance fields are also immutable.

We discuss three mutability analyses:

1. *Signature analysis:* examining access modifiers only; no analysis is performed on method bodies.
2. *Intra-analysis:* processing method bodies and applying intra-procedural dataflow techniques such as marching forests and fencing to get more accurate information on the possible run time types of a field; no CGC is carried out.
3. *Inter-analysis:* enhancing the intra-analysis by applying inter-procedural dataflow techniques to elicit aliasing information.

The above trio treat SXI in the same fashion: it is trivially satisfied for all encapsulated fields and for all **final** fields. Sealing greatly contributes here. As can be seen in Table 1, without sealing, 614 non-**final** fields are identified as encapsulated; with sealing, this number grows by 77% to 1,087.

SII is a simple condition where the analyses differ. With signature analysis, SII holds only for **final** fields. Intra- (and inter-) analysis refines this check by examining instructions that assign values to fields. Our current implementation does not use call graph information to distinguish methods callable only from initialization methods. Thus, sealing does not yet contribute to SII.

Deep immutability, i.e., DII and DXI, is much more challenging. Signature analysis examines the morphism level of the field's declared type in order to assert DII and DXI. Both conditions hold if the static type is oligomorphic, and each concrete heir is classified as an immutable class. Here the role of sealing is in the identification of classes as oligomorphic.

Intra-analysis handles deep immutability issues by checking that all the possible run time types of a field, as derived from a fenced marching forests analysis, are immutable. Here the impact of sealing is through fencing and marching forests.

Inter-analysis makes a stronger attack on deep immutability by conducting inter-procedural alias analysis in all cases where intra-analysis fails. DII is asserted by monitoring all instructions that assign a value to a field and by checking whether the modified object is reachable from a class variable. Similarly, to assert DXI, we monitor potentially leaking instructions, e.g., instructions which return a reference or pass it as a parameter to external code. Here the added duty of sealing is in constructing the call graph, which is instrumental in any inter-procedural analysis.

Let us return now to the mutability and leaking questions as posed by Figure 1. Note that categories C-exp and A-exp (non-**final** exposed fields) are trivially mutable.

The immutability in four leaf nodes, namely categories $\mathsf{C\text{-}exp^F}$, $\mathsf{C\text{-}enc^F}$, $\mathsf{C\text{-}enc}$, and $\mathsf{A\text{-}enc}$, remains to be determined. Out of these categories, the leaking question pertains only to categories $\mathsf{C\text{-}enc^F}$ and $\mathsf{C\text{-}enc}$. (Leaking is not applicable to atomic fields, as in $\mathsf{A\text{-}enc}$, and is irrelevant to exposed fields, as in $\mathsf{C\text{-}exp^F}$). As explained above, leaking may be indicative of programming errors and may even be a source of security breaches.

Examining the four categories in light of the four conditions we find that (i) leaking coincides with failure of DXI, (ii) SII and SXI trivially hold for $\mathsf{C\text{-}exp^F}$ and $\mathsf{C\text{-}enc^F}$, (iii) SXI is tautology for $\mathsf{C\text{-}enc^F}$, $\mathsf{C\text{-}enc}$, and $\mathsf{A\text{-}enc}$, (iv) conditions DII and DXI are applicable to $\mathsf{C\text{-}exp^F}$, $\mathsf{C\text{-}enc^F}$, and $\mathsf{C\text{-}enc}$ only, and (v) SII is only relevant in categories $\mathsf{C\text{-}enc}$ and $\mathsf{A\text{-}enc}$.

Figure 7 reiterates Figure 1 showing the results of the inter-analysis.

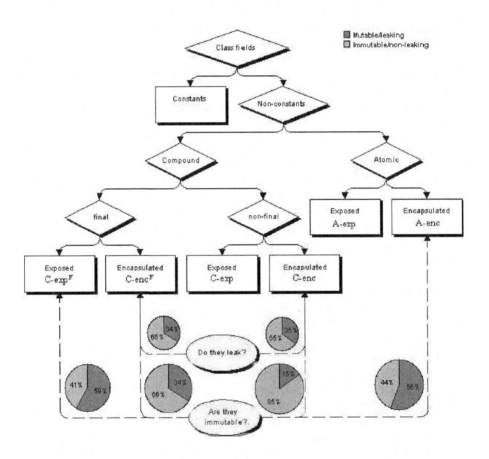

Fig. 7. Results of the inter-analysis with respect to the taxonomy of Figure 1

As can be seen in Figure 7, our analysis finds that a large portion (59%) of $\mathsf{C\text{-}exp^F}$ fields are immutable. This finding is in accordance with our expectation that these fields are nothing but global compound constants. Their sheer number empirically supports the effort to introduce a deep immutability feature into JAVA, e.g., in the manner suggested in [25]. We expect that a more precise analysis would identify as global constants an even greater fraction of this category. However, we found actual modifications to 8% of the fields in this category, which are suspected as being outliers.

In category C-exp^F, language features are lacking with respect to programming practice. In contrast, category A-enc is an example in which programming practice fails to make appropriate use of a valuable language feature. Out of the 195 fields in this category, 109 are found to be immutable. Even though some of these may be modified by native code, most of them are better declared as **final**.

It is somewhat disappointing to find that only for 34% of the C-enc^F fields we could prove that they are immutable. However, we found that in 87% of the fields in this category no state modification was detected in the internal code. Thus, the main reason for labeling the fields in this category as mutable is leaking. Two conclusions follow. First, we notice that as might be expected, there is a relatively small number of fields in this category that are modified by internal code. Second, we observe that it is difficult to prove that fields do not leak.

The second conclusion also applies in category C-enc. We observe a very similar extent of leaking in categories C-enc^F (66%) and C-enc (65%). This is probably an indication that the leaking analysis is not too powerful, and is probably overly conservative in marking fields as leaking.

In comparison, we find that only 30% of the C-enc fields do not undergo modifications within the analysis scope. The huge gap between this percentage and that of category C-enc^F is an indication that the use of **final** is strongly correlated with a deep mutability intention.

In category C-enc, 15% of the fields are provably immutable, which means that both their value and state cannot be modified. These 139 fields are outliers, and should probably be declared as **final**.

Figure 8 explains the impact of sealing in the three analyses.

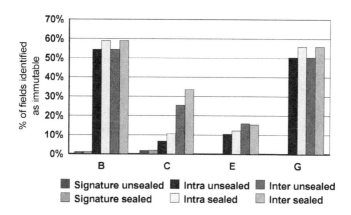

Fig. 8. Percentage of immutable fields identified by the various analysis algorithms in categories C-exp^F, C-enc^F, C-enc, and A-enc

In Figure 8 we first observe that signature analysis produces very poor results, and sealing contributes very little. The other two analyses produce significantly better results, although there is no great difference between intra- and inter-analysis. Sealing improves the results in each of these and in each of the categories by 5 to 7%.

Figure 9 compares the ability of the analyses to prove that fields do not leak.

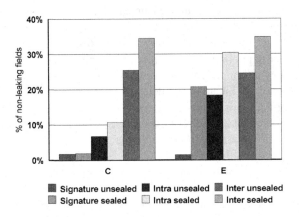

Fig. 9. Percentage of non-leaking fields identified by the various analysis algorithms in categories C-enc^F and C-enc

In Figure 9, we see that most fields are suspect of leakage. This time we see a significant difference between the three analysis levels. Again, we see that sealing improves each of the algorithms, with as much as 12% and even 19% improvement. It is remarkable that in category C-enc, signature analysis with sealing outperforms intra-analysis without sealing.

Finally, we note that the application of sealing changes the breakdown between categories C-exp^F and C-enc^F, C-exp and C-enc, and A-exp and A-enc. Thus Figures 8 and 9 are slightly misleading since the comparison of the algorithms is done on somewhat different sets of fields. When comparing the algorithms based on unified categories: C-exp^F with C-enc^F, C-exp with C-enc, and A-exp with A-enc, similar results were found.

7   Discussion

To our knowledge, this is the first empirical research of this scale on immutability and encapsulation of OO programs. In view of the intractable nature [18] of OO static analysis, our algorithms, just as any other algorithm for problems of this kind, cannot aspire to be more than a *heuristic*. The first criterion for evaluating a heuristic is its run time. In our analyses, this was found to increase almost linearly with the size of the code base.

The accuracy of the analysis is an equally important criterion, but it is much more difficult to evaluate. In the C-enc^F category (Figure 7), for example, we were able to show that about one third of the fields are immutable and do not leak. Our conservative analysis provides little information on the *actual* number of leaking or mutating fields. In many ways, the difficulty here is similar to that of estimating the number of polymorphic call sites, as required for evaluating algorithms for OOTA. It has been standard practice to bound below the number of monomorphic call sites based on execution logs. Applying a similar technique for our problems is more difficult for two reasons. First, checking immutability and leaking by tracing a log is tantamount to the resource consuming task of dynamically maintaining object graphs. Second, a large and diverse suite of programs is required to cover the mammoth and heterogeneous run time library.

As with any other heuristic, ours can be improved by using more sophisticated and accurate techniques. For example, a plausible conjecture is that using some of the alias analysis algorithms common in escape analysis may strengthen some of the measurements. In the realm of OO code analysis, the contribution of this paper is in showing that access level, and in particular sealing, a seemingly innocent mechanism, can be used in a sophisticated, yet efficient manner in code analysis. Two specific mechanisms for doing so are the marching forests and the fencing analysis techniques.

Our work has not yet exhausted the power of sealing for the purpose of code analysis. As hinted above, with sealing, a more precise analysis of instance fields is possible, which in turn will benefit the analysis of class fields. Also, a more accurate construction of the call graph is possible, by aggressively using sealing to determine the externally callable methods.

An even more demanding exploitation of sealing raises several interesting questions. For example, we may want to produce more specialized results, based on the part of the library which is used. Interesting from the program understanding and the language design perspective is the issue of immutability of fields, and the extent to which this property is preserved across inheritance lines. Also valuable is the classification of methods to categories such as *inspectors, mutators,* and *revealers* (returning reference to internal state). A finer categorization could be the classification of parameters as *input-, output-* and *input-output.* We leave all these for continuing research.

A very useful artifact of our analysis is a list of potential mutation- and leaking points of each class field. This list was used by the team behind the reusable JVM project [13] to identify those methods whose invocation requires a reboot. Another application of this list is in guiding programmers to better protect fields that are intended to be encapsulated or immutable.

Manual inspection of this list was also very instructive. We noticed hundreds of cases of lazy initialization of globals, following the pattern

if (x == **null**) x = **new** X(...);

It would be useful to enhance the analysis to recognize this pattern as an initialization rather than modification code.

In many other cases, we found that our analysis was over-conservative. However, it was also a recurring phenomena that only portions, and sometimes very specific portions, of an object were leaked or mutated.

We now highlight some of our finding pertaining to the theoretical language research and to program understanding. We first found that most fields are language constants. We found 68 globally accessible variables, out of which 31 were atomic (A-exp) and 37 were compound (C-exp). We focused on the remaining four categories (C-exp^F, C-enc^F, C-enc, and A-enc) in which we found 2,350 variables (35% of all class fields). We noticed both cases in which some language features were under-used and cases in which they were not sufficient for representing the programmer's intentions.

We identified two new language theoretic notions: oligomorphism and nilmorphism, which are by-products of sealing, and outlined some guidelines on how these might be used in the design. The architecture of the JDK leads us to believe that these concepts might find their use in forthcoming versions.

Acknowledgements Valuable comments made by Bilha Mendelson are gratefully acknowledged. Ronen Lerner implemented parts of this project. We thank Larry Koved for his inspiring comments and for sharing his enthusiasm for this problem. We also thank an anonymous reviewer for his thoughtful comments.

References

[1] P. S. Almeida. Balloon types: Controlling sharing of state in data types. In M. Akşit and S. Matsuoka, editors, *Proceedings of the 11th European Conference on Object-Oriented Programming*, number 1241 in Lecture Notes in Computer Science, pages 32–59, Jyväskylä, Finland, June 9-13 1997. ECOOP'97, Springer Verlag.

[2] K. Arnold and J. Gosling. *The Java Programming Language*. The Java Series. Addison-Wesley, 1996.

[3] E. Bertino, editor. *Proceedings of the 14th European Conference on Object-Oriented Programming*, number 1850 in Lecture Notes in Computer Science, Sophia Antipolis and Cannes, France, June 12–16 2000. ECOOP 2000, Springer Verlag.

[4] B. Blanchet. Escape analysis for Object Oriented languages. Application to Java. In OOPSLA 1999 [30], pages 20–34.

[5] B. Bokowski and J. Vitek. Confined types. In OOPSLA 1999 [30], pages 82–96.

[6] C. Bryce and C. Razafimahefa. An approach to safe object sharing. In OOPSLA 2000 [31], pages 367–381.

[7] B. Calder, C. Krintz, and U. Hölzle. Reducing transfer delay using Java class file splitting and prefetching. In OOPSLA 1999 [30], pages 276–291.

[8] L. Cardelli and P. Wegner. On understanding types, data abstractions, and polymorphism. *ACM Comput. Surv.*, 17(4):471–522, Dec. 1985.

[9] J. D. Choi, M. Gupta, M. Serrano, V. C. Sreedhar, and S. Midkiff. Escape analysis for Java. In OOPSLA 1999 [30], pages 1–19.

[10] D. G. Clarke, J. M. Potter, and J. Noble. Ownership types for flexible alias protection. In *Proceedings of the 13th Annual Conference on Object-Oriented Programming Systems, Languages, and Applications*, pages 48–64, Vancouver, British Columbia, Oct.18-22 1998. OOPSLA'98, ACM SIGPLAN Notices 33(10) Oct. 1998.

[11] T. Cohen and J. Y. Gil. Self-calibration of metrics of Java methods. In *Proceedings of the International Conference on Technology of Object-Oriented Languages and Systems* [37], pages 94–106.

[12] D. Denning. A lattice model of secure information flow. *Commun. ACM*, pages 236–243, 1976.

[13] D. Dillenberger, R. Bordawekar, C. W. Clark, D. Durand, D. Emmes, O. Gohda, S. Howard, M. F. Oliver, F. Samuel, and R. W. S. John. Building a Java Virtual Machine for server

applications: The JVM on OS/390. *IBM Systems Journal*, 39(1):194–210, 2000. Reprint Order No. G321-5723. [8].

[14] K. Driesen and U. Hölzle. The direct cost of virtual functions calls in C++. In *Proceedings of the 11th Annual Conference on Object-Oriented Programming Systems, Languages, and Applications*, pages 306–323, San Jose, California, Oct. 6-10 1996. OOPSLA'96, ACM SIGPLAN Notices 31(10) Oct. 1996.

[15] N. Eckel and J. Y. Gil. Empirical study of object-layout strategies and optimization techniques. In Bertino [3], pages 394–421.

[16] E. Gamma, R. Helm, R. Johnson, and J. Vlissides. *Design Patterns: Elements of Reusable Object-Oriented Software*. Professional Computing. Addison-Wesley, 1995.

[17] S. Ghemawat, K. H. Randall, and D. J. Scales. Field analysis: Getting useful and low-cost interprocedural information. In *Proceedings of the ACM SIGPLAN'00 Conference on Programming Language Design and Implementation (PLDI)*, pages 334–344, Vancouver, BC Canada, June 18-21 2000. ACM SIGPLAN, ACM Press.

[18] J. Gil and A. Itai. The complexity of type analysis of Object Oriented programs. In Jul [24], pages 601–634.

[19] P. Grogono and M. Sakkinen. Copying and comparing: Problems and solutions. In Bertino [3], pages 226–250.

[20] D. Hagimont, J. Mossiere, X. de Pina, and F. Saunier. Hidden software capabilities. In *Proceedings of the 16th IEEE International Conference on Distributed Computing Systems*, pages 282–289, Hong Kong, May 27-30 1996.

[21] H. Hakonen, V. Leppanen, T. Raita, T. Salakoski, and J. Teuhola. Improving object integrity and preventing side effects via deeply immutable references. In *Proceedings of 6th Fenno-Ugric Symposium on Software Technology, (FUSST'99)*, pages 139–150, Sagadi, Estonia, Aug. 19-21 1999.

[22] T. Hill, J. Noble, and J. Potter. Scalable visualisations with ownership types. In *Proceedings of the International Conference on Technology of Object-Oriented Languages and Systems* [37], pages 202–213.

[23] J. Hogg. Islands: Aliasing protection in object-oriented languages. In *Proceedings of the 6th Annual Conference on Object-Oriented Programming Systems, Languages, and Applications*, pages 271–285, Phoenix, Arizona, USA, Oct.6-11 1991. OOPSLA'91, ACM SIGPLAN Notices 26(11) Nov. 1991.

[24] E. Jul, editor. *Proceedings of the 12th European Conference on Object-Oriented Programming*, number 1445 in Lecture Notes in Computer Science, Brussels, Belgium, July 20–24 1998. ECOOP'98, Springer Verlag.

[25] G. Kniesel and D. Theisen. JAC - Java with transitive readonly access control. In *Proceedings of the Intercontinental Workshop on Aliasing in Object-Oriented Systems*[9], Lisbon, Portugal, June 14-18 1999.

[26] T. Lindholm and F. Yellin. *The Java Virtual Machine Specification*. Addison-Wesley Publishing Company, Reading, Massachusetts, second edition, 1999.

[27] B. Meyer. *Object-Oriented Software Construction*. Prentice-Hall, 2nd edition, 1997.

[28] N. H. Minsky. Towards alias-free pointers. In P. Cointe, editor, *Proceedings of the 10th European Conference on Object-Oriented Programming*, number 1098 in Lecture Notes in Computer Science, pages 189–209, Linz, Austria, July 8-12 1996. ECOOP'96, Springer Verlag.

---

[8] Also available as http://www.research.ibm.com/journal/sj/391/-dillenberger.html

[9] Also available as http://cui.unige.ch/ ecoopws/iwaoos/papers/-index.html

[29] J. Noble, J. Vitek, and J. Potter. Flexible alias protection. In Jul [24], pages 158–185.

[30] OOPSLA 1999. *Proceedings of the 14th Annual Conference on Object-Oriented Programming Systems, Languages, and Applications*, Denver, Colorado, Nov. 1–5 1999. ACM SIGPLAN Notices 34(10) Nov. 1999.

[31] OOPSLA 2000. *Proceedings of the 15th Annual Conference on Object-Oriented Programming Systems, Languages, and Applications*, Minneapolis, Minnesota, Oct. 15–19 2000. ACM SIGPLAN Notices 35(10) Oct. 2000.

[32] S. Porat, M. Biberstein, L. Koved, and B. Mendelson. Mutability analysis in Java. In *Proceedings of Centre for Advance Studies Conference (CASCON)*[10], pages 169–183, Mississauga, Ontario, Canada, Nov. 13-26 2000.

[33] C. Skalka and S. Smith. Static enforcement of security with types. In P. Wadler, editor, *Proceedings of the International Conference on Functional Programming (ICFP)*, Montreal, Canada, Sept. 18-20 2000.

[34] A. Snyder. Encapsulation and inheritance in object-oriented programming languages. In N. K. Meyrowitz, editor, *Proceedings of the 1st Annual Conference on Object-Oriented Programming Systems, Languages, and Applications*, pages 38–45, Portland, Oregon, USA, Sept. 29 - Oct. 2 1986. OOPSLA'86, ACM SIGPLAN Notices 21(11) Nov. 1986.

[35] B. Stroustrup. *The C++ Programming Language*. Addison-Wesley, 3rd edition, 1997.

[36] F. Tip and J. Palsberg. Scalable propagation-based call graph construction algorithms. In OOPSLA 2000 [31], pages 281–293.

[37] TOOLS Pasific 2000. *Proceedings of the International Conference on Technology of Object-Oriented Languages and Systems*, Sydney, Australia, Nov. 2000. Prentice-Hall.

[38] J. Whaley and M. Rinard. Compositional pointer and escape analysis for Java programs. In OOPSLA 1999 [30], pages 187–206.

[39] N. Wirth. The programming language Pascal. *Acta Informatica*, 1:35–63, 1971.

[40] A. Zaks, V. Feldman, and N. Aizikowitz. Sealed calls in Java packages. In OOPSLA 2000 [31], pages 83–92.

---

[10] Also available at http://cas.ibm.com/archives/2000/papers/index.shtml

Simple Ownership Types for Object Containment

David G. Clarke[1], James Noble[2], and John M. Potter[3]

[1] Institute of Information and Computing Sciences, Utrecht University
Utrecht, The Netherlands
clad@cs.uu.nl

[2] School of Mathematical and Computing Sciences, Victoria University
Wellington, New Zealand
kjx@mcs.vuw.ac.nz

[3] School of Computer Science and Engineering, University of New South Wales
Sydney, Australia
potter@cse.unsw.edu.au

Abstract. Containment of objects is a natural concept that has been poorly supported in object-oriented programming languages. For a predefined set of ownership contexts, this paper presents a type system that enforces certain containment relationships for run-time objects. A fixed ordering relationship is presumed between the owners.

The formalisation of *ownership types* has developed from our work with *flexible alias protection* together with an investigation of structural properties of object graphs based on dominator trees. Our general ownership type system permits fresh ownership contexts to be created at run-time. Here we present a simplified system in which the ownership contexts are predefined. This is powerful enough to express and enforce constraints about a system's high-level structure.

Our formal system is presented in an imperative variant of the object calculus. We present type preservation and soundness results. Furthermore we highlight how these type theoretic results establish a containment invariant for objects, in which access to contained objects is only permitted via their owners. In effect, the predefined ownership ordering restricts the permissible inter-object reference structure.

Keywords: OO type systems; ownership types; object containment; flexible alias protection.

1   Introduction

Object-oriented programs suffer from a lack of object-level encapsulation. This gives rise to problems with aliasing of objects, leading, in turn, to difficulties with maintaining correct and robust program behaviour To cope with difficulties related to complex control flow, structured programming imposes a single input, single output control-flow discipline. This makes it feasible to abstract the program logic using preconditions and postconditions. Structured programming discipline is so common-place nowadays that the benefits of the approach

J. Lindskov Knudsen (Ed.): ECOOP 2001, LNCS 2072, pp. 53–76, 2001.

are largely presumed. Unfortunately many of the benefits of the structured approach are lost in object-oriented programming: object aliasing leads to a loss of modularity in reasoning about programs.

We aim to encapsulate objects, imposing structure via object containment, yet retaining most of the flexibility and benefits of object-oriented programming. The key ideas have evolved from our work on *flexible alias protection* [34], the recognition of implicit structure in object systems [36], and the ability of type systems to impose this structure [15]. In comparison with flexible alias protection, we provide a formal notion of representation containment with accompanying properties. Our earlier ownership type system [15] was based on a Java-like language, but had a number of restrictions. In particular, the containment structure was defined by objects having a fixed and unique owner, thereby forming an ownership tree. An associated *containment invariant* directly captures the idea that the structure of object systems is reflected in the *dominator tree* for the underlying object-reference graph, as we describe elsewhere [36]. The structural constraints imposed by this earlier ownership type system are too rigid to permit them to be used together with some typical object-oriented programming idioms, such as iterators. Furthermore, we did not address subtyping. In this paper we redress some of these limitations.

We introduce an extra degree of freedom into the ownership type system, separating the notion of *contexts* from objects themselves. In practice, contexts may be associated with static entities such as classes, packages or modules, security domains or network locations. Every object is assigned an *owner* context, which together with the predefined containment ordering, determines which other objects may access it. Objects also have a *representation* context we call simply *rep*; an object's rep determines those objects it may access. To keep things simple, this paper assumes that there is a pre-defined containment ordering on contexts. In other words, we presume the existence of a partial order on a set of fixed contexts, $(\mathcal{C}, \prec:)$. We describe a soundness result and sketch the proof of containment invariance for stored objects. We think of the owner context as providing a domain for the object's external interface, and the representation context as providing a domain for its implementation. We insist that the owner of an object accessible to another contains the other's representation context. Thus our containment invariant states that for a reference from an object with identity ι to one with ι' to exist, it is necessary that $\mathsf{rep}(\iota) \prec: \mathsf{owner}(\iota')$. This is our take on the *no representation exposure* property of flexible alias protection.

The separation of rep and owner context is the key contribution of this paper. Different arrangements of owner and representation contexts within a context ordering allows different configurations of objects, as we demonstrate in Section 3. The resulting type system can model a wide range of alias protection schemes:

- Using per class contexts we can model Sandwich types [18] and a part of the Universes proposal [31].
- Using per Java-style packages we can model Confined Types [8].

- Per object contexts (as evident in the companion to this paper [13]), restricted so that rep contexts are directly inside owner contexts, combined with genericity, allows us to model the containment features of Flexible Alias Protection [34], and so support collections of shared objects, but not iterators acting directly on the representation of those collections. This is effectively our earlier Ownership Types system [15], although the earlier work did not support subtyping or inheritance.
- Separating representations and owners by one or two contexts models the core of the Universes proposal [31], allowing several iterators to access the representation of another object. Universe in addition requires that the iterator has read only access to the other object's representation.
- Finally, further separation of representation and owner contexts allows objects' interfaces to be exported arbirtarily far from their representations in a controlled manner, so that an object's primary interface can belong to some deeply contained subobject. Unlike other systems, this flexibility allows us to model the use of iterators over internal collections as part of a larger abstraction's interface (common in programs using the C++ STL), and COM-style interface aggregation.

We extend the imperative object calculus of Abadi and Cardelli [1] with owner and rep contexts for objects. We chose this formalism to simplify the statement and proof of properties; however the essence of the ownership type system should be easy to translate to any object-oriented notation. The key novelty of our type system is its use of permissions (or capabilities), which are sets of contexts, to govern the well-formedness of expressions. Owners determine which contexts are needed in the permission, and rep determines which permissions are held. Thus the representation context determines which other objects an object can access.

2   Object Calculus with Contexts

In this section we introduce a syntactic variant of the object calculus which captures the essence of our ownership system. First we outline those aspects of the object calculus that are most relevant for our purposes. Next we motivate our key modifications: one deals with owner and rep decorations for objects; the other imposes a syntactic restriction on the form of method call to prevent object references leaking through method closures. Finally we present the syntax for our variant of the object calculus.

2.1   The Object Calculus

The *Theory of Objects* [1] presents a variety of object calculi of increasing complexity. Here we chose an imperative, first-order typed calculus. Being imperative allows us to capture the containment invariant as a property of objects held in the store.

The two basic operations of the object calculus are method select and method update. We review these using the untyped functional object calculus, the simplest presented in [1]. It has the following syntax:

$$
\begin{array}{lll}
a, b ::= & x & \textit{variable} \\
& |\quad [l_i = \varsigma(x_i)b_i{}^{i\in 1..n}] & \textit{object formation (l_i distinct)} \\
& |\quad a.l & \textit{field select/method invocation} \\
& |\quad a.l \Leftarrow \varsigma(x)b & \textit{field update/method update}
\end{array}
$$

An object is a collection of methods labelled l_1 to l_n. Methods take the form $\varsigma(x)b$, where the parameter x refers to the target object, that is *self*, within the method body b. The operational semantics is given by the following reduction rules, where $o \equiv [l_i = \varsigma(x_i)b_i{}^{i\in 1..n}]$:

$$
\begin{array}{ll}
o.l_j \rightsquigarrow b_j\{\!\!\{^o\!/_{x_j}\}\!\!\} & (j \in 1..n) \\
o.l_j \Leftarrow \varsigma(x)b \rightsquigarrow [l_j = \varsigma(x)b, l_i = \varsigma(x_i)b_i{}^{i\in(1..n)-\{j\}}] & (j \in 1..n)
\end{array}
$$

A method invocation $o.l_j$ reduces to the result of substituting the target object o for the self parameter x_j in the body b_j of the method named l_j. A method update $o.l_j \Leftarrow \varsigma(x)b$ reduces to a copy of the target object where the method in slot l_j is replaced by $\varsigma(x)b$. The definition of reduction is completed by allowing reduction to occur at any subexpression within an expression.

In an imperative object calculus, objects are held in a store which is a map from locations to objects. Evaluation of an object expression amounts to the allocation of that object in the store with a particular object identity denoting its location. Object aliasing arises through sharing of object ids. When a method is invoked, its location (or object id) is substituted for the self parameter. Method update changes the object in-place, rather than constructing a new object as for the functional variants of calculus.

Common object-oriented constructs can easily be captured. Fields are modelled as methods which are values that make no reference to the self parameter. Field update employs method update, again with values making no reference to the self parameter. Functions are modelled as objects where a field is used to store the argument to the function. Methods with arguments are modelled as methods which return a function.

2.2   Extending the Calculus with Contexts

Contexts The extension of the object calculus presented here is concerned with controlling object access. Adopting the model discussed in the introduction, we modify objects to include both owner and representation contexts. Objects take the form $[l_i = \ldots{}^{i\in 1..n}]_q^p$, where p is the owner and q is the representation context.

We assume that we are given a fixed collection of contexts which form a partial order $(\mathcal{C}, \prec:)$. The relation $\prec:$ is called *inside*. The converse relation $:\!\succ$ is called *contains*.

Contexts might represent the collection of packages in a Java program. The inside relation $\prec:$ can, for example, represent package nesting. Confined Types [8] use packages as contexts: each package is associated with two contexts, one confined the other not; the confined version of a package is inside the corresponding unconfined version, but no further containment is presumed. A confined type is accessible only through its unconfined version; unconfined types do not restrict access other than via the normal visibility and typing rules for Java. Similarly, contexts could represent a collection of classes where $\prec:$ captures inner class nesting and ϵ corresponds to some ubiquitous system context. Universes take this approach [31]. Alternatively, contexts could represent some combination of these features, or be based on some other scheme, such as machine names on a network, with $\prec:$ representing the subnet relationship.

Evaluation in Context In our system, certain objects may only be accessible within a particular context. Typically computation proceeds by successive method selection and update on a particular target object. Having access to an object means that access is granted to its representation, but only during the evaluation of a selected method. Unfortunately, the object calculus encodes methods with arguments as methods which return a function closure. The resulting closure can be applied, which is fine, or installed as a part of another object via method update, which is not acceptable from our perspective when the closure contains reference to representation. Thus we need to make a second change to the object calculus to distinguish evaluation which may only occur within a context from values which are accessible from without.

The approach we adopt here is simple. As is common in object-oriented programs we presume that all method calls are fully applied, and that no closures are used. So, unlike the object calculus, we actually use a method call syntax, rather than the syntactically simpler method select. A more complex system that associates evaluation contexts with closures is indeed possible, but we prefer to keep our calculus simple.

Thus we modify objects further so that methods take a pre-specified number of arguments: $[l_i = \varsigma(x_i, \Gamma_i)b_i{}^{i \in 1..n}]_q^p$, where Γ denotes the additional formal parameters. Method select now becomes $o.l_j\langle \Delta \rangle$, where Δ is the actual parameter list. Method update is modified in the obvious manner.

2.3   Syntax for an Object Calculus with Ownership

We now present our variant of the object calculus incorporating ownership. Figure 1 gives the syntax for *permissions, types, values, objects, expressions, parameters, stores,* and *configurations*. Contexts were described above. We describe the remainder in turn.

Permissions Permissions denote collections of contexts. A context is only accessible in an expression when it appears in the permission used to type the expression. The permission $\langle p \rangle$ corresponds to the singleton set $\{p\}$, and is the permission required to access objects with owner p. The permission $\langle q \uparrow \rangle$ corresponds to the contexts which contain q, that is, all the context accessible to an object which can access q, for example, objects with representation context q.

$$
\begin{aligned}
p \in \text{CONTEXT} \quad &= \mathcal{C} \\
K \in \text{PERMISSION} \quad &::= \langle p \rangle \\
&\mid \langle p{\uparrow} \rangle \\[1ex]
A, B, C \in \text{TYPE} \quad &::= [l_i : A_i{}^{i \in 1..n}]_q^p \\
&\mid A \to B \\[1ex]
x \in \text{VAR} \\
u, v \in \text{VALUE} \quad &::= x \\
&\mid \iota \\
o \in \text{OBJECT} \quad &::= [l_i = \varsigma(x_i : A_i, \Gamma_i) b_i{}^{i \in 1..n}]_q^p \quad (l_i \ \text{distinct}) \\
a, b \in \text{EXPRESSION} \quad &::= v \\
&\mid o \\
&\mid v.l \langle \Delta \rangle \qquad\qquad where \ \Delta ::= \emptyset \mid v, \Delta \\
&\mid v.l \Leftarrow \varsigma(x : A, \Gamma) b \\
&\mid \textbf{let } x : A = a \textbf{ in } b \\
\Gamma \in \text{PARAM} \quad &::= \emptyset \mid x : A, \Gamma \\[1ex]
\sigma \in \text{STORE} \quad &::= \emptyset \\
&\mid \sigma, \iota \mapsto o \\
s, t \in \text{CONFIG} \quad &::= (\sigma, a)
\end{aligned}
$$

Fig. 1. The Syntax

Types Types include just object and method types.

The object type $[l_i : A_i{}^{i \in 1..n}]_q^p$ lists the names and types of the methods of the object, as well as the owner context p (superscript) and the representation context q (subscript). Objects of this type can only be accessed in expressions possessing at least permission $\langle p \rangle$. We also use the type $[l_i : A_i{}^{i \in 1..n}]^p$ as a shorthand for the type $[l_i : A_i{}^{i \in 1..n}]_p^p$. This can be considered to be the type of an external interface to an object, since it contains only the methods which are accessible to external objects which only have access to context p.

The type $A_1 \to A_2 \to \ldots \to B$ is the type of a method which takes arguments of type $A_1, A_2, \ldots$, which must be object types, and returns a value of object type B. Although the form of method type suggests that partial application is permitted, in fact the rule for well-formed method call forces all arguments to be supplied, as discussed above.

Expressions Expressions are presented in a variant of the *named form* [37]. This amounts to the requirement that the result of (almost) every evaluation step be bound to a variable x which is subsequently used to refer to the result of this computation. While this form does not change the expressiveness of the calculus, it simplifies the statement of its semantics and the proof of its properties.

The language is imperative. Objects evaluate to locations, ι, which are subsequently used to refer to the object in the store. Locations are the only possible result of computation. They do not appear in the expressions a programmer writes.

Objects are given by $[l_i = \varsigma(x_i : A_i, \Gamma_i)b_i{}^{i \in 1..n}]_q^p$. The x_i are the self parameters used in method bodies b_i to refer to the current instance of the object. The type of self A_i is given. The Γ_i are the formal parameters to the method. These are a collection of term variables with their type. The owner context is p and q is the representation context.

Method call $v.l\langle\Delta\rangle$, takes a collection of actual parameters for the method labelled l. The parameters, Δ, are a sequence of values.

Method update, $v.l \Leftarrow \varsigma(x : A, \Gamma)b$, replaces the method labelled l in the object v with that defined by b. Again x is the self parameter and Γ are the formal parameters to the method. As usual, a method can be treated as a field if $x \notin FV(b)$, b is a value, and additionally that $\Gamma = \emptyset$. Thus we do not distinguish between fields and methods.

Let expressions, **let** $x : A = a$ **in** b, are used to define local declarations and to link computations together.

Stores and Configurations The store, σ, is a map from locations to objects for all locations created throughout the evaluation of an expression. A configuration represents a snapshot of the evaluation. It consists of an expression to be evaluated, a, and a store, σ.

3   Examples

The type system explored in this paper allows containment which is specified across an entire system. Objects can be partitioned and contained within contexts which are defined per package or per class or come from some other pre-specified collection. We demonstrate a few example uses of such collections, observing that different partial orders allow for different kinds of restriction, including a partition of objects without any containment.

The first example illustrates the constraints underlying Confined Types [8].

Example 1 (Web Browsers and Applets). Assume there are two packages, *Browser*, abbreviated as B, and *Applet*, abbreviated as A. Let *securityManager* be the object which controls the web browser's security policy. This must be confined to the *Browser* package. The *Applet* package contains the implementation of *applets*. These interact with a *browser* object through which they obtain limited access to the outside world, governed by the *securityManager*. The *browser* object has access to the *securityManager* object to guide its interaction with the *applets*.

The ordering on contexts is:

We can represent this situation above with the following objects:

$$securityManager \mathrel{\widehat{=}} [......]_B^B$$
$$browser \mathrel{\widehat{=}} [securityManager = securityManager, applet = applet, ...]_B^\top$$
$$applet \mathrel{\widehat{=}} [browser = browser, ...]_A^\top$$

In addition, the *browser* can be presented to the *applet* using the interface type $[applet : AppletType, ...]^\top$, rather than its actual type $[securityManager : SecurityManagerType, applet = AppletType, ...]_B^\top$, since the former hides the part of *browser* which contained within the *Browser* package.

This example can be extended so that each *applet* object has its own protected *environment* object if dynamic context creation is added to the type system [13].

Example 2 (General Systems). A system can be partitioned into a collection of subsystems (perhaps using packages or modules). Some objects are not accessible outside a given subsystem, whereas others may belong to a given subsystem, but be accessible by one or more other subsystems. We model this as follows.

Let the set $\mathcal{P} = \{A, B, ...\}$ denote the names of the subsystems. Let the collection of contexts be $\mathcal{C} = \mathbb{P}(\mathcal{P}) - \{\emptyset\}$, where $\mathbb{P}(\mathcal{P})$ is the powerset of $\mathcal{P}$. We will write $ABDF$ to represent the set $\{A, B, D, F\}$. The context ordering $\prec:$ is the defined as follows: for each $A \in \mathcal{P}$, if $A \in P$, where $P \in \mathbb{P}(\mathcal{P})$, then $A \prec: P$, abusing notation slightly. For example, $A \prec: ABC$. Note that this means that the context ordering is a dag, as demonstrated in the following diagram for subsystems $A, B,$ and C:

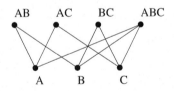

We set an object's representation context to the subsystem in which it resides — that is, A, B, or C — and its owner context to the collection of subsystems which can access it — any context in the diagram above.

Consider the following collection of subsystems, A and C, and objects a, b, and c. The arrows represent the only references allowed between these objects.

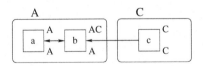

Both a and b come from subsystem A, so their representation context is A. a is contained within subsystem A, so its owner is A. b is also accessible to subsystem

C, so its owner is AC. Finally c has both owner and representation context C. The containment invariant enforces that the references in the figure are the only ones allowed given these contexts and their ordering. Adding more structure, for example, by letting the ordering on contexts be the powerset ordering on sets of subsystem names, allows us to specify in addition the sharing of contained objects among subsystems.

This granularity of the restrictions in the above example resembles Eiffel's export policies, except that in the example the constraints are defined between objects, rather than for individual methods [29].

Example 3 (Class Names as a Partition). The Universes system uses class names as object owners [31]. These can be used to partition the collection of objects, using one partition per class, without providing any containment. All contexts are equally accessible, but objects owned by one class cannot be assigned to a field expecting an object with a different owner.

The contexts required to model this consist of a single context for each class plus the additional context which we denote $\perp$. The partial order on contexts is $\perp \prec: C$, for each class C. An object in partition C has owner C and representation context $\perp$. An example partial order is:

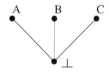

This tree, which is an upside down version of the context ordering used in a previous work [15], could have a top element for the owner of globally accessible objects.

Example 4 (Adding Contained Per Class Contexts).

We can enhance the previous example to allow each class to have objects which are accessible to each instance of the class, but are not accessible outside of the class. To do this we extend the above partial order with $C^* \prec: \perp$ for each class C. The example above becomes:

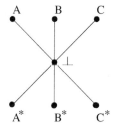

Objects not accessible outside of class C have both owner and representation context C^*. Objects from class C in partition D have owner D and representation context C^*, not $\perp$ as above, so that it can access the elements contained within class C.

4   Formal Presentation of Ownership Types

We begin our formal presentation with a description of how the containment invariant is enforced by the type system. This technique can be applied in more general setting [13]. Then follows the type system.

4.1   Permissions and Containment

Expressions are typed against a given permission: either a point permission $\langle p \rangle$ representing a singleton context $\{p\}$, or an upset permission $\langle q \uparrow \rangle$ denoting all contexts containing q, that is $\{p \mid q \prec: p\}$.

The point permission $\langle p \rangle$ allows access to objects with owner p. An object with rep q is granted the upset permission $\langle q \uparrow \rangle$, thereby giving it (more precisely, its methods) access to any object with owner in that set.

We write $\iota \rightarrow \iota'$ to indicate that one stored object holds a reference to another. The containment invariant is a statement about the well-formedness of stores, in particular the underlying reference structure. It states that:

$$\iota \rightarrow \iota' \Rightarrow \mathsf{rep}(\iota) \prec: \mathsf{owner}(\iota').$$

Let $\iota \mapsto [l_i = \varsigma(x_i : A)b_i{}^{i \in 1..n}]_q^p$ be a location-object binding in some store, so that $\mathsf{owner}(\iota) = p$ and $\mathsf{rep}(\iota) = q$. The locations accessible to ι are those appearing in the method bodies b_i. The containment invariant yields an upper bound on these:

$$\{\iota' \mid \mathsf{owner}(\iota') \in \langle q \uparrow \rangle\}. \tag{1}$$

Now consider the object at location ι' which has owner p'. Access to this object requires permission $\langle p' \rangle$, which corresponds to the singleton set $\{p'\}$. Thus ι' is in the set (1) if

$$\langle p' \rangle \subseteq \langle q \uparrow \rangle. \tag{2}$$

This condition is enforced by our type system.

Consider the following simplified version of our object typing rule:

$$\text{(Val Object-Simplified)} \quad (\text{where } A \equiv [l_i : C_i{}^{i \in 1..n}]_q^p)$$
$$\frac{E, x_i : A; \langle q \uparrow \rangle \vdash b_i : C_i \quad \forall i \in 1..n}{E; \langle p \rangle \vdash [l_i = \varsigma(x_i : A)b_i{}^{i \in 1..n}]_q^p : A}$$

The conclusion states, among other things, that the permission required to access this object is $\langle p \rangle$, where p is the owner. The premises, $i \in 1..n$, each state that the permission governing access in the method bodies b_i is $\langle q \uparrow \rangle$, where q is the representation context. But this is exactly the condition (2). Therefore, the only locations accessible in a method body are those permitted by the containment invariant. This property is formally presented in this paper.

Apart from giving types to the appropriate constructs in the expected manner, the other rules in the type system merely propagate or preserve the constraints we require. Subtyping does not allow the owner information stored in a type to shrink, thus preventing the loss of crucial information. Subtyping was missing from our earlier ownership type system [15], and the keys to regaining it are preventing the loss of the owner and maintaining the ordering between contexts.

The type rules which follow are specified depending on a permission. For the calculus of this paper the minimal required permission can in fact be derived from the types involved, so does not actually need to be explicit. However we adopt the current presentation style, not only because it helps to clarify the role of permissions, but also to cater for extensions such as recursive types, where the permissions can not always be directly inferred [13].

Supplementary Notation The type of an expression depends on a *typing environment*, E, which maps program variables (and locations) to types. The typing environment is organised as a sequence of bindings, where $\emptyset$ denotes the empty environment:

$$E ::= \emptyset \mid E, x : A \mid E, \iota : A$$

The syntax of method formal parameters, Γ, are just a subset of the syntax for environments, which allows them to be treated as environments in the type rules.

The domain of a typing environment $\mathsf{dom}(E)$ extracts the bound in the environment:

$$\mathsf{dom}(\emptyset) \cong \emptyset$$
$$\mathsf{dom}(E, \iota : A) \cong \mathsf{dom}(E) \cup \{\iota\}$$
$$\mathsf{dom}(E, x : A) \cong \mathsf{dom}(E) \cup \{x\}$$

This applies also to Γ.

4.2 The Type System

We define the type system using nine judgements which are described in Figure 2. Judgements concerning constructs which contain no free variables do not require a typing environment in their specification. All judgements concerned with types and expressions are formulated with respect to a permission K.

To simplify the handling of environments, we employ the notation such as $x : A \in E$ to extract assumptions from the typing environment. Well-formedness of the typing environment E is implicit with such assumptions; that is, $E \vdash \diamond$ is part of the assumption.

$E \vdash \Diamond$	E is well-formed typing environment
$K \subseteq K'$	K is a subpermission of K'
$K \vdash A$	A is a well-formed type given K
$K \vdash A{<:}B$	A is a subtype of B given K
$E; K \vdash a : A$	a is a well-typed expression of type A in E given K
$E; K \vdash (A)(\Delta) \Rightarrow C$	The actual parameters Δ match method type A with return type C in E given K
$E \vdash \sigma$	σ is a well-formed store in E
$E; K \vdash (\sigma, a) : A$	(σ, a) is a well-typed configuration with type A in E given K

Fig. 2. Judgements

Well-formed Environments

$$
\text{(Env } \emptyset) \qquad \text{(Env } x) \qquad \qquad \text{(Env Location)}
$$

$$
\frac{}{\emptyset \vdash \Diamond} \qquad \frac{K \vdash A \quad x \notin \mathsf{dom}(E)}{E, x : A \vdash \Diamond} \qquad \frac{\langle p \rangle \vdash [l_i : A_i{}^{i \in 1..n}]_q^p \quad \iota \notin \mathsf{dom}(E)}{E, \iota : [l_i : A_i{}^{i \in 1..n}]_q^p \vdash \Diamond}
$$

Adding a variable to an environment requires that it not be already declared and that its type can be well-formed given some permission (Env x). The permission does not matter at this point, but it will return when x is used in an expression. (Env Location) specifies that locations have object type.

Well-formed Permission and Subpermissions

$$
\text{(SubPerm } p) \qquad \text{(SubPerm } \prec:) \qquad \text{(SubPerm Refl)} \qquad \text{(SubPerm Trans)}
$$

$$
\frac{p \in \mathcal{C}}{\langle p \rangle \subseteq \langle p \uparrow \rangle} \qquad \frac{q \prec: p}{\langle p \uparrow \rangle \subseteq \langle q \uparrow \rangle} \qquad \frac{}{K \subseteq K} \qquad \frac{K \subseteq K' \quad K' \subseteq K''}{K \subseteq K''}
$$

All permissions in PERMISSION, that is $\langle p \rangle$ and $\langle p \uparrow \rangle$ for each $p \in \mathcal{C}$, are valid. The subpermission relation $K \subseteq K'$ is defined in the obvious manner given the interpretation of permissions as sets of contexts.

Well-formed Types

$$
\text{(Type Object) } (l_i \text{ distinct)} \qquad \text{(Type Arrow)} \qquad \text{(Type Allow)}
$$

$$
\frac{\langle q \uparrow \rangle \vdash A_i \quad \forall i \in 1..n \quad q \prec: p}{\langle p \rangle \vdash [l_i : A_i{}^{i \in 1..n}]_q^p} \qquad \frac{K \vdash A \quad K \vdash B}{K \vdash A \rightarrow B} \qquad \frac{K \vdash A \quad K \subseteq K'}{K' \vdash A}
$$

The well-formedness of types depends upon the permission required to access *values* of that type.

The justification for (Type Object) is similar to that for (Val Object) given in Section 4.1. The method types of an object type must be well-formed given permission $\langle q\!\uparrow\rangle$, where q is the representation context. The permission required to access this type is at least $\langle p\rangle$. The condition $q \prec: p$ implies that $\langle p\rangle \subseteq \langle q\!\uparrow\rangle$ ensuring that an object can access itself.

Method types resemble function types, as given by (Type Arrow). Interestingly the permission required to form method types only depends on the argument and result types. It does not depend on the method body, which typically will require a larger permission. This is because the method body can access the object's representation, which in general is not externally accessible.

The rule (Type Allow) states that well-formedness of types is preserved with extended permissions.

Well-formed Subtyping

$$(\text{Sub Object}) \quad (l_i \text{ distinct})$$
$$\frac{\langle q\!\uparrow\rangle \vdash A_i \quad \forall i \in 1..n \quad \langle q'\!\uparrow\rangle \vdash A_i \quad \forall i \in n+1..n+m \quad q' \prec: q \prec: p}{\langle p\rangle \vdash [l_i : A_i^{\,i\in 1..n+m}]_{q'}^p <: [l_i : A_i^{\,i\in 1..n}]_q^p}$$

$$(\text{Sub Allow})$$
$$\frac{K \vdash A<:B \quad K \subseteq K'}{K' \vdash A<:B}$$

The rule (Sub Object) allows methods to be forgotten through subtyping. The owner does not vary, but the representation context can. Firstly, the owner states which context an object resides in. If this information can vary in the type, then we lose the ability to state when two references are not aliases, since references to objects with different owner contexts cannot be aliases. Thus the owner is invariant. Varying the representation context only loses information about which contexts an object can access. These can be considered to be part of an object's implementation and can reasonably be ignored.

A consequence of varying the representation context is that methods which include the initial representation context q' in their type are removed in the supertype. When $q = p$ the only methods present in the type are those accessible to objects which have access to context p. The type in this case will be an interface type $[l_i : A_i^{\,i\in 1..n}]^p$.

Subtypes which are valid given some permission are valid with a larger permission, though not necessarily vice-versa, according to rule (Sub Allow).

Well-typed Expressions

$$(\text{Val } x) \qquad\qquad (\text{Val Location})$$
$$\frac{x : A \in E \quad K \vdash A}{E; K \vdash x : A} \qquad\qquad \frac{\iota : [l_i : A_i^{\,i\in 1..n}]_q^p \in E}{E; \langle p\rangle \vdash \iota : [l_i : A_i^{\,i\in 1..n}]_q^p}$$

Expressions are typed against a typing environment and a permission. Variable typing is by assumption (Val x), though it requires sufficient permission to construct the type. Locations are similarly typed by assumption, where the permission required is at least the point permission for the owner in location's type (Val Location).

$$(\text{Val Object}) \quad (\text{where } A \equiv [l_i : B_i{}^{i\in 1..n}]_q^p \text{ and } B_i \equiv \lfloor \Gamma_i \rfloor_{C_i})$$

$$\frac{E, x_i : A, \Gamma_i; \langle q \uparrow \rangle \vdash b_i : C_i \quad \forall i \in 1..n}{E; \langle p \rangle \vdash [l_i = \varsigma(x_i : A, \Gamma_i)b_i{}^{i\in 1..n}]_q^p : A}$$

The (Val Object) rule requires an auxiliary function $\lfloor \Gamma \rfloor_C$, which converts the method arguments Γ and the return type C into a method type B:

$$\lfloor \emptyset \rfloor_C \,\hat{\cong}\, C$$

$$\lfloor x : A, \Gamma \rfloor_C \,\hat{\cong}\, A \to \lfloor \Gamma \rfloor_C$$

In (Val Object), each method body b_i of method $\varsigma(x_i : A, \Gamma_i)b_i$ is typed against an environment extended with the self parameter x_i with A, the type of the object being formed, and with the formal parameter list Γ_i. The return type of the method body C_i and the formal parameters are combined to make up the method type B_i. The permission $\langle p \rangle$ is required to create an object with owner context p. The permission the method is typed against is $\langle q \uparrow \rangle$, where q is the representation context. Access to self x_i is permitted because $q \prec: p$ can be inferred from the fact that the object's type A appears in environment $E, x_i : A, \Gamma_i$. This means that an objects rep and owner are in the containment relation, with the rep inside the owner.

$$(\text{Val Select})$$

$$\frac{E; K \vdash v : [l_i : A_i{}^{i\in 1..n}]_q^p \quad E; K \vdash (A_j)(\Delta) \Rightarrow C_j \quad j \in 1..n}{E; K \vdash v.l_j\langle \Delta \rangle : C_j}$$

(Val Select) requires that the target have an object type with the appropriate method present. The clause $E; K \vdash (A_j)(\Delta) \Rightarrow C_j$ checks that the arguments are well-typed, correct in number and that access is permitted, and states that the return type is C_j. This form of rule is described below.

$$(\text{Val Update}) \quad (\text{where } A \equiv [l_i : B_i{}^{i\in 1..n}]_q^p \text{ and } B_j \equiv \lfloor \Gamma_j \rfloor_{C_j})$$

$$\frac{E; K \vdash v : A \quad E, x : A, \Gamma_j; K' \vdash b : C_j \quad K' \subseteq \langle q \uparrow \rangle \quad K' \subseteq K \quad j \in 1..n}{E; K \vdash v.l_j \Leftarrow \varsigma(x : A, \Gamma_j)b : A}$$

(Val Update) requires that the target have an object type with the appropriate method present. Firstly, the formal parameter list Γ_j and return type C_j

of the new method must be able to be converted to the method's type B_j, that is, $\lfloor \Gamma_j \rfloor_{C_j} = B_j$. The new method body is typed against a self x with the type of the object being updated, and Γ_j. The expression must have type C_j. The given permission K' is, in effect, at most the intersection between the contexts accessible inside the object, $\langle q \uparrow \rangle$, and the accessible contexts in the surrounding expression, K. This 'intersection' of permissions prevents any illegal locations from being added to object, while maintaining the constraints on the expression performing the method update.

$$
\begin{array}{cc}
\text{(Val Let)} & \text{(Val Subsumption)} \\
\dfrac{E;K \vdash a : A \quad E, x : A; K \vdash b : B}{E;K \vdash \textbf{let } x : A = a \textbf{ in } b : B} & \dfrac{E;K \vdash a : A \quad K' \vdash A{<:}B \quad K \subseteq K'}{E;K' \vdash a : B}
\end{array}
$$

The type rule (Val Let) is standard, except that it carries the same permission through to the expressions.

Finally, (Val Subsumption) allows an expression given one type to be given a supertype, as usual, and to be used with a larger permission.

Well-typed Actual Parameter Lists

$$
\begin{array}{cc}
\text{(Arg Empty)} & \text{(Arg Val)} \\
\dfrac{E \vdash \diamond \quad K \vdash C}{E;K \vdash (C)(\emptyset) \Rightarrow C} & \dfrac{E;K \vdash v : A \quad E;K \vdash (B)(\Delta) \Rightarrow C}{E;K \vdash (A \to B)(v, \Delta) \Rightarrow C}
\end{array}
$$

The judgement $E;K \vdash (B)(\Delta) \Rightarrow C$ guarantees that the actual parameters Δ are correct in number and type, and that the return type is C, all with the same permission K.

Well-typed Stores and Configurations

$$
\begin{array}{cc}
\text{(Store Empty)} & \text{(Store Alloc)} \\
\dfrac{E \vdash \diamond}{E \vdash \emptyset} & \dfrac{E \vdash \sigma \quad E; \langle p \rangle \vdash o : [l_i : A_i{}^{i \in 1..n}]_q^p \quad \iota : [l_i : A_i{}^{i \in 1..n}]_q^p \in E}{E \vdash \sigma, \iota \mapsto o}
\end{array}
$$

$$
\text{(Val Config)}
$$
$$
\dfrac{E \vdash \sigma \quad E;K \vdash a : A \quad \mathsf{dom}(\sigma) = \mathsf{dom}(E)}{E;K \vdash (\sigma, a) : A}
$$

The objects stored at a location must have the same type as the location. Configuration typing is performed in a typing environment whose domain consists of exactly the locations allocated in the store.

5   Dynamic Semantics and Properties

We now consider an operational semantics, and consequent properties, including type preservation and soundness.

5.1   An Operational Semantics

The operational semantics of the calculus are presented in a big-step, substitution-based style in Figure 3. Fundamentally it differs little from the object calculus semantics of Gordon et. al. [19], though the named form of expression allows some minor simplifications.

(Subst Value)   (Subst Object)   where $o \equiv [l_i = \varsigma(x_i : A_i, \Gamma_i)b_i{}^{i \in 1..n}]_q^p$
$$\frac{}{}\qquad \frac{\sigma_1 = \sigma_0, \iota \mapsto o \quad \iota \notin \mathrm{dom}(\sigma_0)}{(\sigma_0, o) \Downarrow (\sigma_1, \iota)}$$

$$\frac{}{(\sigma, v) \Downarrow (\sigma, v)}$$

$$\text{(Subst Select)} \quad \text{where } j \in 1..n$$
$$\frac{\sigma_0(\iota) = [l_i = \varsigma(x_i : A_i, \Gamma_i)b_i{}^{i \in 1..n}]_q^p \quad \{\!\{\Delta/\Gamma_j\}\!\} \text{ is defined}}{\qquad (\sigma_0, b_j\{\!\{{}^{\iota}\!/_{x_j}\}\!\}\{\!\{\Delta/\Gamma_j\}\!\}) \Downarrow (\sigma_1, v)}$$
$$\frac{}{(\sigma_0, \iota.l_j\langle\Delta\rangle) \Downarrow (\sigma_1, v)}$$

$$\text{(Subst Update)} \quad \text{where } j \in 1..n$$
$$\sigma_0(\iota) = [l_i = \varsigma(x_i : A_i, \Gamma_i)b_i{}^{i \in 1..n}]_q^p$$
$$\frac{\sigma_1 = \sigma_0 + (\iota \mapsto [l_i = \varsigma(x_i : A_i, \Gamma_i)b_i{}^{i \in 1..j-1, j+1..n}, l_j = \varsigma(x : A_j, \Gamma)b]_q^p)}{(\sigma_0, \iota.l_j \Leftarrow \varsigma(s : A, \Gamma)b) \Downarrow (\sigma_1, \iota)}$$

$$\text{(Subst Let)}$$
$$\frac{(\sigma_0, a) \Downarrow (\sigma_1, v) \quad (\sigma_1, b\{\!\{{}^v\!/_x\}\!\}) \Downarrow (\sigma_2, u)}{(\sigma_0, \mathbf{let} \ x : A = a \ \mathbf{in} \ b) \Downarrow (\sigma_2, u)}$$

Fig. 3. Big-step, substitution-based operational semantics

The semantics specify an *evaluation relation* between initial and final configurations, $(\sigma, a) \Downarrow (\sigma', v)$. Evaluating expression a with store σ results in a new store σ' and value v.

We use $\sigma, \iota \mapsto o$ to denote extending the store σ with a new location-object binding, where $\iota \notin \mathrm{dom}(\sigma)$. $\sigma + \iota \mapsto o$ denotes updating the store σ so that ι binds to the new object o, where $\iota \in \mathrm{dom}(\sigma)$. In (Subst Select), $b\{\!\{\Delta/\Gamma\}\!\}$, denotes bindings of formal to actual parameters for a method defined as:

$$\{\!\{\emptyset/\emptyset\}\!\} \,\hat{=}\, \epsilon$$
$$\{\!\{v, \Delta/x : A, \Gamma\}\!\} \,\hat{=}\, \{\!\{{}^v\!/_x\}\!\}\{\!\{\Delta/\Gamma\}\!\}$$

where ϵ is the empty substitution. Otherwise $\{\!\{\Delta/\Gamma\}\!\}$ is undefined.

Note that only closed terms are evaluated. Evaluation begins with the configuration $(\emptyset, a)$, that is, some closed expression with an empty store. Variables in **let** expressions and method bodies are always substituted for before they are encountered in evaluation. Expressions either diverge, become stuck, signified by the special configuration WRONG[1], or result in a value which must be a location.

The semantics hold no surprises. Firstly, values require no evaluation (Subst Value). Objects evaluate to a new location, which maps to the original object in the new store (Subst Object). The resulting configuration includes the new store. The evaluation rule (Subst Select) binds the actual parameters Δ to the formal parameters Γ within the body of the selected method, and the resulting expression evaluated. (Subst Update) replaces the method named l from the object at location ι with the one supplied. (Subst Let) evaluates the first expression a, substitutes the result for x in b, which is then evaluated.

5.2   Key Properties

The type system is sound. The proofs have been omitted but generally require straightforward induction.

Soundness depends on the following fundamental lemma.

Lemma 1 (Permissibility).

1. *If $E; K \vdash v : A$ and $K' \vdash A$, then $E; K' \vdash v : A$, where v is a value.*
2. *If $K \vdash A <: B$ and $K' \vdash B$, then $K' \vdash A <: B$.*

The first clause essentially states that the type contains enough information to determine the permission required to access a value. Values can be passed across object boundaries, for example, if the type is well-formed on both the object's inside and outside. This can happen even when the expression computing the value may not have been accessible in both places. This clause is essential for demonstrating type preservation for method select and update.

The second clause states in effect that all subtypes of a given type are accessible wherever the type is accessible. This is required for the validity of substitution and subsumption.

Definition 1 (Extension). *Environment E' is an extension of E, written $E' \gg E$, if and only if E is a subsequence of E'.*

The following type preservation result states that reduction preserves typing:

Theorem 1 (Preservation). *If $E; K \vdash (\sigma, a) : A$ and $(\sigma, a) \Downarrow (\sigma', v)$, then there exists an environment E' such that $E' \gg E$ and $E'; K \vdash (\sigma', v) : A$.*

Soundness states that well-typed expressions do not go wrong:

Theorem 2 (Soundness). *If $\emptyset; K \vdash (\emptyset, a) : A$, then $(\emptyset, a) \not\Downarrow$ WRONG.*

---

[1] These rules presented here only apply when all of the underlying assumptions are specified. Error cases which evaluate to WRONG are captured by the other evaluation rules which we omit. They account for the following errors: message-not-understood error, when the method is not present in the object; an incorrect number of arguments supplied to a method call; and the propogation of errors through subexpressions.

6 The Containment Invariant

The containment invariant is a statement about the well-formedness of stores, in particular the underlying reference structure. The containment invariant states that for well-typed stores the following holds:

$$\iota \to \iota' \;\Rightarrow\; \mathsf{rep}(\iota) \prec: \mathsf{owner}(\iota'),$$

where $\mathsf{owner}(\iota)$ and $\mathsf{rep}(\iota)$ give the owner and representation context of an object.

To prove this formally requires a little more work than suggested by the intuition at the start of Section 4.1. The key aspect to enforcing containment is the use of permissions to control object access to the owner contexts. We define a series of projection functions which collect owner contexts underlying permissions, types, and locations in expressions. In other words, these functions project permissions, types and expressions onto contexts.

The key results state that the owner context for a value is contained in the underlying contexts for its type, and the owner contexts underlying types and expressions are contained within those of any permission that gives access to the types and expressions. In particular, this means that the permission does really bound the owner contexts of locations in an expression. By applying this result to method bodies — more precisely, the locations a method refers to — we obtain the result we desire.

The projection functions are (where $\mathbb{P}(\mathcal{C})$ is the powerset of $\mathcal{C}$):

- $\eta : \textsc{Location} \to \mathcal{C}$.
- $[\![\_]\!] : \textsc{Permission} \to \mathbb{P}(\mathcal{C})$.
- $[\![\_]\!] : \textsc{Type} \to \mathbb{P}(\mathcal{C})$.
- $[\![\_]\!]_\eta : \textsc{Expression} \to \mathbb{P}(\mathcal{C})$.

We use the notation $\eta \models E$ to state that whenever $\iota : [l_i : A_i{}^{i\in 1..n}]_q^p$ occurs in E, then $\eta(\iota) = p$. That is, $\eta(\iota)$ is the same as $\mathsf{owner}(\iota)$. This serves to define η.

The second and third of these functions are defined as follows:

$$[\![\langle p \rangle]\!] \;\widehat{=}\; \{p\}$$
$$[\![\langle q {\uparrow} \rangle]\!] \;\widehat{=}\; \{p \in \mathcal{C} \mid q \prec: p\}$$

$$[\![[l_i : A_i{}^{i\in 1..n}]_q^p]\!] \;\widehat{=}\; \{p\}$$

The final projection (and later the *refers to* relation) depends on the locations present in an expression:

Definition 2 (Locations in a Expression). *The set of locations in an expression, $\mathsf{locs}(a)$, is defined as follows:*

$$\mathsf{locs}(x) \;\widehat{=}\; \emptyset$$
$$\mathsf{locs}(\iota) \;\widehat{=}\; \{\iota\}$$

$$locs([l_i = \varsigma(x_i : A_i, \Gamma_i)b_i{}^{i \in 1..n}]_q^p) \; \hat{=} \; \emptyset$$
$$locs(v.l\langle \Delta \rangle) \; \hat{=} \; locs(v) \cup locs(\Delta)$$
$$locs(\emptyset) \; \hat{=} \; \emptyset$$
$$locs(v, \Delta) \; \hat{=} \; locs(v) \cup locs(\Delta)$$
$$locs(v.l \Leftarrow \varsigma(x : A, \Gamma)b) \; \hat{=} \; locs(v) \cup locs(b)$$
$$locs(\textbf{let } x : A = a \textbf{ in } b) \; \hat{=} \; locs(a) \cup locs(b)$$

Notice this does not look inside objects, because objects define a boundary inside of which the permissions may be different.

The remaining projection is defined as follows:

$$[\![a]\!] \; \hat{=} \; \{\eta(\iota) \mid \iota \in \mathsf{locs}(a)\}$$

The following theorem can be proven by mutual deduction on the structure of typing derivations.

Theorem 3. *We have the following, where in each relevant case $\eta \models E$,*

1. *If $K' \subseteq K$, then $[\![K']\!] \subseteq [\![K]\!]$;*
2. *If $K \vdash A$, then $[\![A]\!] \subseteq [\![K]\!]$;*
3. *If $K \vdash A{<:}B$, then $[\![A]\!] \subseteq [\![B]\!]$;*
4. *If $E; K \vdash a : A$, then $[\![a]\!]_\eta \subseteq [\![K]\!]$;*
5. *If $E; K \vdash v : A$, then $[\![v]\!]_\eta \subseteq [\![A]\!]$; and*
6. *If $E; K \vdash (\Theta)(\Delta) \Rightarrow C$, then $[\![\Delta]\!]_\eta \subseteq [\![K]\!]$.*

It is illuminating to understand the difference between clauses 4 and 5. Clause 4 applies to all expressions including values, stating that permissions control access within expressions. Extending clause 5 to expressions is impossible because an expression may compute using locations which are not captured in the type, yet return a value of a type which only requires a smaller permission to access.

With the notion of a *well-contained store* we capture the containment invariant globally, that is for all stored objects.

Definition 3 (Well-contained Store).

$$\boldsymbol{wf}_\eta(\sigma) \; \hat{=} \; \bigwedge_{\iota \mapsto o \in \sigma} \boldsymbol{wf}_\eta(o)$$

$$\boldsymbol{wf}_\eta([l_i = \varsigma(x_i : A_i, \Gamma_i)b_i{}^{i \in 1..n}]_q^p) \; \hat{=} \; [\![b_i]\!]_\eta \subseteq [\![\langle q \uparrow \rangle]\!]$$

We can use Theorem 3 to easily prove that a well-typed store is well-contained:

Lemma 2. *If $E \vdash \sigma$ and $\eta \models E$ then $\boldsymbol{wf}_\eta(\sigma)$.*

We now convert this result to a local one, that is, one defined between pair of locations, thus demonstrating containment invariance. Firstly, we need the *refers to* relation, which collects the locations present in the bodies of all the methods of an object:

Definition 4 (*refers to*). *The* refers to *relation,* $\to_\sigma$*, for store* σ *is defined as:*

$$\iota \to_\sigma \iota' \text{ iff } \iota \mapsto [l_i = \varsigma(x_i : A_i, \Gamma_i)b_i{}^{i\in 1..n}]_q^p \in \sigma \wedge \iota' \in \textsf{locs}(b_i), \text{ for some } i \in 1..n$$

The functions which give the owner and representation context of an object are defined for a given location-object, $\iota \mapsto [l_i = \varsigma(x_i : A_i, \Gamma_i)b_i{}^{i\in 1..n}]_q^p \in \sigma$, as: $\textsf{owner}_\sigma(\iota) \mathrel{\widehat{=}} p$ and $\textsf{rep}_\sigma(\iota) \mathrel{\widehat{=}} q$,

The containment invariant is now straightforward:

Theorem 4 (Containment Invariant).
   If $E \vdash \sigma$ *then* $\iota \to_\sigma \iota' \Rightarrow \textsf{rep}_\sigma(\iota) \prec: \textsf{owner}_\sigma(\iota')$.

PROOF:

1. ASSUME: $E \vdash \sigma$ and $\iota \to_\sigma \iota'$. In addition, select an η for which $\eta \models E$.
2. By Lemma 2, $\mathbf{wf}_\eta(\sigma)$.
3. So $\iota \mapsto [l_i = \varsigma(x_i : A_i, \Gamma_i)b_i{}^{i\in 1..n}]_q^p \in \sigma$, where $\iota' \in \textsf{locs}(b_i)$ for some i, and $q = \textsf{rep}_\sigma(\iota)$.
4. By 2 and Definition 3, we get $[\![b_i]\!]_\eta \subseteq [\![\langle q \uparrow \rangle]\!]$, where $\eta \models E$.
5. From the definition of $[\![a]\!]_\eta$ for expressions it is clear that $[\![\iota']\!]_\eta \subseteq [\![b_i]\!]_\eta$.
6. But $[\![\iota']\!]_\eta = \{\textsf{owner}_\sigma(\iota')\}$.
7. Therefore $\textsf{owner}_\sigma(\iota') \in [\![\langle q \uparrow \rangle]\!]$, where $q = \textsf{rep}_\sigma(\iota)$.
8. Unravelling the definition of $[\![\langle q \uparrow \rangle]\!]$, we get $\textsf{rep}_\sigma(\iota) \prec: \textsf{owner}_\sigma(\iota')$, as required.

This proof technique generalises to the type system of companion work [13]. This will appear in the first author's thesis [14].

7   Related Work

The pointer structures within object-oriented programs have received surprisingly little examination over the last decade — much less interest than has been lavished on the more tractable problem of inheritance relationships between classes. Good surveys of the problems caused (and advantages gained) by aliasing in object-oriented programming can be found elsewhere [24, 3, 34]. More general notions of references, aggregation, object containment, and ownership have been considered in detail, and are now part of accepted standards [12, 20, 26, 17, 36, 35].

Early work [24], beginning with Islands [23] generally took an informal approach to describing or restricting programs' topologies, based on very simple models of containment. Islands, for example, is based on statically checked mode annotations attached to an object's interface, while the more recent Balloons [3] depends upon sophisticated abstract interpretation to enforce the desired restrictions. Often, these kinds of systems mandate copying, swapping, temporary variables, or destructive reads (rather than standard assignments) to protect their invariants, [5, 10, 21, 28, 30, 9], so they are unable to express many common uses of aliasing in object-oriented programs.

Static alias analysis has similarly long been of interest to compiler writers, even since programming languages began to permit aliasing. Whole programs can be analysed directly to detect possible aliasing [27, 16, 25], or hints may be given to the compiler as to probable aliasing invariants [22]. Static analysis techniques have also been developed to optimise locking in concurrent languages, particularly Java [11, 6, 7, 2, 38]. This work is typically based around escape analysis and removes exclusion from objects that can be shown to be owned by a single thread, although Aldrich et.al.'s work also removes redundant synchronisation due to enclosing locks [2], implying a very simple notion of per-object ownership.

More recent work [33] has attempted to be more practically useful, combining annotations on objects with more flexible models of containment or ownership. Flexible Alias Protection [34] uses a number of annotations to provide nested per-object ownership, while permitting objects to refer to objects belonging to their (transitive) container as well as objects they own directly. A dynamically checked variant has also been proposed [32].

Guava [4] uses a system of annotations on variables and types similar to Flexible Alias Protection, but motivated towards controlling synchronisation in concurrent Java programs, rather than managing aliasing per se. Confined Types [8] use only one annotation to confine objects inside Java packages. This gives a much coarser granularity of ownership than many other proposals, so is advocated mostly for security reasons. Sandwich Types [18] are similar to Confined Types in that they restrict references from instance of one type to instances of another, however they are intended to improve locality by using a separate heap for each Sandwich. Universes [31] are in some way the most similar to the ownership types we have presented here. Their universes are like our representation contexts, and they do incorporate subtyping. However they do not have the clear separation of owner and rep context that we have presented here.

In a companion paper, we develop a more complex ownership type system incorporating dynamic creation of contexts, which allows every object to have its own context, as well as context parameters on methods, and existential quantification over contexts [13]. The simplified rule for object subtyping, (Sub Object), presented in this paper does not appear in the companion work. It would allow existential quantification to be eliminated, simplifying the underlying type system. The present work is simpler and closer to proposals such as Confined Types [8], which depend on a predefined containment model. We believe that this is appropriate particularly for security-sensitive applications.

8   Conclusion

In this paper, we have presented extensions to Abadi and Cardelli's object calculus to describe object ownership. Ownership and representation contexts were added to both objects and object types: the owner context controls which other objects can access an object, while the representation context controls which other objects an object can access. Combined, these form the basis for our containment invariant, which holds for the type system presented here.

The advantage these extensions confer onto the object calculus is simple: the extended calculus can now model containment in a natural and straightforward manner. Due to our static type system, system-level invariants based on containment can be described directly and enforced without any runtime overheads.

The simple type system presented in this paper is restricted in that ownership contexts are fixed: new contexts cannot be created at runtime. While this is sufficient to model systems such as Confined Types [8], we are continuing to develop more powerful (and therefore more complex) type systems that can model systems such as Flexible Alias Protection [34] and its even more flexible successors.

References

[1] Martín Abadi and Luca Cardelli. *A Theory of Objects*. Springer-Verlag, 1996.
[2] Jonathan Aldrich, Craig Chambers, Emin Gun Sirer, and Susan Eggers. Static analyses for eliminating unnecessary synchronization from Java programs. In *Sixth International Static Analysis Symposium*. Springer-Verlag, September 1999.
[3] Paulo Sérgio Almeida. Balloon Types: Controlling sharing of state in data types. In *ECOOP Proceedings*, June 1997.
[4] David F. Bacon, Robert E. Strom, and Ashis Tarafdar. Guava: A dialect of Java without data races. In *OOPSLA'00 Conference Proceedings—Object-Oriented Programming Systems, Languages and Applications*, volume 35, pages 382–400, New York, October 2000. ACM Press.
[5] Henry G. Baker. 'Use-once' variables and linear objects – storage management, reflection and multi-threading. *ACM SIGPLAN Notices*, 30(1), January 1995.
[6] Bruno Blanchet. Escape analysis for object-oriented languages. application to Java. In *OOPSLA Proceedings*, pages 20–34. ACM, 1999.
[7] Jeff Bogda and Urs Hölzle. Removing unnecessary synchronization in Java. In *OOPSLA Proceedings*, pages 35–46. ACM, 1999.
[8] Boris Bokowski and Jan Vitek. Confined Types. In *OOPSLA Proceedings*, 1999.
[9] John Boyland. Alias burying. *Software—Practice & Experience*, 2001. To appear.
[10] Edwin C. Chan, John T. Boyland, and William L. Scherlis. Promises: Limitied specifications for analysis and manipulation. In *IEEE International Conference on Software Engineering (ICSE)*, 1998.
[11] Jong-Deok Choi, M. Gupta, Mauricio Serrano, Vugranam C. Sreedhar, and Sam Midkiff. Escape analysis for Java. In *OOPSLA Proceedings*, pages 1–19. ACM, 1999.
[12] Franco Civello. Roles for composite objects in object-oriented analysis and design. In *OOPSLA Proceedings*, 1993.
[13] David Clarke. An object calculus with ownership and containment. In *Foundations of Object-Oriented Languages (FOOL) 2001*, 2001.
[14] David Clarke. *Object Ownership and Containment*. PhD thesis, School of Computer Science and Engineering, University of New South Wales, Sydney, Australia, 2001. In preparation.
[15] David G. Clarke, John M. Potter, and James Noble. Ownership types for flexible alias protection. In *OOPSLA Proceedings*, 1998.

[16] Alain Deutsch. Interprocedural May-Alias Analysis for Pointers: Beyond k-limiting. In *Proceedigns of the ACM SIGPLAN'94 Conference on Programming Language Design and Implementation*, June 1994.

[17] Jin Song Dong and Roger Duke. Exclusive control within object oriented systems. In *TOOLS Pacific 18*, 1995.

[18] Daniela Genius, Martin Trapp, and Wolf Zimmermann. An approach to improve locality using sandwich types. In *Proceedings of the 2nd Types in Compilation workshop*, number 1473 in Lecture Notes in Computer Science, pages 194–214, Kyoto, Japan, March 1998. Springer-Verlag.

[19] A. D. Gordon, P. D. Hankin, and S. B. Lassen. Compilation and equivalence of imperative objects. *Journal of Functional Programming*, 9(4):373–426, July 1999.

[20] Peter Grogono and Patrice Chalin. Copying, sharing, and aliasing. In *Proceedings of the Colloquium on Object Orientation in Databases and Software Engineering (COODBSE'94)*, Montreal, Quebec, May 1994.

[21] Douglas E. Harms and Bruce W. Weide. Copying and swapping: Influences on the design of reusable software components. *IEEE Transactions on Software Engineering*, 17(5), May 1991.

[22] Laurie J. Hendren and G. R. Gao. Designing programming languages for analyzability: A fresh look at pointer data structures. In *Proceedings of the IEEE 1992 International Conference on Programming Languages*, April 1992.

[23] John Hogg. Islands: Aliasing protection in object-oriented languages. In *OOPSLA Proceedings*, November 1991.

[24] John Hogg, Doug Lea, Alan Wills, Dennis de Champeaux, and Richard Holt. The Geneva convention on the treatment of object aliasing. *OOPS Messenger*, 3(2), April 1992.

[25] Neil D. Jones and Steven Muchnick. Flow analysis and optimization of LISP-like structures. In Steven Muchnick and Neil D. Jones, editors, *Program Flow Analysis: Theory and Applications*. Prentice Hall, 1981.

[26] Stuart Kent and Ian Maung. Encapsulation and aggregation. In *TOOLS Pacific 18*, 1995.

[27] William Landi. Undecidability of static analysis. *ACM Letters on Programming Languages and Systems*, 1(4), December 1992.

[28] K. Rustan M. Leino and Raymie Stata. Virginity: A contribution to the specification of object-oriented software. Technical Report SRC-TN-97-001, Digital Systems Research Center, April 1997.

[29] Bertrand Meyer. *Eiffel: The Language*. Prentice Hall, 1992.

[30] Naftaly Minsky. Towards alias-free pointers. In *ECOOP Proceedings*, July 1996.

[31] P. Müller and A. Poetzsch-Heffter. Universes: A type system for controlling representation exposure. In A. Poetzsch-Heffter and J. Meyer, editors, *Programming Languages and Fundamentals of Programming*. Fernuniversität Hagen, 1999.

[32] James Noble, David Clarke, and John Potter. Object ownership for dynamic alias protection. In *TOOLS Pacific*, Melbourne, Australia, November 1999.

[33] James Noble, Jan Vitek, and Doug Lea. *Report of the Intercontinental Workshop on Aliasing in Object-Oriented Systems*, volume 1743 of *Lecture Notes in Computer Science*. Springer, Berlin, Heidelberg, New York, 2000.

[34] James Noble, Jan Vitek, and John Potter. Flexible alias protection. In Eric Jul, editor, *ECOOP'98— Object-Oriented Programming*, volume 1445 of *Lecture Notes In Computer Science*, pages 158–185, Berlin, Heidelberg, New York, July 1998. Springer-Verlag.

[35] John Potter and James Noble. Conglomeration: Realising aliasing protection. In *Proceedings of the Australian Computer Science Conference (ACSC)*, Canberra, January 2000.

[36] John Potter, James Noble, and David Clarke. The ins and outs of objects. In *Australian Software Engineering Conference*, Adelaide, Australia, November 1998. IEEE Press.

[37] Amr Sabry and Matthias Felleisen. Reasoning about programs in continuation-passing style. In *1992 ACM Conference on LISP and Functional Programming*, pages 288–298, San Francisco, CA, June 1992. ACM.

[38] John Whaley and Martin Rinard. Compositional pointer and escape analysis for Java programs. In *OOPSLA'99 Conference Proceedings—Object-Oriented Programming Systems, Languages and Applications*, volume 34, pages 187–206, New York, October 1999. ACM Press.

Distinctness and Sharing Domains for Static Analysis of Java Programs

Isabelle Pollet[1]*, Baudouin Le Charlier[1], and Agostino Cortesi[2]**

[1] University of Namur, Belgium
[2] Ca' Foscari University, Italy

Abstract. The application field of static analysis techniques for object-oriented programming is getting broader, ranging from compiler optimizations to security issues. This leads to the need of methodologies that support reusability not only at the code level but also at higher (semantic) levels, in order to minimize the effort of proving correctness of the analyses. Abstract interpretation may be the most appropriate approach in that respect. This paper is a contribution towards the design of a general framework for abstract interpretation of Java programs. We introduce two generic abstract domains that express type, structural, and sharing information about dynamically created objects. These generic domains can be instantiated to get specific analyses either for optimization or verification issues. The semantics of the domains are precisely defined by means of concretization functions based on mappings between concrete and abstract locations. The main abstract operations, i.e., upper bound and assignment, are discussed. An application of the domains to source-to-source program specialization is sketched to illustrate the effectiveness of the analysis.

Keywords: Abstract Interpretation, Static Analysis, Type Analysis, Program Specialization.

1 Introduction

The application field of static analysis techniques for object-oriented programming is getting broader, ranging from compiler optimizations to security issues. This leads to the need of methodologies that support reusability not only at the code level but also at higher (semantic) levels, in order to minimize the effort of proving correctness of the analyses.

In this paper we introduce and discuss the foundations of a project aimed at defining and implementing a Java code analyzer based on abstract interpretation [9], a general semantics based methodology for static analysis that has been successfully applied to a large number of purposes mostly in declarative programming languages. In order to derive program properties that hold for every possible execution, an abstract interpreter 'executes' the program over a non

---

* Supported by the Belgian National Fund for Scientific Research (FNRS).
** Partially supported by MURST projects 'Certificazione Automatica di Programmi mediante Interpretazione Astratta' and 'Interpretazione Astratta, Type Systems e Analisi Control-Flow'.

J. Lindskov Knudsen (Ed.): ECOOP 2001, LNCS 2072, pp. 77–98, 2001.

standard domain of (so-called) abstract values. In the case of type analysis, abstract values denote sets of types (i.e., the possible types of the actual instances that may arise at run time). The analysis is conservative, i.e., no erroneus result can be derived, but the results can be inaccurate in some cases. Inaccuracy is an obvious consequence of the fact that any non-trivial property of program execution is undecidable.

The reason to adopt abstract interpretation is twofold. First, the conceptual simplicity and soundness of this technique ensure that most properties of the resulting analysis (precision, completeness, modularity, scalability) depend only upon the choice of a concrete semantics, an abstract domain of properties, and abstract operations that safely approximate the corresponding concrete operations. Second, the design of abstract interpreters has already been successfully developed for other language paradigms (in particular for declarative programming) and we are confident that this approach may have a similar impact on object-oriented programs. Despite the great amount of scientific contributions on object-oriented languages, most of the works on semantics that may support static analyses mainly focused on Data Flow and Type System approaches, while disregarding abstract interpretation. Investigating this methodology for Java programs is thus one of the original contributions of this paper.

The first step in our work has been a precise description of an operational semantics for a sublanguage of Java [22]. The concrete semantics is expressed as a transition system on (finite) graph-descriptions of execution states. A graph-description represents both the environment (i.e., the mapping of each variable to its location), and the store (i.e., the mapping of each location to its value). We do not report on these concrete semantics issues in this paper; we focus instead on the definition of two generic abstract domains for type analysis, namely a distinctness domain and a sharing domain.

These two generic domains share the same key idea: abstract environments and stores look like concrete ones but the values of base types are disregarded (since we focus at this time on type analysis) and types are approximated when needed, keeping the structure as much as possible. This homomorphism between abstract and concrete domain facilitates the understanding of abstract structures.

The two generic abstract domains differ as they correspond to dual ways to look at structural sharing. In the first domain, distinctness of abstract locations can be interpreted as a definite information while structural sharing only means that the corresponding concrete structures may share. In the second domain, structural sharing is a definite information while distinctness of abstract locations only means that the corresponding concrete locations may be distinct. The first approach leads to the 'distinctness domain'. The second one leads to the 'sharing domain'.

Both abstract domains are generic as they are parameterized on a primitive abstract domain whose elements represent sets of concrete types. They can be specialized by a suitable choice of these abstract descriptions to yield specific analysis. They basically integrate type analysis [1, 5] and shape analysis [6, 11, 12, 14, 25].

The rest of the paper is organized as follows. Section 2 outlines the main features of the domains, including a discussion of domain operations (orderings, upper bounds and convergence issues) as well as a discussion of the (abstract) assignment operation, which is one of the most essential and critical step in the design of the abstract semantics. Section 3 presents an application in the area of static detection of dynamic dispatching, describing the use of the abstract domain in program specialization. Sections 4 and 5 discuss related and future work.

We adopt in this paper an intuitive and informal presentation based on examples. Technical material, including definitions, algorithms and proofs, can be found in [22, 23]. We just give here the most basic definitions to provide some feel for the formal treatment behind the intuition.

2   Domains and Operations

The abstract interpretation methodology may be briefly described by the following three steps [9, 21].

1. Define a concrete (operational) semantics, i.e., a formal representation of concrete execution states and of the transition rules corresponding to statement executions. This step, of course, is language-dependent.
2. Define an abstract semantics, i.e., a non-standard domain whose elements represent sets of concrete execution states, and a suite of abstract operations that safely approximate the corresponding concrete ones.
3. Define a generic algorithm, parameterized on the abstract domain, that computes a (post-)fixpoint of the abstract semantics, thus yielding safe information about concrete program executions.

Once points 1 and 3 above are settled, the analysis can be easily tuned according to specific tasks. It just needs to choose a suitable abstract domain, and the correctness of the analysis will follow for free.

In the rest of this section we introduce the main features of concrete and abstract semantics that fit the picture above in the case of object-oriented programs. The abstract domains have been designed for Java but the same approach can be used for other object-oriented languages as well.

2.1   Concrete (Standard) Domain

The concrete domain[1] we consider is a classical product 'environment-store'. Its elements are graphs whose nodes are 'elementary instances' linked, by an edge, to their 'super-instance' and to their fields. Technically, a store is a mapping from an arbitrary and infinite set of *locations* to the set of values (basic values or instances). A *location* can be viewed as the address of a field or of a variable.

---

[1] Usually called 'standard domain'.

Figure 2.1 shows an element of the domain. This situation considers two variables x and y and the current instance. The variable x has a basic type, while y refers to an instance of a simple class whose field ch is equal to null. The current instance is of type C, which extends D. This situation happens, for instance, at the beginning of the execution of the method call c.meth(7,a) (this method is also depicted in Figure 2.1).

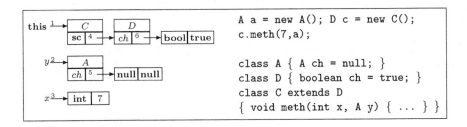

Fig. 2.1. The simple concrete situation S

The mathematical presentation of this domain is given in Definition 1. To complete this definition, we just need to add some constraints to the product $\mathbb{E}nv \times \$tore$ (see [22, 23]). In this definition, $Nclass$ is the set of all class names, while $Nfield$ is the set of possible field names and $Nvar$ the set of (local) variable names.

Definition 1 (Concrete Domain). *The set of **values** is defined as the disjoined union of the **basic values** and the **instances**, i.e., $\mathbb{V}al = \mathbb{B}ase + \mathbb{I}nst$ where $\mathbb{B}ase = \{\mathbf{bool}\} \times \mathbb{B}ool + \{\mathbf{int}\} \times \mathbb{Z} + \{(\mathbf{ni}, \mathbf{ni}), (\mathbf{null}, \mathbf{null})\}$ and $\mathbb{I}nst$ is the largest subset of $Nclass \times (Nfield + \{\mathbf{sc}\} \rightarrowtail \mathbb{L}oc)$ such that if (nc, v) belongs to $\mathbb{I}nst$, then v is one-to-one. The set $\mathbb{E}nv$ of **environments** is defined as the largest subset of $Nvar + \{\mathbf{this}\} \rightarrowtail Type \times \mathbb{L}oc$ such that if e belongs to $\mathbb{E}nv$ and if x and y are two separate elements of the domain of e, then $p_2(e(x)) \neq p_2(e(y))$, with $Type = Nclass + \{\mathbf{null}, \mathbf{int}, \mathbf{bool}, \mathbf{ni}\}$. The set of **stores** is defined as $\$tore = \mathbb{L}oc \rightarrowtail \mathbb{V}al$.*

2.2   Abstract Domains

The abstract domains are very similar to the concrete one but they introduce a new kind of values: the *abstract types*. For each concrete instance, either we keep complete information about its structure at the abstract level, or abstract information about its type, that we call an *abstract type*.

Our framework is completely parametric on the choice of type abstractions. We just need an abstract domain $Type^{\#}$, equipped with an order relation and a least upper bound operator. This domain should be related to the set of types $Type$ by a concretization function $\gamma : Type^{\#} \rightarrow \wp(Type)$. For instance, $Type^{\#}$ may be set equal to the powerset $\wp(Type)$, or to the set $Type$ itself (with $\gamma(t) = \{t' \preceq t\}$, i.e., the set of types specializing t); as a further example, in case of security analyses $Type^{\#}$ may be defined as a partition of $Type$, according to protection domains.

An abstract situation approximating the concrete situation S is depicted in Figure 2.2 (we assume that $Type^{\#} = \wp(Type)$). In this abstract situation, the type of the current instance is approximated and all the structural information concerning this instance is lost.

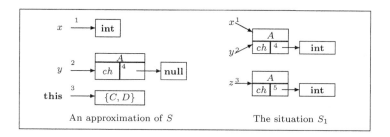

An approximation of S The situation S_1

Fig. 2.2. Two abstract situations

The mathematical presentation of the abstract domains is below. Like in the concrete case, to complete this definition, we just need to add some constraints to the product $Env^{\#} \times \$tore^{\#}$ (see [22, 23]).

Definition 2 (Abstract Domain). *The set of **abstract values** $Val^{\#}$ is defined as $Val^{\#} = Type + Type^{\#} + Inst^{\#}$ where $Inst^{\#}$ is the largest subset of $Nclass \times (Nfield + \{sc\} \longmapsto Loc^{\#})$ such that if (nc, v) belongs to $Inst^{\#}$ then v is one-to-one. The set $Env^{\#}$ of **abstract environments** is defined as the largest subset of $Nvar + \{this\} \longmapsto Type \times Loc^{\#}$, such that if e belongs to $Env^{\#}$ and if x and y are two different elements of the domain of e, then $p_2(e(x)) \neq p_2(e(y))$. The set of **abstract stores** is defined as $\$tore^{\#} = Loc^{\#} \longmapsto Val^{\#}$.*

In the rest of the paper we discuss two generic interpretations of Definition 2, called distinctness and sharing domain, that differ in the way they express information about structural sharing of (concrete) data structures. In the distinctness domain, we assume that two distinct abstract instances always stand for different concrete instances. In the sharing domain, we dually assume that every abstract instance stands for a single concrete one. Such an information is useful notably to improve the accuracy of abstract assignment.

Consider the abstract situation S_1 of Figure 2.2. This situation gives exact type information, but what does it say about structure sharing? Concrete situations potentially (i.e., with the same type information) represented by S_1 (ignoring the exact integer values) are given in Figure 2.3.

In the distinctness domain, the situation S_1 expresses that z is certainly distinct from x and y (but says nothing about the sharing of x and y). Thus the set of situations represented by S_1 in restricted to $\{s_1, s_2\}$. On the contrary, in the sharing domain S_1 expresses that x and y certainly share the same instance (but

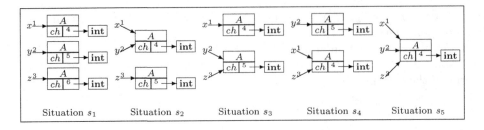

Fig. 2.3. Concrete situations potentially represented by S_1

says nothing about the distinction in regards of z). Thus, the set of represented situations is reduced to $\{s_2, s_5\}$. Briefly, we can say that, in the distinctness domain, the abstract sharing is an approximation, whereas, in the sharing domain it is an exact information.

To capture the intuition, we observe that there are obvious correspondences between concrete and abstract locations. Let us look again at Figure 2.3 and 2.2: in the case of s_1, we have the relation $f_1 = \{(1, a), (2, b), (3, c), (4, d), (5, d), (6, e)\}$, in the case of s_2, the relation $f_2 = \{(1, a), (2, b), (3, c), (4, d), (4, e)\}$ and, in the case of s_5, the relation $f_5 = \{(1, a), (2, b), (3, c), (4, d), (5, e)\}$. The relations f_1 and f_2 are both functions whereas f_2 and f_5 are both one-to-one (precisely the dual property of functionality).

The distinctness domain requires the existence of a (partial but onto) mapping of the concrete locations to the abstract locations, whereas the sharing domain requires a mapping (total but perhaps not onto) of the abstract locations to the concrete ones. These mappings must respect the types and the structure of the instances. The technical definitions of the concretization functions of these two domains rely on these mappings (see [22, 23]). We just give here the definition of the concretization function for the distinctness domain.

Definition 3 (Distinctness Domain: Concretization Function). *Let be* $a = (a_0, a_1)$ *belonging to* $Env^\# \times \$tore^\#$ *and* $d = (d_0, d_1)$ *belonging to* $Env \times \$tore$. *We will say that* a ***approximates*** d ***throughout*** f, *i.e.,* $d \xrightarrow{f} a$, *if and only if* a, d *and* f *satisfy the three following properties.*

1. $f : dom(d_1) \nrightarrow dom(a_1)$
2. $d_0 = \{(v_1, t_1\delta_1), ..., (v_n, t_n\delta_n), (\mathbf{this}, t_{n+1}\delta_{n+1})\}$
   $a_0 = \{(v_1, t_1\alpha_1), ..., (v_n, t_n\alpha_n), (\mathbf{this}, t_{n+1}\alpha_{n+1})\}$
   $\forall i : 1 \le i \le n + 1 : f(\delta_i) = \alpha_i$
3. $\forall l \in dom(f)$,

$$a_1(f(l)) = t \in Type \Rightarrow d_1(l) \in Base \wedge (p_1(d_1(l)) = t$$
$$a_1(f(l)) = e \in Type^\# \Rightarrow p_1(d_1(l)) \in \gamma(e)$$
$$a_1(f(l)) = (nc, va) \in Inst^\# \Rightarrow \begin{cases} d_1(l) = (nc, v) \in Inst \\ dom(v) = dom(va) \\ \forall ch \in dom(v), va(ch) = f(v(ch)) \end{cases}$$

The ***concretization function*** $\gamma_d : \mathbb{D}^\# \to \wp(\mathbb{D})$ *of the distinctness domain is defined in* a *as* $\gamma_d(a) = \{d \mid \exists f, d \xrightarrow{f} a\}$.

Other domains can be defined by assuming other properties for the correspondences between concrete and abstract locations. For instance, requiring that the correspondence is one-to-one and functional leads to the (trivial) domain associating only situations with strictly the same sharing of instances (in our example, $\gamma(S_1) = \{s_2\}$). As another extreme example, accepting any correspondence (respecting the types) leads to a second (trivial) domain without any sharing information (in our example, $\gamma(S_1) = \{s_1, s_2, s_3, s_4, s_5\}$). However, these two domains are less attractive: the first one loses most of the structural information when an upper bound operation is applied, while the second one is very imprecise in the case of abstract assignment.

2.3 Orderings

Both abstract domains are endowed with a relation such that if an element a is smaller than another element a', all situations represented by a are also represented by a'. This means that the preorder is *coherent* with the concretization function. Consequently, the definition of the preorder is very similar to the definition of the concretization function. Again, the key idea is the existence of a relation between the locations of a and the locations of a' respecting the types and the structure.

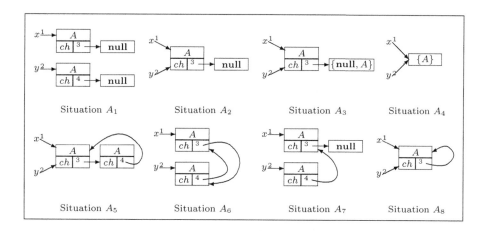

Fig. 2.4. Some abstract situations: which are approximations of others?

We illustrate the preorders on the situations in Figure 2.4. In the case of the distinctness domain, we directly see that $A_1 \leq A_2 \leq A_3 \leq A_4$. Indeed, A_1 gives an exact information about types and sharing whereas A_2 keeps exactly the same type information but loses the information about the distinction between x and y; A_3 is similar to A_2 but approximates the type of ch and A_4 loses all structural information but gives a coherent type information relatively to A_3. The situations A_5 and A_6 give the same type information but are not comparable at the structural level. However, they both can be approximated by A_8, losing the distinction between the two instances but keeping the information that ch refers to one of these two instances. We also have that A_7 and A_8 can both be approximated by A_3, and thus by A_4. As an example, the mapping between A_7 and A_3 is $f = \{(1,1),(2,2),(3,3),(4,3)\}$.

Let us now explore the case of the sharing domain. We directly see that we have the chains $A_2 \le A_1 \le A_4$ and $A_2 \le A_3 \le A_4$. Indeed, A_2 gives exact information about types and sharing whereas A_1 keeps exactly the same type information but loses the information about the sharing between x and y. The situation A_3 is similar to A_2 but approximates the type of ch. Finally, A_4 loses all structural information but gives a coherent type information relatively to A_3, or to A_1. This time, A_3 is not comparable to A_1: A_1 gives and exact type information but says nothing about the sharing of x and y, whereas A_3 says that x shares with y but gives an approximation for the type of $x.ch$. The situation A_8 gives exact type and structural information, whereas the situation A_5 introduces a doubt on the length of the list (length of one or two cells). We have thus that $A_8 \le A_5$ and, for similar reasons, we get $A_8 \le A_6$. We also have that $A_8 \le A_3$ and that all the situations are approximated by A_4. As an example, the mapping between A_8 and A_5 is $g = \{(1,1),(2,2),(3,3),(4,3)\}$.

The technical definitions of the preorders[2] are similar to the respective definitions of the concretization functions. See [22, 23] for these definitions and the coherence proofs.

2.4   Upper Bounds

We now tackle the problem of upper bound operators. A major feature of the distinctness domain is that it has no least upper bound operator[3], as we shall show it immediately on an example. Nevertheless, practically, we are satisfied with an upper bound operator (sufficiently precise however). An algorithm aimed at computing such an operator can be found in [23].

All situations in Figure 2.5 refer to the same environment that uses two variables x and y, of type B. The class B contains one field ch of type C. The class C is extended by D. Let us try to construct the least upper bound of C_1 and C_2. In the situation C_2, x and y share the same instance (i.e., at the concrete level, they can share or not). Thus, in the upper bound, they have to share as well. Furthermore, in the situation C_1, $x.ch$ refers to an instance of type C whereas, in C_2, it refers to an instance of D. Consequently, we approximate the type of $x.ch$ (which is equal to $y.ch$) and we get the situation C_3 as the upper bound. But we can reason in another way: C_1 and C_2 provide the same structure for y. Thus, we keep it in the upper bound. However, in C_2, x shares

---

[2] We do not get orders only because of the arbitrary choice of locations: it can be proven that two abstract elements a_1 and a_2 are *intuitively equivalent* (i.e., the same up to location renaming) if and only if $a_1 \le a_2$ and $a_2 \le a_1$.

[3] With the theoretical consequence that it lacks the property of being a Galois connection.

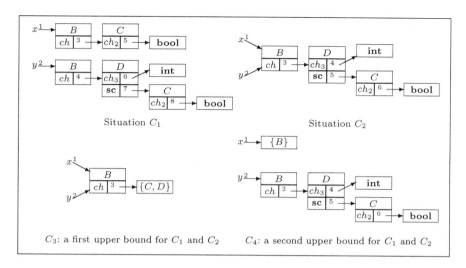

Situation C_1 Situation C_2

C_3: a first upper bound for C_1 and C_2 C_4: a second upper bound for C_1 and C_2

Fig. 2.5. The least upper bound does not exist in the distinctness domain.

with y but the structure of x in C_1 is incompatible with the structure of y. Thus we forget about the structure of x and we get the situation C_4 .

Since the situations C_3 and C_4 are not comparable, we have to conclude that the least upper does not always exist in this domain. Actually, we get a set of 'minimal approximations' instead of a 'minimum approximation'. Intuitively, this 'undesirable' feature stems from the fact that, in general, there are several ways to enforce structure sharing.

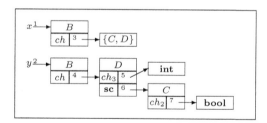

Fig. 2.6. The least upper bound for the sharing domain

We now turn to the sharing domain. We consider the same abstract situations as for the distinctness domain (they do not represent the same sets of concrete situations). In the situation C_1, x and y are referring to two different instances (i.e., just looking at these two instances, we know nothing about the concrete sharing). Thus, any upper bound must keep them different. The complete structure given for y is the same in the two situations, so we keep it. In the situation C_1, $x.ch$ refers to an instance of C whereas in C_2 it refers to an instance of D. Therefore, the type of $x.ch$ has to be approximated and we get the situation C_6 (see Figure 2.6). We obtain here a unique most precise upper bound and, actually, in this domain, the least upper bound always exists. The algorithm computing this least upper bound can be found in [22, 23].

2.5   Convergence

Our abstract domains are both infinite. Hence, the convergence of the induced analysis requires either that the domains satisfy the ascending chain condition (i.e, every infinite ascending chain eventually stabilizes) or that some form of widening can be defined [21].

The distinctness domain satisfies the ascending chain condition. The proof is technical but it can be sketched intuitively. Let $(a_i)_{i \geq 0}$ be an ascending chain. For each couple (a_i, a_{i+1}), there is an onto function from the locations of a_i to the locations of a_{i+1}. This implies that the number of locations decreases and finally stabilizes. The subsequent elements differ only by the (concrete or abstract) types attached to their locations. Moreover, the sequences of types determined by corresponding locations of those elements are all increasing. Therefore they stabilize (if $Type^{\#}$ satisfies the ascending chain condition).

The sharing domain does not satisfy the ascending chain condition. A counter-example is depicted in Figure 2.7. However, the following property holds: every infinite ascending chain either eventually stabilizes, or each of its elements contains a cycle. To prove this property, we first remark that if a_2 contains a cycle and $a_1 \leq a_2$, then necessarily a_1 contains a cycle. Thus, if one element in a chain is cycle-free, so are the following ones. In the cycle-free case, the proof of the ascending chain condition is similar to the proof for the distinctness domain but the stabilization of the number of locations is harder to prove since this number may increase locally. In that case, however, the amount of sharing contained in an element decreases. Technically, the amount of sharing is defined as the 'number of potential new locations' that an element can produce. For instance, the situation A_2 of Figure 2.4 has a potential of one new location (in the sense that the location 3 can be approximated by two locations) whereas its approximation A_1 has a potential of zero new locations. Notice that this number can be defined only if there is no cycle. Finally, the cycle-free characterization of stabilizing chains can be used to define a widening operator that 'breaks the cycles' when the number of locations appears to increase continuously.

2.6   Abstract Assignments

In this section we discuss the most interesting abstract operation: assignment. We explain its abstract semantics by means of significant examples. A more formal presentation of this section can be found in citerapport.

Let us first focus on the distinctness domain. What is the effect of the assignment $x.ch = \mathbf{null}$ on the situations D_1, D_2 and D_3 (see Figure 2.8)? In all these cases, the address of $x.ch$ is 4 and the new value to assign is $\mathbf{null}$. In the

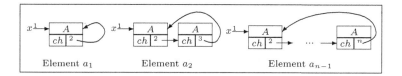

Fig. 2.7. An ascending chain in the sharing domain

case of D_1, the assignment happens exactly like in the concrete case and we get the situation D_4. Indeed, in this situation we know that x is distinct from y and thus the statement $x.ch =$ **null** cannot influence any instance of D_1 different of x. This ideal situation happens when only one location refers to the modified instance.

To the contrary, in the situation D_2, we do not know if x and y are referring to different instances. Thus the assignment can be applied either on x or on both x and y. So the exact type of $y.ch$ is unknown. A correct approximation of the effect of the assignment is, for instance, D_5. The situation is still worse in case D_3, where z may share the same instance. D_6 represents an acceptable solution. Observe that what we have done in the two last cases is to compute an upper bound of the situation before the assignment and the situation that is obtained by simply updating the store like in the concrete case. These are situations where several locations refer to the modified instance.

Moreover, it is not always possible to compute the address of a 'designator' (i.e., a variable or field access expression) as in the previous examples. Indeed, some parts of the structures of the instances may be cut while introducing abstract types. For instance, what is the effect of $z.ch =$ **null** on D_1? The abstract type gives no information about the sharing of any potential instance referred by z. It could share with x or with y (but not with both). Therefore the assignment may affect both instances. A correct approximation of the result in this case is D_7.

As for the 'designator' address, it is not always possible to compute the value of the assigned expression. For instance, we cannot completely evaluate the expression $z.ch$ in the situation D_1. Actually, this means that the situation D_1 gives no information at all about the type of this field. Consequently, the best information we can get is the one given by the type declaration of the field. Assuming that $z.ch$ is declared of type B, the situation D_8 approximates the application of the statement $x.ch = z.ch$ on the situation D_1 ($Cone(B)$ represents the set of types, including the **null** value, specializing B).

We now turn to the sharing domain. What is the effect of $x.ch =$ **null** on E_1 (see Figure 2.9) in this case? Here, we have no information at all about the sharing between the different instances of A. Consequently, we must explore all possibilities of sharing relative to x and we must compute the effect of the assignment for all of them. Actually, it is sufficient to look, on the one hand, at the situation with the weakest sharing and, on the other hand, at the situation with the strongest. These two situations are, after the assignment, E_2 and E_3.

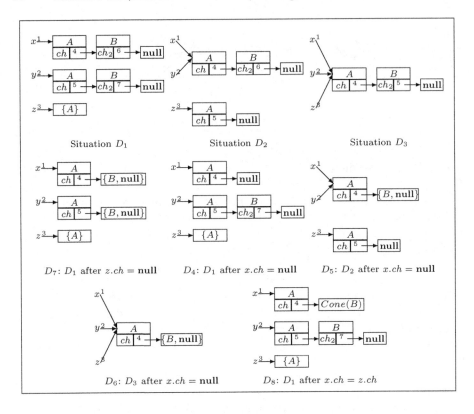

Fig. 2.8. Assignments in the distinctness domain

The abstract result E_4 of the assignment is then obtained by computing the least upper bound of E_3 and E_4. Notice that there is not always a single situation with the strongest possible sharing (like E_3). So, in general, we have to consider all of them.

The treatment of non evaluable addresses and values is similar to the case of the distinctness domain. As an example, the situation E_6 results from the application of the assignment $z.ch = $ **null** to the situation E_5.

3 Application to Program Specialization

In this section, we briefly illustrate how our analysis can be used. The example is about program optimization. More precisely, we focus on program specialization, as getting rid of dynamic dispatching is one of the useful application of static type analysis.

For the sake of the presentation, we adopt a source-to-source approach of these transformations as it may help the reader's intuition about the actual benefits of the analysis. It is obvious that they need not to be implemented this way in a compiler.

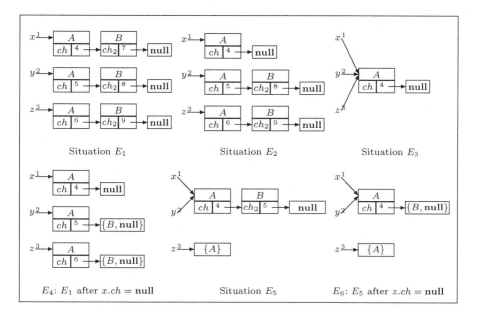

Fig. 2.9. Assignments in the sharing domain

We consider generic lists with only one main operation: the reading of a list (i.e., the method we want to analyze). We look at four Java classes[4] depicted in Figure 3.1: List (generic lists), L2List (lists of lists), StringList (lists of strings), and StringL2List (lists of string lists), with the inheritance relations: null < StringList < List and null < StringL2List < L2List < List.

We now attempt to specialize the generic method readList()[5] in the two concrete classes (i.e., StringList and StringL2List) to obtain more efficient versions.

Let us start with StringList. To perform this analysis, we can use a simple flat type domain: just keeping, for instance, the set of possible types for the variables. The abstract interpretation of newCell(List) applied to a StringList is trivial since it simply returns a new StringList instance. We now examine more cautiously the abstract interpretation of readList() applied to a StringList. Before going into the loop we simply get the mapping this ⤳ {StringList}, 1 ⤳ {StringList} since the method getCell() is applied on a StringList instance. After one iteration, this mapping becomes this ⤳ {StringList}, 1 ⤳ {StringList}, p ⤳ {StringList} and will not be changed by any further iteration. This type information allows us to specialize the method in the StringList class in the following way.

---

[4] We have slightly simplified the actual code to shorten the presentation.

[5] In this example, we use dynamic dispatch to simulate parametric polymorphism: the purpose of the target object of the method readList() is only to provide the exact type of the list to be read, at call time.

```
// Generic Lists                          // Lists of Strings

public abstract class List{               public class StringList
                                                 extends List{
private List next = null;
                                          private String info;
protected abstract List newCell();
protected abstract void getCell();        final protected List newCell() {
                                            StringList sl = new StringList();
private List newCell(List tail) {           return(sl);
  List l = newCell();                       }
  l.next = tail;
  return (l);                             final protected void getCell() {
  }                                         info = SimpleIO.getString();
                                            }
public List readList() {                  }
  List l = newCell(null);
  while (!SimpleIO.isEndOfReading())      // Lists of Lists of Strings
    {
    l.getCell();                          public class StringL2List
    List p = newCell(l);                         extends L2List{
    l=p;
    }                                     final protected List newCell() {
  return (l);                              StringL2List l = new StringL2List();
  }                                        l.info = new StringList();
}                                          return (l);
                                           }
// Lists of Lists
                                          }
public abstract class L2List
      extends List{

protected List info;

final protected void getCell() {
  info = info.readList();
  }
}
```

Fig. 3.1. Classes for list manipulation

```
public List readList()              \\ specialized for StringList
{
   StringList l = (StringList) newCell(null);
   while( SimpleIO.isEndOfReading() == false )
   {
       l.GetCell();
       StringList p = (StringList) newCell(l);
       l = p;
   }
   return(l);
}
```

Finally, we may apply inlining, yielding the following segment of code (without any dynamic dispatching) that directly applies the overriding methods getCell and newCell(List) defined in class StringList.

```
public List readList()                \\ for StringList, after inlining
{
    StringList l = new StringList();
    l.next = null;
    while( SimpleIO.isEndOfReading() == false )
    {
        l.info = SimpleIO.getString();
        StringList p = new StringList();
        p.next = l;
        l = p;
    }
    return(l);
}
```

The case of **StringL2List** is more interesting. In this case, the simple domain used in the previous example is not sufficient, as the analysis must record also structural information. We thus turn now to our domain (we use the distinctness domain here).

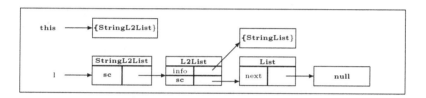

Fig. 3.2. Situation after the statement `List l = newCell(null)`

The type of the current instance is **StringL2List**. Consequently, when executing the call **newCell()** in the statement **List l = newCell(null)**, we surely execute the method of the class **StringL2List** yielding to the (abstract) situation[6] depicted in Figure 3.2. Let us examine the first iteration. We know the exact type of **l** and we apply the method **getCell()** of the class **StringL2List** (inherited from **L2List**). The statement **l.getCell()** does not modify the situation of Figure 3.2 (since we approximated the structure of the field **info**). If we now compute the effect of the sequence **List p = newCell(l); l = p;,** we obtain Figure 3.3. The computation of the body of the **while** statement is iterated and an upper bound operator is applied at each step, until a fixpoint is reached. This fixpoint is depicted in Figure 3.4 (in this case, it is simply an upper bound of the situations in Figures 3.2 and 3.3).

Just as for the **StringList** case, we can first specialize the method and then apply inlining for the calls to the methods **newCell(List)** and **getCell()**.

---

[6] Actually, we get a more precise information for the field **info** since we know its exact structure but we do not represent this structure here in order to simplify the pictures.

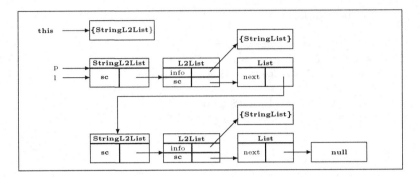

Fig. 3.3. Situation after one iteration

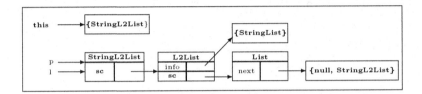

Fig. 3.4. Situation after the while statement

```
public List readList()        // inlining of getCell and newCell
{
   StringL2List l = new StringL2List();
   l.info = new StringList();
   l.next = null;
   while( SimpleIO.isEndOfReading() == false )
   {
       l.info = l.info.readList();
       StringL2List p = new StringL2List();
       p.info = new StringList();
       p.next = l;
       l = p;
   }
   return(l);
}
```

Moreover, we know here the exact type of the field `l.info`. Consequently, the specialized version of the method `readList()` for `StringList` will surely be executed in the statement `l.info = l.info.readList();`. Inlining the body of this method leads to the final version of the code with no dynamic dispatching anymore.

```
public List readList()        // inlining of getCell and newCell
{
   StringL2List l = new StringL2List();
   l.info = new StringList();
   l.next = null;
   while( SimpleIO.isEndOfReading() == false )
   {
      l.info = new StringList();
      l.info.next = null;
      while (SimpleIO.isEndOfReading() == false)
      {
         l.info.info = SimpleIO.getString();
         StringList p_1 = new StringList();
         p_1.next = l.info;
         l.info = p_1;
      }
      StringL2List p = new StringL2List();
      p.info = new StringList();
      p.next = l;
      l = p;
   }
   return(l);
}
```

4   Related Work

A difference between our work and other approaches is that our domains have not
been designed by focusing on a single objective such as type analysis, or shape
analysis, or sharing analysis (to name a few). Our approach is to define abstract
domains that provide natural (i.e., understandable) and generic abstractions of
the standard one. In this section, we explain how the domains can be useful for
specific applications and we compare our work with related one in those areas.

4.1   Static Analysis of Object-Oriented Programs

Static analysis of object-oriented programs has attracted many researchers in
recent years because mainly of the large potential for optimization related to
dynamic dispatch (see e.g., [1, 3, 5]). The main difference between our approach
and most existing work is that we propose a generic framework (for Java program
analysis) explicitly based on abstract interpretation. We believe that this will
allow us 1) to implement a generic and provably correct Java analyzer and 2) to
easily integrate and combine various kinds of analyses in a modular and correct
way. For instance, our approach is able to collect type information not only at the
variable level (as in [5]) but also internally to data structures. The parametric
domain $Type^{\#}$ can be instantiated in many ways to incorporate and improve
upon other work. As an example, we can use the *Type heights* of [3] to perform
escape analysis. (Note however that the approach of [3] is more relational than

ours. It is not clear yet how our abstract domains can be adapted for relational analysis.) As a third example, our approach can be used to perform a sharing analysis fulfilling the objectives of [2].

A main intuition behind our proposal is the idea of explicitly relating abstract and concrete locations by a functional mapping, which makes the interpretation of the abstract domain directly understandable. A similar technique has been recently used in [29] but the mapping between abstract and concrete objects is used to define the semantics of abstract descriptions which are first-order logic formulas, not graph-descriptions. The two approaches can be combined by using abstract locations instead of variable names as arguments in the basic predicates of [29].

4.2   Abstract Interpretation of Logic Programs

The work presented in this paper is greatly inspired by previous work on abstract interpretation of logic programs. Specifically, we apply to (a subset of) Java the same approach as in [4, 19] where a generic framework for the abstract interpretation of Prolog is proposed. Such a framework consists of an abstract semantics and of a general algorithm to compute it. The abstract semantics is proven to approximate safely the standard semantics, once and for all, and the general algorithm is proven to compute the abstract semantics as well. Thus, to get a particular correct analysis it is sufficient to provide an adequate abstract domain and to prove a few safety conditions for this domain. This approach has proven remarkably effective for the analysis of Prolog (see, e.g., [7, 8, 15, 19, 28]). The same approach is now applied for Java. Because of our past experiments with logic programs, we are confident that our approach can scale to 'real' Java programs. This belief must be validated by future work, however.

The abstract domains presented in this paper are similar to the domains presented in [19, 20] but less complex than the domains of [8, 28]; we are therefore confident that the analyses can be made practical. A major difference however is that, in Java, we have to deal with assignments. In the Prolog case, we use the domain `Pattern` [19, 20] which is similar to the sharing domain of this paper: this domain alone is enough to get precise mode analyses for Prolog [19] because instantiated structures cannot be changed; we only have to add a simple component to express distinctness of free variables. This simple component is meaningless in Java where any structure can be updated; this explains the need for the –dual– distinctness domain.

4.3   Pointer and Sharing Analysis

Many authors have worked on abstracting data structures that are dynamically created and modified by programs (see, e.g., [6, 13, 14, 24, 25, 27]). Such abstractions are useful e.g., for compile-time garbage collection, for program understanding, and for statically detecting errors such as `null` dereferencing. Both abstract domains proposed in this paper provide a form of shape analysis of the store (often called the heap) but are less expressive from this point of view than the proposals of e.g., [6, 25, 14]. Nevertheless, our proposal has other strong points:

1. Our domains allow us to combine structural and type analyses, making it possible to infer more precise type information than most existing proposals (e.g., [1, 5]).
2. The information provided by our domains is easier to understand than in e.g., [6, 14, 25, 27] because the abstract store is homomorphic to the concrete one; therefore the domains are convenient for abstract debugging, for instance.
3. Our domains are less expensive to implement because some of the information that is represented by shape graphs in e.g., [6, 14, 25] is replaced by an abstract type information. This is similar to the difference between the abstract domains Pattern [19] and Types[18] in logic programming.
4. Our domains are generic, making it possible to combine them with other approaches in the spirit of [7]. For instance, we could combine the approaches of [6, 14, 25] with ours by using shape graphs as the 'abstract type information' when it becomes impossible to keep a (precise) homomorphic image of the concrete store. This approach has already been experienced for logic programming in [8], where the domains Pattern and Types are efficiently combined.

4.4   Static Detection of Errors

Many authors (and systems) use pointer analyses to statically detect errors in programs (see, e.g., [14, 16, 17]). Some of those proposals use a more powerful shape analysis than ours but our combination of shape and type analysis could allow us to get interesting results as well. (This must be validated experimentally.) Moreover, our type analysis is useful to validate casting conversions, which are unavoidable and error-prone in Java.

4.5   Program Specialization

The general idea of program specialization is to use static information about the program –and possibly about its intended use– to derive another equivalent and hopefully more efficient program [26]. In object-oriented programming this is generally done at the level of object code where dynamic calls to methods can be replaced by static calls and method in-lining [5]. Unfortunately, program specialization may lead to explosion of the program size. We think that our approach will allow us to derive precise type information for program specialization but we currently have no definite idea of how to use it optimally. (Asking the user to annotate the program to help the program specializer may be a solution, in some situations.)

5 Future Work

Our long-term goal is to implement a generic platform for the analysis, the verification, and the optimization of Java programs. We are currently only at the beginning of this undertaking.

At this stage, we have completed the definition of two equivalent concrete operational semantics for a simple yet significant subset of Java and the definition of the two abstract domains presented in this paper. We currently complete the definition of the abstract semantics. We have also started to implement our subset of Java as well as a graphical interface to depict concrete and abstract stores.

Our next step will be to implement a generic analyzer similar to GAIA [7, 8, 15, 19, 28] based on the abstract semantics and the domains. Then we will experiment with the system to evaluate the practical value of the domain and to tune the algorithms.

In the long term, we plan to address the following issues.

1. Variants of the abstract domains will be defined and evaluated. For instance, we can improve the expressiveness of the domains by adding various attributes to abstract locations as in e.g., [14]. More powerful (and expensive) domains can be obtained by introducing some form of 'disjunctive completion' in the domains as in [18], where so-called OR-nodes are used.
2. To get more powerful results, it is convenient to combine the two abstract domains of this paper into a single one by means of reduced product [10] or open product [7] operations. This will be investigated.
3. We will compare the usefulness of purely automatic analyses with respect to analyses of programs annotated by the programmer, in particular for program specialization.

Acknowledgements

The authors thank the ECOOP anonymous referees for their very constructive remarks as well as the reviewers of previous versions of this paper, who helped us a lot to produce this final version.

References

[1] O. Agesen. Constrained-based type inference and parametric polymorphism. In B. Le Charlier, editor, *Proceedings of the First International Symposium on Static Analysis (SAS'94)*, number 864 in LNCS, Namur, September 1994. Springer-Verlag.

[2] P. S. Almeida. Balloon Types: Controlling Sharing of State in Data Types. In *Proceedings of the European Conference on Object-Oriented Programming (ECOOP'97)*, 1997.

[3] B. Blanchet. Escape analysis for object oriented languages. application to java. In *Proceedings of the Conference on Object-Oriented Programming, Systems, Languages and Applications Static Analysis (OOPSLA'99)*, November 1999.

[4] M. Bruynooghe. A practical framework for the abstract interpretation of logic programs. *Journal of Logic Programming*, 10(2):91–124, February 1991.

[5] C. Chambers, J. Dean, and D. Grove. Whole-Program Optimization of Object-Oriented Languages. Technical report, Department of Computer Science and Engineering, University of Washington, Box 352350, Seattle, Washington 98195–2350 USA.

[6] D. R. Chase, M. Wegman, and F. K. Zadeck. Analysis of Pointer and Structures. In *Proceedings of the ACM SIGPLAN'90 Conference on Programming Language and Implementation*, White-Plains, New-York, June 1990.

[7] A. Cortesi, B. Le Charlier, and P. Van Hentenryck. Combination of abstract domains for logic programming. In *Proceedings of the 21th ACM SIGPLAN-SIGACT Symposium on Principles of Programming Languages (POPL'94)*, Portland, Oregon, January 1994.

[8] A. Cortesi, B. Le Charlier, and P. Van Hentenryck. Type analysis of prolog using type graphs. *Journal of Logic Programming*, 23(3):237–278, June 1995.

[9] P. Cousot and R. Cousot. Abstract interpretation: A unified lattice model for static analysis of programs by construction or approximation of fixpoints. In *Conference Record of Fourth ACM Symposium on Programming Languages (POPL'77)*, pages 238–252, Los Angeles, California, January 1977.

[10] P. Cousot and R. Cousot. Systematic design of program analysis frameworks. In *Conference Record of Sixth ACM Symposium on Programming Languages (POPL'79)*, pages 269–282, Los Angeles, California, January 1979.

[11] A. Deutsch. A storeless model of aliasing and its abstraction using finite representations of right-regular equivalence relations. In *Proceedings of the 1992 International Conference on Computer Languages*, pages 2–13, Oakland, California, April 1992. IEEE Computer Society Press, Los Alamitos, California.

[12] A. Deutsch. Interprocedural May-Alias Analysis for Pointers : Beyond k-Limiting. In *Proceedings of the ACM SIGPLAN'94 Conference on Programming Language and Implementation*, pages 230–241, Orlando, Florida, June 1994.

[13] A. Deutsch. Semantic models and abstract interpretation for inductive data structures and pointers. In *Proceedings of the ACM Symposium on Partial Evaluation and Semantics-Based program Manipulation(PEPM'95)*, pages 226–228, New-York, June 1995.

[14] N. Dor, M. Rodeh, and M. Sagiv. Checking cleanness in linked lists. In *Proceedings of the Seventh International Symposium on Static Analysis (SAS'2000)*, LNCS. Springer-Verlag, September 2000.

[15] V. Englebert, B. Le Charlier, D. Roland, and P. Van Hentenryck. Generic abstract interpretation algorithms for prolog: Two optimization techniques and their experimental evaluation. *Software Practice and Experience*, 23(4):419–459, April 1993.

[16] D. Evans. Static detection of dynamic memory errors. In *Proceedings of the ACM SIGPLAN'96 Conference on Programming Language and Implementation*, 1996.

[17] P. Fradet, R. Gaugne, and D. Le Métayer. Static detection of pointer errors: an axiomatisation and a checking algorithm. In *Proceedings of the European Symposium on Programming (ESOP'96)*, LNCS, 1996.

[18] G. Janssens and M. Bruynooghe. Deriving descriptions of possible values of program variables by means of abstract interpretation. *Journal of Logic Programming*, 13(2-3):205–258, 1992.

[19] B. Le Charlier and P. Van Hentenryck. Experimental Evaluation of a Generic Abstract Interpretation Algorithm for Prolog. *ACM Transactions on Programming Languages and Systems (TOPLAS)*, 16(1):35–101, January 1994.

[20] K. Musumbu. *Interprétation Abstraite de Programmes Prolog*. PhD thesis, Institute of Computer Science, University of Namur, Belgium, September 1990. In French.

[21] F. Nielson, H. R. Nielson, and C. Hankin. *Principles of Program Analysis*. Springer-Verlag, 1999.

[22] I. Pollet. Sémantiques opérationnelles et domaines abstraits pour l'analyse statique de Java. DEA thesis, University of Namur, Belgium, September 1999.

[23] I. Pollet, B. Le Charlier, and A. Cortesi. Distinctness and Sharing Domains for Static Analysis of Java Programs. Research Paper RP-01-003, Institute of Computer Science, University of Namur, Belgium, 2001.

[24] M. Sagiv, T. Reps, and R. Wilhelm. Parametric shape analysis via 3-valued logic. In *Proceedings of the 26th ACM SIGPLAN–SIGACT Symposium on Principles of Programming Languages (POPL'99)*, San Antonio, January 1999.

[25] M. Sagiv, T. Reps, and R. Wilhem. Solving shape-analysis problems in languages with destructive updating. *ACM Transactions on Programming Languages and Systems (TOPLAS)*, 20(1):1–50, January 1998.

[26] U. Schultz, J. Lawall, C. Consel, and G. Muller. Towards automatic specialization of Java programs. In *Proceedings of ECOOP'99*, pages 367–390, 1999.

[27] J. Stransky. A Lattice for Abstract Interpretation of Dynamic (lisp-like) Structure. *Information and Computation*, 101:70–102, 1992.

[28] P. Van Hentenryck, A. Cortesi, and B. Le Charlier. Evaluation of *Prop*. *Journal of Logic Programming*, 23(3):237–278, June 1995.

[29] E. Yahav. Verifying Safety Properties of Concurrent Java Programs Using 3-Valued Logic. In *Proc. of the 28th ACM Symposium on Principles of Programming Languages (POPL'2001)*, January 2001.

Precise Constraint-Based Type Inference for Java

Tiejun Wang* and Scott F. Smith

Department of Computer Science
The Johns Hopkins University
Baltimore, MD 21218, USA
{wtj,scott}@cs.jhu.edu

Abstract. Precise type information is invaluable for analysis and optimization of object-oriented programs. Some forms of polymorphism found in object-oriented languages pose significant difficulty for type inference, in particular *data polymorphism*. Agesen's Cartesian Product Algorithm (CPA) can analyze programs with parametric polymorphism in a reasonably precise and efficient manner, but CPA loses precision for programs with data polymorphism. This paper presents a precise constraint-based type inference system for Java. It uses Data-Polymorphic CPA (DCPA), a novel constraint-based type inference algorithm which extends CPA with the ability to accurately and efficiently analyze data polymorphic programs. The system is implemented for the full Java language, and is used to statically verify the correctness of Java downcasts. Benchmark results are given which show that DCPA is significantly more accurate than CPA and the efficiency of DCPA is close to CPA.

1 Introduction

A concrete type inference (also known as a concrete class analysis) is an analysis which infers a set of classes for each expression, representing a conservative approximation of the classes of objects the expression may evaluate to at run-time. Such an analysis is vital for many applications, including call-graph construction [GDDC97, TP00], static resolution of virtual method calls [SHR+00], static verification of type casts, application extraction from libraries [Age96, TLSS99], and various whole program optimizations.

The constraint-based type inference [AW93, EST95] is an effective method whereby a concrete class analysis can be implemented. In constraint-based type inference, subtyping constraints are used to capture the flow information of a program. Type constraints are a more algebraic representation of the flow information, and algebraic manipulations allow for optimizations which lead to more efficient and effective analyses [AFFS98, Pot98, FF97, EST95]. This paper focuses on the construction of a precise constraint-based type inference system for Java.

---

* Partial funding provided by NSF grants CCR-9619843 and CCR-9988491

J. Lindskov Knudsen (Ed.): ECOOP 2001, LNCS 2072, pp. 99–117, 2001.

Polymorphism is widespread in object-oriented programs, and so an accurate analysis must be appropriately polymorphic. For example, a method may apply to arguments of different types, and objects of the same class may have fields assigned with values of different types. A monomorphic type inference algorithm such as 0CFA [Shi91] analyzes each method at the same type across different call sites, and lets all objects created from the same class share the same type, resulting in a significant precision loss on polymorphic programs. A polymorphic analysis is thus needed. But, polymorphic inference is a difficult issue due to subtle trade-offs between expressiveness and efficiency. An expressive algorithm could re-analyze the method for every different method invocation, but this would be very inefficient. The cartesian product algorithm (CPA) [Age95, Age96] addresses this problem, analyzing programs with parametric polymorphism in a manner that makes a reasonable trade-off between expressiveness and efficiency. The basic idea of CPA is to partition the calling context of a method based on the types of the actual arguments passed to the method. If the method is passed arguments of different types at two different invocations, those two different call sites are given different copies of the method type (i.e., different *contours*). And, if the method is invoked on arguments of the same types at two different call sites, those two invocations can efficiently share a contour of the method.

In some cases, an object field can be assigned values of different types, and different objects created from the same class can behave differently. This form of polymorphism is called *data polymorphism*. Data polymorphism occurs quite frequently in object-oriented programs, in particular when generic container classes are used. For example, there might be two instances of **java.util.Vector** created, and the two vectors could contain objects of different types. Since CPA uses a single object type for all objects created from the same class, it loses precision in this case. Here we present a novel type inference algorithm, Data-Polymorphic CPA (DCPA), which extends CPA with the ability to precisely analyze data-polymorphic programs.

We have constructed a prototype implementation of a constraint-based type inference system for the Java language. Several analyses are implemented, including 0CFA, CPA, and DCPA. The system is used as a tool to statically check whether Java type-casts in a program will always succeed at run-time. Cast-checking is a good test of the accuracy of an analysis, since each cast by definition is beyond the Java type system and so represents a more challenging type inference question. DCPA shows good results on benchmark tests: nearly all casts which could be verified statically by a flow-insensitive analysis have been verified by our DCPA implementation. DCPA is shown to be substantially more precise than CPA on Java programs, and to have an efficiency comparable to CPA.

The paper makes several other contributions. We define a generic framework for object-oriented constraint-based type inference that can model parametric polymorphism as well as data polymorphism. This is an object-oriented version of a framework we defined for a functional language with state in [SW00]. We implement 0CFA, CPA and DCPA for the full Java language and get good performance. We also make a series of implementation optimizations to gain a more efficient analysis, including a novel version of the cycle elimination [AFFS98].

2 A Framework for Object-Oriented Constraint Inference

In this section we present a framework for polyvariant constraint-based type inference for objects. It recasts the functional polyvariant framework of [SW00] to handle object-oriented language features. We show how 0CFA and CPA can be expressed as instantiations of the framework. Other frameworks for polyvariant analysis have been proposed, including [PP98, JW95].

2.1 The Types

Our type system is based on Aiken-Wimmers-style set constraints [AW93]. The types are close to those described in [EST95], which gives set constraints for an object-oriented language. The aforecited paper presents constraints for a toy object-oriented language, I-LOOP, which differs in some respects from Java. Here we give a type system designed to specify our implementation of a constraint-based type inference system for Java.

Definition 2.1 (Types): The type grammar is as follows.

$$\tau \quad \in \mathbf{Type} \quad ::= t \mid \tau v \mid (\forall\, \bar{t}.\ \tau \setminus C) \mid [\,l:\tau\,] \mid$$
$$(t_1 \times \ldots \times t_n) \to \tau \mid \mathbf{cast}(\delta, t) \mid$$
$$\mathbf{read}\ \tau \mid \mathbf{write}\ \tau$$

$$t \quad \in \mathbf{TypeVar} \supset \mathbf{ImpTypeVar}$$
$$u \quad \in \mathbf{ImpTypeVar}$$
$$\tau v \quad \in \mathbf{ValueType} \quad ::= \mathbf{int} \mid \mathbf{bool} \mid \ldots \mid \mathbf{obj}(\delta, [\,\overline{l_i : \tau_i}\,])$$
$$\bar{t} \quad \in \mathbf{TypeVarSet} \quad = \mathbf{P}_{\mathrm{fin}}(\mathbf{TypeVar})$$
$$l \quad \in \mathbf{FieldAndMethodIdentifier}$$
$$\delta \quad \in \mathbf{JavaTypeIdentifier}$$
$$\tau_1 <: \tau_2 \in \mathbf{Constraint}$$
$$C \quad \in \mathbf{ConstraintSet} \quad = \mathbf{P}_\omega(\mathbf{Constraint})$$

In this definition, **ValueType** are the types for data values, which includes all Java primitive types (**int** and **bool** are shown as examples) and object types. The type for an object value is of the form $\mathbf{obj}(\delta, [\,\overline{l_i : \tau_i}\,])$, where δ is the identifier of its corresponding class, and the notation $[\,\overline{l_i : \tau_i}\,]$ enumerates the type for every instance field and instance method of the object. Every field or instance method has a field/method identifier. Every instance field of an object is mutable and so is given an imperative type variable u as its type; we distinguish imperative type variables for the presentation of data polymorphism. Every method is given a polymorphic type scheme $(\forall\, \bar{t}.\ \tau \setminus C)$, where $\bar{t}$ is the set of bound type variables, C is the set of constraints bound in this type scheme, and τ is an arrow type. Type schemes are also used for analyzing classes and object creation, as will be explained later. An arrow type $(t_1 \times \ldots \times t_n) \to \tau$ represents a method invocation with t_i as arguments and τ as the result.

Read and write operations on instance fields are analyzed with types **read** τ and **write** τ. Type $[\,l : \tau\,]$ is used for analyzing access of an instance field or invocation of an instance method, where l is the identifier of the field/method, and τ is the type specifying the usage of the field/method. A Java downcast expression is represented with type $\mathbf{cast}(\delta, t)$, where t is the result type of the downcast operation and δ is the identifier of the Java type which the expression is cast to. Casts must be an explicit part of the types because they represent a narrowing of a type. The null value is assigned with a special object type $\mathbf{obj}(\delta_0, [\,])$, which is abbreviated as **null**.

2.2   Constraint Generation

The first phase of constraint-based type inference is to generate a set of initial constraints corresponding to the program being analyzed. This set of constraints captures the immediate flow information corresponding to statements and expressions in the program. A closure computation process must follow this to propagate the initial flow information through the program. Every constraint is of the form $\tau_1 <: \tau_2$, meaning that τ_1 is a subtype of τ_2. This constraint intuitively represents the existence of a "flow" from expressions of type τ_1 to expressions of type τ_2.

We now show how constraints are generated for the key object-oriented features of Java. Analysis of more advanced Java features such as exceptions and inner classes will be discussed later. To ease presentation, the type of every expression will always be a type variable, and the type variable for expression e will be written as $[\![e]\!]$.

For constant expression e of Java primitive type τv, constraint $\tau v <: [\![e]\!]$ is generated. Every static field, local variable or method parameter is assigned a unique type variable. For an assignment expression e1 = e2, if e1 is a static field or a local variable/parameter, $[\![e2]\!] <: [\![e1]\!]$ is generated; if e1 is the access of instance field l, $[\![e1]\!] <: [\,l : \mathbf{write}\ [\![e2]\!]\,]$ is generated, meaning that e1 is expected to be an object that has field l, and this field is written with a value of type $[\![e2]\!]$. Similarly, for a read access of an instance field e.f, $[\![e]\!] <: [\,l : \mathbf{read}\ [\![e.f]\!]\,]$ is generated, where the field named f is identified with abstract field label l.

Every method is given a type of the form $(\forall\ \bar{t}.\ (t_1 \times \ldots \times t_n) \to \tau \setminus C)$, where $t_1, \ldots t_n$ are type variables for the formal arguments, τ is the return type, C collects constraints generated for the method body, and $\bar{t}$ collects type variables locally generated for this method. When the method is an instance method, the last argument t_n is the type of the receiver ("this"). This simple self-passing approach avoids altering the type scheme of an instance method when it is inherited by sub-classes. For method invocation e.m(e1, ..., eN), if a static method is invoked, constraint $(\forall\ \bar{t}.\ \tau \setminus C) <: ([\![e1]\!] \times \ldots \times [\![eN]\!]) \to [\![e.m(e1, ..., eN)]\!]$ is generated, with $(\forall\ \bar{t}.\ \tau \setminus C)$ as the method's type scheme; if an instance method named m, with m having abstract identifier l, is invoked, $[\![e]\!] <: [\,l : ([\![e1]\!] \times \ldots \times [\![eN]\!] \times [\![e]\!]) \to [\![e.m(e1, ..., eN)]\!]\,]$ is generated, meaning that e is an object whose instance method l is invoked with e1, ..., eN as arguments, and the return value "flows-to" program point e.m(e1, ..., eN).

Every class is given two type schemes. First there is a *creation-type-scheme* of the form $(\forall\ \bar{t}.\ t\ \to\ \mathbf{obj}(\delta,[\,l_i\ :\ \tau_i\,])\ \setminus\ \{\})$, which is a type scheme for a function returning an object upon application. In the above object type, every instance field is associated with a fresh imperative type variable u, which is bound in the type scheme. Secondly, there is an *initialization-type-scheme* of the form $(\forall\ \bar{t}.\ t.\ t\ \to\ \mathbf{null}\ \setminus\ C)$, which is a function type scheme taking the object created as argument. The constraint set C collects constraints generated for all the instance initialization code of the class, including a constraint for applying the parent class's initialization-type-scheme. Thus, expression new C() is given initial constraints $\tau_1\ <:\ t\ \to\ [\![\text{new C}()]\!]$, $\mathbf{null}\ <:\ t$, and $\tau_2\ <:\ [\![\text{new C}()]\!]\ \to\ \mathbf{null}$, where τ_1 and τ_2 are the creation-type-scheme and initialization-type-scheme of class C, respectively.

A downcast expression (T)e is given constraint $[\![e]\!]\ <:\ \mathbf{cast}(\delta,[\![(\text{T})e]\!])$, with δ being the identifier associated with the class or interface named T. Similar constraints are used to analyze array element assignments, which also incur run-time typecast checks.

2.3   Computation of the Closure

After generating the initial set of constraints corresponding to the static program text, the inference algorithm computes the complete flow information by applying the set of closure rules of Figure 1 to the constraint set. Each rule specifies a condition under which more constraints are generated; the existence of constraints above the line dictates the generation of constraints below the line. The closure computation starts with the initial constraint set, and the closure rules are applied until no more constraints can be generated. This process is an analysis-time analogy of program execution, and the rules conservatively ensure that all potential program execution paths are covered.

(Trans) $\dfrac{\tau v <: t,\ \ t <: \tau}{\tau v <: \tau}$

(Read) $\dfrac{\mathbf{obj}(\delta,[\,l:u,\dots\,]) <: [\,l:\mathbf{read}\ \tau\,]}{u <: \tau}$

(Write) $\dfrac{\mathbf{obj}(\delta,[\,l:u,\dots\,]) <: [\,l:\mathbf{write}\ \tau\,]}{\tau <: u}$

(Cast) $\dfrac{\mathbf{obj}(\delta,[\,\overline{l_i:\tau_i}\,]) <: \mathbf{cast}(\delta',\tau),\ \ \delta\ \text{Java-subtype-of}\ \delta'}{\mathbf{obj}(\delta,[\,l_i:\tau_i\,]) <: \tau}$

(Message) $\dfrac{\mathbf{obj}(\delta,[\,l:(\forall\ \bar{t}.\ \tau\setminus C),\dots\,]) <: [\,l:(t'_1\times\dots\times t'_n)\to\tau'\,]}{(\forall\ \bar{t}.\ \tau\setminus C) <: (t'_1\times\dots\times t'_{n-1}\times t')\to\tau',\ \ \mathbf{obj}(\delta,[\,l:(\forall\ \bar{t}.\ \tau\setminus C),\dots\,]) <: t'}$

(∀-Elim) $\dfrac{(\forall\ \bar{t}.\ (t_1\times\dots\times t_n)\to\tau\setminus C) <: (t'_1\times\dots\times t'_n)\to\tau',\ \ \tau v_i <: t'_i}{\tau v_i <: \Theta(t_i),\ \ \Theta(\tau) <: \tau',\ \ \Theta(C)}$

Fig. 1. Constraint Closure Rules

The transitivity rule (Trans) models run-time dataflow by propagating value types forward along flow paths. The (Read) rule applies when an object of type $\mathbf{obj}(\delta, [\,l : u, \dots\,])$ reaches a read operation on field l, and the result of the read is of type τ. The (Write) rule applies when a write operation on instance field l is applied to an object whose field l is of type u.

The (Cast) rule enforces the Java run-time typecast mechanism. Recall that type $\mathbf{cast}(\delta', \tau)$ is for a downcast operation casting an expression to Java type δ', and τ is type for the result of the cast operation. The rule applies when an object of type $\mathbf{obj}(\delta, [\,\overline{l_i : \tau_i}\,])$ is subject to the cast operation. If δ is a Java-subtype δ', the cast succeeds and the object becomes the result of the cast expression. Otherwise, the cast fails and the downcast is recorded as unsafe by the inference algorithm.

The (Message) rule applies when an object reaches the receiver position of an instance method invocation. Since the last formal argument of the method's type scheme is for the receiver of the method invocation, a new arrow type is created by putting the type of the actual receiver object as the last argument, and a constraint is generated which invokes the method with the actual arguments specified by the new arrow type.

The most important closure rule is ($\forall$-Elim), which models method invocation or object creation. Constraints $\tau v_i <: t_i'$ indicate that values of type τv_i flow in as the actual arguments. At run-time each method invocation allocates fresh locations on the stack for all variables. To model this behavior in the analysis, a renaming $\Theta \in \mathbf{TypeVar} \xrightarrow{\mathrm{P}} \mathbf{TypeVar}$ is applied to type variables in $\overline{t}$. The partial function Θ is extended to types, constraints, and constraint sets in the usual manner. We call a renaming Θ a *contour*, and we call $\Theta(\tau)$ an *instantiation* of τ. The $\forall$ is eliminated from $(\forall\, \overline{t}.\ t \to \tau \setminus C)$ by applying Θ to C.

The ($\forall$-Elim) rule is parameterized by Θ, which decides for this particular function, call site, and actual argument types, which contour is to be used (*i.e.*, if a new contour is to be created or an existing contour reused). Providing a concrete Θ instantiates the framework to give a concrete algorithm. For example, the monomorphic algorithm 0CFA is defined by letting Θ be the identity renaming.

Besides detecting potentially unsafe downcast expressions, the closure computation outputs the *closure*, the set of constraints closed under the closure rules, as the analysis result. The closure contains complete flow information about the program, and various program properties can be deduced from it. For example, a concrete class analysis can be defined as follows.

Definition 2.2 (Concrete Class Analysis): For an expression e in the program, the set of concrete classes for e, $CC(e)$, is the maximal set of classes, such that if the closure contains constraint $\mathbf{obj}(\delta, [\,\overline{l_i : \tau_i}\,]) <: t$, and t is an instantiation of $[\![e]\!]$, then $\delta \in CC(e)$.

To obtain a CPA instantiation of the framework, Θ in the ($\forall$-Elim) rule is defined as follows:

For each $\alpha \in \overline{t}, \Theta(\alpha) = \alpha^{\tau v_1 \times \dots \times \tau v_n}$.

The contours Θ are generated based on the actual argument types τv_i, thus two applications of the function share the same contour if and only if the actual argument types are the same.

3   Data Polymorphic Analysis

In this section, data polymorphism and our DCPA closure algorithm are defined.

3.1   Motivation

Data polymorphism is defined in [Age96] as the ability of an imperative program variable to hold values of different types at run-time. For example, a field declared to be of type `Object` in Java can store objects of any class. Hence objects created from the same class can behave differently with their fields assigned with values of different types. Recall that object creation `new C()` is analyzed with constraints $(\forall\,\bar{t}.\,\tau\setminus C) <: t \to [\![new\ C()]\!]$ and $null <: t$, where $(\forall\,\bar{t}.\,\tau\setminus C)$ is the creation-type-scheme of class C. For 0CFA and CPA, the ($\forall$-Elim) rule generates only one contour for the creation-type-scheme of every class, and a single object type is assigned to all objects created from a given class. This may lead to a precision loss in the analysis result.

Consider the program of Figure 2. Two instances of `Hashtable` are created

```
import java.util.Hashtable;
class A {
    public static void main(String args[]) {
        Hashtable ht1=new Hashtable();
        Hashtable ht2=new Hashtable();
        ht1.put("zero", new Integer(0));
        ht2.put("true", new Boolean(true));
        Integer i=(Integer)ht1.get("zero");
    }
}
```

Fig. 2. Java program with data polymorphism

and used differently, yet CPA allows them to share the same object type, and the analysis would imprecisely conclude that the result of `ht1.get("zero")` includes `Boolean` objects. If on the other hand two separate object types were used for the two `Hashtable` instances, this downcast would be statically verified as sound.

In order to more accurately analyze such programs, we have developed a Data-Polymorphic CPA (DCPA) algorithm, which extends CPA to effectively analyze data polymorphic programs. The basic idea is to divide CPA contours into two categories: those unrelated to data polymorphism and can be shared without losing precision (the *CPA-safe* or *reusable* contours), and those which may contain data polymorphism and thus sharing such contours might cause a loss of precision (the *CPA-unsafe* contours). The DCPA algorithm is the same as CPA except that: after every contour is generated, it judges the contour to be *CPA-safe* or *CPA-unsafe*; when there is a need to reuse an existing contour, yet the contour is already judged to be *CPA-unsafe*, DCPA would generate a fresh contour instead of reusing the existing one. DCPA aims to be precise by detecting as CPA-unsafe those contours which exhibit data polymorphism, and aims to be efficient by declaring as many contours CPA-safe as possible.

We now discuss the idea in detail. We first consider the analysis of object creations. Recall that an object creation expression **new C()** is analyzed with a pair of constraints $(\forall \; \bar{t}. \; \tau \setminus C) <: t \rightarrow [\![\text{new C()}]\!]$ and **null** $<: t$, where $(\forall \; \bar{t}. \; \tau \setminus C)$ is the creation-type-scheme of class C. We will refer such a pair of constraints as the *creation points* of class C. If a class contains any polymorphic field (a polymorphic field is a field which can store values of different types), DCPA algorithm always judges contours of the creation-type-scheme of such a class as CPA-unsafe. Thus, for any creation point of a class with polymorphic fields, a fresh object type is generated for the class. On the other hand, if a class (e.g. class **java.lang.Integer**) contains no polymorphic fields, DCPA algorithm would judge the contour of the class's creation type scheme as CPA-safe, thus all objects of the class share a single object type.

We now consider contours generated for method invocations. If CPA loses precision because of data polymorphism, there must be multiple objects from the same class such that those objects are used differently at run-time yet CPA let them share the same object type. The goal of DCPA is to generate more object types so that such imprecision can be avoided. Thus, if a method invocation doesn't cause the creation of any objects, the contour for such a method invocation is CPA-safe. For example, consider the program in Figure 3. DCPA would let the two invocations of the method **id** share a single CPA-safe contour.

Furthermore, if a method invocation creates objects, but the objects created do not escape the method scope via the return value, then the contour for such a method invocation is also CPA-safe. Consider the program in Figure 3. Since the two invocations of method **g** have the same argument type, CPA would let them share a single contour. The two invocations create two **Vector** instances, but the two instances escape the scope of **g** only through static field **a**, not through the return values. If two distinct contours were used for the two invocations of method **g**, there would be two creation points of class **Vector**, and there would be two distinct object types generated for **Vector**. But the two object types would both be lower bounds of the type variable for field **a**, forcing them to be equivalent in any case. Thus, for the two invocations of method **g**, generating two contours are not beneficial, and DCPA would let them share a single CPA-safe contour without any loss of precision.

Even if an object created by a method invocation escapes the method scope through the return value, if the fields of the object are already assigned with values of fixed types, such an invocation is also considered CPA-safe. For example, consider method h in Figure 3. A `Vector` object is created and returned by the method. But before it is returned, a `Boolean` object is already put in the vector. Thus the two vectors created by the two invocations of h would both have contents of `Boolean` type. CPA would let the two invocations of method h share a single contour. If two distinct contours were used for the two invocations of method h, there would be two creation points of class `Vector`, and there would be two distinct object types generated for `Vector`. But the two object types would both have `Boolean` as content type. Since all fields of `Boolean` objects are also assigned values of fixed types, we consider that the type for the two vectors as already known and consider generating two distinct contours as not beneficial. Therefore, DCPA would let the two invocations of method h share a single CPA-safe contour.

```
import java.util.*;
class A {
  static Object a;
  static Object id(Object x) { return x;}
  static Object g(Object x) { a=new Vector(); return x;}
  static Object h() {
    Vector v=new Vector();
    v.addElement(new Boolean(true));
    return v;
  }
  public static void main(String args[]) {
    Object obj=new Hashtable();
    id(obj); id(obj); g(obj); g(obj);
    h(); h();
  }
}
```

Fig. 3. Example Program with CPA-Safe Contours

For some programs, even with the above strategy which aims to identify as many CPA-safe contours as possible, there are still too many contours declared as CPA-unsafe. To make the algorithm feasible, an additional unification heuristic is incorporated into DCPA. The idea is that, whenever two object types of the same class "flow together" (*i.e.*, become lower bounds of a single type variable), the algorithm assumes that the data structures represented by the two object types would be used in the same way and it unifies the two object types. Although this unification mechanism could in theory cause precision loss, in practice we have found that such cases are rare.

3.2   The DCPA Algorithm

We now give a definition of the DCPA closure algorithm. The DCPA algorithm computes a constraint closure from the same initial constraints as defined in the previous section, using stack-based algorithm. Whenever a contour is generated for a method invocation, the algorithm checks the return type of the contour to judge if the contour is reusable. To do that, it needs to know the "local" set of constraints corresponding to the local computation of the method invocation. Since contours are nested, in general it must keep a stack of constraints which mirrors the call stack, and the closure computation itself is specified by a state-transition machine where the state is a stack of constraints.

First, we define the representation of contours.

Definition 3.1 (Contour): A contour ρ is a triple of form $(c, \overline{\tau v_i}, \Theta)$, recording information about a $\forall$-elimination, where c is the constraint of form $(\forall \, \overline{t}. \, (t_1 \times \ldots \times t_n) \to \tau \setminus C) <: (t'_1 \times \ldots \times t'_n) \to \tau'$, $\overline{\tau v_i}$ is a vector of the actual argument types, and Θ is the renaming on $\overline{t}$ used by the $\forall$-Elimination.

We define the closure computation as a state transition process, where a state is defined as follows:

Definition 3.2 (Closure State): A *closure state* is a pair (S, Ω). S is a stack with frames of form (ρ, C), where ρ is a contour and C is a set of constraints. Ω is the contour cache, which is a set of pairs of form (ρ, b), where ρ is a contour and b is a boolean value.

A contour is an analysis-time analogy of a run-time activation record, and the state is a stack that corresponds to the run-time stack of activation records. A stack frame (ρ, C) represents a contour with C as the set of local constraints for the contour. Every time a new contour is created, it is pushed onto the stack. When the closure computation is finished for constraints generated by this contour, the contour is popped off the stack. The top frame of the stack corresponds to the current contour. The contour cache Ω stores all contours thus far created. Each contour is associated with a boolean value, which is true iff the contour is reusable. We will write $S \wedge [(\rho, C)]$ to indicate a stack with (ρ, C) as the top frame, and $[(\rho_n, C_n), \ldots, (\rho_1, C_1)]$ as the stack with n frames enumerated from bottom to top. For constraint c and state (S, Ω), we write $c \in S$ if $c \in C_i$ and (ρ_i, C_i) is a frame in S.

Rules for closure state transition are shown in Figure 3.2. Every rule specifies a transition from the closure state above line to the state below the line. The notation (S, Ω) **with** C specifies a closure state where every constraint in C occurs somewhere in S, and there exists at least one constraint in C which occurs in the top frame of S.

The (S-Trans) transitivity rule applies only when at least one constraint amongst $\tau v <: t$ and $t <: \tau$ is in set C_1 (the constraint set in the top frame of the state stack), and the constraint $\tau v <: \tau$ generated by the transitivity is added to C_1. This serves to maintain the invariant that any constraints generated from the constraint set in the stack top will also become part of the constraint set in the stack top. The rules (S-Read), (S-Write), (S-Cast), (S-Message) can

(S-Trans) $\dfrac{(S \wedge [(\rho_1, C_1)], \Omega) \text{ with } \{\tau v <: t, t <: \tau\}}{(S \wedge [(\rho_1, \{\tau v <: \tau\} \cup C_1)], \Omega)}$

(S-Read) $\dfrac{(S \wedge [(\rho_1, C_1)], \Omega) \text{ with } \{\mathbf{obj}(\delta, [l : u, \dots]) <: [l : \mathbf{read}\ \tau]\}}{(S \wedge [(\rho_1, \{u <: \tau\} \cup C_1)], \Omega)}$

(S-Write) $\dfrac{(S \wedge [(\rho_1, C_1)], \Omega) \text{ with } \{\mathbf{obj}(\delta, [l : u, \dots]) <: [l : \mathbf{write}\ \tau]\}}{(S \wedge [(\rho_1, \{\tau <: u\} \cup C_1)], \Omega)}$

(S-Cast) $\dfrac{(S \wedge [(\rho_1, C_1)], \Omega) \text{ with } \{\mathbf{obj}(\delta, [\overline{l_i : \tau_i}]) <: \mathbf{cast}(\delta', \tau)\}, \delta \text{ Java-subtype-of } \delta'}{(S \wedge [(\rho_1, \{\mathbf{obj}(\delta, [\overline{l_i : \tau_i}]) <: \tau\} \cup C_1)], \Omega)}$

(S-Message) $\dfrac{(S \wedge [(\rho_1, C_1)], \Omega) \text{ with } \{\mathbf{obj}(\delta, [l : (\forall\ \overline{t}.\ \tau \setminus C), \dots]) <: [l : (\times_n^{i=1} t_i') \to \tau']\}}{(S \wedge [(\rho_1, \{(\forall\ \overline{t}.\ \tau \setminus C) <: ((\times_{n-1}^{i=1} t_i') \times t') \to \tau', \atop \mathbf{obj}(\delta, [l : (\forall\ \overline{t}.\ \tau \setminus C), \dots]) <: t'\} \cup C_1)], \Omega)}$

(S-∀-Reuse) $\dfrac{(S \wedge [(\rho_1, C_1)], \Omega) \text{ with } \{(\forall\ \overline{t}.\ (\times_n^{i=1} t_i) \to \tau \setminus C) <: (\times_n^{i=1} t_i') \to \tau', \tau v_i <: t_i'\}, \atop (((\forall\ \overline{t}.\ (\times_n^{i=1} t_i) \to \tau \setminus C) <: (\times_n^{i=1} t_i'') \to \tau'', \overline{\tau v_i}, \Theta), \mathbf{true}) \in \Omega}{(S \wedge [(\rho_1, C_1 \cup \{\Theta(\tau) <: \tau'\})], \Omega)}$

(S-∀-Begin) $\dfrac{\begin{array}{l}(S \wedge [(\rho_1, C_1)], \Omega) \text{ with } \{(\forall\ \overline{t}.\ (\times_n^{i=1} t_i) \to \tau \setminus C) <: (\times_n^{i=1} t_i') \to \tau', \tau v_i <: t_i'\}, \\ (((\forall\ \overline{t}.\ (\times_n^{i=1} t_i) \to \tau \setminus C) <: \times_n^{i=1} t_i'' \to \tau'', \overline{\tau v_i}, \Theta''), \mathbf{true}) \notin \Omega, \\ (((\forall\ \overline{t}.\ (\times_n^{i=1} t_i) \to \tau \setminus C) <: \times_n^{i=1} t_i' \to \tau', \overline{\tau v_i}, \Theta'), b) \notin \Omega\end{array}}{(S \wedge [(\rho_1, C_1), (\rho, \{\tau v_i <: \Theta(t_i)\} \cup \Theta(C))], \Omega)}$
where $\rho = ((\forall\ \overline{t}.\ (\times_n^{i=1} t_i) \to \tau \setminus C) <: (\times_n^{i=1} t_i') \to \tau', \overline{\tau v_i}, \Theta)$,
and Θ is a fresh renaming on type variables in $\overline{t}$

(S-∀-End) $\dfrac{(S \wedge [(\rho_2, C_2), (\rho_1, C_1)], \Omega)}{(S \wedge [(\rho_2, C_2 \cup C_1 \cup \{\Theta(\tau) <: \tau'\})], \Omega \cup \{(\rho_1, b)\})}$
where for $\rho_1 = ((\forall\ \overline{t}.\ (\times_n^{i=1} t_i) \to \tau \setminus C) <: (\times_n^{i=1} t_i') \to \tau', \overline{\tau v_i}, \Theta)$,
b is true iff ρ_1 is reusable in $(S \wedge [(\rho_2, C_2), (\rho_1, C_1)], \Omega)$

(S-Unify) $\dfrac{(S, \Omega) \text{ with } \{\mathbf{obj}(\delta, [\overline{l_i : \tau_i}]) <: t, \mathbf{obj}(\delta, [\overline{l_i' : \tau_i'}]) <: t\}}{\Theta((S, \Omega)), \text{ where } \Theta = U(\mathbf{obj}(\delta, [\overline{l_i : \tau_i}]), \mathbf{obj}(\delta, [\overline{l_i : \tau_i'}]))}$

Fig. 4. DCPA Constraint Closure Rules

be understood similarly. In (S-Message) and subsequent rules, notation $\times_n^{i=1} t_i$ abbreviates $t_1 \times \dots \times t_n$.

The (∀-Elim) rule of the framework corresponds to three DCPA closure rules. (S-∀-Reuse) is used in the case that the ∀-elimination reuses an existing contour. A contour ρ is reusable for this application if $(\rho, \mathbf{true}) \in \Omega$ and ρ has the same argument types as this application. According to the (∀-Elim) closure rule, this ∀-elimination would generate such a set of constraints: $\{\tau v_i <: \Theta(t_i), \Theta(\tau) <: \tau'\} \cup \Theta(C)$. Since this is a reuse of an existing contour, all those constraints except for the constraint $\Theta(\tau) <: \tau'$ have already been generated and those constraints are already in the constraint sets of the stack. Thus, only constraint $\Theta(\tau) <: \tau'$ is added to the constraint set in the top frame of the stack.

The rule (S-∀-Begin) creates a new contour. The condition $(\forall\ \overline{t}.\ (t_1 \times \dots \times t_n) \to \tau \setminus C) <: t_1'' \times \dots \times t_n'' \to \tau'', \overline{\tau v_i}, \Theta''), \mathbf{true}) \notin \Omega$ means that there is no reusable (CPA-safe) contour for the same function applied to the same argument type τv_i in the contour cache. The condition $(((\forall\ \overline{t}.\ (t_1 \times \dots \times t_n) \to \tau \setminus C) <: t_1' \times \dots \times t_n' \to \tau', \overline{\tau v_i}, \Theta'), b) \notin \Omega$ means that it is not the case that there is already a contour generated for this application. When the two conditions are satisfied, a fresh contour is generated for the application. The local constraint set of the new contour is initialized to include constraints $\tau v_i <: \Theta(t_i)$ and the fresh copy of all bound constraints, $\Theta(C)$. The constraint $\Theta(\tau) <: \tau'$ corresponding to the flow from the return value of the function to the application result is not considered a local constraint of the contour. Finally, the new contour along with its local constraint set is pushed on to the stack.

The rule (S-∀-End) ends the creation of a contour. It pops the current contour off the stack, merges the local constraints of this contour with those in the new top frame of the stack, generates constraint $\Theta(\tau) <: \tau'$ corresponding to the flow from the return value to the application result, and checks if the contour is reusable and records it in the contour cache. The definition of *reusable* is now defined, via the notions of *local type* and *complete type*.

Definition 3.3 (Local Types): Object type $\mathbf{obj}(\delta, [\overline{l_i : \tau_i}])$ is *local* to state $([(\rho_n, C_n), \dots, (\rho_1, C_1)], \Omega)$ if $\mathbf{obj}(\delta, [\overline{l_i : \tau_i}])$ does not appear as a subterm of some constraint in C_i for any $i \neq 1$.

Type $\mathbf{obj}(\delta, [\overline{l_i : \tau_i}])$ is declared local if and only if it is created locally by the current contour.

Definition 3.4 (Complete Types): Type τ is *complete* in state (S, Ω) iff any of the following cases holds:

1. τ is a primitive Java type, e.g. **int** or **bool**;
2. $\tau = t$, $\tau v_1 <: t \in S$, $\tau v_2 <: t \in S$, and $\tau v_1 \neq \tau v_2$;
3. $\tau = t$, $\tau' <: t \in S$, and τ' is complete in (S, Ω);
4. $\tau = \mathbf{obj}(\delta, [\overline{l_i : \tau_i}])$, and for any τ_i which is imperative type variable u_i, u_i is complete in (S, Ω);
5. $\tau = \mathbf{obj}(\delta, [\overline{l_i : \tau_i}])$, and $\mathbf{obj}(\delta, [\overline{l_i : \tau_i}])$ is not local to (S, Ω).

In the first case above, **int** and **bool** and all other Java primitive types are judged complete. In cases 2. and 3., a type variable is considered complete if it has a complete type or at least two different value types as lower bounds. In cases 4. and 5., object type $\mathbf{obj}(\delta, [\overline{l_i : \tau_i}])$ is complete if the type variables for all its fields are complete, or it is not created locally by the current contour. The above definition is subtle, and the details are critical in obtaining an accurate and efficient analysis.

Definition 3.5 (Reusable Contour): A contour $((\forall\ \overline{t}.\ (t_1 \times \dots \times t_n) \rightarrow \tau \setminus C) <: (t'_1 \times \dots \times t'_n) \rightarrow \tau', \overline{\tau v_i}, \Theta)$ is *reusable* in state (S, Ω) iff $\Theta(\tau)$ is complete in (S, Ω) and there does not exist $(((\forall\ \overline{t}.\ (t_1 \times \dots \times t_n) \rightarrow \tau \setminus C) <: t''_1 \times \dots \times t''_n, \overline{\tau v_i}, \Theta'), \mathtt{false}) \in \Omega$.

The above definition judges a contour ρ as not reusable if the return type of the contour is not complete.

The rule (S-Unify) unifies two object types when they are from the same class, making them lower bounds of the same type variable. The unification algorithm is defined as follows.

Definition 3.6 (Unification of Object Types): The unifier of the two object types of same class l, $U(\mathbf{obj}(\delta, [\overline{l_i : \tau_i}]), \mathbf{obj}(\delta, [\overline{l_i : \tau'_i}]))$, is a composition of substitutions $\lfloor \tau_i / \tau'_i \rfloor$ for each i s.t. τ_i is an imperative type variable.

We now define the closure process itself, via a state transition relation which is prioritized to make sure a contour is not popped until its analysis has finished.

Definition 3.7 (DCPA State Transition Relation $\mapsto$): $s_1 \mapsto s_2$ iff closure state s_1 transits to s_2 by a rule in Figure 3.2, and one of the following three cases hold: the rule is neither (S-$\forall$-Begin) nor (S-$\forall$-End); the rule is (S-$\forall$-Begin), and the only other applicable rule on s_1 is (S-$\forall$-End); or, the rule is (S-$\forall$-End), and no other rules are applicable on s_1. $\overset{*}{\mapsto}$ is the transitive, reflexive closure of $\mapsto$.

The closure computation is a state-transition process via relation $\mapsto$ until a fixed point is reached.

Definition 3.8 (DCPA Closure Computation): Given a constraint set C, if $([(\rho_0, C)], \{\}) \overset{*}{\mapsto} ([(\rho_0, C')], \Omega)$, (where ρ_0 is a special dummy contour), and for any state s such that $([(\rho_0, C')], \Omega) \mapsto s$, we have $s = ([(\rho_0, C')], \Omega)$, then we say $([(\rho_0, C)], \{\}) \overset{\text{DCPA}}{\longmapsto} ([(\rho_0, C')], \Omega)$, and also will write $C \overset{\text{DCPA}}{\longmapsto} C'$, meaning C' is the DCPA closure of C.

Now the type inference with DCPA Algorithm can be defined as follows:

Definition 3.9 (DCPA Algorithm): For a program e with initial constraint set C, if $C \overset{\text{DCPA}}{\longmapsto} C'$, then C' is a DCPA closure for e.

4 Implementation

In this section, we discuss our implementation of 0CFA, CPA and DCPA for Java. The system is itself written in Java. It takes Java source code as input and statically checks the validity of all down-casts in the program. For each Java downcast of the form (T)e, casting expression e to Java class or interface T, the system computes a set of Java classes which are conservative approximations of the classes which e can take on at run-time. If the algorithm discovers that e might evaluate to an object of class C, and C is not a Java subtype of T, then the downcast is reported as *unsafe*; otherwise the cast is *safe*. If a downcast is judged as safe by the system, it is guaranteed to succeed at run-time. The system currently can handle all standard Java language features, including objects, classes, interfaces, inner classes, and exceptions. The only feature the system cannot handle automatically is the reflection mechanism of Java.

Though our system is built as a downcast checker, it is essentially a concrete class analysis tool for Java. So, it could also be used as an analysis tool for static resolution of virtual method calls and other compiler optimizations.

4.1 Java Language Issues

We have up to now ignored several features of Java; here we provide a sketch of how they are handled by the implementation. Recall that an extra "this" argument is added for the type scheme of every instance method. Type schemes for constructors also have an extra "this" argument. Because of this, the processing of inheritance is simple: no classes, methods or constructors are re-analyzed upon inheritance. Every class is represented as a class object, which has the following components: a reference to the class object for the parent class, a method-lookup-table containing type schemes for instance methods defined in this class, type schemes for constructors and static methods, and the class's creation-type-scheme and initialization-type-scheme. Such a class object implements the "class identifier" concept in our type system, and is shared by all object types created from the class.

For each abstract method of a Java interface, a hashtable is built, which associates every concrete class implementing this interface with the an instance method of the class, corresponding to the abstract method. Such hashtables are used during closure computation to determine the type scheme of the target method for a virtual method call through an interface.

Array objects are analyzed as special object types with a single field representing the array contents. Array store expressions in Java require a run-time check to ensure the type safety. Thus those expressions are analyzed in a similar way as down-cast expressions. And, the system also statically checks the type safety of every array store expression.

Inner Classes are analyzed as follows. In Java, from an instance of the inner class, an instance of every enclosing class is accessible. Thus, for every enclosing class, an additional field is added to the object types of the inner class, representing the enclosing instance. Similarly, the creating-type-scheme of an inner class contains an extra "this" argument for every enclosing class. An inner class may also access local variables in the surrounding lexical context. For every local variable accessed, we add a special field in the inner class for it, and thus convert the variable access to a field access. In this way, all type schemes generated in our system enjoy the following property: bound type variables of one type scheme never appear in the scope of another type scheme. Namely, no nested type schemes are. Thus, when instantiating a type scheme by renaming all types and constraints in its scope, no type scheme needs to be renamed.

Java exception-handling features are analyzed in a simple manner. Each exception class (*i.e.*, subclass of java.lang.Throwable) is represented by a unique type variable. If exception class A is a subclass of exception class B, constraint $t_1 <: t_2$ is generated, where t_1 and t_2 are type variables for classes A and B respectively. A statement throw e produces a special constraint $[\![e]\!] <: \mathbf{exception}$, where $\mathbf{exception}$ is a special type such that for any object type τ of an exception class becoming a lower-bound of $\mathbf{exception}$, a constraint $\tau <: t$ is generated with t as the type variable corresponding to the exception class of τ. A statement of form try {...} catch(T e) {...} produces constraint $t <: [\![e]\!]$, where t is the type variable for the exception class T.

We also make special effort to accurately analyze a common Java programming idiom:

```
if (x instanceof A) {
    A c = (A) x;    ...
}
```

At the entry point of the true branch, it is certain that values of variable x are instances of class A. The analysis uses a simple algorithm to conservatively estimate whether the boolean condition of an if statement further constrains the class of any object by presence of instanceof, and if so uses that fact in the analysis.

Since our analysis is a whole program analysis, libraries must be included in program analysis. We use the Sun JDK library source. Native library methods were manually replaced with type-compatible Java code. The reflection features of Java pose a significant difficulty for any static analysis. For example, it is impossible for a static analysis to determine precisely which class is dynamically loaded. Our solution is to manually replace library code using reflection with type-compatible code without reflection. For example, the code fragment Class.forName(x).newInstance() can be replaced with new A() if it is certain that class A is loaded.

4.2   Optimizations

We now discuss some optimizations implemented in our system to improve the performance for analyzing realistic Java applications.

Optimization with Monomorphic Types Monomorphic types include Java primitive types (*e.g.*, int, boolean) and object types of monomorphic classes. Monomorphic classes (*e.g.*, String, Integer) are those classes which do not have subclasses and only have fields capable of storing values of monomorphic values. If according to the Java static type declaration, a variable or expression is of a monomorphic type, we use the monomorphic type directly as the type for such a variable or expression without any type inference effort.

Additional Contour Sharing DCPA as defined will in fact not always terminate on recursive programs. We previously formalized a provably terminating CPA algorithm [SW00]. Since no nested type schemes are generated in our current system, CPA would always terminate without any special termination mechanism. To ensure the termination of DCPA, our system performs online recursion detection, and always treats contours for recursive methods as CPA-safe.

Another issue is to prevent the algorithm from creating too many contours on certain pathological cases. Agesen [Age96] defines the notion of *megamorphism*, which means too many different value types flow to a single call site as arguments. To prevent CPA from blowing up, the number of contours generated for a megamorphic call site is reduced. This idea is also employed in our system. In theory, DCPA may also blow up when too many contours are judged as CPA-unsafe. To prevent DCPA from blowing up in this case, a contour is regarded as CPA-safe when too many object types are created locally by the contour.

Online Cycle Elimination Partial online cycle elimination [AFFS98] is another optimization incorporated in our system. The basic idea is to detect cycles of the form $t_1 <: t_2 \ldots <: t_n <: t_1$, and collapse all type variables on such cycles into a single variable. We have implemented the cycle elimination mechanism using a novel approach. Instead of performing cycle detection as a separate operation at every update of the constraint system, as in [AFFS98], we piggyback the cycle detection operation on the process of propagating value types along flow paths. Whenever the (Trans) closure rule is applied on constraint $\tau v <: t$, τv also needs to be propagated to type variables which are upper bounds of t. Our system performs cycle detection on t while propagating τv forward. It keeps track of type variables visited on the current flow path so an already-visited variable will be discovered. In this way, the overhead of cycle detection is reduced.

Automatic Constraint Garbage Collection Constraints which will induce no future closure computation have served their purpose and can be garbage collected. It is possible to precisely detect which constraints are garbage [EST95, Pot98], but these algorithms are nontrivial and the act of detecting the garbage itself slows down the analysis. We use a simpler form of garbage collection which is automatic: constraints are represented in the implementation in a manner such that many unreachable constraints will be automatically collected by the Java run-time garbage collector.

There are additional constraint-based optimizations which could be included in our system to further improve its performance, including constraint graph minimization [FF97] and precise garbage collection.

5   Experimental Results

Benchmark results are presented in Table 6. The following benchmark programs were used: $jlex^1$ is a lexical analyzer generator; $toba^2$ is a Java-to-C code translator; $javacup^3$ is a Java parser generator; $jtar^4$ is an archive utility; $bloat^5$ is a Java bytecode optimizer; $self$ is our system itself used as a benchmark; $sablecc^6$ is a compiler generator; $javac$ and $javadoc$ are standard tools in Sun's Java SDK.

The column "lines" shows the number of lines of source code in the benchmark program only. Since our system is a whole-program analysis, every benchmark was analyzed along with the reachable library code. The column "methods" shows the number of reachable methods in the whole program including libraries detected by DCPA algorithm; The column "casts" shows the number of downcasts in the benchmark program only. Downcasts reachable in the library code are also checked, but checking downcasts in user code is the goal of the system and only those casts are reported. Each benchmark is analyzed with

---

[1] see www.cs.princeton.edu/~appel/modern/java/JLex/
[2] see www.cs.arizona.edu/sumatra/toba/
[3] see www.cs.princeton.edu/~appel/modern/java/CUP/
[4] see www.angelfire.com/on/vkjava/
[5] see www.cs.purdue.edu/homes/hosking/bloat
[6] see www.sable.mcgill.ca/sablecc/

Program	lines	methods	casts	0CFA		CPA			DCPA		
				safe	time	safe	time	Θ	safe	time	Θ
jlex	7835	398	65	10.8%	3.3	16.9%	3.5	1.5	100%	3.8	2.3
toba	6417	777	63	4.8%	4.8	4.8%	5.1	1.6	22.2%	6.4	2.7
javacup	10592	532	459	8.1%	3.6	8.1%	3.9	1.4	89.3%	4.5	3.6
jtar	11904	1446	10	0%	6.7	0%	7.1	1.5	100%	11.0	2.4
bloat	18841	1053	205	7.8%	5.3	8.8%	5.9	1.5	30.2%	7.1	4.3
self	23122	1304	130	36.9%	4.5	51.5%	5.9	1.9	93.8%	10.7	3.4
javadoc	–	2314	310	25.3%	10.1	40.8%	13.0	1.9	77.7%	23.6	4.3
sablecc	23111	2811	519	34.5%	10.9	35.2%	10.9	2.5	61.7%	21.3	4.1
javac	–	2933	606	17.1%	12.5	30.5%	30.0	2.5	50.1%	74.8	7.1

Table 1. Benchmark Data

0CFA, CPA and DCPA. The columns labeled "safe" indicate the percentage of total user downcasts which have been statically verified. The columns labeled "time" report system execution time in seconds, including time for parsing, type inference and closure computation. For CPA and DCPA, columns labeled "Θ" report the average number of contours generated for each type scheme; this is always 1 for 0CFA.

The benchmark results were obtained using the Sun JDK 1.3 on a PC with a 866MHZ Pentinum processor and 512M of memory. All benchmarks except *javac* were analyzed with a 80M maximum heap size. *javac* has a very complex inheritance hierarchy, and its analysis is significantly more complex than the other benchmarks. The results for *javac* with 0CFA, CPA, DCPA were obtained with 80M, 96M and 160M maximum heap size, respectively.

As can be seen in the benchmarks, DCPA can verify significantly more downcasts than either CPA or 0CFA. For example, all downcasts in user code of *jlex* and *jtar* have been statically verified. This shows that CPA and 0CFA are not precise enough for downcast checking, and in general, DCPA is a much more precise type inference algorithm for object-oriented languages. We have manually studied the downcasts which cannot be verified by DCPA for some benchmark programs. Nearly all of them cannot be verified even with an analysis that would generate a fresh contour for every function application. Some of the remaining downcasts could be verified by a flow-sensitive analysis, but most are fundamentally "dynamic", with safety that depends on the state of execution, and thus not verifiable by any static analysis of this variety. For example, DCPA can only verify 22.2% of the downcasts in toba, but a manual inspection shows that nearly all of the remaining downcasts are fundamentally dynamic. In summary, DCPA appears to produce nearly optimal results as a flow-insensitive static analysis for downcast checking on the programs we have tested. DCPA also has good efficiency: comparing the time and the average number of contours of CPA and DCPA, we can see that DCPA's efficiency is comparable to CPA; furthermore, realistic Java applications can be analyzed.

6   Related Work

Plevyak and Chien's iterative flow analysis (IFA) [PC94] is a precise constraint-based analysis of object-oriented programs. To the best of our knowledge, IFA is the only system in the literature capable of analyzing data polymorphic programs precisely. IFA uses an iterative approach in which the whole analysis must be iterated multiple times. Compared to IFA, our system detects data polymorphism online, and does not need generational iteration.

O'Callahan [Cal99] has built a system for the analysis of Java bytecode. The system is used for static verification of Java downcasts. His type schemes are much more compact yet less precise than the constraint-based type schemes used in our system. While our system aims to reuse contours across different call sites and only produces a few contours on average for each type scheme, his system is fully context-sensitive and always instantiates a type scheme differently in every different context. Duggan has also proposed a system to automatically detect polymorphic Java classes [Dug99]. His proposal does not appear to be as precise as ours. It is currently not implemented or tested with benchmarks and so its feasibility and performance are unclear.

The analysis we produce here is perhaps the most precise constraint-based analysis for object-oriented programs thus far developed. We are going opposite the common trend today, which is toward less expressive (but more efficient) analyses (e.g., [SHR+00, TP00]). These fast analyses are getting popular because for many purposes it has become clear that a fine-grained analysis is not needed. But, this paper shows that there still are purposes, including cast-checking, where it is critical to have a very fine-grained analysis.

References

[AFFS98]   Alexander Aiken, Manuel Fhndrich, Jeffrey S. Foster, and Zhendong Su. Partial online cycle elimination in inclusion constraint graphs. In *ACM SIGPLAN Conference on Programming Language Design and Implementation (PLDI)*, 1998.

[Age95]   Ole Agesen. The cartesian product algorithm. In *Proceedings ECOOP'95*, volume 952 of *Lecture notes in Computer Science*, 1995.

[Age96]   Ole Agesen. *Concrete Type Inference: Delivering Object-Oriented Applications*. PhD thesis, Stanford University, 1996. Available as Sun Labs Technical Report SMLI TR-96-52.

[AW93]   A. Aiken and E. L. Wimmers. Type inclusion constraints and type inference. In *Proceedings of the International Conference on Functional Programming Languages and Computer Architecture*, pages 31–41, 1993.

[Cal99]   Robert O' Callahan. Optimizing a solver of polymorphism constraints: SEMI. Technical Report CMU-CS-99-136, CMU, June 1999.

[Dug99]   Dominic Duggan. Modular type-based reverse engineering of parameterized types in java code. In *ACM SIGPLAN Symposium on Object-Oriented Programming: Systems, Languages and Applications (OOPSLA)*, 1999.

[EST95]   Jonathan Eifrig, Scott Smith, and Valery Trifonov. Sound polymorphic type inference for objects. In *OOPSLA '95*, pages 169–184, 1995.

[FF97]   Cormac Flanagan and Matthias Felleisen. Componential set-based analysis.
            In *Proceedings of the ACM SIGPLAN Conference on Programming Lan-
            guage Design and Implementation (PLDI-97)*, volume 32, 5 of *ACM SIG-
            PLAN Notices*, pages 235–248, New York, June 15–18 1997. ACM Press.

[GDDC97]   David Grove, Greg DeFouw, Jeffrey Dean, and Craig Chambers. Call graph
            construction in object-oriented languages. In *ACM Conference on Object-
            Oriented Programming Systems, Languages, and Applications (OOPSLA)*,
            1997.

[JW95]   Suresh Jagannathan and Stephen Weeks. A unified treatment of flow anal-
            ysis in higher-order languages. In *Conference Record of the Twenty-Second
            Annual ACM Symposium on Principles of Programming Languages*, pages
            393–408, 1995.

[PC94]   John Plevyak and Andrew Chien. Precise concrete type inference for
            object-oriented languages. In *Proceedings of the Ninth Annual ACM Con-
            ference on Object-Oriented Programming Systems, Languages, and Appli-
            cations*, pages 324–340, 1994.

[Pot98]   François Pottier. A framework for type inference with subtyping. In *Pro-
            ceedings of the third ACM SIGPLAN International Conference on Func-
            tional Programming (ICFP'98)*, September 1998.

[PP98]   Jens Palsberg and Christina Pavlopoulou. From polyvariant flow informa-
            tion to intersection and union types. In *POPL*, 1998.

[Shi91]   Olin Shivers. *Control-Flow Analysis of Higher-Order Languages*. PhD the-
            sis, Carnegie-Mellon University, 1991. Available as CMU Technical Report
            CMU-CS-91-145.

[SHR+00]   V. Sundaresan, L. Hendren, C. Razafimahefa, R. Valee-Rai, P. Lam,
            E. Gagnon, and C. Godin. Practical virtual method call resolution for
            java. In *ACM Conference on Object-Oriented Programming Systems, Lan-
            guages, and Applications (OOPSLA)*, 2000.

[SW00]   Scott Smith and Tiejun Wang. Polyvariant flow analysis with constrained
            types. In Gert Smolka, editor, *Proceedings of the 2000 European Symposium
            on Programming (ESOP'00)*, volume 1782 of *Lecture Notes in Computer
            Science*, pages 382–396. Springer Verlag, March 2000.

[TLSS99]   F. Tip, C. Laffra, P. Sweeney, and D. Streeter. Practical experience with
            an application extractor for java. In *ACM Conference on Object-Oriented
            Programming Systems, Languages, and Applications (OOPSLA)*, 1999.

[TP00]   F. Tip and J. Palsberg. Scalable propagation-based call graph construction.
            In *ACM Conference on Object-Oriented Programming Systems, Languages,
            and Applications (OOPSLA)*, 2000.

CCC: User-Defined Object Structure in C

Yasunori Harada[1], Kenichi Yamazaki[2], and Richard Potter[3]

[1] Japan Science and Technology Corporation / NTT
NTT CSLabs, Wakamiya 3-1, Morinosato, Atsugi-City, Kanagawa-Pref., Japan.
hara@acm.org, http://www.brl.ntt.co.jp/people/hara
[2] NTT DoCoMo
yamazaki@nue.org
[3] Japan Science and Technology Corporation
potter@is.s.u-tokyo.ac.jp

Abstract. Traditional object-oriented programming languages do not support user-level object structure definition, so it is impossible to treat external or low-level data structures (like an integer, an array and a pointer) as actual objects. To overcome this, we apply Predicate Dispatching to arbitrary data of C to create CCC. CCC is a simple language extension of C and features user-level object structure definitions, conditional-style dispatching, multi-methods, and class scoped macros.

1 Introduction

There is a need to introduce several object-oriented (OO) technologies into programs that manipulates low-level or external data structure. Low-level programming can take advantages of the special data structures. For example, an implementation of a Lisp-like language can use a tag-embedded pointer structure that indicates object types, and most C programming uses null (zero) pointer to show termination of a list structure. Moreover, a program that manipulates external data like a structured file or a protocol packet must use formats that are to fit an external or a standard object structure.

Traditional OO programming languages (PLs) cannot define such a data structure as their own object. C++ can define an object from only a structure that has a pointer of its class' virtual function table. So OO technologies cannot be applied to low-level or external data structure.

To overcome this problem, we apply Predicate Dispatching [3] to arbitrary data of C. Predicate Dispatching and the previous works by these authors [1,2] feature dispatching by a predicate associated with a method. Because of the independence between a method dispatching mechanism and the defining of an object structure, any data structure can be treated as an object.

We propose a small language extension of C, which we call CCC (C with Condition Classes). In CCC, a class that is defined by a condition expression plays a role in method dispatching and inheritance, but not data abstraction. The defining of a data structure mechanism is just the same as that in C. Any data structure (including low-level and external data) that can be represented by

J. Lindskov Knudsen (Ed.): ECOOP 2001, LNCS 2072, pp. 118–129, 2001.

C can be treated as an object in CCC. For each method signature, the CCC compiler generates a corresponding generic function that can dynamically determine a class and do multi-method dispatching.

In the next section, we overview CCC with an example. Section 3 shows how generic functions are generated from class and method definitions. Section 4 discusses about precise CCC features.

2 CCC Overview

CCC is a small extension of C. For a rough understanding, we give examples of the inputs and outputs of the CCC compiler.

2.1 Conditionally Defined Classes

Let

    @class *Name* [(*Arguments*)] [if (*Condition*)] { *Body* }

be the syntax of a conditionally defined class[1]. *Name* is a class name that identifies the class. *Arguments*, the class-arguments, is a C-style argument list, a comma separated sequence of type and variable pairs. *Condition*, the class-condition, is a Boolean C-expression. *Body*, the class-body, includes method, macro and subclass definitions. A variable defined in class-arguments is accessible in the class-conditions and class-bodies of the class and its subclasses. Method definitions in the class-body take the same form as C function definitions.

An anonymous class can be defined by making *Name* be _. *Arguments* and its outer parentheses can be omitted if there are no class arguments. If *Condition* is always true (i.e. non zero), "if (*Condition*) " can be omitted.

An example of class definitions is as follows:

```
@class integer (int x) {
  int abs() { return x; }
  @class negint if (x < 0) {
    int abs() { return -x; }
  }
}
```

This CCC code defines two classes, integer and its subclass negint. Each class has a method abs() that replies the absolute value of a class argument int x. Once these classes are defined, any C integer can be treated as an object in the class hierarchy by invoking the method with the class argument as follows:

---

[1] In this paper, we use type-face letters for terminal symbols, italics for non-terminal symbols, and square brackets to indicate an eliminatable sequence.

```
void foo() {
  int y = abs(-10);
}
```

Class definitions are translated by the CCC compiler into a C program as follows.

```
int integer_abs(int x) { return x; }
int negint_abs(int x) { return -x; }
int abs(int x) {
  if (1) {
    if (x < 0) {
      return negint_abs(x);
    }
    return integer_abs(x);
  }
}
void foo() {
  int y = abs(-10);
}
```

A method M in a class L is translated to a C function named L_M that has arguments that are a concatenation of the class arguments and the method's local arguments (blank in this example). For each unique method signature (as defined by C's function signature), one method dispatch function (abs() in this example) is generated. It takes class arguments (x) and method local arguments (blank), checks conditions of each class (1 and x < 0), and calls the corresponding method body (integer_abs() or negint_abs()). Note that meaningless code segments like if (1) are not an efficiency concern because they can be removed by most C compilers during optimization.

2.2 Class Types

CCC has three different types of class definitions: an if-class, a switch/case-class, and an elsif-class. These are the same except for the type of a conditional statement that is generated in the dispatch function. By choosing class types, a programmer can optimize dispatching behavior.

An elsif-class must have a previous if or elsif-class. For each method in an elsif-class, the CCC compiler generates a dispatch function using an else if statement. When conditions do not overlap, an if-class can be more efficient than an elsif-class. When there is doubt about overlap, the elsif-class is more safe. This will be discussed later in the paper.

A switch/case-class is used for fast dispatching by constants. A switch/case-class consists of one switch-class and its subclasses, which must all be case-classes. For each method in a switch/case-class, the CCC compiler generates a dispatch function using switch/case statements. A switch-class takes one argument, which is used as the expression for a switch-statement. A case-class takes one argument, which is used as the constant for a `case` label. The switch-class itself may have a method that is used for `default` label of the `switch-case` statement. The class definitions

```
@class A(int x) switch(x) {
  @class B case(1) { }
  @class C case(2) { }
}
```

are semantically the same as

```
@class A(int x) {
  @class B if (x==1) { }
  @class C elsif (x==2) { }
}
```

2.3 Examples

The following example from an interpreter for a Lisp-like language demonstrates tricky object implementation using tag-embedded pointers and fast method dispatching.

First, we must design the memory structure for implementing CONS and the primitive data types:

```
typedef unsigned int ptr;
@class object (ptr self) {
  // bits 1-2 are for data type.
  @class data switch (self & 0x6) {
    @class nil_or_cons case (0x0) {
      @class nil if (self == 0) { }
      @class cons elsif (1) { }
    }
    @class number case (0x2) { }
    @class string case (0x4) { }
    @class other  case (0x6) { }
  }
}
```

This defines the basic object classification hierarchy. An object is specified as a single `ptr` and is referenced in the CCC code as `self`. To check a class, `self` is masked with the bit mask `0x6`, and according to the masked value, class `nil_or_cons`, `number`, `string` and `other` are distinguished. If `self` is zero in `nil_or_cons`, the object class is `nil`, otherwise `cons`.

Now we can define macros for data access for a cons structure that is implemented as a pair of `ptr`s, CAR and CDR.

```
@+cons {
  macro CAR {(*((ptr *)self))}
  macro CDR {(*((ptr *)self+1))}
}
```

Here,

> @+*Class* { *Segment* }

is syntax sugar called insertion, which inserts *Segment* into a previously defined *Class* body. *Segment* can include any methods and subclass definitions.

> macro *Name* [(*Macro-Arguments*)] { *Body* }

is a class local macro definition. This is similar to C's macros except there is no need to use escape codes for carriage returns, because brackets must balance. Like methods, a class local macro can be accessed from its class and subclasses, and may be redefined in subclasses[2].

Using such macros, safe methods that check errors can be defined.

```
@+object {
  ptr car() { return 0; }
  ptr cdr() { return 0; }
}
@+cons {
  ptr car() { return CAR; }
  ptr cdr() { return CDR; }
}
```

CCC takes these incremental definitions and compiles them into unified dispatch functions. For example, the car() method is compiled to the following:

```
ptr object_car(ptr self) { return 0; }
ptr cons_car(ptr self) { return (*((ptr *)self)); }
ptr car(ptr self) {
  if (1) {
    switch ((self & 0x6)) {
      case (0):
      if (self == 0x0) {
      } else if (1) {
        return cons_car(self);
      }
    }
    return object_car(self);
  }
}
```

This compiled code checks minimum conditions to access a CONS structure. With a reasonable C compiler this will produce efficient, fast code.

---

[2] Although macro is a dangerous mechanism, we choose this because it is simple and can take any code segment of programs. In our experience of CCC, a class local encapsulated control structure using macro is convenient.

Using this class hierarchy, a simple pretty printer is defined as

```
@+number { void pprint() { printf("%d", value);} }
@+nil    { void pprint() { printf("nil"); } }
@+cons {
  void pprint() {
    putchar('('); pprint(CAR); cdrprint(CDR); }
}
@+object {
  void cdrprint() {
    printf(" . "); pprint(self); putchar(')');  }
}
@+cons {
  void cdrprint() {
    putchar(' '); pprint(CAR); cdrprint(CDR);  }
}
@+nil {
  void cdrprint() { putchar(')'); }
}
```

This produces output like

```
(-10 11)
(-12 (-10 11) . 13)
```

3 Generating Dispatch Functions

This section describes how the CCC compiler generates dispatch functions. The CCC compiler collects the code segments of class definitions, builds a large class tree, extracts a method tree for each method signature, and generates the dispatch codes. Each node of the tree is a class, and each branch of the tree leading to a node is a condition. The root of a tree is a virtual root class that has no name, no class-arguments, and a condition that is always true. A class that is in the top level of CCC's source code is a subclass of the virtual root class. A class L is connected into its direct super class with L's condition branch. Subclasses of the same class are ordered according to the order of the class definitions in the sequence of input files.

For each method signature M, CCC builds, according to following rules, a method tree T that is a subset of the class tree. 1) If a class L defines the method M, then L is in the subtree T. 2) If a class L's subclass is in the tree T, then L is in the tree T. 3) And if an elsif-class L is in the tree T, then L's elder sibling classes[3] are in T. Fig.1 shows an example of class and method trees.

The CCC compiler generates a dispatch function according to a method tree. A dispatch function is a tree of condition statements that have a one to

---

[3] They share the same super class as L and are defined earlier than L

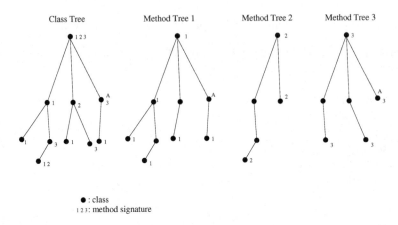

Fig. 1. Class Tree and Method Trees: According to method tree rules, three method trees are generated. For example, class A is included in method tree 1 (because of rule 2) and method tree 3 (because of rule 1).

one correspondence to its method tree's nodes and branches, according to the class type (if-class, switch/case-class or elsif-class).

The CCC compiler generates dispatch functions using the following recursive algorithm:

Assume T is a node in a method M's tree.

```
generate(Method M, MethodTree T) {
  /* generate its condition */
  switch (T's class type) {
    case if-class:  write "if" statement with T's condition.
    case elsif-class:  write "else" and "if" statement
                                       with T's condition.
    case switch-class:  write "switch" statement
                                       with T's expression.
    case case-class: write "case" label with T's constant.
  }
  write open block "{"
  /* generate its subclasses */
  for each child C of T in order {
    generate(M, C);
  }
  if T has Method M {
    write method-function-call with a "return" statement
  }
  write close block "}"
}
```

In this algorithm summary, some error checks (for example switch-class's subclass must be case-class and so on) are omitted.

4   Discussion

4.1   Combining with User-Level Classes

Using CCC, a programmer can combine several levels of classes into a single hierarchy. Based on the Section 2.3 example, let's define a user-level class onto implementation-level data structures.

```
ptr atomPoint;
@+cons {
  @class point if (CAR == atomPoint) {
    macro x {car(CDR)}
    macro y {car(cdr(CDR))}
    ptr pointX() { return x; }
    ptr pointY() { return y; }
    void pprint() {
      pprint(x); putchar('@'); pprint(y);
    }
  }
}
```

Here atomPoint is a global variable containing a pointer to the atomic Lisp symbol point. A Lisp data structure (point 10 20) becomes a CCC point object, and methods pointX(), pointY(), and pprint() can be used for this object. The output of pprint() of (point 10 20) is 10@20. This is helpful for combining Lisp- and C-based programming.

4.2   Overlapped Conditions

The CCC compiler cannot compute whether conditions overlap or not, so a programmer must be sure to use the correct type of class, if-class or elsif-class.

Let's compare if-class with elsif-class. If the condition sets are overlapped, for example, (x > 100) and (x > 0), the class definitions for each case are

```
1.    @class A (int x) {
        @class B if (x > 100) { }
        @class C if (x > 0) { }
      }
2.    @class A (int x) {
        @class B if (x > 100) { }
        @class C elsif (x > 0) { }
      }
```

Assume a method M is defined in only classes A and C in both cases. We would expect class B to inherit method M from class A. But, the generated C codes are

```
1.    void M(int x, ..) {
         if (1) {
            if (x > 0) { C_M(x, ..); return; }
            A_M(x, ..); return;
         }
      }
2.    void M(int x, ..) {
         if (1) {
            if (x > 100) {
            } else if (x > 0) { C_M(x, ..); return; }
            A_M(x, ..); return;
         }
      }
```

The `elsif` version (case 2) works correctly, because for class B (ex. x = 101), A_M() is called. However, the `if` version (case 1) does not work correctly, because for class B (ex. x = 101) class C's method C_M() is called.

On the other hand, for the case of non-overlapped conditions, both cases work correctly, but the `elsif` version is not efficient because unnecessary condition checks are generated.

Cecil [1,2] can handle such overlapped conditions and eliminate such unnecessary condition checks.

4.3   Condition Reuse

To check whether an object belongs to a certain class, CCC generates class checking functions and allows the reuse of class conditions. As an example, a generated class checking function is shown here for the class `nil` in Section 2 (instead of a real output, a macro expanded result is shown),

```
int nil_p(ptr self) {
   return (1) && (1) && ((self & 0x6)==0) && (self ==0);
}
```

Using such a function, we can define new classes

```
@+cons {
   @class singleton if (nil_p(CDR)) { }
   @class list if (nil_p(CDR) || list_p(CDR)) { }
}
```

The class `singleton` is a cons and its cdr slot is nil. Class `list` is a nil terminated sequence of one or more conses. This `list` checker is a recursive function.

4.4   Non-OO Application

Polymorphism and inheritance mechanisms are also useful for non-OOPL.

```
@class fullBattery {
  @class lowBattery if (gBattery < 20) {
    void playSound(Sound s) {
      /* be silent to save a battery */
    }
  }
  void playSound(Sound s) {
    /* normal play s */
  }
}
```

In this example, there are two classes that have no class arguments. The class condition of class `lowbattery` checks the global variable `gBattery`. This code defines a method that can be invoked with the simple call `playSound(s)`. There is no object but class `lowbattery` is still able to inherit class `fullBattery`'s other behavior through polymorphism.

4.5   Multi-method Dispatching

CCC can also generate a multi-method dispatching function using the same Predicate Dispatching mechanism. Condition-based multi-method dispatching has more power than class-based ones like CLOS and Cecil. For example,

```
@class plane (int x, int y) {
  @class halfplane (x > y) { }
}
```

defines class `halfplane` as a relation of two objects. In Cecil, a relation object is needed for this kind of dispatching.

4.6   Method Search Direction

A running CCC program searches for methods in a different direction than a dynamic OOPL like Smalltalk[6]. In a dynamic OOPL, an object class is determined using class ID, then the system searches the method from its class to the root class, and executes the first one it finds. In CCC, the system checks the conditions of branches of the method subtree in a depth-first manner and if a class that has no branch satisfying the condition is found, its method is executed. Even though the techniques are different, the semantics are the same, except that the conditions in CCC can be more general than the simple test-for-subclass conditions of an OOPL.

4.7   C++ as Target Language

CCC can generate C++ code instead of C code using a compiler option. This changes CCC's method signature semantics. A C function name must be globally unique, so CCC's method names must be unique for different types of class arguments. On the other hand, in C++ we can use the same function name for different types of return values and arguments, so CCC treats method names with different argument and return types as different method signatures.

4.8   CCC Implementation

The CCC compiler is a 2500-line C language program. It can be installed easily on any UNIX system.

We have developed several useful applications using CCC. One major application is a shared-memory-based language interpreter that processes objects in a shared memory. The interpreter uses a graph rewriting paradigm and several interpreter processes can attach to the shared memory and manipulate objects. In this implementation, CCC has been useful for defining tricky object encodings in shared memory. The object-oriented and incremental programming features of CCC make it easy to extend the interpreter in an orderly way that is compatible with older shared memory.

5   Related Work

The e language [10] combines object-oriented and constraint-oriented mechanisms. It is used for microchip modeling and verification. The language has when inheritance and constraints that are similar to Predicate Classes [2] but more declarative for use in testing.

EU-Lisp [8] and SchemeXerox [9] extend Lisp-like languages to treat low-level data structures. The differences between these languages and CCC are CCC has an object-oriented method dispatch, and CCC's methods are more flexible than those "accessors".

6   Conclusion

We presented a new language called CCC, which is a small extension of C with Predicate Dispatching. Using CCC, a programmer can attach a class hierarchy onto arbitrary data structures expressed in C. So CCC can express a program that treats low-level and external data structures as objects, including a tag-embedded pointer, a null pointer, the X-Window XEvent structure, several graphics file formats, and so on. The paper showed a small Lisp implementation with a type tag-embedded pointer by CCC. With a traditional language, OO technologies are awkward to apply to these examples, because only classical programming constructions such as macro and if statements can be used.

CCC gives programmers simple and efficient views. CCC-generated code is easily predictable and a programmer can control it efficiently.

Examples and implementation of CCC can be found at our Web site [11].

Acknowledgments

The authors are grateful for the constructive suggestions of the reviewers.

References

1. Chambers, C.: *Object-Oriented Multi-Methods in Cecil*, Proc.ECOOP'92.
2. Chambers, C.: *Predicate Classes*, Proc.ECOOP'93.
3. Ernst, M., Kaplan, C., and Chambers, C.: *Predicate Dispatching: A Unified Theory of Dispatch*, ECOOP'98.
4. Harada, Y., Yamazaki, K.: *Condition Classes: Polymorphism and Inheritance without Data Abstraction*, PRO, IPSJ, Jan. 1996 (In Japanese).
5. Steele, G.L.: Common Lisp: *The Language*, Digital Press, Bedford MA, 1990. Second edition.
6. Goldberg, A. and Robson, D. *Smalltalk-80: The Language and Its Implementation*. Addison-Wesley, Reading, MA, 1983.
7. Ellis, M.A., Stroustrup, B.: *The Annotated C++ Reference Manual.*, Addison-Wesley, Reading, MA, 1990.
8. Queinnec, C., Cointe, P.: *An Open-Ended Data Representation Model for EuLisp*, Proc. 1988 ACM Conference on LISP and Functional Programming.
9. Adams, N., Curtis, P., Spreitzer, M.: *"First-class Data-type Representation in SchemeXerox*, Proc. 1993 ACM Conference on Programming Language Design.
10. Hollander, Y., Morley, M., Noy, A.: *The e Language: A Fresh Separation of Concerns*, 38th International Conference on Technology of Object-Oriented Languages: TOOLS-38 Europe 2001, Ed. Wolfgang Pree.
11. Harada, Y.: CCC web page, `http://www.brl.ntt.co.jp/people/hara/ccc/`.

Appendix: CCC Syntax

Class := (*If-Class* | *Switch-Case-Class*) [*Elsif-Class*].
Class-Head := @class *Name* [(*Class-Arguments*)].
If-Class := *Class-Head* [if (*Expression*)] { *Body* }.
Elsif-Class := *Class-Head* elsif (*Expression*) { *Body* } [*Elsif-Class*].
Switch-Case-Class := *Class-Head* switch (*Expression*) { *Switch-Body* }.
Case-Class := *Class-Head* case (*Const-Expression*) { *Body* }.
Body := (*Class* | *Macro* | *Method*)*.
Switch-Body := (*Case-Class* | *Macro* | *Method*)*.
Macro := macro *Name* [(*Macro-Arguments*)] { *Macro-Body* }.
Method := C function definition.
Expression := C expression.
Const-Expression := C constant expression.
Macro-Body := C any code segment with balanced parentheses.
Class-Arguments := C Argument list (Comma separeted sequence of pair of type and variable).
Macro-Arguments := C Macro Argument list (Comma seperated sequence of variable).

$\mathcal{F}ickle$: Dynamic Object Re-classification[*]

Sophia Drossopoulou[1], Ferruccio Damiani[2], Mariangiola Dezani-Ciancaglini[2],
and Paola Giannini[3]

[1] Department of Computing, Imperial College
[2] Dipartimento di Informatica, Università di Torino
[3] DISTA, Università del Piemonte Orientale

Abstract. *Re-classification* changes at run-time the class membership
of an object while retaining its identity. We suggest language features for
object re-classification, which could extend an imperative, typed, class-
based, object-oriented language.

We present our proposal through the language $\mathcal{F}ickle$. The imperative
features combined with the requirement for a static and safe type system
provided the main challenges. We develop a type and effect system for
$\mathcal{F}ickle$ and prove its soundness with respect to the operational semantics.
In particular, even though objects may be re-classified across classes
with different members, they will never attempt to access non-existing
members.

1 Introduction

In class-based, object-oriented programming, an object's behaviour is determined by its class. Case or conditional statements should be avoided when differences can be expressed through different classes. Thus, students paying reduced
and employees paying full conference fees are best described through distinct
classes Stdt and Empl with different methods fee().

However, this elegant approach does not scale when objects change classification. For example, how can we represent that mary, who was a Stdt, became an
Empl? Usually, class based programming languages do not provide mechanisms
for objects to change their class membership. Two solutions are possible: Either
to replace the original Stdt object by an Empl object, or to merge the two classes
Stdt and Empl into one, *e.g.* StdtOrEmpl.

Neither solution is satisfactory. The first solution needs to trace and inform all
references to mary. The second solution blurs in the same class the differences
in behaviour that were elegantly expressed through the class system. In fact,
[28] lists the lack of re-classification primitives as the first practical limitation of
object oriented programming.

We suggest language features which allow objects to change class membership
dynamically, *e.g.* the object pointed at by variable aWindow belonged to class

---

[*] This research was supported in part by MURST Cofin '99 TOSCA Project, CNR-
GNSAGA, and the EPSRC (Grant Ref GR/L 76709).

J. Lindskov Knudsen (Ed.): ECOOP 2001, LNCS 2072, pp. 130–149, 2001.

OpenedWindow   but now belongs to class IconifiedWindow. We combine these features with a strong type system.

Our approach therefore directly supports the state pattern [18], avoiding the explicit delegation of behaviour to another object.

The idea of object re-classification is not new. From a foundational perspective, in [1] method overriding explains field update and delegation in an object-based calculus, while in [15] method extensions represent class inheritance. From a databases perspective, [6] suggests multiple most specific classes, while in [19] objects may accumulate several roles in a functional setting. From a programming perspective, in [30] classes have "modes" representing different states, *e.g.* opened vs. iconified window. Wide classes [29] allow an object to be temporarily "widened" or "shrunk", *i.e.* become an object of a subclass or superclass, requiring run-time tests for the presence of fields. Predicate classes [10, 14] extend multimethods, suggesting method dispatch depending on predicates on the receiver and argument.

We take a programming perspective, and base our approach on an imperative, class-based language, where classes are types and subclasses are subtypes,[1] and where methods are defined inside classes and selected depending on the class of the receiver. We achieve dynamic re-classification of objects by explicitly changing the class membership of objects.

We describe our approach through the language $\mathcal{F}ickle$. A *re-classification* operation changes the class membership of an object while preserving its identity; it maintains all fields declared as common to the original and the target class and initializes the extra fields. *State* classes are possible targets of re-classifications; in that sense, they represent object's possible states. *Root* classes are the superclasses of such state classes and declare all the members common to them. Only non-state classes may appear as types of parameters or fields. $\mathcal{F}ickle$ is statically typed, with a type and effect system [24, 31], which determines the re-classification effect of an expression on the receiver and on all other objects. The type system is sound, so that terminating execution of a well-typed expression produces a value of the expected type, or a null-pointer exception, but does *not* get stuck.

This paper is organized as follows: In Section 2 we introduce $\mathcal{F}ickle$ informally using an example. In Section 3 we outline $\mathcal{F}ickle$: the syntax, operational semantics, typing rules, and we state type soundness. In Section 4 we compare our proposal with other approaches. In Section 5 we describe design alternatives. In Section 6 we draw some conclusions.

$\mathcal{F}ickle$ has been presented at FOOL'8 (London, January 20). A full version of this paper is available at http://www.di.unito.it/~damiani/papers/dor.html.

---

[1] Even though the object-based paradigm may be more fundamental [1] and though classes should not be types, and subclasses should not imply subtypes [8], current praxis predominantly uses languages of the opposite philosophy.

```
class StackException  extends Exception{
   StackException(String str) { } {super(str); }
}


abstract root class Stack extends Object{
   int capacity;    // maximum number of elements

   abstract bool isEmpty() {  } ;
   abstract int top() {  } throws StackException;
   abstract void push(int i) { Stack } throws StackException;
   abstract void pop()  { Stack } throws StackException;
}


state class EmptyStack extends Stack{
   EmptyStack(int n) {  } {capacity:= n; }

   bool isEmpty() {  } {return true; }
   int top() {  } throws StackException
      {thrownewStackException("StackUnderflow"); }
   void push(int i) { Stack }
      {this⇓NonEmptyStack; a:= newint[capacity]; t:= 0; a[0]:= i; }
   void pop() {  } throws StackException
      {thrownewStackException("StackUnderflow"); }
}


state class NonEmptyStack extends Stack{
   int[] a;    // array of elements
   int t;        // index of top element

   NonEmptyStack(int n, int i) {  }
      {capacity:= n; a:= newint[capacity]; t:= 0; a[0]:= i; }

   bool isEmpty() {  } {return false ; }
   int top() {  } {return a[t]; }
   void push(int i) {  } throws StackException
    {t:= t + 1;
      if (t == capacity) thrownewStackException("StackOverflow");  else a[t]:= i; }
   void pop() { Stack }
      {if (t == 0) this⇓EmptyStack;  else t:= t − 1;   }
}
```

Fig. 1. Program P_{st}- stacks with re-classifications

2   An Example

In Figure 1 we define, using a Java-like syntax, a class Stack, with subclasses EmptyStack and NonEmptyStack. A stack has a capacity (field int capacity) that is the maximum number of integers it can contain and the usual functions characterizing stacks, *i.e.* stack: isEmpty, top, push, and pop.

In $\mathcal{F}ickle$ we introduced two new kinds of classes: **state** and **root**. State classes may serve as targets of re-classifications, and *cannot* be used as types for fields or parameters; in our example, EmptyStack and NonEmptyStack. Root classes define the fields and methods common to their state subclasses; in our example, Stack. The subclasses of root classes must be state classes.[2] A state class c must have a (possibly indirect) root superclass c′; objects of class c may be re-classified to any subclass of c′.

Annotations like { } and { Stack } before throws clauses and method bodies are called *effects*. Effects list the root classes of all objects that may be re-classified by invocation of that method.

Methods with the empty effect { }, *e.g.* isEmpty, may not cause any re-classification. Methods with non-empty effects, *e.g.* pop and push with effect { Stack }, may re-classify objects of a subclass of their effect; in our case of Stack. Such re-classifications may be caused by *re-classification expressions*, *e.g.* this⇓EmptyStack, or by further method calls.

The method body of push in class EmptyStack contains the re-classification expression this⇓NonEmptyStack. At the start of the method the receiver is an object of class EmptyStack, therefore it contains the field capacity and does not contain the fields a and t. After execution of this⇓NonEmptyStack the receiver is of class NonEmptyStack, and therefore the fields a and t are accessible, while the field capacity retains its value. This mechanism allows the transmission of some information from the object before the re-classification to the object after the re-classification.

Consider example (1):

$$
\begin{array}{ll}
& \text{Stack s;} \\
1. & \text{s:= } \textbf{new} \text{ EmptyStack(100);} \\
2. & \text{s.push(3);} \\
3. & \text{s.push(5);}
\end{array}
\qquad (1)
$$

After line 1. the variable s is bound to an EmptyStack object, after line 2. the object (not the binding) is re-classified to NonEmptyStack. Therefore, the call of push in line 2. selects the method from EmptyStack, while the call of push in line 3. selects the method from NonEmptyStack. With the re-classification we allocate array a and initialize a and t.

---

[2] A root class is almost the same as the first non-state superclass of a state class. The property that *all* its subclasses are state classes allows for a simpler type system. Enforcing this property, *i.e.* enforcing that all subclasses of a class with a state subclass are state classes, is impossible in a system with separate compilation. This is why we introduce root classes as a separate kind of class.

Re-classification is transparent to aliasing. For instance, in example (2)

> Stack s1, s2;
> 1. s1:= **new** NonEmptyStack(100, 3);
> 2. s2:= s1;   (2)
> 3. s1.pop();
> 4. s2.isEmpty();

line 4. returns **true**. Re-classification removes from the object all fields that are not defined in its root superclass and adds the remaining fields of the target class. *E.g.* after line 3. in example (2) the object pointed at by s1 does not have the fields t and a.

Through aliasing one re-classification might affect *several* variables; in example (2) the re-classification after line 3. affects both s1 and s2. For this reason, we prevent variables from accessing members declared in a state class, and we do that by forbidding state classes appearing in field or parameter declarations. Therefore, example (3) is illegal:

> Stack s;
> NonEmptyStack ns;   //   illegal!
> 1. ns:= **new** NonEmptyStack(100, 3);
> 2. s:= ns;   (3)
> 3. s.pop();
> 4. ns.t;   //   error!

If the declaration of ns were legal, then, after line 3. the object bound to s and ns would be re-classified to EmptyStack, and the field access ns.t in line 4. would raise a fieldNotFound error.[3]

Therefore, members of state classes are only accessible via **this** either from methods of the particular state class if there is no previous mutation (*e.g.* access t in pop of class NonEmptyStack before the re-classification), or from methods of other state classes after appropriate re-classifications (*e.g.* access t in method push of NonEmptyStack after the re-classification).

State classes are used as types when typing the receiver, **this**. This supports accessing members from state classes, *e.g.* **this**.t in push in NonEmptyStack.

3   The Language $\mathcal{F}$*ickle*

3.1   Syntax

A $\mathcal{F}$*ickle* program is a sequence of class definitions, consisting of field and method definitions. Method bodies are sequences of expressions. We limit methods to have only one parameter called x. The syntax is similar to that of Java, and can be found in the Appendix.

---

[3] A less satisfactory approach would forbid the assignment on line 2., *c.f.* **c2**(d) in Section 5.

Class definitions may be preceded by the keyword **state**, or **root**. State classes describe the properties of an object while it satisfies some conditions; when it does not satisfy these conditions any more, it can be explicitly re-classified to another state class. For example, NonEmptyStack describes non-empty stacks; if these become empty, then they are re-classified to EmptyStack. Root classes abstract over state classes.[4] Any subclass of a state or a root class must be a state class. Objects of a state class c may be re-classified to class c′, where c′ must be a subclass of the uniquely defined root superclass of c. For example, Stack abstracts over EmptyStack and NonEmptyStack; objects of class EmptyStack may be re-classified to NonEmptyStack, and vice versa.

Objects of a non-state, non-root class c behave like regular Java objects, *i.e.* are never re-classified. However, objects pointed at by a variable x of type c *may* be re-classified. Namely, if c had two state subclasses d and d′ and x referred to an object of class d, the object may be re-classified to d′. Our type system insures that this re-classification will not cause accesses to fields or methods that are not defined for the object.

Fields, parameters and values returned by methods have declared types which are either boolean types or non-state classes; we call these types *variable types*. Thus, such fields and parameters may point to objects which do change class, but these changes do *not* affect their type. Instead, the type of this *may be a state class* and *may change*.

Objects are created with the expression **new**c – c may be *any* class, also a state class. Re-classification expressions, this⇓c, set the class of this to c – c must be a state class.

Method declarations have the shape:

$$\text{t m } (\text{t}_1 \text{ x}) \{ \text{c}_1, ..., \text{c}_n \} \{ \text{ e } \}$$

where t is the result type, t_1 is the type of the formal parameter x, and e the body. The effect consists of root classes $\text{c}_1,..., \text{c}_n$, with $n \geq 0$.

We require root classes to extend only non-root and non-state classes, and state classes to extend either root classes or state classes. The judgment $\vdash P \diamond_a$ expresses that program P satisfies these conditions, as well as the more obvious requirements for acyclic inheritance and unique definitions.

Remark 1. Section 2 follows a more liberal syntax: any number of parameters, abstract classes and methods, user defined constructors, local variables, exceptions, types **int** and **void**.

3.2 Operational Semantics

We give a structural operational semantics that rewrites pairs of expressions and stores into pairs of values, exceptions, or errors, and stores - in the context of a

---

[4] Root classes are not necessarily abstract classes and state classes may be super-classes. Thus, our proposal is orthogonal to the "abstract superclass rule" discussed in [21].

given program. Stores map the unique parameter name x and the receiver this to values and addresses to objects. Values are booleans or addresses.

We discuss the two most significant rewrite rules of $\mathcal{F}ickle$: method call and re-classification. Other rewrite rules of $\mathcal{F}ickle$ are listed in the Appendix.

For method calls, $e_0.m(e_1)$, we evaluate the receiver e_0, obtaining an address, say ι. We then evaluate the argument, e_1. We find the appropriate body by looking up m in the class of the object at address ι – we use the function $\mathcal{M}(P, c, m)$ that returns the definition of method m in class c (going through the class hierarchy if needed). We then execute the body, after substituting this with the current object, and assigning to the formal parameter the value of the actual parameter. After the call, we restore the original receiver and parameter.[5]

$$
\frac{
\begin{array}{l}
e_0, \sigma \rightsquigarrow \iota, \sigma_0 \\
e_1, \sigma_0 \rightsquigarrow v_1, \sigma_1 \\
\sigma_1(\iota) = [\![...]\!]^c \\
\mathcal{M}(P, c, m) = t\ m(t_1\ x)\ \phi\ \{\ e\ \} \\
\sigma' = \sigma_1[\text{this} \mapsto \iota][x \mapsto v_1] \\
e, \sigma' \rightsquigarrow v, \sigma''
\end{array}
}{
e_0.m(e_1), \sigma \rightsquigarrow v, \sigma''[\text{this} \mapsto \sigma(\text{this}), x \mapsto \sigma(x)]
}
$$

For re-classification expressions, $\text{this} \Downarrow d$, we find the address of this, which points to an object of class c. We replace the original object by a new object of class d. We preserve the fields belonging to the root superclass of c and initialize the other fields of d according to their types. The term $\mathcal{R}(P, c)$ denotes the least superclass of c which is not a state class: If c is a state class, then $\mathcal{R}(P, c)$ is its unique root superclass, otherwise $\mathcal{R}(P, c) = c$. For example, $\mathcal{R}(P_{st}, \text{NonEmptyStack}) = \text{Stack}$, and $\mathcal{R}(P_{st}, \text{StackException}) = \text{StackException}$. Moreover $\mathcal{F}s(P, c)$ denotes the set of fields defined in class c, $\sigma(\iota)(f)$ the value of the field f in the object at address ι, and $\mathcal{F}(P, c, f)$ the type of field f in class c.

$$
\frac{
\begin{array}{l}
\sigma(\text{this}) = \iota \\
\sigma(\iota) = [\![...]\!]^c \\
\mathcal{F}s(P, \mathcal{R}(P, c)) = \{f_1, ..., f_r\} \\
\forall l \in 1, ..., r : \quad v_l = \sigma(\iota)(f_l) \\
\mathcal{F}s(P, d) \setminus \{f_1, ..., f_r\} = \{f_{r+1}, ..., f_{r+q}\} \\
\forall l \in r+1, ..., r+q : \quad v_l\ \text{initial for}\ \mathcal{F}(P, d, f_l)
\end{array}
}{
\text{this} \Downarrow d, \sigma \rightsquigarrow \iota, \sigma[\iota \mapsto [\![f_1 : v_1, ..., f_{r+q} : v_{r+q}]\!]^d]
}
$$

Take for instance program P_{st} from Figure 1. For a store σ_1, with $\sigma_1(s) = \iota$, and $\sigma_1(\iota) = [\![\text{capacity} : 100, a : \{3\}, t : 0]\!]^{\text{NonEmptyStack}}$ we have $s.\text{pop}(), \sigma_1 \rightsquigarrow_{st} \iota, \sigma_2$ where $\sigma_2 = \sigma_1[\iota \mapsto [\![\text{capacity} : 100]\!]^{\text{EmptyStack}}]$ *i.e.* we obtain an object of class EmptyStack with unmodified capacity.

Note that the rule for re-classification uses the types of the fields to initialize the fields, as the object creation does. In a well-typed program we always have

---

[5] We restore the references, but not the contents: thus, after a method call the receiver is the same, but any side effects caused by execution of the method body survive after the call.

$\mathcal{R}(P, c) = \mathcal{R}(P, d)$ (and both c and d are state classes). This implies that re-classification depends only on the target class d, not on the class c of the receiver. Therefore a compiler could fold the type information into the code, by generating specific re-classification code for each state class.

3.3 Typing

Widening, Environments, Effects It is useful to define some assertions: $P \vdash c \Diamond_s$ means that c is a state class, $P \vdash c \Diamond_r$ means that c is a root class, $P \vdash c \Diamond_{nsr}$ means that c is a non-state, non-root class, $P \vdash c \Diamond_c$ means that c is any class, $P \vdash t \Diamond_{vt}$ means that t is a variable type *i.e.* either **bool**, or a non-state class, $P \vdash t \Diamond_t$ means that t is a type, *i.e.* any class or **bool**. Finally, $P \vdash t \leq t'$ means that type t' widens type t, *i.e.* t is a subclass of, or identical with, t'. In our example, $P_{st} \vdash$ Stack $\Diamond_r$ and $P_{st} \vdash$ Stack $\Diamond_{vt}$, and $P_{st} \vdash$ EmptyStack $\Diamond_s$, but $P_{st} \nvdash$ EmptyStack $\Diamond_{vt}$.

Environments, Γ, map the parameter x to variable types, and the receiver this to classes. Lookup, $\Gamma(id)$, update, $\Gamma[id \mapsto t]$, and well-formedness, $P \vdash \Gamma \Diamond$, have the usual meaning.

An effect, ϕ, is a set $\{ c_1, ..., c_n \}$ of root classes; it means that any object of a state subclass of c_i may be re-classified to any state subclass of c_i. The empty effect, $\{ \}$, guarantees that no object is re-classified. Effects are well formed, *i.e.* $P \vdash \{ c_1, ..., c_n \} \Diamond$, iff $c_1,...,c_n$ are distinct root classes. Thus, $P \vdash \{ c_1, ..., c_n \} \Diamond$ implies that c_i are not subclasses of each other.

Typing Specialities We motivate the typing rules through two examples.

The type of this may change within a method body. In Example (4):

```
root class  A { }
state class  B  extends  A { bool j; }
state class  C  extends  A {
    bool i;
    bool m(){ A }{
        this.i := false;    // type correct, this is currently a C        (4)
        this.j := false;    // type incorrect, this is currently a C
        this⇓B;
        this.i := false;    // type incorrect, this is currently a B
        this.j := false     / *  type correct, this is currently a B  * / }
}
```

this has type C before the re-classification, and it has type B afterwards.

Changes to the type of this are caused either by explicit re-classification, as in Example (4), or by potential, indirect re-classification, as in methods h and k of Example (5).

```
root class  A { bool g(){ A }{  true }    }
state class  B  extends  A {  }
state class  C  extends  A {
   bool g(){ A } { this⇓B; true }
   bool m(bool x){ }{ x }
   bool h(D aD){ A }{
      this.m(true);                    //  type correct
      aD.f();                          //  might re-classify this
      this.m(true)                     / *  type error * /  }
   bool k(D aD){ A }{
      this.m(true);                    //  type correct
      this.m(aD.f())                   / *  type error * /  }
}


class  D {
   A anA;
   bool f(){ A }{  anA.g() }
}
```
$$(5)$$

If in method h, in (5), before aD.f() the field aD.anA happened to be an alias
of the receiver, this, then this would be re-classified to B. In order to capture
such potential re-classifications, each method declares as its effect the set of root
classes of objects that may be re-classified through its execution. In our case, f
has effect { A }. Therefore, after the call aD.f() the type of this is A, *i.e.* the
application of the effect { A } to class C.

Thus, typing an expression e, in the context of program P, and environment
Γ involves three components, namely

$$P, \Gamma \vdash e : t \parallel c \parallel \phi$$

where t is the type of the value returned by evaluation of e, where c is the
class of this after evaluation of e, and where ϕ conservatively estimates the
re-classification effect of the evaluation of e.

For example, let P_4 and P_5 be the programs from examples (4), and (5), and
environments, Γ_0, Γ_1, Γ_2, with $\Gamma_0(\text{this})$=C, $\Gamma_1(\text{this})$=B, and $\Gamma_2(\text{this})$=A. At
the beginning of the body of m in (4), we have: $P_4, \Gamma_0 \vdash$ this.i : bool $\parallel$ C $\parallel$ { };
then, the re-classification is typed as $P_4, \Gamma_0 \vdash$ this⇓B : B $\parallel$ B $\parallel$ { A }. Therefore,
afterwards we use environment Γ_1, with $P_4, \Gamma_1 \vdash$ this.j : bool $\parallel$ B $\parallel$ { A }.[6]
In h we have $P_5, \Gamma_0 \vdash$ aD.f() : bool $\parallel$ A $\parallel$ { A }, and therefore the next term,
this.m(true), is checked in environment Γ_2, where it is type incorrect.

The point from which effects modify the type of this is important. In method
calls, the argument may affect the receiver. In example (5), in method k the first
call of the method m is type correct, but the second is not. Namely, evaluation
of the argument, aD.f(), may re-classify objects of subclasses of A, and therefore

---

[6] Here the effect ({ A }) is the root superclass of the type of this (B). In the general
case effects are sets of root classes, and need not contain the root superclass of this.

might re-classify this. Thus, the effect of the argument must be taken into account when looking-up the method. Because $P_5, \Gamma_0 \vdash$ this : $C \parallel C \parallel \{\ \}$, and $P_5, \Gamma_0 \vdash$ aD.f() : **bool** $\parallel A \parallel \{A\}$, we look-up the method m in class A; none is found, and so this.m(aD.f()) is type incorrect in environment Γ_0.

Typing Rules are given in Figure 5 of the Appendix, using look-up functions. The functions $\mathcal{FD}(P, c, f)$, $\mathcal{MD}(P, c, m)$ search for fields and methods only in class c itself, while $\mathcal{F}(P, c, f)$, $\mathcal{M}(P, c, m)$ go through the class hierarchy.

We only discuss the rules for re-classification and for method call.

The re-classification this$\Downarrow$c is type correct if c, the target class, is a state class, and if c and the class of this before the re-classification(the class Γ(this)) are subclasses of the same root class.

$$\frac{P \vdash c \ \Diamond_s \qquad \mathcal{R}(P, c) = \mathcal{R}(P, \Gamma(\text{this}))}{P, \Gamma \vdash \text{this}\Downarrow c \ : \ c \parallel c \parallel \{\mathcal{R}(P, c)\}}$$

Consider method calls, $e_0.m(e_1)$. The evaluation of the argument e_1 may modify the class of the object e_0, as shown in example (5). This could happen if a superclass of the original class of e_0 is among the effects of e_1. (Existence of such a class implies uniqueness, since effects are sets of root classes.) The definition of m has to be found in the new class of the object e_0. For this purpose, we define the application of effects to classes:

$$\{c_1, ..., c_n\}@_P c = \begin{cases} c_i & \text{if } \mathcal{R}(P, c) = c_i \text{ for some } i \in 1, ..., n \\ c & \text{otherwise.} \end{cases}$$

For example, $\{\text{Stack}\}@_{P_{st}} \text{NonEmptyStack} = \text{Stack}$, and $\{\text{Stack}\}@_{P_{st}} \text{Object} = \text{Object}$.

For method call we lookup the definition of method m in the class obtained by applying the effect of the argument to the class of the receiver (which in general is not this):

$$\frac{\begin{array}{l} P, \Gamma \vdash e_0 \ : \ c \parallel c_0 \parallel \phi_0 \\ P, \Gamma[\text{this} \mapsto c_0] \vdash e_1 \ : \ t_1' \parallel c_1 \parallel \phi_1 \\ \mathcal{M}(P, \phi_1@_P c, m) \ = t \ m(t_1 \ x) \ \phi \ \{ \ ... \ \} \\ P \vdash t_1' \leq t_1 \end{array}}{P, \Gamma \vdash e_0.m(e_1) \ : \ t \parallel \phi@_P c_1 \parallel \phi \cup \phi_0 \cup \phi_1}$$

Well-Formed Programs A program is well formed (*i.e.* $\vdash P \ \Diamond$) if all its classes are well-formed (*i.e.* $P \vdash c \ \Diamond$): Methods may override superclass methods only if they have the same name, argument, and result type, and their effect is a subset of that of the overridden method. Method bodies must be well formed, return a value appropriate for the method signature, and their effect must be a subset of that in the signature. See Figure 5 of the Appendix, where $\mathcal{C}(P,c)$ returns the definition of class c in program P.

Soundness Figure 2 introduces agreement notions between programs, stores, and values:

- $P, \sigma \vdash v \lhd t$ means that value v agrees with type t in the context of program P and store σ;
- $P, \Gamma \vdash \sigma \diamond$ means that store σ agrees with environment Γ and program P.

$$\frac{}{P, \sigma \vdash \texttt{true} \ \lhd \texttt{bool}} \qquad \frac{}{P, \sigma \vdash \texttt{false} \ \lhd \texttt{bool}} \qquad \frac{P \vdash t \diamond_c}{P, \sigma \vdash \texttt{null} \lhd t}$$

$$\frac{\sigma(\iota) = [\![...]\!]^c \qquad P \vdash c \leq t}{\forall f \in \mathcal{F}s(P, c) : \ P, \sigma \vdash \sigma(\iota)(f) \lhd \mathcal{F}(P, c, f)}{P, \sigma \vdash \iota \lhd t}$$

$$\frac{\sigma(\iota) = [\![...]\!]^c \implies P, \sigma \vdash \iota \lhd c, \ \text{for all addresses } \iota,}{P, \sigma \vdash \sigma(\texttt{this}) \lhd \Gamma(\texttt{this}), \qquad P, \sigma \vdash \sigma(x) \lhd \Gamma(x)}{P, \Gamma \vdash \sigma \diamond}$$

Fig. 2. Agreement between programs, stores, and values

The type system is sound in the sense that a converging well-typed expression returns `nullPntrExc`, or a value which agrees with the expression's type; but is *never* stuck. The resulting state agrees with the program and the environment (taking the effect into account):

Theorem 1 (Type Soundness) *For well-formed program* P, *environment* Γ, *expression* e, *and type* t, *such that*

$$P, \Gamma \ \vdash \ e \ : \ t \parallel c \parallel \phi$$

if $P, \Gamma \vdash \sigma \diamond$, *and* e, σ *converges then*

- $e, \sigma \rightsquigarrow v, \sigma', \quad P, \sigma' \vdash v \lhd t, \quad and \quad P, \Gamma[\texttt{this} \mapsto c] \vdash \sigma' \diamond,$
  or
- $e, \sigma \rightsquigarrow \texttt{nullPntrExc}, \sigma', \quad and \quad P, \Gamma[\texttt{this} \mapsto (\phi @_P \Gamma(\texttt{this}))] \vdash \sigma' \diamond.$

Proof outline We introduce a notion of agreement requiring receivers to remain the same, and re-classifications to be between subclasses of the effect:

$P, \phi \vdash \sigma \lhd \sigma'$ iff
- $\sigma(\texttt{this}) = \sigma'(\texttt{this}),$ and
- $\sigma(\iota) = [\![...]\!]^c \implies \sigma'(\iota) = [\![...]\!]^{c'}, \ \phi @_P c = \phi @_P c'.$

We prove the following stronger theorem:

If $P, \Gamma \ \vdash \ e \ : \ t \parallel c \parallel \phi$, and $P, \Gamma \vdash \sigma \diamond$, and e, σ converges, then
- $e, \sigma \rightsquigarrow v, \sigma', \quad P, \sigma' \vdash v \lhd t, \quad P, \phi \vdash \sigma \lhd \sigma', \quad P, \Gamma[\texttt{this} \mapsto c] \vdash \sigma' \diamond,$ or
- $e, \sigma \rightsquigarrow \texttt{nullPntrExc}, \sigma', \quad P, \phi \vdash \sigma \lhd \sigma', \quad P, \Gamma[\texttt{this} \mapsto (\phi @_P \Gamma(\texttt{this}))] \vdash \sigma' \diamond.$

The proof is by induction on the derivations of the operational semantics. The full proof can be found at http://www.di.unito.it/~damiani/papers/dor.html. □

Remark 2. As far as divergent expressions go, the theorem does not say anything. However, the operational semantics forces convergence for standard typing errors or access to members undefined for an object. Therefore, Theorem 1 suffices to ensure that for a well-typed expression such errors will not occur.

Remark 3. The weaker guarantee of well-formedness for the resulting store σ' in the second case of Theorem 1, is due to the fact that the interruption of execution of e might prevent setting the type of this to c. For instance, for program P_0, state classes d', d'', which are not subclasses of each other, and d their root superclass, σ_0, Γ_0 and e_0 with $\sigma_0(\text{this}) = [[\cdots]]^{d'}$ and $\Gamma_0(\text{this}) = d'$, and $e_0 = \text{null.f}; \text{this}\Downarrow d''$, typing produces:

$$P_0, \Gamma \vdash e_0 : d'' \| d'' \| \{d\},$$

whereas execution produces:

$$e_0, \sigma_0 \underset{P_0}{\rightsquigarrow} \text{nullPntrExc}, \sigma_0.$$

In σ_0 the receiver this is bound to an object of class d'. So, $P_0, \Gamma[\text{this}\mapsto d''] \nvdash \sigma_0 \diamond$.
However, $\{d\}@_{P_0}\Gamma_0(\text{this}) = d$, and $P_0 \vdash d' \sqsubseteq d$. Thus,
$P_0, \Gamma_0[\text{this}\mapsto\{d\}@_P\Gamma_0(\text{this})] \vdash \sigma_0 \diamond$ holds.

4   Related Work

The Foundational Perspective Most foundational work is based on functional object-based languages. In [1] method overriding models field update and delegation. In [15] method extensions represent class inheritance, while [7, 12, 26, 16, 27] enhance the above representation by introducing a limited form of method subtyping. These calculi deal with questions of width-subtyping over breadth-subtyping, the use of MyType, method extension and overriding, and were primarily developed for modelling inheritance and delegation.

Object extension in these calculi can be seen as the promotion of an object of class c to an object of a subclass of c. In [16, 26, 12, 19, 7], unrestricted subtyping followed by object expansion might cause messageNotUnderstood errors, and so type soundness is recovered by imposing certain restrictions on the use of subtyping, with the consequence that an object cannot be promoted to a superclass and then to the original subclass.

For databases, [6] suggests multiple most specific classes, thus in a way allowing multiple inheritance, while [19] allows objects to accumulate different roles in a functional setting. They model non-exclusive roles (*e.g.* female and professor), whereas we model objects changing mutually exclusive classes (*e.g.* opened window versus iconified window).

Refinement types in functional languages distinguish cases through subtypes, see [17]. The main questions in [17] are type inference, and establishing that functions are well defined, that is they cover all possible cases. Side-effects are not considered, therefore questions like aliasing that are central to our development do not arise.

The Practical Perspective Predicate classes [10, 14], on an imperative setting, suggest multi-method dispatch depending on predicates on the receiver and arguments. Code is broken down per-function while $\mathcal{F}ickle$ follows the mainstream, whereby code is broken down per-class. In [10] the term "re-classification" denotes changes in attribute values which imply changes in predicates when calculated next. Thus, re-classification in [10, 14] is implicit and lazy, whereas in $\mathcal{F}ickle$ re-classification is explicit and eager. In [10, 14] different methods may dispatch depending on different predicates, *e.g.* insert depends on priority vs. precedence lists, whereas print depends on empty vs. non-empty lists. This is not possible in $\mathcal{F}ickle$, unless perhaps, extended with multiple inheritance.

For single method dispatch, in [30] classes have "modes" representing different states, *e.g.* opened vs. iconified window. Wide classes [29] are the nearest to our approach, and allow an object to be temporarily "widened" or "shrunk". However they differ from $\mathcal{F}ickle$, by dropping the requirement for a strong type system, and requiring run-time tests for the presence of fields – not amazing, since wide classes were primarily developed to exploit significant changes in objects' structure to obtain a better memory usage.

Modula-3 [9] supports limited change of objects' behaviour, by allowing objects' method suites to be determined at object creation time. Self [2] allows dynamic inheritance among prototypes, thus making type inference difficult [3]. In BETA [23] nested patterns model dynamic state changes, but require dynamic type checking.

For concurrent objects [25] gives behavioural types that guarantee that every message has a chance of being received if it requires a method that may be enabled at some point in the future.

$\mathcal{F}ickle$ is the successor of our earlier proposal, $\mathcal{F}ickle$–99 [13], which addressed the same requirement. $\mathcal{F}ickle$ improves $\mathcal{F}ickle$–99 in at least two respects. Firstly, in $\mathcal{F}ickle$–99 we needed to prevent objects from mutating while executing a method, and achieved this either through run-time locks or through an effect system. Secondly, in $\mathcal{F}ickle$–99 we had to distinguish three kinds of methods, two kinds of objects and two kinds of types.

5   Design Alternatives

Our aim was to develop language features supporting re-classification of objects in an imperative setting, allowing aliasing. Thus, we fixed the operational semantics very early. However, the design of a safe type system was by no means as straightforward. The main challenges were:

c1 The type of this inside method bodies containing re-classifications; – *c.f.* Example (4), Section 3.3.
c2 Re-classification of an aliased object may remove members, which the object needs in another context– *c.f.* Example (3), Section 2.

c3 Re-classification of an object while it executes a method which uses members removed by a re-classification further down the call stack – *c.f.* Example (5), Section 3.3.

We have considered, and experimented with several ideas:

For c1 The type of this changes after re-classifications; we express that through the second component of our typing scheme.

For c2 We considered several solutions, and have chosen (e):

(a) Check the existence of members at run-time, as in [29]; but this is type-unsafe.

(b) An object should have all members for all possible state subclasses of its root superclass, as in [14]. Although type safe, this does not allow compact representations as required in [29], and does not express our intention of exclusive cases.

(c) Require all state subclasses of a root class to have exactly the same members, and differ in the method bodies only. However, this requirement is too strong, *e.g.* does not hold for empty and non-empty stacks.

(d) In *Fickle*-99, we avoid the aliasing introduced through line 2. in Example (3). Types are either non-state, non-root classes, or sets of state classes. Subtyping for such sets of state classes is only the identity. Accessing a member of an expression with type a set of state classes is only legal if all state classes define this member.

(e) In *Fickle*, we forbid the use of state classes as types, except for the type of this. Thus state classes may have different members, but all state subclasses of the same root class offer the same interface to all their clients.

For c3 We reconsidered the solutions **c2**(a)-**c2**(e), and chose (e).

(a)-(c) With any of the approaches described in **c2**(a), **c2**(b), or **c2**(c), the problem would not arise; but we have rejected these solutions in **c2**.

(d) In *Fickle*-99 we "lock" an object of a state class when it starts executing a method, and "unlock" when it finishes. Attempting to re-classify a locked object throws an exception; *e.g.* Example (5) could throw such an exception. This is too restrictive, and has the draw-back that it allows run-time errors.

(e) In *Fickle* the type system ensures against the problem; the effects from any called methods are applied to the type of this; therefore, after a call which may modify the receiver, the type of this will be the root superclass, and so, access to state class members will be type incorrect.

6   Conclusions

Fickle is the outcome of several designs and successive improvements. In the process, we also developed an interesting typing scheme, where typing an expression affects the environment in which the following or enclosing expressions are typed.

We are now satisfied that the suggested approach is useful and usable. Even though *Fickle* requires methods to be annotated by their re-classification effects, the burden on the programmer can be alleviated through conventions (*e.g.* absence of annotation indicates the empty effect, overriding methods need not mention their effects since these have to be subsets of the effect of the overridden method), or through type inference.

We have several examples, *e.g.* accounts, linked lists, adventure games, and cases delineating the typing rules [22]. The most immediate limitation of *Fickle* is perhaps its lack of direct support for threads, since effects calculated for invocations spawning children threads may happen *after* the point when the type of this has changed in the parent thread.

We are working on an implementation of *Fickle* through a preprocessor [5, 4]. Type correct *Fickle* programs are mapped into equivalent Java programs, where root classes are represented by wrapper classes, containing a field value, which points to an object of one of its state subclasses. Method calls are forwarded from the wrapper object to its value field, and re-classifications are implemented by overwriting the value field.

In a production compiler one can avoid the wrapper object and the indirection in method dispatch, if one knows the maximal size of state subclasses of any given rootclass[7]. The constraint that the target and source of re-classification have a common root superclass allows the standard, efficient implementation of method call, where we lookup through an offset into the method dispatch table of the receiver. The fact that sources and targets of re-classifications have the same maximal size allows to implement re-classification through simple in-place overwriting of the source object.

A direct implementation would manipulate the object tables, as available in Java or Smalltalk implementations *c.f.* Chapter 30 in [20], and would avoid the restriction on the maximal size of state subclasses.

Further work includes the incorporation of *Fickle* into a full language, the refinement of the effect system *e.g.* through data-flow analysis techniques, the incorporation of myType and multiple inheritance, the distinction of subclassing from subtyping, and the modelling of irreversible re-classifications (*e.g.* pupa to butterfly), the support a limited form of concurrency, and extensions allowing parameters, result types, and fields to be of state classes.

Acknowledgements

Fickle has greatly benefited from constructive criticism on *Fickle*–99 from Walt Hill, Viviana Bono, Luca Cardelli, Andrew Kennedy, Giorgio Ghelli, and the POPL'00 reviewers. Christopher Anderson, Lorenzo Bettini, Ross Jarman, and the FOOL'8 and ECOOP'01 referees gave us useful feedback on *Fickle*.

---

[7] Restrictions on possible subclasses can be found in several systems, *e.g.* in [11].

References

[1] M. Abadi and L. Cardelli. *A Theory of Objects*. Springer, 1996.

[2] O. Agesen, L. Bak, C. Chambers, B.W. Chang, U. Hölzle, J. Maloney, R.B. Smith, and D. Ungar. The SELF programmers's reference manual, version 2.0. Technical report, SUN Microsystems, 1992.

[3] O. Agesen, J. Palsberg, and M.I. Schwartzbach. Type inference of Self: Analysis of objects with dynamic and multiple inheritance. *Software - Practice and Experience*, 25(9):975–995, 1995.

[4] D. Ancona, C. Anderson, F. Damiani, S. Drossopoulou, P. Giannini, and E. Zucca. An Effective Translation of Fickle into Java, April 2001. Technical Report, DISI University of Genova and Imperial College. Available from http://www.di.unito.it/~damiani/dor.html.

[5] C. Anderson. Implementing Fickle, Imperial College, final year thesis - to appear, June 2001.

[6] E. Bertino and G. Guerrini. Objects with Multiple Most Specific Classes. In *ECOOP'95*, volume 952 of *LNCS*, pages 102–126. Springer, 1995.

[7] V. Bono, M. Bugliesi, M. Dezani-Ciancaglini, and L. Liquori. Subtyping Constraints for Incomplete Objects. In *CAAP'97*, volume 1214 of *LNCS*, pages 465–477. Springer, 1997.

[8] P. Canning, W. Cook, W. Hill, and W. Olthoff. Interfaces for Strongly Typed Object Oriented Languages. In *OOPSLA'89*, pages 457–467. ACM press, 1989.

[9] L. Cardelli, J. Donahue, L. Glassman, M. Jordan, B. Kalsow, and G. Nelson. Modula-3 report (revised). Technical report, DEC System Research Center, 1989.

[10] C. Chambers. Predicate Classes. In *ECOOP'93*, volume 707 of *LNCS*, pages 268–296. Springer, 1993.

[11] C. Chambers and G. Leavens. Type Checking Modules for Multimethods. *ACM Transactions on Programming Languages and Systems*, 17(6):805–843, 1995.

[12] P. Di Gianantonio, F. Honsell, and L. Liquori. A Lambda Calculus of Objects with Self-inflicted Extension. In *OOPSLA'98*, pages 166–178. ACM press, 1998.

[13] S. Drossopoulou, M. Dezani-Ciancaglini, F. Damiani, and P. Giannini. Objects Dynamically Changing Class. Technical report, Imperial College, August 1999. Available from http://www.di.unito.it/~dezani/odcc.html.

[14] M.D. Ernst, C. Kaplan, and C. Chambers. Predicate Dispatching: A Unified Theory of Dispatch. In *ECOOP'98*, volume 1445 of *LNCS*, pages 186–211. Springer, 1998.

[15] K. Fisher, F. Honsell, and J.C. Mitchell. A Lambda Calculus of Objects and Method Specialization. In *Nordic Journal of Computing 1(1)*, pages 3–37, 1994.

[16] K. Fisher and J.C. Mitchell. A Delegation-based Object Calculus with Subtyping. In *FCT'95*, volume 965 of *LNCS*, pages 42–61. Springer, 1995.

[17] T. Freeman and F. Pfenning. Refinement types for ML. In *SIGPLAN '91*, pages 268–277. ACM Press, 1991.

[18] E. Gamma, R. Helm, R. Johnson, and J. Vlissidis. *Design Pattersn*. Addison-Wesley, 1994.

[19] G. Ghelli and D. Palmerini. Foundations of Extensible Objets with Roles. In *FOOL'06*, 1999. Available from
http://www.cs.williams.edu/~kim/FOOL/FOOL6.html.

[20] A. Goldberg and D. Robson. *Smalltlak-80: The Language and its Implementation*. Addison-Wesley, 1985.

[21] W.L. Hürsch. Should Superclasses be Abstract? In *ECOOP'94*, volume 821 of *LNCS*, pages 12–31. Springer, 1994.

[22] R. Jarman and S. Drossopoulou. Examples in Fickle. Available from http://www.di.unito.it/~damiani/papers/dor.html.

[23] B.B. Kristensen, O.L. Madsen, B. Moller-Pederson, and K. Nygaard. The BETA programming language. In *Research Directions in Object-Oriented Programming*, pages 7–48. MIT Press, 1987.

[24] M. Lucassen and D.K. Gifford. Polymorphic effect systems. In *POPL'88*, pages 47–57. ACM press, 1988.

[25] A. Ravara and V.T. Vasconcelos. Typing non-uniform concurrent objects. In *CONCUR'00*, volume 1877 of *LNCS*, pages 474–488. Springer, 2000.

[26] D. Rémy. From Classes to Objects via Subtyping. In *ESOP'98*, volume 1381 of *LNCS*, pages 200–220. Springer, 1995.

[27] J.C. Riecke and C.A. Stone. Privacy via Subsumption. In *FOOL'98*, 1998. Available from http://www.cs.williams.edu/~kim/FOOL/FOOL5.html.

[28] T. Scheer and S. Pringle. Ten Practical Limitations of Object Orientation, November 1998. OOPSLA Poster Session, Available from http://www.acm.org/sigplan/oopsla/oopsla98/fp/posters/10.htm.

[29] M. Serrano. Wide Classes. In *ECOOP'99*, volume 1628 of *LNCS*, pages 391–415. Springer, 1999.

[30] A. Tailvasaari. Object Oriented Programming with Modes. *Journal of Object Oriented Programming*, pages 27–32, 1992.

[31] J.-P. Talpin and P. Jouvelot. Polymorphic Type, Region and Effect Inference. *Journal of Functional Programming*, 2(3):245–271, 1992.

Appendix

More on Syntax A $\mathcal{F}ickle$ program is a sequence of class declarations, according to Figure 3. Non terminals appear as *nonTerm*, keywords appear as **keyword**, literals appear as `literal` and identifiers appear as identifier. We omit separators like **;** or **,** where they are obvious. We use standard extended BNF, where a [-] pair means optional, and A^* means zero or more repetitions of A. For simplicity, all methods have one parameter, called x.

More on Operational Semantics The operational semantics rewrites pairs of expressions and stores into pairs of values, exception or errors, and stores - in the context of a given program.

The store maps the parameter x to a value, `this` to an address, and addresses to objects. Values are the source language values, *sVal, i.e.* `true`, `false`, and `null`, or addresses. Addresses may point to objects, but *not* to other addresses, primitive values, or `null`. Thus, in $\mathcal{F}ickle$, as in Java, pointers are implicit, and there are no pointers to pointers. The signature of the rewriting relation $\rightsquigarrow$ is:

$$
\begin{array}{rcl}
\rightsquigarrow & : & progr \longrightarrow expr \times store \longrightarrow (val \cup dev) \times store \\
store & = & (\{\texttt{this}\} \longrightarrow addr) \cup (\{\texttt{x}\} \longrightarrow val) \cup (addr \longrightarrow object) \\
val & = & sVal \cup addr \\
dev & = & \{\texttt{nullPntrExc}, \texttt{stuckErr}\} \\
object & = & \{ [[f_1 : v_1, ..., f_r : v_r]]^c \mid f_1, ..., f_r \text{ are fields identifiers}, \\
& & \qquad v_1, ..., v_r \in val, \text{ and } c \text{ is a class name} \}
\end{array}
$$

$progr$	$::=$	$class^*$
$class$	$::=$	[**root** | **state**] **class** c **extends** c { $field^*$ $meth^*$ }
$field$	$::=$	$type\ f$
$meth$	$::=$	$type\ m\ (type\ \times\ )\ eff$ { e }
$type$	$::=$	**bool** | c
eff	$::=$	{ c^* }
e	$::=$	**if** e **then** e **else** e | $var := e$ | $e\ ;\ e$ | $sVal$ |
		var | $e.m(\ e\ )$ | **new** c | **this** | **this**$\Downarrow c$.
var	$::=$	x | $e.f$
$sVal$	$::=$	**true** | **false** | **null**

$$\text{with the identifier conventions}$$

$c ::= \mathsf{c} \mid \mathsf{c}' \mid \mathsf{c_i} \mid \mathsf{d} \mid \ ...$	for class names
$f ::= \mathsf{f} \mid \mathsf{f}' \mid \mathsf{f_i} \mid \ ...$	for field names
$m ::= \mathsf{m} \mid \mathsf{m}' \mid \mathsf{m_i} \mid \ ...$	for method names

Fig. 3. Syntax of $\mathcal{F}ickle$

We define some operations on objects and stores.

Definition 2 *For object* $\mathsf{o} = [[\mathsf{f}_1 : \mathsf{v}_1...\mathsf{f}_l : \mathsf{v}_l...\mathsf{f}_r : \mathsf{v}_r]]^{\,c}$, *store* σ, *value* v, *address* ι, *identifier or address* z, *field identifier* f, *we define:*

- field access $\mathsf{o}(\mathsf{f})$ *as* $\quad \mathsf{o}(\mathsf{f}) = \begin{cases} \mathsf{v}_l & \textit{if } \mathsf{f} = \mathsf{f}_l \textit{ for some } l \in 1,...,r, \\ \mathcal{U}df & \textit{otherwise} \end{cases}$
- object update $\mathsf{o}[\mathsf{f}\mapsto\mathsf{v}]$, *as* $\quad \mathsf{o}[\mathsf{f}\mapsto\mathsf{v}] = [[\mathsf{f}_1 : \mathsf{v}_1...\mathsf{f}_l : \mathsf{v}...\mathsf{f}_r : \mathsf{v}_r]]^{\,c}$ *if* $\mathsf{f}_l = \mathsf{f}$ *for some* $l \in 1,...,r$,
- store update $\sigma[\mathsf{z}\mapsto\mathsf{v}]$, *as* $\quad \sigma[\mathsf{z}\mapsto\mathsf{v}](\mathsf{z}) = \mathsf{v}, \quad \sigma[\mathsf{z}\mapsto\mathsf{v}](\mathsf{z}') = \sigma(\mathsf{z}')$ *if* $\mathsf{z}' \neq \mathsf{z}$.

Figure 4 lists all the rewrite rules of $\mathcal{F}ickle$ except those discussed in Section 3.2 and those for propagation of exceptions and errors.

More on Typing A first use of the information about the class of the receiver appears in the rule for typing the composition $e\ ;\ e'$ of two expressions. The second expression, e', is typed in the updated environment $\Gamma[\mathsf{this}\mapsto c]$ where c is the class of **this** after the evaluation of the first expression, e. So, the effect of the composition is the union of the effects of the components.

With $c \sqcup_P c'$ we denote the least upper bound of c, c' in P with respect to $\sqsubseteq$. This is used in the rule for typing **if** e **then** e_1 **else** e_2, to determine a conservative approximation of the type of **this** after the evaluations of the conditional. The two branches may cause two different re-classifications for **this**, *i.e.* c_1 and c_2. So, after the evaluation we can only assert that **this** belongs to the least upper bound of c_1 and c_2. The other rules are either explained in Section 3.3 or are standard.

$$v, \sigma \rightsquigarrow v, \sigma$$

$$\frac{e_1, \sigma \rightsquigarrow v', \sigma''\quad e_2, \sigma'' \rightsquigarrow v, \sigma'}{e_1; e_2, \sigma \rightsquigarrow v, \sigma'}$$

$$\frac{e, \sigma \rightsquigarrow true, \sigma''\quad e_1, \sigma'' \rightsquigarrow v, \sigma'}{\text{if } e \text{ then } e_1 \text{ else } e_2, \sigma \rightsquigarrow v, \sigma'}$$

$$\frac{e, \sigma \rightsquigarrow false, \sigma''\quad e_2, \sigma'' \rightsquigarrow v, \sigma'}{\text{if } e \text{ then } e_1 \text{ else } e_2, \sigma \rightsquigarrow v, \sigma'}$$

$$\frac{}{x, \sigma \rightsquigarrow \sigma(x), \sigma}$$
$$\text{this}, \sigma \rightsquigarrow \sigma(\text{this}), \sigma$$

$$\frac{e, \sigma \rightsquigarrow \iota, \sigma'}{e.f, \sigma \rightsquigarrow \sigma'(\iota)(f), \sigma'}$$

$$\frac{e, \sigma \rightsquigarrow v, \sigma'}{x := e, \sigma \rightsquigarrow v, \sigma'[x \mapsto v]}$$

$$\frac{\begin{array}{c} e, \sigma \rightsquigarrow \iota, \sigma'' \\ e', \sigma'' \rightsquigarrow v, \sigma''' \\ \sigma'''(\iota)(f) \neq \mathcal{U}df \\ \sigma' = \sigma'''[\iota \mapsto \sigma'''(\iota)[f \mapsto v]] \end{array}}{e.f := e', \sigma \rightsquigarrow v, \sigma'}$$

$$\frac{e, \sigma \rightsquigarrow null, \sigma'}{e.f := e', \sigma \rightsquigarrow \mathbf{nullPntrExc}, \sigma'}$$
$$e.f, \sigma \rightsquigarrow \mathbf{nullPntrExc}, \sigma'$$
$$e.m(e_1), \sigma \rightsquigarrow \mathbf{nullPntrExc}, \sigma'$$

$$\frac{\begin{array}{c} \mathcal{F}s(P, c) = \{f_1, ..., f_r\} \\ \forall l \in 1, ..., r: \quad v_l \text{ initial for } \mathcal{F}(P, c, f_l) \\ \iota \text{ is new in } \sigma \end{array}}{\mathbf{new}\ c, \sigma \rightsquigarrow \iota, \sigma[\iota \mapsto [\![f_1 : v_1, ..., f_r : v_r]\!]^c]}$$

$$\frac{\begin{array}{c} e, \sigma \rightsquigarrow v, \sigma' \\ \sigma'(v)(f) = \mathcal{U}df \end{array}}{e.f, \sigma \rightsquigarrow \mathbf{stuckErr}, \sigma'}$$
$$e.f := e', \sigma \rightsquigarrow \mathbf{stuckErr}, \sigma'$$

$$\frac{\begin{array}{c} e, \sigma \rightsquigarrow v, \sigma' \\ v \neq true \text{ and } v \neq false \end{array}}{\text{if } e \text{ then } e_1 \text{ else } e_2, \sigma \rightsquigarrow \mathbf{stuckErr}, \sigma'}$$

$$\frac{\begin{array}{c} e_0, \sigma \rightsquigarrow v, \sigma_0 \\ v \neq null \\ \sigma_0(v) = \mathcal{U}df \text{ or } v \notin addr \end{array}}{e_0.m(e_1), \sigma \rightsquigarrow \mathbf{stuckErr}, \sigma_0}$$

$$\frac{\begin{array}{c} e_0, \sigma \rightsquigarrow \iota, \sigma_0 \\ e_1, \sigma_0 \rightsquigarrow v_1, \sigma_1 \\ \sigma_1(\iota) = [\![...]\!]^c \\ \mathcal{M}(P, c, m) = \mathcal{U}df \end{array}}{e_0.m(e_1), \sigma \rightsquigarrow \mathbf{stuckErr}, \sigma_1}$$

Fig. 4. Execution of expressions

$$\frac{P \vdash c \diamond_s \qquad \mathcal{R}(P,c) = \mathcal{R}(P,\Gamma(\mathsf{this}))}{P,\Gamma \vdash \mathsf{this}{\Downarrow}c \;:\; c \parallel c \parallel \{\,\mathcal{R}(P,c)\,\}}$$

$$\frac{\begin{array}{l} P,\Gamma \vdash e_0 \;:\; c \parallel c_0 \parallel \phi_0 \\ P,\Gamma[\mathsf{this}{\mapsto}c_0] \vdash e_1 \;:\; t_1' \parallel c_1 \parallel \phi_1 \\ \mathcal{M}(P, \phi_1@\mathsf{pc}, m) = t\; m(t_1\, x)\, \phi\, \{\,...\,\} \\ P \vdash t_1' \leq t_1 \end{array}}{P,\Gamma \vdash e_0.m(e_1) \;:\; t \parallel \phi@\mathsf{pc}_1 \parallel \phi \cup \phi_0 \cup \phi_1}$$

$$\frac{P \vdash \Gamma \diamond}{\begin{array}{l} P,\Gamma \vdash \mathsf{true} \;:\; \mathsf{bool} \parallel \Gamma(\mathsf{this}) \parallel \{\ \} \\ P,\Gamma \vdash \mathsf{false} \;:\; \mathsf{bool} \parallel \Gamma(\mathsf{this}) \parallel \{\ \} \\ P,\Gamma \vdash x \;:\; \Gamma(x) \parallel \Gamma(\mathsf{this}) \parallel \{\ \} \\ P,\Gamma \vdash \mathsf{this} \;:\; \Gamma(\mathsf{this}) \parallel \Gamma(\mathsf{this}) \parallel \{\ \} \end{array}}$$

$$\frac{P \vdash \Gamma \diamond \qquad P \vdash c \diamond_c}{\begin{array}{l} P,\Gamma \vdash \mathsf{null} \;:\; c \parallel \Gamma(\mathsf{this}) \parallel \{\ \} \\ P,\Gamma \vdash \mathsf{new}\ c \;:\; c \parallel \Gamma(\mathsf{this}) \parallel \{\ \} \end{array}}$$

$$\frac{P,\Gamma \vdash e \;:\; c \parallel c' \parallel \phi \qquad \mathcal{F}(P,c,f) = t}{P,\Gamma \vdash e.f \;:\; t \parallel c' \parallel \phi}$$

$$\frac{P,\Gamma \vdash e \;:\; t \parallel c \parallel \phi \qquad P,\Gamma[\mathsf{this}{\mapsto}c] \vdash e' \;:\; t' \parallel c' \parallel \phi'}{P,\Gamma \vdash e;\ e' \;:\; t' \parallel c' \parallel \phi \cup \phi'}$$

$$\frac{\begin{array}{l} P,\Gamma \vdash x \;:\; t \parallel c \parallel \{\ \} \\ P,\Gamma[\mathsf{this}{\mapsto}c] \vdash e \;:\; t' \parallel c' \parallel \phi' \\ P \vdash t' \leq t \end{array}}{P,\Gamma \vdash x{:=}e \;:\; t' \parallel c' \parallel \phi'}$$

$$\frac{\begin{array}{l} P,\Gamma \vdash e \;:\; c' \parallel c'' \parallel \phi \\ P,\Gamma[\mathsf{this}{\mapsto}c''] \vdash e' \;:\; t \parallel c \parallel \phi' \\ \mathcal{F}(P, \phi'@\mathsf{pc}', f) = t' \\ P \vdash t \leq t' \end{array}}{P,\Gamma \vdash e.f{:=}e' \;:\; t \parallel c \parallel \phi \cup \phi'}$$

$$\frac{\begin{array}{l} P,\Gamma \vdash e \;:\; \mathsf{bool} \parallel c \parallel \phi \\ P,\Gamma[\mathsf{this}{\mapsto}c] \vdash e_1 \;:\; t_1 \parallel c_1 \parallel \phi_1 \\ P,\Gamma[\mathsf{this}{\mapsto}c] \vdash e_2 \;:\; t_2 \parallel c_2 \parallel \phi_2 \\ P \vdash t_i \leq t \text{ for } i \in 1,2 \end{array}}{P,\Gamma \vdash \mathsf{if}\ e\ \mathsf{then}\ e_1\ \mathsf{else}\ e_2 \;:\; t \parallel c_1 \sqcup \mathsf{pc}_2 \parallel \phi \cup \phi_1 \cup \phi_2}$$

$$\frac{\begin{array}{l} \vdash P \diamond_a \\ \mathcal{C}(P,c) = [\mathsf{root}\ |\ \mathsf{state}\ ]\mathsf{class}\ c\ \mathsf{extends}\ c'\ \{...\} \\ \forall f : \mathcal{FD}(P,c,f) = t_0 \implies \quad P \vdash t_0 \diamond_{vt} \quad \text{and} \quad \mathcal{F}(P,c',f) = \mathcal{U}df \\ \forall m : \mathcal{MD}(P,c,m) = t\; m(t_1\, x)\, \phi\, \{\ e\ \} \implies \\ \quad P \vdash t \diamond_{vt} \qquad\qquad P \vdash t_1 \diamond_{vt} \\ \quad P \vdash \phi \diamond \qquad\qquad P,\{t_1\, x, c\ \mathsf{this}\} \vdash e \;:\; t' \parallel c'' \parallel \phi' \\ \quad P \vdash t' \leq t \qquad\qquad \phi' \subseteq \phi \\ \quad \mathcal{M}(P,c',m) = \mathcal{U}df \quad \text{or} \quad (\mathcal{M}(P,c',m) = t\; m(t_1\, x)\, \phi''\, \{\,...\,\} \quad \text{and} \quad \phi \subseteq \phi'') \end{array}}{P \vdash c \diamond}$$

$$\frac{\forall c : \mathcal{C}(P,c) \neq \mathcal{U}df \implies P \vdash c \diamond}{\vdash P \diamond}$$

Fig. 5. Typing rules for expressions and well-formed classes and programs

Scripting .NET Using Mondrian

Erik Meijer[1], Nigel Perry[2], and Arjan van Yzendoorn[3]

[1] Microsoft
erik@microsoft.com
[2] Massey University
N.Perry@massey.ac.nz
[3] Utrecht University
affie@cs.uu.nl

Abstract. We introduce the design of Mondrian, a functional script-ing language for glueing together components on the .NET platform. Mondrian is monadic statement centric with pure expressions and non-strict evaluation and explores the melding of the OO and the purely lazy functional paradigms.

1 Introduction

This paper introduces Mondrian, a functional scripting language designed espe-cially for the new Microsoft .NET platform. Mondrian is aimed at two different audiences. One is existing functional programmers who would like to be able to inter-work more closely with other languages that target the .NET Common Language Runtime (CLR), the other is existing OO programmers who would like to explore being able to write and access objects written in functional languages.

Mondrian inherits "just-in-time" (lazy) evaluation, higher order functions and monadic commands from Haskell, and classes, threads, and exceptions from the CLR (although influenced by Massey Hope+C [15] and Haskell [16]). The syntax of Mondrian is a melding of C$^\sharp$ [2] and Haskell.

The formal semantics and type rules of Mondrian are yet to be defined precisely, and indeed as an experimental language are in a state of flux. Ultimately, Mon-drian's type system will depend on the availability of generics in the CLR [9]. Therefore this paper only presents a semi-formal description of the language.

The current implementation of Mondrian is highly experimental, its main goal is to explore interoperability in the .NET space, often at the expense of raw execution speed. We do however use the underlying CLR features where possible, and "encode" only features such currying and lazy evaluation that the CLR does not directly support.

J. Lindskov Knudsen (Ed.): ECOOP 2001, LNCS 2072, pp. 150–164, 2001.

2   Mondrian

The semantics of Mondrian are based of those of lazy functional programming with monadic I/O, with modifications and additions to suit an OO environment and to inter-work well with other languages that target the CLR. We describe Mondrian by highlighting the differences between it and a traditional functional language.

2.1   History and Context

We started to explore the possibility of a pure functional scripting language for glueing together software components [5] in the original Mondrian paper [13]. Along the way however, we had to encountered several other interesting research problems such as foreign function interfaces [12, 10, 14, 4, 3, 8] and type system issues [18, 11] that needed to be solved before we could continue the actual implementation on Mondrian. In the mean time, Microsoft announced its new .NET platform, which made it much easier to build our experimental compiler as we could leverage on the high-level services of the Common Language Runtime (CLR) such as garbage collection, threading, language interoperability, etc.

The name *Mondrian* honors the Dutch painter Piet Mondrian (1872-1944) and reflects the purity, minimalism, orthogonality and simplicity of the language design.

The Mondrian compiler is available for download at the Mondrian web site `http://www.mondrian-script.org`. The compiler also accepts GHC's "Core" intermediate language as input, hence it can serve as a portable back end for Haskell as well.

2.2   Functions and Expressions

As a functional language, functions and pure expressions are central to the semantics of Mondrian, in contrast to object oriented languages where objects and methods are fundamental. Within Mondrian functions and expressions have a pure and lazy semantics. When viewed from another language executing on the .NET platform a Mondrian function appears as an object with a specific method `Apply` as its entry point, which conforms to the object-oriented view of the world (section 6).

Expression evaluation in Mondrian is lazy. Functions are defined using lambda notation and to simplify the language no pattern matching on arguments is provided. Function application is curried. Unusually the typical "\" used to denote the start of a lambda expression is also omitted. Top level names are bound by simple assignment syntax. For example, the addition function is defined by:

```
add = a -> b -> a + b;
```

Apart from the built-in operators, overloading (ad-hoc polymorphism) is not supported.

2.3 Types

Mondrian provides the same primitive types as the .NET platform; such as integers, floats and characters. Strings are also directly supported.

Parametric polymorphism is provided in the usual functional language manner. For example a function to evaluate the length of a list (see below) is typed as:

```
length : forall a. List<a> -> Integer
```

The CLR (and C♯) do not yet provide generics or parametric polymorphism and function types [9]. Therefore when viewed from C♯ a polymorphic Mondrian function appears as a function over `Object` (ie all type variables are erased and replaced by `Object`), hence the signature of the function `length` appears in C♯ as:

```
Integer length(List as);
```

This mapping clearly involves some static type information loss; while there can be many distinct type variables in Mondrian there is only one `Object` in .NET. Further work is required in this area to determine the most appropriate mapping and division between static and dynamic type checking.

Functional languages typically provide type products, disjoint unions and parametric polymorphism. Object-oriented languages usually are based around type products and subtype polymorphism. To bridge this gap Mondrian's type system provides products, subtypes, and parametric polymorphism.

Uses of disjoint unions in traditional functional languages are replaced by the use of classes and subclasses in Mondrian. For example, the standard list type:

```
data List a = Nil | Cons a (List a)
```

is defined in Mondrian by defining an abstract base class `List` and two subclasses `Nil` and `Cons`:

```
abstract class List<a> {};
class Nil<a> extends List<a> {};
class Cons<a> extends List<a> {
  head : a;
  tail : List<a>;
};
```

To construct an instance of a `List` you call either `new Nil {}` to obtain an empty list, or `new Cons{ head = a; tail = as; }` to cons an element `a` on an existing list `as`. For convenience both the use of `new` and the empty field list `{}` are optional.

2.4   Multi-choice Selection and Pattern Matching

For multi-choice selection and pattern matching a switch expression is provided. The syntax is reminiscent of C$^\sharp$ while the semantics comes from Haskell.

For primitive types, such as integers and characters, selection is based on the value of the predicate. For class types the selection is based on the subtype of the predicate and equates to the use is in C$^\sharp$.

The following example, which implements the standard list map function, illustrates the switch expression on subtypes:

```
map : forall a,b . (a -> b) -> List<a> -> List<b>;
map = f -> as -> switch (as) {
  case Nil :
    Nil;
  case Cons { a = head; as = tail; } :
    Cons { head = f(a); tail = map(f)(as); };
};
```

2.5   Namespaces

Mondrian currently inherits the concept namespaces (and the syntax) of C$^\sharp$, however, the notion of namespace does not really exist in the CLR, which instead is based on the notion of modules and assemblies. We are currently considering changing Mondrian to reflect this more directly.

2.6   Commands

Mondrian inherits monadic I/O from Haskell [21], the syntax follows Haskell except the do keyword is omitted in keeping with the minimal approach of Mondrian.

For example, a simple "hello world" program in Mondrian may be written as:

```
main : IO<()>;
main = {
  Console.WriteLine("Please enter you name: ");
  name <- Console.ReadLine();
  Console.WriteLine("Hello " + name);
}
```

Note: Strings in Mondrian have type String rather than the list of characters as in Haskell. The operator "+" is also overloaded to represent string concatenation as in C$^\sharp$.

Commands are first class citizens in Mondrian, that means you can pass them as arguments to and return them from functions, put them in list, etc. In combination with lazy evaluation, this allows you to define your own control structures.

For instance, the function forEver executes a command forever. You can easily define forEver using the standard functions repeat : a -> List<a> that takes an element a and generates an infinite list of copies of a, and the function sequence_ : List<IO<a>> -> IO<()> that takes a list of commands and runs them in sequence:

```
forEver : IO<a> -> IO<()>;
forEver = ma -> sequence_ (repeat (ma));

sequence_ : List<IO<a>> -> IO<()>;
sequence_ = mas -> switch (mas) {
  case Nil:
    { return Nil; };
  case Cons{ ma = head; mas = tail; }:
    { ma; sequence_ mas; };
}

repeat : a -> List<a>;
repeat = a -> new Cons{ head = a; tail= repeat a; };
```

3   Exceptions

The execution of I/O statements within the monadic system of Mondrian has a well defined temporal order, in common with similar mechanisms in Hope+C [15] and Haskell [19]. This execution model also has direct parallels with that of the exception mechanism provided by the CLR.

3.1   Handling Exceptions

In the CLR, all exceptions are treated uniformly by replacing the current execution with the execution of an exception handler. We adopt this same model within the Mondrian monadic I/O system, and borrow most of the syntax from C# by adding a monadic "try/catch/finally" construct to Mondrian's commands:

```
try{
  ...
} catch(e : Exception) {
  ...
} finally {
  ...
}
```

For programmatically generated exceptions we also adopt the CLR model adding a keyword throw of type:

```
throw : forall a. Exception -> a
```

By adopting the same exception model as .NET we also gain inter-language exceptions. If .NET code invoked from Mondrian throws an exception then it can be caught by Mondrian code, and vice-versa.

3.2   Example

The function `readLinesFromURL` attempts to open a URL and returns the response as a list of Strings using the helper function `readLines : Stream -> IO<List<String>>`. Any failure to do this is caught in a try-catch block, which then returns an empty list of strings.

```
readLinesFromURL :: String -> IO<List<String>>;
readLinesFromURL = host -> {
  try {
    url <- WebRequest.Create(host);
    resp <- HttpWebRequest.GetResponse() url;
    str <- HttpWebRequest.GetResponseStream() resp;
    readLines str;
  } catch (e : Exception) {
    result Nil;
  };
};
```

4   Concurrency

Mondrian supports concurrent programming using threads. So it can inter-work closely with other .NET languages it builds directly on the threads and synchronization primitives of these environments. In particular:

- A Mondrian thread is a (subclass of a) .NET thread. This not only provides an obvious implementation solution but also trivially supports a mix of Mondrian and .NET threads inter-working with each other.
- Mondrian monadic commands can be enclosed within a monitor (synchronized block), and have access to the same synchronization primitives (wait, notify/pulse).
- Mondrian has access to the same IPC mechanisms as other .NET languages. This includes monitors as above and also standard classes for pipes, object streams, etc. Using these mechanisms IPC works seamlessly between Mondrian threads or between a Mondrian thread and one written in another .NET language.

The first two points are supported by additions to Mondrian, the last is already provided through the Mondrian to foreign language calling interface.

4.1 Threads in Mondrian

Mondrian provides its own `MondrianThread` class which parallels the one provided by the CLR. To match the function orientation of Mondrian the `Thread` class provides a number of functions whose names and purpose follow those of the CLR, but which take a `MondrianThread` object as argument:

```
CreateThread : forall a. IO<a> -> IO<MondrianThread<a>>
```

This creates a thread which executes the given Mondrian command and returns a Mondrian thread object. The returned object is a subtype of the .NET `Thread` and contains all the standard methods.

As in .NET once created a thread must be started using the function:

```
Start : Thread<a> -> IO<a>
```

Note this function takes a `Thread` and not a `MondrianThread`, so it can start either a Mondrian or foreign language thread. Standard methods on threads such as `join` and `suspend` are similarly provided.

The following simple example creates two threads that write an infinite stream of "a" respectively "b"'s on the screen, and then runs them in parallel:

```
main = {
  as <- CreateThread { forEver(Console.Write("a")); };
  bs <- CreateThread { forEver(Console.Write("b")); };
  Start(as); Start(bs);
}
```

4.2 Inter-thread Synchronization and Communication

Mondrian provides a direct equivalent to C#'s synchronized blocks:

```
synchronized (e){ ...statements... }
```

with type:

```
forall a, b. Lock -> IO<b> -> IO<b>
```

and the associated functions:

```
getLock : IO<Lock>
wait : Lock -> IO<()>
notify : Lock -> IO<()>
notifyAll : Lock -> IO<()>
```

To preserve Mondrian's functional semantics, we cannot lock on an arbitrary object, but have to obtain a lock explicitly via the monadic call `getLock`. The execution of a synchronized statement first evaluates the expression e to WHNF to obtain the object to lock and the statements are executed. On completion the lock on the object is released. The semantics of the functions `wait`, `notify` and `notifyAll` directly mirror their .NET counterparts.

4.3   Other IPC Methods

Mondrian also provides a library of constructs ranging from the low-level semaphore through typed channels constructed over .NET pipes so that distributed systems can easily be constructed. Even Haskell's MVars [7] are provided. We stress though that all these are simple constructions provided as a library and involve no extensions to the Mondrian language or its primitive operations.

5   Implementation

Implementing a functional language such as Mondrian on the .NET platform requires a number of issues to be tackled, the main ones being:

- How are values and parametric polymorphism represented?
- How are functions are represented?
- How is partial function application (currying) handled?
- How are "just in time" computations (thunks) represented?

All these issues are well understood and methods have been developed for efficient implementation on standard machine architectures. However the CLR differs from traditional machines in a number of ways, including:

- It is a typed machine. The type system for any language implemented on .NET has to map to the .NET type system.
- It is object-oriented, the key building blocks are objects with methods. Mondrian is function-oriented, it's key building blocks are functions. Currently, the CLR does not yet natively support closures.

We choose to implement Mondrian by using features of the .NET platform wherever possible and resorting to well-known techniques for implementing functional languages, the Spineless Tagless G-Machine (STG)[6] or the so-called *PUSH/ENTER* model, in case there is no direct support for a semantic feature in the CLR.

5.1   The Representation of Values and Functions

All values in Mondrian are first class and exist as long as required (referenced). The standard method of implementing such values in any language is to use a garbage collected heap. The object system of .NET is heap based and automatically managed by the system. The obvious mapping is therefore taken, a Mondrian value is represented as a .NET object.

Mondrian, in common with other functional languages, is built around functions. Functions can be defined statically in the program; functions are first class values and can be passed as arguments, returned as results, and stored in data structures; and functions can be created at runtime based on other dynamic values.

In .NET an object possess all the properties of a function in Mondrian. We therefore map a Mondrian function to a .NET object that implement the `Code` interface that contains a method `ENTER` that is used to evaluate the function by the Mondrian runtime:

```
interface Code {
  public Object ENTER();
}
```

For example, given the Mondrian function definition:

```
Foo = x -> ...
```

is represented by the following .NET class[1] Foo that implements the `Code` interface:

```
class Foo : Code {
  public Object ENTER() {
    ... code for body of Foo ...
  }
}
```

To handle nested functions, we simply create an object with private fields to store any values that are needed to construct the function (a *closure*), and compile code for the method which performs the computation using these values. A closure also implements the `Code` interface and can be used just like a compile-time defined function.

The design space of representing function closures in an object oriented framework is a surprisingly large, and we describe only a tiny slice of that here, in particular we will not discuss the duel *EVAL/APPLY* method that has been investigated by other functional languages that target the CLR such as ML.NET [1]. We also are looking in representing closures using delegates.

---

[1] We show our target code in C$^\sharp$ for readability

5.2   Function Arguments and Partial Applications

A powerful feature of Mondrian, in common with many functional languages, is the ability to "partially apply" (or curry) a function, that is call a function with fewer arguments than it is defined to accept. If fewer arguments are supplied the result is a partially applied function, which is just a dynamically generated function with some argument values already wired in. These partial applications can therefore be represented just like any other function.

However a method is needed to actually pass the arguments to a function in the first place. As .NET is strongly typed simply missing out some of the arguments and then calling the function will not work. In other words, the CLR does not directly support curried functions, and hence we have to implement this semantic feature ourselves. One possible solution is to create a separate stack object to pass function arguments. A function call then becomes: place arguments on stack using Mondrian.PUSH, call the ENTER method of the function's object passing no arguments (an obvious optimization is to have several overloaded ENTER methods that serve as fast entry points when a known function is called with a known number of arguments).

For example, adding more detail to the Foo function given above its definition becomes:

```
class Foo : Code {
  public Object ENTER() {
    Object arg = Mondrian.POP();
    ... rest of body of Foo ...
  }
}
```

A call to this function will be compiled to C$^\sharp$ code which is equivalent to:

```
Foo f = new Foo();
Mondrian.PUSH(<argument>);
result = f.ENTER();
```

5.3   "Just in Time" Computations

Mondrian is a lazy language and does not actually perform a computation until its result is needed, it does computation "just in time". This means any value may in fact be either a real value or a computation which when performed will produce the real value (a so called *thunk*). The essence of lazy evaluation is to update thunks with their values after they have been evaluated for the first time. Like currying, lazy evaluation is not a semantic feature that is directly supported by the CLR, so we have to implement it explicitly.

Again, the design space for implementation thunks is surprisingly big. We have experimented with various implementations, and have not yet decided which one is best. The one sketched below using exceptions in an interesting way.

The standard STG implementation method solves this problem by wrapping JIT computations using a helper function which pushes a special value on a "mark stack" which encodes the current stack depth and a reference to the thunk object being evaluated. Now on every entry to a function a check is made on the number of arguments available and the value on top of the mark stack. When either the argument stack is empty (computation complete), or there are insufficient arguments (JIT computation has produced a partial application), the value on the mark stack can be removed, the thunk updated to hold its value, and then the process repeated on the new top of the mark stack.

All this may sound a bit complicated and indeed it is! However using the facilities of .NET we developed a simple solution for lazy evaluation. Rather than wrap a JIT computation in a small function which pushes a value onto a mark stack, we use one which does a function call and starts up a new *trampoline*, thereby effectively using the runtime stack instead of maintaining an explicit marker stack. A trampoline is a small iterative loop, that makes repeated calls to a function until the value returned indicates the computation has completed.

As explained the mark stack method iterates down the mark stack updating as many thunks as needed and handles the case of partial applications. If it did not then the trampoline would have to distinguish between three possible return types; a simple value, a continuing computation, and a partial computation. This is where we can now use the features of .NET to simplify the implementation. We wrap the trampoline in an exception (try/catch) block and then on function entry throw an exception, carrying a partial application value, if there are insufficient arguments. The trampoline/exception block catches this and updates the JIT object. The exception is then re-thrown, which has the same effect as the iterative compare/update/pop cycle of the mark stack method.

The resultant code is a lot simpler than the mark stack method, and does not require a special stack and the overhead of maintaining it.

A sketch of this code in C$^\sharp$ is as follows, if a function does not find enough arguments on the argument stack, it throws and *partial application exception*:

```
class Foo : Code {
  public Object ENTER()
    { if(!Mondrian.AVAILABLE(1)) throw PAP_Exception(this);
      Object a = Mondrian.POP();
      <body of Foo>
    }
}
```

And the JIT trampoline follows the following schema:

```
try {
  // Trampoline loop
        while(f is Code) { f = f.ENTER(); }
} catch(PAP_exception e) {  /
```

```
    ... update thunk with ...
    ... partial application f ...
    throw e;
}
```

Thunks and Exceptions It is possible for the execution of I/O to cause the evaluation of a thunk. If an exception occurs during the evaluation of the thunk then the thunk must be left in a suitable state. This issue can be a thorny one to deal with [17], however due to Mondrian being based on the CLR model which does not support asynchronous exceptions the problem is easily handled. Within the thunk evaluation code we catch any exception, update the thunk with a closure which throws the same exception value, and then re-throw the exception.

Thunks and Threads Once multiple evaluation threads are running there is the possibility that two, or more, threads may attempt to evaluate a thunk. As the evaluation of a thunk can take an arbitrarily large amount of time it is best to avoid multiple evaluation. To handle this we make the evaluation method for a thunk a synchronised one. The first thread to attempt to evaluate the thunk will acquire the lock and undertake the work. Any subsequent threads will block until the lock is released and then find the work done and use the already computed result.

6   Interop

6.1   Calling C♯ from Mondrian

C♯, or any other .NET language, are invoked from Mondrian through the I/O system to preserve Mondrian's purely functional semantics. To call a constructor the `create` construct is used which returns a monadic function closure which when executed invokes the foreign language constructor to create an object.

To enable the calling of a foreign method, the `invoke` (and `invokeStatic`) construct is provided. This returns a monadic function closure which takes an object along with any method arguments and calls the foreign method. This style of method calling where the object is passed explicitly differs from the C♯ model but is reminiscent of the Ada 95 OO model [20].

The function closures returned by `create` and `invoke` evaluate any argument values to WHNF before invoking the foreign constructor/method. This is done to bridge the gap between the lazy world of Mondrian and the strict world of .NET. However should a structured value need to be passed then either it must be fully evaluated before the inter-language call (using Mondrian's strict function, see below), or the foreign function must call back to Mondrian to evaluate any suspensions it finds.

The following simple example demonstrates `create` and `invoke`:

```
main = {
  gen <- create System.Random();
  n <- invoke System.Random.Next(Int32) 10 gen;
  putStrLn ("Random 1..10: " + show n);
}
```

Note that `create` and `invoke` take both the foreign constructor/method and it's argument type(s), if any. The Mondrian type system does not support overloading so these constructs use the argument types to uniquely identify the constructor/method to be called.

Accessing the fields and properties of a foreign object is provided by the `get` and `set` constructs in a similar manner as for constructors and methods.

6.2   Calling Mondrian from C♯ and Other .NET Languages

Programmers calling Mondrian from other .NET languages should not need to know how Mondrian works under the hood. In particular, partial application is not normally used by other .NET languages and when they need to call Mondrian code to perform some algorithm, they will usually therefore supply a full set of arguments to the Mondrian function. To handle this common scenario, we simply add a `Apply` method with the full number of arguments to the function object, which is then used by other .NET languages as the function's entry point.

For example, our function `Foo`, with the method added for calling from other .NET languages it now looks something like:

```
class Foo : Code {
  // used by Mondrian runtime
  public Object ENTER() {
    ... as before ...
  }

  // used when called externally .NET languages
  public Object Apply(Object x) {
    Code f = this;
    ...evaluate f in Mondrian specific way...
    return f;
  }
}
```

And a call from C$^\sharp$ becomes something like:

```
Foo foo = new Foo();
result = foo.Apply(4);
```

Note that `Apply` is not a static method on `Foo` as evaluating `foo.Apply(3)` may trigger thunk updates. Indeed calling `foo` a subsequent time might return its result faster than calling `foo` the first time.

References

[1] The SML.NET Compiler. http://research.microsoft.com/Projects/SML.NET/.

[2] Ben Albahari, Peter Drayton, and Brad Merrill. *C$^\sharp$ Essentials*. O'Reilly, 2001.

[3] Sigbjorn Finne, Erik Meijer, Daan Leijen, and Simon Peyton Jones. Calling Hell from Heaven and Heaven from Hell. In *Proceedings of ICFP'99*.

[4] Sigbjorn Finne, Erik Meijer, Daan Leijen, and Simon Peyton Jones. HDirect: A Binary Foreign Function Iinterface for Haskell. In *Proceedings of ICFP'98*.

[5] J. Hughes. Why Functional Programming Matters. *Computer Journal*, 32(2):98–107, 1989.

[6] Simon Peyton Jones. Implementing Lazy Functional Languages on Stock Hardware: the Spineless Tagless G-Machine. *Journal of Functional Programming*, 2(2), April 1992.

[7] Simon Peyton Jones, Andy Gordon, and Sigbjorn Finne. Concurrent Haskell. In *POPL*, 1996.

[8] Simon Peyton Jones, Erik Meijer, and Daan Leijen. Scripting COM components from Haskell. In *Proceedings of ICSR5*, 1998.

[9] Andrew Kennedy and Don Syme. Design and Implementation of Generics for the .NET Common Language Runtime. In *PLDI*, 2001.

[10] Daan Leijen, Erik Meijer, and Jim Hook. *Haskell as an Automation Controller*, volume 1608 of *LNCS*. 1999.

[11] Jeff Lewis, Mark Shields, Erik Meijer, and John Launchbury. Implicit Arguments: Dynamic Scoping with Static Types. In *Proceedings of POPL'00*.

[12] Erik Meijer. Server-side Scripting in Haskell. *Journal of Functional Programming*, 2000.

[13] Erik Meijer and Koen Claessen. The Design and Implementation of Mondrian. In *Haskell Workshop*, 1997.

[14] Erik Meijer, Daan Leijen, and Jim Hook. Client-side Web Scripting with HaskellScript. In *PADL*, 1999.

[15] Nigel Perry. *Massey Hope+C*, 1992. Massey University.

[16] Simon Peyton-Jones, John Hughes, and (eds). Report on the Language Haskell'98. http://www.haskell.org/report, February 1998.

[17] Alastair Reid. Putting the Spine back in the Spineless Tagless G-Machine: An Implementation of Resumable Blackholes. In *IFL*, 1998.

[18] Mark Shields and Erik Meijer. Type Iindexed Records. In *Proceedings of POPL'01*.

[19] Andy Moran Simon Marlow, Simon Peyton Jones and John Reppy. Asynchronous Exceptions in Haskell. In *PLDI*, 2001.

[20] S. Tucker Taft and Robert A. Duff, editors. *ADA 95 Language and Standard Libraries : ISO/IEC 8652:1995(E)*. Springer Verlag, 1997.

[21] Philip Wadler. Monads for Functional Programming. In *Advanced Functional Programming*, volume 925 of *LNCS*, 1995.

A Quasi Optimal Bit-Vector Encoding of Tree Hierarchies.
Application to Efficient Type Inclusion Tests

Olivier Raynaud and Eric Thierry

LIRMM, 161 rue Ada, 34392 Montpellier Cedex 5, France
raynaud@lirmm.fr,thierry@lirmm.fr

Abstract. Type inclusion tests consist in determining whether a type is a subtype of another. An efficient implementation of type inclusion is an important feature of object oriented programming languages.

A well-known method to achieve these tests is to associate to each type a subset of a set $S = \{1, \dots, k\}$ such that type inclusion coincides with subset inclusion. Such an embedding of types into 2^S (the lattice of all subsets of S) is called a bit-vector encoding of the type hierarchy. These encodings are known for several interesting features. Bit-vector encodings are perfectly appropriate for hierarchies with single subtyping as well as hierarchies with multiple subtyping. Subset inclusion tests can be performed very efficiently.

Several works have studied bit-vector encodings from a theoretical point of view ([6, 7, 10, 14, 16, 18, 19]) and from a practical point of view ([3, 8, 9, 17]), in particular in order to minimize the size of the encoding, i.e. the size of S.

In this article, we present a new algorithm which computes bit-vector encodings for single subtyping hierarchies, also called tree hierarchies.

Our algorithm is simple, it computes the bit-vector encoding very quickly and gives good results for the size of the encoding. In particular, we have significantly improved the best bounds known for the encoding sizes of some benchmarks presented in [9].

1 Introduction

Performances of object-oriented programs in a run time environment are strongly linked with the techniques which are used to solve the problem of dispatching methods. When invoked, a generic function executes its most appropriate method based on the class of its arguments. Determining such a method usually requires to execute some subtype tests [11, 12]. For instance, such tests occur in C++ where dynamic casting is allowed, or in the execution with JAVA or SMALLTALK languages.

J. Lindskov Knudsen (Ed.): ECOOP 2001, LNCS 2072, pp. 165–180, 2001.

The type inclusion relation (or subtype relation) is a transitive, reflexive anti-symmetric relation, thus it is a partial order on the types of the program, also called the hierarchy of types. In order to check the inclusion of types, many techniques called **hierarchical encodings** have been developed [1, 3, 4, 5, 6, 9]. Figure 1 represents such an encoding for the Petra hierarchy. Petra is a generic application for the modelisation of telephone networks. The usual requirements for these encodings are the runtime efficiency, so that type tests should be fast, and the minimization of the space used to store the encoding.

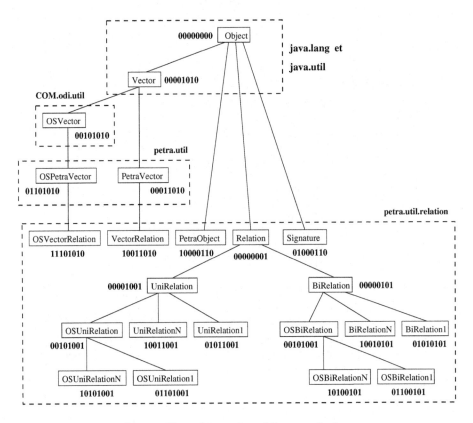

Fig. 1. Type hierarchy of Petra relations

A classical way to encode a hierarchy of N types is to index these types with integers from 1 to N and store the subtype relation in a binary matrix M of size $N \times N$ where $M[x, y] = 1$ if the type indexed by y is a subtype on the one indexed by x, and $M[x, y] = 0$ otherwise. With this method, type inclusion tests can be performed in constant time. But the main drawback is the quadratic space needed to store the matrix.

Another method consists in associating with each type the list of its direct subtypes (a direct subtype of A is a subtype B of A such that there is no other type between A and B for the subtype relation). This method which saves space is however slow for checking whether a type is a subtype of another.

More generally it is difficult to optimize both speed and space, and it is necessary to choose an encoding with a good compromise, depending of the needs (see for instance [17] for an evaluation of several kinds of encodings).

In this article, we will study a well-known kind of hierarchical encoding, called **bit-vector encoding**. The idea is to associate with each type a subset of a fixed set $S = \{1, \ldots, k\}$ such that type inclusion coincides with subset inclusion. More formally, we denote by $P = (X, \leq)$ the type hierarchy where X is the set of the types and $x \leq y$ if and only if y is a subtype of x. A **bit-vector encoding** of P is an application ϕ from X into 2^S (the lattice of all the subsets of S) such that: $x \leq y$ if and only if $\phi(x) \subseteq \phi(y)$. The **size** of the encoding ϕ is the cardinal of S. The elements of S are sometimes called **colors** or **genes** ([3]).

In order to describe the hierarchies, we also introduce the next definitions. Let x be a type in the hierarchy $P = (X, \leq)$, $Anc(x) = \{y \in X \mid y \neq x,\ y \leq x\}$ is the set of the **ancestors** of x and $Desc(x) = \{y \in X \mid y \neq x,\ x \leq y\}$ is the set of the **descendants** of x. A direct subtype y of the type x is called a **child** of x and x is a **parent** of y. A **chain** is a sequence $x_0, x_1, \ldots, x_h$ of types such that $x_0 \leq x_1 \leq \ldots \leq x_h$, the **height** of this chain is h. The **height** of the hierarchy P is the maximal height of all the chains of P, it is denoted by $height(P)$. The **degree** of a type x is the number of direct subtypes of x, it is denoted by $deg(x)$.

A **single subtyping hierarchy** is a hierarchy where each type has at most one parent. The other hierarchies are called **multiple subtyping hierarchies**. Conventionally the hierarchies will be drawn in a top-down fashion. The edges represent the direct subtype relation with the subtypes below their parent types. Figure 2 shows three different representations of a unique bit-vector encoding ϕ of size $|S| = 6$ for a given hierarchy P. The first one associates to each type x its code $\phi(x)$ which is a subset of $S = \{1, 2, 3, 4, 5, 6\}$. The second one associates with each type x its **reduced code** $\phi_r(x)$ defined by $\phi_r(x) = \phi(x) \backslash \bigcup_{y \in Anc(x)} \phi(y)$. The last one associates to each type x a vector of $|S|$ bits where bit i is equal to 1 if $i \in \phi(x)$ and equal to 0 otherwise. This is a way to implement bit-vector encodings and it uses $|S|$ bits per type. These three representations are perfectly equivalent. The complete code is obtained from the reduced code by propagating the colors of the types to their descendants. The encoding of Figure 1 represents a bit-vector encoding of the Petra hierarchy.

Several known encoding methods compute bit-vector encodings [3, 9, 13, 19]. We enumerate below the strong points of bit-vector encodings:

1. Appropriate for single subtype hierarchies and multiple subtype hierarchies.
2. Economical with space (good compression compared to the binary matrix encoding).
3. Fast type inclusion tests (constant time for bit-vectors of bounded size)

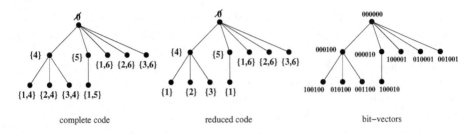

Fig. 2. The three different representations of a bit-vector encoding

For a given hierarchy, the smallest bit-vector encodings are very compact encodings with sizes usually closer to $\log_2(N)$ bits rather than N bits (where N is the number of types in the hierarchy). It represents a very important saving of space in comparison with the binary matrix storage which requires N bits per type. Unfortunately finding the minimum size of a bit-vector encoding for a given hierarchy (a parameter which is also called the **2-dimension** of the hierarchy [2, 16]) is known to be a NP-hard problem [15] and recently it has been shown that approximating the 2-dimension is equivalent to approximating the optimal coloration of a graph [13]. A consequence of this result is that there does not exist an algorithm which approximates the 2-dimension up to a constant factor unless P=NP. Fortunately, it is possible to propose heuristics that produce very compact bit-vector encodings for practical cases. It is actually the aim of this article.

Concerning the speed of the type inclusion tests, checking whether $x \leq y$ is equivalent to check whether $\phi(x)$ OR $\phi(y) = \phi(y)$. These are elementary boolean operations and if we consider that the size of the bit-vectors is bounded (for instance if we known that it can be stored on two machine words), it is a constant time test (for a discussion about "constant time" tests, see [17] where several techniques of tests are presented with their implementation using RISC instructions).

In this article, we present a new algorithm to compute a near optimal bit-vector encoding for single subtyping hierarchies. Without loss of generality, we only consider **tree hierarchies** which are single subtyping hierarchies with a root type (a top element). The types with no subtype are called leaves. Such hierarchies of types often occur in object oriented languages, even in the ones that allow multiple subtyping. The motivation of this study is to improve the size bounds for people using the framework of bit-vector encodings. We show how to take into account the tree structure in order to minimize the encoding size.

In Section 2, we give a short overview of the previous works dealing with tree hierarchies. We present bit-vector encoding algorithms as well as other encoding algorithms for comparison. Our algorithm is described in Section 3. This is a simple greedy algorithm with no preprocessing step and no setting of parameters for optimization. The Section 4 evaluates the performances of this algorithm. We show that we have obtained the optimal balancing strategy for trees. Finding this optimal balancing was conjectured to be feasible for trees in [9]. As a result, we have significantly improved the encoding sizes of some benchmarks coming from [9]. This section contains a comparison of the encoding sizes of known algorithms on these benchmarks and on generic tree hierarchies (complete trees and comb trees). We conclude this article in Section 5.

2   Previous Works

Many techniques are known to achieve type inclusion tests for tree hierarchies. First we must present a well-known encoding called Schubert's numbering or Relative Numbering which is optimal in time and space. This algorithm finds a good numbering of the types. For each type x of the hierarchy, a couple of integers $(l(x), r(x))$ are computed as follows: traverse the tree with a Depth First Search and for each new type increment a counter c. When a type x is first encountered, store c in $l(x)$. When the traversal leaves the type store the current value of c in $r(x)$. Then a type x is a subtype of a type y if and only if $l(y) \leq l(x)$ and $r(x) \leq r(y)$. In order to store an encoding of N types, we can say that this encoding uses $2\lceil \log_2(N) \rceil$ bits per type and a type inclusion test just requires two integer comparisons (constant time comparisons). Figure 3 shows a example of such an encoding.

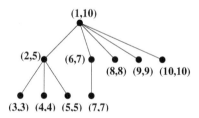

Fig. 3. Schubert's numbering (also called Relative Numbering).

Among the studies about tree hierarchies, we also can mention the Cohen's algorithm [11] which proposes constant type tests and uses a matrix $N \times H$ of integers where H is the height of the hierarchy. It represents $H * \log_2(N)$ bits per type, it is usually better than the binary matrix method but it still may be costly in space, especially compared to bit-vector encodings.

Relative Numbering which is used in programming languages such as MODULA-3, is clearly an optimal encoding for time and space when we deal with single subtyping hierarchies. However we decided to focuss on bit-vector encodings for this class of hierarchies. Such a study aims at increasing our knowledge about bit-vector encodings and developing new heuristics for single subtyping hierarchies that could be extended later to encode multiple subtyping hierarchies.

One naive method to compute a bit-vector encoding associates with each type a different index and consider this single color as the reduced bit-vector encoding. The corresponding encoding after propagation of the colors has size N where N is the number of types. It needs the same space as the binary matrix method. The space cost is extremely expensive compared to the near optimal bit-vector encodings as we will see.

Caseau is the first to have studied bit-vector encodings in the special case of tree hierarchies [3]. He focussed on a particular class of bit-vector encodings: those whose reduced encoding have at most one color per type. His method computes a conflict graph from the hierarchy then colors the graph and finally computes a bit-vector encoding with the colors used for the graph. His encoding makes a interesting reuse of colors and he was able to precise the size of its encoding for tree hierarchies. Let C be a chain $x_0, x_1, \ldots, x_p$ of a tree hierarchy T, he defines the *weight* of this chain by $weight(C) = \sum_{0 \le i \le p} deg(x_i)$. The size of Caseau's encoding of T is the maximum weight for all the chains of T. Figure 5 shows an example of the reduced encoding produced by this method (the chain of maximum weight is in bold).

In their article [9], Vitek, Krall and Horspool have revisited this approach. They also construct a conflict graph and compute a bit-vector encoding from a coloration of this graph. The reduced encoding also has at most one color for each type, but they start by modifying the initial hierarchy in order to get smaller bit-vector encodings. They have better results thanks to this preprocessing, but their algorithm still depends on the performance of coloring algorithms which determines the size of the encoding. They included the idea of "balancing" the hierarchy during preprocessing, we will come back to this point in Section 4.

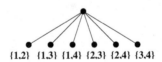

{1.2} {1.3} {1.4} {2.3} {2.4} {3.4}

Fig. 4. The optimal bit-vector encoding for a type and its 6 children

In [19], Caseau, Habib, Nourine and Raynaud went back to the conflict graph method in order to encode any hierarchy but they proposed to use a special algorithm if the input appends to be a tree hierarchy. They present an algorithm especially designed for tree hierarchy. In order to give the size of their encoding, we have to define a function $cmin(n)$ which is the minimum number of colors needed to encode a type with n direct subtypes. It is known that $cmin(n) = \min\{k \mid C_k^{k/2} \ge n\}$ and it is approximately $\lceil log_2(n) \rceil$ (for all $n \le 40000$, $\lceil log_2(n) \rceil \le cmin(n) \le \lceil log_2(n) \rceil + 2$) . For instance $cmin(6) = 4$ as it is shown on Figure 4. We redefine a weight function for a chain C by

$weight(C) = \sum_{0 \le i \le p} cmin(deg(x_i))$. The size of their encoding of T is the maximum of the weight function taken over all the chains of T. Figure 5 shows such an encoding. This algorithm is clearly a amelioration of Caseau's algorithm in the case of tree hierarchies.

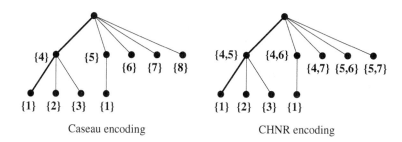

Fig. 5. Encodings generated by Caseau's method and CHNR's method

The next section presents our algorithm, it is based on two ideas that were already raised in [3] and [9]: splitting and balancing.

3 The Encoding Algorithm

We present here a new algorithm for computing a very compact bit-vector encoding of tree hierarchies. First in order to formalise the "splitting and balancing" strategies, we introduce a particular class of bit-vector encodings: the **dichotomic encodings**. Then we describe our algorithm which compute a compact dichotomic encoding. As we will see in Section 4, it produces the smallest dichotomic encoding for the input tree hierarchy.

3.1 Dichotomic Encodings

The idea consists in splitting in two parts the initial tree and giving a different color to the codes of each subtree. By repeating this operation on each part recursively until each subtree is empty, we are able to produce what we call a dichotomic encoding.

Let T be a hierarchy with a bit-vector encoding, let x be a color of this encoding, we will call T_x the set of the elements of T which contain x in their code. We give a recursive definition of a *dichotomic encoding* .

Definition 1. *Let T be a hierarchy, we will say that an encoding of T is dichotomic if there exist two elements x and y such that:*

- *Every element of T, with a non empty code, contains either x or y in its code.*

- The codes of T_x minus x form a dichotomic encoding of T_x.
- The codes of T_y minus y form a dichotomic encoding of T_y.
- If T is composed by an unique vertex, the empty code is considered as a dichotomic encoding.

Let us first remark that a dichotomic encoding is equivalent to an embedding of the hierarchy into a binary tree. We call this technique *dichotomic* because we split the tree in two differents parts which can be encoded independently. Secondly note that there exist many dichotomic encodings for a unique tree. We will show that our algorithm produces the most compact one.

3.2   The Algorithm

This is a bottom-up greedy algorithm which basically constructs a binary tree from the input hierarchy T by introducing intermediate nodes (symbolising "splitting" operations) and it carries weights on the nodes in order to "balance" this binary tree. The weight of a node s denoted by $weight(s)$ corresponds to the number of colors necessary to encode the subtree composed of s and its descendants (this subtree is denoted by $T(s)$). The computation of the weights follows a bottom-up topological order of the hierarchy: we need to calculate the weights of the children before that of the parent.

At the beginning, only the leaves carry a weight equal to zero. Then, assuming that all the children of a node s are carrying a weight, three cases can occur.

1. If s has only one child v, the subtree $T(s)$ needs $weight(v) + 1$ colors to be encoded. One color to encode the vertex v and $weight(v)$ to encode the subtree $T(v)$.

2. If s has exactly two children u and v such that $weight(u) \leq weight(v)$, we encode $T(u)$ with colors dedicated to $T(v)$ and we encode vertices u and v with two news colors. This encoding of $T(s)$ will use $weight(v) + 2$ colors.

3. If s has more than two children, to ensure that our method produces the most compact dichotomic encoding, we will merge the two subtrees $T(u)$ and $T(v)$ whose weights are minimal. We introduce a new node w having u and v as children. This node w replaces u and v in the list of the children of s and with the same method as above we can encode $T(w)$ with $\max(weight(u), weight(v)) + 2$ colors.

The algorithm 1 follows this strategy. It computes a binary tree T' where the input tree T is embedded. At the end every node s of T' (the nodes of T and the new intermediate nodes) has a unique color stored in $c(s)$, it corresponds to the reduced encoding of our bit-vector encoding and the last step consists in propagating these colors through the hierarchy to obtain the final encoding.

Algorithm 1: Dichotomic encoding generation for a given tree T

Data : A tree T.

Result: A dichotomic encoding of T.

begin

Each leaf v is given a weight: $weight(v) \leftarrow 0$;

Other vertices are not given any weight;

while *There exist a node s without weight such that all his children have a weight* **do**

if *s has a unique child v* **then**

Give to v the color : $c(v) \leftarrow weight(v) + 1$;

Give to s the weight : $weight(s) \leftarrow weight(v) + 1$;

if *s has exactly 2 children u and v* **then**

Give to u the color : $c(u) \leftarrow \max(weight(u), weight(v)) + 1$;

Give to v the color : $c(v) \leftarrow \max(weight(u), weight(v)) + 2$;

Give to s the weight :

$weight(s) \leftarrow \max(weight(u), weight(v)) + 2$;

if *s has more than 3 children* **then**

Choose u and v two children whose weights are minimal;

Introduce a new node w whose children are u and v, and which is the child of s;

Give to u the color: $c(u) \leftarrow \max(weight(u), weight(v)) + 1$;

Give to v the color : $c(v) \leftarrow \max(weight(u), weight(v)) + 2$;

Give to w the weight :

$weight(w) \leftarrow \max(weight(u), weight(v)) + 2$;

1   Let T' be the tree generated from T, associate to each node s of T the following encoding : $code(s) = \{c(s')|s' \in T' \text{ and } s' \leq_{T'} s\}$;

end

Figure 6 shows an execution of Algorithm 1 which generates the tree T' from T. Intermediate nodes are in white, the color $c(s)$ of a node s is given by an integer, the integer given between parenthesis corresponds to the weight carried by the node. The last drawing represents the initial tree with its final bit-vector encoding (after step

Computing the weight of a node from the weight of its k children can be done in $O(k * log_2 k)$ time by sorting the weights of the children. Algorithm 1 can be implemented in a bottom-up way running in $O(n * log_2 \Delta)$ time with $O(n)$ space, where n is the number of nodes of the tree and Δ is the maximum degree of a node of the tree.

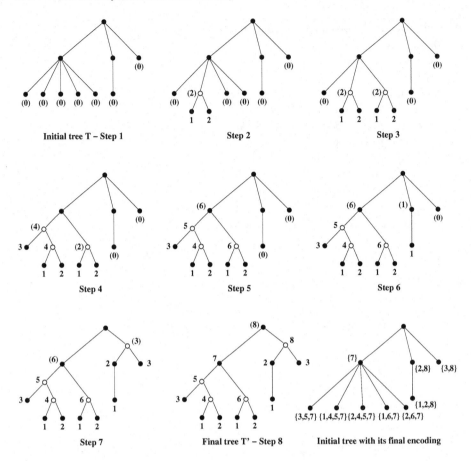

Fig. 6. Initial tree T, the binary tree T' and the final *dichotomic encoding* computed by algorithm 1

4   Results

First we will develop in this section the theorical aspects of our results. We will discuss about optimality and give some bounds for the size of the encoding computed by our algorithm. We will also study the case of two special shapes of tree hierarchies. Secondly we will sum up some pratical tests carried out on class hierarchies of oriented objects languages like Visualworks2 or Digitalk3.

4.1   Theoretical Results

Optimality result. The next theorem garanties that in the framework of "splitting and balancing" strategies, our algorithm provides a bit-vector encoding of optimal size. Vitek and al. conjectured it was feasible in [9].

Theorem 1. *Algorithm 1 produces a dichotomic encoding of minimal size.*

Proof. Producing a dichotomic encoding of a tree T is equivalent to embedding T into a binary tree T'. Then the size of the dichotomic encoding is equal to the maximal weight of a chain in the binary tree in the sense of Caseau (the weight of a chain is the sum of the degrees of the nodes of this chain). Moreover we can associate with each node s of T' a weight which is the maximal weight of a chain starting from s. This is equivalent to the number of colors encoding the subtree rooted at s in the dichotomic encoding.

To prove that our algorithm computes the smallest size for a dichotomic encoding, we just have to prove locally that it makes the best construction for a *level*, namely a node with its weighted children.

Suppose that all the children of a node s carry a weight. We are going to prove that our construction minimizes the weight that will be propagated to the node s.

1. Consider an embedding of this level into a binary tree BT. We associate with each node x its height $h(x)$ in BT and each leaf x of BT carries a weight $w(x)$. The weight of BT, denoted by $weight(BT)$ is the maximum of $w(x) + 2 * h(x)$ for all the leaves of BT.
2. Suppose that two leaves α and β of BT with the smallest weights $w(\alpha)$ and $w(\beta)$ are not "married" (the children of the same node). Then we can construct another binary tree BT' embedding the level such that α and β are married and $weight(BT') \leq weight(BT)$. Figure 7 describes this initial situation. The nodes α and β have a first common ancestor which is s', the weight α is "married" with the node γ and β is "married" with the node δ. The height of the parent of α and γ (resp. β and δ) from s' is denoted by h_γ (resp. h_δ). Now suppose that $h_\gamma \leq h_\delta$, by inverting δ and α we have a new binary tree BT' such that $weight(BT') \leq weight(BT)$ (if we had $h_\gamma \geq h_\delta$, we would have inverted γ and β).
3. Suppose now that we suppress two "married" leaves of BT with weights α and β and we associate with the new leaf (their common parent) the weight $\max(w(\alpha), w(\beta)) + 2$. Then it is clear that this new binary tree BT' verifies $weight(BT') = weight(BT)$.

Given a level with weights on the leaves, consider an embedding BT of minimum weight $weight(BT)$. By alternatively using the transformations 2 and 3, we transform BT into another binary tree BT' with the same optimal weight and which is an embedding that can be constructed by Algorithm 1 (and all the embeddings that can be constructed by Algorithm 1 have the same weight). $\square$

Remark 1. the algorithm does not provide the optimal size of all the bit-vector encoding (as it will be seen on the generic examples of the next paragraph or in figure 4). As far as we know, finding polynomially this minimum size remains an open problem.

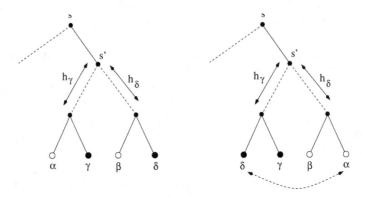

Fig. 7. Transformation of the embedding when $h_\gamma \leq h_\delta$.

Evaluation for two particular instances of tree hierarchies. Our interest focusses on two generic examples illustrated by Figure 8 and Figure 9. A *complete d-tree* is a tree hierarchy such that all the nodes have a degree equal to d and all the chains from the root to the leaves have the same height (see Figure 8). A *comb d-tree* is a tree hierarchy such that all the nodes have a degree equal to d and the leaves are the children of a unique chain (see Figure 9). These generic examples give a good idea of the behaviour of known encoding algorithms. In Table 1, the encoding sizes of three algorithms are compared: Caseau's encoding [3], CHNR's encoding [19] (these two methods were mentionned in Section 2) and the encoding of algorithm 1. The method described in [9] does not appear in this table because it is not possible to predict the output size. We also give the number of nodes. In CHNR's column, the exact value is in fact obtained by replacing $\lceil \log_2(d) \rceil$ by $cmin(d)$ but we leave $\lceil \log_2(d) \rceil$ because it is approximately the real value. The parameter h is the height of the hierarchy.

Instance	Number of nodes	Caseau's method	CHNR's method	Dichotomy
Complete d-tree	$(d^{h+1}-1)/(d-1)$	$h*d$	$h*\lceil log_2 d \rceil$	$2*h*\lceil log_2 d \rceil$
Comb d- tree	$(h*d)+1$	$h*d$	$h*\lceil log_2 d \rceil$	$2(h-1+\lceil log_2 d \rceil)$

Table 1. Comparison of different bit-vector methods (the number of bits per type in the encoding)

Some bounds on the encoding size. If we look at the examples of the table 1, our algorithm provides encodings with a size close to $\log_2(N)$ bits (where N is the number of nodes), especially when the height h is smaller than $\log_2(N)$. For these cases, the space cost is close to the encoding schemes which minimize the space storage and are not bit-vector encodings (such as the one presented in Section 2). The next proposition bounds the encoding size of our algorithm

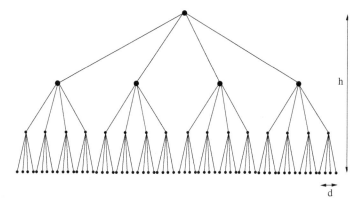

Fig. 8. Complete d-tree of height h with $d = 4$ and $h = 3$.

with usual paramaters of hierarchies. Let T be a tree hierarchy, the height of T is denoted by h and the maximal degree of a node of T is denoted by Δ. The number of nodes of T is N.

Proposition 1. *Let $size(T)$ be the size of the bit-vector encoding generated by Algorithm 1 for T. Then:*

$$\max(h, \lceil \log_2(N) \rceil) \leq size(T) \leq 2 * h * \lceil \log_2(\Delta) \rceil$$

On practical examples, we can expect the size to be far from the upper bound. We have experimented our algorithm on a set of benchmarks in the next subsection.

4.2 Practical Results

In order to evaluate the performance of Algorithm 1, it has been applied to a collection of benchmarks. These benchmarks have been used by Vitek, Krall and Horspool in [9] and [17] for the analysis of several hierarchical encoding algorithms.

The benchmarks that we have used are four examples of hierarchies from object oriented languages like Smalltalk or C++. These class libraries contain from 311 to 1956 classes and have a tree structure.

Table 2 recapitulates the encoding size that were obtained for each of the four hierarchies: Visualworks3 (Smalltalk-80), Digitalk3 (Smalltalk-80), NeXTStep (Objective-C), ET++ (C++). The second column indicates the number of classes in the hierarchy. The next two columns have been picked up from the article [9]. The "Caseau" column gives the size of a bit-vector encoding obtained with the method described in [3] for tree hierarchies. The "KVH" column gives the best results obtained by the heuristics of Vitek and al. [9]. Their heuristics can use

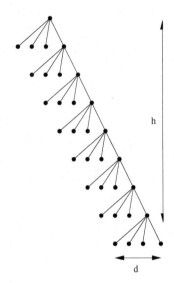

Fig. 9. Comb d-tree of height h with $d = 4$ and $h = 8$.

different preprocessing steps and different optimization routines. The results presented here correspond to the best choices in their strategy. We recall that their heuristics also apply to multiple subtyping hierarchies. The "CHNR" column presents the improvement of Caseau's method which was described in [19]. And the last column gives the size of our bit-vector encoding. Drawings of these hierarchies can be found in the Appendix, with some complements concerning the format of the benchmarks and our implementation.

Benchmark	Classes	*Caseau's method*	*KVH's method*	*CHNR's method*	*Dichotomy*
Visualworks2	1956	420	50	58	32
Digitalk3	1357	325	36	52	29
NeXTStep	311	177	23	28	20
ET++	371	181	30	41	20

Table 2. Encoding sizes for benchmarks

5   Conclusion

If several types are added to a tree hierarchy deleting its tree structure, then computing a bit-vector encoding of the new hierarchy from a dichotomic encoding of the old one is a difficult problem when we want to keep minimizing the size of the encoding. More generally, dealing with incrementality for bit-vector encodings remains a difficult problem as far as we know.

However we intend to apply the main routine used in Algorithm 1 to encode multiple subtyping hierarchies: by decomposing the hierarchy into modules, the algorithm used to compute the weight of a node from the weights of its children could be used to compute an encoding size of the whole hierarchy from encoding sizes of its modules, not all the time but for special cases of decomposition. This could be one application of the dichotomic encoding algorithm.

Acknowledgements

We must thank Lhouari Nourine and Michel Habib for their advice, Yoav Zibin for its careful reading and the referees for their comments and suggestions.

References

[1] H. At-Kaci, R. Boyer, P. Lincoln, and R. Nasr. Efficient implementation of lattice operations. *ACM Transactions on Programming Langages and Systems*, 11(1):115–146, january 1989.

[2] A. Bouchet. Codages et dimensions de relations binaires. *Annals of Discrete Mathematics 23, Ordres: Description and Roles, (M. Pouzet, D. Richard eds)*, 1984.

[3] Yves Caseau. Efficient handling of multiple inheritance hierarchies. In *OOP-SLA'93*, pages 271–287, 1993.

[4] G. Ellis. Efficient retrieval from hierarchies of objects using lattice operations. In *Conceptual Graphs for knowledge representation, (Proc. International conference on Conceptual Structures, Quebec City, Canada, August 4-7, 1993), G. W. Mineau, B. Moulin and J. Sowa, Eds, Lecture Notes in Artificial Intelligence 699, Springer, Berlin*, 1993.

[5] A. Fall. The foundations of taxomic encoding. in International KRUSE Symposium: Knowledge Retrieval, Use and Storage for Efficiency, University of Santa-Cruz., August 1995.

[6] M. Habib, M. Huchard, and L. Nourine. Embedding partially ordered sets into chain-products. In *International KRUSE Symposium: Knowledge Retrieval, Use and Storage for Efficiency. University of Santa-Cruz.*, pages 147–161, August 1995.

[7] M. Habib and L. Nourine. Bit-vector encoding for partially ordered sets. In Proc. of International Workshop ORDAL'94, editor, *Orders, Algorithms and Applications*, number 831, pages 1–12, Lyon, France, July 1994. LNCS.

[8] M. Habib, L. Nourine, and O. Raynaud. A new lattice-based heuristic for taxonomy encoding. In *International KRUSE Symposium: Knowledge Retrieval, Use and Storage for Efficiency. Vancouver .*, pages 60–71, August 1997.

[9] A. Krall, J. Vitek, and R.N. Horspool. Near optimal hierarchical encoding of types. In *Ecoop'97, LNCS*, number 1241, pages 128–145.

[10] G. Markowsky. The representation of posets and lattices by sets. *Algebra Universalis*, 11:173–192, 1980.

[11] N.H.Cohen. Type-extension type tests can be performed in constant time. *Programming languages and systems*, 13(4):626–629, July 1991.

[12] C. Quiennec. Fast and compact dispatching for dynamic object-oriented languages. *Information Processing Letters (accepted for publication)*, 1997.

[13] O. Raynaud and E. Thierry. Calcul de la 2-dimension d'un ensemble ordonn. Research Report 00082, LIRMM, Montpellier, France, 2000.

[14] M. Skorsky. *Endliche Verbnde Diagramme und Eigenschaften*. PhD thesis, (written in English) Darmstadt, Germany, 1992.

[15] J. Stahl and R. Wille. Preconcepts of contexts. *in Proc. Universal Algebra (Sienna)*, 1984.

[16] William T. Trotter. Embedding finite posets in cubes. *Discrete Mathematics*, 12:165–172, 1975.

[17] J. Vitek, R.N. Horspool, and A. Krall. Efficient type inclusion tests. In *OOPSLA'97*, number 1241, pages 128–145.

[18] R. Wille. Restructuring lattice theory: An approach based on hierarchies of contexts. *in Ordered sets,I. Rival, Eds. NATO ASI No 83, Reidel, Dordecht, Holland*, pages 445–470, 1982.

[19] M. Habib Y. Caseau, L. Nourine, and O. Raynaud. Encoding of mutiple inheritance hierarchie and partial orders. *Computational Intelligence*, 15:50–62, N1, 1999.

On the Usefulness of Liveness
for Garbage Collection and Leak Detection

Martin Hirzel[1], Amer Diwan[1], and Antony Hosking[2]

[1] University of Colorado
Boulder, CO 80309
{hirzel, diwan}@cs.colorado.edu
[2] Purdue University
West Lafayette, IN 47907
hosking@cs.purdue.edu

Abstract. The effectiveness of garbage collectors and leak detectors in identifying dead objects depends on the "accuracy" of their reachability traversal. Accuracy has two orthogonal dimensions: (i) whether the reachability traversal can distinguish between pointers and non-pointers (type accuracy), and (ii) whether the reachability traversal can identify memory locations that will be dereferenced in the future (liveness accuracy). While prior work has investigated the importance of type accuracy, there has been little work investigating the importance of liveness accuracy for garbage collection or leak detection. This paper presents an experimental study of the importance of liveness on the accuracy of the reachability traversal. We show that while liveness can significantly improve the effectiveness of a garbage collector or leak detector, the simpler liveness schemes are largely ineffective. One must analyze globals using an interprocedural analysis to get significant benefit.[0]

1 Introduction

Garbage collection (GC), or automatic storage reclamation, has many well-known software engineering benefits [29]. First, it eliminates memory management bugs, such as dangling pointers. Second, unlike explicit deallocation, GC does not compromise modularity since modules do not need to know the memory management philosophies of the modules that they use. It is therefore no surprise that even though C and C++ do not mandate GC as part of the language definition, many C and C++ programmers are now using it either for reclaiming memory or for *leak detection*. It is also no surprise that many newer programming languages (e.g., Java [14], Modula-3 [21], SML [20]) require garbage collection. This increased popularity of garbage collection makes it more important than ever to fully understand the tradeoffs between different garbage collection alternatives.

---

[0] This work was supported by NSF ITR grant CCR-0085792. Any opinions, findings and conclusions or recommendations expressed in this material are the authors' and do not necessarily reflect those of the sponsors.

J. Lindskov Knudsen (Ed.): ECOOP 2001, LNCS 2072, pp. 181–206, 2001.
© Springer-Verlag Berlin Heidelberg 2001

An *ideal* garbage collector or leak detector identifies all heap-allocated objects[1] that are not *dynamically live*. A dynamically-live heap object is one that will be used in the future of the computation. More operationally, a dynamically-live heap object is one that can be reached by following pointers that will be dereferenced in the future of the computation (*dynamically-live pointers*). In order to retain only dynamically-live objects, the ideal garbage collector must be able to exactly identify what memory locations contain dynamically-live pointers. Unfortunately, a real garbage collector or leak detector has no way of knowing what pointers will be dereferenced in the future; thus it may use compiler support to identify an approximation to dynamically-live pointers. The precision of the garbage collector or leak detector in identifying dynamically-live objects depends on the *accuracy* of the compiler support.

There are two dimensions to accuracy: the extent to which the compiler information is able to distinguish pointers from non-pointers (*type accuracy*) and the extent to which the compiler information identifies live pointers (*liveness accuracy*). Prior work [17] has mostly focused only on type accuracy and liveness accuracy has received only a little attention in the literature [1]. In this paper we investigate the effect of different levels of liveness accuracy; in prior work we investigated the effect of different levels of type accuracy [17]. Our approach is to modify a garbage collector (particularly the Boehm-Demers-Weiser collector [7, 9]) to accept and use different combinations of type and liveness accuracy information.

One way to conduct this study is to implement a large number of accuracy schemes in a compiler and garbage collector and to compare their performance. However, accuracy schemes are difficult to implement and thus the above mentioned approach would be infeasible. We therefore take a different approach: we implement the accuracy schemes as a upper-bound approximation in a highly parameterized run-time analysis. This approach is easier since at run time we have perfect alias and control-flow information. However, our approach is limited in that it gives us only an upper bound on the usefulness of accuracy schemes and also requires two identical runs of each program. We do not intend our approach to be used directly for leak detection or garbage collection: the goal of our approach is to collect experimental results that will help to drive subsequent work in leak detection and garbage collection.

To increase the applicability of this study, some of our benchmarks use explicit deallocation while others use garbage collection. Benchmarks in the former group include many C programs from the SPECInt95 benchmark suite. Benchmarks in the latter group include Eiffel programs and some C programs that were designed to be used with a customized or conservative garbage collector.

Our results demonstrate that liveness accuracy significantly improves a garbage collector or leak detector's ability to identify dead objects. However we also find that simple liveness analyses (e.g., intraprocedural analysis of local variables [1]) are largely ineffective for our benchmark programs. In order to get a significant benefit one must use a more aggressive liveness analysis that is interprocedural and can analyze global variables. We also show that our most aggressive liveness analysis is able to identify small leaks in several of our benchmark programs.

---

[1] We use the term *object* to include any kind of contiguously allocated data record, such as C structs and arrays as well as objects in the sense of object-oriented programming.

The remainder of the paper is organized as follows. Section 2 defines terminology for use in the remainder of the paper. Section 3 further motivates this work. Section 4 reviews prior work in the area. Section 5 describes our experimental methodology and particularly our liveness analysis. Section 6 presents the experimental results. Section 7 discusses the usefulness of our approach in debugging garbage collectors and leak detectors. Section 8 suggests directions for future work and Section 9 concludes.

2 Background

A garbage collector or leak detector identifies unreachable objects using a *reachability traversal* starting from local and global variables of the program.[2] All objects not reached in the reachability traversal are dead and can be freed. In order to identify the greatest number of dead objects, only *live pointers*, that is, pointers that will be dereferenced in the future, must be traversed. Unfortunately, without prior knowledge of the future of the computation it is impossible to precisely identify live pointers. Thus, reachability traversals use conservative approximations to the set of live pointers. In other words, a realistic reachability traversal may treat a non-pointer or a non-live pointer as a live pointer, and may therefore fail to find all the dead objects. The *accuracy* of a reachability traversal refers to its ability to precisely identify live pointers.

There are two dimensions to accuracy: *type accuracy* and *liveness accuracy*. Type accuracy determines whether or not the reachability traversal can distinguish pointers from non-pointers. Liveness accuracy determines whether or not the reachability traversal can identify variables whose value will be dereferenced in the future. Both dimensions require compiler support.

Figure 1 gives an example of the usefulness of type accuracy. Let's suppose the variables *hash* and *ptr* hold the same value (bit pattern) at program point p_3 even though one is a pointer and the other is an integer. If a reachability traversal is not type accurate it will find that the object allocated at p_2 is reachable at point p_5 since *hash* "points to" it. If, instead, the traversal was type accurate, it would not treat *hash* as a pointer and could reclaim the object allocated at p_2 (garbage collection) or report a leak to the programmer (leak detection).

p_1: **int** *hash* = *hashValue*(...);
p_2: **int** *ptr* = (**int**)(*malloc*(...));
p_3: ⟨code using *∗ptr*⟩
p_4: *ptr* = **null**;
p_5: ...

Fig. 1. Type accuracy example

---

[2] For simplicity, we do not discuss generational collectors which may also do a reachability traversal starting from selected regions of the heap.

Figure 2 gives an example of the usefulness of liveness accuracy. Let's suppose *parse* returns an abstract syntax tree and that after p_6 *ast* holds the only pointer to the tree. Let's suppose that the variable *ast* is not dereferenced at or after program point p_8 (in other words, it is dead). A reachability traversal that does not use liveness information will not detect that the object returned by *parse* is garbage at program point p_8. On the other hand a reachability traversal that uses liveness information will find that *ast* is dead at program point p_8 and will reclaim the tree returned by *parse* (garbage collection) or report it as a leak to the programmer (leak detection).

p_6: *Tree ∗ast = parse*();
p_7: *CFG ∗cfg = translate*(*ast*);
p_8: ⟨code that does not use *ast*⟩

Fig. 2. Liveness accuracy example

A major hindrance to both type or liveness accuracy is that they require significant compiler support. In the case of type accuracy the compiler must preserve type information through all the compiler passes and communicate it to the reachability traversal [12]. In the case of liveness accuracy the compiler must conduct a liveness analysis and communicate the liveness information to the reachability traversal. Unlike type information, a compiler does not need to preserve liveness information through its passes if the liveness analysis is the last pass before code generation.

3   Motivation

Prior work has focused almost exclusively on one aspect of accuracy – the ability to distinguish pointers from non-pointers – and has considered liveness only as an afterthought. By separating the two aspects of accuracy, we can identify accuracy strategies that are different from any that have been proposed before and are worth exploring. For example, consider the problem of garbage collecting C programs. Prior work has simply noted that C is unsafe and thus the garbage collector must be conservative (type-inaccurate). While this is true with respect to the pointer/non-pointer dimension of accuracy, it is not true with respect to the liveness dimension. A collector for C and C++ programs which considers all variables with appropriate values to be pointers would improve (both in efficiency and effectiveness) if it knew which variables were live; variables that are not live need not be considered as pointers at GC time even if they appear to be pointers from their value (see example in Figure 2).

Table 1 enumerates a few of the possible variations in each of the two dimensions of accuracy. If prior work has proposed a particular combination of accuracy, the table also references some of the relevant prior work. Many papers have proposed the *no liveness information/full type accuracy* scheme and so we cite only a few of the relevant papers in the table.

Even in this incomplete table, five out of nine combinations are unexplored in the literature. Several of the unexplored combinations have significant potential for advancing

Table 1. Some variations in the two dimensions of garbage collector accuracy

Level of liveness accuracy	Level of type accuracy		
	None	Partial	Full
None	[6]	[4, 10]	[3, 18, 28]
Intraprocedural for local vars			[1, 2, 12, 27]
Interprocedural for local and global vars	(a)	(b)	(c)

the state of the art in leak detection and garbage collection. For example, consider the combination of *interprocedural liveness for local and global variables* with the three possibilities for *pointer information* (marked (a), (b), and (c) in table). Possibility (a) will be useful for unsafe languages, such as C, since it will allow even a type-inaccurate reachability traversal to ignore certain pointers and thus improve both its precision and efficiency. Possibility (c) will improve over the best type-accurate schemes used for type-safe languages such as Java and Modula-3 [1, 12, 27] since it incorporates liveness of globals which we expect to be much more useful than liveness for local variables. Finally, possibility (b) may be useful for either safe or unsafe languages (with some programmer support).

This paper explores a significant part of the accuracy space in order to better understand the different possibilities for liveness and their usefulness in leak detectors and garbage collectors.

4 Related Work

In this section we review prior work on comparing different garbage collection alternatives, type and liveness accuracy for compiled languages, and leak detection.

Shaham *et al.* [23] and Hirzel and Diwan [17] present work that is most relevant to this paper. Shaham *et al.* evaluate a conservative garbage collector using a limit study: They find that the conservative garbage collector is not effective in reclaiming objects in a timely fashion. However, unlike our work, they do not experimentally determine how much of this is due to type inaccuracy versus liveness inaccuracy, or which level of accuracy would make their underlying garbage collector more effective. Hirzel and Diwan [17] present an investigation of different levels of type accuracy using an earlier version of our framework. They demonstrate that the usefulness of type accuracy in reclaiming objects depends on the architecture. In particular, type accuracy is more important for 32-bit architectures than for 64-bit architectures. Hirzel and Diwan investigate only one dimension of accuracy, namely type accuracy, and ignore liveness accuracy in their study.

Bartlett [4], Zorn [32], Smith and Morrisett [24], and Agesen *et al.* [1] compare different garbage collection alternatives with respect to memory consumption. Bartlett [4] describes versions of his mostly-copying garbage collector that differ in stack accuracy. Zorn [32] compares the Boehm-Demers-Weiser collector to a number of explicit memory management implementations. Smith and Morrisett [24] describe a new mostly-copying garbage collector and compare it to the Boehm-Demers-Weiser collector. All these studies focus on the total heap size. Measuring the total heap size is useful for comparing collectors with the same accuracy, but makes it difficult to tease apart the effects of fragmentation, allocator data structures, and accuracy. Since we are counting bytes in reachable objects instead of total heap size, we are able to look at the effects of garbage collector accuracy in isolation from the other effects. Agesen *et al.* investigate the effect of intraprocedural local variable liveness on the number of reachable bytes after an accurate garbage collection. Besides intraprocedural local-variable liveness we also consider many other kinds of liveness.

Zorn [32], Smith and Morrisett [24], and Hicks *et al.* [16] compare different memory management schemes with respect to their efficiency. Zorn [31] looks at the cache performance of different garbage collectors. We do not look at run-time efficiency but instead concentrate on the effectiveness of garbage collectors in reclaiming objects.

Boehm and Shao [8] describe a technique for obtaining type accuracy for heap objects without compiler support which requires a moderate amount of programmer support. Boehm and Shao do not report any results for the effectiveness of their scheme.

Diwan *et al.* [12], Agesen *et al.* [1], and Stichnoth *et al.* [25] consider how to perform accurate garbage collection in compiled type-safe languages. Diwan *et al.* [12] describe how the compiler and run-time system of Modula-3 can support accurate garbage collection. Agesen *et al.* [1] and Stichnoth *et al.* [25] extend Diwan *et al.*'s work by incorporating liveness into accuracy and allowing garbage collection at *all* points and not just safe points. Even though these papers assume type-safe languages, type accuracy is still difficult to implement especially in the presence of compiler optimizations. Our work identifies what kinds of accuracy are useful for reclaiming objects, which is important for deciding what kinds of accuracy to obtain by compiler analysis. Also, our approach can be used in its current form for identifying leaks in both type-safe and unsafe languages.

Hastings and Joyce [15], Dion and Monier [11], and GreatCircle [13] describe leak detectors based on the Boehm-Demers-Weiser collector [9]. The Boehm-Demers-Weiser collector can also be used as a leak detector [7]. Our scheme uses more accurate information than these detectors and is thus capable of finding more leaks in programs.

5   Methodology

One approach to this study is to implement several different levels of accuracy in a compiler and communicate this information to a reachability traversal. However, because we wanted to experiment with many different levels of accuracy the implementation effort would have been prohibitive since implementing even a single accuracy scheme is a challenging undertaking [12]. We therefore chose a different tactic.

Our basic approach (Figure 3) is to analyze a running program to determine different levels of type and liveness information. This approach is easier than actually building several levels of accuracy since at run time we have perfect aliasing and control flow information. Moreover, at run time we do not have to worry about preserving any information through later optimization passes. An additional advantage is that we can do a direct, detailed, and meaningful comparison between the different memory management schemes. Section 5.1 describes our methodology for collecting type information, and section 5.2 describes our methodology for collecting different levels of liveness information. Section 5.3 introduces the different accuracy levels that we consider in this paper. Section 5.4 shows how we compare the effectiveness of reachability traversals with different levels of accuracy information. Section 5.5 discusses the limitations of our approach. Section 5.6 describes and gives relevant statistics about our benchmark programs.

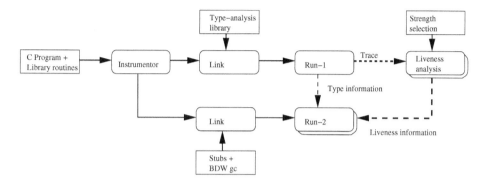

Fig. 3. Framework

5.1 Approach for Type Accuracy

We use the same infrastructure for type accuracy as our previous study on type accuracy [17] so we describe it only briefly here. We convert our C source programs into the SUIF representation [26, 30], instrument the SUIF representation to make calls to a run-time *type-analysis library*, link and run the program (*Run-1*). The type-analysis library precisely tracks the flow of pointers at run time and determines which locations contain pointers. At the end of Run-1, the instrumentation outputs type information in the form of tables that describe which memory locations contain pointers. This information is similar to compiler output in a real garbage collection system for a type-safe language.

Then, we link the same instrumented program with empty stubs instead of the type analysis library and with the Boehm-Demers-Weiser (BDW) garbage collector [7]. We have modified BDW so that it can use the type information during *Run-2*. Since memory addresses of objects may be different in the second run, Run-1 assigns unique identifiers to each heap-allocated object and global variable and uses these identifiers to refer to objects. Run-1 communicates type-accurate information to Run-2 using *location descriptors*, which take one of the following forms:

- $\langle global\_id, offset \rangle$: the global variable identified by *global_id* contains a pointer at *offset*.
- $\langle heap\_id, offset \rangle$: the heap allocated object identified by *heap_id* contains a pointer at *offset*.

– $\langle$proc_name, offset$\rangle$: activation records for the procedure identified by proc_name contain a pointer at offset.

We output the above information for every call and allocation point. We do not output any information about pointers in registers since we force all variables to live in memory; registers serve only as scratch space and never contain pointers to objects that are not also reachable from pointers in memory.

The set-up for type accuracy differs slightly from our earlier work on type accuracy [17] in a few aspects. We exclude the activation records of the BDW garbage collector itself from the root set of the reachability traversal. We found and fixed a leak in the BDW collector. Finally, we force the heap to start at a slightly higher address in Run-2 to minimize interference with the data structures needed by our infrastructure.

5.2 Approach for Liveness

Besides generating type information, Run-1 also outputs a trace of events. We analyze this trace to obtain liveness information. In addition to type information, Run-2 can also use the liveness information to improve the precision of its reachability traversals.

Our analysis of the trace mirrors the actions of a traditional backward-flow liveness analysis in a compiler. Like a traditional data-flow liveness analysis, there are two main events in our run-time analysis: uses and definitions. Uses, such as pointer dereferences, make a memory location live at points immediately before the use. Definitions, such as assignments, make the defined memory location dead just before the definition. The run-time analysis is parametrized so that it can realistically simulate a range of static analyses.

Format of the Trace. The trace consists of a sequence of events that are recorded as the program executes. Table 2 describes the kinds of events in a trace. The events in the trace are designed to enable different flavors of liveness analysis.

Some events (such as "assign") refer to memory locations. The trace represents the memory locations using *location descriptor instances* instead of location descriptors as described in Section 5.1, because we need to distinguish between multiple instances of a local variable. Each global location descriptor has only one instance but local location descriptors have multiple instances, one for each invocation of the local variable's enclosing procedure. Each local location descriptor instance, besides identifying its location descriptor, has an attribute, *Home*, which identifies the activation record for which the instance was created. Section 5.2 demonstrates how maintaining location descriptor instances avoids imprecision in analyzing recursive calls.

Basic Algorithm. To obtain liveness information, we perform an analysis on the event trace. In a nutshell, we read the sequence of events in reverse order and keep track of which locations are live at any point during program execution. This approach reflects the fact that liveness of pointers depends on the future, not the past, of the computation.

Our algorithm maintains two data structures: *currentlyLive* and *resultingLiveness*. For each location descriptor instance ℓ, *currentlyLive*(ℓ) indicates whether it is live at

Table 2. Trace events

Event	Example	Description
$assign(lhs, rhs_1, \ldots, rhs_n)$	$x = y + z$	Assignment to location *lhs* from the locations $rhs_1 \ldots rhs_n$. Used to represent normal assignments, parameter passing, and assignment of return value of a call.
$use(rhs)$	$\ldots * x \ldots$	Use of location *rhs*. A pointer dereference is a use. Also passing a parameter to an external function is a use of the parameter.
$call()$	$\overset{\rightarrow}{} f(\ldots)$	Call to a procedure.
$return()$	$\rightarrow f(\ldots)$	Return from a procedure. (For a longjmp, we generate several *return*-events.)
$allocation(p)$	$malloc(\ldots)$	Allocation of heap object number p (numbered consecutively since program startup).

the current point in the analysis. In other words, as the analysis processes the trace events in reverse order, it keeps track of what is live at any given point of the original execution of the benchmark. The *resultingLiveness* data structure maintains liveness information that will be output at the end of the program. When the liveness analysis finishes, for a stack location descriptor s, $resultingLiveness(s) \equiv \{cs_1, \ldots, cs_n\}$ is the set of call sites where s is live, and for a global location descriptor g, $resultingLiveness(g) \equiv \{p_1, \ldots, p_m\}$ is the set of dynamic calls to malloc where g is live (these include the points where we do reachability traversals in Run-2). We use stack location descriptors rather than stack location descriptor instances in *resultingLiveness* to keep the output of the analysis manageable. Note that we output more precise information for globals than for stack variables since maintaining such detailed information for stack locations was infeasible.

As the liveness analysis is processing the trace, it also also tracks the call point at which each active procedure is stopped. For instance, if procedure p calls q, within the body of q the stopping point for the activation record of p will be the call to q within p. Given location description instance x, $HomeCS(x)$ gives the stopping point of the *Home* activation record of x.

Our analysis never directly reads the *currentlyLive* flags, but instead uses the function *isLive*, which defaults to

$$\textbf{proc } isLive(\ell) \; \{ \; \textbf{return } currentlyLive(\ell); \; \}$$

In Section 5.2, we describe how *isLive* helps to obtain selective liveness.

Table 3 gives the actions that the liveness analysis performs on each event. The actions for *assign* and *use* are similar to the corresponding transfer functions that a compile-time liveness analysis would use. The actions for *call* are, however, more complex, and we motivate and describe them in Section 5.2.

Our algorithm works by keeping the *currentlyLive* flags up-to-date for all locations ℓ. The intuition here is that ℓ must be live prior to any potential dereference of the value it contains; i.e., a *use*, *assign* to another live location, or *call* of an external function that sees ℓ. When the analysis has completed, it outputs each location descriptor along with its *resultingLiveness*.

Table 3. Liveness analysis

Event	Action
$assign(lhs, rhs_1, \ldots, rhs_n)$	If $isLive(lhs) \equiv$ **true**, then make $currentlyLive(rhs_1), \ldots,$ $currentlyLive(rhs_n)$ true. If none of the rhs_i is the same as the lhs, make $currentlyLive$ false for lhs.
$use(rhs)$	Make $currentlyLive$ true for the location descriptor instance rhs.
$call()$	If this is an external call, for each externally visible location ℓ, make $currentlyLive(\ell)$ true. Then, for each stack location descriptor instance s with $isLive(s) \equiv$ **true**, add $HomeCS(s)$ to the *resultingLiveness* of s's location descriptor.
$return()$	Initialize data structures (such as ones that record the stopping points).
$allocation(p)$	For each global location ℓ with $isLive(\ell) \equiv$ **true**, add the dynamic program point p to the *resultingLiveness* of ℓ.

Analyzing Call Events. To understand the reason for the complexity in analyzing calls, consider the a run of the code segment in Figure 4 where f calls itself recursively just once. Consider the most recent invocation of f (which must be in the *else* branch, since in this example, f recurses just once). The expression $**b$ dereferences the variable c but *from the previous call to f*. Thus, c from the previous invocation of f is live at the recursive call to f. However, even though $**b$ dereferences c, it does not dereference the most recent instance of c and thus, c is not live at the call to g. Calls are the most complex to analyze since that's where we handle such situations precisely.

```
int a;
int **b;
void f(){
    int *c;              /* uninitialized */
    if(...){
        b = &c;
        f();
    else{
        *b = &a;
        g();             /* call site cg */
        ... **b ...;
    }
}
```

Fig. 4. Recursive call example

The intuition for how we handle calls is as follows. The liveness analysis maintains the *currentlyLive* flags for all location descriptor instances based on the actions in Table 3. When the liveness analysis encounters a call event, it updates the *resultingLiveness* of all stack instances that are live at that call. To update the *resultingLiveness* for a live instance x, it adds $HomeCS(x)$ to $resultingLiveness(x)$. In other words, call events are the points where we summarize the information in *isLive* into *resultingLiveness*.

Let's consider what happens when we apply our method to the execution of the code in Figure 4. As before, consider a run of the code in where f calls itself recursively just once. Table 4 shows an event trace (in reverse order) of the above program along with the actions our liveness analysis will take. For some events (such as returns) we do not list any actions since these events serve to simply initialize auxiliary data structures. During the trace generation we create two instances of the location descriptor for local variable c: c_1 for the first call to f and c_2 for the second call to f. Note however that our algorithm adds to the *resultingLiveness* of c on behalf of c_1 and not on behalf of c_2. This is correct and precise since c_2 is not dereferenced (or assigned to a variable that is dereferenced) in this run.

Table 4. Processing a trace of the example program

Event	Comment	Analysis action
11: *return*()	outer f returns	
10: *return*()	inner f returns to outer f	
9: *use*(b)	deref of b	$currentlyLive(b) \leftarrow$ **true**
8: *use*(c_1)	deref of $*b \equiv c_1$	$currentlyLive(c_1) \leftarrow$ **true**
7: *return*()	g returns to inner f	
6: *call*()	inner f calls g	add $HomeCS(c_1)$ to $resultingLiveness(c)$
5: *use*(b)	deref of b	$currentlyLive(b) \leftarrow$ **true**
4: *assign*(c_1)	assign to $*b \equiv c_1$	$currentlyLive(c_1) \leftarrow$ **false**
	else-part in inner f	
3: *call*()	outer f calls inner f	no locals live, nothing happens!
2: *assign*(b)	assign to b	$currentlyLive(b) \leftarrow$ **false**
	then-part in outer f	
1: *call*()	call to outer f	

Selective Liveness. We consider three dimensions that determine the precision of liveness: (i) the region of memory for which we have liveness information (stack, heap, and globals), (ii) whether we compute liveness only for scalar variables or also for record fields and array elements (i.e., *aggregates*), and (iii) whether we compute liveness information intraprocedurally or interprocedurally. We now describe how we vary the above dimensions in the algorithm from Section 5.2.

By changing the implementation of *isLive* we can select the precision level of the first two dimensions. For example, suppose we wish to compute liveness information for scalars in the stack, then we use the implementation of *isLive* in Figure 5. In other words, for those regions of memory and kinds of variables where we do not want liveness information, we assume they are always live.

```
proc isLive(ℓ){
    if(ℓ ∈ Stack and ℓ ∈ ScalarVars)
        then return currentlyLive(ℓ);
        else return true;
}
```

Fig. 5. *isLive* when computing liveness for scalars in stack

By changing what calls are to external routines we can select the precision of the third dimension. For example, if we wish to mimic intraprocedural analysis then we consider all calls as being to external routines. The action for the *call()*-event in Table 3 will therefore make all externally visible locations (heap locations, global locations, or stack locations whose address gets taken) live at all calls. For interprocedural analysis all calls are to non-external routines. We handle library routines by providing stubs that mimic their behavior.

5.3   Accuracy Levels in This Paper

Table 5. Schemes evaluated

	Area of memory	
	Stack	Stack+Globals
No type accuracy		
None	(N, N)	(N, N)
Intraprocedural scalars	(N, i_s^{scalar})	$(N, i_{sg}^{\text{scalar}})$
Intraprocedural all	(N, i_s^{all})	(N, i_{sg}^{all})
Interprocedural scalars	(N, I_s^{scalar})	$(N, I_{sg}^{\text{scalar}})$
Interprocedural all	(N, I_s^{all})	(N, I_{sg}^{all})
With type accuracy		
None	(T, N)	(T, N)
Intraprocedural scalars	(T, i_s^{scalar})	$(T, i_{sg}^{\text{scalar}})$
Intraprocedural all	(T, i_s^{all})	(T, i_{sg}^{all})
Interprocedural scalars	(T, I_s^{scalar})	$(T, I_{sg}^{\text{scalar}})$
Interprocedural all	(T, I_s^{all})	(T, I_{sg}^{all})

Table 5 gives the schemes that we evaluate in this paper along with abbreviations for the schemes. The first part of the table lists schemes that do not include type accuracy but may include liveness accuracy. The second part of the table lists schemes that include type accuracy and may also include liveness. The entries in the table are pairs, the first element of which gives the level of type accuracy ($(N, \cdot)$ are schemes with no type accuracy and $(T, \cdot)$ are schemes with type accuracy) and the second element gives the level of liveness accuracy. The "intraprocedural" configurations $(\cdot, i.)$ assume the worst case for all externally visible variables (globals and locals whose address has been taken) while the "interprocedural" configurations $(\cdot, I.)$ analyze across procedure boundaries for externally visible variables. The "scalars" $(\cdot, \cdot^{\text{scalar}})$ configurations compute liveness information only for scalar variables whereas the "all" $(\cdot, \cdot^{\text{all}})$ configurations compute it for all scalar variables, record fields, and array elements. The "stack" configurations $(\cdot, \cdot_s)$ compute liveness information only for stack variables whereas the "stack and globals" $(\cdot, \cdot_{sg})$ configurations compute it for locations on the stack and for statically allocated variables. While the abbreviations from Table 5 identify accuracy levels, we will sometimes use them to mean the number of bytes occupied by reachable objects when using that accuracy level.

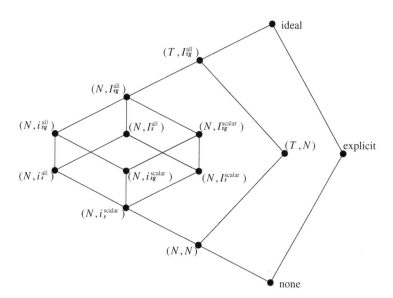

Fig. 6. Memory Management Schemes. Each node in this graph is a memory management scheme. An edge indicates that the scheme with the lower vertical position is strictly weaker than the scheme with the higher vertical position.

Figure 6 presents accuracy schemes organized as a lattice. The order is by strength, with the strongest scheme at the top and the weakest scheme at the bottom.

Note that we decided not to look at liveness for the heap. To see why, let us first imagine what it would mean in our context. Let $\langle heap\_id, offset \rangle$ be a heap location. If we had heap-accurate liveness for aggregates, we might for example know that even though the heap object $heap\_id$ contains a pointer at $offset$, that pointer will not be used in the future. But getting this information poses at least two challenges. First, in order to compute heap liveness we need a precise pointer analysis which is often prohibitively expensive. Second, how to communicate the heap liveness information to the garbage collector? A precise pointer analysis may create many instances of each allocation site and the information may therefore get to be very large. With our trace-based approach, we could of course have obtained heap liveness information, but given the difficulty of obtaining it at compile time, our results would have been a very loose upper bound. Thus, we omitted a study of heap liveness for this paper.

5.4 Measurement Methodology

To collect our numbers, we execute Run-2 multiple times for each benchmark, once for each liveness scheme. To facilitate comparison of the different accuracy schemes, we trigger the reachability traversal at the same time for each level of accuracy. For this study we trigger a reachability traversal every A/n bytes of allocation where A is the total allocation throughout the benchmark run and $n = 50$. Thus for each program and accuracy scheme we end up with a vector of approximately 50 numbers representing the reachable bytes found at each traversal. To compare two liveness schemes, we simply subtract their vectors to determine how they compare at each traversal. The numbers we present in Section 6 are typically averages computed over the difference vectors.

Here is an example for our metric, where for simplicity we assume $n = 3$. Let the conservative garbage collector (N, N) encounter $(100, 200, 200)$ bytes in reachable heap objects after its three collections. Let our strongest liveness scheme (N, I_{sg}^{all}) encounter $(100, 180, 160)$ bytes in reachable heap objects after its three collections. We write $\text{avg} \frac{(N,N)-(N,I_{sg}^{all})}{(N,N)}$ to mean $\frac{1}{n} \left(\frac{(N,N)_1-(N,I_{sg}^{all})_1}{(N,N)_1} + \ldots + \frac{(N,N)_n-(N,I_{sg}^{all})_n}{(N,N)_n} \right)$, which is $\frac{1}{3} \left(\frac{100-100}{100} + \frac{200-180}{200} + \frac{200-160}{200} \right) = 10\%$ in our concrete example. In other words, with strong liveness accuracy, the heap would on average be 10% smaller after garbage collections.

An alternative metric is to measure the heap size (including fragmentation and GC data structures) or the process footprint instead of bytes in reachable heap objects. These are useful metrics but unfortunately not ones we can measure easily in our infrastructure since our instrumentation and extensions to the Boehm-Demers-Weiser collector increase the memory requirements of the host program.

5.5 Limitations

The two main limitations of our approach are: (i) it is a limit study and thus not guaranteed to expose the *realizable* potential of liveness, and (ii) our instrumentation may perturb program behavior and thus, we could suffer from Heisenberg's uncertainty principle.

Our results are an upper bound on the usefulness of liveness information because our analysis has perfect alias information, and because a location may not be live in a particular run, even though there exists a run where it is live. To reduce the possibility of having large errors of this sort, we ran a selection of our benchmarks on multiple inputs and compared the results across the inputs. Section 6.5 presents these results.

Also, we spent significant time manually inspecting the output of our liveness analysis when it yielded a significant benefit. While our manual inspection was not exhaustive (or anywhere close), we found no situations where our liveness analysis' results were specific only to a particular run.

The methodology that we use to obtain our data influences the results itself because we force all local variables to live on the stack, even when they could otherwise have been allocated in registers. Register allocation in a conventional compiler may use its own liveness analysis and may reuse the register assigned to a variable if that variable is dead. Thus, at garbage collection time the dead pointer is not around anymore. In other words, the compiler is passing liveness information to the garbage collector implicitly by modifying the code rather than explicitly. Since register allocators typically use only intraprocedural liveness analysis of scalars, this effect is likely to be strictly weaker than our intraprocedural liveness scheme for scalars on the stack.

5.6 Benchmarks

We used three criteria to select our benchmark programs. First, we picked benchmarks that performed significant heap allocation. Second, we picked benchmarks that we thought would demonstrate the difference between accurate and inaccurate garbage collection. For example, we picked *anagram* since it uses bit vectors which may end up looking like pointers to a conservative garbage collector. Third, we included a number of object-oriented benchmarks.

Table 6 describes our benchmark programs. *Lang.* gives the source language of the benchmark programs. *Lines* gives the number of lines in the source code of the program (including comments and blank lines). *Total alloc.* gives the number of bytes allocated throughout the execution of the program. Two of our benchmarks, *gctest* and *gctest3*, are designed to test garbage collectors [4, 5]. These benchmarks both allocate and create garbage at a rapid rate. The original version of these programs contained explicit calls to the garbage collector. We removed these calls to allow garbage collection to be automatically invoked. The benchmarks *bshift*, *erbt*, *ebignum*, and *gegrep* are Eiffel programs that we translated into C with the GNU Eiffel compiler SmallEiffel. We used the option -no_gc and linked the generated C code up with our collector. Likewise, we disabled the garbage collector included in the Lisp interpreter *li* from the SPECInt95 benchmark suite to use our collector instead. The remaining programs use standard C allocation and deallocation to manage memory. We conducted all our experiments on a AMD Athlon workstation.

Due to the prohibitive cost of our analyses,[3] we had to pick relatively short runs for most of the programs. However, for those programs where we were able to do both shorter and longer runs, we found little difference between the two runs as far as our results are concerned.

---

[3] Some of these benchmarks take over 24 hours on a 850 MHz Athlon with 512MB of memory to run all the configurations.

Table 6. Benchmarks

Name	Lang.	Lines	Total alloc.	Main data structures	Workload
Programs written with gc in mind:					
gctest3	C	85	2 200 004	lists and arrays	loop to 20,000
gctest	C	196	1 123 180	lists and trees	only repeat 5 in listtest2
bshift	Eiffel	350	28 700	dlists	scales 2 through 7
erbt	Eiffel	927	222 300	red-black trees	50 trees with 500 nodes each
ebignum	Eiffel	3 137	109 548	arrays	twice the included test-stub
li	C	7 597	9 030 872	cons cells	`nqueens.lsp`, $n = 7$
gegrep	Eiffel	17 185	106 392	DFAs	`'[A-Za-z]+\-[A-Za-z]+'` t
Programs with explicit deallocation:					
anagram	C	647	259 512	lists and bitfields	`words < input.in`
ks	C	782	7 920	D-arrays and lists	`KL-2.in`
ft	C	2 156	166 832	graphs	`1000 2000`
yacr2	C	3 979	41 380	arrays and structures	`input4.in`
bc	C	7 308	12 382 400	abstract syntax trees	find primes smaller 500
gzip	C	8 163	14 180	Huffman trees	`-d texinfo.tex.gz`
ijpeg	C	31 211	148 664	various image repn.	`testinput.ppm -GO`

6   Results

We now present experimental results to answer the following questions about the usefulness of liveness for garbage collection and leak detection:

1. Does liveness enable us to identify more garbage objects?
2. How does liveness accuracy compare to type accuracy in reclaiming objects?
3. How powerful should a liveness analysis be before it is useful?
4. Do our more powerful liveness schemes allow us to find more memory leaks in our benchmarks?

Sections 6.1, 6.2, 6.3, and 6.4 present results to answer the above questions. Section 6.5 validates our methodology. Section 6.6 discusses the implications of our results for garbage collectors and leak detectors. Finally, Section 6.7 summarizes our results.

6.1   Usefulness of Liveness

In this section we consider whether liveness enables the reachability traversal to detect more of the dead objects as compared to a reachability traversal that does not use liveness information. Table 7 compares our strongest liveness scheme, (N, I_{sg}^{all}), to no liveness, (N, N). To make this and other tables in this paper easier to read we leave all zero entries blank. Note that there are still some "0" entries in the table: these entries represent values that are less than 1% but not zero.

The first column of Table 7 gives the benchmark program. The second column gives the additional unreachable bytes that (N, I_{sg}^{all}) identifies over (N, N) as a percent of the bytes that (N, N) identifies as reachable. The data in this column is an average over the data collected at each of the reachability traversals. A non-empty cell in this column means that (N, I_{sg}^{all}) identified more unreachable bytes than (N, N). An empty cell in this column means that (N, N) performed as well as (N, I_{sg}^{all}). The third column gives an indication of the increased memory requirement of (N, N) over (N, I_{sg}^{all}): it compares the maximum number of bytes that are reachable with the two schemes as a percent of the maximum number of bytes that are reachable with (N, N). The fourth column gives the percent of reachability traversals after which (N, I_{sg}^{all}) retained fewer objects than (N, N). Recall that we trigger reachability traversals approximately 50 times for each benchmark run (Section 5.4). A non-empty cell in this column means that at some traversals (N, I_{sg}^{all}) identified more unreachable bytes than (N, N).

Table 7. Usefulness of liveness

Benchmark avg	$\frac{(N,N)-(N,I_{sg}^{all})}{(N,N)}$%	$\frac{\max(N,N)-\max(N,I_{sg}^{all})}{\max(N,N)}$%	$\frac{\text{Traversals different}}{\text{Num traversals}}$%
gctest3	0	0	79
gctest			
bshift	42	23	94
erbt	19	6	98
ebignum	13	18	87
li	0		2
gegrep	59	43	98
anagram			
ks			
ft			
yacr2	21	15	90
bc	2	0	98
gzip	11	17	50
ijpeg	1		20

From Table 7 we see that (N, I_{sg}^{all}) benefits 10 out of our 14 benchmark programs. For two of the programs (*gctest3* and *li*) the improvement due to liveness is small. For six of the programs (*bshift*, *erbt*, *ebignum*, *gegrep*, *yacr2*, and *gzip*) liveness reduces the maximum number of reachable bytes by up to 43%. From the fourth column we see that several of the programs leak memory for most of the execution (i.e., the leaks, on average, are not short lived). Thus from these numbers we conclude that liveness (at least in its most aggressive form) has the potential to significantly improve the effectiveness of garbage collectors and leak detectors.

6.2   Liveness versus Type Accuracy

In this section we investigate the individual and cumulative benefits of type and liveness accuracy. Table 8 compares reachability traversals using type accuracy only $((T, N))$, liveness accuracy only $((N, I_{sg}^{all}))$, and both type accuracy and the best liveness accuracy

$((T, I_{sg}^{all}))$. The columns of this table present the difference between the bytes retained by (N, N) and the bytes retained by (T, N), (N, I_{sg}^{all}), and (T, I_{sg}^{all}) as a percent of the bytes retained by (N, N). As with Table 7, the data in Table 8 is an average across all the reachability traversals in a program run. Column 3 of this table is the same as Column 2 of Table 7.

Table 8. Liveness and type accuracy. All benchmarks that see no benefit from liveness or type accuracy are omitted.

Benchmark	avg $\frac{(N,N)-(T,N)}{(N,N)}$ %	avg $\frac{(N,N)-(N,I_{sg}^{all})}{(N,N)}$ %	avg $\frac{(N,N)-(T,I_{sg}^{all})}{(N,N)}$ %
gctest3		0	0
bshift		42	42
erbt		19	19
ebignum	0	13	13
li		0	0
gegrep		59	59
yacr2		21	21
bc		2	2
gzip	1	11	12
ijpeg	1	1	1

From Table 8 we see that just adding type information to a reachability traversal yields relatively modest improvements for these benchmark runs (though type accuracy may yield greater benefits on other architectures [17]). In comparison there is a significant benefit to using liveness information in a reachability traversal. From Column 4 we see that there is little benefit to adding type information to liveness for identifying dead objects. In other words, the information that the aggressive liveness analysis computes is sufficient for identifying live pointers. There may, however, be performance benefits to type information since a type-accurate collector can compact reachable memory and thus affect its memory system behavior.

6.3   Strength of Liveness Analysis

In this section we investigate the usefulness of different levels of liveness. Since more precise liveness information is more difficult to implement and expensive to compute, it is important to determine the point of diminishing return for liveness. Table 9 gives the impact of the precision of liveness information on the reachability traversal's ability to identify dead objects. Table 9 is divided into two parts: *Stack liveness* presents the data when we compute liveness only for variables on the stack and *Stack and global liveness* presents the data when we compute liveness for variables on the stack and global variables. Each part has three columns. The first column of each part is the baseline: it shows the benefit of computing simple liveness (i.e., only for scalar variables and using an intraprocedural analysis). We compute the first column of each section in the same manner as the columns of Table 8. The second and third columns of each section indicate how the value in the first column would increase if we used interprocedural liveness and computed liveness for elements of aggregate variables (i.e., record fields and array elements). There was no benefit to analyzing aggregates in an intraprocedural analysis of stack or global variables and thus we omitted those columns from the table.

Table 9. Varying the strength of the liveness analysis. Columns 2 and 5 (baseline) give the benefit of intraprocedural liveness of scalars for stack and globals. Columns 3, 4, 6, and 7 give the additional benefit of interprocedural analysis and analysis of aggregates over their corresponding baselines. All benchmarks that see benefit from neither liveness nor type accuracy are omitted.

Program	Stack liveness			Stack and global liveness		
	avg $\frac{(N,N)-(N,i_s^{\text{scalar}})}{(N,N)}$%	+IP	+IP+aggr	avg $\frac{(N,N)-(N,i_{sg}^{\text{scalar}})}{(N,N)}$%	+IP	+IP+aggr
gctest3	0			0		
bshift	0			0	3	42
erbt					1	19
ebignum	13	0	0	13	0	0
li					0	0
gegrep	0	9	9	0	23	58
yacr2	0			1	20	20
bc	0			0	1	2
gzip		11	11			11
ijpeg			1			1

From Table 9 we see that there is little or no benefit from adding intraprocedural stack liveness for our benchmarks. This is consistent with behavior observed by Agesen *et al.* [1]. Indeed, until we do an interprocedural analysis we get almost no benefit from stack liveness. Note that once we have added interprocedural liveness, analyzing aggregates helps only slightly. Thus, if one is implementing only a stack analysis, then the best bet is to implement an interprocedural liveness analysis and not bother with analyzing non-scalars.

The majority of the benefit of liveness analysis comes from analyzing global variables (see second set of columns in Table 9). The relative importance of local and global variable liveness is not too surprising: unlike local variables, global variables are around for the entire lifetime of the program and thus a dead pointer in a global variable will have a much bigger impact on reachability traversal than a dead pointer in a (relatively short lived) local variable. However, even for global variables, liveness analysis yields little benefit unless the liveness analysis is interprocedural. The cumulative impact of adding aggregate and interprocedural analysis is greater than the sum of the parts. For example, in benchmark *bshift* the benefit of interprocedural analysis is 3% and the benefit of analyzing aggregates is 0%, but the benefit of adding both is 42%.

Figure 7 illustrates how the combined effect of analyzing aggregates and interprocedural analysis is greater than the sum of their parts. In this example s is a global record. Assume for this example that the fields of s are used consistently with their types. If we analyze procedure f using an interprocedural analysis without aggregates then we would have to conclude that the two fields of s may contain pointers at the call to g since the analysis is conservative about record fields. If we analyze procedure f using an intraprocedural liveness analysis that analyzes aggregates then once again we would have to conclude that the fields of s may contain live pointers at the call to g since the intraprocedural analysis assumes the worst case for calls. Only when we analyze procedure f using an interprocedural liveness analysis that analyzes aggregates are we able to determine that the fields of s do not contain pointers.

> **var** s : **record** i : **ref int**; j : **ref int**; **end**
> **proc** $f()$
> $\ldots$
>   **call** $g()$
> $\ldots$

Fig. 7. Example of the synergy between analyzing aggregates and doing interprocedural analysis

To summarize, Figure 8 shows both the theoretical (Figure 8(a)) and experimental (Figure 8(b)) relationship between the different liveness analyses. Figure 8(a) is the segment of Figure 6 that contains the liveness accurate memory management schemes. Figure 8(b) is the same graph, but with a different interpretation of vertical position. For each scheme S in (b), the vertical position corresponds to the metric $\mathrm{avg}\frac{(N,N)-S}{(N,N)}\%$, which is explained in Section 5.4. The horizontal lines in Figure 8(b) connect accuracy schemes that differ in strength only theoretically but not in our experiments.

6.4   Effectiveness in Finding Leaks

The previous sections shed light on the impact of different kinds of liveness information on garbage reclamation or leak detection. In this section we discuss whether or not liveness was able to identify leaks in any of our benchmark programs. We define a *leak* as an object that is never deallocated by the original program but could have been deallocated before the program ended. This is a rather weak notion of leaks, however, since it does not incorporate *timeliness* of deallocation. For example, if an object becomes useless early in the program and is not explicitly deallocated till much later it would not qualify as a leak under our definition.

Of our seven benchmarks that use explicit deallocation (*anagram, ks, ft, yacr2, bc, gzip,* and *ijpeg*) (N, I_{sg}^{all}) found leaks in *yacr2, bc,* and *ijpeg*. Of these, the leaks in *bc* and *ijpeg* are an insignificant percentage of total allocation (less than 1%). The leak in *yacr2* however is significant and accounts for 60% of total allocation (i.e., 60% of of the space is leakage). Since *yacr2* does only a modest amount of total allocation in our run, a leak of 60% is not as critical as it sounds. However, it is important to keep in mind that most of the benchmarks we used (particularly the C codes) are well-established and well-studied programs; thus it would have been surprising to find significant leaks in them.

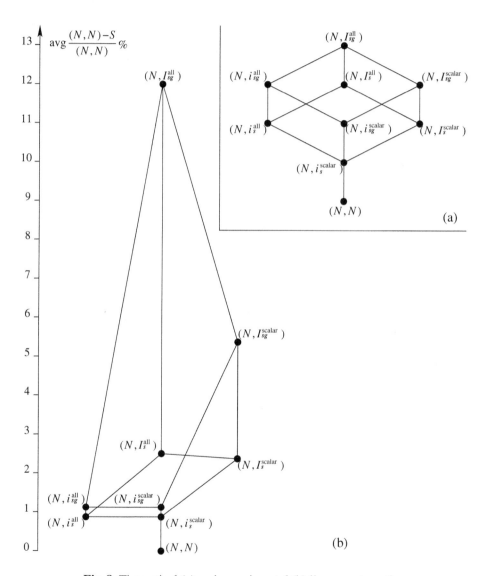

Fig. 8. Theoretical (a) and experimental (b) liveness strength.

6.5   Validation of Our Methodology

Our approach extracts liveness information from a single run of the program and thus it is possible that the liveness information is specific only to that run. In this section we consider how the liveness information varies across runs. A high variation means that our methodology is computing loose upper bounds and thus is severely limited in its usefulness.

To investigate the variation across runs, we ran three benchmarks with a different input and compared the results to our previous runs. If a stack or global location had a different liveness at any point in the two runs we counted that location as "different". Table 10 gives the stack and global locations that are different as a percent of total stack and global locations when using (N, I_{sg}^{all}). The results for other levels of accuracy are similar or better. As with our other tables, we leave the "0" entries blank; 0.0 in this table means that the value is smaller than 0.1% but not 0.

Table 10. Number of stack and global locations that are different as a percent of total static stack and global locations

Benchmark	Stack Count	Stack % different	Global Count	Global % different
gegrep	30484	0.7	48717	0.0
yacr2	586	2.7	384	
gzip	2075	1.3	84158	2.2

From Table 10 we see that there is little difference between the liveness information for our two runs. We also measured the effectiveness of different levels of accuracy in identifying dead objects (similarly to Table 7). We found that the results were identical for the two runs in terms of the relative usefulness of the different accuracy schemes. The number of bytes that each liveness scheme was able to identify as dead was of course different between the two runs. Thus, it is likely that our run-time methodology is computing a tight upper bound.

6.6   Implications for Leak Detection and GC

Our results demonstrate that a liveness-accurate reachability traversal will find many more dead bytes than one that is not liveness accurate *even if it is type accurate*. Particularly, even garbage collectors and leak detectors written for unsafe programs can be much more effective with strong liveness information.

A significant advantage of liveness accuracy over type accuracy is that it is more widely applicable since it does not require a compiler to propagate liveness information across its optimization passes and also it does not require type-safe languages. One could even imagine using it to null out pointers in the source code instead of communicating it to the garbage collector in form of tables. Yet the benefits (in reclaiming objects) of liveness information are even greater than the benefits of type information.

Thus, we believe that a liveness analysis deserves to become an integral part of garbage collectors and leak detectors.

6.7 Summary of Results

Our results demonstrate that while liveness accuracy significantly improves a reachability traversal's ability to identify dead objects, the simpler liveness analyses are rarely useful. For liveness accuracy to have a significant impact, the liveness analysis must analyze both local and global variables and use an interprocedural analysis. Adding analysis of aggregate variables further improves interprocedural liveness of local and global variables but has no impact on intraprocedural liveness.

7 Experiences

Besides demonstrating that certain kinds of liveness can be valuable in identifying dead objects, our experiments also had an unexpected side effect: they enabled us to identify leaks in the BDW collector [7]. The BDW collector is a mature and extremely useful tool that has been used heavily by a large user community for over 10 years and there are even commercial leak detection products that are based on this collector [11]. Thus we were surprised to find any leaks in this collector. Our experience leads us to believe that experiments such as ours may be valuable to implementors of garbage collectors and leak detectors in fine tuning their systems.

Broadly speaking there are two kinds of bugs in a garbage collector or leak detector: (i) it can incorrectly identify a live object as dead and (ii) it can fail to identify a dead object. The existence of a bug of the first kind, particularly in a garbage collector, will probably be exposed quickly since freeing a live object will cause the program to exhibit unexpected behavior or to crash. The existence of a bug of the second kind is much harder to detect since it does not cause the program to crash: it just causes the program to use more memory. Since most programmers treat a garbage collector as a black box, they will not realize if the leak is due to a bug in the garbage collector or if it is due to an unfortunate pointer in their own code. All bugs we found in the BDW collector were of the second kind.

How did our experiments help us in finding leaks in the BDW collector? We experimented with a wide range of variations in the BDW collector, some of which minor (such as intraprocedural liveness of local scalar variables) and some of which significant (such as ones involving interprocedural analysis). We discovered the leaks when we saw behavior in one of our variations that did not make sense. For instance, in one case we found that incorporating intraprocedural liveness of global and local variables found many more dead objects than intraprocedural liveness for just local variables. When we tried to imagine how such a situation could happen we ended up with contrived examples which seemed unlikely to appear in real programs. Thus, we investigated further and found the source of the problem: the BDW collector was mistakenly using some of its own global variables as roots. When we provided liveness information for globals to the BDW collector it circumvented BDW's mechanism for finding roots in global variables and thus avoided this problem.

To summarize, garbage collectors and leak detectors are notoriously hard to write and debug. Our experimental methodology provides implementors of these tools with an additional mechanism for identifying potential performance problems.

8   Future Work

Our work demonstrates that while liveness is useful for both garbage collection and leak detection our method is not practical for real-world applications since it requires two identical runs. To remedy this we are working on a compiler support for computing liveness information that obviates the need for two runs at the loss of some precision. We expect that this will not only result in a reachability traversal that users can use for leak detection or garbage collection but it will also allow us to run much larger experiments with liveness. The results in this paper will guide us in determining what kinds of compiler analyses to build in order to improve the effectiveness of reachability traversals.

A limitation of our current infrastructure is that it can handle only C programs or programs that can be converted into C. Given that Java is the current mainstream language that uses garbage collection it would be worthwhile to repeat a similar set of experiments for Java programs. Java programs may behave quite differently from C or Eiffel programs and thus the results may be different for Java programs. We tried using Toba [22] to translate Java programs to C and then use them as benchmarks for this study. Unfortunately the C code that Toba generates even for tiny applications is too large for our infrastructure (since it includes not just the user program but also the Java standard libraries). We are now moving our analysis infrastructure to the Jalapeño JVM [2] which will allow us to experiment with Java programs.

9   Conclusions

We describe a detailed investigation of the impact of liveness and type accuracy on the effectiveness of garbage collectors and leak detectors. By separating the two dimensions of accuracy—*type accuracy* and *liveness accuracy*—we are able to identify interesting new accuracy schemes that have not been investigated in the literature. We use a novel methodology that uses a trace-based analysis to enable us to easily experiment with a wide range of liveness schemes.

Our experiments reveal that liveness can have a significant impact on the ability of a garbage collector or leak detector in identifying dead objects. However, we show that the simple liveness schemes are largely ineffective: we need to use an aggressive liveness scheme that incorporates interprocedural analysis of global variables before we see a significant benefit. Our aggressive liveness schemes are also able to find memory leaks in our suite of well-studied benchmarks.

Acknowledgements

We thank the anonymous reviewers for their helpful comments and suggestions. We also thank Michael Hind and Urs Hoelzle for comments on a draft of this paper, and John DeTreville for fruitful discussions about our methodology and results.

References

[1] Ole Agesen, David Detlefs, and J. Eliot B. Moss. Garbage collection and local variable type-precision and liveness in Java virtual machines. In *ACM conference on programming language design and implementation*, pages 269–279, Montreal, Canada, June 1998.

[2] Bowen Alpern *et al.* The Jalapeño virtual machine. *IBM Systems Journal*, 39(1):211–238, February 2000.

[3] Andrew W. Appel. A Runtime System. *Lisp and Symbolic Computation*, 3(4):343–380, November 1990.

[4] Joel F. Bartlett. Compacting garbage collection with ambiguous roots. Technical Report 88/2, DEC Western Research Laboratory, Palo Alto, CA, February 1988. Also in *Lisp Pointers* 1(6):2-12, April-June 1988.

[5] Joel F. Bartlett. Mostly-copying garbage collection picks up generations and C++. Technical report, DEC Western Research Laboratory, Palo Alto, CA, October 1989.

[6] Hans Boehm, Alan Demers, and Scott Shenker. Mostly parallel garbage collection. In *ACM conference on programming language design and implementation*, pages 157–164, Minneapolis, MN, November 1991.

[7] Hans Boehm, Alan Demers, and Mark Weiser. A garbage collector for C and C++. http://www.hpl.hp.com/personal/Hans_Boehm/gc/.

[8] Hans Boehm and Zhong Shao. Inferring type maps during garbage collection. In *OOPSLA '93 Workshop on Memory Management and Garbage Collection*, September 1993.

[9] Hans Boehm and Mark Weiser. Garbage collection in an uncooperative environment. *Software—Practice and experience*, pages 807–820, September 1988.

[10] Dominique Colnet, Philippe Coucaud, and Olivier Zendra. Compiler support to customize the mark and sweep algorithm. In *Proceedings of the International Symposium on Memory Management*, pages 154–165, Vancouver, October 1998.

[11] Jeremy Dion and Louis Monier. Third degree. http://research.compaq.com/wrl/projects/om/third.html.

[12] Amer Diwan, J. Eliot B. Moss, and Richard L. Hudson. Compiler support for garbage collection in a statically typed language. In *ACM conference on programming language design and implementation*, pages 273–282, San Francisco, CA, July 1992.

[13] Great Circle – Real-time error detection and code diagnosis for developers. http://www.geodesic.com/products/greatcircle.html.

[14] James Gosling, Bill Joy, and Guy Steele. *The Java language specification*. Addison-Wesley, 1996.

[15] Reed Hastings and Bob Joyce. Fast detection of memory leaks and access errors. In *Proceedings of the Winter '92 USENIX conference*, pages 125–136, 1992.

[16] Michael Hicks, Jonathan Moore, and Scott Nettles. The measured cost of copying garbage collection mechanisms. In *Functional Programming*, pages 292–305, June 1997.

[17] Martin Hirzel and Amer Diwan. On the type accuracy of garbage collection. In *Proceedings of the International Symposium on Memory Management*, pages 1–12, Minneapolis, MN, October 2000.

[18] Richard L. Hudson, J. Eliot B. Moss, Amer Diwan, and Christopher F. Weight. A language-independent garbage collector toolkit. Technical Report 91-47, University of Massachusetts at Amherst, September 1991.

[19] Richard Jones and Rafael Lins. *Garbage collection: algorithms for automatic dynamic memory management*. John Wiley & Sons, 1st edition, 1997.

[20] Robin Milner, Mads Tofte, and Robert Harper. *The Definition of Standard ML*. MIT Press, Cambridge, Massachusetts, 1990.

[21] Greg Nelson, editor. *Systems Programming with Modula-3*. Prentice Hall, New Jersey, 1991.

[22] Todd Proebsting, Gregg Townsend, Patrick Bridges, John Hartman, Tim Newsham, and Scott Watterson. Toba: Java for applications – a way ahead of time (WAT) compiler. In *USENIX COOTS*, pages 41–53, June 1997.

[23] Ran Shaham, Elliot K. Kolodner, and Mooly Sagiv. On the effectiveness of GC in Java. In *Proceedings of the International Symposium on Memory Management*, pages 12–17, Minneapolis, MN, October 2000.

[24] Frederick Smith and Greg Morrisett. Comparing mostly-copying and mark-sweep conservative collection. In *Proceedings of the International Symposium on Memory Management*, pages 68–78, October 1998.

[25] James Stichnoth, Guei-Yuan Lueh, and Michael Cierniak. Support for garbage collection at every instruction in a Java compiler. In *ACM conference on programming language design and implementation*, pages 118–127, May 1999.

[26] Stanford University SUIF Research Group.   Suif compiler system version 1.x. http://suif.stanford.edu/suif/suif1/index.html.

[27] David Tarditi, Greg Morrisett, P. Cheng, C. Stone, Robert Harper, and Peter Lee. TIL: A type-directed optimizing compiler for ML. In *ACM conference on programming language design and implementation*, pages 181–192, May 1996.

[28] David Ungar. Generation scavenging: A non-disruptive high performance storage reclamation algorithm. In *Proceedings of the ACM SIGSOFT/SIGPLAN Software Engineering Symposium on Practical Software Development Environments*, pages 157–167, 1984.

[29] Paul R. Wilson, Michael S. Lam, and Thomas G. Moher. Caching considerations for generational garbage collection. In *1992 ACM Conference on Lisp and Functional Programming*, pages 32–42, San Francisco, California, June 1992.

[30] Robert P. Wilson, Robert S. French, Christopher S. Wilson, Saman P. Amarasinghe, Jennifer-Ann M. Anderson, Steven W. K. Tjiang, Shih-Wei Liao, Chau-Wen Tseng, Mary W. Hall, Monica S. Lam, and John L. Hennessy. SUIF: An infrastructure for research on parallelizing and optimizing compilers. *ACM SIGPLAN Notices*, 29(12):31–37, December 1984.

[31] Benjamin Zorn. The effect of garbage collection on cache performance. Technical Report CU-CS-528-91, University of Colorado at Boulder, May 1991.

[32] Benjamin Zorn. The measured cost of conservative garbage collection. In *Software–Practice and Experience*, pages 733–756, July 1993.

Concurrent Cycle Collection
in Reference Counted Systems

David F. Bacon and V.T. Rajan

IBM T.J. Watson Research Center
P.O. Box 704, Yorktown Heights, NY 10598, U.S.A.
dfb@watson.ibm.com, vtrajan@us.ibm.com

Abstract. Automatic storage reclamation via reference counting has important advantages, but has always suffered from a major weakness due to its inability to reclaim cyclic data structures.

We describe a novel cycle collection algorithm that is both *concurrent* — it is capable of collecting garbage even in the presence of simultaneous mutation — and *localized* — it never needs to perform a global search of the entire data space. We describe our algorithm in detail and present a proof of correctness.

We have implemented our algorithm in the Jalapeño Java virtual machine as part of the Recycler, a concurrent multiprocessor reference counting garbage collector that achieves maximum mutator pause times of only 6 milliseconds. We present measurements of the behavior of the cycle collection algorithm over a set of eight benchmarks that demonstrate the effectiveness of the algorithm at finding garbage cycles, handling concurrent mutation, and eliminating global tracing.

1 Introduction

Forty years ago, two methods of automatic storage reclamation were introduced: reference counting [7] and tracing [23]. Since that time tracing collectors and their variants (mark-and-sweep, semispace copying, mark-and-compact) have been much more widely used due to perceived deficiencies in reference counting.

Changes in the relative costs of memory and processing power, and the adoption of garbage collected languages in mainstream programming (particularly Java) have changed the landscape. We believe it is time to take a fresh look at reference counting, particularly as processor clock speeds increase while RAM becomes plentiful but not significantly faster. In this environment the locality properties of reference counting are appealing, while the purported extra processing power required is likely to be less relevant.

At the same time, Java's incorporation of garbage collection has thrust the problem into the mainstream, and large, mission critical systems are being built in Java, stressing the flexibility and scalability of the underlying garbage collection implementations. As a result, the supposed advantages of tracing collectors — simplicity and low overhead — are being eroded as they are being made ever more complex in an attempt to address the real-world requirements of large and varied programs.

Furthermore, the fundamental assumption behind tracing collectors, namely that it is acceptable to periodically trace all of the live objects in the heap, will not necessarily scale to the very large main memories that are becoming increasingly common.

J. Lindskov Knudsen (Ed.): ECOOP 2001, LNCS 2072, pp. 207–235, 2001.

There are three primary problems with reference counting, namely:

1. storage overhead associated with keeping a count for each object;
2. run-time overhead of incrementing and decrementing the reference count each time a pointer is copied; and
3. inability to detect cycles and consequent necessity of including a second garbage collection technique to deal with cyclic garbage.

The inability to collect cycles is generally considered to be the greatest weakness of reference counting collectors. It either places the burden on the programmer to break cycles explicitly, or requires special programming idioms, or requires a tracing collector to collect the cycles.

In this paper, we present first a synchronous and then a concurrent algorithm for the collection of cyclic garbage in a reference counted system. The concurrent algorithm is a variant of the synchronous algorithm with additional tests to maintain safety properties that could be undermined by concurrent mutation of the data structures.

Like algorithms based on tracing (mark-and-sweep, semispace copying, and mark-and-compact) our algorithms are linear in the size of the graph traced. However, our algorithms are able to perform this tracing locally rather than globally, and often trace a smaller subgraph.

These algorithms have been implemented in a new reference counting collector, the Recycler, which is part of the Jalapeño Java VM [1] implemented at the IBM T.J. Watson Research Center. Jalapeño is itself written in Java.

In concurrently published work [3] we describe the Recycler as a whole, and provide measurements showing that our concurrent reference counting system achieves maximum measured mutator pause times of only 6 milliseconds. End-to-end execution times are usually comparable to those of a parallel (but non-concurrent) mark-and-sweep collector, although there is occasionally significant variation (in both directions).

In this paper we concentrate on describing the cycle collection algorithm in sufficient detail that it can be implemented by others, and give a proof of correctness which gives further insight into how and why the concurrent algorithm works. We also provide measurements of the performance of the cycle collection algorithms for a suite of eight Java benchmarks.

The rest of the paper is organized as follows: Section 2 describes previous approaches to cycle collection; Section 3 describes our synchronous algorithm for collection of cyclic garbage; Section 4 then presents our concurrent cycle collection algorithm. Section 5 contains proofs of correctness for the concurrent cycle collection algorithms. Section 6 presents our measurements of the effectiveness of the algorithms. Section 7 describes related work on concurrent garbage collection. Finally, we present our conclusions.

Subsections 3.1 and 4.4 contain detailed pseudocode of the algorithms and can be skipped on a first reading of the paper.

2   Previous Work on Cycle Collection

Previous work on solving the cycle collection problem in reference counted collectors has fallen into three categories:

- special programming idioms, like Bobrow's groups [5], or certain functional programming styles;
- use of an infrequently invoked tracing collector to collect cyclic garbage [8]; or
- searching for garbage cycles by removing internal reference counts [6, 22].

An excellent summary of the techniques and algorithms is in chapter 3 ("Reference Counting") of the book by Jones and Lins [17]. The first algorithm for cycle collection in a reference counted system was devised by Christopher [6]. Our synchronous cycle collection algorithm is based on the work of Martínez et al [22] as extended by Lins [20], which is very clearly explained in the chapter of the book just mentioned.

There are two observations that are fundamental to these algorithms. The first observation is that garbage cycles can only be created when a reference count is decremented to a non-zero value — if the reference count is incremented, no garbage is being created, and if it is decremented to zero, the garbage has already been found. Furthermore, since reference counts of one tend to predominate, decrements to zero should be common.

The second observation is that in a garbage cycle, all the reference counts are internal; therefore, if those internal counts can be subtracted, the garbage cycle will be discovered.

As a result, when a reference count is decremented and does not reach zero, it is considered as a candidate root of a garbage cycle, and a local search is performed. This is a depth-first search which subtracts out counts due to internal pointers. If the result is a collection of objects with zero reference counts, then a garbage cycle has been found and is collected; if not, then another depth-first-search is performed and the counts are restored.

Lins [20] extended the original algorithm to perform the search lazily by buffering candidate roots instead of exploring them immediately. This has two advantages. Firstly, after a time, the reference count of a candidate root may reach zero due to other edge deletions, in which case the node can simply be collected, or the reference count may be re-incremented due to edge additions, in which case it may be ignored as a candidate root. Secondly, it will often prevent re-traversal of the same node.

Unfortunately, in the worst case Lins' algorithm is quadratic in the size of the graph, as for example in the cycle shown in Figure 1. His algorithm considers the roots one at a time, performing the reference count subtraction and restoration passes for that root before moving on.

Therefore, Lins' algorithm will perform a complete scan from each of the candidate roots until it arrives at the final root, at which point the entire compound cycle will be collected.

3   Synchronous Cycle Collection

In this section we describe our synchronous cycle collection algorithm, which applies the same principles as those of Martínez et al and Lins, but which only requires $O(N + E)$ worst-case time for collection (where N is the number of nodes and E is the number of edges in the object graph), and is therefore competitive with tracing garbage collectors.

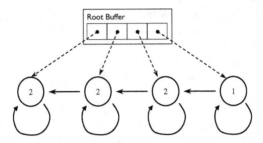

Fig. 1. Example of compound cycle that causes Lins' algorithm to exhibit quadratic complexity.

We also improve the practicality of the algorithm by allowing resizing of collected objects, and show how significant constant-time improvements can be achieved by ruling out inherently acyclic data structures.

Our synchronous algorithm is similar to Lins' algorithm: when reference counts are decremented, we place potential roots of cyclic garbage into a buffer called Roots. Periodically, we process this buffer and look for cycles by subtracting internal reference counts.

There are two major changes that make the algorithm linear time: first of all, we add a *buffered* flag to every object, which is used to prevent the same object being added to the root buffer more than once per cycle collection. This in turn places a linear bound on the size of the buffer.

Secondly, we analyze the entire transitive closure of Roots as a single graph, rather than as a set of graphs. This means that the complexity of the algorithm is limited by the size of that transitive closure, which in turn is limited by $N + E$ (since Roots is bounded by N by the use of the buffered flag). Of course, in practice we hope that the transitive closure will be significantly smaller.

In practice we found that the first change (the use of the buffered flag) made almost no difference in the running time of the algorithm; however, the second change (analyzing the entire graph at once) made an enormous difference in run-time. When we applied Lins' algorithm unmodified to large programs, garbage collection delays extended into minutes.

3.1   Pseudocode and Explanation

We now present detailed pseudocode and an explanation of the operation of each procedure in the synchronous cycle collection algorithm.

In addition to the buffered flag, each object contains a color and a reference count. For an object T these fields are denoted buffered(T), color(T), and RC(T). In the implementation, these quantities together occupy a single word in each object.

Color	Meaning
Black	In use or free
Gray	Possible member of cycle
White	Member of garbage cycle
Purple	Possible root of cycle
Green	Acyclic
Red	Candidate cycle undergoing Σ-computation
Orange	Candidate cycle awaiting epoch boundary

Table 1. Object Colorings for Cycle Collection. Orange and red are only used by the concurrent cycle collector and are described in Section 4.

All objects start out black. A summary of the colors used by the collector is shown in Table 1. The use of green (acyclic) objects will be discussed below. The algorithm is shown in Figure 2. The procedures are explained in detail below. Increment and Decrement are invoked externally as pointers are added, removed, or overwritten. CollectCycles is invoked either when the root buffer overflows, storage is exhausted, or when the collector decides for some other reason to free cyclic garbage. The rest of the procedures are internal to the cycle collector. Note that the procedures MarkGray, Scan, and ScanBlack are the same as for Lins' algorithm.

Increment(S) When a reference to a node S is created, the reference count of T is incremented and it is colored black, since any object whose reference count was just incremented can not be garbage.

Decrement(S) When a reference to a node S is deleted, the reference count is decremented. If the reference count reaches zero, the procedure Release is invoked to free the garbage node. If the reference count does not reach zero, the node is considered as a possible root of a cycle.

Release(S) When the reference count of a node reaches zero, the contained pointers are deleted, the object is colored black, and unless it has been buffered, it is freed. If it has been buffered, it is in the Roots buffer and will be freed later (in the procedure MarkRoots).

PossibleRoot(S) When the reference count of S is decremented but does not reach zero, it is considered as a possible root of a garbage cycle. If its color is already purple, then it is already a candidate root; if not, its color is set to purple. Then the *buffered* flag is checked to see if it has been purple since we last performed a cycle collection. If it is not buffered, it is added to the buffer of possible roots.

CollectCycles() When the root buffer is full, or when some other condition, such as low memory occurs, the actual cycle collection operation is invoked. This operation has three phases: MarkRoots, which removes internal reference counts; ScanRoots, which restores reference counts when they are non-zero; and finally CollectRoots, which actually collects the cyclic garbage.

MarkRoots() The marking phase looks at all the nodes S whose pointers have been stored in the Roots buffer since the last cycle collection. If the color of the node is purple (indicating a possible root of a garbage cycle) and the reference

```
Increment(S)
  RC(S) = RC(S) + 1
  color(S) = black

Decrement(S)
  RC(S) = RC(S) - 1
  if (RC(S) == 0)
    Release(S)
  else
    PossibleRoot(S)

Release(S)
  for T in children(S)
    Decrement(T)
  color(S) = black
  if (! buffered(S))
    Free(S)

PossibleRoot(S)
  if (color(S) != purple)
    color(S) = purple
    if (! buffered(S))
      buffered(S) = true
      append S to Roots

CollectCycles()
  MarkRoots()
  ScanRoots()
  CollectRoots()

MarkRoots()
  for S in Roots
    if (color(S) == purple)
        and RC(S) > 0
      MarkGray(S)
    else
      buffered(S) = false
      remove S from Roots
      if (RC(S) == 0)
        Free(S)

ScanRoots()
  for S in Roots
    Scan(S)
```

```
ScanRoots()
  for S in Roots
    Scan(S)

CollectRoots()
  for S in Roots
    remove S from Roots
    buffered(S) = false
    CollectWhite(S)

MarkGray(S)
  if (color(S) != gray)
    color(S) = gray
    for T in children(S)
      RC(T) = RC(T) - 1
      MarkGray(T)

Scan(S)
  if (color(S) == gray)
    if (RC(S) > 0)
      ScanBlack(S)
    else
      color(S) = white
      for T in children(S)
        Scan(T)

ScanBlack(S)
  color(S) = black
  for T in children(S)
    RC(T) = RC(T) + 1
    if (color(T) != black)
      ScanBlack(T)

CollectWhite(S)
  if (color(S) == white
      and ! buffered(S))
    color(S) = black
    for T in children(S)
      CollectWhite(T)
    Free(S)
```

Fig. 2. Synchronous Cycle Collection

count has not become zero, then `MarkGray(S)` is invoked to perform a depth-first search in which the reached nodes are colored gray and internal reference counts are subtracted. Otherwise, the node is removed from the `Roots` buffer, the `buffered` flag is cleared, and if the reference count is zero the object is freed.

`ScanRoots()` For each node `S` that was considered by `MarkGray(S)`, this procedure invokes `Scan(S)` to either color the garbage subgraph white or re-color the live subgraph black.

`CollectRoots()` After the `ScanRoots` phase of the `CollectCycles` procedure, any remaining white nodes will be cyclic garbage and will be reachable from the `Roots` buffer. This procedure invokes `CollectWhite` for each node in the `Roots` buffer to collect the garbage; all nodes in the root buffer are removed and their `buffered` flag is cleared.

`MarkGray(S)` This procedure performs a simple depth-first traversal of the graph beginning at `S`, marking visited nodes gray and removing internal reference counts as it goes.

`Scan(S)` If this procedure finds a gray object whose reference count is greater than one, then that object and everything reachable from it are live data; it will therefore call `ScanBlack(S)` in order to re-color the reachable subgraph and restore the reference counts subtracted by `MarkGray`. However, if the color of an object is gray and its reference count is zero, then it is colored white, and `Scan` is invoked upon its children. Note that an object may be colored white and then re-colored black if it is reachable from some subsequently discovered live node.

`ScanBlack(S)` This procedure performs the inverse operation of `MarkGray`, visiting the nodes, changing the color of objects back to black, and restoring their reference counts.

`CollectWhite(S)` This procedure recursively frees all white objects, re-coloring them black as it goes. If a white object is buffered, it is not freed; it will be freed later when it is found in the `Roots` buffer.

3.2 Acyclic Data Types

A significant constant-factor improvement can be obtained for cycle collection by observing that some objects are inherently acyclic. We speculate that they will comprise the majority of objects in many applications. Therefore, if we can avoid cycle collection for inherently acyclic objects, we will significantly reduce the overhead of cycle collection as a whole.

In Java, dynamic class loading complicates the determination of inherently acyclic data structures. We have implemented a very simple scheme as part of the class loader. Acyclic classes may contain:

- scalars;
- references to classes that are both acyclic and □nal; and
- arrays of either of the above.

Our implementation marks objects whose class is acyclic with the special color green. Green objects are ignored by the cycle collection algorithm, except that when

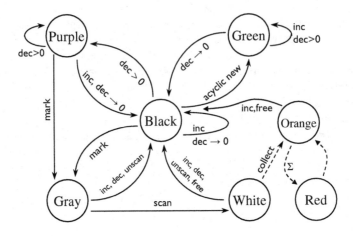

Fig. 3. State transition graph for cycle collection.

a dead cycle refers to green objects, they are collected along with the dead cycle. For simplicity of the presentation, we have not included consideration of green objects in the algorithms in this paper; the modifications are straightforward.

While our determination of acyclic classes is very simple, it is also very effective, usually reducing the objects considered as roots of cycles by an order of magnitude, as will be shown in Section 6. In a static compiler, a more sophisticated program analysis could be applied to increase the percentage of green objects.

4   Concurrent Cycle Collection

We now describe a concurrent cycle collection algorithm based on the principles of our synchronous algorithm of the previous section.

For the purposes of understanding the cycle collection algorithm, the multiprocessor reference counting system can be viewed very abstractly as follows: as mutators create and destroy references to objects (either on the stack or in the heap), corresponding increment and decrement operations are enqueued into a local buffer, called the *mutation buffer*. Periodically, the mutators send these mutation buffers to the *collector*, which applies the reference count updates, frees objects whose counts drop to zero, and periodically also performs cycle collection.

Time is divided into *epochs*, and each mutator must transfer its mutation buffer to the collector exactly once per epoch. However, aside from this requirement, in normal operation no synchronization is required between mutators and the collector.

When all mutation buffers for an epoch have been transferred to the collector, the increments for the just-completed epoch are applied; however, the decrements are not applied until the next epoch boundary. This prevents freeing of live data which might otherwise occur due to race conditions between the mutators. The advantage of this approach is that it is never necessary to halt all the mutators simultaneously.

In its implementation, the Recycler only tracks pointer updates to the heap, and snapshots pointers in the stack at epoch boundaries. Our algorithm is similar to Deutsch-Bobrow deferred reference counting [9], but is superior in a number of important respects. Our implementation of concurrent reference counting is most similar to the reference counting collector of DeTreville [8]. The Recycler is described in detail by Bacon et al [3].

4.1   Two Phase Cycle Collection

Now that we have abstracted the concurrent system to a collection of mutators emitting streams of increment and decrement operations, and a reference counting collector which merges and applies these operations, we can describe in overview how the algorithm operates.

The concurrent cycle collection algorithm is more complex than the synchronous algorithm. As with other concurrent garbage collection algorithms, we must contend with the fact that the object graph may be modified simultaneously with the collector scanning it; but in addition the reference counts may be as much as a two epochs out of date (because decrements are deferred by an epoch).

Our algorithm relies on the same basic premise as the synchronous algorithm: namely, that given a subset of nodes, if deleting the internal edges between the nodes in this subset reduces the reference count of every node in the subset to zero, then the whole subset of nodes is cyclic garbage. (The subset may represent more than one independent cycles, but they are all garbage cycles.)

However, since the graph may be modified, we run into three basic difficulties. Firstly, since we can not rely on being able to retrace the same graph, the repeated traversal of the graph does not define the same set of nodes. Secondly, the deletion of edges can disconnect portions of the graph, thus making the global test by graph traversal difficult. Thirdly, reference counts may be out of date.

Our algorithm proceeds in two phases. In the first phase, we use a variant of the synchronous algorithm as described in Section 3 to obtain a candidate set of garbage nodes. We then wait until an epoch boundary and then perform the second phase in which we test these to ensure that the candidates do indeed satisfy the criteria for garbage cycles.

The two phases can be viewed as enforcing a "liveness" and a "safety" property. The first phase enforces liveness by ensuring that potential garbage cycles are considered for collection. The second phase ensures safety by preventing the collection of false cycles induced by concurrent mutator activity.

4.2   Liveness: Finding Cycles to Collect

Essentially, we use the synchronous algorithm to find candidate cycles. However, due to concurrent mutator activity, the graph may be changing and the algorithm may produce incorrect results.

To perform the concurrent cycle collection, we need a second reference count for each object, denoted CRC(S). This is a hypothetical reference count which may become incorrect due to concurrent mutator activity. In the implementation, we are able to fit both reference counts, the color, and the buffered flag into a single header word by using a hash table to hold count overflows, which occur very rarely.

The liveness phase of the concurrent algorithm proceeds in a similar manner to the synchronous cycle collection algorithm, except that when an object is marked gray its cyclic reference count (CRC) is initialized to its true reference count — the "true" reference count (RC) is not changed. Henceforward, the mark, scan, and collect phases operate upon the cyclic reference count instead of the true reference count. In the CollectWhite procedure, instead of collecting the white nodes as garbage, we color them orange and add them to a set of *possible* garbage.

By using the cyclic reference count we ensure that in the event of concurrent mutator activity, the information about the true reference count of the objects is never lost.

In absence of mutator activity, the liveness phase will yield the set of garbage nodes, and the safety phase will certify that this indeed is a set of garbage of nodes and we can collect them.

However, the presence of concurrent mutator activity can cause live nodes to enter the list in three different ways. Firstly, the mutator can add an edge, thus causing the MarkGray procedure to incorrectly infer that there are no external edges to a live object. Secondly, the mutator can delete an edge, thus causing scan procedure to incorrectly infer a live object to be garbage. Thirdly, the deletion of edges concurrent to running of the MarkGray and scan procedure can create gray and white nodes with various values of cyclic reference counts. While eventually the reporting of the mutator activity will cause these nodes to be detected and re-colored, if these nodes are encountered before they are re-colored they can mislead the runs of the above procedures into inferring that they are garbage.

The output of phase one is a set of nodes believed to be garbage in the Cycle-Buffer data structure. The CycleBuffer is divided into discrete connected components, each of which forms a potential garbage cycle. Due to mutator activity, the contents of the CycleBuffer can be a superset of the actual set of garbage nodes and can contain some nodes that fail tests in the safety phase (this is discussed in detail in Section 5).

4.3 Safety: Collecting Cycles Concurrently

The second ("safety") phase of the algorithm takes as input a set of nodes and determines whether they form a garbage cycle. These nodes are marked with a special color, orange, which is used to identify a candidate set in the concurrent cycle collector.

The safety phase of the algorithm consists of two tests we call the Σ-test and the Δ-test. If a subset of nodes of the object graph passes both the Σ-test and the Δ-test, then we can be assured that the nodes in the subset are all garbage. Thus, correctness of the safety phase of our algorithm is not determined by any property of the output of the liveness phase which selects the subgraphs. This property of the safety phase of the algorithm considerably simplifies the proof of correctness as well as modularizing the code.

In theory, it would be possible to build a cycle collector which simply passed random sets of nodes to the safety phase, which would then either accept them as garbage or reject them as live. However, such a collector would not be practical: if we indeed pick a random subset of nodes from the object graph, the chances that they form a complete garbage subgraph is very small. The job of the liveness phase can be seen as finding likely sets of candidates for garbage cycles. If the mutator activity is small in a given epoch, this would indeed be very likely to be true.

The Σ-test consists of two parts: a *preparation* and an actual *test*. In the preparation part, which is performed immediately after the candidate cycles have been found, we iterate over the subset and initialize the cyclic reference count of every node in the subset to the reference count of the node. Then we iterate over every node in the subset again and decrement the cyclic reference count of any children of the node that are also in the subset. At the end of the preparation computation, the cyclic reference count of each node in the subset represents the number of references to the node from nodes external to the subset. In the actual test, which is performed after the next epoch boundary, we iterate over every node in the subset and test if its cyclic reference count is zero.

If it is zero for every member of the set, then we know that there exists no reference to this subset from any other node. Therefore, any candidate set that passes the Σ-test is garbage, unless the reference count used during the running of the preparation procedure is outdated due to an increment to one of the nodes in the subset.

This is ascertained by the Δ-test. We wait until the next epoch boundary, at which point increment processing re-colors all non-black nodes and their reachable subgraphs black. Then we scan the nodes in the candidate set and test whether their color is still orange. If they are all orange, we know that there has been no increment to the reference count during the running of the preparation procedure and we say that the candidate set passed the Δ-test.

Any subset of garbage nodes that does not have any external pointers to it will pass both the tests. Note that we do not have to worry about concurrent decrements to the members of the subset, since it is not possible for the reference count of any node to drop below zero.

However, it is possible for a set of garbage to have pointers to it from other garbage cycles. For example in Figure 1, only the candidate set consisting of the last node forms isolated garbage cycle. The other cycles have pointers to them from the cycle to their right.

We know that the garbage cycles in the cycle buffer cannot have any forward pointers to other garbage cycles (if they did, we would have followed them and included them in a previous garbage cycle). Hence, we process the candidate cycles in the cycle buffer in the reverse of the order in which we found them. This reasoning is described more formally in Lemma 3 in Section 5.

When a candidate set passes both tests, and hence is determined to be garbage, then we free the nodes in the cycle, which causes the reference counts of other nodes outside of the cycle to be decremented. By the stability property of garbage, we can decrement such reference counts without concern for concurrent mutation.

When we decrement a reference count to an orange node, we also decrement its cyclic reference count (CRC). Therefore, when the next candidate cycle is considered (the previous cycle in the buffer), if it is garbage the Σ-test will succeed because we have augmented the computation performed by the preparation procedure.

Hence when we reach a candidate set, the cyclic reference count does not include the count of any pointers from a known garbage node. This ensures that all the nodes in Figure 1 would be collected.

A formalism for understanding the structure of the graph in the presence of concurrent mutation, and a proof of correctness of the algorithm is presented in Section 5.

4.4 Pseudocode and Explanation

We now present the pseudocode with explanations for each procedure in the concurrent cycle collection algorithm. The pseudocode is shown in Figures 4 and 5. The operation of `CollectCycles` and its subsidiary procedures is very similar to the operation of the synchronous algorithm of Figure 2, so for those procedures we will only focus on the differences in the concurrent versions of the procedures.

`Increment(S)` The true reference count is incremented. Since the reference count is being incremented, the node must be live, so any non-black objects reachable from it are colored black by invoking `ScanBlack`. This has the effect of re-blackening live nodes that were left gray or white when concurrent mutation interrupted a previous cycle collection.

`Decrement(S)` At the high level, decrementing looks the same as with the synchronous algorithm: if the count becomes zero, the object is released, otherwise it is considered as a possible root.

`PossibleRoot(S)` For a possible root, we first perform `ScanBlack`. As with `Increment`, this has the effect of re-blackening leftover gray or white nodes; it may also change the color of some purple nodes reachable from S to black, but this is not a problem since they will be considered when the cycle collector considers S. The rest of `PossibleRoot` is the same as for the synchronous algorithm.

`ProcessCycles()` Invoked once per epoch after increment and decrement processing due to the mutation buffers from the mutator threads has been completed. First, `FreeCycles` attempts to free candidate cycles discovered during the previous epoch. Then `CollectCycles` collects new candidate cycles and `SigmaPreparation` prepares for the Σ-test to be run in the next epoch.

`CollectCycles()` As in the synchronous algorithm, three phases are invoked on the candidate roots: marking, scanning, and collection.

`MarkRoots()` This procedure is the same as in the synchronous algorithm.

`ScanRoots()` This procedure is the same as in the synchronous algorithm.

`CollectRoots()` For each remaining root, if it is white a candidate cycle has been discovered starting at that root. The `CurrentCycle` is initialized to be empty, and the `CollectWhite` procedure is invoked to gather the members of the cycle into the `CurrentCycle` and color them orange. The collected cycle is then appended to the `CycleBuffer`. If the root is not white, a candidate cycle was not found from this root or it was already included in some previously collected candidate, and the buffered flag is set to false. In either case, the root is removed from the `Roots` buffer, so that at the end of this procedure the `Roots` buffer is empty.

```
Increment(S)
  RC(S) = RC(S) + 1
  ScanBlack(S)

Decrement(S)
  RC(S) = RC(S) - 1
  if (RC(S) == 0)
    Release(S)
  else
    PossibleRoot(S)

Release(S)
  for T in children(S)
    Decrement(T)
  color(S) = black
  if (! buffered(S))
    Free(S)

PossibleRoot(S)
  ScanBlack(S)
  color(S) = purple
  if (! buffered(S))
    buffered(S) = true
    append S to Roots

ProcessCycles()
  FreeCycles()
  CollectCycles()
  SigmaPreparation()

CollectCycles()
  MarkRoots()
  ScanRoots()
  CollectRoots()

MarkRoots()
  for S in Roots
    if (color(S) == purple
        and RC(S) > 0)
      MarkGray(S)
    else
      remove S from Roots
      buffered(S) = false
      if (RC(S) == 0)
        Free(S)
```

```
ScanRoots()
  for S in Roots
    Scan(S)

CollectRoots()
  for S in Roots
    if (color(S) == white)
      CurrentCycle = empty
      CollectWhite(S)
      append CurrentCycle
        to CycleBuffer
    else
      buffered(S) = false
    remove S from Roots

MarkGray(S)
  if (color(S) != gray)
    color(S) = gray
    CRC(S) = RC(S)
    for T in children(S)
      MarkGray(T)
  else if (CRC(S) > 0)
    CRC(S) = CRC(S) - 1

Scan(S)
  if (color(S) == gray
      and CRC(S) == 0)
    color(S) = white
    for T in children(S)
      Scan(T)
  else
    ScanBlack(S)

ScanBlack(S)
  if (color(S) != black)
    color(S) = black
    for T in children(S)
      ScanBlack(T)

CollectWhite(S)
  if (color(S) == white)
    color(S) = orange
    buffered(S) = true
    append S to CurrentCycle
    for T in children(S)
      CollectWhite(T)
```

Fig. 4. Concurrent Cycle Collection Algorithm (Part 1)

```
SigmaPreparation()
  for C in CycleBuffer
    for N in C
      color(N) = red
      CRC(N) = RC(N)
    for N in C
      for M in children(N)
        if (color(M) == red
          and CRC(M) > 0)
          CRC(M) = CRC(M)-1
    for N in C
      color(N) = orange

FreeCycles()
  last = |CycleBuffer|-1
  for i = last to 0 by -1
    C = CycleBuffer[i]
    if (DeltaTest(C)
      and SigmaTest(C))
      FreeCycle(C)
    else
      Refurbish(C)
  clear CycleBuffer

DeltaTest(C)
  for N in C
    if (color(N) != orange)
      return false
  return true

SigmaTest(C)
  externRC = 0
  for N in C
    externRC = externRC+CRC(N)
  return (externRC == 0)
```

```
Refurbish(C)
  first = true
  for N in C
    if ((first and
        color(N)==orange) or
        color(N)==purple)
      color(N) = purple
      append N to Roots
    else
      color(N) = black
      buffered(N) = false
    first = false

FreeCycle(C)
  for N in C
    color(N) = red
  for N in C
    for M in children(N)
      CyclicDecrement(M)
  for N in C
    Free(N)

CyclicDecrement(M)
  if (color(M) != red)
    if (color(M) == orange)
      RC(M) = RC(M) - 1
      CRC(M) = CRC(M) - 1
    else
      Decrement(M)
```

Fig. 5. Concurrent Cycle Collection Algorithm (Part 2)

MarkGray(S) This is similar to the synchronous version of the procedure, with adaptations to use the cyclic reference count (CRC) instead of the true reference count (RC). If the color is not gray, it is set to gray and the CRC is copied from the RC, and then MarkGray is invoked recursively on the children. If the color is already gray, and if the CRC is not already zero, the CRC is decremented (the check for non-zero is necessary because concurrent mutation could otherwise cause the CRC to underflow).

Scan(S) As with MarkGray, simply an adaptation of the synchronous procedure that uses the CRC. Nodes with zero CRC are colored white; non-black nodes with CRC greater than zero are recursively re-colored black.

ScanBlack(S) Like the synchronous version of the procedure, but it does not need to re-increment the true reference count because all reference count computations were carried out on the CRC.

CollectWhite(S) This procedure recursively gathers white nodes identified as members of a candidate garbage cycle into the CurrentCycle and colors them orange as it goes. The buffered flag is also set true since a reference to the node will be stored in the CycleBuffer when CurrentCycle is appended to it.

SigmaPreparation() After the candidate cycles have been collected into the CycleBuffer, this procedure prepares for the execution of the Σ-test in the next epoch. It operates individually on each candidate cycle C. First, each node S in C has its CRC initialized to its RC and its color set to red. After this only the nodes of C are red. Then for any pointer from one node in C to another node in C, the CRC of the target node is decremented. Finally, the nodes in C are re-colored orange. At the end of SigmaPreparation, the CRC field of each node S contains a count of the number of references to S from outside of C.

FreeCycles() This procedure iterates over the candidate cycles in the reverse order in which they were collected. It applies the safety tests (the Σ-test and the Δ-test) to each cycle and if it passes both tests then the cycle is freed; otherwise it is refurbished, meaning that it may be reconsidered for collection in the next epoch.

DeltaTest(C) This procedure returns true if the color of all nodes in the cycle are orange, which indicates that their have been no increments to any of the nodes in the cycle.

SigmaTest(C) This procedure calculates the total number of external references to nodes in the cycle, using the CRC fields computed by the SigmaPreparation procedure. It returns true if the number of external references is zero, false otherwise.

Refurbish(C) If the candidate cycle has not been collected due to failing a safety test, this procedure re-colors the nodes. If the first node in the candidate cycle (which was the purple node from which the candidate was found) is still orange, or if any node has become purple, then those nodes are colored purple and placed in the Roots buffer. All other nodes are colored black and their buffered flags are cleared.

FreeCycle(C) This procedure actually frees the members of a candidate cycle that has passed the safety tests. First, the members of C are colored red; after this, only the nodes in C are red. Then for each node S in C, CyclicDecrement decrements reference counts in non-red nodes pointed to by S.

CyclicDecrement(M) If a node is not red, then it either belongs to some other candidate cycle or not. If it belongs to some other candidate cycle, then it is orange, in which case both the RC and the CRC fields are decremented (the CRC field is decremented to update the computation performed previously by the SigmaPreparation procedure to take the deletion of the cycle pointing to M into account). If it does not belong to some other candidate cycle, it will not be orange and a normal Decrement operation is performed.

For ease of presentation, we have presented the pseudocode in a way that maximizes readability. However, this means that as presented the code makes more passes over the nodes than is strictly necessary. For instance, the first pass by `SigmaPreparation` can be merged with `CollectWhite`, and the passes performed by `DeltaTest` and `SigmaTest` can be combined. In the implementation, the passes are combined to minimize constant-factor overheads.

5   Proofs

In this section we prove the correctness of the concurrent cycle collection algorithm presented in Section 4.

5.1   The Abstract Graph

For the purpose of the proof of correctness of the above tests for garbage it is useful to define an abstract graph G_i for the ith epoch of the garbage collector. At beginning of each epoch the collector thread gets a set of increments and decrements from each of the mutator threads. If the increment refers to a new node, it implies the creation of that node. In addition, each increment implies addition of a directed edge between two nodes and each decrement implies deletion of an edge. The increments and decrements do not provide the source of the edges, so in practice we cannot build this graph, nor do we need to build it for the purpose of the algorithm. But for the purposes of the proof it is useful to conceptualize this graph. The graph G_i denotes the graph that is generated by adding nodes for each reference to a new node, and inserting and deleting edges to G_{i-1} corresponding to the increments and decrements at the beginning of ith epoch. In addition, when a node is determined to be garbage and is freed, it is deleted from G_i. At the beginning of the first epoch we start with an empty graph G_0.

We can similarly define an abstract set of roots R_i for each epoch i. The roots are either in the mutator stacks or in global (class static) variables. The roots in the mutator stacks are named by the increments collected from the stack snapshots of each mutator for the epoch. The roots from the global variables are the sources in edges implied by increment and decrement operations whose source is a global variable instead of a heap variable. R_i is simply the union of these two types of roots.

Given G_i and R_i, we can then define the set of garbage objects in G_i, which we denote Γ_i, as

$$\Gamma_i = G_i - R_i^\star$$

that is, the set difference G_i minus the transitive closure of the roots R_i.

5.2   Safety: Proof of Correctness

A garbage collector is *safe* if every object collected is indeed garbage. In this section we prove the safety of our algorithm.

At the end of epoch $i+1$, the procedure `ProcessCycles` invokes `FreeCycles` to collect the cycles identified as potential garbage during epoch i.

Let the set B_i denote the contents of the `CycleBuffer` generated during the cycle collection in epoch i. This is the collection of orange nodes generated by the concurrent variant of the synchronous cycle detection algorithm, which used the set of purple nodes (denoted P_i) as roots to search for cyclic garbage.

B_i is partitioned into the disjoint sets $B_{i1} \ldots B_{in}$. Each B_{ik} is a candidate garbage cycle computed by the cycle collection algorithm from a particular purple node in P_i.

Due to concurrent mutation, B_i may contain nodes from $G_i \cup G_{i+1}$.

Lemma 1. *Any set B_{ik} containing nodes that do not exist in G_i (that is, $B_{ik} - G_i \neq \emptyset$) will fail the Δ-test.*

Proof. The only way for new nodes to be added to G_i in G_{i+1} is by increment operations. However, all concurrent increment operations will have been processed before we apply the Δ-test. Processing an increment operation invokes ScanBlack, so that if the node in question is in B_{ik}, then that node (at least) will be re-colored from orange to black. The presence of that black node in B_{ik} will cause the Δ-test to fail.   □

Therefore, for a given epoch i with G_i, R_i, and Γ_i, let

Ω_i denote the set containing the sets $B_{ik} \in B_i$ that passed the Δ-test. The sets in Ω_i are denoted Ω_{ik}. Since all Ω_{ik} have passed the Δ-test, all $\Omega_{ik} \subseteq G_i$.

C denote one of the sets Ω_{ik}, namely a set of nodes believed to be a garbage cycle that has passed the Δ-test.

S denote a specific node in that collection ($S \in C$).

$RC(S)$ denote the reference count at a node S in the ith epoch. By definition RC(S) is the reference count of node S in graph G_i.

$RC(S, C)$ denote the number of references to S from nodes within C.

$RC^{\Sigma}(S, C)$ denote the number of references to S from nodes within C as determined by the Σ-test.

$CRC(S)$ denote the hypothetical reference count for $S \in C$ as computed by the Σ-test.

$\overline{C}$ denote $G_i - C$, the complement of C in G_i.

Theorem 1. *If C passes the Σ-test, that is if we have computed the values of $CRC(S)$ for each $S \in C$ as described in the procedure SigmaPreparation in Section 4 and*

$$\sum_{S \in C} CRC(S) = 0$$

then C is a set of garbage nodes ($C \subseteq \Gamma_i$).

Proof. From the above definitions, for every $S \in C$,

$$RC(S) = RC(S, C) + RC(S, \overline{C})$$

Since we delay the processing of the decrements by one epoch, this ensures that the following properties are true:

$RC(S)$ is non-negative and if it is zero, then S is a garbage node.

$RC(S, \overline{C})$ is non-negative and if it is zero for every node S in C then C is a collection of garbage nodes.

During the Σ-test, we determine the number of references to node S from nodes within C. Therefore by definition,

$$CRC(S) = RC(S) - RC^{\Sigma}(S, C).$$

The $RC^{\Sigma}(S, C)$ may differ from the $RC(S, C)$ because there may be new references to S from nodes within C that were added to G_i, thereby increasing $RC^{\Sigma}(S, C)$; or because there may be references to S from nodes in C that were deleted from G_i, thereby decreasing $RC^{\Sigma}(S, C)$. If the collection passes the Δ-test, then no references were added to S at any time during the last epoch.

Therefore,

$$RC(S, C) \geq RC^{\Sigma}(S, C)$$

and

$$\begin{aligned} CRC(S) &= RC(S) - RC^{\Sigma}(S, C) \\ &\geq RC(S) - RC(S, C) = RC(S, \overline{C}) \end{aligned}$$

If $CRC(S)$ is zero from the Σ-test, since $RC(S, \overline{C})$ is non-negative, it follows that $RC(S, \overline{C})$ has to be zero too. Further, if $RC(S, \overline{C}) = 0$ for every node in the collection C, then the whole collection C is garbage.   □

Lemma 1 and Theorem 1 show that the Δ-test and the Σ-test are sufficient to ensure that any set C of nodes that passes both tests is garbage. The following theorem shows that both the tests are necessary to ensure this as well.

Theorem 2. *Both Δ-test and Σ-test are necessary to ensure that a candidate set B_{ij} contains only garbage nodes.*

Proof. We will prove by example. Consider the graph of nodes shown in Figure 6 (a). The cycle was detected from the purple node a, which is the starting point from which cycle collection is run. If the edge between nodes c and d is cut between the MarkGray and the Scan routines, then the nodes a and b will be collected by the CollectWhite routine and form a set B_{ij}. These nodes are not garbage. However, since there have been no increments to the reference counts of either of these nodes, this set will pass Δ-test.

The decrements will be processed an epoch later, at epoch $i + 2$, so the decrement to node d will not have an effect on the nodes a and b in the FreeCycles operation performed in epoch $i + 1$. Even waiting for an additional epoch does not guarantee that the fact that nodes a and b will be detected by Δ-test, since during epoch $i + 1$ the edge from d to e could be cut. Indeed, by making the chain of nodes $\{c, d, e\}$ arbitrarily long and having a malicious mutator cut edges at just the right moment, we can have the non-garbage set of nodes B_{ij} pass the Δ-test for arbitrarily many epochs. Hence the Δ-test alone cannot detect all live nodes in B_i.

Now consider the graph of nodes shown in Figure 6 (b). The cycle is detected starting with the purple node f, from which cycle collection is run. If a new edge is added

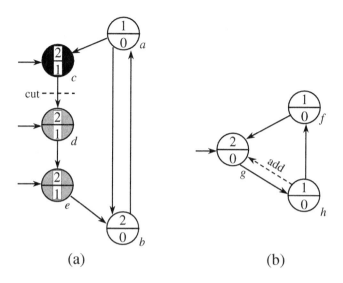

(a)   (b)

Fig. 6. Race conditions uniquely detected (a) by the Σ-test, and (b) by the Δ-test. The purple nodes from which cycle collection started were a and f. Inside of each node is shown the reference count, or RC (top) and the cyclic reference count, or CRC (bottom).

from node h to node g before the MarkGray routine is run (shown as the dashed line in the figure), the reference count of the node g will be out of date. If the cycle collector observes the newly added edge, the sum of the reference counts in $\{f, g, h\}$ will equal the sum of the edges. Hence the set of nodes $\{f, g, h\}$ will be collected by the CollectWhite routine and form the set B_{ik}. If the increments are not processed before the Σ-test is done, then B_{ik} will pass the Σ-test. Hence Σ-test alone cannot detect all live nodes in B_i.   □

Notice that we are not claiming that the two race conditions shown in Figure 6 are an exhaustive list of all possible race conditions that our algorithm will face. But these two are sufficient to show the necessity of both the tests. Thus the two tests are both necessary and sufficient to ensure the safety of the algorithm.

Finally we prove here the following Lemma that will be used in the next section, since the proof uses the notation from the present section. We define a *complete* set of nodes as one which is closed under transitive closure in the transpose graph; that is, a complete set of nodes includes all of its parents.

Lemma 2. *If $C \subseteq \Gamma_i$ is a complete set of nodes, then C will pass both the Σ-test and the Δ-test.*

Proof. By the stability property of garbage, there can be no changes to the reference counts of the nodes $S \in C$, since $S \in \Gamma_i$. Therefore, C passes the Δ-test.

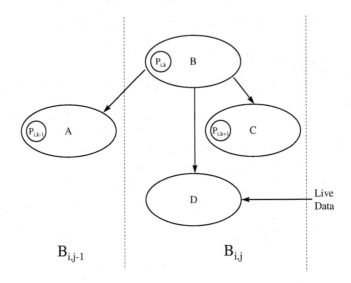

Fig. 7. Concurrent mutation of the nodes in D can cause candidate sets $B_{i,j-1}$ and $B_{i,j}$ to become undiscovered garbage.

By the same reasoning,

$$RC(S,C) = RC^\Sigma(S,C).$$

Since C is a complete set,

$$RC(S) = RC(S,C).$$

Therefore,

$$\begin{aligned} CRC(S) &= RC(S) - RC^\Sigma(S,C) \\ &= RC(S) - RC(S,C) \\ &= 0 \end{aligned}$$

Hence, C will pass the Σ-test.   □

5.3   Liveness: Proof of Correctness

A garbage collector is *live* if it eventually collects all unreachable objects. Our concurrent algorithm is subject to some extremely rare race conditions, which may prevent the collection of some garbage. Therefore, we prove a weak liveness condition which holds provided that the race condition does not occur in every epoch.

We can only demonstrate weak liveness because it is possible that a candidate cycle $C \in \Omega_i$ contains a subset which is a complete garbage cycle, and some nodes in that subset point to other nodes in C which are live (see Figure 7). This is a result of our running a variant of the synchronous cycle collection algorithm while mutation continues, thus allowing race conditions such as the ones shown in Figure 6 to cause `Collect-Cycles` to occasionally place live nodes in a candidate set B_{ik}. The resulting candidate set B_{ik} will fail either the Σ-test or the Δ-test for that epoch. If this occurs, the cycle will be reconsidered in the following epoch. Therefore, unless the race condition occurs indefinitely, the garbage will eventually be collected.

Any garbage nodes that are not collected in epoch i are called the *undiscovered garbage* of epoch i.

In practice, we have been unable to induce the race condition that leads to undiscovered garbage, even with adversary programs. However, this remains a theoretical limitation of our approach.

We have solutions to this problem (for instance, breaking up a set that fails either of the two tests into strongly connected components), but have not included them because they complicate the algorithm and are not required in practice. We are also investigating another alternative, in which the entire cycle collection is based on performing a strongly-connected component algorithm [4]; this alternative is also promising in that the number of passes over the object graph is substantially reduced.

In this section we will prove that if a set of garbage nodes is free from the race condition leading to undiscovered garbage, it will be collected in the epoch i; otherwise it will be considered again in the epoch $i + 1$.

We previously defined P_i as the set of purple nodes in epoch i, that is the set of nodes from which the cycle detection algorithm begins searching for cyclic garbage in `CollectCycles`.

Theorem 3. *The purple set is maintained correctly by the concurrent cycle collection algorithm: every garbage node is reachable from some purple node. That is,*

$$\Gamma_i \subseteq P_i^{\star}.$$

Proof. The `Decrement` procedure ensures that the only garbage in the set G_i is cyclic garbage. In addition, `Decrement` adds all nodes having decrement to non-zero to the purple set. Thus we know that any cyclic garbage generated during the processing of increments and decrements in epoch i is reachable from the purple set. What remains to be proved is that the purple set contains roots to any uncollected cyclic garbage from the previous epochs.

We know this to be trivially true for epoch 1. We assume that it is true for epoch i and prove that, after running the `CollectCycles` routine, it is true for epoch $i + 1$. The result then follows by induction.

Let P be a member of the purple set in epoch i that is the root of a garbage cycle. The `CollectRoots` routine ensures that the root of each cycle generated by it is stored in the first position in the buffer and takes all white nodes that are reachable from it and unless it has been collected before (therefore reachable from another root node) puts it in the current cycle. Since `CollectCycles` is a version of the synchronous garbage collection algorithm, and there can be no concurrent mutation to a subgraph of garbage nodes, all such garbage nodes will be in the current cycle. In addition, any other uncollected purple node reachable from P and the cycle associated with will be added to the current cycle. If this latter purple node is garbage, then it will continue to be reachable from P and hence proper handling of P will ensure proper handling of this node and its children.

The Refurbish routine will put this first node back into the purple root set unless: a) the current cycle is determined to be garbage, in which case the entire cycle is freed or b) the first node is determined to be live, in which case it is not the root of a garbage cycle.

Hence the purple set P_{i+1} will contain the roots of all the garbage cycles that survive the cycle collect in epoch i.   □

Corollary 1. *The cycle buffer generated in the ith epoch contains all the garbage nodes present in G_i. That is,*

$$\Gamma_i \subseteq B_i \subseteq P_i^{\star}.$$

Proof. By Theorem 3, the root of every garbage cycle is contained in P_i. The procedure CollectCycles is a version of the synchronous garbage collection algorithm. There can be no concurrent mutation to a subgraph of garbage nodes. Therefore, all garbage nodes will be in put into the cycle buffer B_i.   □

Unfortunately, due to concurrent mutation B_i may contain some live nodes too. Let $B_{ij} \in B_i$ denote a set of nodes that were collected starting from a root node $P_{ik} \in P_i$. If all the nodes in B_{ij} are live, then it will fail one of the two tests (Δ-test or Σ-test) and its root will be identified as a live node and discarded.

It is however possible that B_{ij} contains a set of garbage nodes as well as a set of live nodes as shown in Figure 7. There are three purple nodes $P_{i,k-1}, P_{i,k}, P_{i,k+1}$. CollectWhite processes $P_{i,k-1}$ first and creates the candidate set $B_{i,j-1}$ which contains the nodes in A. Then CollectWhite processes $P_{i,k}$ and creates the candidate set $B_{i,j}$ which contains the nodes in B, C, and D. This includes both the garbage nodes in C reachable from another purple node not yet considered ($P_{i,k+1}$) and live nodes in D.

In this case B_{ij} will fail one of the two safety tests and the algorithm will fail to detect that it contained some garbage nodes. Furthermore, the algorithm will fail to detect any other garbage nodes that are pointed to by this garbage, such as $B_{i,j-1}$ in the figure. The roots $P_{i,k-1}$ and P_{ik} will be put into P_{i+1}, so the garbage cycles will be considered again in $(i+1)^{st}$ epoch, and unless a malicious mutator is able to fool CollectCycles again, it will be collected in that epoch. But the fact remains that it will not be collected during the current epoch.

Let U_i be the set of nodes undiscovered garbage in epoch i. That is, every member of U_i either has a live node in its cycle set or its cycle set is pointed to by a member of U_i. We will show that all the other garbage nodes (i.e. the set $\Gamma_i - U_i$) will be collected in epoch i.

Lemma 3. *There are no edges from garbage nodes in B_{ik} to B_{il} where $k < l$.*

Proof. The CollectRoots routine takes all white nodes that are reachable from the root of the current cycle, colors them orange, and places them in a set B_{il}. Any nodes that it reaches that were previously colored orange are not included in the set because they have already been included in some previous set B_{ik}. Thus all nodes that are reachable from the current root exist in the current cycle or in a cycle collected previously. Since the nodes in B_{ik} were collected before the nodes in B_{il} there can be no forward pointers from the first to the second set, unless some edges were added after the running of the `CollectRoots` routine. However, since there can be no mutation involving garbage nodes, this is not possible. □

Let K_i be the set of all nodes collected by the procedure `FreeCycles`.

Theorem 4. *All the garbage that is not undiscovered due to race conditions will be collected in the ith epoch. That is,*

$$K_i = \Gamma_i - U_i.$$

Proof. From Corollary 1 above, we know that every node in Γ_i is contained in B_i.

If a cycle B_{ij} fails the Δ-test, then we know that it has a live node. In that case, a node in this cycle is either live, in which case it does not belong to Γ_i, or it is a garbage node that is undiscovered garbage, hence it belongs to U_i. Thus none of these nodes belong to $\Gamma_i - U_i$.

If a cycle B_{ij} fails the Σ-test, it means that there is some undeleted edge from outside the set of nodes in B_{ij}. By Lemma 3, it cannot be from a garbage node that comes earlier in the cycle buffer. If this is from a live node or from a garbage node that is undiscovered garbage, then garbage nodes in this cycle, if any, belong to the set U_i. If it is not from an undiscovered garbage node, then that garbage node belongs to a discovered garbage set later in the cycle buffer.

But in the `FreeCycles` routine we process the cycles in the reverse of the order in which they were collected. As we free garbage cycles, we delete all edges from the nodes in it. By Lemma 3, the last discovered garbage set cannot have any external pointers to it. Therefore it will pass the Σ-test also. In addition, when we delete all edges from this set, the next discovered garbage set will pass the Σ-test. Hence, every discovered garbage cycle set B_{ij} will pass both the tests. □

Corollary 2. *In the absence of the race condition leading to undiscovered garbage, namely a mixture of live and garbage nodes in some set B_{ik}, all garbage will be collected. That is,*
$$K_i = \Gamma_i.$$

Proof. In this case, there are no live nodes in any B_{ik} that contains garbage and hence U_i is a null set. The result follows from Theorem 4. □

6   Measurements

We now present measurements of the effectiveness of our concurrent cycle collection algorithm within the Recycler, a reference counting garbage collector implemented as part of, Jalapeño, a Java virtual machine written in Java at the IBM T.J. Watson Research Center.

Program	Description	Applic. Size	Threads	Objects Allocated	Percent Acyclic
201_compress	Compression	18 KB	1	0.2 M	73%
202_jess	Java expert system	11 KB	1	17.4 M	19%
209_db	Database	10 KB	1	6.6 M	10%
227_mtrt	Multithreaded raytracer	571 KB	2	14.2 M	87%
228_jack	Parser generator	131 KB	1	16.8 M	78%
portbob	Business Object Benchmark	138 KB	3	7.9 M	61%
jalapeño	Jalapeño compiler	1378 KB	1	19.2 M	7%
ggauss	Cyclic torture test (synth.)	8 KB	1	32.5 M	< 1%

Table 2. Benchmarks and their overall characteristics.

The measurements in this section concentrate on the operation of the reference counting system within the Recycler. In concurrently published work [3] we present detailed measurements of the system as a whole, including a comprehensive performance evaluation which shows that with sufficient resources, the Recycler achieves a maximum 6 millisecond pause time without appreciably slowing down the applications.

6.1 Benchmarks

Table 2 summarizes the benchmarks we used. Our benchmarks consist of a mixture of SPEC benchmarks and other programs: portbob is an early version of the benchmark recently accepted by SPEC under the name jbb; jalapeño is the Jalapeño optimizing compiler compiling itself; and ggauss is a synthetic benchmark designed as a "torture test" for the cycle collector: it does nothing but create cyclic garbage, using a Gaussian distribution of neighbors to create a smooth distribution of random graphs.

Since we did no have source code for all benchmarks, application size is given as the total class file size in kilobytes.

SPEC benchmarks were run with "size 100" for exactly two iterations, and the entire run, including JIT time, was counted.

We ran the benchmarks with one more CPU than there are threads; the extra CPU ran the concurrent collector.

The largest benchmark is jalapeño, the Jalapeño optimizing compiler compiling itself. It allocates 19 million objects, of which only 8% are determined by the classloader to be acyclic (and therefore marked green). The optimizer represents the worst-case type of program likely to be seen by the cycle collector in practice: its data structures consist almost entirely of graphs and doubly-linked lists.

6.2 Cycle Collection

Table 3 summarizes the operation of the concurrent cycle collection algorithm. Cycle collection was performed every eight epochs or when the Roots buffer exceeded a threshold size; usually the latter condition triggered cycle collections sooner. They seem to occur once every four to five epochs.

Program	Ep.	Cyc. Coll.	Roots Checked	Cycles Found			Marked			Refs. Traced	Trace/ Alloc.
				Coll.	Σ	Δ	Gray	White	Orange		
201_compress	40	9	12153	97	0	0	13020	726	484	62971	0.42
202_jess	127	33	155507	0	13	0	293995	14523	52	2281521	0.13
209_db	275	61	1261177	0	0	0	2793425	14551	0	23737713	3.57
227_mtrt	152	29	467334	10	0	2	3097618	1122418	654137	18558847	1.31
228_jack	230	47	151160	782	0	0	231356	75610	49141	875234	0.05
portbob	50	16	434071	0	0	5	678077	2279	5	6345488	0.80
jalapeño	476	106	6382521	279790	0	0	7621940	3049754	2019731	49571627	2.58
ggauss	489	105	7111449	266666	0	0	7511620	6782726	6484782	37715868	1.16

Table 3. Cycle Collection. "Ep." is the number of epochs; "Cyc. Coll." is the number of cycle collections. For "Cycles Found", the number collected, and rejected due to the Σ- and Δ-tests.

There were a number of surprising results. First of all, despite the large number of roots considered, the number of garbage cycles found was usually quite low. Cyclic garbage was significant in jalapeño and our torture test, ggauss. It was also significant in compress, although the numbers do not show it: multi-megabyte buffers hang from cyclic data structures in compress, so the application runs out of memory if its 97 cycles are not collected in a timely manner.

The Jalapeño optimizing compiler and the synthetic graph generator both freed about 20% of their objects with the cycle collector. We were surprised that the number was not higher, given that virtually all of the data structures were potentially cyclic. However, it appears that even so, a large proportion of objects are simple (rather than cyclic) garbage.

Of more than half a million candidate cycles found for the eight benchmarks, concurrent mutation introduced only 20 false candidate cycles, with most of the false cycles being rejected by the Σ-test in jess. None of these rejected cycles was undiscovered garbage that was collected later (that is, part of a set U_i as described in Section 5).

In fact, we were unable to create false cycles artificially when we tried modifying the ggauss program to turn it into a malicious mutator designed solely for the purpose of fooling the CollectCycles algorithm. This demonstrates conclusively that undiscovered garbage is a problem only in theory, and not in practice.

Table 3 also shows how the different phases of the cycle collection algorithm proceeded: marking (gray), looking like cyclic garbage (white), and provisionally identified as cyclic garbage (orange). The amount of marking varied widely according to the benchmarks.

Finally, Table 3 shows the number of references that must be followed by the concurrent reference counting collector ("Refs. Traced"). We have also normalized this against the total number of objects allocated ("Trace/Alloc"). The db benchmark required the most tracing per object. Apparently it performs far more modification of its potentially cyclic data structures than other programs – presumably inserting and removing database objects into its index data structure.

Compared to tracing garbage collectors, the reference counting collector has an advantage in that it only traces locally from potential roots, but has a disadvantage in that the algorithm requires multiple passes over the subgraph. Furthermore, if the root of a large data structure is entered into the root buffer frequently and high mutation rates force frequent epoch boundaries, the same live data structure might be traversed multiple times.

Our measurements show that a reference-counting based collector using our cycle collection technique may perform very little tracing, or a large amount of tracing, and that this is very application dependent.

Over all, the measurements presented here show that our cycle collection algorithm is practical and capable of handling large programs, and in many cases should provide significantly increased locality and reduction in memory traffic over tracing-based collectors.

The Recycler is described in greater detail and compared quantitatively to a parallel mark-and-sweep collector by Bacon et al [3].

7   Related Work on Concurrent Collection

While numerous concurrent, multiprocessor collectors for general-purpose programming languages have been described in the literature [8, 10, 11, 14, 15, 18, 19, 21, 26, 27], the number that have been implemented is quite small and of these, only a few actually run on a multiprocessor [2, 8, 14, 11, 13, 24].

DeTreville's work on garbage collectors for Modula-2+ on the DEC Firefly workstation [8] is the only comparative evaluation of multiprocessor garbage collection techniques. His algorithm is based on Rovner's reference counting collector [26] backed by a concurrent tracing collector for cyclic garbage. Unfortunately, despite having implemented a great variety of collectors, he only provides a qualitative comparison. Nevertheless, our findings agree with DeTreville's in that he found reference counting to be highly effective for a general-purpose programming language on a multiprocessor. The Recycler differs in its use of cycle collection instead of a backup mark-and-sweep collector.

Huelsbergen and Winterbottom [15] describe a concurrent algorithm (VCGC) that is used in the Inferno system to back up a reference counting collector. They report that reference counting collects 98% of data; our measurements for Java show that the proportion of cyclic garbage is often small but varies greatly. The only measurements provided for VCGC were on a uniprocessor for SML/NJ, so it is difficult to make meaningful comparisons.

The only other concurrent, multiprocessor collector for Java that we know of is the work of Domani et al [13, 12]. This is a generational collector based on the work of Doligez et al [11], for which generations were shown to sometimes provide significant improvements in throughput.

The other implemented concurrent multiprocessor collectors [2, 14, 11, 24] are all tracing-based algorithms for concurrent variants of ML, and generally have significantly longer maximum pause times than our collector. In addition, ML produces large amounts of immutable data, thereby simplifying the collection process.

The garbage collector of Huelsbergen and Larus [14] for ML achieved maximum pause times of 20 ms in 1993, but only for two small benchmarks (Quicksort and Knuth-Bendix). Their collector requires a read barrier for mutable objects that relies on processor consistency to avoid locking objects while they are being forwarded. Read barriers, even without synchronization instructions, are generally considered impractical for imperative languages [17], and on weakly ordered multiprocessors their barrier would require synchronization on every access to a mutable object, so it is not clear that the algorithm is practical either for imperative languages or for the current generation of multiprocessor machines.

Lins has presented a concurrent cycle collection algorithm [21] based on his synchronous algorithm. Unlike the Recycler, Lins does not use a separate reference count for the cycle collector; instead he relies on processor-supported asymmetric locking primitives to prevent concurrent mutation to the graph. His scheme has, to our knowledge, never been implemented. It does not appear to be practical on stock multiprocessor hardware because of the fine-grained locking required between the mutators and the collector. Our algorithm avoids such fine-grained locking by using a second reference count field when searching for cycles, and performing safety tests (the Σ-test and the Δ-test) to validate the cycles found.

Jones and Lins [16] present an algorithm for garbage collection in distributed systems that uses a variant of the lazy mark-scan algorithm for handling cycles. However, they rely on much more heavy-weight synchronization (associated with message sends and receives and global termination detection) than our algorithm. The algorithm has never been implemented.

In terms of cycle collection systems that have been implemented, the closest to our work is that of Rodrigues and Jones [25], who have implemented an algorithm for cycle collection in distributed systems. However, they use a tracing collector for local cycles and assume that inter-processor cycles are rare, and they use considerably more heavy-weight mechanisms (such as lists of back-pointers) than we do; on the other hand they also solve some problems that we do not address, like fault tolerance.

8 Conclusions

We have presented algorithms for the collection of cyclic data structures in reference counted systems, starting with a synchronous algorithm which we then extended to handle concurrent mutation without requiring any but the loosest synchronization between mutator threads and the collector.

We presented detailed pseudocode and a proof of correctness of the concurrent algorithm. We have implemented these algorithms as part of the Recycler, a concurrent multiprocessor reference counting garbage collector for Java, and we presented measurements that show the effectiveness of our algorithm over a suite of eight significant Java benchmarks.

Our work is novel in two important respects: it represents the first practical use of cycle collection in a reference counting garbage collector for a mainstream programming language; and it requires no explicit synchronization between the mutator threads or between the mutators and the collector.

Another contribution of our work is our proof methodology, which allows us to reason about an abstract graph that never exists in the machine, but is implied by the stream of increment and decrement operations processed by the collector. In effect we are able to reason about a consistent snapshot without ever having to take such a snapshot in the implementation.

Our cycle collection algorithm forms a key part of the Recycler, a garbage collector for Java, which achieves end-to-end execution times competitive with a parallel mark-and-sweep collector while holding maximum application pause times to only six milliseconds.

Acknowledgements

We thank Dick Attanasio, Han Lee, and Steve Smith for their contributions to the implementation of the reference-counting garbage collector in which we implemented the algorithms described in this paper, and the entire Jalapeño team, without which this work would not have been possible. We also thank the anonymous referees for their comments which helped us to improve the paper.

References

[1] ALPERN, B., ET AL. Implementing Jalapeño in Java. In *OOPSLA'99 Conference Proceedings: Object-Oriented Programming Systems, Languages, and Applications* (Denver, Colorado, Oct. 1999). *SIGPLAN Notices, 34*, 10, 314–324.

[2] APPEL, A. W., ELLIS, J. R., AND LI, K. Real-time concurrent collection on stock multiprocessors. In *Proceedings of the SIGPLAN Conference on Programming Language Design and Implementation* (Atlanta, Georgia, June 1988). *SIGPLAN Notices, 23*, 7 (July), 11–20.

[3] BACON, D. F., ATTANASIO, C. R., LEE, H. B., RAJAN, V. T., AND SMITH, S. Java without the coffee breaks: A nonintrusive multiprocessor garbage collector. In *Proceedings of the SIGPLAN Conference on Programming Language Design and Implementation* (Snowbird, Utah, June 2001). *SIGPLAN Notices, 36*, 5 (May).

[4] BACON, D. F., KOLODNER, H., NATHANIEL, R., PETRANK, E., AND RAJAN, V. T. Strongly-connected component algorithms for concurrent cycle collection. Tech. rep., IBM T.J. Watson Research Center and IBM Haifa Scientific Center, Apr. 2001.

[5] BOBROW, D. G. Managing re-entrant structures using reference counts. *ACM Trans. Program. Lang. Syst. 2*, 3 (July 1980), 269–273.

[6] CHRISTOPHER, T. W. Reference count garbage collection. *Software – Practice and Experience 14*, 6 (June 1984), 503–507.

[7] COLLINS, G. E. A method for overlapping and erasure of lists. *Commun. ACM 3*, 12 (Dec. 1960), 655–657.

[8] DETREVILLE, J. Experience with concurrent garbage collectors for Modula-2+. Tech. Rep. 64, DEC Systems Research Center, Palo Alto, California, Aug. 1990.

[9] DEUTSCH, L. P., AND BOBROW, D. G. An efficient incremental automatic garbage collector. *Commun. ACM 19*, 7 (July 1976), 522–526.

[10] DIJKSTRA, E. W., LAMPORT, L., MARTIN, A. J., SCHOLTEN, C. S., AND STEFFENS, E. F. M. On-the-fly garbage collection: An exercise in cooperation. In *Hierarchies and Interfaces*, F. L. Bauer et al., Eds., vol. 46 of *Lecture Notes in Computer Science*. Springer-Verlag, New York, 1976, pp. 43–56.

[11] DOLIGEZ, D., AND LEROY, X. A concurrent generational garbage collector for a multi-threaded implementation of ML. In *Conference Record of the Twentieth ACM Symposium on Principles of Programming Languages* (Charleston, South Carolina, Jan. 1993), ACM Press, New York, New York, pp. 113–123.

[12] DOMANI, T., ET AL. Implementing an on-the-fly garbage collector for Java. In *Proceedings of the ACM SIGPLAN International Symposium on Memory Management* (Minneapolis, MN, Oct. 2000). *SIGPLAN Notices, 36*, 1, 155–166.

[13] DOMANI, T., KOLODNER, E. K., AND PETRANK, E. A generational on-the-fly garbage collector for Java. In *Proceedings of the SIGPLAN Conference on Programming Language Design and Implementation* (June 2000). *SIGPLAN Notices, 35*, 6, 274–284.

[14] HUELSBERGEN, L., AND LARUS, J. R. A concurrent copying garbage collector for languages that distinguish (im)mutable data. In *Proceedings of the Fourth ACM Symposium on Principles and Practice of Parallel Programming* (May 1993). *SIGPLAN Notices, 28*, 7 (July), 73–82.

[15] HUELSBERGEN, L., AND WINTERBOTTOM, P. Very concurrent mark-&-sweep garbage collection without fine-grain synchronization. In *Proceedings of the ACM SIGPLAN International Symposium on Memory Management* (Mar. 1999). *SIGPLAN Notices, 34*, 3, 166–174.

[16] JONES, R. E., AND LINS, R. D. Cyclic weighted reference counting without delay. In *PARLE'93 Parallel Architectures and Languages Europe* (June 1993), A. Bode, M. Reeve, and G. Wolf, Eds., vol. 694 of *Lecture Notes in Computer Science*, Springer-Verlag, pp. 712–715.

[17] JONES, R. E., AND LINS, R. D. *Garbage Collection*. John Wiley and Sons, 1996.

[18] KUNG, H. T., AND SONG, S. W. An efficient parallel garbage collection system and its correctness proof. In *IEEE Symposium on Foundations of Computer Science* (1977), IEEE Press, New York, New York, pp. 120–131.

[19] LAMPORT, L. Garbage collection with multiple processes: an exercise in parallelism. In *Proceedings of the 1976 International Conference on Parallel Processing* (1976), pp. 50–54.

[20] LINS, R. D. Cyclic reference counting with lazy mark-scan. *Inf. Process. Lett. 44*, 4 (Dec. 1992), 215–220.

[21] LINS, R. D. A multi-processor shared memory architecture for parallel cyclic reference counting. *Microprocessing and Microprogramming 35*, 1–5 (Sept. 1992), 563–568. *Proceedings of the 18th EUROMICRO Conference* (Paris, France).

[22] MARTÍNEZ, A. D., WACHENCHAUZER, R., AND LINS, R. D. Cyclic reference counting with local mark-scan. *Inf. Process. Lett. 34*, 1 (1990), 31–35.

[23] MCCARTHY, J. Recursive functions of symbolic expressions and their computation by machine. *Commun. ACM 3* (1960), 184–195.

[24] NETTLES, S., AND O'TOOLE, J. Real-time garbage collection. In *Proceedings of the SIGPLAN Conference on Programming Language Design and Implementation* (Albuquerque, New Mexico, June 1993). *SIGPLAN Notices, 28*, 6, 217–226.

[25] RODRIGUES, H. C. C. D., AND JONES, R. E. Cyclic distributed garbage collection with group merger. In *Proceedings of the Twelfth European Conference on Object-Oriented Programming* (Brussels, July 1998), E. Jul, Ed., vol. 1445 of *Lecture Notes in Computer Science*, Springer-Verlag, pp. 249–273.

[26] ROVNER, P. On adding garbage collection and runtime types to a strongly-typed, statically-checked, concurrent language. Tech. Rep. CSL–84–7, Xerox Palo Alto Research Center, July 1985.

[27] STEELE, G. L. Multiprocessing compactifying garbage collection. *Commun. ACM 18*, 9 (Sept. 1975), 495–508.

A Bytecode Translator for Distributed Execution of "Legacy" Java Software

Michiaki Tatsubori[1], Toshiyuki Sasaki[1]*, Shigeru Chiba[1,2]**, and Kozo Itano[1]

[1] University of Tsukuba, Japan
[2] PRESTO, Japan Science and Technology Corporation

Abstract. This paper proposes a system named Addistant, which enables the distributed execution of "legacy" Java bytecode. Here "legacy" means the software originally developed to be executed on a single Java virtual machine (JVM). For adapting legacy software to distributed execution on multiple JVM, developers using Addistant have only to specify the host where instances of each class are allocated and how remote references are implemented. According to that specification, Addistant automatically transforms the bytecode at load time. A technical contribution by Addistant is that it covers a number of issues for implementing distributed execution in the real world. In fact, Addistant can adapt a legacy program written with the Swing library so that Swing objects are executed on a local JVM while the rest of objects are on a remote JVM.

1 Introduction

Object-oriented distributed software can be developed with various programming tools and environments. For example, a number of object request brokers have been proposed[8,9,10,21], just to mention a few, and they allow programmers to easily make an object accessed by a remote host through a network. The programmers only have to define the interface of the object in an interface definition language. Another example is to use a distributed programming language like Emerald[3]. Such a language provides language constructs for creating objects on remote hosts, migrating them to another host, and so on.

However, these programming tools and environments are mainly for developing new distributed software from scratch; they are not for adapting "legacy" software to distributed execution on multiple hosts. Here, "legacy" means that the software was originally developed with intent to be executed on a single host. The existing tools or environments are not helpful in modifying the legacy software so that part of the software can be executed on a remote host. The programmers have to manually modify the source text of the program to follow a programming conventions specified by the tools, or to use special language constructs. This modification takes long time and it is error-prone. It is even impossible if the program text is not available or modifiable. Practical demands

---

* Currently, Hitachi Ltd., Japan.
** Currently, Tokyo Institute of Technology, Japan.

J. Lindskov Knudsen (Ed.): ECOOP 2001, LNCS 2072, pp. 236–255, 2001.

for adapting legacy software to distributed execution will never disappear. While there is already a number of such legacy software, programmers will continue to develop legacy software since non-distributed software is easier to develop than distributed software.

To support distributed execution of legacy software written in Java[7], we have developed a system named *Addistant*. Addistant helps developers modify legacy Java programs to run on multiple Java virtual machines (JVM)[14]. It performs:

- Letting developers specify where to allocate the instances of each class among multiple hosts, in a policy file separated from the original program. All the instances of a class must be subject to the same allocation policy. Since real software contains a large number of objects, it is not realistic to individually specify where each object is allocated.
- Translating the bytecode of the legacy Java software according to the specification above so that specified classes are executed on the JVM running on a remote host. Addistant does not need source code for the translation. The translated bytecode is the regular Java bytecode. No custom JVM is needed for execution. And,
- Delivering the translated bytecode to remote JVM. This delivery is also performed by the runtime system of Addistant.

The translation by Addistant has been implemented by a synthesis and re-engineering of ideas found in existing programming tools and environments for distributed software. It is based on the proxy-master model, in which a proxy object forwards method invocations to a remote object through a network although the generation of the classes for proxy objects automatically managed by Addistant; it is hidden from the developers. A technical contribution by Addistant is rather that it covers all the issues that we encounter if applying the proxy-master model to real software development in Java. For example, since the JVM does not allow modifying the bytecode of the system classes at load time, the proxy-master model cannot be implemented with only a well-known straightforward translation, which requires the bytecode translation of all related classes including the system classes. To avoid these problems, Addistant provides multiple implementation approaches, which developers can choose for each class.

A typical application of Addistant is to apply functional distribution to a legacy Java program so that some modules of that program are executed on a remote host suitable for the functionality of those modules. For example, Addistant can be used to adapt a legacy program using the Swing class library[22], which is Java's graphical user interface (GUI) library, so that GUI objects are executed on a host in front of the user while other objects are on a remote high-performance host. The resulting program produced by Addistant achieves good performance. Although the same effects can be achieved by using the X Window System[18], which enables the program to show windows on a remote display, our experiments showed that Addistant could achieve better response time of the GUI than the X Window System. This is because the X Window

System implements distribution at the level of runtime library and thus it needs network communication for every drawing primitive. On the other hand, Addistant implements distribution by translating a whole program including both library code and user code. This higher-level distribution significantly reduces the amount of network communication. This fact suggests that a distributed program developed with a program translator can give better performance than one with a runtime library.

In the rest of this paper, Section 2 presents the architecture of Addistant. Section 3 describes Java-related implementation issues. In Section 4, we show how Addistant can be used for adapting legacy software using the Swing class library to distributed execution. Section 5 discusses related work. Finally, section 6 concludes the paper.

2 Addistant

Addistant is a Java programming tool for adapting legacy software, which was developed with intent to be executed on a single JVM, to distributed execution so that some objects of that software are executed on a remote host. This adaptation is performed by a bytecode translator at load time. This section first mentions design issues of the tools like Addistant, and then presents how Addistant deals with them.

2.1 Design Goal

Unlike developing distributed software from scratch, adapting legacy software written in Java to distributed execution needs special tool support. Without such tool support, programmers would have to read the program of that software and modify it so that some objects should be allocated on a remote host and method invocations be specially treated as if they are across a network. Since manual modification is troublesome and error-prone, a programming tool should automate this modification.

Although a number of researchers have been proposing Java-based distributed languages[12,17,19], those languages are not suitable for this purpose. Using such a distributed language, the programmer needs to obtain the source code of the program, which is usually unavailable if supplied by a third party. Moreover, she has to modify the program to use special syntax provided by that language. For example, in case of a language proposed by Nagaratnam[17], a regular Java statement for creating an object:

```
Frame f = new Frame("The Great Encyclopedia");
```

must be replaced with a statement:

```
Frame f = remotenew Frame("The Great Encyclopedia");
```

using special syntax `remotenew`. She has to obtain the source code and edit all such statements.

Existing object request brokers (ORB)[4,8,9,10,21] are not suitable as well. They are mainly for making legacy software as a component of larger distributed software. To use such an ORB for distributing some modules of that software to a remote host, a programmer has to manually split the software into several modules and modify the program so that interactions among the modules are subject to the protocols of the ORB. For example, the Java RMI requires that all remote method invocations be performed through interface types. Suppose a method `show()` is called on a remote instance `f` of a class Frame. First, the programmer must declare a new interface DistributedFrame and modify the declaration of the class Frame so that the class Frame implements the interface DistributedFrame. Then she has to substitute DistributedFrame for occurrences of the class name Frame in the program. Also, she has to care about a number of issues such as remote object creation and polymorphism.

An ideal tool for adapting legacy software to distributed execution must provide the following features:

- **Remote reference:** The tool must hide implementation details of remote-object references from the programmers. The programmers should not have to modify the program so that remote references in the program follow a particular protocol specified by the tool.
- **Policy of object allocation:** The tool must allow the programmers to easily specify whether each object is allocated on a local host or a remote host. Since the programmers may not know details of the program of legacy software, the object allocation should be specified at an appropriate abstract level.
- **Program delivery:** The tool must be able to automatically deliver the program of modules to a remote host if those modules are executed on that host.

In the rest of this section, we first focus on the implementation of the remote reference. Then we describe how the users of Addistant specify the policy of object allocation. We also describe how Addistant implements the program delivery.

2.2   Remote Reference

Addistant implements remote references by bytecode translation at load time. To run the translated software, no custom JVM is needed; Addistant only needs that the regular JVM is running on every host.

Addistant employs the proxy-master model, which is also known as the Remote Proxy pattern[6,20], so that a remote method can be transparently invoked with the same syntax as a local method. In this model, an object whose methods can be invoked from a remote host is associated with an object called proxy existing on that remote host. For distinction, we call the former object master.

A proxy provides the same set of methods as its master and delegates every method invocation to its master. It encapsulates details of network communication necessary for the remote method invocations.

Unfortunately, any single implementation approach of the proxy-master model cannot deal with all kinds of classes. Each approach covers only the classes satisfying the criteria peculiar to that approach. Since we design a programming tool for legacy software, which someone else may have written, we cannot choose a single approach and enforce the criteria on the whole program. For example, one of the approaches needs to modify the declaration of the class of master objects. Since the JVM does not accept modified system classes, if an instance of a system class is a remote object, that approach cannot be used. A different approach must be used for that case.

To avoid this problem, Addistant provides several different approaches for implementing the proxy-master model. It currently provides four approaches: *replace*, *rename*, *subclass*, and *copy*. The developers can choose one from the four for each class of master. The differences among the four approaches are mainly how a proxy class is declared, how caller-side code, that is, expressions of remote method invocations, is modified, and how a master class is modified. The four approaches cover most of cases in practical development according to our experiences with the Swing library. To choose one from these four approaches, the developers must know whether a given class of master meets some of the following features or not:

- **Call by reference:** The master object must be passed to a remote method as a parameter in the call-by-reference manner. It cannot be passed in the call-by-value manner.
- **Heterogeneity:** A variable with that class type must be able to hold both local and remote references. Some kinds of master objects do not require this feature. For example, all the instances of a GUI class would exist on the same host in front of the user. If so, all the references to those instances are local on that host while they are remote on the other host. In this case, local and remote references do not coexist on a single host.
- **Unmodifiable bytecode:** The implementation must be done without transforming the unmodifiable bytecode. This is required as JVM prohibits the developers from modifying or replacing the bytecode of the system classes such as java.util.Vector. This feature is divided into three sub-features: the class declaration of the master objects (*original class*) is unmodifiable, other master classes accessing the master objects (*referrer classes*) are, or other master classes creating the master objects (*factory classes*) are, respectively.

The remainder of this subsection presents details of the four approaches, and conditions in which the approaches can be used. The summary of the conditions is listed in Table 1.

Replace Approach. The first approach is the *replace* approach. It is available unless the heterogeneity feature is required or the original class is unmodifiable.

Table 1. Applicability of the four approaches. The mark of x ([x]) indicates that the approach is (probably) unavailable in case the feature is required.

	Replace	Rename	Subclass	Copy
Call by reference				x
Heterogeneity	x	x		
Unmodifiable bytecode of original class	x		[x]	[x]
referrer classes		x		
factory classes		x	x	

Developers should apply this approach to non-system classes whose masters are allocated at the same host.

Suppose that the class of a master object is Widget. Since the heterogeneity feature is not required, all the references to the Widget objects are either local or remote. Therefore, Addistant uses the original Widget class for local references on one host while it generates another version of the Widget class for remote references on the other hosts (Table 2). This version corresponds to a proxy class for the original Widget class. Addistant sends the bytecode of this proxy class to the host where there are remote references to Widget masters.

Table 2. The proxy class for a class Widget used by each approach. Here, we assume that the original Widget is a subclass of Object.

	Replace	Rename	Subclass
Proxy class	Widget†	WidgetProxy	WidgetProxy
Superclass of proxy	Object	Object	Widget
Variable type for proxy	Widget†	WidgetProxy	Widget

†A different version of the Widget class.

Rename Approach. The second approach is the *rename* approach. The replace approach is not available if the declaration of the original class is not modifiable. The rename approach can be used in that case although it requires that the referrer classes and the factory classes are modifiable. As the replace approach, the rename approach is not available if the heterogeneity feature is required. Developers should apply this approach to classes like java.awt.Window.

In the rename approach, Addistant generates a proxy class of the original class Widget with a different name such as WidgetProxy. Then Addistant uses that proxy class for remote references. It modifies the bytecode of all the referrer classes on the hosts where references to the Widget objects are remote so that all the occurrences of the original class name Widget are replaced with the proxy class name WidgetProxy. Addistant does not modify the other referrer classes on the host where references to the Widget objects are local.

Addistant also modifies the factory classes if they are used on the host where references to the Widget objects are remote. Since the Widget objects must be created on the other host, Addistant also replaces all the occurrences of Widget with WidgetProxy in the bytecode of the factory classes. For example, it translates the following statement:

```
Frame w = new Frame();
```

into this statement:

```
FrameProxy w = new FrameProxy();
```

The latter statement creates a proxy object, which requests a remote host to create a master object.

Subclass Approach. The third approach is the *subclass* approach. It is available even if the heterogeneity feature is required. Developers should apply this approach to classes like java.util.Vector.

In this approach, a proxy class WidgetProxy is a subclass of the original class Widget. Both local and remote references have the reference type to Widget so that they can coexist on the same host. If a reference is local, it points to a Widget object. If a reference is remote, it points to a WidgetProxy object.

However, as the rename approach, this approach needs to modify the factory classes if they are used on the host on which references to master objects are remote. Furthermore, this approach may require that the original class is modifiable. First, if the original class is a **final** class or it includes a **final** method, it must be modified to be a non-**final** class and to include no **final** method. Otherwise, the proxy class cannot be a subclass of the original class or override methods declared in the original class. Second, if the constructor of the original class causes inappropriate side-effects and fails to create an object, Addistant must add to that class another constructor performing nothing so that the constructor of the proxy class can call it. Remember that a constructor must call a constructor of the super class in Java. For example, the original constructor of the class Widget may access a local graphic device. If it is called by the constructor of WidgetProxy (since WidgetProxy is a subclass of Widget), it may throw an error because of the absence of the graphic device on the host where the WidgetProxy object is created.

Note that the subclass approach does not require that the original class is modifiable if the original class is not a **final** class and the constructors do not cause inappropriate side-effects. For instance, the bytecode of a system class java.io.File is unmodifiable. Since that class is used by other system classes, the referrer classes are also unmodifiable. Thus, even if the heterogeneity feature is not required, either the replace or rename approaches cannot be used for java.io.File. On the other hand, the subclass approach can be used for that class.

Copy Approach. The last is the *copy* approach. This approach can be used for primitive types such as **int** and classes like java.lang.String, instances of which are immutable.

If the copy approach is chosen for a class C, a remote reference to an instance of C cannot exist. If a local reference to an instance of C is passed to a remote method, Addistant makes a *shallow* copy of that instance on the remote host. A local reference to that copy is passed to the method. Thus, the copy approach cannot be used if a reference must be passed to a remote method in the call-by-reference manner. However, the copy approach does not need to modify bytecode at all.

Addistant also provides a slightly different version of the copy approach: the *write-back* copy approach. If this approach is chosen, the contents of the copy passed to the remote method are written back to the master object after executing that remote method. For example, suppose that the write-back copy approach is chosen for an array of **byte**. Then in the following code:

```
byte[] buf = ... ;
inputstream.read(buf);
```

the call to **read()** on a remote object **inputstream** makes a copy of **buf** on the remote host. A local reference to that copy is passed to **read()**. Since the write-back copy approach is chosen, the contents of that copy are written back to **buf** after executing **read()**. Therefore, the byte data read from the input stream are eventually stored in **buf**.

2.3   Object Allocation

Addistant allows the developers to specify a policy of object allocation for each class. It does not allow to use a different policy for each object because Addistant is a tool for modifying legacy software; it is not realistic for the developers to specify a policy for every occurrence of "new" (the operator of object creation) appearing in a program, which someone else may have written.

The developers can declare that all the instances of a class are allocated on a specific host. If a host D is specified for a class C, an expression "new C()" (create an instance of C) executed on any host is interpreted as that an instance of C is created on the (probably remote) host D. On the other hand, if any host is not specified for the class C, an expression "new C()" executed on a host D' is interpreted as that an instance of C is locally created on the host D'.

The declaration by the developers is written in a policy file, which Addistant reads at startup time. The policy file is written in an XML-like syntax. For example, a declaration below:

```
<import proxy="rename" from="display">
      java.awt.*
</import>
```

means that all the instances of classes included in the **java.awt** package are allocated on a host specified by a variable **display**. Remote references to these instances are implemented with the rename approach. The variable **display** is bound to a real host name at run time. If the "from" attribute is not given, the instances of a class C are allocated on a host where an expression "new C()" is executed.

Note that java.awt.* means all the classes included in the java.awt package. It does not mean sub-packages of java.awt, such as java.awt.image because sub-packages are irrelevant to the parent package with respect to the language semantics. For example, the access rights of a class in a sub-package are equivalent to ones in other packages than the parent package of that sub-package. To specify all the classes and sub-packages in java.awt, java.awt.- should be used.

Besides all classes included in a package, all subclasses of a class in a package can be specified. For example, a declaration below:

```
<import proxy="rename" from="display">
    subclass@java.awt.Component
</import>
```

means that the rename approach is used for all the subclasses of the class Component, including Component itself. To specify only the subclasses excluding the parent class, exactsubclass should be used instead of subclass.

Some implementation approaches of remote references restrict policies of object allocation. Since the replace and rename approaches require that local and remote references do not coexist, the "from" field must be specified so that instances are created on the same host. On the other hand, the copy approach does not allow the developers to specify the "from" field since it does not deal with remote references.

2.4 Bytecode Delivery

Addistant provides a mechanism for automatically distributing bytecode from a host to other hosts. The users have to only run a class loader of Addistant on every host. If a program starts on a host A and creates an object on a remote host D, the class loader on the host A sends necessary bytecode to the class loader on the host D so that the object can be created on the host D. If the bytecode must be modified, it is modified by the class loader on the host A before it is sent to the host D. If the bytecode is of system classes, the class loader on the host D loads it from a local file system instead of the host A.

Although the regular class loader of Java fetches bytecode on demand, the class loader of Addistant may fetch the bytecode of certain classes in advance. For example, suppose that the rename approach is specified for all subclasses of a class C. If the class loader of Addistant loads a class U, it must read the bytecode of the class specified by every name appearing in the bytecode of U and examine whether each class is a subclass of C. If so, the class name must be replaced with the name of the proxy class. Thus, while the class loader of Addistant loads a class U, it may fetch a number of other classes as well as the class C and subclasses of C.

3 Implementation Issues

3.1 Single System Image

There are several implementation issues for keeping the semantics of the Java language in distributed program execution, that is, providing a single system image with multiple JVMs. This sub section describes how Addistant deals with those issues.

Remote Field Access. Although a naive implementation of the proxy-master model cannot support remote field accesses, Addistant translates a field access at the bytecode levelinto a static method invocation on that class and thereby enables remote field accesses. Suppose that a class Point declares a field x and the field is accessed as follows:

```
Point p;
..   = p.x ..
..   p.x = 100 ..
```

If remote references to Point objects are implemented by the rename approach, the code above is translated into the code below:

```
PointProxy p;
.. = PointProxy.read_x(p) ..
.. PointProxy.write_x(p, 100) ..
```

The static methods read_x() and write_y() implement the remote field accesses. They are declared in the proxy class produced by Addistant.

The translation above must be applied to all the remote field accesses. Therefore, Addistant cannot deal with remote field accesses embedded in the unmodifiable bytecode, for example, the bytecode of the system classes.

Equality between Remote References. Addistant preserves the semantics of the equality operators such as "==" and "!=" with respect to remote references. To do that, Addistant maintains a table of proxy objects on every host so that there exists only a single proxy object referencing to each master object. Addistant gives a unique identifier to every master object and sends this identifier when a reference to the master object is passed as a parameter across the network to a remote method. Then it looks up the corresponding proxy object in the table and passes a reference to that proxy object to the destination method. If the proxy object is not found in the table, Addistant creates and registers it in the table.

Self Deadlock Avoidance. In Addistant, any host can invoke a method on a remote object and receive a method invocation from a remote object. Therefore, a remote method call from a host A to a host D may cause another method call back from D to A. In this case, the latter method call must be handled by the same thread that requested the former method call on the host A. Otherwise, a deadlock may occur if the methods are synchronized ones.

Suppose that a Button object and a Listener object exist on different hosts D (display host) and A (application host), respectively. The declarations of class Button and Listener are as follows:

```
class Button {
    Listener listener;
    synchronized void push() {
        listener.pushed(this);
    }
    synchronized ButtonState getState() { ... }
}

class Listener {
    void handlePush(Button button) {
        .. button.getState() ..
    }
}
```

If push() is invoked on the Button object, it calls handlePush() on the remote Listener object. Then getState() is called back on the Button object. If push() and getState() are executed by different threads, a deadlock occurs since the two threads try to lock the Button object at the same time. The deadlock never occurs if the two objects exist on the same host because all the methods are executed by the same thread.

In order to ensure the same thread executes all the methods called back, Addistant establishes a one-to-one communication channel between the thread executing push() on D (T_D^i) and the one executing handlePush() on A (T_A^i). This communication channel is stored in a thread local variable implemented with java.lang.ThreadLocal. A thread always uses the same channel for every remote method invocation and it waits for not only the result of the invocation but also another request of invocation from a remote thread sharing the same channel. When handlePush() calls getState(), the thread T_A^i sends a request of getState() to the remote thread T_D^i connected through the communication channel, which is the thread executing push() on D and blocking to wait for the result of handlePush(). The thread T_D^i invokes the requested getState() to send the result of getState() through the channel, and then it continues to wait for the result of the original handlePush(). Thereby, both push() and getState() are executed by the same thread T_D^i. A deadlock is avoided.

Distributed Garbage Collection. Addistant maintains a table of objects exported to a remote host. While there exists a proxy object on a remote host, the master object is recorded in that table so that it is not garbage collected. If all the proxy objects are garbage collected, then the master object is removed from the table. If there are no other references to the master object, then the master object is garbage collected.

The table of proxy objects for checking the equality between remote references is implemented with the weak reference mechanism of Java[1]. An element of the table is a weak reference to a proxy object. Thus, the proxy object is garbage collected when the garbage collector determines that nothing except that table refers to the proxy object.

Currently, Addistant cannot collect all objects if remote references make cycles. Although several algorithms are known for dealing with distributed cycles, efficiently implementing those algorithms is not straightforward without modifying the JVM. For example, if using a distributed mark-sweep algorithm, we would need a mechanism for tracing object references. However, Java's reflection API does not provide such a mechanism. We expect that weak references and object finalizers might help to solve this problem but implementation details are still open.

3.2 Bytecode Modification

Bytecode Translation Toolkit. One of the research aims of the development of Addistant was to examine the expressive power of Javassist[5], which is our toolkit for implementing a bytecode translator for Java. Unlike other similar toolkits, Javassist provides a source-level view of bytecode for the developers, who can manipulate bytecode without detailed knowledge of the bytecode specifications. Javassist is easier to use than other naive toolkits as a source-level debugger is easier to use than an assembly-level debugger. On the other hand, Javassist restricts the ability to modify bytecode. It does not allow bytecode modification that is difficult to express with a source-level view.

To show that the expressive power of Javassist is powerful enough to implement a real application, we have developed Addistant within the confines of the Javassist API (Application Programming Interface). No undocumented low-level API was used. All the bytecode modification that Addistant needs could be easily implemented with a source-level abstraction provided by Javassist.

Bootstrap Classes. If we use a command-line option provided by Sun's JVM, we can modify the bytecode of system classes and have the JVM load the modified bytecode at bootstrap time. Hence using this option extends the range of the classes that the approaches provided by Addistant for implementing the proxy-master model are applicable to. However, we did not modify the bytecode of the system classes because Sun's license terms prohibit the modification. Even if we could modify, consistently modifying the system classes is difficult since runtime systems such as a system class loader depends on the definition of the system classes.

4   Distributed Swing Applications

This section presents that Addistant can adapt legacy software using the Swing class library so that GUI objects are allocated on a remote host and the users can interact with the software through the GUI shown on a remote display. The Swing class library is a GUI library included in the standard Java runtime environment. Although the same effects can be achieved with the X Window system[18], Addistant can achieve better performance since drawing operations are directly performed on the host with a display. This is typical benefit of functional distribution. The X Window system needs network communication for every primitive drawing operation and hence communication overheads tend to be a performance bottleneck.

In this section, we first present a policy file for adapting legacy software using the Swing class library to distributed execution. Then we show the results of our performance measurement.

4.1   Policy File

The following is a typical policy file for adapting software using the Swing class library:

```
<policy>
    <import proxy="rename" from="display">
        subclass@java.awt.-
        subclass@javax.swing.-
        subclass@javax.accessibility.*
        subclass@java.util.EventObject                       </import>
    <import proxy="rename" from="application">
        exactsubclass@java.io.[InputStream|OutputStream|Reader|Writer]
        exactsubclass@javax.swing.filechooser.*      </import>
    <import proxy="subclass">
        subclass@java.util.[Dictionary|AbstractCollection|AbstractMap]
        subclass@java.util.BitSet                            </import>
    <import proxy="writeBackCopy">
        array@-                                               </import>
    <import proxy="replace" from="application">
        user@-                                                </import>
    <import proxy="copy">
        -                                                     </import>
</policy>
```

Here, the variable display indicates the host where the GUI objects are allocated. The variable application indicates the other host where the rest of the objects are allocated. An import declaration listed above has a higher priority.

This policy file specifies that GUI objects are allocated on the display host and remote references to those objects are implemented with the rename approach. Any array type (array@-) is processed with the write-back copy approach. The instances of classes except the system classes (user@-) are allocated on the application host and remote references to them are implemented with the replace approach. The rest of the classes are processed with the copy approach.

4.2 Performance Measurement

For performance measurement, we used two host computers. One is a machine with a 500MHz PentiumIII and Linux 2.2. It is a display server for executing GUI objects. The other is a machine with a 440MHz UltraSparcII and Solaris 2.7. It is an application server for executing the other objects. We used the HotSpot JVM (JDK 1.3) for both machines. For connecting the two machines, we used two kinds of network: 100Base-TX full-duplex and 10Base-T half-duplex.

Remote Method Invocation. Before measuring the performance of a GUI, we compared the execution time of remote invocations of empty methods among Addistant (AD) and other Java-based object request brokers (ORB), which are HORB[10] version 2.0.1, Java RMI (JRMI) included in JDK 1.3, and Java Class Broker[8] (JCB) version 1.2. We changed the number and types of parameters and measured the elapsed time of each remote method invocation. We also changed the network connecting the two hosts.

Table 3. Elapsed Time (milliseconds) for a remote method invocation. AD indicates Addistant.

(ms)	(100Base-TX full-duplex)				(10Base-T half-duplex)			
	HORB	JRMI	JCB	AD	HORB	JRMI	JCB	AD
void f()	0.33	0.52	0.71	0.28	0.48	0.69	0.86	0.40
void f(int)	0.33	0.53	0.78	0.48	0.48	0.69	0.93	0.61
int f(int)	0.34	0.54	1.20	0.54	0.49	0.71	1.42	0.68
void f(int,int,int)	0.34	0.54	0.75	0.76	0.49	0.71	0.91	0.91
int f(int,int,int)	0.34	0.55	1.17	0.83	0.50	0.72	1.40	0.99
void f(String)	0.34	0.58	0.83	0.36	0.50	0.75	1.00	0.48
String f(String)	0.35	0.63	0.94	0.37	0.52	0.81	1.11	0.50
void f(String[])	0.58	0.87	1.26	0.66	0.77	1.08	1.46	0.85
String[] f(String[])	0.84	1.22	1.66	0.79	1.10	1.50	1.94	0.99
void f(byte[])	0.69	0.94	1.26	2.76	1.51	1.73	2.08	2.93

Table 3 lists the results. The results showed that Addistant achieved a comparable performance to other ORB except the case that a byte array was passed. This is because the parameter encoder/decoder of Addistant had not been tuned and because Addistant used the write-back copy approach for passing an array as a parameter although the other ORB did not write the updated contents of the array back after executing a method. In the measurement, all String type parameters included 10 ASCII characters. The size of String array was three. The size of byte array was 1024.

Window Drawing. To measure the performance of a GUI, we prepared three Java programs. The first one displays a single window (a java.awt.Frame object) containing no components. The second displays a single empty internal window (a javax.swing.JInternalFrame object) in a window (a javax.swing.JFrame object). The third displays a single internal window containing twenty buttons (a javax.swing.JButton object) in a window. The size of the window is 600 by 600 while the size of the internal window is 500 by 500.

We compared the X Window system[18], Rawt[11], and Addistant by measuring the elapsed time that each program took for creating and drawing a window (and internal windows) on a remote display. The X Window system showed a window on a remote display by connecting a remote X server. Rawt is a GUI library that is compatible to the Swing class library but enables to show a window on a remote display. Addistant showed a window on a remote display by allocating GUI objects on the remote host with that display.

Table 4 listed the results. As a drawing image becomes more complex, Addistant showed better performance against Rawt because Rawt allocates only part of instances of the Swing classes on the remote host with a display and thus it needs a larger number of remote method invocations for drawing a window. On the other hand, Addistant allocates all instances of the Swing classes on the remote host and thus the interactions among the Swing objects are local method invocations. This is because Addistant is a general-purpose bytecode translator and it allows the developers to easily customize object allocation for maximizing performance. Rawt cannot do that since the implementation of Rawt is a black box.

Table 4. The elapsed time (seconds) for drawing a window.

	X Window	Rawt	Addistant
(100base-TX full-duplex)			
No components	0.005	0.041	0.044
1 internal window	0.156	1.814	0.276
20 buttons	0.873	17.599	0.955
(10base-T half-duplex)			
No components	0.006	0.041	0.045
1 internal window	0.612	1.988	0.281
20 buttons	1.895	21.322	0.971

Since the X Window system asynchronously executes an X server and an X client, the elapsed time listed in the table indicates the time needed for sending all the requests from the client to the server. It does not indicate the actual elapsed time of drawing a window. In fact, we observed that the response time of the GUI implemented on top of the X Window system was considerably slower than one on top of Addistant.

To confirm our observation above, we conducted another experiment. We wrote a Java program that displays a button in a window and, if that button is clicked, then a graphic image (1148 by 778) is shown in the window. Table 5 listed the results of our experiment. We measured the elapsed time after the button was clicked by mouse until the image was shown. The time was measured by hand. 0.0 means that the response time was too short to measure. Since the Swing class library caches a drawn image, Rawt and Addistant responded quicker than the X Window to a mouse click at the second time. The X Window must transfer the drawn image every time from the client to the server. Even at the first time, Addistant achieved the best performance if the network is 10Base-T since the X Window system and Rawt had to transfer a larger amount of data between the hosts. Table 6 listed the results of our measurement of the size of the data exchanged through a network during the above interaction. The X Window system needs a few megabytes whereas Addistant does less than a hundred kilobytes. The large amount of exchanged data can be a performance bottleneck.

Table 5. The response time (seconds) to a mouse click.

(sec.)	(100Base-TX full-duplex)			(10Base-T half-duplex)		
	X Window	Rawt	Addistant	X Window	Rawt	Addistant
1st	1.6	2.6	2.0	5.6	3.2	2.0
2nd	1.4	0.0	0.0	5.6	0.0	0.0

Table 6. The size of the data (Kbyte) exchanged through a network.

	X Window	Rawt	Addistant
1st	3493.57	116.20	81.88
2nd	3438.96	10.95	0.06

5   Related Work

5.1   Transparent Distribution

To run a Java program on a distributed environment, several extended Java virtual machines have been developed. These virtual machines such as cJVM[2], Java/DSM[23], and JESSICA[16] provide a single-machine image on several network-connected computers, that is, a workstation/PC cluster. Thus, multiple threads are executed in parallel as if they were running on a multi-processor machine with shared memory. These virtual machines do not need to modify a program at all to run it. A difference between Addistant and these virtual machines is that Addistant uses the standard JVM and hence it is mainly for functional distribution, where objects run on the most suitable host for the computation by the objects.

   JavaParty[19] extended the Java language for parallel distributed computing. They introduced only the extended modifier "remote" for class declarations. Although the users of Addistant do not have to modify a program, the users of JavaParty have to append an extended modifier "remote" to a class declaration if an instance of that class is accessed through a remote reference.

There are a number of object request brokers for Java. Most of them, including the Java RMI[21], require that a remote object be accessed through an interface type. Thus, developers may have to largely modify programs if they adapt legacy software to distributed execution. Java Class Broker[8] avoids this problem by a technique similar to our subclass approach. However, it requires developers to modify a program to follow another programming convention. For example, the following regular Java program:

```
Frame f = new Frame("The Great Encyclopedia");
Button b = new Button();
f.add(b);
```

must be translated into a program using a runtime distribution manager object objectBroker:

```
Object[] params = {"The Great Encyclopedia"};
Frame f = (Frame) objectBroker.create("Frame", params);
Button b = (Button) objectBroker.getProxy("Button", new Button());
f.add(b);
```

5.2   Remote Display

The X Window System[18] enables a Java program to show a graphical output on the display of a remote host. Like Addistant, the X Window System does not require developers to modify their programs to use a remote display. However, as shown in Section 4, the X Window System is often less efficient than Addistant.

Rawt[11] is a GUI library that is compatible to the standard Java GUI library. If substituting Rawt for the standard library, developers can extend their programs without any other modifications to use a remote display for output. Underlying network communication is encapsulated by that library. Addistant can be regarded as a tool for semi-automatically producing a library like Rawt from the standard Java GUI library. Since the production by Addistant is based on both the library and user code, however, the resulting software can often achieve better performance than Rawt.

5.3   Aspect-Oriented Programming

With Addistant, developers describe a policy file for adapting software to distributed execution. This policy file can be considered as a separate description of a distribution aspect in the context of aspect-oriented programming (AOP). In this context, Addistant is a tool for *weaving* a Java program written for a single JVM and a description separately written about a distribution aspect.

Proposing a distribution aspect is not new. For example, D[15] provides an aspect language for distribution. However, it allows programmers to separately describe how a parameter is passed to a remote procedure whereas Addistant allows to describe where objects are allocated and how proxy objects are implemented. Furthermore, it seems that the design goal of D is to support the development of distributed software from scratch. The goal of Addistant is to add a new aspect on existing software for adaptation. Thus, the description in a policy file is not a part of program text but rather *meta-level* instructions to modify an existing program.

6   Conclusion

This paper presented Addistant, which is a programming tool for adapting legacy Java software to distributed execution. Addistant performs this adaptation by bytecode translation at load time. No source code is needed for the adaptation. The users of Addistant have only to write a policy file for specifying where the instances of each class are allocated and how remote references to those instances are implemented. The users can select an implementation approach from the four provided by Addistant.

Although the four implementation approaches are not new, a contribution of this paper is that it reveals that letting developers select an implementation approach for each class is necessary for adapting legacy Java software in the real world to distributed execution. This paper presented several practical issues that we must consider for the adaptation. However, the ability of Addistant still has a few limitations. Although the developers using Addistant do not need to read or modify source code, they must have some knowledge of source code, for example, which class of objects should be allocated on a remote host. Moreover, Addistant provides only class-based distribution: all the instances of a class must be allocated on the same host. These limitations are acceptable in our GUI examples although it is an open question in other contexts.

This paper also showed that Addistant could adapt a Java program using the Swing class library so that GUI objects could be allocated on a remote host with a display. This functional distribution with Addistant showed better response time of the GUI than the distribution with the X Window System and the Rawt class library. This fact suggests that library-level functional distribution could not give good performance since only the library code is split and distributed to multiple hosts. On the other hand, Addistant can split a whole program including both user and library code and then it can distribute objects so that the maximum performance could be obtained.

Acknowlegement

The authors thank anonymous reviewers for their advice on this paper. Kenichi Kourai and Yasushi Shinjo gave helpful comments on the drafts of this paper. This research was supported in part by the Japan Science and Technology Corporation.

References

1. Ken Arnold, James Gosling and David Holmes, Garbage Collection and Memory, Chapter 12, In *The Java Programming Language Third Edition*, Addison Wesley, pp.313–327, 2000.
2. Yariv Aridor, Michael Factor and Avi Teperman, CJVM: a Single System Image of a JVM on a Cluster, In *Proceedings of ICPP 99*, IEEE, 1999.
3. Andrew Black, Norman Hutchinson, Eric Jul, Henry Levy, and Larry Carter, Distribution and Abstract Types in Emerald, In *IEEE Transactions on Software Engineering, Vol.SE-13, No.1*, IEEE, pp.65–76, 1987.
4. Denis Caromel, Wilfried Klauser and Julien Vayssièra, Towards Seamless Computing and Metacomputing in Java, In *Concurrency: Practice & Experience, Vol.10, No.11-13*, Wiley, pp.1043–1061, 1998.
5. Shigeru Chiba, Load-time Structural Reflection in Java, In *Proceedings of ECOOP 2000, LNCS 1850*, Springer Verlag, pp.313–336, 2000.
6. Erich Gamma, Richard Helm, Ralph Johnson, and John Vlissides, *Design Patterns - Elements of Reusable Object-Oriented Software*, Addison-Wesley, 1994.
7. James Gosling, Bill Joy, and Guy Steele, *The Java Language Specification*, Addison-Wesley, 1996.
8. Zvi Har'El and Zvi Rosberg, Java Class Broker - A Seamless Bridge from Local to Distributed Programming, In *Journal of Parallel and Distributed Computing, Vol.60, No.11*, Academic Press, pp.1223–1237, 2000.
9. Michael Hicks, Suresh Jagannathan, Richard Kelsey, Jonathan T. Moore, and Cristian Ungureanu, Transparent Communication for Distributed Objects in Java, In *Proceedings of the ACM 1999 conference on Java Grande*, pp.160–170, 1999.
10. Satoshi Hirano, HORB: Distributed Execution of Java Programs, In *Lecture Notes in Computer Science 1274*, Springer, pp.29–42, 1997.
11. IBM, *Remote Abstract Windowing Toolkit (RAWT)*, Online publishing, URI `http://www.s390.ibm.com/java/rawt.html`, 2000.
12. Laxmikant V. Kalé, Milind Bhandarkar, and Terry Wilmarth, Design and Implementation of Parallel Java with Global Object Space, In *Proceedings of PDPTA '97, Conference on Parallel and Distributed Processing Technology and Applications*, 1997.
13. Sheng Liang and Gilad Bracha, Dynamic Class Loading in the Java Virtual Machine, In *Proceedings of OOPSLA '98, ACM SIGPLAN Notices, Vol.33, No.10*, pp.36–44, 1998.
14. Tim Lindholm and Frank Yellin, *The Java Virtual Machine Specification*, Addison-Wesley, 1997.
15. Cristina V. Lopes and Gregor Kiczales, D: A Language Framework for Distributed Programming, In *Technical report SPL97-010*, pp.50–67, Xerox Palo Alto Research Center, 1997.
16. Matchy J. M. Ma, Cho-Li Wang, and Francis C. M. Lau, JESSICA: Java-Enabled Single-System-Image Computing Architecture, In *Journal of Parallel and Distributed Computing, Vol.60, No.11*, Academic Press, pp.1194–1222, 2000.
17. Nataraj Nagaratnam, Arvind Srinivasan, and Doug Lea, Remote Objects in Java, In *Proceedings of IASTED '96, International Conference on Networks*, 1996.
18. Robert Scheifler and Jim Gettys, The X Window System, In *ACM Transactions on Graphics, Vol.5, No.2*, pp.79–109, 1986.
19. Michael Philippsen and Matthias Zenger, JavaParty - Transparent Remote Objects in Java, In *Concurrency: Practice & Experience, Vol.9, No.11*, Wiley, pp.1225–1242, 1999.

20. Hans Rohnert, The Proxy Design Pattern Revisited, In *Pattern Languages of Program Design 2*, Addison-Wesley, pp.105–118, 1995.
21. Sun Microsystems, Inc., *The Java Remote Method Invocation Specification*, Online publishing, URI `http://java.sun.com/products/jdk/rmi/`, 1997.
22. Sun Microsystems, Inc., *Java Foundation Classes*, Online publishing, URI `http:-//java.sun.com/products/jfc/index. html`, 2000.
23. Weimin Yu and Alan Cox, Java/DSM: A Platform for Heterogeneous Computing, In *Concurrency: Practice & Experience, Vol.9, No.11*, Wiley, pp.1213–1224, 1997.

Reflections on MOPs, Components, and Java Security

Denis Caromel and Julien Vayssière

INRIA - CNRS - I3S
Université de Nice Sophia-Antipolis
{First.Last}@sophia.inria.fr

Abstract. This article investigates the security issues raised by the use of meta-programming systems with Java. For each possible type of MOP (compile-time, load-time, etc.), we study the permissions required for both the base and the meta-level protection domains, taking into account the flow of control between the different parts of the application.
We show that the choice of a particular MOP architecture has a strong impact on security issues. Assuming a component-based architecture with code from various origins having different levels of trust, we establish a set of rules for combining the permissions associated with each protection domain (integration, base-level, meta-level, etc.).

1 Introduction

In this article we investigate how Meta-Object Protocols (MOPs) [15] may be combined with Java's security architecture, especially in the context of component-based applications.

Java is the first mainstream programming language to take security into account from scratch, however it has also given birth to quite a large number of meta-programming extensions. Since its initial public release in 1995, Java has arguably become one of the most popular implementation platforms for researchers in the field of meta-programming with object-oriented languages. There now exist Java implementations of many different types of MOP.

Specifying a security policy for a Java application means determining the different protection domains involved and granting permissions to each of them, the goal being to run each piece of code using the smallest set of permissions necessary. As monolithic programs are now being gradually replaced with programs that are made up of a number of components, the above *principle of least privilege* becomes even more relevant. Furthermore, within the framework of meta-programming, one can use standard (base-level), meta-level, and MOP components, together with application-specific code, each of them having a specific origin and a different level of trust. The question of what happens to the specific security permissions of base-level and meta-level components when used together presents itself. This article tackles the more general problem of combining reflection and security in component-based Java applications.

J. Lindskov Knudsen (Ed.): ECOOP 2001, LNCS 2072, pp. 256–274, 2001.

The organization of the paper is as follows. In section 2 we successively give an overview of the security architecture of Java, introduce a classification of MOPs in four distinct categories, and identify a typical reflective component architecture. For that application, section 3 investigates the consequences of the MOP architecture on the original permission sets. Analyzing the different types of MOPs results in the development of a set of rules that govern the combination of the permission sets. We demonstrate that the different MOPs raise different security issues. This section also takes into account the `doPrivileged` construct. Section 4 presents related but orthogonal research: assuming that a MOP is secure, how can one use it to implement security policies? Finally, Section 5 summarizes and further generalizes the results.

2   Security, MOPs, and Components

In this section provide some background information on the security architecture of Java and meta-programming in Java, we then present a typical component-based application which will be used as a reference for the remainder of the paper.

2.1   The Security Architecture of Java

What follows is a short introduction to the security architecture of Java. A more detailed presentation can be found in [13].

The development of a security architecture for Java was motivated by the need to protect local resources from Java applets downloaded from untrusted sites. This explains why the current version of Java is heavily focused on *access control*, i.e. protecting access to critical local resources such as files, sockets, or the windowing system. The security architecture of Java is not concerned however with issues such as controlling the flow of information between the different pieces of code running inside a virtual machine [21], a problem of great importance, for example, in the JavaCard environment [4]. The Java language also has built-in security features, such as strong typing, enforcement of access modifiers, and no pointer arithmetic, which we will not address in this paper because they do not raise major problems when used with MOPs.

Central to the security architecture of Java is the notion of *protection domain*. A protection domain corresponds to either a URL from which classes can be downloaded, or a set of certificates that can be used for signing classes, or to any combination of both. This enables the mapping of protection domains to *principals* (persons or organizations on behalf of whom some code is distributed, and who can be held responsible if the code misbehaves). Each protection domain has an associated set of *permissions*. Each permission consists of a resource (for example, a file) that we want to protect access to, and an access mode (such as read, write, or execute).

Specifying a security policy for a Java application means determining the different protection domains involved and granting permissions to each of them.

This enables an application to run in accordance with the *principle of least privilege* [25], which states that a piece of code "should operate using the least set of privileges necessary to complete the job". This principle is of equal importance for both computer security and software engineering since it limits the damages that can result from a security attack and also protects a program from the consequences of a bug unwantingly introduced by a programmer.

At runtime, each of the classes loaded inside the virtual machine is associated with a specific protection domain. Whenever a thread performs a call that requires a specific permission, the security manager computes the *intersection* of the permission sets of all the protection domains on the execution stack of the thread. If this intersection contains the permission needed for accessing the resource, then access is granted, otherwise it is denied. This means that it is not sufficient for a given class to belong to a protection domain that has the right permissions in order to be granted access, all the other classes on the stack need to have this set of permissions as well.

In the context of a MOP-based application, with calls on the stack going successively back and forth between the base-level and the meta-level, the fact that it is the intersection of the set of permissions on the stack that determines whether or not access is granted is of great importance for our discussion.

However, the security architecture of Java provides a way to reduce this constraint. The `doPrivileged` construct enables us to limit the computation of the intersection to the protection domain from which the `doPrivileged` call is made and the protection domains subsequently called from it. The signature of the method is as follows:

```
public static Object doPrivileged (PrivilegedAction action)
```

The parameter of type `PrivilegedAction` encapsulates the code that is executed with the permissions of the new intersection of the protection domains. In other words, it means that the class that uses this `doPrivileged` construct takes responsibility for the classes that called it.

2.2   Meta-programming and Java

Since its initial public release in 1995, Java[1] has arguably become the implementation platform of choice for researchers in the field of meta-programming with object-oriented languages. There now exist Java implementations of all the major types of MOPs, from compile-time and load-time MOPs to run-time MOPs. We identify three main reasons why Java has become such an appealing platform for implementing meta-programming systems.

First of all, Java is an interpreted language and interpreters have proven to be an appropriate model for thinking about and implementing reflective features into programming languages [10]. Interpreters provide a natural separation between how an application is written in a given language and the description of

---

[1] by *Java*, we mean the whole *Java Platform*, which encompasses the *Java Virtual Machine* [17] (JVM), the *Java Language* [14] itself, and all the *Java Core APIs*.

how this language is executed. Interpreters allow us to alter the execution of a program simply by modifying the interpreter, without having to modify the program itself. This is the approach taken by sych runtime-MOPs as MetaXa[2][16], Guarana [22] and Iguana/J [23].

Seconfly, Java comes with a set of built-in reflective features, both structural and behavioral, which can be used as basic building blocks by designers of meta-programing systems. The best-known reflective feature of Java is the *Reflection API* [20]. This API was introduced with JDK 1.1 and provides structural reflection: Java programs can discover at runtime what types[3] exist inside a JVM and can inquire about all the constructors, methods, and variables for a given type. The Reflection API also provides a limited possibility to dynamically invoke those reflected members; however this does not come close to full-fledged *behavioral reflection* [10].

A third reason why Java is an interesting platform for implementing meta-programming systems is that Java classes are loaded and linked on demand at runtime. This class-loading mechanism is itself reflected through objects of type `ClassLoader`, which provides the indispensable hook for implementing load-time MOPs. MOPs in this category usually modify the bytecode for a class at the moment it is loaded into the JVM.

For these three reasons, a significantly large number of MOPs have been written for Java. Depending on when meta-level code is executed, MOPs can be broadly sorted into four categories:

- *Compile-time MOPs* reflect language constructs available at compile-time by creating metaobjects to represent things such as classes, methods, loops, statements, etc. The meta-level code is executed at compile-time in order to perform a translation on the source code of a program.
- *Load-time MOPs* reflect on the bytecode and make use of a modified class loader in order to modify the bytecode at the moment it is loaded into the JVM. Their behavior if somehow similar to compile-time MOPs, except that they operate on bytecode rather than on source code.
- *VM-based runtime MOPs* rely on a modified version of the JVM in order to intercept things that only exist at runtime such as method invocations and read or write operations on fields. When such events occur, control is transferred to meta-level objects that are standard Java objects.
- *Proxy-based runtime MOPs* introduce hooks into the program, either at compile-time or load-time, in order to reify runtime events, mostly method invocation. They do not require any modification to the VM, which explains why some low-level events cannot be reified.

2.3   Component-Based Architecture and MOPs

As observed in [27], monolithic programs are now being gradually replaced with programs that are made up of a number of components, originating from various

---

[2] formerly known as MetaJava

[3] By *type* here we mean primitive types, arrays, classes, and interfaces.

sources and with various levels of trust, plus some application-specific code for gluing pieces together. This is especially true for Java applications, thanks to the JavaBeans component model [19] which provides a standardized way to describe and compose reusable Java components. However, it may happen that a third-party component lacks a specific non-functional property, such as support for transactions, persistence, or security. Meta-level protocols have proven to be a solution of choice for adding non-functional properties to third-party components [31], and so we will focus on component-based applications for the remainder of the article.

We will now illustrate the notion of component-based architecture with an example of a typical application (see Fig.1). This application is composed of five different components. The application-specific code, which is itself treated as a component named A, glues together two third-party components, $B1$ and $B2$. As $B2$ lacks some non-functional property, it is extended with a meta-level behavior described in component $MetaB2$ by using a metaobject protocol encapsulated inside component MOP. It is important to note that both the MOP and the meta-level classes are considered as components of the application, and as such are granted some permissions but not necessarily all permissions.

We would like to stress that this example, however typical, does not pretend to describe or model all possible applications that can be built using MOPs and meta-level classes. Rather, it should be seen as a first step in the direction of a general model for talking about the security properties of such applications. Building such a model is a subject for future research and is beyond the scope of this paper.

Nevertheless, we think this example is typical enough to describe most interesting cases. First of all, we have three base-level components with all direct and transitive chains of calls and callbacks between them. Moreover, one of the base-level components is extended with a meta-level component while the other is not. One of the components is implicitly using a reified component, and the example also includes some integration code, which is also packaged as a component.

Arrows on the figure represent possible method calls from one component to another component. We assume a one-to-one mapping between components and protection domains, since each component was written by a possibly different principal. Hence, performing method calls from a component to another component means crossing the boundaries of protection domains. For example, $MetaB2$ calls the methods of $B2$ for executing reified calls originally sent to $B2$, as represented by the arrow from $MetaB2$ to $B2$. It is worthwhile to mention here that the absence of an arrow from $B2$ to $MetaB2$ is due to the fact that classes inside $B2$ are not MOP-aware. We now list all the potential calls between protection domains for this typical application. This is essential for determining the protection domains that may appear together on the stack.

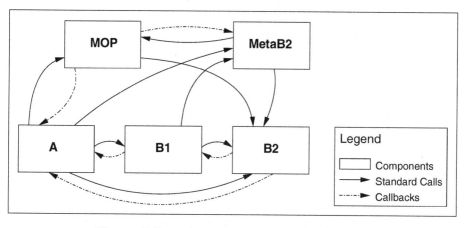

Fig. 1. Calls and callbacks between components

$A \to B1$, $A \to B2$, $A \to MOP$, $B1 \to B2$, $MetaB2 \to MOP$	A client component uses the service provided by another component.
$B1 \to A$, $B2 \to A$, $MOP \to A$, $B2 \to B1$, $MOP \to MetaB2$	Callbacks from a component to one of its client components.
$A \to MetaB2$, $B1 \to MetaB2$	Calls initially sent to $B2$ intercepted by the MOP for meta-level processing by $MetaB2$.
$MetaB2 \to B2$	$MetaB2$ executes a reified call originally sent to $B2$.
$MOP \to B2$	The MOP instantiates a reified instance of $B2$.

For completeness, we also list the calls that will not happen and explain why.

$B1 \nrightarrow MOP$, $MOP \nrightarrow B1$, $MetaB2 \nrightarrow B1$	$B1$ is not MOP-aware. It does not know that the calls it sends to $B2$ are reified.
$B2 \nrightarrow MOP$, $B2 \nrightarrow MetaB2$	$B2$ does not have to be MOP-aware either, which is one of the advantages of using MOPs for adapting third-party components.
$MetaB2 \nrightarrow A$	No callback from meta-level code to client code.

In the figure and the two tables above, all method calls could be considered equally important, because we assumed that any chain of calls might trigger an access check. However, it is not quite true. There are a couple of assumptions that we can make which help reduce the number of possible chains of calls that we must consider.

First, let us notice that calls such as $A \to MOP$ and $MOP \to B2$ are only concerned with creating reified instances of types in $B2$. We can expect object creation and initialization not to perform security-sensitive actions, as these usually happen later on in the life cycle of the object.

Rule 1 *The instantiation of reified objects should not perform actions that require access checks. If such actions must be performed, they should be delayed until after the construction of the object, for example until the first method call to the reified object is made (lazy initialization).*

The second assumption we would like to make is concerned with callbacks. Callbacks are method calls sent from a component to one of its client components through a specific interface in order to notify the client of the occurrence of an event. Event-based components originated in the realm of graphical user interface components and are becoming increasingly popular, thanks to the event model of JavaBeans. Although callbacks are standard method calls, their function is simply to deliver an event and then return, as opposed to calls from a client to a component in which a request for a service is made[4]. As it is not possible to guarantee that a method, called as part of the delivering of an event, does not perform an action that requires an access check, the specifications of the event model strongly recommend that one should perform such actions in a separate dedicated thread, and thus in a different security context. As callbacks are normal method calls, the security architecture of Java treats them just like any other method call. We believe that callbacks, when used according to the following rule, do not have any consequence security-wise.

Rule 2 *Callbacks should not perform actions that may trigger an access check. If such an action must be performed as the consequence of the callback, it should rather be done in a separate thread that was created and launched by the component that received the callback.*

Let us present the immediate benefits of applying this rule in a simple case with no MOP and no meta-level code. The only components we consider here are A, $B1$, and $B2$. They are connected together as in figure 1. If we call P, the function that maps components to the set of permissions of their protection domain, a call from A to $B1$ and then to $B2$ results in the following constraint on the permission sets of the protection domains:

$$P(A) \supseteq P(B1) \supseteq P(B2)$$

If callbacks need to perform actions that require access checks, callbacks from $B2$ to $B1$, and from $B1$ to A, respectively, add the two following equations:

$$P(B2) \supseteq P(B1)$$

---

[4] Although there is no way to actually enforce this property, it is considered in the Java community to be sound programming practice to do so.

and

$$P(B1) \supseteq P(A)$$

and hence, together with the first equation above, this leads to:

$$P(A) \equiv P(B1) \equiv P(B2)$$

If the rule above is enforced, we are back to the first constraint, which is far better as it allows us to maintain the specific permission sets, and hence abide by the least privilege principle. In the remainder of this article we will use this example architecture together with the two rules above in order to investigate the permission issues raised by the use of different kinds of MOPs.

3 Combining Permission Sets with Reflection

We now detail how the different categories of MOPs work and investigate their impact on security. We will present compile-time MOPs, load-time MOPs, VM-based runtime MOPs, and proxy-based runtime MOPs. In general, we will consider the most static solution for each MOP. For instance, a compile-time MOP could be used for implementing a proxy-based runtime MOP, however we will only consider the case of translations that do not introduce metaobjects at run-time.

3.1 Compile-Time MOPs

The typical MOP in this category is OpenJava[5] [7][28], which inherits most of the design philosophy of its direct ancestor Open C++ Version 2 [6]. OpenJava can be seen as an "advanced macro processor" that performs a source-to-source translation of a set of classes written in a possibly extended version of Java into a set of classes written in standard Java.

The translation to be applied to a base class is described in a metaclass associated with the base class. The metaclass is written in standard Java using a class library that extends the Java Reflection API with new classes for reflecting language constructs such as assignments, conditional expressions, field accesses, method calls, variables, type casts, etc. As a result, the object-oriented design of the library makes writing translations easier and more natural than with Open C++ where the sole abstraction available to the meta-level programmer is bare abstract syntax trees.

At first sight, the use of OpenJava does not break the security model of Java in any way: OpenJava outputs standard Java classes that compile and run within the standard Java environment and are subject to the same security restrictions as any Java class. Nevertheless, there is still a little security concern

---

[5] We should also mention *Reflective Java* [32], a compile-time MOP for intercepting method invocations.

with OpenJava. Even though it does not introduce any breach of security as such, it weakens the protection one might expect because it goes against the principle of least privilege. OpenJava allows a translation associated with a given base class to affect classes that may belong to different protection domains than the protection domain of the base class, and this may blur the fine-grained protection policy of the security architecture.

OpenJava defines the scope of the translation, expressed in the metaclass associated with a base class, according to the following rule: a translation can only affect the base class itself (*callee-side* translation) or the classes that perform method calls to the base class (*caller-side* translation)[6].

As a consequence, a caller-side translation may introduce, into all the client classes of a base class, code that may require additional permissions in order to run (figure 2). In the typical component-based application presented in figure 1, this means that the meta-level component $MetaB2$ will be incorporated into both the application code A and the MOP-unaware component $B1$ because the base-level component $B2$ is reified.

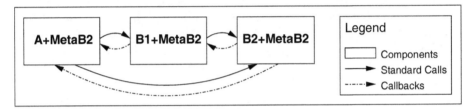

Fig. 2. Pure compile-time MOP

As OpenJava does not provide a way to tell what are the permissions required by the bits of code inserted by $MetaB2$ into the other components, we have to take the most conservative approach. In order to ensure that the resulting program does not raise security-related exceptions, the permission sets to be assigned to the resulting components are:

$$P(A + MetaB2) = P(A) \cup P(MetaB2)$$

$$P(B1 + MetaB2) = P(B1) \cup P(MetaB2)$$

$$P(B2 + MetaB2) = P(B2) \cup P(MetaB2)$$

Which means that the permission set of $MetaB2$ has to spread to the whole program. This goes against the principle of least privilege and defeats the purpose of a fine-grained security architecture.

There is also a problem with the requirement that as soon as a piece of code is modified by the meta-level (either caller- or callee-side) its set of permissions is

---

[6] Performing caller-side translation implies that all the client classes of the base class on which the translation is performed are known at the time of the translation.

expanded to include the permissions of the meta-level code. That is because there is no way to know what are the permissions required by the code inserted by the meta-level into the base-level code. Hence the most conservative approach has to be taken and all the permissions of the meta-level have to be added to the base-level classes. In the security literature, this problem is known as the *composite principal problem* and is of great importance to access control in distributed systems [1]. We will see that it also appears in run-time MOPs.

As a conclusion to this section, compile-time MOPs present inherent incompatibility issues with security but do not raise major security problems. What might be needed is a companion tool that would help the user understand how the translations expressed with the MOP affect the permission sets of the caller and callee protection domains, and also help the user dispatch the permissions needed by all the different components.

3.2   Load-Time MOPs

In load-time MOPs, meta-level computations take place either only at load-time or at both load-time and run-time. This leads to two different kinds of load-time MOPs: pure load-time MOPs and load-time MOPs that are used for implementing run-time MOPs.

Pure load-time MOPs [8] are close to compile-time MOPs, except that they operate on the bytecode representation of a class instead of on its source code. We call these kind of MOPs *pure* because metaobjects only exist at load-time, as opposed to load-time MOPs used for implementing run-time MOPs, like Kava [29], where meta-objects also exist at runtime.

As we can expect, the consequences in terms of permissions are similar to what we obtained with compile-time MOPs. However, there is one important difference. A transformation applied to a class in a compile-time MOP may also affect the client classes for the class, this is what we called caller-side translation in section 3.1. This is not possible for load-time MOPs since translations have to be performed at load-time on a class-by-class basis: client classes may have been loaded before the class the translation is performed on, and it is not allowed to modify classes after they are loaded inside the JVM [12].

Figure 3 illustrates the situation at runtime. The components MOP and $MetaB2$ have disappeared, since they only exist at load-time. For pure load-time MOPs we have

$$P(B2 + MetaB2) = P(B2) \cup P(MetaB2)$$

and hence

$$P(A) \supseteq P(B1) \supseteq P(B2 + MetaB2)$$

Again, the problem of the composite principal ($B2 + MetaB2$ in the above two statements) appears. It is actually a harder problem than one might first imagine because the meta-level transformation performed on $B2$ may add some code that requires permissions that are not needed for the execution of either $B2$

or $MetaB2$. For instance, $MetaB2$ might include, within a string, the instruction to be added into $B2$, for example `new File().write(...)`. It seems impossible to correctly determine the set of permissions required by $B2 + MetaB2$ without the cooperation of the meta-level code.

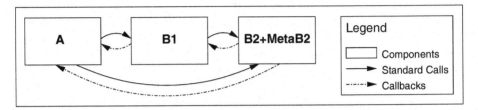

Fig. 3. Pure load-time MOP

The second category of load-time MOPs contains MOPs, such as Kava [29], which modify the bytecode of a class at load-time in order to introduce hooks that implement a shift from the base-level to the meta-level at some specific reification points in the code, usually on entering or leaving a method, or on reading from or writing to a field. This is why we say Kava is a run-time MOP implemented through load-time transformations of the code.

We can assume that the code inserted into the base-class does not trigger any security check, since it is simply responsible for sending calls to the meta-level. In our example, this means that the permission set required by $B2$ remains the same, and the scenario at runtime is close to the one presented in figure 1. However there is one assumption made by the authors of Kava that greatly simplifies the problem: both the MOP classes (MOP) and the meta-level classes ($MetaB2$) are assumed to be part of the "trusted computing base", which means that these classes are granted the same permissions as the classes in packages `java.*`, namely all permissions.

As a result, computing the intersection of the permission sets on the stack at any moment no longer depends on the permissions of components MOP and $MetaB2$, and so we are back to a scenario without any meta-level components, as is illustrated in figure 4. This means that base-level access checks remain the same as in a non MOP-enabled version of the application. Meta-level access checks will not be a problem, as long as they are performed inside `doPrivileged` blocks, so as to exclude base-level classes when computing the intersection of the permission sets.

To conclude this section, load-time MOPs either suffer almost from the same problem as compile-time MOPs or manage to solve the problem with permissions at the expense of granting meta-level classes with all permissions.

3.3   VM-Based Runtime MOPs

MetaXa [16] and Guaraná [22] are two examples of VM-based run-time MOPs. They both rely on a modified version of the JVM. Guaraná is implemented using

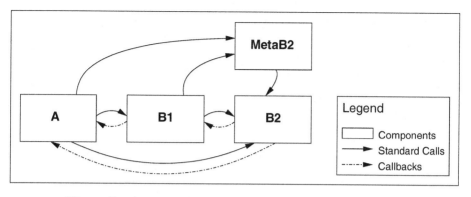

Fig. 4. Load-time MOP for implementing a run-time MOP

a modified version of the freely-available Kaffe virtual machine and MetaXa extends the virtual machine with a collection of native methods put together in a dynamic C library.

If our example application were run using such a MOP, there would be no modification to the set of permissions required by $B2$ because the interception mechanism is no longer visible as a standard call on meta-objects, but instead is buried deep inside the JVM.

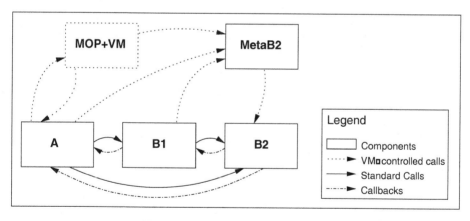

Fig. 5. VM-based Runtime MOPs

It is difficult to express relations between the different permission sets as we did for the previous kinds of MOPs since run-time MOPs have the power to alter the security architecture because they have access to the inner workings of the JVM. The very fact that these MOPs rely on a modified version of the JVM is not necessarily a security problem, instead it is actually a software diffusion problem.

Even if we trust the implementers of the MOPs, how can we control the enormous power given to the meta-level developer by letting him access and modify the internal data structures of the virtual machine, for example the state of the execution stack of a thread which is central to the decision-making algorithm of the security architecture of Java ?

If we assume that these potentially dangerous mechanisms are only used for intercepting the events that we want to see reified, then we are back to the security constraints of load-time MOPs used for implementing run-time MOPs. One hidden assumption about Java's security architecture is that all actions are performed through method calls. If a meta-level method is called as the consequence of, for example, reading a field or releasing a lock on an object, the behavior of the security architecture is not clear. To the best of our knowledge, all VM-based runtime MOPs were designed for versions of Java prior to Java 2, which explains why no attention at all has been paid to this problem.

3.4   Proxy-Based Runtime MOPs

Just like VM-based runtime-MOPs, *Proxy-based runtime MOPs* such as *RJava* [9] or ProActive[5], reify things that only exist at runtime, like object creation or method calls. The difference is that proxy-based runtime-MOPs are targeted at the standard Java runtime environment and do not rely on a specialized VM. As a consequence, there are things that VM-based MOPs can reify that proxy-based MOPs cannot, such as field access or operations on object locks.

The interception mechanism usually follows the *Proxy* design pattern [11]: a surrogate object with the same interface as the reified object acts as the reified object for its clients, intercepts method calls, and sends reified method calls to the meta-level.

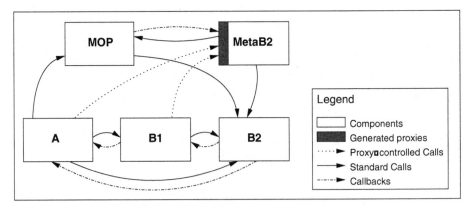

Fig. 6. Proxy-based Runtime MOPs

One can further differentiate *polymorphic* run-time MOPs when the reference returned by the MOP on the instantiation of a reified object is compatible with the original class of the reified object. For instance, a standard class C can be instantiated with a MOP together with a meta-object of type M, and assigned to a variable of type A. The Java pseudo-code for this would be:

```
C c = (C) MOP.newReified (''C'', ''M'');
```

This feature is quite important if one wants to be able to use reified instances of C in a component that was originally designed to be a client of objects of type C[7]. In *ProActive*, for example, the objects that intercept method calls are called *stubs*. They are instances of classes that are subtypes of the class of the object that is reified. Stub classes are generated and compiled on demand at runtime. As all classes involved in a reified call are normal Java classes and the execution environment is absolutely standard, all the protection domains involved appear on the stack.

As a result, in the general case of proxy-based runtime MOPs, the meta-level component has to include the permission sets of the component it reflects on:

$$P(MetaB2) \supseteq P(B2)$$

Note that, by contrast with the VM-based case, there seems to exist no means to avoid it. However, such a restriction is quite fair and moderate and should not be an obstacle to the use of reflection in secure component-based architectures.

Also, as can be seen from the chain of calls in the case of reified object creation, we call the MOP component to trigger the creation, then the meta-level code $MetaB2$, and finally the base code $B2$. Hence, the permissions of the MOP have to be at least equal to the permissions of $MetaB2$, which should be enough. So we have:

$$P(MOP) \supseteq P(MetaB2)$$

To generalize, the permissions of the MOP in that case have to be at least the union of the permission sets of all the meta-level components.

3.5 doPrivileged and Summary

As explained in section 2.1, the doPrivileged construct allows us to limit the computation of the intersection of the permissions to the current protection domains after doPrivileged is invoked. We now examine how this feature may influence the constraints on the permission sets of our example application.

Usually, doPrivileged calls are found in standard libraries in order to execute security-sensitive method calls which are well-understood (such as reading font files from a fonts directory) and are not a security threat, whatever the permission set of the class that calls the method is.

For compile-time and pure load-time MOPs, one might be tempted to add doPrivileged calls into $MetaB2$ in order to alleviate the need to take the

---

[7] Note that the new *dynamic proxy* feature of the Reflection API only allows dynamic stub generation for interfaces but not for classes.

union of $P(B2)$ and $P(MetaB2)$ for the set of permissions of the resulting class. However, this does not work because at runtime the resulting class belongs to a single composite principal.

On the other hand, using the `doPrivileged` construct proves interesting for run-time MOPs as it alleviates the following constraint:

$$P(A) \supseteq P(B1) \supseteq P(MetaB2)$$

An example of this is when $MetaB2$ requires permissions that we do not want to give to the principal of $B1$. This means that $MetaB2$ no longer has to worry about the permission sets of the classes that perform reified calls, and the constraint above is no longer required to hold.

Let us now summarize the constraints on permission sets that we obtained for all the different kinds of MOPs:

Compile-time

$$(P(A) \cup P(MetaB2)) \supseteq (P(B1) \cup P(MetaB2)) \supseteq (P(B2) \cup P(MetaB2))$$

Pure load-time

$$P(A) \supseteq P(B1) \supseteq (P(B2) \cup P(MetaB2))$$

Run-time VM-based

$$P(A) \supseteq P(B1) \supseteq P(MetaB2) \supseteq P(B2)$$

Run-time proxy-based

$$P(A) \supseteq P(B1) \supseteq P(MOP) \supseteq P(MetaB2) \supseteq P(B2)$$

Fig. 7. Summary of the constraints on the permission sets

4   Related Work: MOP-Based Security Enforcement

The idea of using MOPs for expressing and implementing security policies is not a new one. The security aspect of an application has long been recognized as fairly orthogonal to functional code, although this point has never, to the best of our knowledge, been thoroughly investigated.

A metaobject that intercepts method invocations for an object that represents a resource to be secured is the ideal place for implementing access control checks without having to mix functional code with security-related code. In a model based on capabilities, a metaobject attached to a reference can control the propagation of the capability across protection domains. Riechmann [24], for example, proposes a model in which metaobjects, attached to the boundary of a component, control how references to objects that live inside the component are transmitted to other components. It dynamically attaches security metaobjects to these references according to the level of trust of the component the reference is transmitted to.

A similar idea was developed with the concept of *Channel Reification* [18, 2]. This model enhances the message reification model with the notion of history (or state). The model was implemented in Java as part of a history-dependent access control mechanism [3] that goes beyond the well-known access matrix model [25], which is essentially a stateless access control mechanism. The channel reification model is also claimed to be superior to the meta-object model where a single metaobject monitors all access to a resource because it works with method-level granularity and can be used for implementing *role-based access models* [26] which are particularly well-suited to distributed object-oriented computing.

Another instance of using MOPs for implementing security policy is presented in [30]. The idea here is to use the load-time MOP Kava (see 3.2) in order to adapt third-party components to meet real-world security requirements. The authors contrast their approach with the wrapper-based approach adopted by the Enterprise Java Beans framework and argue that load-time MOPs provide a cleaner implementation of meta-level security policies. In addition, having a separate meta-level for the security policy attached to a component eases the expression of any kind of high-level security mechanisms, while the wrapper-based approach seems less expressive and is in fact only appropriate for enforcing access control on resources.

These experiments proved the feasibility of using MOPs for implementing security policies. Another issue is to know if this approach is worthwhile, i.e. if the expression of a security policy at the metalevel is orthogonal enough to functional code for this approach to be used in real-world applications.

In the context of Java, the very fact that the declaration of which permissions are granted to which piece of code (the *policy* file) is separated from the source code might be interpreted as a proof that functional code and the declaration of security policies are orthogonal. However, there is at least one hint that functional code and security are not that orthogonal. In practice, the security policy as described in the *policy* file is unworkable if the code does not make use of the `doPrivileged` call for bypassing part of the security mechanism.

5   Conclusion

We first defined a classification of MOPs based on the time of reflection shift (compile-time, load-time, run-time VM-based, run-time proxy-based). From that basis, and within a typical component-based reflective application, we have demonstrated that the type of MOP being used greatly impacts the constraints on permission sets.

A compile-time MOP globally imposes the constraint that the permissions of a meta component have to be added to the corresponding base-level component, and moreover, to all its client components. More generally, if a meta component reflects on several base components, the former permissions will have to spread to all the base components and to all their clients. This fact might be an important security concern as meta-level code can potentially require high permissions (for instance in order to write persistent data on disk) that would be dangerous to associate to untrusted reflected-on components.

A similar problem, but with less consequences, occurs with load-time MOPs as the meta-level permissions only need to spread to the base-level class, and not to all the clients. That is still an important issue to take into account.

In the case of run-time proxy-based MOPs, the only constraint seems to be the inclusion of the meta-level permission set within its base-level permission set. Indeed, this is a rather reasonable constraint. When the technique of generated proxies is used, the proxy code must also have at least the base-code permissions. Furthermore, if several meta-level components are used, the permissions of the MOP have to be at least the union of all their permissions.

Finally, a run-time VM-based MOP in theory implies similar constraints as a run-time proxy-based MOP. However, as the MOP is actually within the modified VM, the constraints can be alleviated by the MOP implementer if needed. This MOP architecture, besides its specific software diffusion limitation, raises the problem of letting the meta-level control the inner working of the VM. A solution might be to define specific MOP permissions to provide the integrator with the ability to control and enforce, in a declarative manner, what can be reflected on within the VM.

References

[1] Martin Abadi, Michael Burrows, Butler Lampson, and Gordon Plotkin. A calculus for access control in distributed systems. *ACM Transactions on Programming Languages and Systems*, 15(4):706–734, September 1993.

[2] M. Ancona, W. Cazzola, and E. B. Fernandez. Reflective authorization systems: Possibilities, benefits, and drawbacks. *Lecture Notes in Computer Science*, 1603:35–50, 1999.

[3] Massimo Ancona, Walter Cazzola, and Eduardo B. Fernandez. A history-dependent access control mechanism using reflection. In *Proceedings of the 5th ECOOP Workshop on Mobile Object Systems (MOS'99)*, Lisbon, Portugal, June 1999.

[4] Pierre Bieber, Jacques Cazin, Virginie Wiels, Guy Zanon, Pierre Girard, and Jean-Louis Lanet. Electronic purse applet certification: extended abstract. In Steve Schneider and Peter Ryan, editors, *Electronic Notes in Theoretical Computer Science*, volume 32. Elsevier Science Publishers, 2000.

[5] D. Caromel, W. Klauser, and J. Vayssiere. Towards Seamless Computing and Metacomputing in Java. *Concurrency Practice and Experience*, 10(11–13):1043–1061, November 1998.

[6] Shigeru Chiba. A metaobject protocol for C++. In *OOPSLA '95 Conference Proceedings: Object-Oriented Programming Systems, Languages, and Applications*, pages 285–299. ACM Press, 1995.

[7] Shigeru Chiba and Michiaki Tatsubori. Yet another java.lang.class. In *ECOOP'98 Workshop on Reflective Object-Oriented Programming and Systems*, Brussels, Belgium, July 1998.

[8] Geoff A. Cohen, Jeffrey S. Chase, and David L. Kaminsky. Automatic program transformation with JOIE. In *Proceedings of the USENIX 1998 Annual Technical Conference*, pages 167–178, Berkeley, USA, June 15–19 1998. USENIX Association.

[9] José de Oliveira Guimarães. Reflection for statically typed languages. In Eric Jul, editor, *ECOOP '98—Object-Oriented Programming*, volume 1445 of *Lecture Notes in Computer Science*, pages 440–461. Springer, 1998.

[10] J. Ferber. Computational reflection in class based object-oriented languages. *ACM SIGPLAN Notices*, 24(10):317–326, October 1989.

[11] E. Gamma, R. Helm, R. Johnson, and J. Vlissides. *Design Patterns: Elements of Reusable Object-oriented Software*. Addison Wesley, Reading, 1996.

[12] Li Gong. Secure Java class loading. *IEEE Internet Computing*, 2(5):56–61, 1998.

[13] Li Gong. *Inside Java 2 platform security: architecture, API design, and implementation*. Addison-Wesley, Reading, MA, USA, june 1999.

[14] J. Gosling, B. Joy, and G. Steele. *The Java Language Specification*. Addison-Wesley, Reading, USA, 1997.

[15] Gregor Kiczales and Jim des Rivieres. *The art of the metaobject protocol*. MIT Press, Cambridge, MA, USA, 1991.

[16] Juergen Kleinoeder and Michael Golm. Metajava: An efficient run-time meta architecture for java. Techn. Report TR-I4-96-03, Univ. of Erlangen-Nuernberg, IMMD IV, 1996.

[17] Tim Lindholm and Frank Yellin. *The Java Virtual Machine Specification*. Addison-Wesley, Reading, USA, 1997.

[18] Gabriella Dodero Massimo Ancona, Walter Cazzola and Vittoria Gianuzzi. Channel reification: A reflective model for distributed computation. In *Proceedings of IEEE International Performance Computing, and Communication Conference (IPCCC'98)*, pages 32–36, Phoenix, Arizona, USA, Feb 1998.

[19] Sun Microsystems. The JavaBeans API Specification, July 1997.

[20] Sun Microsystems. The Java Core Reflection API, 1998.

[21] Andrew C. Myers. JFlow: Practical mostly-static information flow control. In *Proceedings of the 26th ACM Symposium on Principles of Programming Languages (POPL)*, pages 228–241, San Antonio, Texas, Jan 1999.

[22] Alexandre Oliva and Luiz Eduardo Buzato. The design and implementation of Guaraná. In *Proceedings of the Fifth USENIX Conference on Object-Oriented Technologies and Systems*, pages 203–216. The USENIX Association, 1999.

[23] Barry Redmond and Vinny Cahill. Iguana/J: Towards a dynamic and efficient reflective architecture for java. In *ECOOP 2000 Workshop on Reflection and Metalevel Architectures*, June 2000.

[24] T. Riechmann and J. Kleinoeder. Meta objects for access control: Role-based principals. In C. Boyd and E.Dawson, editors, *Proceeding of the Third Australasian Conference on Information Security and Privacy*, number 1438 in Lecture Notes in Computer Science, pages 296–307. Springer, July 1998.

[25] Jerome H. Saltzer and Michael D. Schroeder. The protection of information in computer systems. *Proceedings of the IEEE*, 63(9), September 1975.

[26] Ravi S. Sandhu, Edward J. Coyne, Hal L. Feinstein, and Charles E. Youman. Role-based access control models. *Computer*, 29(2):38–47, February 1996.

[27] Peter Sewell and Jan Vitek. Secure composition of insecure components. In *Proceedings of the Computer Security Foundations Workshop, CSFW-12*, 1999.

[28] Michiaki Tatsubori. An extension mechanism for the Java language. Master's thesis, Graduate School of Engineering, University of Tsukuba, 1999.

[29] I. Welch and R. Stroud. From Dalang to Kava — the evolution of a reflective Java extension. In Pierre Cointe, editor, *Proceedings of the second international conference Reflection'99*, number 1616 in Lecture Notes in Computer Science, pages 2 – 21. Springer, July 1999.

[30] I. Welch and R. J. Stroud. Using reflection as a mechanism for enforcing security policies in mobile code. In *Proceedings of ESORICS'2000*, number 1895 in Lecture Notes in Computer Science, pages 309–323, October 2000.

[31] Ian Welch and Robert Stroud. Using metaobject protocols to adapt third-party components. Work-in-Progress paper presented at Middleware'98, Lake District England, September 1998.

[32] Zhixue Wu and Scarlet Schwiderski. Reflective Java: Making Java even more flexible. Technical report, ANSA, 1997.

The Optimistic Readers Transformation

Robert Strom and Joshua Auerbach

IBM T.J. Watson Research Center,
30 Saw Mill River Rd.
Hawthorne, NY 10532, USA
{strom, jsa}@watson.ibm.com

Abstract. Monitors, such as Java classes with synchronized methods, are a convenient and safe abstraction for designing and reasoning about multithreaded object-oriented programs. However, the straightforward implementation of monitors can be inefficient, particularly in programs in which the majority of calls are to read-only methods. We introduce the optimistic readers program transformation, which may be implemented either as a compiler optimization, or as a "design pattern." This transformation produces an implementation whose observable behavior is equivalent to that of a monitor, but in which read-only methods do not acquire locks or perform any shared writes. As a result, programmers can reason about their programs as if each shared object were implemented using mutual exclusion, while achieving the performance benefits of unsynchronized reads. We present the program transformation using the platform-independent abstraction CRF. We then demonstrate the performance of this transformation as applied to benchmarks derived from the core module of a practical system – a Java-based publish-subscribe router. We compare the performance of the optimistic readers transformation to unoptimized synchronized methods and to reader and writer locks.

1 · Introduction

There is an apparent tension between efficiency and ease of use in multithreaded programming. In particular, the discipline of communication between threads using *monitor* objects is easy to program, and easy to reason about. Each method acquires an exclusive lock on the monitor; the system as a whole executes methods serially, and any invariant maintained by the object is preserved in any execution. Monitors are straightforward to code – for example in Java, one merely attaches the `synchronized` attribute to all methods of a class. On the other hand, monitors are often inefficient in practice, especially when the majority of calls are to read-only methods. It would appear more efficient to allow unsynchronized reads. Unfortunately, if this is allowed, reasoning about program behavior suddenly becomes much more difficult. The execution results may be surprising and architecture-dependent. Checking even simple programs for correctness can be complex, and may depend on fine details of the implementations of the classes, which goes against the spirit of object-oriented programming. A way out

J. Lindskov Knudsen (Ed.): ECOOP 2001, LNCS 2072, pp. 275–301, 2001.
© Springer-Verlag Berlin Heidelberg 2001

of this dilemma is to design programs and reason about them using monitors and then to systematically *transform* an implementation using monitors into an equivalent but more concurrent program.

This paper presents one such transformation, called the optimistic readers transformation. The optimistic readers transformation

- distinguishes between read and update methods,
- updates a version count each time an update method executes,
- executes read methods without synchronizing, but performs extra operations before and after executing the body of the read method to detect whether the read method read a consistent version,
- aborts and re-executes the read method whenever an inconsistent version was read.

The optimistic readers transformation meets two criteria that we have required of any solution to our problem:

- *Correctness:* A transformed class may not deliver any results that the original synchronized program could not deliver.
- *Performance:* When reads predominate, the measured performance is comparable to the performance of an unsynchronized program.

The Optimistic Readers transformation was originally proposed in conjunction with Guava [1], a Java dialect in which monitor classes are distinguished from other classes, in which read methods are distinguished from update methods, and in which compile-time checking rules out the use of unsynchronized sharing between multiple threads. For Guava, the transformation can be realized as part of the optimization step of a compiler. However, this transformation can be applied equally well in other languages. Although we will illustrate our examples using standard Java, our methodology will apply to any object-oriented or object-based language or environment supporting the concept of multiple threads and synchronization. The optimistic readers transformation can be applied by programmers as a "design pattern," rather than by compilers as an optimization step.

In Sect. 2, we define the problem and present the optimistic readers transformation, simplified for purposes of exposition by assuming sequential consistency and ignoring aborts. In Sect. 3, we complete the exposition by relaxing the sequential consistency assumption and showing how aborts are handled. We employ the platform-independent Commit/Reconcile/Fence (CRF) model in order to specify the transformation precisely. Section 4 discusses further refinements and special cases: nested monitor calls, "usually read" methods, fine-grained optimism, and single-write methods. Section 5 outlines a toolkit that can aid in applying the optimistic readers transformation to complex programs. Section 6 presents measurements derived from a case study in which the optimistic readers transformation was applied to a preexisting application, resulting in a considerable performance improvement. We compare the result of the optimistic readers transformation with (1) the unoptimized, fully synchronized program, and with (2) a version of the program that acquires separate read and write locks. Section 7 discusses related work.

2   Definitions and Overview

Consider the following Java class:

```java
class Foo {
  private int a = 0;
  private int b = 0;

  synchronized void inc(int x) {
    a += x;
    b += x;
  }

  synchronized int prod() {
    int t1 = a;
    int t2 = b;
    return (t1*t2);
  }
}
```

Method `inc` updates the instance variables of `Foo` – it is an *update* method; method `prod` only reads them – it is a *read* method. Notice that in any execution in which multiple threads access an instance of `Foo`, only square numbers will be returned from method `prod`.

A method is defined to be a read method provided it meets these conditions:[1]

1. It does not write instance variables, or write fields of instance variables, or call update methods of instance variables.
2. It may write fields of parameters or call update methods of parameters provided that (a) these methods do not access any monitors for which locks are not already held, and (b) these methods do not update any objects accessible from instance variables.

The above restrictions limit writes to stack variables and to thread-local objects passed in by the caller of the read method. A corollary of this definition is that there are no read-write or write-write conflicts between read methods executed by concurrent threads. Any method not meeting these restrictions is considered to be an update method. In the Guava proposal, there are compile-time checks to validate these rules; in most languages, these checks must be performed manually.

Now consider the following transformed program:

```java
class Foo {
  private int a = 0;
  private int b = 0;
  private int vno = 0; // added
```

---

[1] The same definition was used in Guava.

```
synchronized void inc(int x) {
  vno++; /* pre-increment */
  a += x;
  b += x;
  vno++; /* post-increment */
}

/* unsynchronized */
int prod() {
  int v1 = vno; /* pre-inspect*/
  int t1 = a;
  int t2 = b;
  int v2 = vno; /* post-inspect */
  if (v1 == v2 && v1%2 == 0)
    return(t1*t2); /* commit */
    else ... /* abort */
  }
 }
}
```

This code is only a first approximation to the correct transformed code, since it ignores reorderings permitted by the Java memory model, and it ignores various problems that can occur on a path that aborts. These issues are discussed in detail in the next section.

We define version 0 to be the initial state of the monitor. We define version v to be the state after v update methods have completed execution.

Recall that a transformed program is considered to be correct provided the sequences of values observed by other objects correspond to those that could have been observed in some execution of the original program. As applied to our example, the above condition requires that only square numbers should be returned from calls to **prod**.

Since the original program always executes all methods sequentially, the transformed program must also behave as if all methods were executed sequentially. This entails: (1) that values read by a read method must always be from some version v, never from an intermediate result of an update method, and (2) that if a read method reads multiple values, they all must come from the same version v. Otherwise, the execution is said to have a *read-write conflict*, and the execution is no longer equivalent to a sequential execution of the read and update methods.

For the purposes of this section only, we will assume a memory model based on sequential consistency [2]. Under this assumption:

- each thread executes the instructions in the order specified by the source code, and
- shared memory performs reads and writes in a global total order consistent with some interleaving of the instructions contributed by each thread.

Applying the assumption of sequential consistency and remembering that the update methods are still constrained by mutual exclusion to execute sequentially, it is easy to verify that:

1. All writes to version v occur at a time when variable vno has value $2v - 1$.
2. Therefore, whenever vno is read and yields an even result $2v$, all the writes previously executed by the first v executions of the update method have been written to shared memory, and no writes executed by execution $v + 1$ have been written to shared memory; therefore
3. subsequent reads are guaranteed to see versions no earlier than v, and
4. previous reads are guaranteed to see versions no later than v, therefore
5. if the if test succeeds, meaning that vno contained the even number $2v$ both before and after all the reads in that read method, the reads are guaranteed to be all from version v.

The above shows that any read method that commits will have read a consistent version (subject to the assumption of sequential consistency). Therefore any read method that commits has no read-write conflicts with any update method. And as a corollary of our definition of read method, a read method never has any conflicts with any other read method. Hence all committed read methods give the same effects as if they were executed by the untransformed, synchronized program.

This reasoning applies regardless of the semantics of the methods being optimized. Therefore, assuming that read and update methods can be distinguished, it is always valid to perform this transformation by inserting exactly one pre-increment before the first write to a variable owned[2] by the class being optimized, exactly one post-increment after the last write to an owned variable, one pre-inspect before the first read of an owned variable, and one post-inspect after the last read of an owned variable. The case where a transformed read method of one class calls a nested transformed read method will be discussed in Sect. 4.

3   Refinement

Having presented an idealized situation in which the memory model is sequentially consistent, and aborts are ignored, we now refine the transformation to deal with realistic memory models, and with aborts.

3.1   Memory Model

A memory model guaranteeing sequential consistency is easy to reason about, but is usually weakened in practice for two reasons:

---

[2] The notion of ownership is formalized in the Guava paper. For the purposes of this discussion, a variable is owned by a monitor if it is an instance variable or it is reachable by a chain of references from an instance variable. Stack variables and arguments passed in are not owned by a monitor.

– Multiprocessors read from caches, and asynchronously flush changed cache lines to memory, causing values to appear in shared memory in a different order than the order in which they were assigned by the thread. Barrier instructions must be used when stronger guarantees are needed.
– Compilers reorder operations in order to reuse computations, and to exploit parallelism in functional units. Suppressing these reorderings would also pay a penalty, the more so since most classes are not shared across multiple threads.

Many languages are not precise about the assumed memory model underlying multithreaded implementations. However, since threading is an integral part of the Java language, and since Java program behavior must be understood independent of platform, the Java Language Specification precisely defines the permissible effects of concurrent access [3]. The implications of this model have been surprising [4], and revisions have been proposed [5,6].

In this section, we define the ordering constraints for the optimistic readers transformation using the CRF notation [7]. The CRF notation has been described as a memory model; but it can also be thought of as a platform-independent language capable of specifying different memory models. It has, in fact, been used to shed light on the Java memory model [6].

In CRF each thread has a local semantic cache or *sache*. Each location in the sache corresponds to a global memory location. The CR part of the model augments operations **LoadL** from the sache and **StoreL** to the sache with **Reconcile** operations that force the sache to follow global memory, and **Commit** operations that force global memory to follow the sache; these operations are presumed to occur atomically in a merged global order. The F part of the model adds the operations $\mathbf{Fence}_{rr}$, $\mathbf{Fence}_{rw}$, $\mathbf{Fence}_{wr}$, and $\mathbf{Fence}_{ww}$. These operations take a pair of memory locations as arguments. They specify an ordering constraint between preceding operations on the first location and following operations on the second. For example, $\mathbf{Fence}_{rr}(\mathbf{a},\mathbf{b})$ means that a preceding **Reconcile** of location **a** may not be reordered with respect to a **Reconcile** of location **b**. A similar meaning applies to a **w** subscript and a **Commit**. A course-grained notation is offered to allow a single **Fence** instruction to suppress the reordering of operations on a collection of variables. Even in the absence of fences, reorderings always respect data dependencies.

Since the write methods are synchronized, it is unnecessary to issue **Reconcile** operations before the second or subsequent read of any variable; similarly it is unnecessary to issue **Commit** operations after any writes other than the last write to any variable, with the exception of vno, which must be committed as part of the pre-increment. In the read methods, it is unnecessary to issue **Reconcile** operations before second or subsequent reads to any variable except vno. In this section, we will concentrate on the **Fence** operations, since these are essential to the correctness of the transformation. We introduce only those fences that are needed to preserve the conditions for applying the steps in the correctness argument of Sect. 2.

First, we introduce those fences needed to assure that any thread that acquires a lock will see all the writes to shared variables made by the thread that released the lock and all earlier writes visible to that thread. This guarantee is independent of the optimistic readers transformation; it is built into the Java semantics of synchronized methods.

The prolog of the update method is:

```
Fenceww *L,mylock
Lock mylock
Fencewr mylock,*MV
Fenceww mylock,*MV
```

The notation ***L** in an argument to **Fence** denotes all lock variables. Similarly, ***M** denotes all shared variables owned by the monitor, and ***MV** denotes all these variables plus the introduced variable vno. This code guarantees that previous monitors executed by this thread are not reordered after this one, and that reads and/or writes of variables owned by the monitor are not reordered before the lock acquisition.

The epilog of the update method is:

```
Fenceww *MV, mylock
Fencerw *MV, mylock
Unlock mylock
```

This code similarly guarantees that operations of the monitor are not moved to a place where the lock is no longer held.

The interior of method inc is:

```
// pre-increment
Reconcile vno
temp = LoadL vno
StoreL vno,temp+1
Commit vno
Fenceww vno,*M
// body
Reconcile a
temp1 = LoadL a
StoreL a,temp1+x
Commit a
Reconcile b
temp2 = LoadL b
StoreL b,temp2+x
Commit b
// post-increment
Fenceww *M,vno
StoreL vno,temp+1
Commit vno
```

The effect of the fences at the end of the pre-increment and the beginning of the post-increment is to "corral" the writes to variables a and b between the pre-increment and the post-increment so that step 1 of the argument of Sect. 2 continues to hold.

Similarly, the read method now looks like this:

```
// pre-inspect
Reconcile vno
v1 = LoadL vno
Fence_rr vno,*MV
// body
Reconcile a
t1 = LoadL a
Reconcile b
t2 = LoadL b
// post-inspect
Fence_rr *MV,vno
Reconcile vno
v2 = LoadL vno
if (v1 == v2 && v1%2 == 0)
return t1*t2; else /* abort */
```

The fences here similarly corral the reads of a and b so that they occur between the successive reads of vno, preserving the argument of steps 2 and 3 of Sect. 2, and hence the conclusions as well.

Now since Java programmers cannot currently write CRF directly, some discussion is in order on how to express the above in Java. The precise answer depends upon the resolution of proposals to repair the Java memory model. The complexity of the current model and the controversies surrounding its replacement are beyond the scope of this paper. The former is well summarized by Bill Pugh [4], and the latter by the Java Memory Model Workshop at OOPSLA 2000 [8].

In Pugh's latest proposal, most of the desired fences are generated as a result of declaring vno with the attribute volatile. In his model, writes are allowed to move (subject to constraints related to locks and volatile variables), but not reads. Writes may not be moved past writes to volatile variables or before reads to volatile variables; and reads and writes of volatiles are totally ordered with respect to one another. Unfortunately, nothing prevents the writes to a and b from being moved ahead of the write in the pre-increment of vno. So in Pugh's model, the optimistic transformation must be realized by both declaring vno as volatile and inserting the additional operation int bogus = vno following the pre-increment, to act as a barrier to moving prescient stores of a and b too early.

In Maessen, Arvind, and Shen's proposal [6], an explicit CRF translation is given for Java volatile and Java locking. Their translation also requires the insertion of the operation int bogus = vno following the pre-increment in the update method. However, since they generate read-read fences only after loads of volatiles and not before, it is necessary to precede the post-test with an empty `synchronized` block to force a read fence.

The current Java memory model restricts only the reordering of operations on `volatile` variables themselves, and does not restrict reordering of other reads and writes with respect to volatile variables. So, empty `synchronized` blocks are required in even more places. In our case study implementation described in Sect. 6, we use a `VersionNumber` class with `native` methods to precisely control the mapping of CRF onto the machine architecture.

In other languages, comparable calls to the thread package or inserted assembler instructions would be needed to achieve the necessary fence operations.

3.2   Aborts

Up until now, we have only dealt with the cases in which the thread executing the read method is "lucky" and the post-test succeeds. If the thread is "unlucky," we have the following problems:

- Although we know from the above reasoning that the post-test will fail if a consistent version is not read, we must still ensure that execution reaches the post-test without first looping, aborting, or crashing.
- We must ensure that it is always possible to correctly re-execute the method after an abort.

Let us deal with each of these issues in turn.

Reaching the Post-Test. If the execution of a reading thread overlaps the execution of a writing thread, then it is possible for the reader to see inconsistent values from multiple versions, and in the case of multiword variables (such as Java `long` integers), possibly even corrupted values of a single variable. These bad values may cause a loop to fail to terminate, or may cause an unexpected action, such as a null pointer or array bounds exception that the original method did not handle. In both cases the post-test would not be reached. Therefore it is necessary for the transformed code to guard against these possibilities.

All loops (or recursive calls) whose number of executions depend on shared variables and are not statically known to be bounded must be replaced by guarded loops that periodically issue the post-inspect test and abort if this fails, continuing the loop if it succeeds. All contexts where exceptions might be raised must be guarded by constructs that handle the exception by repeating the post-inspect test and aborting if it fails. In Java this would mean enclosing the body in a `try` block. The exception handler must then issue a post-inspect test, and then re-raise the exception on success and abort on failure. In the case study described in Sect. 6, we used static analysis to satisfy ourselves that loops were bounded and added a `try` block to catch stray exceptions.

A nastier possibility exists if an unsynchronized read could cause data of the wrong type to be read. In Java, which allows unsynchronized reads but promises type-safety, this problem cannot occur. Although a thread may observe a partially initialized object or even an incompletely loaded class, the Java virtual machine promises to provide a legal value for each field accessed (e.g., a zero or a null pointer) or else throw a well-defined exception, even if concurrent threads fail to synchronize when they should. But in other languages, this can be a problem. For instance, tagged variants can be written by one thread, while another thread sees the old tag but the updated variant. Or storage can be freed, and reallocated without being cleared to a standard "safe" value (like zero). In these languages optimistic readers need to be cautious by either recovering from the resulting faults, or by repeating the post-inspect test after reading but before dereferencing a pointer that came from a place whose type can vary. These restrictions probably mean that optimistic readers should only be attempted in these languages when aided by a program transformation tool.

Performing the Abort. When the post-inspect test fails, the abort action is simply to re-execute the read method. However, to guarantee liveness, we must make sure that a read eventually commits. Usually this means that there is some bound of the number of retries permitted before an optimistic read method "gives up" and reverts to pessimism by acquiring the lock on the object and re-invoking the method. In the case study of Sect. 6, we gave up extremely easily – if an optimistic read aborted once, it was immediately retried using a pessimistic read.

Undoing Side-Effects. We have up to now assumed that read methods are idempotent – that if they are aborted, they can simply be re-executed and the effects of any writes they performed can be ignored. For Java, this is true of methods that only write to the stack and not to parameters – any stack variables written will simply be overwritten when the operation is retried, and any objects created will just become garbage and will be collected in due course. For languages without garbage collection, the abort operation must begin by freeing any allocated objects to avoid memory leaks.

Recall that by our definition of a read method, it is permitted for a read method to update parameters passed by reference, provided that they are local to the caller. If this occurs, e.g. the method appends to a `StringBuffer` parameter, then the operation is no longer idempotent. Either the writes must be saved and delayed until the operation commits, or else the parameter object must support additional operations to remember its state on entry to the read operation and to restore the state in the event of an abort.

4   Special Situations

4.1   Nested Reads

By our definition of a read method, it is impossible for a read method on a monitor to invoke update methods on other monitors. However, it is possible for a read method of one monitor to issue one or more *nested* invocations of read methods of other monitors. If both the outer and the nested read methods are implemented with the optimistic readers transformation, we need to make sure that the dynamic behavior of the entire invocation still meets the assumptions used in the proof of correctness, namely that all pre-inspects precede all post-inspects. A naive implementation will not work in the case in which the outer method makes two or more nested calls. Suppose that method `prod` of class `Foo` of our earlier example is the inner read, and that we have the following outer read method:

```
class Bar {
  private Foo f;

  Bar (Foo initial) {
    f = initial;
  }
  ...
  synchronized int diff() {
    int t1 = f.prod();
    int t2 = f.prod();
    return (t2-t1);
  }
}
```

Now suppose that we have an instance `myfoo` of `Foo`, and an instance `mybar` of `Bar` constructed with parameter `myfoo`. Suppose that thread 1 invokes `myfoo.inc(1)`, while threads 2 and 3 each invoke `mybar.diff()`. In the unoptimized program, the two invocations of `diff` must run sequentially, and since `myfoo` is incremented exactly once, at most one of them can return non-zero. But in a naive implementation in which each separate call to `prod` performs its own pre-inspect and post-inspect, it would be possible for both reader threads to read an old value into `t1` and a new value into `t2`, thus violating the correctness condition, even though none of the post-tests failed.

This is the exact same problem as occurs in database concurrency control, and the solution is exactly the same [9]. The correctness guarantee requires that the issuing of pre-reads and post-tests must be *two-phase*, and that therefore the post-test of the first call to `prod` must be deferred until the completion of the second call to `prod`. The desired effect can be accomplished by inlining `prod` and moving the post-test to the appropriate place. For simple cases like this one, this kind of inlining can be done by hand. For the general case, however, assuming the transformation is being applied without benefit of a compiler or program transformer, the toolkit described in Sect. 5 may be employed: its `VersionContext` class is used to maintain the two-phase property across any number of nested checks.

4.2 "Usually Read" Methods

So far we have assumed that each method is designated as either a read or as an update method. However it is possible that a method can be an update method when analyzed statically, and still have one or more execution paths that are read only. If the read only execution paths are executed sufficiently frequently, it is advantageous for the method to be executed optimistically whenever a read only path is taken, requesting a lock only when actually behaving as an update method. A real-life instance of this situation occurred in our publish-subscribe system, the subject of the case study in Sect. 6. Lookup operations would first check a cache to see if an identical lookup had been performed since the last time the subscriptions had changed; only if it had not would the more lengthy computation be performed, in which case the result might be stored into the cache. Most lookups did not result in cache updates. The ones that did would have the effect of promoting the "usually read" method to an update method.

We can achieve this result by delayed acquisition of a lock. Consider the following method of class Foo that is sometimes an update method and sometimes read only:

```
synchronized int mixed(int x) {
  int t = a - b;
  if (t <= x) return t;
  else {
    b++;
    return t - 1;
  }
}
```

Here, we can read a and b, and perform the computation a - b before deciding whether to acquire a lock. Here is the transformed program:

```
/* unsynchronized */
int mixed(int x) {
  int v1 = vno; /* pre-inspect */
  int t = a - b;
  if (t <= x) {
    int v2=vno; /* post-inspect */
    if (v1 == v2 && v1%2 == 0)
      return(t); /* commit */
      else ... /*abort*/
  }
```

```
      else synchronized (this) {
        int v2=vno; /* post-inspect */
        if (v1 != v2 || v1%2 != 0)
          ... /* abort */
        vno++; /* pre-increment */
        b++;
        vno++; /* post-increment */
        return t - 1;
      }
}
```

In the above example, if the method takes the path where t <= x, then it behaves exactly like an ordinary read method. If the method takes the path where t > x, then it acquires a lock on this. If the post-test succeeds, then we are sure that the information read so far is consistent based upon the current version – which is the same as saying that the state is the same as it would have been had the lock on this been acquired on entrance to the method. We can then proceed to continue execution as if this method had been invoked as a regular update method.

It should be noted that no shared memory accesses should occur after the synchronized block is exited (otherwise, the two-phase property would be violated). Thus, the example shown cannot be nested. The nesting of "usually read" methods can be accomplished using the toolkit described in Sect. 5. Or, if the optimistic readers transformation is performed by a compiler, it can translate this nested case to a continuation-passing form to achieve the correct result. It is also possible to eagerly abort a nested "usually read" method that discovers the need to write, forcing it to be re-executed with a lock. Studying the tradeoffs between these solutions is left for future work.

4.3   Multi-partition Objects

The optimistic readers transformation presented in Sect. 3 assumes that an update method modifies the entire state of the monitor, and potentially conflicts with any read method that reads any part of the state. This assumption, though conservative, simplifies the transformation, and usually yields considerable performance improvement. However, in certain applications, there could be an excessive rate of phantom aborts that occur because a reader reads one part of the state, while a writer updates another part of the state.

For instance, suppose a hash table monitor is implemented as an array of BucketList objects, where each BucketList is a linked list of buckets containing keys and values. Suppose further that the buckets are not shared across multiple BucketList objects. Each separate BucketList now constitutes a disjoint *partition* of the state of the hash table. Each insert, delete, or modify of the hash table modifies a single partition (depending upon the hash code of the key); similarly, each lookup of the hash table reads a single BucketList. Then, provided one is willing to allocate a version number array with one entry per partition, one can reduce contention and therefore frequency of aborts by replacing the monitor-wide version number with separate version numbers for each partition.

Fine-grained version numbering will also work when methods access more than one partition, provided that the pre-increment and post-increment operations, and the pre-read and the post-test operations follow the two-phase discipline discussed above.

It is clear, of course, that managing a large number of version numbers in a complex data structure (particularly when nesting is involved) can become complex. The toolkit describe in Sect. 5 addresses some of these concerns.

4.4   Single Word Write

Under certain conditions, it is permissible to optimize away the pre- and post-increment operations, and the pre-read and post-test operations. The usual case in which this is possible must meet these conditions:

1. the monitor state (or in a multi-partition monitor, the partition state) consists of a single word that can be atomically written (in Java, this would mean a 32-bit volatile),
2. the write to the single-word partition follows all other writes (if any),
3. there is only one such single-word partition, and
4. no read method ever accesses the single-word partition more than once.

The transformed code looks like the regular transformed code except:

1. The single word in the single-word partition is a `volatile` variable on its own, with no version number, no pre-increment, and no post-increment.
2. There is no pre-inspect, post-inspect, or test for the single-word partition. The order of operations must be: pre-inspects, then read of the single-word, then read of all the other words, then post-inspects.

Because of these conditions, it is impossible to have a read-write conflict. It is impossible for a read method to see an incomplete version since it must either see the new or the old value. It is impossible for multiple reads of the single-write partition to see values from different versions, since there can be no multiple reads. And since the value is volatile and written last, it is impossible to see a new version of the variable and old versions of variables in other partitions. It is possible to see an old version of the variable and new values of variables written earlier, but then the post-inspect test for one of these other partitions will fail. (The pre-inspect for the partition that saw the new version must have seen an old version number, since it preceded the read of the single-write variable that saw an old value. But the post-inspect for that same partition must see a new version number, since it followed a read that saw a new value.)

It is possible for the single-write field to be a reference to an object, provided that the whenever a reference is assigned, it is a reference to a newly allocated object not visible from anywhere else. It is not permitted to update an already accessible object and then store its address into the reference, since it could then be possible for readers to see the old value of the reference via other copies of the reference.

5   A Toolkit

To aid in applying optimistic readers to non-trivial programs without the benefit of a specialized compiler or program transformation tool, we created a toolkit consisting of the following classes and methods.

```
public class VersionNumber {
  public VersionNumber();
  public void preIncrement();
  public void postIncrement();
  public int preInspect();
  public int postInspect();
}

public class ConflictException
  extends Exception {...}

public class VersionContext {
  // no public constructor
  public static VersionContext allocate(int numReads,
                                        int numPush);
  public void free();
  public void bePessimistic();
  public void pushMonitorContext(Object monitor,
                                 int maxWrites);
  public void popMonitorContext();
  public void useVersion(VersionNumber toUse)
             throws ConflictException;
  public void modifyVersion(VersionNumber toModify)
             throws ConflictException;
  public boolean isConsistent();
}

public class OptimisticThread
  extends Thread {
  // public constructors mimic those of Thread
}
```

The VersionNumber class, already mentioned, encapsulates one version number and the four methods needed to manipulate it. This is done to ensure that the necessary CRF **Fence** operations are imposed on all accesses to the value. The pure Java embodiment of this class uses vacuous **synchronized** blocks before post-incrementing and after pre-inspecting to (rather crudely) accomplish this goal. The class also loads an ancillary `native` code library (if provided) which replaces the pure Java implementation with a more precise match to the CRF requirements. The measurements of Sect. 6 were taken using a `native` implementation for PowerPC (employing the `lwarcx`, `stwcx`, `sync` and `isync` instructions), thus avoiding any lock activity whatsoever. In preliminary measurements we saw some differences between the pure Java and native implementations, though these were small until the number of processors (and threads) grew to eight or more, at which point the native implementation continued to scale while the pure Java implementation did not. This suggests that the excess synchronization imposed by the Java memory model was starting to be significant. Under a proposed revision to the memory model [5], less over-synchronization would occur in a pure Java implementation of `VersionNumber`.

The `VersionContext` class is used for three purposes.

1. It helps maintain the needed two-phase property when there are nested reads as described in Sect. 4.1 or simply many different `VersionNumber` instances per object (as can happen with the multi-grained optimism strategy of Sect. 4.3).
2. It helps with late lock acquisition and coordinated lock release, which are required when "usually read" methods are nested.
3. When optimism must be abandoned and locks acquired after all, it allows the identical code to be used for both optimistic and pessimistic execution.

Use of `VersionContext` is optional in programs that are simple enough. For example, it was not used in the experiment described in the next section.

An outer read method (one that is not called by another optimistically transformed method) allocates a `VersionContext` object. An inner read method uses the `VersionContext` supplied by the outer method. For modularity, it is a good practice to supply both an outer and inner version of every read (and "usually read") method, as in this transformation of the original `Foo` class.

```
class Foo {
  ...
  private VersionNumber vno = new VersionNumber();

  synchronized void inc(int x) {
    vno.preIncrement();
    a += x;
    b += x;
    vno.postIncrement();
  }
```

```
// Used when prod() is an outer method
int prod() {
  VersionContext vc = VersionContext.allocate(1, 0);
  try {
    try {
      int ans = prod(vc);
      if (vc.isConsistent())
        return ans;
    } catch (ConflictException e) {
    } catch (RuntimeException e) {
      if (vc.isConsistent())
        throw e;
    } catch (Error e) {
      if (vc.isConsistent())
        throw e;
    }
    // Optimistic execution failed due to
    // read-write conflict
    synchronized(this) {
      vc.bePessimistic();
      return prod(vc);
    }
  } finally {
    vc.free();
  }
}

// Used when prod() is called by another transformed
// read method
int prod(VersionContext vc) throws ConflictException {
  vc.useVersion(vno);
  int t1 = a;
  int t2 = b;
  return (t1*t2);
}
}
```

The preceding example illustrates the use of VersionContext when only pure read methods are being transformed. The useVersion method is called to perform each pre-inspect, passing the VersionNumber associated with the partition being read. It automatically checks whether the same VersionNumber was earlier touched by the same method and does nothing in that case. It throws ConflictException if the VersionNumber is odd (meaning a modification is in progress). Otherwise, it records the VersionNumber's current value for later. The isConsistent method post-inspects all VersionNumber objects that have been touched during the lifetime of the VersionContext. The bePessimistic method resets the `VersionContext` and establishes "pessimistic" mode. In pessimistic mode, the `useVersion` method does nothing and the `isConsistent` method always returns `true`, allowing the transformed code to execute efficiently when the monitor lock is held. When only read methods are transformed, only one `VersionContext` object is required per thread.

When methods of the "usually read" type are nested, some other methods of `VersionContext` come into play, as is illustrated by the following transformation of the `mixed` method introduced in Sect. 4.2.

```
// The outer version (not shown) follows the same pattern
// as was illustrated for the prod method.
// This is the inner version.
int mixed(int x, VersionContext vc) throws ConflictException {
  vc.useVersion(vno);
  vc.pushMonitorContext(this, 1);
  try {
    int t = a - b;
    if (t <= x) return t;
    else {
      vc.modifyVersion(vno);
      b++;
      return t-1;
    }
  } finally {
    vc.popMonitorContext();
  }
}
```

A method that might turn into an update method must call `pushMonitorContext` at the beginning and `popMonitorContext` in a `finally` clause. The `useVersion` method is used just as it would be in a pure read method. The `modifyVersion` method is called with every `VersionNumber` that guards state about to be modified by the method.

The first time `modifyVersion` is called, the `VersionContext` enters pessimistic mode. Using the stack of object references saved during previous calls to `pushMonitorContext`, it acquires all locks that would have been acquired had all these monitor objects been locked from the start. It checks consistency of all `VersionNumbers` used up to that point and throws `ConflictException` upon observing any inconsistency (releasing the locks first, of course). If all the used versions are consistent, it holds the locks it has just acquired, and pre-increments the supplied `VersionNumber`.

Once in pessimistic mode, each `modifyVersion` call pre-increments a version number. Each `pushMonitorContext` call immediately locks its argument. Each `popMonitorContext` call post-increments all the version numbers that were pre-incremented under the monitor context about to be popped, then unlocks that monitor.

The monitor context stack just described cannot be implemented in the Java *source* language because that language forces `monitorenter` and `monitorexit` JVM instructions to nest lexically, while the JVM only requires them to nest dynamically. We employ a tiny class implemented via raw Java byte codes to get around the source language restriction. Improper monitor states are avoided provided the `pushMonitorContext` and `popMonitorContext` calls are nested as shown in the example.

Note that update methods do not use `VersionContext` but call the `VersionNumber.preIncrement` and `postIncrement` methods directly. When an update method calls a read method of a transformed monitor it does so through the outer version of the method, which allocates a new `VersionContext`. Thus, when a "usually read" method (in a portion statically known to be updating the object) invokes an update method which invokes a read method, there can be a stack of `VersionContext` objects active in a thread. This is safe because all but the innermost `VersionContext` will have become pessimistic, and only the innermost must be two-phase in order to achieve correctness.

The `OptimisticThread` class maintains a per-thread stack of preallocated and pre-formatted `VersionContext` objects so that the gains of the optimistic reader transformation are not counteracted by increased heap allocation overhead. The `VersionContext.allocate` method automatically uses this stack if `OptimisticThread` is being employed. The parameters to `allocate` are advisory, and further reduce heap allocation overhead when the number of calls to certain `VersionContext` methods can be predicted.

6   Experimental Results

6.1   Background and Methodology

Our experimental results were collected using the Gryphon publish-subscribe system [10]. A publish-subscribe system takes an event and delivers it to that subset of subscribers whose prior subscriptions indicated interest in that event. Although it began as a research project, Gryphon has been used as middleware in support of real applications (for example, IBM-developed web-sites for Wimbledon 2000 and the 2000 Olympics).

Gryphon employs a network of specialized routers called *brokers*. At the heart of each broker is a shared object called `MatchSpace`, containing all the subscriptions of which the broker is aware, along with the associated routing information. We decided to evaluate the optimistic readers transformation for Gryphon's `MatchSpace` after observing scalability limitations on PowerPC multiprocessor machines that fell short of an application requirement. As a result of this study, the optimistic version of `MatchSpace` is now the production version.

For our present purposes, a `MatchSpace` has three methods, `subscribe` (which registers a new subscription), `unsubscribe` (which removes a subscription), and `route` (which examines a message and returns the list of matching subscriptions). The first two are write methods, while the third is a "usually read" method as discussed in Sect. 4.2. It usually does not change `MatchSpace`, but it sometimes does so in order to maintain a cache.

To achieve high performance, brokers create a pool of concurrent threads. Threads repeatedly pick up a message, determine a destination list by invoking the `route` method of `MatchSpace`, and then deliver the message to each destination on that list. Intermittently, a thread will receive a request to add or remove a subscription and will call `subscribe` or `unsubscribe`.

In the original `MatchSpace`, all three methods were `synchronized`. However, prior to this study, synchronization on the `route` method was dropped in favor of a reader-writer locking design (detailed below). We were thus able to compare three implementations of `MatchSpace`: the original "pure monitor" implementation which we call "pessimistic," the reader-writer locks implementation, and the optimistic readers implementation. Rather than examining earlier versions of Gryphon (which differed in other ways), we reworked all three `MatchSpace` implementations to fit the latest version of Gryphon.

To provide a baseline for comparison of these three implementations, we also measured an implementation that was identical to the pessimistic implementation except that the `route` method was unsynchronized. Such an implementation would not be practical, since it could potentially produce wrong results. However, we treated this implementation as providing an upper limit on the performance of any correct implementation, and as a way to quantify our claim of Sect. 1 that when reads predominate, the optimistic program should perform comparably to an unsynchronized program.

To implement the optimistic readers transformation, we employed the `VersionNumber` class from the toolkit. Because of the simplicity of the application, the other toolkit classes were not used.

An instance variable of type `VersionNumber` was added to `MatchSpace`. The `subscribe` and `unsubscribe` methods were augmented with a call to `preIncrement` at the beginning and a call to `postIncrement` at the end. Those methods remained `synchronized` and otherwise unchanged.

The original route method was renamed to `pessimisticRoute` (and remained `synchronized`) while a new unsynchronized `route` method was created.

The new route method began by determining whether the cache needed to updated. If so, it invoked the method `pessimisticRoute`, which was revised to bracket cache updates with calls to methods `preIncrement` and `postIncrement`. In the case of a pure read, `route` obtained the current version number using `preInspect`. An odd number again resulted in a call to `pessimisticRoute`. Otherwise, `route` executed the pure read path excerpted from the original `route` method. Finally, `route` called `postInspect`. If the version numbers differed, the results were discarded and `pessimisticRoute` invoked instead. If the version numbers matched, the results were trusted and no lock ever had to be acquired.

This methodology deviates in minor ways from what a compiler would have done automatically, but is clearly equivalent. It illustrates that a human being can apply this methodology as a design pattern in simple cases, deviating from the purely mechanical in minor ways, and preserving code readability. We leave for future work the evaluation of this approach with a more complex application, employing the full toolkit.

The reader-writer locking code employed three methods as follows.

```
synchronized
void obtainReadLock() {
  readers++;
}

synchronized
void releaseReadLock() {
  readers--;
  if (readers == 0 && waiters > 0)
    notifyAll();
}

void obtainWriteLock() {
  while (readers > 0) {
    waiters++;
    wait();
    waiters--;
  }
}
```

The `route` method was made unsynchronized, and a call to `obtainReadLock` was inserted at the beginning and a call to `releaseReadLock` was inserted at the end. The two (`synchronized`) write methods were augmented with calls to `obtainWriteLock` at the beginning. [3]

Measurements were obtained using an existing Gryphon performance testing "harness" called the "I/O-free test." This test includes the code of the CPU-intensive parts of Gryphon, including `MatchSpace`, together with a message generator. A "read" in this benchmark consists of creating a message, invoking the "usually read" method `route` to determine a destination set, and pretending to deliver the message without recourse to actual network I/O. An "update" consists of invoking `subscribe` followed by `unsubscribe`, to create write-interference without actually changing the number of subscriptions in match space during a run. A multithreaded version of the test was developed in which the pattern of updates to `MatchSpace` and the pattern of reads were controlled by separate Poisson distributions. For a given number of threads and a given write rate, the throughput was measured as the maximum read rate at which the processors just approached saturation. A run was considered to cause saturation if during the last 10% of the 30 second run, no thread was able to drain its input queue.

---

[3] We also measured the performance with an alternative reader-writer discipline in which readers were not allowed to obtain locks if another thread was waiting to obtain a write lock. This alternative discipline never performed better and often performed worse than the original one, and hence was dropped from the comparison.

6.2   Results

The measurements for Fig. 1 and Fig. 2 were made on a 4-way PowerPC Model 270 running the AIX operating system version 4.3, running Java 2, JDK version 1.3.0 from IBM.

Figure 1 shows the read throughput for four threads at update rates varying from 0.5 updates per second per thread to 2000 updates per second per thread. As the figure illustrates, both optimistic reading and reader-writer locking start out with a substantial advantage over the pure monitor implementation at low update rates. However, as the update rate increases, the reader-writer locking implementation gradually degrades to nearly the same throughput as the fully synchronized implementation, while the optimistic readers implementation degrades much more slowly and keeps its advantage in throughput. We speculate that the overhead of `wait` and `notifyAll` is responsible for this and we cannot rule out the possibility that the results might be different using a different machine architecture or Java implementation. Even at 2000 writes per second per thread, which is a rate far beyond the rates likely in a real Gryphon deployment, the throughput of optimistic readers is only about 10% worse than that of the unsynchronized algorithm. At more realistic write rates, the difference between optimistic readers and unsynchronized readers is considerably less.

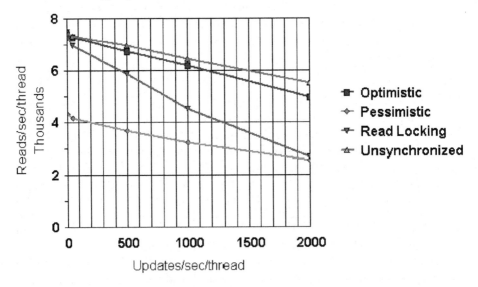

Fig. 1. Read throughput as a function of update frequency

Figure 2 plots essentially the same data as Fig. 1 but in terms of speedup (using the rate for a single thread as a baseline). Notice that the pure monitor barely achieves twofold speedup on a four-way multiprocessor. The optimistic readers implementation maintains a threefold or greater speedup even at 2000 writes per second per thread.

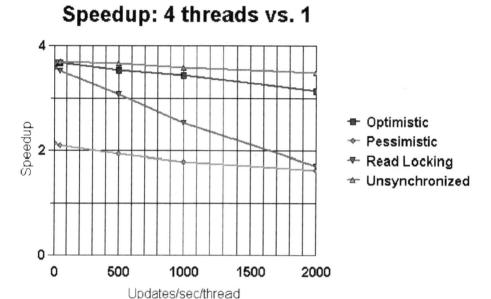

Fig. 2. Speedup as a function of update frequency

The measurements for Fig. 3 and Fig. 4 employed a 24-way PowerPC Model S80 server, running the identical operating system and Java environment.

Figure 3 shows what happens when the update rate is held constant at 500 updates per second per thread and the number of threads is varied from 1 to 13. Optimistic readers maintains an increasing advantage as the number of threads increases. Note that the line for reader-writer locking eventually crosses the line for the pure monitor, indicating that, at high degrees of parallelism, this well-known technique is no longer viable. Again, it is possible that `wait` and `notify` have overheads that outstrip those of simple lock contention in the architecture and operating system chosen for this study.

It is worth pointing out that when only a single thread is running, the performance of all algorithms is for all practical purposes the same. This follows from the fact that in the IBM Java implementation, the overhead of locking and unlocking is negligible when there is no contention. Therefore the reduced performance of the pessimistic algorithm in the multi-threaded case is attributable to real lock contention, and not to any inherent inefficiency in acquiring and releasing locks.

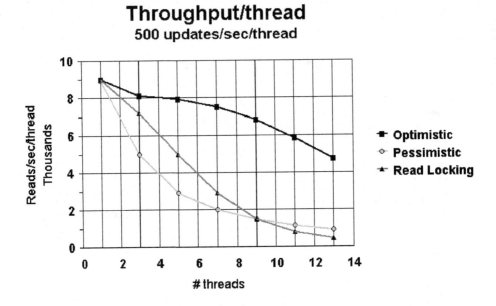

Fig. 3. Maximum throughput/thread as a function of number of threads

Figure 4 provides the speedup data for the same data as in Fig. 3, also plotting the "ideal" speedup curve. Notice that the optimistic readers implementation tracks the ideal curve closely, peaking at 11 threads before beginning to decline.

7   Related Work

The optimistic readers transformation follows the same philosophy as does the *optimistic concurrency control* proposed by Kung and Robinson [11] and extensively explored since. Computation is allowed to proceed in parallel and is aborted if the results are found to be inconsistent with a serial execution order. Optimistic concurrency control contemplates a transactional database environment in which the *commit* and *abort* operations are provided by a transaction manager. We show how *commit* and *abort* are readily implemented without a transaction manager for the special case of read operations as defined here.

Of course, the observation that reads may be safely and concurrently executed in the absence of writes is well-known. It is the basis of the popular *concurrent-read exclusive-write* (CREW) model and the reader-writer locking optimization that was earlier used in Gryphon. Characteristics of this model have been extensively studied (see, for example, [12]). What we have contributed is a general

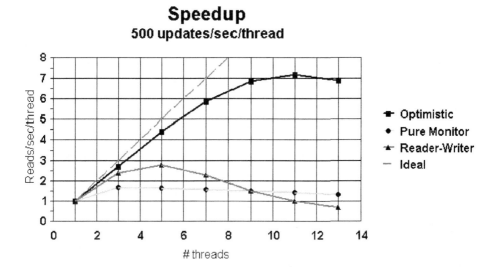

Fig. 4. Speedup as a function of number of threads

technique for achieving CREW semantics with a mixture of synchronized and unsynchronized methods without using the potentially expensive monitor `wait` and `notify` methods.

Our transformation is also in the spirit of Herlihy's general methodology [13] for implementing concurrent data objects using the `load_linked` and `store_conditional` primitives. We do not require these primitives (though we do rely on the more generic CRF `Fence` operation), because our transformation is limited to optimizing the reads, leaving the mutators to be handled via traditional locking.

8   Discussion

We have shown that it is not necessary to give up a simple correctness specification for the sake of efficiency. For example, in the Gryphon case study, the result of every `route` call reflects an actual state of the subscriptions in `MatchSpace`, yet the performance over a wide range of conflict rates is still comparable to the performance of an unsynchronized program and outperforms other techniques such as reader and writer locks.

The optimistic readers transformation vindicates the monitor model, but also depends on the consistent use of the monitor model. For the transformation to work, it must be possible to partition the state of the entire system into disjoint monitor objects. This is straightforward in the case of objects like hash tables or Gryphon's `MatchSpace`. But if objects in one monitor can contain references to objects in another, then unique version numbers can no longer be associated with changes to a single object. A tool, the Guava dialect of Java, has been proposed by one of the authors to make such checking automatic. In today's object-oriented languages, it is necessary to design the application from the beginning using a methodology centered around monitors.

It is relatively straightforward to implement our transformation as a compiler optimization for a proposed monitor-based dialect such as Guava. Alternatively, it is straightforward to implement the transformation as a post-processor for standard Java provided that the programmer is satisfied that the code has been written using a monitor discipline. In order for application writers to code optimistic monitors directly, it is desirable for programmers to employ the utility classes `VersionNumber` for platform-independent reading and updating of version counts with proper synchronization, and `VersionContext` for correct generation of the two-phase post-inspect tests. Aided by these, and employing a type-safe language like Java, doing optimistic reader transformations as a design pattern becomes feasible.

In the absence of type-safety, it is more doubtful whether the technique is practical. Ironically, it may be easier to assure that an optimistic reader is safe in a lower-level language like C, where every memory access is visible to the user, than in a higher-level language like C++. In these languages, the technique is probably only practical in controlled environments where type-safety is not dependent on values read from shared memory.

Finally, it is of interest that the `VersionNumber` object can only be implemented efficiently in a platform-dependent way. Even in Java, a platform-independent implementation would perform excessive synchronization. In other languages lacking an explicit memory model, `VersionNumber` would of necessity be implemented differently depending upon the memory model of each architecture. It is worth noting that in some proposed revisions of the Java memory model, a platform-independent implementation would be efficient.

References

1. Bacon, D. F., Strom, R. E., and Tarafdar, A., "Guava: A Dialect of Java without Data Races", In OOPSLA 2000 Conference Proceedings, pp. 382-400, October 2000.
2. Gharachorloo, K. "Memory Consistency Models for Shared Memory Multiprocessors," PhD thesis, Stanford University, 1995.
3. Gosling, J., Joy, B., and Steele, G., The Java Language Specification. Addison Wesley, Menlo Park, CA, 1996.
4. Pugh, W., "Fixing the Java Memory Model". In Proceeedings of the ACM Java Grande Conference, June 1999.
5. Pugh, W., "Semantics of Multithreaded Java", URL:
   http://www.cs.umd.edu/~pugh/java/memoryModel/semantics.pdf
6. Maessen, J-W., Arvind, and Shen, X., "Improving the Java Memory Model Using CRF", In OOPSLA 2000 Conference Proceedings, pp. 1-12., October 2000.
7. Shen, X., Arvind, and Rudolph, L. "Commit-Reconcile and Fences (CRF): A New Memory Model for Architects and Compiler Writers" In Proceedings of the 26th International Symposium On Computer Architecture, Atlanta, Georgia, May 1999.
8. Java Memory Model Workshop, URL:
   http://www.cs.umd.edu/~pugh/java/memoryModel/workshop.

9. Eswaran, K.P., Gray, J., Lorie, R. A., Traiger, I.L., "The Notions of Consistency and Predicate Locks in a Database System." CACM 19(11), pp. 624-633, 1976.

10. Banavar, G., Chandra, T., Mukherjee, B., Nagarajarao, J., Strom, R., and Sturman, D., "An Efficient Multicast Protocol for Content-based Publish-Subscribe Systems", In Proceedings of the International Conference on Distributed Computing Systems, 1999.

11. Kung, H.T., and. Robinson, J.T., "On Optimistic Methods for Concurrency Control", ACM TODS, v. 6, no. 2, pp. 213-226, June 1981.

12. Reiman, M., and. Wright, P.E., "Performance analysis of concurrent-read exclusive-write". In Joint International Conference on Measurement and Modeling of Computer Systems (ACM SIGMETRICS) San Diego, CA, Pages 168-177, May 1991.

13. Herlihy, M. "A Methodology for Implementing Highly Concurrent Data Objects." ACM Transactions on Programming Languages and Systems, v. 15, no. 5, pp. 745-770, November 1993.

Invited Talk:

People and the Limits of Methodology

Alistair Cockburn

Humans and Technology
7691 Dell Rd.
Salt Lake City, UT 84121
alistair.cockburn@acm.org

Abstract. People have a nasty habit of ruining neatly drawn up methodologies. It's not that they intend to, it is just that people are packaged as "individuals" while methodologies are packaged in "roles." We shall explore principles that follow methodologies versus those that follow people, see how far methodologies can take us versus where we have to give in to the characteristics of people, and how to concoct an agile-but-sufficient methodology on the fly, using a view of software development as a cooperative game of invention and communication.

J. Lindskov Knudsen (Ed.): ECOOP 2001, LNCS 2072, pp. 302-302, 2001.

Family Polymorphism

Erik Ernst

Department of Computer Science
University of Aalborg, Denmark
eernst@cs.auc.dk

Abstract. This paper takes polymorphism to the multi-object level. Traditional inheritance, polymorphism, and late binding interact nicely to provide both *flexibility* and *safety* – when a method is invoked on an object via a polymorphic reference, late binding ensures that we get the appropriate implementation of that method for the actual object. We are granted the flexibility of using different kinds of objects and different method implementations, and we are guaranteed the safety of the combination. Nested classes, polymorphism, and late binding of nested classes interact similarly to provide both safety and flexibility at the level of multi-object systems. We are granted the flexibility of using different *families* of kinds of objects, and we are guaranteed the safety of the combination. This paper highlights the inability of traditional polymorphism to handle multiple objects, and presents family polymorphism as a way to overcome this problem. Family polymorphism has been implemented in the programming language gbeta, a generalized version of BETA, and the source code of this implementation is available under GPL.[1]

1 Introduction

Imagine a hotel lobby with a few people standing around, waiting. The receptionist decides to get things going by asking a man "Are you a husband?" and asking a woman "Are you a wife?". Upon receiving two affirmative – though slightly baffled – answers, those two people are assigned to the same room, together with the little girl who said "Erm, yeah, and I'm a daughter!"

The reason why this might not be entirely appropriate is that those people may very well be 'husband', 'wife', and 'daughter', but it makes a big difference whether or not they play these roles in the *same family*.

Family polymorphism is a programming language feature that allows us to express and manage multi-object relations, thus ensuring both the flexibility of using any of an unbounded number of families, and the safety guarantee that families will not be mixed. It is, in a sense, a programming language feature that solves problems with the same structure as the hotel room assignment problem.

Traditional inheritance, polymorphism, and late binding of methods provide both flexibility and safety in the following sense. A polymorphic reference x may at run-time refer to an object which is an instance of some class C_i chosen from

---

[1] http://www.cs.auc.dk/~eernst/gbeta/.

J. Lindskov Knudsen (Ed.): ECOOP 2001, LNCS 2072, pp. 303–326, 2001.

a set of classes $\mathcal{C} = \{C_0 \ldots C_k\}$. We may invoke a method m on x, typically using syntax such as x.m(), and each of the classes may provide its own method implementation for m or inherit an implementation defined elsewhere. Late binding ensures that the chosen implementation of m is the one associated with C_i (if any), i.e., the appropriate implementation for the actual object. Static type checking may be used to ensure that there is indeed an implementation for every invocation.

All in all, this provides the flexibility of using several classes and several method implementations, and the safety of ensuring that the chosen method implementation is always appropriate for the actual object. It is important to note that the same call-site, x.m(), is *reused* with all those pairs consisting of a class and a method implementation; that it does not depend on the exact class of x or the exact choice of implementation of m; and moreover that the set of class/method pairs is open-ended.

Now consider the situation where two or more objects are involved, for instance where one object is given as an argument to a method on the other object, x.m(y). In this case, traditional object-oriented languages such as the Java™ programming language [2] and C++ [25] will only allow us to associate two compile-time constant classes with this expression, namely the statically known class of x, C_x, and the statically known argument type of m, the class C_m. At run-time, x may refer to an instance of any subclass of C_x and y may refer to an instance of any subclass of C_m. There is no way to ensure statically that a particular subclass C'_x of C_x is always paired up with a particular subclass C'_m of C_m.

Note that multiple dispatch [5,10,23] solves a *different* problem: With multiple dispatch it is possible to choose a method implementation based on the actual classes of x and y – but we do not want to choose a method implementation for an arbitrary combination of classes, we want to ensure that the combinations of classes are *not* arbitrary.

The fact is that the traditional notion of polymorphism is unable to capture relations between several objects and their methods – it only handles the case with one object and its methods, and multi-object relations are always specified in terms of a fixed number of compile-time constant classes, i.e., essentially monomorphically. As we shall see in Sect. 3, this means that we must give up either flexibility or safety, we cannot have both at the same time.

We use the term *family polymorphism* to describe a generalized kind of polymorphism that will allow us to statically declare and manage relations between several classes polymorphically, i.e., in such a way that a given set of classes may be known to constitute a family – that family being characterized by having certain relations between its members – but it is not known statically exactly what classes they are.

The contributions of this work are the concept of family polymorphism, the underlying programming language mechanism, the associated static analysis techniques, and the implementation in a full-scale programming language, gbeta [13]. The notion of dependent types that makes family polymorphism possible has been present in some form in the BETA [19] community for many years (it is described informally in [19]), but the static analysis and the implementation have not been complete before gbeta.

The rest of this paper is structured as follows: Section 2 argues that the multi-class perspective is becoming more and more important. Section 3 describes the problems with current approaches in more detail, by means of a running example in Java and C++. The way these problems are solved with family polymorphism is described in Sect. 4. Finally, Sect. 5 covers related work, and Sect. 6 concludes.

2 We Need Class Families

Traditional object-orientation allows us to express a concept and several variations and/or implementations thereof by means of the class and inheritance mechanisms. However, there are many signs that this single-class perspective is becoming obsolete or at least insufficient.

A main motivational point of generative programming [12] and software product line approaches (e.g. [4]) is that modern software engineering must support variability at a more global scale than the individual class. This means that variants must be composed consistently across an application.

Languages and systems supporting advanced separation of concerns – such as aspect-oriented programming [14], composition filters [1], and multi-dimensional separation of concerns [26] – often emphasize the handling of cross-cutting concerns, i.e., issues involving more than one class. This means that they add support for the creation of class family variants.

Even in more traditional languages like Java and C++ it is possible to express class families, and the momentum behind the abovementioned research efforts supports the claim that the multi-class perspective cannot be ignored.

When a system contains more than one variant of a class family at the same time, it becomes necessary to maintain consistency in the usage of family members, i.e., to avoid mixing the families inappropriately. In this case it is not sufficient to be able to choose variants statically, there must also be support for management of multiple class family variants at run-time. As described in the next section, this causes a dilemma. Family polymorphism is a mechanism that can be used to resolve this dilemma.

3 Handling Graphs with Traditional Polymorphism

In this section we will present an example of a class family, and draw the attention to an unfortunate choice between safety and flexibility in reuse that we are forced to make. It is a property of the type systems of Java and C++ that we cannot have both safety and reuse flexibility at the same time, but this property is shared with more advanced type systems such as those of GJ [6] and Cecil [11,15]. We will return to this topic in Sect. 3.3 and 4.2.

Consider the concept of a *graph*, consisting of a set of *nodes* connected in some way by a set of *edges*. The graph concept plays the "organizing" role, offering a common frame of reference under which the concept of node and the concept of edge make sense. Moreover, there are many different kinds of graphs – colored graphs, weighted graphs, labelled graphs, etc.

In this context we will concentrate on a simple `Graph` and an `OnOffGraph`. The latter adds support for switching each edge on and off, for instance to model communication networks where individual links may now and then be broken.

A `Graph` is not just one graph in the usual sense, it represents all nodes and edges of a particular *kind*, and these nodes and edges may then be organized and reorganized into any number of concrete graphs. In Sect. 4 we shall look at some data structures that may be used to hold the nodes and edges of a concrete graph.

3.1   The Naïve Approach

It is not hard to express graphs by means of two families of classes as described in the previous section. A definition of such class families in Java is given in Fig. 1. The first family consists of the classes `Node` and `Edge`, and the second family consists of the classes `OnOffNode` and `OnOffEdge`. A sample class `Main` contains code to show usage of these class families. It might seem more natural to express a class family by means of inner classes in Java, but since they would add syntactic complexity and would exhibit the same problems, we chose to avoid inner classes in this example.

The method `touches` on `Node` tests whether or not a given `Edge` is connected to the receiver `Node`. It would presumably be used to find paths through the graph. In a simple `Graph` the answer only depends on the graph structure, but in an `OnOffGraph` it also depends on the enabledness of the `Edge`.

The `main` method in `Main` invokes a method `build` three times, with different arguments. The method `build` expects to receive a `Node` and an `Edge`, both from the same class family. It then proceeds to connect the `Node` and the `Edge`, and finally invokes the method `touches` on the `Node` with the `Edge` as an argument. The third argument to `build` is a `boolean` which shows the expected result.

In the first two cases, `build` is used as it was intended, and it produces the expected result. However, in the third case we break the "rules" and invoke `build` with two objects from different class families. This causes a `ClassCastException` at run-time. The fourth case is confusing and probably unintended, but does not directly cause run-time errors.

The third invocation is type correct, since an `OnOffNode` is-a `Node` and an `Edge` is-an `Edge`. And if the `OnOffNode` had only been known statically as a `Node`, the failing third invocation of `build` would have looked just like the successful first invocation, according to the type system.

The problem is obviously that we have been unable to express the *actual* requirements. As we can see in the implementation of `touches` in the class `OnOffNode`, the argument of type `Edge` must really be an `OnOffEdge` – otherwise the dynamic cast will fail. Since method arguments in Java are in-variant, we must use `Edge` as the argument type and then use a dynamic cast in the method body. Of course, we may then invoke the method with an instance of `Edge` as

```
class Node {
  boolean touches(Edge e) { return (this==e.n1) || (this==e.n2); }
}

class Edge { Node n1,n2; }

class OnOffNode extends Node {
  boolean touches(Edge e) {
    return ((OnOffEdge)e).enabled? super.touches(e) : false;
  }
}

class OnOffEdge extends Edge {
  boolean enabled;
  OnOffEdge() { this.enabled=false; }
}

public class Main {
  static void build(Node n, Edge e, boolean b) {
    e.n1=e.n2=n;
    if (b == n.touches(e)) System.out.println("OK");
  }
  public static void main(String[] args) {
    build(new Node(), new Edge(), true);
    build(new OnOffNode(), new OnOffEdge(), false);
    build(new OnOffNode(), new Edge(), true); // ClassCastException!
    build(new Node(), new OnOffEdge(), true); // "works"
  }
}
```

Fig. 1. Reuse: Yes – Safety: No

argument, and the error will only be detected at run-time. The type system will not allow us to express the connection between the members of a class family, it will only allow us to create a type hole such that all *combinations* of members of these families, including the correct combinations, are allowed.

It may be argued that this is not a "type hole", it is a dynamic cast, and the people who use dynamic casts deserve what they get. The point is that the programmer is forced into writing a program with incomplete compile time type checking because the discipline which *should* be imposed on the choice of arguments cannot be expressed. So it is a type hole, even if it is one we have explicitly asked for.

Apart from this, the example exhibits the very nice property that the method build works both for a simple Graph and for an OnOffGraph. In other words, we are allowed to reuse the method build with several different class families, without any static dependency on the actual choice of family.

3.2   Working Out Safety

We have the option of shifting the trade-off in favor of safety, giving up on some reuse opportunities. An alternative expression of the class families is given in Fig. 2, and it is obviously a bit less straightforward than the previous version.

In this case we use the language C++, because Java does not (currently) support genericity and hence does not allow this kind of solution. For brevity, we use the keyword `struct` and not `class`, thus avoiding the need for accessibility declarations.

In this approach, we use type parameters to establish "pre-families", i.e., sets of type parameterized classes such that mutually recursive families of classes can be created by template instantiation, as with `Node` and `Edge`, and with `OnOffNode` and `OnOffEdge`.

In line with Fig. 1 there is a `main` function where the two class families are used, and the usage is expressed in two almost identical functions, `build1` and `build2`. These two functions have the same functionality as the method `build` in Fig. 1.

The difference between the situation in Fig. 1 and the situation in Fig. 2 is that the members of the class families are related in different ways according to the type systems.[2] In Fig. 1, `OnOffNode` is a subclass of `Node` and `OnOffEdge` is a subclass of `Edge`. This is not the case in Fig. 2. In other words, in the first figure the families are related by a memberwise subclass relation, and in the second figure the families consist of unrelated classes.

Since there is no relation between a member of one family and a member of another family, there is no danger of mixing members of different families. Hence, this closes the type hole – as we should also expect, given that the second example is expressed without dynamic casts. Statements mixing the two families, like the two function calls which are commented out in `main`, will cause the program to be rejected at compile time.

The result is that we have gained safety and lost reuse.

Note that we could also have achieved the same trade-off in Java by textually copying the inherited material from `Node` to `OnOffNode`, and from `Edge` to `OnOffEdge`, and then removing the 'extends' clauses – except of course that textual copying creates maintenance and comprehension problems.

At this point, C++ programmers would immediately remark that the loss of reuse is a non-problem: We could simply change `build` into a template function with the argument types being template arguments. That would make it possible to write just one (template) function `build` with textually the same body as `build1` and `build2`. We could then invoke it in place of both `build1` and `build2` in `main`.

The reason why this is *not* a solution is that each call-site for this `build` template function would be associated with a compile-time fixed choice of family. E.g., the first call-site in `main` would then be an invocation of `build<Node,Edge>`,

---

[2] Since types and classes may be considered to coincide for the subset of Java and C++ that we are concerned with, we will sometimes use expressions such as 'the class X' where 'the type associated with the class X' would have been more precise.

```
template <class N, class E> struct NodeF;
template <class N, class E> struct EdgeF { N *n1,*n2; };
template <class N, class E> struct NodeF {
    virtual bool touches(E* e)
      { return (this==e->n1) || (this==e->n2); }
};

struct Edge;
struct Node: public NodeF<Node,Edge> {};
struct Edge: public EdgeF<Node,Edge> {};

template <class ON, class OE>
struct OnOffEdgeF: public EdgeF<ON,OE> {
    bool enabled;
    OnOffEdgeF(): enabled(false) {}
};
template <class ON, class OE>
struct OnOffNodeF: public NodeF<ON,OE> {
    bool touches(OE* e) {
        return e->enabled? NodeF<ON,OE>::touches(e) : false;
    }
};

struct OnOffEdge;
struct OnOffNode: public OnOffNodeF<OnOffNode,OnOffEdge> {};
struct OnOffEdge: public OnOffEdgeF<OnOffNode,OnOffEdge> {};

void build1(Node* n, Edge* e, bool b) {
    e->n1=e->n2=n;
    if (b == n->touches(e)) cout << "OK\n";
}

void build2(OnOffNode* n, OnOffEdge* e, bool b) {
    e->n1=e->n2=n;
    if (b == n->touches(e)) cout << "OK\n";
}

int main(int argc, char *argv[]) {
    build1(new Node(), new Edge(), true);
    build2(new OnOffNode(), new OnOffEdge(), false);
    // build1(new OnOffNode(), new Edge(), false); // type error
    // build2(new OnOffNode(), new Edge(), false); // type error
    return 0;
}
```

Fig. 2. Safety: Yes – Reuse: No

and the second call-site an invocation of build<OnOffNode,OnOffEdge>, even though there is no need to explicitly write the part in angle brackets.

In spite of the fact that the template function call would look very much like a function taking dynamically polymorphic arguments, the difference has far-reaching consequences:

1. First, whenever a node and an edge should be delivered to a template function such as build via a number of intermediate functions, every function in the entire call chain must be a template function, and the exact types of those objects must be known statically at the original call-site (either exactly Node and Edge, or exactly OnOffNode and OnOffEdge, never anything like "any pair of classes that makes up a consistent subfamily of Graph").
2. Second, a template function may be a member function, but it cannot be a virtual member function. This means that we must not only know the exact type of every node and edge everywhere, we must also know statically what methods implementations *of other classes* are being used on them.
3. Third, we cannot have lists, sets, hash tables, or other data structures containing nodes and edges belonging together. We can only have data structures containing members of one, statically selected and then fixed family of nodes and edges.
4. Finally, it is perfectly reasonable to assume that a sub-family of Node and Edge would provide an implementation of an interface specified by Node and Edge. When using this implementation sub-family in a large, complex system, the template based approach would make large parts of this complex system statically dependent on that sub-family, because all usages of nodes and edges would have to be performed in a context where the exact classes of the members of the sub-family are known statically. This would make the system as a whole more fragile, as would any forced dependency on implementation details.

In short, the lack of dynamic polymorphism in multi-object settings causes the same kinds of problems that would arise if we were to give up dynamic polymorphism in the well-known single-object setting.

3.3   The Scope of This Problem

If the problems outlined in the previous sections were specific for the Java and C++ language designs and well-known solutions were available elsewhere, the issue would not be of much interest. We will therefore argue that those problems arise in many different language designs, and no good solutions are known to us – apart from the family polymorphism which is the main topic of this paper.

An approach which is similar to the one taken in Fig. 2 can be used in other languages with support for genericity based on type parameterization. In the following we will consider the relation between these approaches.

Many different proposals have been made for the addition of genericity to Java based on parametric polymorphism [21,6,9,24, and others]. F-bounds [8] make it possible to design the genericity mechanism in such a way that a type parameterized class may be type checked once and for all – as opposed to C++ templates where type checking must essentially be performed from scratch at each instantiation. Moreover, using a homogeneous translation scheme (as in GJ [6]) just one version of the code is generated for one generic entity, thus making it possible to support "virtual template methods" in Java (late binding is by default used for all methods in Java, so an ordinary Java method would correspond to a virtual member function in C++). This is the approach taken in GJ. Hence, the problem with virtual template member functions is less serious than the other problems – it is a consequence of the macro-like nature of the C++ template mechanism.

As described in [7], a somewhat more involved technique than the one used in Fig. 2 must be employed in order to express families of mutually recursive classes with genericity based on F-bounds, but it is still possible.

Note, however, that the C++ approach where each template instantiation is statically analyzed separately is in a sense the maximally flexible approach. Any kind of constraints that could be specified on type parameters of a generic entity in order to enable type checking of the entity as such (and not per instantiation) would only be able to reduce the flexibility, compared to the C++ approach. This is because constraints on the type arguments will only be sufficiently strict if every possible choice of type arguments will actually make the implementation type safe, and in those cases the C++ style per-instantiation checking would also succeed. In other words, there is no hope that constrained type arguments could afford us greater flexibility at instantiation sites than what we have already seen in C++.

On the other hand, it is possible in very advanced type systems such as the one used in Cecil [15] to explicitly declare that a given parameterized class is, e.g., co-variant in a given type argument and contra-variant in another type argument. The problem is, however, that this would not help us. For instance, EdgeF<N,E> is in-variant in N, and NodeF<N,E> is contra-variant in E. Hence, any attempt to declare that NodeF<N,E> and EdgeF<N,E> are co-variant in N and E would simply make their implementations type incorrect. So any approach based on (possibly constrained) type parameterization of individual classes and methods will not allow us to obtain polymorphism at the level of class families.

This should not be a surprise, since any mechanism in a type system that would establish a memberwise subtyping relation between the members of class families would also allow us to mix classes from different families, as it was done in Fig. 1, in the last invocation of build. In other words, if we could do such a thing, the type system in question would be unsound.

In summary, the approach taken in Fig. 2 can be used in other languages with genericity mechanisms based on type parameterization, but it does not solve the problems associated with: excessive propagation of templatization; the lack of type safe data structures for class family member instances (except for data structures statically bound to *one* particular family); the widespread propagation of static dependencies on implementation details; and the lack of dynamic polymorphism.

Hence, in order to achieve a safe and flexible mechanism, we must strive for something other than memberwise subtyping. In the next section we shall see how the notion of classes as attributes makes it possible to establish a safe and useful kind of family polymorphism.

4   Handling Graphs with Family Polymorphism

The main problem in the approaches considered so far is that the family itself is not represented explicitly. As long as the family is only implicitly present, it is hard to conceive of any other kind of polymorphism for families of classes than the one based on a memberwise subtype relationship.

However, if we introduce the notion of classes as attributes of objects then it is suddenly possible to use an object as a repository of classes – a class family. If we moreover introduce the notion of late binding of such class attributes then it becomes possible to specify a number of families of classes by means of an ordinary inheritance network describing variants of the enclosing object, the *family object*. For each such family object it is statically known that it is a repository for *some* variant of the class family declared in the statically known type of the family object, but it is not statically known *which* class family it is.

This is the approach taken in gbeta. The gbeta type system is consistent with the type system design for BETA[3] that is described informally in [19], but it is stricter than the actual implementation of type checking in the Mjølner implementation of BETA [29]. In the languages gbeta and BETA, classes and methods (and more) have been unified into the single abstraction called a *pattern*. This means that we may use words like 'class' and 'method', but the denoted entities will in both cases be patterns, so these words are simply synonyms for the word 'pattern' with an added hint to the reader about how to understand the role played by that pattern in the given context. Consequently, class attributes are really pattern attributes and late binding of class attributes is late binding of pattern attributes, normally designated as *virtual patterns*.

To make this concrete, we will present and discuss a version of our class family example written in gbeta, as shown in Fig. 3.

In the gbeta version of the class family example, the two class families are declared explicitly as the pattern Graph and the subpattern (think 'subclass') OnOffGraph. Each instance of Graph or a subpattern of Graph will have two attributes named Node and Edge. These two attributes will be patterns ('classes'), and they are known to belong together, forming a family of mutually recursive patterns ('classes'). That is, an object myGraph is known to contain a class family whose members are accessible as myGraph.Node and myGraph.Edge, respectively.

As we shall see below, the type system does *not* allow us to mix members of different class families – in other words, when myGraph and yourGraph are

---

[3] The gbeta type system is considerably more expressive than the BETA type system, but the BETA type system comes out as a special case.

```
(# Graph:
    (# Node:<
        (# touches:<
            (# e:^Edge; b:@boolean
            enter e[]
            do (this(Node)=e.n1) or (this(Node)=e.n2) -> b
            exit b
            #);
        exit this(Node)[]
        #);
        Edge:< (# n1,n2:^Node exit this(Edge)[] #)
    #);
    OnOffGraph: Graph
        (# Node::<(#touches::<!(# do (if e.enabled then INNER if)#)#);
        Edge::<(#enabled:@boolean #)
        #);
    build:
        (# g:< @Graph; n:^g.Node; e:^g.Edge; b:@boolean
        enter (n[],e[],b)
        do n->e.n1[]->e.n2[];
            (if (e->n.touches)=b then 'OK'->putline if)
        #);
    g1:@Graph; g2:@OnOffGraph
do
    (g1.Node, g1.Edge, true) -> build(#g::@g1#);
    (g2.Node, g2.Edge, false) -> build(#g::@g2#);
    (* (g2.Node, g1.Edge, false) -> build(#g::@g1#); type error *)
    (* (g2.Node, g1.Edge, false) -> build(#g::@g2#); type error *)
#)
```

Fig. 3. Reuse: Yes – Safety: Yes

not statically known to be the *exact same object*, the patterns myGraph.Node
and yourGraph.Node are considered to be unrelated (unless of course they are
statically known, e.g., because of a type exact reference to the enclosing object,
and those statically known patterns are related). Also note that the type system
will distinguish between an unbounded number of class families because they
are associated with *instances* (e.g., myGraph) and not with *classes* (e.g., Graph).
If they had been associated with classes then the type system would at most
have been able to distinguish between a fixed number of families, determined
at compile-time – increasing the danger that objects could be mixed inappropriately, because conceptually separate families would have to be treated as one
family by the type system.

To continue with the example, Node and Edge are specified with the same
attributes as they were in Fig. 1 and Fig. 2. The further-binding of Node and
Edge in OnOffGraph, corresponding to the classes OnOffNode and OnOffEdge, are

also incrementally specified in a similar manner as previously. The expressions `exit this(···)[]` specify that the result of evaluating a `Node` or an `Edge` is a reference to that object itself (in BETA and gbeta the evaluation semantics of a class must be specified explicitly).

Finally, a method `build` is defined, one instance of each kind of graph is declared, and `build` is invoked twice, once with members of the `Graph` family and once with members of the `OnOffGraph` family. The two last statements are commented out; they demonstrate mixing of families, and if they are included the type system detects that they are not type safe.

We have to clarify a few points about the example. First, argument passing to methods and functions, assignment, and other evaluations are expressed in BETA and gbeta with the '`->`' operator, and the direction of the dataflow is left-to-right (where most other languages employ a right-to-left direction, opposite to the reading direction). It might help to think of the '`->`' as similar to the pipe symbol used on the command line in many operating systems.

Second, BETA and gbeta provide a kind of *transparency*: it is invisible in many places whether a result is stored or computed. Thus, `g1.Node` denotes a pattern, but when it is used in an evaluation context it gives rise to an object instantiation, and the new object is the result of the expression; in other words, a 'new' operator is implicitly added to the expression.

Third, `build` accepts four arguments, namely g, n, e, and b; n and e are received by reference, b is received by value, and g is a constant attribute of each invocation of `build`.

There are many reasons why the different argument modes are specified syntactically the way they are (some of them historic), but for the purposes of this discussion we will just mention that a syntactic form like the following might work better to communicate the actual semantics of the invocations of `build`; note that this is for illustration, it is not valid gbeta syntax:

```
build(g1, new g1.Node(), new g1.Edge(), true);
build(g2, new g2.Node(), new g2.Edge(), false);
```

It is essential to ensure that the first argument to `build` (g1 and g2, respectively) is constant throughout the evaluation of the arguments and the execution of the method. Only then is it known for sure that we are not mixing different families. If we were to provide this argument as an ordinary (assignable) by-reference argument, then the gbeta type analysis would not accept the implementation of `build` as type safe.

On the other hand, it makes no difference whether the graph given as an argument to `build` is an instance of `Graph`, of `OnOffGraph`, or of any other subpattern of `Graph`. We just need to know that it is *some* kind of a repository for a family consisting of `Node` and `Edge`, i.e., that it is an instance of a pattern that is less than or equal to `Graph`. This means that `build` can be reused with an unbounded number of different subfamilies of `Graph`, and it means that each invocation is guaranteed to not mix up different families. That amounts to the conclusion that the class family example has now been expressed with both safety and reuse opportunities preserved.

4.1 Revisiting the Problems

Let us reconsider the issues described near the end of Sect. 3.2, associated with the template method based approach:

1. Type checking with family polymorphism is based on an ordinary subtype constraint on the family object, so there is no need for exact static knowledge about any of the involved classes. The *relations* between the involved classes must be captured, but that may be expressed by means of the identity of the family object.
2. There are no special considerations about the methods of other classes – build could as well have been a virtual method. As mentioned, this problem can also be solved in other ways.
3. Data structures may be constructed to hold nodes and edges from a family whose family object is an instance of an arbitrary (not statically known) subpattern of Graph. Such data structures are 'family polymorphic'.
4. Since it is easy to hide the actual class of the family object by ordinary dynamic polymorphism, there is no need to propagate static knowledge about every subfamily of Graph to all usage points in a large system.

For instance, if we wish to operate on a list of nodes and a list of edges belonging together in the same subfamily of Graph, then we may use the following data structure:

```
NodesAndEdges:
  (# g:< @Graph;
     nodes: @list(# element::g.Node #);
     edges: @list(# element::g.Edge #)
  #)
```

This pattern is parameterized by the immutable object reference **g**, and it contains the list **nodes** with elements of type **g.Node**, and the list **edges** with elements of type **g.Edge**. In essence, it is a package containing two lists holding instances of members of a class family.

We can create a subpattern of this data structure to hold some nodes and edges belonging to a family object **myGraph** which is an instance of a subpattern of Graph, say LabelledGraph:

```
myGraph: @LabelledGraph;
myNodesAndEdges: @NodesAndEdges(# g::@myGraph #)
```

This declares **myNodesAndEdges** to be an object which is an instance of a subpattern of NodesAndEdges where the attribute **g** is immutably bound to **myGraph**. At this point we can pass **myNodesAndEdges** as an argument to methods such as this one:

```
listBuild:
  (# ne:< @NodesAndEdges;
     n: ^ne.g.Node; e: ^ne.g.Edge
```

```
do ne.nodes.head -> n[];
   ne.edges.head -> e[];
   (n,e,true) -> build(#g::@ne.g#)
#)
```

This method receives **ne** as a constant argument and thereby provides access to a class family object – namely **ne.g** – and a list of nodes belonging to that family – **ne.nodes** – and finally a list of edges belonging to the same family – **ne.edges**. The method starts by calling **head** twice, extracting the first element of the two lists (and omitting the check for an empty list...) and then invokes **build**. Note that we could have threaded **ne** through any number of method invocations as an ordinary by-reference argument, known only as an instance of a pattern that is less than or equal to **NodesAndEdges**. For example:

```
m1: (# x:^NodesAndEdges enter x[] do listBuild(# ne::@x #)#);
m2: (# x:^NodesAndEdges enter x[] do x[]->m1 #);
m3: (# x:^NodesAndEdges enter x[] do x[]->m2 #)
```

In this example, m3 calls m2 which calls m1, each time passing x – known as an instance of NodesAndEdges or a subpattern – to the next method. None of these methods depend on the exact classes in the class family and, of course, neither does listBuild nor build. We could invoke it with ne[]->m3, where ne is any reference whose declared type is NodesAndEdges or a subpattern thereof, e.g., myNodesAndEdges[]->m3.

This shows that we can package and re-package a family of classes and some instances of those classes, and we can statically ensure that the classes belong to the same family and the objects belong to the classes – without knowing statically *what* classes the family contains.

4.2   Revisiting the Alternative

In an approach based on parametric polymorphism, i.e., type parameterization, type safety in the management of class families is achieved by avoiding subtyping relationships between families. This implies that every individual piece of code dealing with a class family is either monomorphic (statically tied to one particular class family) or it is inside a generic entity with the family members as type parameters. In the first case, reuse opportunities are obviously lost. Let us consider the second case more closely.

Any execution of code inside a type parameterized entity corresponds to a ground instantiation of that entity – a direct or indirect instantiation having actual type parameters all of which are types not containing type variables. This is enforced by the design of such type parameterization mechanisms: (1) a parameterized class is not a class, it is a function from types to classes, and it is only possible to create objects as instances of classes, such as a parameterized class *applied to some type arguments*; (2) a type parameterized method may be called from another type parameterized method, but the call stack has finite depth and it does not start with a type parameterized method, so at some point the type parameters to the method are received from some other source than the caller-method, i.e., as ground types or depending on type parameters of an enclosing parameterized class – which brings us back to the first case. Note that if the types are type variables, they must be the type parameters of the *same* enclosing generic entity for *all* members of the class family; otherwise they cannot be mutually recursive.

This strict discipline is necessary for the soundness of the static analysis; if it were possible to have a mutable entity (an object) at run-time which is parametrically polymorphic (i.e., an instance of a type parameterized class which has *not* received all of its type arguments as ground types), then it would be possible to interpret the "free type variable" differently at different times and thereby destroy the overall type correctness of the program. This is well-known from functional languages with mutable references, such as Standard ML [20] and Caml [30].

This means that *every* run-time call-chain of methods passing instances of members of a class family as arguments or looking them up in their receiver object includes a call-site which is monomorphic in the class family, and any method which is type parameterized by the family is eventually called from such a monomorphic site. In other words, a call chain can only access a class family polymorphically after a certain point where the access is monomorphic.

Now compare this to the well-known case of traditional dynamic polymorphism used with single objects (not families). Consider for example the case where we have an inheritance hierarchy rooted in `GraphicalObject`, containing subclasses such as `Circle` and `Rectangle`, and supporting a (virtual) method `draw`. With this design it is possible to create a number of instances of various subclasses of `GraphicalObject`, and to store them all in a `List` whose elements are typed as `GraphicalObject`. Now we may traverse the list and execute `draw` on each element. Note that the call-stack in this case does *not* include a monomorphic access before the polymorphic access. In fact, there may not exist *any* pointers typed by the actual class to each object in the list in the entire program execution state (a `this` pointer typed by the actual class may be created *later*, in the execution of the `draw` method).

This makes a big difference.

The big difference is not unlike the effects of manual memory management – it is a global phenomemon. In systems without garbage collection, it is necessary to design intricate, global management schemes such that the following question can be answered correctly at certain points: "Is it possible that there exists another live pointer to this object?" If the answer is incorrectly "No!" there will be dangling pointers, and if the answer is incorrectly "Yes!" there may be memory leaks. In a similar fashion, to be able to perform an operation on a group of objects which are instances of some members of a class family, it is necessary to design management schemes to ensure that there is at least one monomorphic pointer to each of those objects somewhere in the system, and we must be able to find that pointer in order to initiate a (possibly parametrically polymorphic) call-chain that will perform the operation.

In the single-object case, we can collect `GraphicalObjects` in a polymorphic data structure and then forget about their precise classes, and the definition and usage of the data structure is strictly isolated from static dependencies on the individual subclasses such as `Circle` etc.

But in the multi-object case, we cannot create a similar polymorphic collection of nodes and edges and perform operations on them without creating dependencies on their actual classes. This means that we will have to change our collection every time we want to put objects from a new sub-family into it.

One possible approach would be to use wrapper classes like `NodesAndEdges` – the difference is that, with parametric polymorphism, creation of these objects and insertion of nodes and edges would have to happen monomorphically. We could then have lists of these wrapper objects etc. However, it would be necessary to *rediscover* the exact actual subclass of `NodesAndEdges` for each wrapper in such a list we intend to use, because the contained nodes and edges can *only* be made accessible with monomorphic access. The rediscovery could be achieved with `instanceof` or similar means, but the rediscovery site would depend specifically on each class family that it is capable of rediscovering. Add a new subfamily, and this piece of source code must be changed.

Hence, even though there seems to be only a subtle difference between the approach based on parametric polymorphism and the approach based on family polymorphism, we claim that the difference has far-reaching consequences, especially for large scale systems where the propagation of static dependencies have the most devastating effects.

As mentioned, in the approach based on family polymorphism we exploit the features of *virtual patterns* in gbeta, which are a generalization of virtual patterns in BETA [18,19]. The next section discusses some properties of the underlying type system.

4.3   Aspects of the gbeta Static Analysis

It has been claimed that virtual types are inherently not type safe [7]. The reason why this opinion has emerged is probably that the community behind virtual patterns has not expressed with sufficient clarity that virtual patterns are attributes of *objects*, not attributes of classes. Consequently, virtual types are not attributes of types. In particular, this point was not emphasized in [27], where a design of virtual types in Java is proposed, inspired by the notion of virtual patterns in BETA. Also, virtual patterns may have been confused with unchecked covariance. However, virtual patterns have a kind of existential type, so potential covariance – in the type of a method argument, say – is always known statically, at all call-sites.

Let us briefly outline why it would be unsound to let virtual types be attributes of types. Assume that a type system for a language with virtual attributes (be it virtual classes or virtual patterns) would have the following property: If an object x is known to have type T and V is a virtual attribute associated with T and declared to have type T_V, then $x.V$ has the type $T.V$; $T.V$ would be an existential type such as $\exists T_V' \leq T_V . T_V'$, i.e., a type T_V' that is a characteristic of T, but only known by its upper bound T_V. If this type T'_V is assumed to be a property of the type of the enclosing object, T, then two different objects x and y both having type T would have the *same* virtual type, i.e., $x.V$ and $y.V$ would have the same type. That would obviously be unsound in a type system with subsumption, since x could be an instance of a class having most specific type T, and y could be an instance of a subclass whose virtual V could be furtherbound to a strict subtype T^y_V of T_V. An assignment from a reference $x.r$ to a reference $y.r$ referring to the same declaration of r, having the type of V, would then be an assignment from a reference of type T_V to a reference of type T^y_V (a strict subtype of T_V), i.e., the assignment would be type incorrect – but such a type system would consider it to be an assignment between references having the *same* type.

Conversely, if a virtual V declared in a class having type T should be an existential type $\exists T'_V \leq T_V . T'_V$ that is treated is such a way in the type analysis that *no* assignments between references of type $T.V$ were allowed – thus avoiding the abovementioned type hole – then it would be impossible to write useful implementations involving virtual types. For instance, a method accepting an argument of type V would not be able to invoke another method accepting an argument of type V as an invocation on the current receiver object (a "self-send").

Of course, neither of these approaches is used in gbeta. In fact, as it was already stated very clearly for BETA in [19, p. 133], a pattern declaration Q inside another pattern declaration P declares a distinct Q pattern for *each instance* of P. This means that the static analysis of BETA and gbeta must consider pattern attributes, including virtual pattern attributes, as having composite types, consisting of two kinds of information. The space constraints do not permit a detailed description of the gbeta type system here; please refer to Chap. 13 and App. E of [13] for more details. We will however extract some salient features of this type system, in order to support the claims made about its properties.

The first kind of information in a gbeta type is the usual kind of static representation of object types: maps from names to types, indicating that any instance having the given type will have attributes with some specified names having specified types. The second kind of information is a relative representation of an enclosing object of a pattern, represented as a path leading from the current object to that enclosing object of the pattern. Moreover, every gbeta type is characterized as being exact, or known by upper bound only, or known by upper and lower bound. Types which are known by upper bound could be characterized as existential types, but it should be noted that they are also dependent types, depending on their enclosing objects.

We should mention that if Q is a pattern attribute of two objects a and b, it is often the case that $a.Q$ and $b.Q$ are indeed statically known to be the same pattern – gbeta and BETA would hardly be practically useful otherwise. But $a.Q$ and $b.Q$ generally cannot be assumed to be the same pattern if any of them are only known by upper bound, not even if a and b are known to be instances of the same pattern.

Both patterns and objects have types in gbeta. Two pieces of syntax denoting patterns have different types if they are not known to be associated with the exact same maps from names to types *and* the same enclosing objects, and two pieces of syntax denoting objects have different types unless they are guaranteed to denote the exact same object at run-time. It is *not* sufficient to know that two objects are exactly an instance of the same pattern, they would still have different types if they might be different objects.

To put this into context of the examples given above, the virtuals $x.V$ and $y.V$ discussed above would be known to have certain attributes (declared in the statically known maps from names to types), and they would moreover be known to be the V virtual of exactly the object denoted by x and the object denoted by y, respectively. In the (typical) case where x and y are not guaranteed to be the exact same object, $x.V$ and $y.V$ will generally have assignment incompatible types – no subtyping relation exists between them, they are just possibly different.

Note that this means that a virtual pattern known only by upper bound which is reached via a mutable reference is "not even equal to itself"; for instance, if z is a mutable reference then two different occurrences of z may refer to two different objects – not even flow analysis could have guaranteed that no assignments to z will happen between two usages of z, because there could be other threads having access to the current object.

In practical BETA and gbeta programming it is very often the case that a virtual pattern occurs as an attribute of an object that is accessed via an immutable reference. As described in [28], virtual types can be changed into ordinary types (whose structure is known completely at compile-time) by means of so-called final bindings. This is possible in BETA and gbeta, but an immutable reference to the enclosing object is an equally valid and more common way to make references with virtual types assignable. Note that the approach based on an immutable reference works both when the virtual in question is known exactly and when it is known only by upper bound. Actually, an example of the latter is the element types of the lists in NodesAndEdges.

A special case is the source code in a pattern declaration P containing a virtual pattern declaration V, i.e., the code executed in a context where V is an attribute of an enclosing object (think: V is an attribute of 'this'). An enclosing object is accessed via an immutable reference, usually implicit at the source code level, but available as this(X) for an appropriate identifier X. This means that the name V used on its own has a type that is the same everywhere in the declaration of P.[4] This in turn means that it is both dynamically safe and recognized as type safe by the static analysis to assign between different references having the type of V.

Hence, a virtual attribute V of a pattern P can inside P be treated in much the same way as a constrained type argument inside a type parameterized class: The statically known upper bound of the virtual yields a certain available interface and allows for assignment to all non-existentially typed references having

---

[4] For those who know that this isn't quite true: In the enclosing MainPart.

supertypes of the upper bound of the virtual, and the virtual is known to be "equal to itself" such that assignments between references with the type of V are also allowed. This makes it safe and convenient to program patterns containing virtuals.

Finally, we can apply this knowledge about the typing of gbeta in general and gbeta virtuals in particular to the example shown in Fig. 3 and the method listBuild shown near the end of Sect. 4.1. Whenever an immutable reference to an object is established (e.g., with a constant argument like g:<@Graph), all references to virtual attributes in that object are then known to be the virtuals of exactly that object. This means that references declared to have the same virtual type, i.e., the type of the same virtual pattern, are assignment compatible. For instance, the elements of ne.nodes in the method listBuild are known to have the type of ne.g.Node, exactly like the local attribute n of listBuild. Hence, it is safe to assign an element from ne.nodes to n, even though we have no static knowledge about the exact pattern of which ne is an instance. Similarly, n may safely be given to build as an argument, because that argument is declared to have type g.Node – and g is known to be the same object as ne.g, because of the binding g::@ne.g in the invocation of build.

In this description we have used the term 'type' to denote the knowledge established by static analysis about each of the entities – patterns and objects – accessible in the run-time environment (patterns are, at least conceptually, available at run-time).

In particular, the type of a virtual pattern is a compile-time description that restricts the possible actual patterns denoted by a given virtual attribute to a well-defined (but generally unbounded) set of patterns. This description is parameterized by a run-time context; in other words, it is a function that maps a run-time context into a run-time entity, in this case a pattern.

From this notion of the type of a virtual pattern it might be possible to derive a notion of virtual types, defined without referring to virtual patterns or similar concepts. There is an ongoing debate as to whether 'virtual X' should be 'virtual types' or 'virtual classes', also touched upon in [7]. The approach taken in gbeta is a kind of 'virtual classes' approach, because patterns may (also) be considered as classes.

The main difference between virtual patterns and (pattern-less) virtual types, considered from a practical point of view, would be that virtual types can not be used to create new instances, whereas virtual classes/patterns can be used just like other classes/patterns to create objects. As a result it is, e.g., possible to create nodes and edges in a given subfamily of Graph, and to compose them into a graph, again without having any static dependency links between the graph creation code and the exact Graph subfamily being used. It is our experience that the constructive use of virtual patterns is extremely useful. It is also yet another example of a situation where it is possible to use (in this case enlarge or create) a Graph without creating monomorphic dependencies; with an approach based on type parameterization or even virtual types, it would be necessary to refer to the exact classes of one particular class family in order to create new nodes and edges.

5   Related Work

The language gbeta has been developed as a generalized version of BETA, so the design of BETA is an immensely important starting point for gbeta, and the community around BETA has provided lots of valuable feed-back. Moreover, as mentioned in Sect. 4, the informal understanding of types in BETA as described in [19] matches the actual type system of gbeta quite well, apart from the fact that the basic concepts are more general in gbeta. However, the implementation of gbeta is very different from the implementation of BETA. In particular, the static analysis of virtual patterns in BETA – as described in [17] – does actually not suffice to handle family polymorphism correctly. The problem is that this static analysis in too many cases considers a virtual pattern in two different objects to be the same pattern. Even though the author had used BETA for years at this point, this problem with the static analysis of BETA only became apparent after a close inspection of [17]. This underscores the importance of formalizing the semantics and static analysis – a task which has unfortunately not yet been completed. However, the gbeta static analysis is the first one to solve this problem in the static analysis of BETA, and moreover it handles the added generality of gbeta.

In Sect. 3.3 and 4.2 it has already been discussed in what ways and to what extent parametric genericity can provide both type safety and reuse opportunities with class families. Our general conclusion is that either safety or reuse opportunities must be compromised, and in particular the almost-solution based on type parameterized methods will cause widespread static dependencies on the exact class families being managed. We should mention that the proposal in [7] is based on having type exact references to the members of a class family, thus making family polymorphism impossible at the outset.

In [22] it is described how families of mutually recursive classes may be expressed in OCaml, and how subfamilies may be created by inheritance. The structural type equivalence and the sophisticated support for type inference in this language makes it possible to decouple the classes in families, and in some cases to avoid the heavy notation for type arguments associated with some other approaches based on parametric polymorphism. However, this is only possible when the types of the members of the family are known in one type checking context, such as a single `let` statement. If we were to create one member of a family and store it in a variable and later create another member of that family, the types would have to be expressed explicitly. Moreover, this approach has the same problem as all the other approaches based on parametric polymorphism, namely that there must be a monomorphic call site on the call stack whenever a polymorphic piece of code is working with members of any class family.

In the area of functional languages there is a large body of work concerned with dependent types (see, e.g. [31]). A dependent type is a type that is allowed to depend on run-time values in program executions, and it is typically used to express and prove detailed properties of the outcome of computations, such as "reverse is a function that accepts an argument of type 'a list(n) and returns a result of type 'a list(n)", meaning that it returns a list of the same type *and* *length* (n) as the argument. Often, dependent types are made less useful because support for general usage of program values in types makes type checking undecidable (as in Cayenne [3]), and often it is required that programmers provide proofs manually, using some kind of theorem prover.

The gbeta type system has not yet been proved correct, but the implementation certainly does not require manual intervention. This type system employs dependent types in that it is part of each pattern type that this pattern is defined in one particular run-time context, and the type system only accepts two pattern types as being equivalent if they are associated with the same run-time context, in addition to having the same attributes with the same types, of course. No flow analysis is made to discover what expressions will denote the same object – we do not consider flow analysis to be an acceptable tool as part of type checking – so object 'sameness' is only detected in the case where the object is accessed via equivalent paths of immutable references. This approach seems to work very well in practice, so there are no immediate plans to extend the analysis in order to discover further occurrences of object sameness.

Finally, it is instructive to compare the usage of objects in gbeta as class repositories with the usage of structures, signatures, and functors in SML [16] to provide packages of types and values. A *structure* in SML is a package of types and values which may be created at top-level and referred to by means of structure names (they are not first class values). A *signature* is a structure specification, listing required names and kinds of types, and names and types of values. By applying a signature to a structure, it may be ensured that the structure conforms to the given specification, and all parts of the structure not specified in the signature will thereafter be invisible outside the structure. Finally, a functor is a function from structures to structures (again: not a first class function). It may take a structure constrained by a signature as an argument, and it will itself have a signature. An application of the functor to a structure which matches the required signature will then produce a structure with the promised resulting signature.

Tentatively, the following concepts are related: A gbeta object is similar to an SML structure; subtype polymorphism performs a similar role in gbeta as signatures in SML; and a gbeta mixin may play a role similar to the one played by a functor in SML.

The first difference between gbeta objects and the SML module system is that gbeta objects are (partially) mutable, first-class entities, whereas SML structures are immutable entities that may only be used at top-level, in their own, separate name space. Moreover, it causes differences at many levels that the SML type system is oriented toward structural equivalence, whereas the gbeta type system distinguishes between two different declarations of the same name, except where these two declarations are explicitly declared to be related.

On the other hand, subsumption (subtype polymorphism) makes it possible for a gbeta object to present a subset of the actually implemented interface, similar to a structure with a declared signature. A mixin may be used to enhance a pattern which may then be instantiated, yielding an object which is an enhanced version of the object that the original pattern would have produced; when the object is used as a class repository, this is similar to the effect of applying a functor to a structure. Note that this may happen at run-time in gbeta.

In summary, the basic concepts in the SML module system may be useful as a starting point for the understanding of the usage of gbeta objects in the management of class families. However, there are so many and so deep differences that the analogy should not be taken too far.

6 Conclusion

This paper has presented the notion of family polymorphism. It has been demonstrated that traditional notions of polymorphism – dynamic, single-object subsumption and parametric polymorphism, with or without F-bounds – do not allow us to treat groups of objects belonging to mutually recursive families of classes in a safe manner without causing widespread dependencies on the exact classes involved, thereby prohibiting reuse with other families of classes.

The virtual pattern mechanism in gbeta supports polymorphic access to such groups of objects based on a notion of types depending on the identity of objects used as class repositories. This solves the abovementioned problems with safety and loss of reuse opportunities, and it only requires the explicit passing of the class family repository object together with the instances of members of that class family.

We believe that the correct but polymorphic management of multiple related objects is a natural and inevitable development in the area of object-orientation, on top of the well-established polymorphic usage of single objects. In particular, we expect various approaches to systematic production of variants of more than one class, including systems for advanced separation of concerns, to become more and more pervasive. Consequently, variants of groups of mutually dependent classes will also become more and more important. Family polymorphism is needed to ensure the traditional benefits of object-orientation, also when using these class families.

Acknowledgments. Thanks to the anonymous referees for their valuable and detailed comments, and to participants in various workshops on separation of concerns, aspect orientation, and related topics for the inspiration to focus on these ideas.

References

1. M. Aksit, K. Wakita, J. Bosch, and L. Bergmans. Abstracting object interactions using composition filters. *Lecture Notes in Computer Science*, 791:152++, 1994.

2. Ken Arnold and James Gosling. *The Java^{TM} Programming Language*. The Java^{TM} Series. Addison-Wesley, Reading, MA, USA, 1998.

3. L. Augustsson. Cayenne – a language with dependent types. In *Proceedings of the 3rd ACM SIGPLAN International Conference on Functional Programming*, pages 239–250, 1998.

4. Don Batory, Rich Cardone, and Yannis Smaragdakis. Object-oriented frameworks and product lines. In P. Donohoe, editor, *Proceedings of the First Software Product Line Conference*, pages 227–247, August 2000.

5. B. Bobrow, D. DeMichiel, R. Gabriel, S. Keene, G. Kiczales, and D. Moon. *Common Lisp Object System Specification*. Document 88-002R. X3J13, June 1988.

6. Gilad Bracha, Martin Odersky, David Stoutamire, and Philip Wadler. Making the future safe for the past: Adding genericity to the Java programming language. In Craig Chambers, editor, *Proceedings OOPSLA'98, ACM SIGPLAN Notices*, volume 33, 10, pages 183–200, Vancouver, BC, October 1998.

7. K. Bruce, M. Odersky, and P. Wadler. A statically safe alternative to virtual types. *Lecture Notes in Computer Science*, 1445:523–549, 1998.

8. Peter Canning, William Cook, Walter Hill, John Mitchell, and Walter Olthoff. F-bounded polymorphism for object-oriented programming. In *Fourth International Conference on Functional Programming and Computer Architecture*. ACM, September 1989. Also technical report STL-89-5, from Software Technology Laboratory, Hewlett-Packard Laboratories.

9. Robert Cartwright. Compatible genericity with run-time types for the Java^{tm} programming language. In Craig Chambers, editor, *Proceedings OOPSLA'98, ACM SIGPLAN Notices*, volume 33, 10, Vancouver, October 1998. ACM Press.

10. Craig Chambers. Object-oriented multi-methods in Cecil. In O. Lehrmann Madsen, editor, *Proceedings ECOOP'92*, LNCS 615, pages 33–56, Utrecht, The Netherlands, June 1992. Springer-Verlag.

11. Craig Chambers. *The Cecil Language, Specification and Rationale*. Dept. of Comp.Sci. and Eng., Univ. of Washington, Seattle, Washington, 1997.

12. Krzysztof Czarnecki and Ulrich Eisenecker. *Generative Programming: Methods, Tools, and Applications*. Addison-Wesley, 1st edition, 2000.

13. Erik Ernst. *gbeta – A Language with Virtual Attributes, Block Structure, and Propagating, Dynamic Inheritance*. PhD thesis, DEVISE, Department of Computer Science, University of Aarhus, Aarhus, Denmark, June 1999.

14. Gregor Kiczales, John Lamping, Anurag Mendhekar, Chris Maeda, Cristina Lopes, Jean-Marc Loingtier, and John Irwin. Aspect-oriented programming. In Mehmet Aksit and Satoshi Matsuoka, editors, *Proceedings ECOOP'97*, LNCS 1241, pages 220–242, Jyväskylä, Finland, 9–13 June 1997. Springer.

15. Vassily Litvinov. Constraint-based polymorphism in Cecil: Towards a practical and static type system. In Craig Chambers, editor, *Proceedings OOPSLA'98, ACM SIGPLAN Notices*, volume 33, 10, Vancouver, October 1998. ACM Press.

16. D. MacQueen. Modules for standard ML. In *Proceedings of the 1984 ACM Symposium on Lisp and Functional Programming*, pages 198–207, New York, August 1984. ACM Press.

17. Ole Lehrmann Madsen. Semantic analysis of virtual classes and nested classes. In Linda M. Northrop, editor, *Proceedings OOPSLA'99, ACM SIGPLAN Notices*, volume 34, 10, Denver, October 1999. ACM Press.

18. Ole Lehrmann Madsen and Birger Møller-Pedersen. Virtual classes: A powerful mechanism in object-oriented programming. In *Proceedings OOPSLA'89, ACM SIGPLAN Notices*, volume 24, 10, pages 397–406, October 1989.

19. Ole Lehrmann Madsen, Birger Møller-Pedersen, and Kristen Nygaard. *Object-Oriented Programming in the BETA Programming Language.* Addison-Wesley, Reading, MA, USA, 1993.
20. R. Milner, M. Tofte, R. W. Harper, and D. MacQueen. *The Definition of Standard ML.* MIT Press, 1997.
21. Martin Odersky and Philip Wadler. Pizza into Java: Translating theory into practice. In *Conference Record of POPL '97: The 24th ACM SIGPLAN-SIGACT Symposium on Principles of Programming Languages*, pages 146–159, Paris, France, 15–17 January 1997.
22. Didier Rémy and Jérôme Vouillon. On the (un)reality of virtual types. Work in progress, available from `http://pauillac.inria.fr/~remy/`, 2001.
23. Andrew Shalit. *The Dylan Reference Manual: The Definitive Guide to the New Object-Oriented Dynamic Language.* Addison-Wesley, Reading, Mass., 1997.
24. Jose H. Solorzano and Suad Alagić. Parametric polymorphism for Java^{tm}: A. In Craig Chambers, editor, *Proceedings OOPSLA'98, ACM SIGPLAN Notices*, volume 33, 10, Vancouver, October 1998. ACM Press.
25. Bjarne Stroustrup. *The C++ Programming Language.* Addison-Wesley, 3rd edition, 1997.
26. Peri Tarr, Harold Ossher, William Harrison, and Stanley M. Sutton. N degrees of separation: Multi-dimensional separation of concerns. In *Proceedings of the 1999 International Conference on Software Engineering (ICSE'99)*, pages 107–119, Los Angeles, May 1999. Association for Computing Machinery.
27. Kresten Krab Thorup. Genericity in Java with virtual types. In *Proceedings ECOOP'97*, LNCS 1241, pages 444–471, Jyväskylä, June 1997. Springer-Verlag.
28. Mads Torgersen. Virtual types *are* statically safe. In *5th Workshop on Foundations of Object-Oriented Languages (FOOL)*, at `http://pauillac.inria.fr/~remy/fool/program.html`, January 1998.
29. Mjølner Informatics, Århus, Denmark: `http://www.mjolner.dk/`.
30. Pierre Weis, María-Virginia Aponte, Alain Laville, Michel Mauny, and Ascánder Suárez. The CAML reference manual, Version 2.6. Technical report, Projet Formel, INRIA-ENS, 1989.
31. Hongwei Xi. *Dependent Types in Practical Programming.* PhD thesis, Department of Mathematical Sciences, Carnegie Mellon University, Pittsburgh, PA 15213, September 1998.

An Overview of AspectJ

Gregor Kiczales[1], Erik Hilsdale[2], Jim Hugunin[2], Mik Kersten[2],
Jeffrey Palm[2] and William G. Griswold[3]

[1] Department of Computer Science, University of British Columbia,
201-2366 Main Mall, Vancouver, BC V6T 1Z4 Canada
gregor@cs.ubc.ca
[2] Xerox Palo Alto Research Center
3333 Coyote Hill Road, Palo Alto, CA 94304 USA
(hilsdale, hugunin, mkersten, palm)@parc.xerox.com
[3] Department of Computer Science and Engineering, University of California, San Diego
La Jolla, CA 92093 USA
wgg@cs.ucsd.edu

Abstract. AspectJ™ is a simple and practical aspect-oriented extension to Java™. With just a few new constructs, AspectJ provides support for modular implementation of a range of crosscutting concerns. In AspectJ's dynamic join point model, join points are well-defined points in the execution of the program; pointcuts are collections of join points; advice are special method-like constructs that can be attached to pointcuts; and aspects are modular units of crosscutting implementation, comprising pointcuts, advice, and ordinary Java member declarations. AspectJ code is compiled into standard Java bytecode. Simple extensions to existing Java development environments make it possible to browse the crosscutting structure of aspects in the same kind of way as one browses the inheritance structure of classes. Several examples show that AspectJ is powerful, and that programs written using it are easy to understand.

1 Introduction

Aspect-oriented programming (AOP) [14] has been proposed as a technique for improving separation of concerns in software.[1] AOP builds on previous technologies, including procedural programming and object-oriented programming, that have already made significant improvements in software modularity.

The central idea of AOP is that while the hierarchical modularity mechanisms of object-oriented languages are extremely useful, they are inherently unable to modularize all concerns of interest in complex systems. Instead, we believe that in the

---

[1] When we say "separation of concerns" we mean the idea that it should be possible to work with the design or implementation of a system in the natural units of concern – concept, goal, team structure etc. – rather than in units imposed on us by the tools we are using. We would like the modularity of a system to reflect the way "we want to think about it" rather than the way the language or other tools force us to think about it. In software, Parnas is generally credited with this idea [29, 30].

J. Lindskov Knudsen (Ed.): ECOOP 2001, LNCS 2072, pp. 327-353, 2001.

implementation of any complex system, there will be concerns that inherently crosscut the natural modularity of the rest of the implementation.

AOP does for *crosscutting concerns* what OOP has done for object encapsulation and inheritance—it provides language mechanisms that explicitly capture crosscutting structure. This makes it possible to program crosscutting concerns in a modular way, and achieve the usual benefits of improved modularity: simpler code that is easier to develop and maintain, and that has greater potential for reuse. We call a well-modularized crosscutting concern an *aspect*.[2] An example of how such an aspect crosscuts classes is shown in Figure 1.

AspectJ is a simple and practical aspect-oriented extension to Java. This paper presents an overview of AspectJ, including a number of core language features, the basic compilation strategy, the development environment support, and several examples of how AspectJ can be used.[3] The examples show that using AspectJ we can code, in clear form, crosscutting concerns that would otherwise lead to tangled code.

The main elements of the language design are now fairly stable, but the AspectJ project is not nearly finished. We continue fine-tuning parts of the language, building a third-generation compiler, expanding the integrated development environment (IDE) support, extending the documentation and training material, and building up the user community. We plan to work with that user community to empirically study the practical value of AOP.

The next section describes the basic assumptions behind the AspectJ language design. Section 3 presents the core language. Section 4 outlines the compiler. Section 5 describes the AspectJ-aware tool extensions we have developed. Section 6 shows that AspectJ can capture crosscutting structure in elegant and easy to understand ways. We conclude with a discussion of related and future work. As an overview, detailed design rationale and detailed compiler and tool implementation issues are outside the scope of this paper.HYPERLINK

2   Basic Design Assumptions

AspectJ is the basis for an empirical assessment of aspect-oriented programming. We want to know what happens when a real user community uses an AOP language. What kinds of aspects do they write? Can they understand each other's code? What kinds of idioms and patterns emerge?   What kinds of style guidelines do they develop? How effectively can they work with crosscutting modularity? And, above all, do they develop code that is more modular, more reusable, and easier to develop and maintain?

Because these are our goals, designing and implementing AspectJ is really just part of the project. We must also develop and support a substantial user community. To

---

[2] AOP support can be added to languages that are not object-oriented. The key property of an AOP language is that it provides crosscutting modularity mechanisms. So when we add AOP to an OO language, we add constructs that crosscut the hierarchical modularity of OO programs. If we add AOP to a procedural language, we must add constructs that crosscut the block structure of procedural programs [4, 6].

[3] This paper is written to correspond with AspectJ version 0.8.

make this possible, we have chosen to design AspectJ as a *compatible* extension to Java so that it will facilitate adoption by current Java programmers. By compatible we mean four things:

- *Upward compatibility* — all legal Java programs must be legal AspectJ programs.
- *Platform compatibility* — all legal AspectJ programs must run on standard Java virtual machines.
- *Tool compatibility* — it must be possible to extend existing tools to support AspectJ in a natural way; this includes IDEs, documentation tools, and design tools.
- *Programmer compatibility* — Programming with AspectJ must feel like a natural extension of programming with Java.

The programmer compatibility goal has been responsible for much of the feel of the language. Whereas our previous AOP languages were domain-specific, AspectJ is a general-purpose language like Java. AspectJ also has a more Java-like balance between declarative and imperative constructs. AspectJ is statically typed, and uses Java's static type system. In AspectJ programs we use classes for traditional class-like modularity structure, and then use aspects for concerns that crosscut the class structure.

There are several potentially valuable AOP research goals that AspectJ is not intended to meet. It is not intended to be a "clean-room" incarnation of AOP ideas, a formal AOP calculus or an aggressive effort to explore the AOP language space. Instead, AspectJ is intended to be a practical AOP language that provides, in a Java compatible package, a solid and well-worked-out set of AOP features.

3   The Language

AspectJ extends Java with support for two kinds of crosscutting implementation. The first makes it possible to define additional implementation to run at certain well-defined points in the execution of the program. We call this the *dynamic crosscutting* mechanism. The second makes it possible to define new operations on existing types. We call this *static crosscutting* because it affects the static type signature of the program. This paper only presents dynamic crosscutting.

Dynamic crosscutting in AspectJ is based on a small but powerful set of constructs. *Join points* are well-defined points in the execution of the program; *pointcuts* are a means of referring to collections of join points and certain values at those join points; *advice* are method-like constructs used to define additional behavior at join points; and *aspects* arc units of modular crosscutting implementation, composed of pointcuts, advice, and ordinary Java member declarations.

This section of the paper presents the main elements of the dynamic crosscutting support in the language. The presentation is informal and example-based.

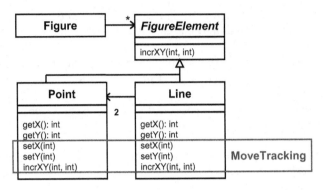

Fig. 1. UML description of a simple figure editor. The box labeled "MoveTracking" shows an aspect that crosscuts methods in the Point and Line classes. This aspect is discussed in detail in Section 3

3.1 Join Point Model

The join point model is a critical element in the design of any aspect-oriented language mechanism. This model provides the common frame of reference that makes it possible for execution of a program's aspect and non-aspect code to be properly coordinated.

In previous work, we have used several different kinds of join point model, including primitive application nodes in a dataflow graph [13, 18, 23, 27] and method bodies [27, 28]. Early versions of AspectJ used a model in which the join points were principled places in the source code.

The dynamic crosscutting elements of AspectJ are now based on a model in which join points are certain well-defined points in the execution of the program. This model gives us important additional expressive power, discussed in Section 3.9. In this model join points can be considered as nodes in a simple runtime object call graph. These nodes include points at which an object receives a method call and points at which a field of an object is referenced. The edges are control flow relations between the nodes. In this model control passes through each join point twice, once on the way in to the sub-computation rooted at the join point, and once on the way back out.

We illustrate join points using a simple figure editor, the kernel of which is shown in Figure 1, and which also serves as a running example. (Complete code from the paper is at aspectj.org/doc/papers/ecoop2001.) Based on these classes, executing the first three lines of code in Figure 2 builds the objects shown below. In this picture large circles represent objects, square boxes represent methods and small numbered circles represent join points. Executing the last line starts a computation that proceeds through the join points labeled below. In each case the join point is first reached just before the action described begins executing. Control passes back through the join point when the action described returns.

```
Point pt1 = new Point(0, 0);
Point pt2 = new Point(4, 4);
Line  ln1 = new Line(pt1, pt2);

ln1.incrXY(3, 6);
```

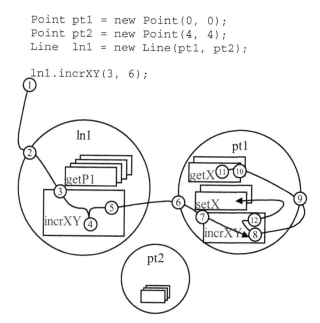

Fig. 2. The first three lines of code build the objects shown as large circles below. The rectangles represent methods.Executing the final line of code starts a computation that includes the sequence of join points shown as small numbered circles.

1. A method call join point corresponding to the incrXY method being called on the object ln1.
2. A method call reception join point at which ln1 receives the incrXY call.
3. A method execution join point at which the particular incrXY method defined in the class Line begins executing.
4. A field get join point where the _p1 field of ln1 is read.
5. A method call join point at which the incrXY method is called on the object pt1.
   ...
8. A method call join point at which the getX method is called on the object pt1.
   ...
11. A field get join point where the _x field of point pt1 is read.

   Control returns back through join points 11, 10, 9 and 8.
12. A method call join point at which the setX method is called on p1.
   ... and so on, until control finally returns back through 3, 2 and 1

The different kinds of join points provided by AspectJ are shown in Table 1. Note that while AspectJ defines a number of kinds of join points, only a few kinds suffice for many programs, and all kinds of join points behave the same with respect to other

Table 1. The dynamic join points of AspectJ. Join points marked with * are not used in further examples in this paper.

kind of join point	points in the program execution at which...
method call constructor call*	a method (or a constructor of a class) is called. Call join points are in the calling object, or in no object if the call is from a static method.
method call reception constructor call reception	an object receives a method or constructor call. Reception join points are before method or constructor dispatch, i.e. they happen inside the called object, at a point in the control flow after control has been transferred to the called object, but before any particular method/constructor has been called.
method execution* constructor execution*	an individual method or constructor is invoked.
field get	a field of an object, class or interface is read.
field set	a field of an object or class is set.
exception handler execution*	an exception handler is invoked.
class initialization*	static initializers for a class, if any, are run.
object initialization*	when the dynamic initializers for a class, if any, are run during object creation.

language features.[4] This substantially reduces the complexity of learning to program with AspectJ.

3.2 Pointcut Designators

A *pointcut* is a set of join points, plus, optionally, some of the values in the execution context of those join points. AspectJ includes several primitive *pointcut designators*. Programmers can compose these to define anonymous or named user-defined pointcut designators. Pointcuts are not higher order, nor are pointcut designators parametric.

A simple way to think of pointcut designators is in terms of matching certain join points at runtime. For example, the pointcut designator

```
receptions(void Point.setX(int))
```

matches all method call reception join points at which the Java signature of the method call is void Point.setX(int) Intuitively, this refers to every time a point receives a call to change its x coordinate. Similarly

---

[4] There is one exception to this rule. It is not possible to define before or around advice on constructor reception or constructor execution join points.

```
receptions(void FigureElement.incrXY(int, int))
```

intuitively refers to every time any kind of figure element (i.e. an instance of `Point` or `Line`) receives a call to shift a certain distance.

Pointcuts can be combined using and, or and not operators ('&&', '||' and '!'). The following compound pointcut designator refers to all receptions of calls to a `Point` to change its x or y coordinate.

```
receptions(void Point.setX(int)) ||
receptions(void Point.setY(int))
```

Primitive Pointcut Designators

AspectJ includes a variety of primitive pointcut designators that identify join points in different ways. Some primitive pointcut designators only identify pointcuts of one kind, for example `receptions` only matches method call reception join points. Others match any kind of join points at which a certain property holds. For example, `instanceof(Point)` matches all join points at which the currently executing object (the value of `this`) is an instance of `Point` or a subclass of `Point`.

These two kinds of join point designators can be combined to identify join points in useful ways. For example:

```
!instanceof(FigureElement) &&
calls(void FigureElement.incrXY(int, int))
```

matches all method calls to `incrXY` that do not come from an object that is a figure element. This will mean calls that come from an object of another type, as well as calls that come from static methods.[5]

The primitive pointcut designators are summarized in Table 2. They are explained further as they are used in the paper.

User-Defined Pointcut Designators

User-defined pointcut designators are defined with the `pointcut` declaration. The declaration:

```
pointcut moves():
    receptions(void FigureElement.incrXY(int, int)) ||
    receptions(void Line.setP1(Point))             ||
    receptions(void Line.setP2(Point))             ||
    receptions(void Point.setX(int))               ||
    receptions(void Point.setY(int));
```

defines a new pointcut designator, moves(), that identifies whenever a figure element receives a call of a method that can move it. User-defined pointcut designators can be used wherever a pointcut designator can appear.

---

[5] Because there is no currently executing object in static methods, the `instanceof(FigureElement)` will not match such join points.

Table 2. Primitive pointcut designators. Any ...*TypeName* position does normal sub-type matching. Any ...*id* position does matching by string equality. See section 3.9 for information about more sophisticated wild card matching in these positions

`calls(`*signature*`)`
 `receptions(`*signature*`)`
 `executions(`*signature*`)`
 	
 Matches call/reception/execution join points at which the method or constructor called matches *signature*. The syntax of a method signature is:
 	
 ResultTypeName RecvrTypeName.meth_id`(`*ParamTypeName,* ...`)`
 	
 The syntax of a constructor signature is:
 	
 *NewObjectTypeName.*new`(`*ParamTypeName,* ...`)`

`gets(`*signature*`)`
 `gets(`*signature*`)[`*val*`]`
 `sets(`*signature*`)`
 `sets(`*signature*`)[`*oldVal*`]`
 `sets(`*signature*`)[`*oldVal*`][`*newVal*`]`
 	
 Matches field get/set join points at which the field accessed matches the signature. The syntax of a field signature is:
 	
 FieldTypeName ObjectTypeName.field_id

`handles(`*ThrowableTypeName*`)`   Matches exception handler execution join points of the specified type.

`instanceof(`*CurrentlyExecutingObjectTypeName*`)`
 `within(`*ClassName*`)`
 `withincode(`*signature*`)`
 	
 Matches join points of any kind at which the currently executing:
    - object is of type *CurrentlyExecutingObjectTypeName*
    - code is contained within *ClassName*
    - code is contained within the member defined by the method or constructor
 signature

`cflow(`*pointcut_designator*`)`   Matches join points of any kind that occur strictly within the dynamic extent of any join point matched by pointcut_designator.
`callto(`*pointcut_designator*`)`   Matches method call join points that in one step lead to any reception or execution join points matched by pointcut_designator.

`staticinitializations(`*TypeName*`)`
 `initializations(`*TypeName*`)`
 	
 Matches class or object initializations of the specified type.

3.3 Advice

Advice is a method-like mechanism used to declare that certain code should execute at each of the join points in a pointcut. AspectJ supports *before, after,* and *around* advice. Additionally, there are two special cases of after advice, *after returning* and *after throwing*, corresponding to the two ways a sub-computation can return through a join point. Both before advice and all three kinds of after advice are strictly additive with respect to the normal computation at the join point. Around advice has the special capability of selectively preempting the normal computation at the join point. This advice framework is based on the declarative method combination mechanism in CLOS [11] (which itself was modeled on the demon methods of Flavors [8, 10, 31]).

Advice declarations define advice by associating a code body with a pointcut, and a time, relative to each join point in the pointcut, when the code should be executed. The advice declaration

```
after(): moves() {
   flag = true;
}
```

defines after advice on the pointcut moves(). The '()' between 'after' and the ':' means the advice has no parameters. The effect of this declaration is to ensure that the flag variable is set to true whenever a figure element finishes handling a move method call. (The declaration of the variable is shown in the example in Section 3.4.)

A simple model for the behavior of advice is in terms of runtime dispatch. (Section 4 outlines the techniques the compiler uses to ensure that most if not all of the matching overhead happens at compile time.) Upon arrival at a join point, all advice in the system are examined to see whether any apply at the join point. Any that do are collected, ordered according to specificity (described in Section 3.5), and executed as follows:

1. First, any around advice are run, most-specific first. Within the body of an around advice, calling proceed() invokes the next most specific piece of around advice, or, if no around advice remain, goes to the next step.
2. Then all before advice are run, most-specific first.
3. Then the computation associated with the join point proceeds.
4. Execution of after returning and after throwing advice depends on how the computation in step 3 and prior after returning and after throwing advice terminate.
   - If they terminate normally, all after returning advice are run, least specific first.
   - If they terminate by throwing an exception, all after throwing advice that match the exception are run, least specific first. (This means after throwing advice can handle exceptions thrown by less specific after returning and after throwing advice.)
5. Then all after advice are run, least-specific first.
6. Once all after advice have run, the return value from step 3, if any, is returned to the innermost call to proceed from step 1, and that piece of around advice continues running.

7. When the innermost piece of `around` advice returns, it returns to the surrounding `around` advice.
8. When the outermost piece of `around` advice returns, control continues back from the join point.

3.4 Aspects

Aspects are modular units of crosscutting implementation. Aspects are defined by aspect declarations, which have a form similar to that of class declarations. Aspect declarations may include pointcut declarations, advice declarations, as well as all other kinds of declarations permitted in class declarations.

The following declaration defines an aspect that implements the behavior of keeping track of whether a figure element has moved recently. This aspect might be used by the screen update mechanism to find out whether anything has changed since the last time the screen was updated. (More sophisticated versions of this aspect will be presented as the paper proceeds.)

```
aspect MoveTracking {

  static boolean flag = false;

  static boolean testAndClear() {
    boolean result = flag;
    flag = false;
    return result;
  }

  pointcut moves():
      receptions(void FigureElement.incrXY(int, int))
      receptions(void Line.setP1(Point))
      receptions(void Line.setP2(Point))
      receptions(void Point.setX(int))
      receptions(void Point.setY(int));

  after(): moves() {
    flag = true;
  }
}
```

Advice of an aspect are similar to methods in that they have access to all members of the class. So in this case the after advice can reference the static variable `flag`.

Aspect Instances

In AspectJ, the default behavior of non-abstract aspects is to have a single instance. Advice run in the context of this instance. The `aspect` declaration accepts a modifier, called 'of' that provides other kinds of aspect instance behavior. Discussion of this functionality is outside the scope of this paper.

3.5 Aspect Precedence

In general, more than one piece of advice may apply at a join point. The different advice can come from different aspects or even the same aspect. The relative order in which such advice executes is well defined. The ordering is based on the fact that aspects are the primary units of crosscutting functionality. So advice ordering, or specificity, is resolved with respect to the relative precedence of the aspects in which the advice is defined.

For two pieces of advice, a_1 and a_2, defined in aspects A_1 and A_2 respectively, the relative specificity is determined as follows:

- If A_1 and A_2 are the same, whichever piece of advice appears first in that aspect declaration's body is more specific. This rule exists because one aspect may need to define multiple advice that apply at the same join point. This commonly happens when there are matching before and after advice, but it can also happen with two pieces of advice of the same kind.
- If A_1 directly or indirectly extends A_2, then a_1 is more specific than a_2. This rule is a natural extension of method overriding rules in OO languages. It supports the common case where the related advice are defined in aspects that naturally exist in an extends relationship. (Section 3.8 discusses aspect inheritance and overriding in more detail.)
- If the declaration of A_1 includes a dominates modifier that mentions A_2, then a_1 is more specific than a_2. This rule exists because, in some cases, the programmer needs to control precedence between aspects that do not exist in an extends relationship.
- In all other cases the relative specificity between a_1 and a_2 is undefined. This is the most common case – two conceptually and semantically independent aspects define advice that apply at the same join point – and the programmer does not need to control the relative ordering of such advice.

The following mobility aspect is an example of the use of the dominates modifier. This simple aspect implements a global flag that freezes all figure elements so that they cannot move. The aspect works by checking the flag before any move operation, and simply doing a "quiet abort" of the operation if moves are disabled.

```
aspect Mobility dominates MoveTracking {
  private static boolean enableMoves = true;

  static void enableMoves()  { enableMoves = true;  }
  static void disableMoves() { enableMoves = false; }

  around() returns void: MoveTracking.moves() {
    if ( enableMoves ) {
      proceed();
    }
  }
}
```

It would not make sense for this aspect to extend MoveTracking, because it doesn't define a more specialized version of the move tracking functionality. But it is essential that it have precedence over MoveTracking, so that it can abort a move before it gets registered. Note that the code for this aspect shows that one aspect can refer to a pointcut defined in another aspect in the same way that static fields are referred to in Java.

3.6 Pointcut Parameters

In many cases it is useful for advice to have access to certain values that are in the execution context of the join points. For example, a more sophisticated version of the move tracking aspect might record the specific figure elements that have moved recently rather than just a single bit saying that some figure element has moved recently.

AspectJ provides a parameter mechanism that makes it possible for advice to see a subset of the values in the execution context of join points. This mechanism operates in both advice and pointcut declarations. In advice declarations values can be passed from the pointcut designator to the advice. In pointcut declarations values can be passed from the constituent pointcut designators to the user-defined pointcut designator. In both cases, the flow of values is from the right of the ':' to the left. The net effect is that values made available by primitive pointcut designators can be used in the body of advice.

For example, the following piece of advice has access to both the object receiving the method call and the argument to that call:

```
before(Point p, int nval):
    receptions(void p.setX(nval)) {
  System.out.println("x value of " + p +
                      " will be set to " + nval + ".");
}
```

The parameter mechanism uses a combination of positional and by-name matching. The list of parameters to the left of the ':' declares that this piece of advice has two parameters, of type `Point` and `int`, named `p` and `nval` respectively. Then, to the right of the colon, those two parameter names can be used in the same position that a type name would normally appear to say that the parameter should get the corresponding value. So, the `p` and `nval` in `p.setX(nval)` mean that the effective signature is `Point.setX(int)`, and that `p` should get the object receiving the call, and `nval` should get the value of the first argument to the call.

Definition and use of parameters works in a similar way in user-defined pointcuts. In this code

```
pointcut incrXYs(FigureElement fe):
    receptions(void fe.incrXY(int, int));

after(FigureElement figElt): incrXYs(figElt) {
    <'figElt' is bound to the figure element here>
}
```

the pointcut declaration says that `incrXYs(FigureElement)` exposes a single parameter, of type `FigureElement`, and that it is the receiver of the `incrXY` method call. The advice declaration says that figElt should be bound to the first parameter of incrXYs, which is the figure element being moved. Note that the name of the parameter in the pointcut declaration does not have to be the same as within the advice declaration.

Values can be exposed from other primitive pointcut designators as well. A common case is to use instanceof with a parameter to provide access to the object making a call, as follows:

```
pointcut gets(Object caller):
    instanceof(caller) &&
    (calls(int Point.getX())      ||
     calls(int Point.getY())      ||
     calls(Point Line.getP1())    ||
     calls(Point Line.getP2()));
```

The primitive pointcut designators expose values as suggested by the naming convention in Table 2. The RecvrTypeName position in method signatures exposes the object receiving the method call and so on.

Static Typing of Receiver

In a *highly polymorphic* pointcut designator like moves, there is no common super type that accepts all of the method calls in the pointcut (i.e. there is no type that accepts all of incrXY, setP1, setP2, setX and setY). That means it isn't possible to write moves to expose the figure element that is moving by simply plugging a common parameter into the receiver position of each receptions. One cannot write something like:

```
pointcut moves(FigureElement fe):
    receptions(void fe.incrXY(int, int))  ||
    receptions(void fe.setP1(Point))      ||
    receptions(void fe.setP2(Point))      ||
    . . .
```

because setP1 is not defined on FigureElement. Instead, the object receiving the calls must be picked up using instanceof as follows:

```
pointcut moves(FigureElement fe):
    instanceof(fe) &&
    (receptions(void FigureElement.incrXY(int, int)) ||
     receptions(void Line.setP1(Point))      ||
     receptions(void Line.setP2(Point))      ||
     receptions(void Point.setX(int))        ||
     receptions(void Point.setY(int)));
```

Access to Return Values

In some cases, after returning advice may want to access the value being returned through the join point. This is done with special syntax, to make it clear that the return value is only present in after returning advice:

```
after(Point p) returning (int x):
    receptions(int p.getX()) {
  System.out.println(p + " returned " +
                     x + " from getX().");
}
```

Parameters and Proceed

Within an `around` advice that has parameters, `proceed` accepts parameters with the same signature as the `around` advice itself. Calling `proceed` with different actual values for those parameters will cause all remaining advice and the rest of the computation to see the new values. This can be used to implement advice that does pre-processing on the values as follows:

```
around(int nv) returns void:
    receptions(void Point.setX(nv)) ||
    receptions(void Point.setY(nv)) {
  proceed(Math.max(0, nv));
}
```

The effect of this advice is to ensure that any method call to change the x or y coordinate of a point has its parameter clipped to greater than zero before the change proceeds.

3.7 Reflective Access to Join Point

To make certain kinds of advice easier to write, AspectJ provides simple reflective access to information about the current join point. Within the body of an advice declaration, the special variable `thisJoinPoint` is bound to an object representing the current join point. The join point object provides information common to all join points, such as what kind of join point it is and the signature of the surrounding method. It also provides information specific to each kind of join point, i.e. a field reference join point provides access to the field signature.

3.8 Inheritance and Overriding of Advice and Pointcuts

To support aspect-libraries, AspectJ provides a simple mechanism of pointcut overriding and advice inheritance. To use this mechanism a programmer defines an *abstract aspect*, with one or more *abstract pointcuts*, and with advice on the pointcut(s). This, then, is a kind of library aspect that can be parameterized by aspects that extend it. For example, the following defines a simple library of tracing functionality.

```
abstract aspect SimpleTracing {

  abstract pointcut tracePoints();

  before(): tracePoints() {
    printMessage("Entering", thisJoinPoint);
  }
  after(): tracePoints() {
    printMessage("Exiting", thisJoinPoint);
  }

  void printMessage(String when, JoinPoint tjp) {
    code to print an informative message
    using information from the join point
  }
}
```

Using the library aspect in a specific situation just requires extending the aspect and supplying a concrete definition for the abstract pointcut.

```
aspect IncrXYTracing extends SimpleTracing {

  pointcut tracePoints():
      receptions(void FigureElement.incrXY(int, int));

}
```

Making the abstract pointcut concrete in the sub-aspect has the effect of inheriting the advice declaration from the super-aspect into the sub-aspect. If the sub-aspect includes a `dominates` modifier, that modifier affects the precedence of the inherited advice.

3.9 Property-Based Crosscutting

The pointcuts presented above are all defined in terms of an explicit enumeration of method signatures. Although this is appropriate in many cases, we have found that it is useful to be able to define a pointcut by means of certain other properties of join points. To enable such property-based crosscutting, AspectJ includes two kinds of features, wildcarding in pointcut designators and control-flow based pointcut designators.

Wildcarding in Pointcut Designators. AspectJ includes a very simple wildcarding mechanism in pointcut designators. Examples of what this mechanism allows the programmer to say are:

- `receptions(* Point.*(..))`
  matches receptions of calls to any method defined on the class `Point` (i.e. `incrXY(int, int),getX(),getY(),setX(int),setY(int))`.[6]
- `receptions(Point.new(..))`
  matches receptions of calls to any constructor for an object of type `Point` (i.e. the `Point(int, int)` constructor).
- `receptions(public * com.xerox.scanner.*.*(..))`
  matches receptions of calls to any public method defined on any type in the `com.xerox.scanner` package.
- `receptions(* Point.get*())`
  matches receptions of calls to any method defined on `Point` for which the the id starts with `get` and which accepts zero arguments – i.e. the nullary getters `getX()` and `getY()`

Control-Flow Based Crosscutting. AspectJ also includes two primitive pointcut designators that allow picking out join points based on whether they are in a particular control-flow relationship with other join points. In order to do this, these designators differ from others in that they accept pointcut designators as parameters.

The `cflow(pcd)` pointcut designator matches all join points that are strictly within the dynamic extent of the join points matched by *pcd*. The points matched by *pcd* itself are not matched by `cflow(pcd)`. A canonical use of `cflow` is to distinguish between top-level versus recursive calls of a method. So, for example,

```
pointcut moves(FigureElement fe): <as above>;

pointcut topLevelMoves(FigureElement fe):
    moves(fe) && !cflow(moves(FigureElement)));
```

The definition of `topLevelMoves` reads as any join point matched by `moves`, but not within the control flow of `moves`. In other words, if the move operation invokes another move operation recursively, that recursive operation will not be matched.

4   Implementation

This section briefly outlines the current language implementation.

The main work of any AOP language implementation is to ensure that aspect and non-aspect code run together in a properly coordinated fashion. This coordination process is called *aspect weaving* and involves making sure that applicable advice runs at the appropriate join points. As is the case with most other language features, aspect weaving can be done by a special pre-processor [7], during compilation, by a post-compile processor [14], at load time, as part of the virtual machine, using residual runtime instructions, or using some combination of these approaches.

---

[6] This will also match calls to methods defined in the class `Object`. If the programmer explicitly wants to exclude these they could write: `receptions(* Point.*(..)) && !receptions(* Object.*(..))`.

The AspectJ language design strives to be silent on the issue of when aspect weaving should be done. We provide a compiler-based implementation of the language that does almost all weaving work at compile-time. This exposes as many programming errors as possible at compile time and avoids unnecessary runtime overhead. Certain special cases of advice involve residual dispatch overhead at runtime.

The compiler uses a pay-as-you-go implementation strategy. Any parts of the program that are unaffected by advice are compiled just as they would be by a standard Java compiler.

The compiler transforms the source program in three ways: the body of every advice declaration is compiled into a standard method, parts of the program where advice applies are transformed to insert static points corresponding to the dynamic join points, and code to implement any residual dynamic dispatch is inserted at those static points.

4.1 Compilation of Advice Bodies

Every before or after advice body is compiled into a standard method and the advice is run by a call to the method from appropriate points in the code. This potentially means that the use of advice will add the overhead of a single method-call. But, these methods are always either static or final, so they can easily be inlined by most JVMs [11]. This means there should generally be no observable performance overhead from these additional method calls.

An around advice body is compiled into one method body for each corresponding static point in the code. This allows us to pass the needed state for the around efficiently on the call-stack and to implement the proceed statement without needing to use Java's reflection mechanisms. This implementation strategy trades an increase in bytecode size for significantly reduced runtime overhead.

4.2 Corresponding Method

The compiler transforms the source program into a form in which there is an explicit *corresponding method* for each dynamic join point that might have advice at runtime. This transformation is only performed for join points that might have advice, not all join points. So, for example, in a program that has advice on the pointcut designated by gets(int Point._x), the compiler would transform references of the form p._x, where p is a Point, to Point.jp0$(p), and add the following method to the class Point:

```
private static int $jp$0(Point obj) {
  return obj._x;
}
```

Once this corresponding method has been generated, before and after advice are implemented by making the corresponding method call the advice methods, as needed.

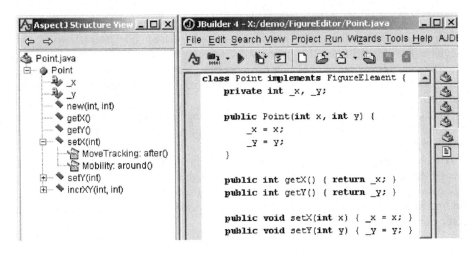

Fig. 3. A portion of the screen when using the AJDE extension to JBuilder 4. The main window on the right shows the code for the class Point. The structure view on the left shows the class Point, and shows that setX, setY and incrXY are all crosscut by advice; setX is further expanded to show what advice crosscuts it. The user can click on the advice to jump there.

There are many cases, including this one, where the compiler will add additional method calls in order to create corresponding methods. This happens for method call, method call reception and field access join points. Extra method calls are also added as part of the implementation strategy for around advice. The overhead of these methods is small in any JVM, and again since they are all static or final, they will be optimized away by good JVMs. We expect a future version of the AspectJ compiler to provide optimizing modes that will eliminate some of these minor overheads.

4.3 Dynamic Dispatch

The use of certain pointcut designators, like cflow, callsto, and instanceof, can require a run-time test to determine whether a particular corresponding method actually matches a particular join point designator. In such cases, the corresponding method includes residual testing code that guards the execution of the advice. This overhead is relatively small.

5   Tool Support

In object-oriented programming, development tools typically allow the programmer to easily browse the class structure of their programs. Such support enables the programmer to see the inheritance and overriding structure in their program, as well as seeing compact representations of the contents of individual classes [13, 18, 23].

```
emacs@SILVER                                                    _ □ ✕

Buffers  Files  Tools  Edit  Search  Mule  Classes  JDE  Aspectj  Java  Help
class Point implements FigureElement {
  private int _x, _y;

  public Point(int x, int y) {
    _x = x;
    _y = y;
  }

  public int getX() { return _x; }
  public int getY() { return _y; }

  public void setX(int x) { _x = x; }    [MoveTracking, Mobility]
  public void setY(int y) { _y = y; }    [MoveTracking, Mobility]

  public void incrXY(int dx, int dy) {   [MoveTracking, Mobility]
    setX(getX() + dx);
    setY(getY() + dy);
  }
}
--\--   Point.java            (JDE AspectJ)--L18--Bot--[M:incrXY]----
```

Fig. 4. A portion of the screen when using the AspectJ-aware extension to emacs. The text in [Square Brackets] following the method declarations is automatically generated, and serves to remind the programmer of the aspects that crosscut the method.

For AspectJ, we are developing analogous support for browsing aspect structure. This enables the programmer to see the crosscutting structure in their programs. It works by showing a bi-directional coupling between aspects (and their advice), and the classes (and their members) that the advice affect. Figure 3 shows one of the extensions we have made to JBuilder 4. This extension to the structure view tool allows the programmer to easily see a summary of all the crosscutting affecting the class Point. If the structure view window is focused on an aspect, it will show all the targets of that aspect's advice.

A second kind of environment extension provides a more light-weight reminder of the aspect structure. This extension works by annotating the source code, as seen in the editor, with an indication of whether aspects crosscut that code. Figure 4 shows how we have extended emacs with this functionality. The automatically generated annotations name the aspects that crosscut the method. A keystroke command can be used to pop up a menu of the advice, choose one, and jump to it.

We currently support AspectJ-aware extensions to emacs, JBuilder and Forte for Java. Additional tool support includes debugger extensions to understand that advice, display it correctly on the stack etc., as well as extensions to Javadoc [17] to make it understand crosscutting structure and generate appropriate hyper-links etc.

All of these extensions work by consulting a database that is maintained by the compiler. Once the API stabilizes, we intend to make it public so that others can develop tools that use it as well.

6   Understanding Crosscutting Structure

One of the most important questions we must answer is how easy is it to program with AspectJ. In particular, is crosscutting structure, implemented with AspectJ, something that appears easy to understand and work with? We do not yet have enough experience to say for sure, but our experience to date suggests that the answer is yes.

6.1 Modular, Concise, and Explicit

Consider the following simple aspect, which is not part of the figure editor example. This aspect implements a simple error logging functionality, in which every public method defined on any type in the com.xerox.printers package logs any errors it throws back to its caller.

```
aspect SimpleErrorLogging {
  Log log = new Log();

  pointcut publicEntries():
      receptions(public * com.xerox.printers.*.*(..));

  after() throwing (Error e): publicEntries() {
    log.write(e);
  }
}
```

This aspect appears to be better than the plain Java implementation of the same functionality in several ways:

- The aspect is *more modular*. In the ordinary Java implementation, code for this aspect would be spread across every public method.
- The aspect is *more concise*. In the plain Java version something like six lines of code would be added to each public method to wrap the body in a "try... catch..." statement.
- The aspect is *more explicit*. In this code, the *structural invariant* underlying the crosscutting is clear. A quick look at the code is all it takes to understand that all the public methods defined in the com.xerox.printers package should do error logging.

Consider a program maintenance scenario in which a programmer must work with a system with this kind of functionality. In the plain Java implementation, the programmer would discover the logging code one method at a time. After seeing several such methods the programmer might guess that logging was being done by all public methods of that class or perhaps even the package. But they would have to make careful use of a tool like grep to be sure. And of course they might not even make this guess.

In the AspectJ implementation, every public method would carry an annotation, similar to that in Figures 3 and 4, so that when the programmer look at the first public method they would see an annotation, something like that in Figures 3 and 4, which would tell them that the method was crosscut by the SimpleErrorLogging aspect. They could quickly go to the aspect, read the ten lines of code, and understand the intent of the code. The structural invariant underlying the functionality – that all public methods must log – would be clear and enforced.

Aspects that use explicit enumeration of method signatures can also be more modular, concise and explicit than their plain Java counterparts. Consider the now familiar moves pointcut:

```
pointcut moves(FigureElement fe):
    instanceof(fe) &&
    (receptions(void FigureElement.incrXY(int, int)) ||
     receptions(void Line.setP1(Point))            ||
     receptions(void Line.setP2(Point))            ||
     receptions(void Point.setX(int))              ||
     receptions(void Point.setY(int)));
```

Even though this pointcut is enumeration rather than property-based, putting the complete set of method signatures in a single place makes the crosscutting structure explicit and clear. When reading the MoveTracking aspect it is easy to tell what invariant it preserves – whenever something moves it records that fact. Writing the Mobility aspect in terms of MoveTracking.moves, makes it clear that multiple aspects of the implementation crosscut all the move operations. The IDE support ensures that when we happen to be looking at the setX method for Point, we see that Mobility and MoveTracking crosscut there. Navigating to either aspect will show their structure and the fact that Mobility is defined in terms of MoveTracking.

This clarity is preserved when enumeration-based crosscutting is used together with property-based crosscutting. This is evident in the topLevelMoves pointcut.

```
pointcut topLevelMoves(FigureElement fe):
    moves(fe) && !cflow(moves(FigureElement));
```

Our experience is that the cflow pointcut designator takes only a short while for people learning AspectJ to learn, and once they do so, they find it quite easy to understand this code. It is certainly much easier than to understand what is going on from the middle of the classic tangled implementation of this functionality.

Clear explicit crosscutting structure can come from the way multiple advice declarations interact as well. In the SimpleTracing aspect of Section 3.8, there are two advice declarations:

```
before(): tracePoints() {
  printMessage("Entering", thisJoinPoint);
}
after(): tracePoints() {
  printMessage("Exiting", thisJoinPoint);
}
```

Even without knowing what join points tracePoints will match, we understand something important about the structure of this code – the entering and exiting messages happen in pairs, on the way into and back out of join points matched by tracePoints.

6.2 The Role of IDE Technology

IDE technology plays an important role in these scenarios. In the course of preparing the paper we encountered a bug in which `MoveTracking` and `Mobility` had inconsistent moves pointcuts. The bug was immediately apparent, because the environment showed numerous methods tagged with the `Mobility` and `MoveTracking` aspects and one method tagged with just `MoveTracking`.

Because it is now standard practice for OO programmers to use some kind of IDE support and because it is so easy to incorporate AspectJ support into an IDE, we believe it is reasonable to expect programmers to have IDE support available for such scenarios.

The ability of the IDE to present the structure of the program depends on the degree to which the code declaratively captures that structure. OO IDEs do a good job of presenting inheritance structure because code in OO programming languages captures inheritance explicitly. The AspectJ IDE support works well because code in AspectJ captures crosscutting explicitly.

7   Related Work

In earlier work we proposed aspect-oriented programming [24] and presented three examples of domain-specific [1] AOP languages [5] that we had developed. AspectJ differs from those three systems in that it is a general-purpose language, it is integrated with Java, it has a dynamic join point model, and we are developing a full compiler, rather than just a pre-processor.

7.1 Other Work in AOP

Adaptive Programming [27] provides a special-purpose declarative language for writing class structure traversal specifications. Using this language prevents knowledge of the complete class structure from becoming tangled throughout the code. Adaptive Components [36] build on adaptive programming by using similar graph-language techniques to allow flexible linking of aspectual components and classes. This makes aspectual components reusable. AspectJ supports reusable aspects using the pointcut-overriding and advice-inheritance mechanism, neither of which requires a special graph language.

Composition Filters [28] wrap objects inside of filters that operate on the messages the objects receive. The filters have crosscutting access to the messages received by an object. But attachment of filters to objects is done as part of class definitions, so composition filters are less well suited than AspectJ for crosscuts that involve more than one class.

De Volder has proposed a logic meta-programming (LMP) approach that can serve as kind of an AOP language toolkit [32, 33]. In this approach, the equivalent of our pointcut designators use logical queries to specify crosscuts. This approach can take advantage of unification to define parametric pointcut designators. It supports higher-order pointcut designators as well. We have considered extending AspectJ with this kind of power, but have decided not to do so, in order to keep the language simpler and easier for Java developers to learn quickly. We may re-consider this issue in release 2.0 or later; we believe the current pointcut designator syntax leaves us room to do so in an upward compatible way.

7.2 Multi-dimensional Separation of Concerns

Subject-oriented programming is a means for composing and integrating disparate class hierarchies (subjects), each of which might represent different concerns [9]. More recent work on multi-dimensional separation of concerns (MDSOC) [2, 19] is intended to separate concerns along multiple dimensions at once. Hyper/J [15] is a specific proposal for MDSOC. Hyper/J works by having the programmer write two kinds of meta-declarations: The first describes how to slice concerns out of a set of classes; the second describes how to re-compose those concerns into a new program. Hyper/J has the potential to slice a concern out of code without re-factoring the classes. By comparison, in AspectJ the separation of crosscutting concerns is done in the original code, by writing it as an aspect. We believe re-factoring the code with an aspect will be easier to maintain than slicing concerns out, but it is too soon to know.

7.3 Reflection

Computational reflection [19-22, 26, 38] enables crosscutting programs. For example, it is possible to write a small piece of meta-code that runs for all methods. Smalltalk-76 included meta-level functionality [12]. CommonLoops and 3-KRS proposed different meta-level architectures for OO languages [3] PCL provided the first efficient metaobject-protocol [25]. Much of the research in reflection has explored varying the meta-level architecture to support different kinds of crosscutting [2] and to achieve flexibility without sacrificing performance [34].

With the exception of reflective access to `thisJoinPoint`, AspectJ has been designed so that the semantics of advice is not a meta-programming nor a reflective semantics. In particular, AspectJ the identifiers in pointcut designators do not refer to program representation or interpreter state – they do not involve reification.

7.4 Object-Oriented Programming

Flavors [35], New Flavors [37], CommonLoops [16] and CLOS [34] all support multiple-inheritance, declarative method combination and open classes. C++ supports multiple inheritance [35]. While AspectJ includes elements of these, AspectJ also provides more powerful and modular support for crosscutting than can be achieved with these features.

Declarative method combination, as in the CLOS line of languages, is not sufficient for AOP, because it lacks the pointcut mechanisms that enable crosscutting.

Ordinary multiple-inheritance (MI) is not sufficient for AOP for two reasons. First, a single aspect can include advice for all the different participants in a multi-class interaction. Using MI, a separate mixin-class must be defined for each participant class. Second, aspects work by *reverse-inheritance* – the aspect declares what classes it should affect rather than vice-versa. This means that adding or removing aspects from the system does not require editing affected class definitions.

Completely unstructured open classes, as in CLOS and its ancestors, enable some degree of crosscutting modularity, but they do so in a totally unstructured way. In AspectJ, classes and aspects are modular units, even if an aspect can crosscut classes.[7]

7.5 Other Work

Walker and Murphy have proposed a system based on implicit context that is also intended to improve separation of concerns [37]. Implicit context is similar to AspectJ in that the separation is made explicit in the source code. But it differs from AspectJ in that it provides reflective access to the entire call history of a system. Thus explicit context can reason about a wider dynamic context than is possible with cflow. AspectJ programmers could write aspects to manually gather call history information and thereby duplicate some explicit context functionality.

Implicit parameters provide dynamically scoped variables within a statically typed Hinley Milner framework [16]. Implicit parameters are lexically distinct from regular identifiers, and are bound by a special construct whose scope is dynamic, rather than static as with let. Implicit parameters have some of the power of using cflow to pass dynamic context. Implicit parameters are more powerful, in that the binding they create can be set from any reference site. But they do not have explicit crosscutting modularity support because references to the parameter are still spread throughout the code. Many implementations of Scheme provide the fluid-let construct that dynamically binds variables by side-effect, and then re-instates the previous binding after evaluation of the body is completed.

8   Future Work

We plan to use AspectJ as the basis of an empirical assessment of aspect-oriented programming. We want to develop a real AOP user community, and work with them to understand the practical effects of AOP. Our main focus now is building up and supporting the user community. To enable this, we are focusing on fine-tuning the language design and improving the quality of the compiler, IDE extensions and documentation.

The compiler has three main limitations that we are currently working on: it uses javac as a back-end rather than generating class files directly; it requires access to all the source code for the system; and it performs a full recompilation whenever any part of the user program changes. We believe we know how to build an incremental compiler that will perform reasonably well on modestly large systems, but fast

---

[7] Flavors, New Flavors and CLOS use the Common Lisp module system, called the package system. It is typically used in only very coarse-grained ways, certainly not at the level of single classes as in Java, and usually not even at the level of single packages in Java.

incremental compilation for a language like AspectJ is definitely an area for future research.

In the tools area, we plan to support more IDEs. We will also make a crosscutting structure browsing API that will allow others to develop tools that understand AspectJ code. Our existing navigation model doesn't capture the structure of `cflow` pointcuts as well as we would like, so this will also be an area for future work.

Beyond the 1.0 release we plan to explore new kinds of pointcut designators based on dataflow properties of the program. Our goal with this functionality, which we call dflow, is to be able to capture crosscuts such as the extent of a value and control boundary crossings.

9 Summary

AspectJ is a seamless aspect-oriented extension to Java. Programming with AspectJ feels like a small extension of programming with Java. AspectJ programs are largely ordinary Java programs in which we use ordinary Java for class-like modularity, and use aspects to implement crosscutting modularity.

Implementing crosscutting concerns using AspectJ benefits in three ways over a plain Java implementation of the same functionality: the implementation is more modular and concise; the structure of the crosscutting is captured in a more explicit form; and because of the first two properties, programming environment tools can help the programmer navigate and understand that structure.

Looking forward, our goal is to work with the AspectJ user community to assess the benefits of using aspect-oriented programming, in more complex systems as well as to continue to explore language design, methodological and other issues.

10 Acknowledgements

We thank the AspectJ users most of all. Their suggestions, questions and bug reports have been invaluable in getting the project to where it is today. Without the users, this project would not be possible.

Brian de Alwis, Yvonne Coady, Chris Dutchyn and Gail Murphy helped us with detailed comments on the paper. Extensive comments from Bob Filman, Robert Hirschfeld and the anonymous reviewers we also very helpful.

Our work builds on contributions from numerous past members of our research group. In particular John Lamping and Cristina Lopes played major roles in getting AOP and AspectJ to where they are today.

This work was partially supported by the Defense Advanced Research Projects Agency under contract number F30602-C-0246. This work was also partially supported by the Natural Sciences and Engineering Research Council (NSERC) of Canada, Xerox Canada Limited and Sierra Systems. Java and Forte are trademarks of Sun Microsystems. JBuilder is a trademark of Inprise Corporation.

References

1. Proceedings of the Conference on Domain-Specific Languages (DSL). USENIX,Santa Barbara, California, USA (1997)
2. Bobrow, D.G., et al.: CommonLoops: Merging Lisp and Object-Oriented Programming. In: Proceedings of the Conference on Object-Oriented Programming Systems, Languages, and Applications (OOPSLA). ACM, Portland, Oregon (1986) 17-29
3. Cannon, H.: Flavors: A non-hierarchical approach to object-oriented programming. Symbolics Inc.(1982)
4. Coady, Y., G. Kiczales, and M. Feeley: Exploring an Aspect-Oriented Approach to Operating System Code. In: Position paper for the Advanced Separation of Concerns Workshop at the Conference on Object-Oriented Programming Systems, Languages, and Applications (OOPSLA). ACM, Minneapolis, Minnesota, USA (2000)
5. DeVolder, K.: Aspect-Oriented Logic Meta Programming. In: Meta-Level Architectures and Reflection, Reflection'99. Springer, Saint-Malo, France (1999) 250-272
6. Filman, R.E. and D.P. Friedman: Aspect-Oriented Programming is Quantification and Obliviousness. In: Position paper for the Advanced Separation of Concerns Workshop at the Conference on Object-Oriented Programming Systems, Languages, and Applications (OOPSLA). ACM, Minneapolis, Minnesota, USA (2000)
7. Friendly, L.: Design of Javadoc. In: The Design of Distributed Hyperlinked Programming Documentation (IWHD). Springer-Verlag, Montpellier, France (1995)
8. Goldberg, A.: Smalltalk-80: The Interactive Programming environment. Addisson-Wesley, Reading MA (1984)
9. Goldberg, A. and D. Robson: Smalltalk-80: The Language and Its Implementation. Addison-Wesley, (1983)
10. Green, T.R.G. and M. Petre: Usability analysis of visual programming environments: a 'cognitive dimensions' approach. Journal of Visual Languages and Computing. 7,2. (1996) 131-174
11. Griswold, D.: The Java HotSpot Virtual Machine Architecture. Sun Microsystems, Inc.(1998)
12. Ichisugi, Y., S. Matsuoka, and A. Yonezawa: RbCl: A reflective object-oriented concurrent language without a run-time kernel. In: International Workshop on New Models for Software Architecture (IMSA): Reflection and Meta-Level Architecture. Tama City, Tokyo (1992) 24-35
13. Irwin, J., et al.: Aspect-Oriented Programming of Sparse Matrix Code. In: Proceedings of the International Symposium on Computing in Object-Oriented Parallel Environments (ISCOPE). Springer, Marina del Rey, CA, USA (1997) 249-256
14. Kiczales, G., et al.: Aspect-Oriented Programming. In: Proceedings of the European Conference on Object-Oriented Programming (ECOOP). Springer-Verlag, Finland (1997)
15. Kiczales, G. and L. Rodriguez: Efficient Method Dispatch in PCL. In: LISP and Functional Programming. ACM Press, Nice, France (1990) 99-105
16. Lewis, J., et al.: Implicit Parameters: Dynamic Scoping with Static Types. In: Proceedings of the 27th Annual ACM SIGPLAN-SIGACT Symposium on Principles of Programming Languages. Boston, Massachusetts (2000) 108-118
17. Lieberherr, K.J.: Adaptive Object-Oriented Software: The Demeter Method with Propagation Patterns. PWS Publishing Company, Boston (1996)
18. Lopes, C.V. and G. Kiczales: D: A Language Framework for Distributed Programming. Technical Report SPL97-010, P9710047. Xerox Palo Alto Research Center,Palo Alto, CA (1997)
19. Maes, P.: Concepts and Experiments in Computational Reflection. In: Proceedings of the Conference on Object-Oriented Programming Systems, Languages, and Applications (OOPSLA). ACM, Orlando, Florida (1987) 147-155

20. Masuhara, H., S. Matsuoka, and A. Yonezawa: Designing an OO reflective language for massively-parallel processors. In: Position paper for the workshop on Object-Oriented Reflection and Metalevel Architectures at the Conference on Object-Oriented Programming Systems, Languages, and Applications (OOPSLA). Washington, DC (1993)
21. Matsuoka, S., T. Watanabe, and A. Yonezawa: Hybrid group reflective architecture for object-oriented concurrent reflective programming. In: Proceedings of the European Conference on Object-Oriented Programming (ECOOP). Springer, Geneva, Switzerland (1991) 231-250
22. McAffer, J.: The CodA MOP. In: Position paper for the workshop on Object-Oriented Reflection and Metalevel Architectures at the Conference on Object-Oriented Programming Systems, Languages, and Applications (OOPSLA),. Washington, DC (1993)
23. Mendhekar, A., G. Kiczales, and J. Lamping: RG: A Case-Study for Aspect-Oriented Programming. Technical Report SPL97-009, P9710044. Xerox Palo Alto Research Center,Palo Alto, CA (1997)
24. Mezini, M. and K.J. Lieberherr: Adaptive Plug-and-Play Components for Evolutionary Software Development. In: Proceedings of the Conference on Object-Oriented Programming Systems, Languages, and Applications (OOPSLA). ACM, Vancouver, British Columbia, Canada (1998) 97-116
25. Moon, D.A.: Object-Oriented Programming with Flavors. In: Proceedings of the Conference on Object-Oriented Programming Systems, Languages, and Applications (OOPSLA). ACM, Portland, Oregon (1986) 1-8
26. Okamura, H., Y. Ishikawa, and M. Tokoro: Metalevel Decomposition in AL-1/D. In: International Symposium on Object Technologies for Advanced Software. Springer Verlag, (1993) 110-127
27. Ossher, H., et al.: Subject-Oriented Composition Rules. In: Proceedings of the Conference on Object Oriented Programming Systems, Languages, and Applications (OOPSLA). ACM, Austin, Texas (1995) 235-250
28. Ossher, H. and P.L. Tarr: Hyper/J: multi-dimensional separation of concerns for Java. In: Proceedings of the International Conference on Software Engineering (ICSE). ACM, Limerick, Ireland (2000) 734-737
29. Parnas, D.L.: On the Criteria To Be Used in Decomposing Systems Into Modules. Communications of the ACM. 15,12. (1972) 1053-1058
30. Parnas, D.L.: Software Engineering or Methods for the Multi-Person Construction of Multi-Version Programs. Lecture Notes in Computer Science. Programming Methodology. (1974)
31. Shneiderman, B.: Direct Manipulation: A step beyond Programming languages, In: Human-Computer Interaction: A Multidisciplinary Approach, R.M. Baecker and W.A.S. Buxton, Editors. Morgan Kaufmann Publishers, Inc.: Los Altos, CA (1983) 461-467
32. Smith, B.C.: Reflection and Semantics in a Procedural Language, PhD Thesis. M.I.T(1982)
33. Smith, B.C.: Reflection and Semantics in LISP. In: Proceedings of the Symposium on Principles of Programming Languages (POPL). ACM, (1984) 23-35
34. Steele, G.L.: Common Lisp the Language. 2nd ed. Digital Press, (1990) 1029
35. Stroustrup, B.: The C++ Programming Language. 3rd ed. Addison-Wesley, (1997)
36. Tarr, P.L., et al.: N Degrees of Separation: Multi-Dimensional Separation of Concerns. In: Proceedings of the International Conference on Software Engineering (ICSE). ACM, Los Angeles, CA (1999) 107-119
37. Walker, R. and G. Murphy: Implicit Context: Easing Software Evolution and Reuse. In: Proceedings of the Conference on Foundations of Software Engineering (FSE). ACM, San Diego, California (2000)
38. Watanabe, T. and A. Yonezawa: Reflection in an object-oriented concurrent language. In: Proceedings of the Conference on Object-Oriented Programming Systems, Languages, and Applications (OOPSLA). ACM, San Diego, CA (1988) 306-315

True Modules for Java-like Languages

Davide Ancona and Elena Zucca*

DISI - Università di Genova
Via Dodecaneso, 35, 16146 Genova (Italy)
{davide,zucca}@disi.unige.it

Abstract. We present JAVAMOD, a true module system constructed on top of a Java-like language. More in detail, this means that basic modules are collections of Java classes and specify in their interface the imported and exported classes with their types; furthermore, it is possible to write structured module expressions by means of a set of module operators and a type system at the module level ensures type safety.

In designing such a type system, one has to face non trivial problems, notably the fact that a module M which extends an imported class C can be correctly combined only with modules exporting a class C which, besides providing the expected services, causes no interferences with its subclasses defined in M.

What we obtain is a module language which is extremely flexible and allows to express (without any need of enriching the syntax of the core level, that is, the Java language), for instance, generic types as in Pizza and GJ, mixin classes (that is, subclasses parametric in the direct superclass) and mutually recursive class definitions split in independent modules.

1 Introduction

Widely used object-oriented languages, like Java and C++, typically provide only weak module systems. Java packages, for instance, are basically just a mean for structuring the namespace, while there is no support for the following features which are highly desirable for a modular approach to software development.

Module interfaces A module interface is a specification of the services a given module both needs from and provides to others. As it is well-known, these specifications serve as a formal contract [26] between server and client. Hence, the client can rely on the server specification without any need at looking at the implementation; on the other side, the correctness of an implementation w.r.t. the specification can be separately checked.

Module interfaces also allow to handle in a flexible way visibility levels, specifying that only a subset of the components defined in a module (classes

---

* Partially supported by Murst - TOSCA Teoria della Concorrenza, Linguaggi di Ordine Superiore e Strutture di Tipi and APPlied SEMantics - Esprit Working Group 26142.

J. Lindskov Knudsen (Ed.): ECOOP 2001, LNCS 2072, pp. 354–380, 2001.

in the case we are considering) are exported and possibly with a restricted interface.

Note that in object-oriented languages visibility levels and other modularity related aspects are often handled at the class level, making the class mechanism more complex. A separation of concerns allows a more clean and powerful language design, as already pointed out in [30]; see also [17] for an extended discussion on this point.

Separate type-checking A code fragment (module) which needs some services from others should be possibly typed in isolation, by just specifying these services, and it should be possible to provide only later their actual implementation. On the contrary, in Java a class whose definition relies on the specification of other classes can be typed only if all these classes actually *exist* (as either source or bytecode) in the environment.

Module expressions A principle which has recently become popular in the programming language community (see, e.g., [25]) is that a module system should have two linguistic levels: a *module language* providing operators for combining software components, constructed on top of a *core language* (following the terminology introduced with Standard ML) for defining module components. The module language should have its own typing rules and be as independent as possible from the core language; even more, it could be in principle instantiated over different core languages (see [4]).

Despite of the considerable effort has been invested in the last years in studying theoretical foundations and developing new forms of module systems[1], there is relatively little amount of effort spent until now, both on the theoretical and implementation side, on applying these ideas to the case of object-oriented languages.

In particular, at our knowledge there has been no attempt at integrating a rich module system supporting the three features mentioned above with the Java language, apart from the simple extension of the package system proposed in [6].

In this paper, we face one important part of this integration problem, that is, the design of a typed module system on top of a Java-like language as core language (see the Conclusion for a brief discussion on application to a realistic Java extension). We choose Java as a paradigmatic and real example of a typed object-oriented language where classes are types, hence subtyping coincides with inheritance. In designing such a type system, one has to face non trivial problems, notably the fact that a module M which extends an imported class C can be correctly combined only with modules exporting a class C which, besides providing the expected services, causes no interferences with its subclasses defined

---

[1] Let us mention the wide literature about foundations and improvements of Standard ML module system (see, e.g. [24, 22]), the notions of *mixin* (see, e.g. [8, 9, 20, 2, 1]) and *unit* [19] and the type-theoretical analysis of recursion between modules proposed in [12].

in M^2. We can propose at least two solutions for this problem; that developed in this paper has the advantage of allowing a simpler type system.

The resulting language, which we call JAVAMOD, allows to express (without any need of enriching the syntax of the core level, that is, the Java language), for instance, generic types as in Pizza [28] and GJ [10], mixin classes (that is, subclasses parametric in the direct superclass [20, 7, 1]) and mutually recursive class definitions split in independent modules. The language has two (stratified) levels. At the module level there are *module expressions*, constructed from basic modules by the three operators of *merge* (putting together two modules connecting their imported and exported classes), *hiding* (making totally or partially invisible from the outside some exported classes) and *renaming* (changing the name of some exported classes). A basic module is a collection of Java classes, that is, the core level is pure Java.

In the extended version of this paper [5] we provide a simple and intuitive reduction semantics for module operators of JAVAMOD by translation in a simple module calculus, called MINIJAVAMOD, and show that the type system we have defined actually guarantees that well-typed module expressions behave correctly w.r.t. this semantics. At the module level MINIJAVAMOD can be seen as a superset of JAVAMOD, in the sense that it is more expressive and module expressions in JAVAMOD can be easily seen as expressions in MINIJAVAMOD. The core level is a minimal Java fragment enriched by the possibility of annotating superclasses with the required class type in `extends` clauses.

The design of both JAVAMOD and MINIJAVAMOD at the module level is largely based on our previous work on CMS[4, 3], a simple and powerful calculus of modules, generic w.r.t. the underlying core calculus and suitable for encoding various existing mechanisms for composing modules (including parameterized modules like ML functors and mutually recursive modules), in the same way λ-calculus provides a theoretical basis for functional languages.

The paper is organized as follows. In Sect.2 we informally describe the module operators of JAVAMOD by some examples and illustrate their flexibility for expressing (keeping as core language pure Java) different language constructs; in particular, we show how to express generic types as in Pizza [28] and GJ [10], mixin classes as in [20, 7, 1], and mutually recursive class definitions split in independent modules. In Sect.3 we discuss in detail the typing problems related to imported superclasses, and describe the solution chosen in JAVAMOD. Sect.4 is devoted to the formal definition of a type system for JAVAMOD. In Sect.5 we compare the approach taken in this paper with related work. Finally, in the Conclusion we summarize the relevance of the work and outline directions for further developments.

---

[2] An example of interference is when C contains some method which is also defined in some subclass in M, causing unexpected overriding

2   A True Module Language for Java

In this section we informally present our proposal for adding modules to Java; we call JAVAMOD the language obtained through this extension. The aim is to give an informal overview of the language (see Sect.4 for the formal definitions), to show the benefits of the approach in terms of software reuse and modification and to discuss the main theoretical issues that have to be tackled when adding modules to Java.

2.1   Basic Modules

Roughly speaking, a basic module in JAVAMOD is a collection of Java classes, exactly as happens for packages. However, there are three main differences that make JAVAMOD a true module system.

The first distinguishing feature is that modules in JAVAMOD are *typed*, in the sense that each module has a unique *module interface* (not to be confused with Java interfaces). Accordingly to the classical ADT approach, the interface of a module M is logically separate from the implementation of M. In practice, interfaces could either be automatically generated from module definitions, or provided by the programmer in separate files. Taking the latter approach, it would make sense that several modules could implement the same interface, instead of always having the same name for both interface and implementation as we assume here for simplicity. Moreover, keeping separate interface files has the advantage that a module can be safely recompiled if it is modified in a way that still implements the same interface.

The second major difference with Java packages is that a module M can be parametric, in the sense that it can depend on a number of *imported* classes whose definition is not known at time of definition of M, but rather must be provided from other modules in a proper way that will be better specified in the sequel.

For instance, let us consider the following example of basic module definition in JAVAMOD:

```
interface PairMod;
import
 Elem:{}
export
 Pair:{
  Pair(Elem fst,Elem snd);
  void set(Elem newfst,Elem newsnd);
  Elem fst();
  Elem snd();
 }

module PairMod;
class Pair{
```

```
Elem fst;
Elem snd;
Pair(Elem fst, Elem snd){
   this.fst=fst;
   this.snd=snd;
}
void set(Elem newfst, Elem newsnd){
   fst=newfst;
   snd=newsnd;
}
Elem fst(){return fst;}
Elem snd(){return snd;}
}
```

A basic module consists of an interface (keyword `interface`) and an implementation (keyword `module`), which are assumed to be defined in separate files but have the same name (this is a convenient name convention for matching interfaces with implementations).

The interface of a module is made up of an *import* and an *export* list. For simplicity in this paper we consider only classes and not interfaces. The interface for `PairMod` specifies an imported class named `Elem` and an exported class `Pair`.

Imported classes are used as formal parameters in the corresponding implementation (i.e., in the definition of module `PairMod`), whereas exported classes must be defined in the implementation and are the class which are visible from the outside (we call them *exported* or also *public* in analogy with Java packages). The classes defined in the implementation which are not exported are local to the implementation.

Intuitively, `PairMod` is a generic module which takes as parameter a class called `Elem` and returns a class called `Pair`: in other words, `PairMod` is equivalent to a generic class in Pizza or GJ [28, 10] or to a functor in ML [27]. However, note that in JAVAMOD instances of `PairMod` are not obtained by functional application (as happens in Pizza, GJ and ML), but rather by merging with other modules (see the paragraph devoted to the *merge* operator below), hence mutual dependencies can be expressed.

We require the set of the names of the imported classes to be disjoint from the set of the names of the (both public and non public) classes declared in the body of the module. As happens for Java packages, it is possible to access public classes of a module through the dot notation; however, this is correct only for non parametric modules (i.e., modules with no imported classes).

Each class in the import/export lists must be associated with a *class type*; a class type is a collection of field declarations and method and constructor headers[3][21]. Note that class types could be not expressed as Java interfaces, which only may contain instance method headers.

---

[3] In general, module interfaces can contain also information about the class hierarchy, as shown in Sect.3; this is not the case for the module `PairMod` where both `Elem` and `Pair` implicitly extend `Object`.

Class types are introduced in JAVAMOD for allowing separate type-checking of modules; for instance, the imported class `Elem` is associated with the empty class type, therefore it can be used inside `PairMod` only as an abstract type (in other words, the only information about `Elem` is that `Elem` is a subclass of `Object`.). The definition of class `Pair` must implement the associated type in the export list; more precisely, the exact type of `Pair` that can be inferred from the class definition must be a subtype of the type in the export list of the interface. *Width* class subtyping is allowed, that is a class can have more members than those listed in its exported type, whereas *depth* subtyping is not correct, that is, exported members must keep their exact type, accordingly with the fact that in Java types cannot be changed in overridden methods.

In the example above, the class `Pair` is exported with a proper supertype of its exact type, since the two fields `fst` and `snd` have been omitted; access to these two fields is forbidden outside the module. For this reason, the Java access modifier `public` is redundant for modules in JAVAMOD: members which are listed in the interface are public, whereas members which are omitted in the interface are only visible inside the module, as happens with the package visibility level of Java[4]. Note that all classes mentioned in the class types of the export list must be public; this is a notable difference with Java packages, where a class can be not `public` but still appear as type in public classes.

2.2   Module Expressions

We illustrate now the third main difference with Java packages. JAVAMOD supports module expressions in the sense that it is possible to write complex expressions denoting structured modules, even though modules are not first class values. Such expressions are built on top of basic modules by means of three operators for combining modules: merge, hiding and renaming.

Merge The merge operator allows the user to combine together two modules. Informally speaking, let M_1 and M_2 be two basic modules which are type compatible for merging (see the next paragraph); then their merge is equivalent to a basic module M where each imported class of M_1 matching a public class C of M_2 has been bound to C and conversely. The imported classes of M are those of M_1 and M_2 that do not match any public class, whereas the public (resp. non public) classes are the public (resp. non public) classes of M_1 and M_2.

Type compatibility is defined as follows: the sets of public classes of M_1 and M_2 must be disjoint[5] in order to avoid name clashes; furthermore, the types of classes imported in both M_1 and M_2 must match. Finally, the imported classes of M_1 and M_2 matching the name of a public class C in the other module must also match the type of C. When merging two modules, matching between class types must be exact; see Sect.3 for more details about this choice.

---

[4] For reasons of space and simplicity in this paper we do not consider the `private` and `protected` access modifiers.

[5] Note that this requirement does not apply to non public classes, where accidental name clashes can be resolved by α-renaming [5].

As informally described above, merge is not only an operator for putting modules together, but also for instantiating imported classes. For example, let us consider the following module, where the class Elem represents points:

```
interface ElemMod;
export
 Elem:{}

module ElemMod;
class Elem{
    int x,y;
    void move(int dx,int dy){
      x=x+dx;
      y=y+dy;
    }
}
```

Then we can define

```
interface LineMod;
export
 Elem:{}
 Pair:{
  Pair(Elem fst,Elem snd);
  void set(Elem newfst,Elem newsnd);
  Elem fst();
  Elem snd();
 }

module LineMod;
PairMod merge ElemMod;
```

The module LineMod defines the two public classes Pair and Elem and imports no classes. The class Elem represents points, and is exported with the empty type, whereas the class Pair represents pairs of points which determine a line.

We turn now to consider a more meaningful example showing how it is possible in JavaMod to split mutually recursive data types into different modules. To this aim, consider the following module implementing trees:

```
interface TreeMod;
import
 Forest:{
   Forest();
   Forest add(Tree t);
   boolean equals(Forest f);
 }
```

```
  Node:{boolean equals(Node e);}
 export
  Tree:{
   Tree(Node e);
   Tree addChild(Tree t);
   boolean equals(Tree t);
  }

module TreeMod;
class Tree {
 Node root;
 Forest children;
 Tree(Node e){this(e,new Forest());}
 Tree(Node e, Forest f){ root=e; children=f;}
 Tree addChild(Tree t){ return new Tree(root,children.add(t));}
 boolean equals(Tree t){
  return root.equals(t.root) && children.equals(t.children);
 }
}
```

The module TreeMod provides a highly generic implementation for trees since it is parametric in both the data type forest representing the children of a given tree and the type of the elements labelling the nodes. The constructor Tree(Node e) corresponds to the ability of creating trees with a single node and, therefore, no children.

Assume now to have a module ForestMod implementing forests as lists defined as follows:

```
interface ForestMod;
import
 Tree:{
   Tree(Node e);
   Tree addChild(Tree t);
   boolean equals(Tree t);
 }
 Node:{boolean equals(Node e);}
export
 Forest:{
  Forest();
  Forest add(Tree e);
  boolean equals(Forest f);
 }

module ForestMod;
class Forest {
  Tree tree;
```

```
Forest next;
Forest(){}
Forest(Tree tree, Forest next){
  this.tree=tree;
  this.next=next;
}
Forest add(Tree t){
  return new Forest(t,this);
}
boolean equals(Forest f){
  return tree.equals(f.tree) && next.equals(f.next)
}
}
```

The module ForestMod is independent of the implementation of the data type tree. Note that the default constructor Forest() is visible from the outside, whereas the visibility of the constructor Forest(Tree tree, Forest next) is limited to the module.

We can now bind the imported class Tree of ForestMod to the corresponding public class of TreeMod and, conversely, bind the imported class Forest of TreeMod to the corresponding public class of ForestMod.

```
interface TreeInst;
...
```

```
module TreeInst;
TreeMod merge ForestMod;
```

The module TreeInst we obtain is still parametric in the type of the labels represented by the two imported classes Node in TreeMod and ForestMod which are shared in TreeInst; however, the implementation for the type forest has been fixed. As a matter of fact we have combined together two generic types to produce two mutually recursive types, following a schema rather natural and intuitive. Note that this is much more than the simple possibility offered in Java of defining mutually recursive classes (even in different packages), since in this case the dependency is *fixed* once for all, hence it is impossible to use two different instances of TreeMod in the same program (for instance, if we need to deal with both integer labelled and string labelled trees). On the other side, existing languages with true module systems, like ML, usually do not support recursive modules [15].

Renaming The renaming operator allows a bijective renaming of the exported classes of a given module. Such an operation is useful especially to solve name clashes or to bind imported classes when merging two modules.

For example, a module implementing the data type of points is unlikely to have the interface of the module ElemMod previously defined, but it is more reasonable to think of ElemMod as being obtained by renaming a module PointMod with the following interface:

```
interface PointMod;
export
 Point:{}
```

Therefore, `ElemMod` could be more reasonably defined by:

```
interface ElemMod;
 ...
```

```
module ElemMod;
PointMod rename Point to Elem;
```

We can take advantage of the renaming operator also for giving a more meaningful name to the class `Pair` obtained by merging `PairMod` with `ElemMod`:

```
module LineMod;
(PairMod merge ElemMod) rename Elem to Point, Pair to Line;
```

In this way, the interface of `LineMod` has been changed into:

```
interface LineMod;
export
Point:{}
Line:{
  Line(Point fst,Point snd);
  void set(Point newfst,Point newsnd);
  Point fst(); Point snd();}
```

Hiding Hiding is a standard module operator used for abstracting implementation details. Roughly speaking, hiding in JAVAMOD corresponds to signature matching in ML [27] and is based on the notion of *subtyping* between interfaces. More formally, a module interface I_1 is a subtype of a module interface I_2 iff:

- the set of imported classes of I_1 is included in the set of imported classes of I_2 (width subtyping for imported classes);
- the set of exported classes of I_2 is included in the set of exported classes of I_1 (width subtyping for exported classes);
- if the imported class C has type $C\tau$ in I_1 and $C\tau'$ in I_2, then $C\tau'$ must be a subtype $C\tau$ (depth subtyping for imported classes);
- if the exported class C has type $C\tau$ in I_1 and $C\tau'$ in I_2, then $C\tau$ must be a subtype $C\tau'$ (depth subtyping for exported classes).

Subtyping between class types corresponds to the usual width subtyping between record types, as formalized in Sect.4.2.

According to this definition of subtyping, by means of the hiding operator it is possible either to completely hide a public class (i.e., make it non public) or to only hide some of its members (fields, methods and constructors). This operator is particularly useful in conjunction with the merge operator. Consider, for instance, the more realistic situation where the previously mentioned module `PointMod` has the following interface:

```
interface PointMod;
export
 Point:{void move(int dx,int dy);}
```

Then the module `ElemMod` obtained by renaming `Point` by `Elem` in `PointMod` could no longer be correctly merged with the module `PairMod` since, accordingly to the type rule for merge, the type of `Elem` in `PairMod` must coincide with the type of `Elem` in `ElemMod`. However, we can solve this problem by means of the hiding operator:

```
interface LineMod;
...
module LineMod;
PairMod merge (ElemMod show {export Elem:{}});
```

The expression `ElemMod show {export Elem:{}}` corresponds to hide the method `move` of the class `Elem` in the module `ElemMod`; in other words, the module `ElemMod` has been coerced to an interface where `Elem` has the empty type.

We conclude this section by briefly discussing some other renaming/hiding mechanisms which are not considered in this paper. A useful possibility would be that of renaming class members, for instance methods. However, this would be fairly more core-dependent than the `show` operator. On the contrary, a complementary hiding operator specifying what is hidden instead of what is visible and the possibility of coercing a module to an existing named module interface are standard possible extensions.

3   An Open Issue: Extending Imported Classes

In Sect.2 we have presented some interesting features of JavaMod by means of several examples; in particular, we have shown that JavaMod supports generic classes and the ability of splitting mutually recursive data types in different modules.

This section is devoted to another interesting feature: mixin classes. A mixin class does not extend a fixed superclass, but simply specifies the set of fields and methods a generic superclass should provide. In this way, the same mixin can be instantiated on many superclasses, producing different subclasses, thus avoiding code duplication and largely improving modularity and reuse. Several papers have investigated mixins and their usefulness (see, for instance, [20, 16, 7, 1, 14]).

The expressive power of mixins can be recovered in JavaMod, since classes defined in a module can extend imported classes. As an example, consider the definition of the following module `OrdPairMod`:

```
interface OrdPairMod;
import
 Elem:{boolean less(Elem e);}
```

```
Pair:{Pair(Elem fst,Elem snd);
       void set(Elem newfst,Elem newsnd);
       Elem fst(); Elem snd();}
export
 OrdPair:{OrdPair(Elem fst,Elem snd);
          void set(Elem newfst,Elem newsnd);
          Elem fst(); Elem snd(); void ord();}

module OrdPairMod;
class OrdPair extends Pair{
 OrdPair(Elem fst,Elem snd){
  super(fst,snd);
 }
 void ord(){
  if (snd().less(fst())) set(snd(),fst());
 }
}
```

The class `OrdPair` can be regarded as a both generic and mixin class, so that we would be tempted to call it a *generic mixin*; indeed, `OrdPair` can be considered a mixin class since it extends the imported class `Pair`, hence, in principle, it can be instantiated on different superclasses, yielding different subclasses. On the other hand, `Pair` is generic in `Elem` and, therefore, the same holds for `OrdPair`.

We can now instantiate the generic mixin represented by `OrdPair` by merging the module `OrdPairMod` with the module `PairMod` defined in Sect.2. By definition of the merge operator, the resulting module still has an imported class, `Elem`; in other words, we have instantiated `OrdPairMod` on a generic class and, hence, as a result, we have obtained another generic class.

Until now everything seems to work fine; however, the ability of extending imported classes introduces some challenging issues involving both the type system and the semantics of the language.

A first problem that has to be considered is the possibility of introducing cycles in the inheritance hierarchy; it is not hard to figure out a possible scenario where a user tries to merge together two modules M1 and M2, the former defining a public class B which extends an imported class A, the latter defining a public class A which extends an imported class B. Clearly, in this case the semantics of the resulting mixin is not well-defined, therefore these kinds of situation should be statically avoided by considering ill-typed the expression M1 merge M2. In order to do this, information about the inheritance hierarchy must be introduced in the module interfaces.

For example, the interface of the module `OrdPairMod` should be changed as follows:

```
interface OrdPairMod;
import
 Elem:{boolean less(Elem e);}
 Pair:{Pair(Elem fst,Elem snd);
```

```
        void set(Elem newfst,Elem newsnd);
        Elem fst(); Elem snd();}
export
 OrdPair:extends+ Pair
        {OrdPair(Elem fst,Elem snd);
         void set(Elem newfst,Elem newsnd);
         Elem fst(); Elem snd(); void ord();}
```

In other words, besides the class type of OrdPair, the interface of OrdPairMod must expose also the imported superclass of OrdPair. We use the keyword extends+ rather than extends, since the type information C extends+ C' does not imply that C is a direct subclass of C'; indeed, if C directly extends C'' which, in turns, directly extends C' and C is public, C'' is not public and C' is imported, than the needed information is that C is a subclass of C'.

We can better formalize the considerations above as follows; for each public class C of a given module M, the following mutually exclusive kinds of information about the inheritance hierarchy can be found in the interface of M:

- C extends+ C', where C' is a imported class of M. This information is essential for avoiding cycles in the inheritance hierarchy when merging M with other modules. Note that removal of this information from the interface is unsafe since it can lead to undetected cycles. Similar considerations apply also when C extends a class $M'.C'$ of another module M' (see Sect.4.2).
- C extends+ C', where C' is a public class of M. This information is not needed for avoiding cycles, but it is useful for type-checking expressions, since we can rely on the information that C is a subtype of C'. This information can be safely hidden. For sake of simplicity we do not consider this possibility in the full formalization of the language given in Sect.4.2.
- No hierarchy information. This implicitly means that C extends+ Object.

Note that in principle we could specify inherited classes not only for public but also for imported classes; for instance, it could be useful to specify that a certain imported class C extends another imported class C'. Despite its obvious utility, for sake of simplicity here we do not consider this further feature whose introduction in the language would not be trivial.

As a final remark, note that information about the class hierarchy of a given module can be easily inferred by the compiler.

A second major problem related to the extension of imported classes consists in the definition of matching between class types when imported classes are instantiated with public classes (i.e., when merging modules in JAVAMOD). As already stated in Sect.2, in this case we require type matching between imported and public classes to be exact; this seems to be quite a strict constraint, since at first glance one would be tempted to use the structural subtyping relation $\sqsubseteq$ between class types used for the hiding operator. Unfortunately, this would lead to type inconsistencies. To see this, assume to merge the module OrdPairMod with another module AnotherMod defining a public class Pair having the following type:

```
{Pair(Elem fst,Elem snd);
 void set(Elem newfst,Elem newsnd);
 Elem fst(); Elem snd();
 Pair ord();
}
```

According to the definition of ⊑, the type of `Pair` in `AnotherMod` is a subtype of the type of `Pair` in `OrdPairMod`. But, if we merge the two modules together, then we obtain a type inconsistency since the method `Pair ord()` in `Pair` cannot be correctly overridden by the method `void ord()` in `OrdPair`, since the return types are not compatible[6]. A different kind of problem arises if `Pair` has a method `void ord()`; in this case, there is no type inconsistency, since the method *can* be correctly overridden by the method `void ord()` in `OrdPair`, but this overriding is *unexpected*, in the sense that it has not been planned by the designer of the module `OrdPairMod`. Hence, one can wonder whether in this case it is sensible to keep standard semantics (that is, the method in `OrdPair` overrides that in `Pair`) or to define an alternative semantics preventing this unwanted effect. Note that this problem is not peculiar of Java, but common to every typed object-oriented language; however, in Java also overloading is a source of problems, since the extension of an imported class may introduce unwanted method overloading and change the overloading resolution of method calls in the body of the subclasses.

In literature several proposals for solving this problem can be found; we refer to Sect.5 for a survey. However, the use of subtyping on class types in conjunction with parametric subclasses seems to be still an open issue.

The solution presented in this paper gives up to use subtyping on class types, forcing exact type matching. However, this rule is not so restrictive as it may seem, since, when possible, exact matching can be obtained through the hiding operator. For example, before merging `AnotherMod` with `OrdPairMod`, it is possible to hide the method `Pair ord()` of class `Pair` in `AnotherMod`, so that it is not visible in the subclass `OrdPair` and no conflicts arise. This approach has the main advantage of being simple from the type-theoretical point of view; also the semantics is intuitively clear, even though its formalization requires some care. The basic problem is that a call `p.ord()` where p has dynamic type `OrdPair` must invoke the method in `Pair` rather than that in `OrdPair` in a context where the static type of the receiver is `Pair` and this method is visible, analogously to what happens for `private` methods in Java; see [5] for the technical solution. A choice based on hiding extra-methods is also taken in [17, 18].

An alternative solution to hiding methods can be provided by a mechanism for renaming methods, as supported, for instance, by Eiffel [26].

Another possible solution consists in avoiding to hide the extra-members of classes used for instantiating imported classes in favor of a more powerful (but also complex) type system being able to reject all the instantiations which would lead to the inconsistencies mentioned above. Indeed, in practice our approach

---

[6] More precisely, in Java the return type of an overridden method cannot be changed at all.

can be considered not so adequate from the point of view of software reuse. Reconsider, for example, the modules PointMod and LineMod as defined in the paragraph devoted to the hiding operator in Sect.2. Since the method move of class Point is not visible in the class Line of LineMod, we fail to have a real implementation of lines, since we cannot invoke the point-specific method move upon the two components fst and snd of a line.

A type system able to solve this problem has not been fully investigated yet, though a solution following the principle of forbidding unwanted interferences can be found in [7, 1]. This corresponds to the simplified situation where each imported superclass is extended by exactly one subclass. However, the general problem arising when the language supports both parametric modules and classes (as in JavaMod) and not simply mixin classes turns out to be more challenging.

4   Type-Checking Modules in JavaMod

In this section we make some considerations on how a compiler for JavaMod should work in practice and we specify a type system which formalizes the static semantics of the language. We refer to [5] for the formal definition of the dynamic semantics of JavaMod. However, note that our concern here is mainly on type-checking, therefore we avoid any consideration on code generation issues, even though this topic is far from being simple and deserves a deep investigation (see the Conclusion).

We first give an idea of how a compiler for JavaMod could be designed in practice, and then turn to specify a type system for it.

4.1   A Compiler for JavaMod

The first issue we need to address is how a module can be defined in practice. As already explained in Sect.2, we take the rather classical ADT approach which requires the notion of module interface and implementation to be strongly separated. Therefore, the definition of a module M is split into at least two files: the *interface* (containing the type of M visible to all other modules) and the *implementation* file (containing the source code for M).

Note that the interface file is not produced by the compiler, but must be provided by the programmer, therefore the compilation for M fails if no interface file for M is available. The interface file is unique for any module; on the contrary, the implementation of a basic module M can be split in several files each of them containing the declaration of a subset of the classes of M. Therefore, basic modules can be structured in the same way as packages. Finally, structured modules (i.e., those built on top of basic modules) are defined by a unique implementation file containing the corresponding module expression.

We can adopt the same name conventions of Java packages: the notation $M.C$ is used for referring to a class C defined in another module M; if no ambiguities arise, it is possible to use the import directive in order to omit M.

We specify now how the compiler for JAVAMOD is expected to behave. First of all, the user should be able to invoke compilation on a given module M (for instance, by mentioning the interface file or one of the implementation files of M); the compilation fails if the interface or the implementation for M are not available. Otherwise, the source code of M is parsed and type-checked; the compilation is *separate* in the sense that the compilation of M can be accomplished without any need for the source code of the modules M depends on. In most cases, the compiler looks only for the interface files of the modules mentioned in M, but there are cases where also a check of the existence of some binary file is required, in order to avoid mutually recursive definition of modules whose semantics would be undefined.

For instance, consider the following two module definitions:

```
module M1;
M2 rename C1 to C2;
```

```
module M2;
M1 rename C2 to C1;
```

Clearly, M1 and M2 have no semantics, therefore we expect the compilation of these two modules to fail. Indeed, in order to avoid these kinds of cycles, the compiler must check that if module M1 is defined in terms of M2, then M2 must be compiled prior to M1; an effective way to enforce this compilation order is to require the presence of the binary of M2 for successfully compiling M1. Following this approach it is not possible to successfully compile the two modules defined above (see the type system defined in Sect.4.2).Note that this checking could be performed at the source level if all sources were available, but here we are interested in a separate compilation framework where each module can be type-checked without looking at (and even in absence of) the code of other modules.

On the other hand, note that there are some other kinds of mutual dependencies which are safe and should not been rejected by the compiler. For instance, module interfaces can be mutually recursive, as in the following example:

```
interface M1;
...
export
 C : { M2.C m();}
...
```

```
interface M2;
...
export
C : { M1.C m();}
...
```

Basic module definitions can be mutually recursive as well:

```
module M1;
...
 class C { ... new M2.C()...}

module M2;
...
 class C{ ... new M1.C()...}
```

These examples are easily recognized as safe by the compiler, since in these cases module M1 (and M2 too) does not refer to the whole module M2 (resp. M1), but rather to a single member of its (for more details, see Sect.4.2).

If all required interface and binary files are present, then the compiler can type-check the code of M. Finally, if the source code of M turns out to be statically correct, then the compiler needs to check whether the definition of M is really an implementation of the corresponding interface specified by the user (this is formally captured by a subtyping relation between module types, see Sect.4.2).

4.2   A Type System for JavaMod

The abstract syntax and the types for JAVAMOD are given in Fig.1. For reasons of space, we focus only on modules and omit all definitions and rules related to the core language (see [13, 23, 1] for the definitions of type systems for subsets of Java closely related to the core language of JAVAMOD).

$$
\begin{array}{lll}
MD ::= & \textbf{module } M; \; ME & \text{(module declaration)} \\
ME ::= & M & | \quad \text{(module name)} \\
 & CD_j^{j \in J} & | \quad \text{(basic module)} \\
 & ME_1 \textbf{ merge } ME_2 & | \quad \text{(merge)} \\
 & ME \textbf{ rename } C_1 \textbf{ to } C_2 & | \quad \text{(renaming)} \\
 & ME \textbf{ show } M\tau & \text{(hiding)} \\
M\tau ::= & C_i{:}C\tau_i{}^{i \in I} \to C_j{:}\widehat{C\tau}_j^{\,j \in J} & \text{(module type)} \\
\widehat{C\tau} ::= & \textbf{extends+}\widehat{C} \; C\tau \mid C\tau & \text{(extended class type)} \\
C\tau ::= & \{\tau_i \; f_i^{i \in I} \; \tau_j \; m_j(\bar{\tau}_j)^{j \in J} \; C(\bar{\tau}_l)^{l \in L}\} & \text{(class type)} \\
\widehat{C} ::= & C \mid M.C & \text{(extended class name)} \\
\tau ::= & \widehat{C} & \text{(Java type)} \\
\bar{\tau} ::= & \tau_i^{i \in I} & \text{(arguments type)} \\
CD ::= & \textbf{class } C \dots & \text{(class declaration)} \\
\vdots
\end{array}
$$

Fig. 1. Abstract syntax and types of JAVAMOD.

A module declaration consists of a module name and a module expression. Module expressions are inductively defined on top of module names and basic modules (which are collections of class declarations) by means of the three operators of merge, renaming and hiding. Module declarations and expressions coincide with those informally introduced in Sect.2, except for one difference: renaming is restricted to a single class name. However, this restriction is minimal, since an expression like M `rename A to B, C to D` can be considered as a syntactic abbreviation for M `rename A to B rename C to D`.

Module types specify two sets of imported and exported classes; the notation $C_i{:}C\tau_i{}^{i \in I}$ denotes the map associating with each class C_i the type $C\tau_i$ (for any $i \in I$), hence it is well-formed even in case of repetitions, but not when classes are overloaded. Imported classes are associated with *class types*, i.e. types where no superclass is specified (recall from Sect.3 that this kind of information is essential only for exported classes). Class types contain field names with the corresponding types, method names with the corresponding headers (result and arguments type) and constructor headers (class name and arguments type). On the contrary, an *extended class type* is a class type which may contain also a reference to a superclass (denoted by an *extended class name*); exported classes are associated with extended class types, hence for them it is possible to derive information about their ancestors from the module type.

As already explained, an extended class name of the form $M.C$ is used inside a module M' for referring to a class C defined in another module M. For sake of simplicity, we do not model the `import` directive so classes defined in other modules can be mentioned only by using their extended name. Finally, note that Java types and extended class names coincide, since we have omitted interfaces.

The typing rules for module declarations and expressions are defined in Fig.2.

The first typing rule defines well-formed module declarations. The main judgment $\Gamma \vdash MD \diamond$ has the following meaning: the module declaration MD is statically correct in the module environment Γ. A module environment Γ is a sequence of the form $M_i{:}{<}M\tau_i, K_i{>}^{i \in I}$ associating a module type $M\tau_i$ and a *compilation flag* K_i with each module name M_i ($i \in I$). The types $M\tau_i$ correspond to the interface files associated with each module M_i. The compilation flag K_i is true if and only if M_i has already been compiled (i.e., its binary file is available to the compiler); as previously explained, compilation flags are used for avoiding cycles in the module expressions (see also the comments on the typing rules below). If $\Gamma = M_i{:}{<}M\tau_i, K_i{>}^{i \in I}$, then Γ_T and Γ_C denote $M_i{:}M\tau_i{}^{i \in I}$ and $M_i{:}K_i{}^{i \in I}$, respectively; furthermore, the expression $\Gamma_T(M)$ denotes $M\tau$ if $M{:}M\tau$ is in Γ_T, is undefined otherwise. An analogous notation is used for Γ_C.

The type-checking of M succeeds if the environment Γ is well-defined (judgment $\vdash \Gamma \diamond$, defined in Fig.3), the method expression ME is well-typed (judgment $\Gamma; M \vdash ME{:}M\tau'$) and has a module type $M\tau'$ which is a subtype of the interface $M\tau$ of M declared by the user (judgment $\Gamma \vdash M\tau' \sqsubseteq_M M\tau$, defined in Fig.4). This last requirement ensures that the declaration for M really implements its interface specified in the environment Γ.

$$\dfrac{\begin{array}{c} \vdash \Gamma \diamond \\ \Gamma; M \vdash ME{:}M\tau' \\ \Gamma \vdash M\tau' \sqsubseteq_M M\tau \end{array}}{\Gamma \vdash \texttt{module } M \texttt{ is } ME \diamond} \quad \Gamma_T(M) = M\tau$$

$$\dfrac{}{\Gamma; M' \vdash M{:}M\tau} \quad \dfrac{\Gamma_C(M)}{\Gamma_T(M) = M\tau}$$

$$\dfrac{\Gamma; M \vdash CD_j{:}{<}C_j, \widehat{C\tau_j}{>} \ \forall j \in J}{\Gamma; M \vdash CD_j^{j \in J}{:}C_i{:}C\tau_i{}^{i \in I} \to C_j{:}\widehat{C\tau_j}^{j \in J}} \quad \Gamma_T(M) = C_i{:}C\tau_i{}^{i \in I} \to C_l{:}\widehat{C\tau_l}^{l \in L}$$

$$\dfrac{\begin{array}{c} \Gamma; M \vdash ME_1{:}(C_i{:}C\tau_i{}^{i \in I_1}, C_b{:}C\tau_b{}^{b \in B_1} \to C_j{:}\widehat{C\tau_j}^{j \in J_1}, C_b{:}\widehat{C\tau_b}^{b \in B_2}) \\ \Gamma; M \vdash ME_2{:}(C_i{:}C\tau_i{}^{i \in I_2}, C_b{:}C\tau_b{}^{b \in B_2} \to C_j{:}\widehat{C\tau_j}^{j \in J_2}, C_b{:}\widehat{C\tau_b}^{b \in B_1}) \\ \Gamma \vdash \widehat{C\tau_i} \lhd C\tau_i \ \forall i \in B_1 \cup B_2 \end{array}}{\Gamma; M \vdash ME_1 \texttt{ merge } ME_2{:}(C_i{:}C\tau_i{}^{i \in I_1 \cup I_2} \to C_j{:}\widehat{C\tau_j}^{j \in J_1 \cup B_2}, C_j{:}\widehat{C\tau_j}^{j \in J_2 \cup B_1})} \quad (*)$$

$(*) \ \forall i, j \in I_1 \cup I_2 \ C_i = C_j \implies C\tau_i = C\tau_j$

$$\dfrac{\Gamma; M \vdash ME{:}M\tau}{\Gamma; M \vdash ME \texttt{ rename } C_k \texttt{ to } C_l {:}M\tau[C_l/C_k]} \quad \begin{array}{c} M\tau = C_i{:}C\tau_i{}^{i \in I} \to C_j{:}\widehat{C\tau_j}^{j \in J} \\ k \in J, l \notin I \cup J \end{array}$$

$$\dfrac{\begin{array}{c} \Gamma; M \vdash ME{:}M\tau' \\ \Gamma; M \vdash M\tau \diamond \\ \Gamma \vdash M\tau' \sqsubseteq_M M\tau \end{array}}{\Gamma \vdash ME \texttt{ show } M\tau{:}M\tau}$$

Fig. 2. Typing rules for module declarations and expressions

The following typing rules define well-formed module expressions.

The rule for module names is straightforward; note that type-checking succeeds only if M has been already compiled, so that it is not possible to type-check mutually recursive module expressions, as already explained in Sect.4.1.

The typing rule for basic module depends on the core level judgment $\Gamma; M \vdash CD{:}{<}C, \widehat{C\tau}{>}$ used for typing class declarations, which is not defined here but assumed to correspond to some of the existing formalization of the Java type system (see, e.g., [13]). For any correct class declaration CD this judgment returns the name C and the extended class type of the class defined by CD with all members, either inherited or declared in C. The environment Γ and the module name M are used for retrieving information about classes defined in other modules and in M, respectively. The side condition is only used for retrieving the imported classes of the module. Note that the exported classes inferred by the rule may be different from those associated with M in the module environment.

In the rule for the `merge` operator, the sets of indexes B_1 and B_2 correspond to the imported classes of M_1 and M_2, respectively, which are bound in the merge process while I_1 and I_2 correspond to those which are not bound; J_1 and

J_2 correspond to unbound exported classes. The notation $C_i:C\tau_i^{i\in I}$, $C_j:C\tau_j^{j\in J}$ denotes disjoint union of maps, hence is well-formed only when $\{C_i \mid i \in I\}\cap\{C_j \mid j \in J\} = \emptyset$. The rule can be instantiated under the implicit side conditions that all disjoint unions are well-defined; for instance the way is written the resulting type of the expression ME_1 merge ME_2 ensures that exported classes do not conflict. The only explicit side condition ensures that imported classes are not overloaded in the resulting module. The third premise ensures that for each class which is bound the exported type matches the imported type (judgment $\Gamma \vdash \widehat{C\tau_i} \lhd C\tau_i$ defined in Fig.4).

The side conditions for the **renaming** operator ensure that only exported classes can be renamed and that the renaming is bijective. The notation $M\tau[C_l/C_k]$ denotes the type obtained by renaming C_k by C_l in $M\tau$.

The rule for hiding is straightforward (see Fig.4 for the definition of the subtyping relation $\sqsubseteq_M$).

Fig.3 contains the rules for well-defined environments and types.

A module environment $M_i:<M\tau_i, K_i>^{i\in I}$ is well-defined if for every $i \in I$, the module type $M\tau_i$ is well-defined in the same environment (recall that module types can be mutually dependent) and in the module M, if module names are not overloaded (first side condition) and there are no cycles in the inheritance hierarchy involving classes belonging to different modules (the straightforward definition of the auxiliary function $noCycles$ has been omitted).

A module type $M\tau$ is well-defined in a module environment Γ and in a module M ($\Gamma; M \vdash M\tau \diamond$) if (first and second hypothesis) the (extended) class type of every imported/exported class C is well-defined in the same environment and module and in the class C (needed for checking the correctness of constructor headers), if imported and exported classes are disjoint (first side-condition) and imported/exported class names are not overloaded (second and third side-condition).

An extended class type $\widehat{C\tau}$ is well-defined in a module environment Γ, a module M and a class C ($\Gamma; M; C \vdash \widehat{C\tau} \diamond$), if its corresponding extended class name is well-defined in the same environment and module (first hypothesis) and if its corresponding class type is well-defined in the same environment, module and class (second hypothesis). Note that for sake of simplicity, the extended class name of the ancestor class can only denote either an exported class of another module or an imported class of M (see the side-conditions and the comments below on well-defined extended class names); this corresponds to maintain only the minimal information needed for avoiding cycles in the inheritance graph (recall the considerations in Sect.3).

A class type $C\tau$ is well-defined in a module environment Γ, a module M and a class C ($\Gamma; M; C \vdash C\tau \diamond$), if fields and methods are not overloaded[7] (first and second side conditions) and if all the types and arguments types mentioned in $C\tau$ are well-defined in the same environment and module and w.r.t. all classes imported/exported in M (first and second hypothesis).

---

[7] For simplicity we avoid method overloading of Java.

$$\frac{M_i:<M\tau_i, K_i>^{i\in I}; \; M_i \vdash M\tau_i \diamond \; \forall i \in I}{\vdash M_i:<M\tau_i, K_i>^{i\in I} \diamond} \quad \begin{array}{l} \forall i,j \in I \; M_i = M_j \implies M\tau_i = M\tau_j, K_i = K_j \\ noCycles(M_i:M\tau_i^{i\in I}) \end{array}$$

$$\frac{\begin{array}{c} \Gamma; M; C_i \vdash C\tau_i \diamond \; \forall i \in I \\ \Gamma; M; C_i \vdash \widehat{C}\tau_j \diamond \; \forall j \in J \end{array}}{\Gamma; M \vdash C_i:C\tau_i^{i\in I} \to C_j:\widehat{C}\tau_j^{j\in J} \diamond} \quad \begin{array}{l} C_i^{i\in I} \cap C_j^{j\in J} = \emptyset \\ \forall i,j \in I \; C_i = C_j \implies C\tau_i = C\tau_j \\ \forall i,j \in J \; C_i = C_j \implies \widehat{C}\tau_i = \widehat{C}\tau_j \end{array}$$

$$\frac{\dfrac{\Gamma; M; \vdash \widehat{C} \diamond}{\Gamma; M; C \vdash C\tau \diamond}}{\Gamma; M; C \vdash \text{extends+}\widehat{C}\, C\tau \diamond} \quad \begin{array}{l} \Gamma_T(M) = C_i:C\tau_i^{i\in I} \to C_j:\widehat{C}\tau_j^{j\in J} \\ (\widehat{C} = M.C_k \vee \widehat{C} = C_k) \implies k \in I \end{array}$$

$$\frac{\begin{array}{c} \Gamma; M \vdash \tau_i \diamond \; \forall i \in I \cup J \\ \Gamma; M \vdash \bar{\tau}_i \diamond \; \forall i \in J \cup L \end{array}}{\Gamma; M; C \vdash \{\tau_i\, f_i^{i\in I}\; \tau_j\, m_j(\bar{\tau}_j)^{j\in J}\; C(\bar{\tau}_l)^{l\in L}\} \diamond} \quad \begin{array}{l} \Gamma_T(M) = C_i:C\tau_i^{i\in I} \to C_j:\widehat{C}\tau_j^{j\in J} \\ \forall i,j \in I \; f_i = f_j \implies i = j \\ \forall i,j \in J \; m_i = m_j \implies i = j \end{array}$$

$$\frac{}{\Gamma; M \vdash C_k \diamond} \quad \begin{array}{l} \Gamma_T(M) = C_i:C\tau_i^{i\in I} \to C_j:\widehat{C}\tau_j^{j\in J} \\ k \in I \cup J \end{array}$$

$$\frac{}{\Gamma; M \vdash M.C_k \diamond} \quad \begin{array}{l} \Gamma_T(M) = C_i:C\tau_i^{i\in I} \to C_j:\widehat{C}\tau_j^{j\in J} \\ k \in I \cup J \end{array}$$

$$\frac{}{\Gamma; M' \vdash M.C_k \diamond} \quad \begin{array}{l} M' \neq M \\ \Gamma_T(M) = \epsilon \to C_j:\widehat{C}\tau_j^{j\in J} \\ k \in J \end{array}$$

$$\frac{\Gamma; M \vdash \tau_j \diamond \; \forall j \in J}{\Gamma; M \vdash \tau_j^{j\in J} \diamond}$$

Fig. 3. Well-defined environments and types

An extended class name $\widehat{C}$ is well-defined in a class environment Γ and a module M, if $\widehat{C}$ refers either to one of the classes in $C_i^{i\in I\cup J}$ (either using the plain name, in the first rule, or prefixing the name of M, in the second rule) or to an exported class of another module which has no imported classes (third rule).

The typing rule for arguments types is straightforward.

Finally, Fig.4 contains the rules defining the matching and the subtyping relation between (extended) class types and the subtyping relation between module types.

As already stated, in our approach matching is exact (first two rules); note that the extended class name in extended class types is simply ignored.

Subtyping on module types and on (extended) class types are clearly structural.

The rule for module types allows both *width* and *depth* subtyping: in a subtype there can be more exported classes and less imported classes w.r.t. the supertype (width subtyping), whereas the types of the exported classes already present in the supertype can be refined and the types of the imported classes already present in the supertype can be less specific (depth subtyping). Note the contravariance between imported and exported classes.

The rule for extended class types expresses the fact that the information about the ancestor class cannot be forgotten via subsumption.

The rule for class types allows width but not depth subtyping: in a subtype there can be some additional field/method/constructor, but the types of the members already present in the supertype cannot change.

$$\frac{\Gamma \vdash C\tau \lhd C\tau'}{\Gamma \vdash \mathtt{extends+}\widehat{C}\, C\tau \lhd C\tau'}$$

$$\frac{}{\Gamma \vdash C\tau \lhd C\tau}$$

$$\frac{\begin{array}{c}\Gamma \vdash C\tau'_i \sqsubseteq_C C\tau_i \ \forall i \in I \\ \Gamma \vdash \widehat{C\tau}_j \sqsubseteq_C \widehat{C\tau}'_j \ \forall j \in J'\end{array}}{\Gamma \vdash C_i{:}C\tau_i{}^{i\in I} \to C_j{:}\widehat{C\tau}_j{}^{j\in J} \sqsubseteq_M C_i{:}C\tau'_i{}^{i\in I'} \to C_j{:}\widehat{C\tau}'_j{}^{j\in J'}} \quad \begin{array}{c} I \subseteq I' \\ J' \subseteq J \end{array}$$

$$\frac{\Gamma \vdash C\tau \sqsubseteq_C C\tau'}{\Gamma \vdash \mathtt{extends+}\widehat{C}\, C\tau \sqsubseteq_C \mathtt{extends+}\widehat{C}\, C\tau'}$$

$$\frac{}{\Gamma \vdash \{\tau_i \ f_i^{i\in I} \ \tau_j \ m_j(\bar{\tau}_j)^{j\in J} \ C(\bar{\tau}_l)^{l\in L}\} \sqsubseteq_C \{\tau_i \ f_i^{i\in I'} \ \tau_j \ m_j(\bar{\tau}_j)^{j\in J'} \ C(\bar{\tau}_l)^{l\in L'}\}} \quad \begin{array}{c} I' \subseteq I \\ J' \subseteq J \\ L' \subseteq L \end{array}$$

Fig. 4. Matching and subtyping relations

5 Related Work

In this section we discuss other existing proposals for defining module systems on top of object-oriented languages and, more in general, other approaches which tackle the problems mentioned in Sect.3 which arise when extending imported superclasses.

As mentioned in the Introduction, there are no attempts, for what we know, at integrating a true module system with Java, apart from the simple extension of the package system proposed in [6]. There are, however, some proposals of languages including both modules and classes; at our knowledge, these are MzSCHEME [19], OCAML [29] and MOBY [17]. In MzSCHEME the module language provides basic modules (called *units*) and operators which are similar to those of CMS, in particular allowing mutual recursion; however the core language is an object-oriented extension of Scheme, that is, an untyped language. In OCAML and MOBY classes are integrated with an ML-like module system; in other words, the module language is a small applicative language, where the unique module combinator is function application. Moreover, both support *structural* object types[8] (that is, an object type is essentially a record of typed fields and methods, and there is some fixed rule to determine when a type is a subtype of another), following the long tradition in theoretical object calculi.

We analyze now how the above mentioned proposals and others tackle the problems mentioned Sect.3 which arise when extending imported superclasses.

We briefly recall the main issues. As mentioned there, in order to get a correct instantiation of a mixin (a class which extends an imported class) on a given superclass, it is not enough to require this superclass to provide all the components specified in the mixin. Indeed, extra-components of the superclass could interfere with components defined in the mixin. The most typical situation of interference is when the superclass has some extra-method with the same name and type of some method in the mixin, leading to unexpected overriding. However, other similar situations can arise depending on the language; for instance in Java unexpected hiding of fields and static components and unexpected overloading (see [1] for a solution tailored to Java). In all these cases, one has to decide whether the unexpected interference has to be accepted or rejected.

There are basically two approaches to solve this problem.

The first possibility consists in requiring the matching between the expected superclass type in the mixin and the actual type of the superclass to be exact. In this case, extra-components in the superclass have to be either implicitly or explicitly hidden. This approach has the advantage of keeping simpler the type system; the semantics is intuitively clear, even though its formalization requires some care (see the definition of method look-up in [5]).

The second possibility consists in allowing extra-components, checking at instantiation time that there are no interferences. This approach requires a more involved type system: in particular we need more type information in module interfaces (for each imported class the types of all its subclasses inside the module), and a mechanism for type propagation, since the type of a subclass of an imported class depends on the type of the actual superclass.

In MZSCHEME, the core language is untyped, so the problem simply does not arise. The solution of both OCAML and MOBY follows the first approach mentioned above, as this paper does, in the sense that extra-components of the superclass are hidden.

In OCAML the solution is even more restrictive in the sense that there is no way of hiding public methods.

In MOBY, hiding is implicit: application of a parametric module requires that, in the argument, the type of each class is a structural subtype of the expected type, and extra-methods are not part of the resulting type. In dynamic semantics, the fact that method look-up must take into account hiding of inherited methods

---

[8] In [18] both structural and named types are considered.

can be achieved by adding in run-time configurations the information on the static type of the receiver in method calls, as we do in [5], and splitting the association from method names to method bodies in two parts (a dictionary and a method suite).

The above discussed proposals, and this paper as well, all focus on constructing a flexible module system on top of an object-oriented language, without changing the underlying core level. In particular, mixin classes are obtained indirectly as classes whose superclass is an imported class.

Other proposals, on the contrary, add mixin classes as a new construct at the core level.

In [1], an extension of Java with mixin classes is proposed, called Jam (together with an implementation by translation in pure Java). The language has been designed with the main objective in mind to obtain, rather than a new theoretical language, a working and smooth extension of Java.

The interference problems are solved by the second kind of approach. In particular, interferences which would produce an ill-formed Java class are forbidden at instantiation time (for instance, methods with the same name and arguments type but different return type or incompatible `throws` clause).

An analogous solution, in the context of an object calculus, is taken in [7].

In [20], the authors describe MIXEDJAVA, a language with a Java-like syntax where it is only possible to declare either mixins or interfaces, while usual classes are seen as particular mixins which define all the components. In MIXEDJAVA, there are two kinds of mixins, atomic and compound. The declaration of an atomic mixin is of the form `mixin M extends I { ... }` , where I is an interface which specifies the expected superclass type. Instantiation of a mixin on a superclass is generalized to mixin composition. Overriding takes place only for the methods which are explicitly mentioned in the interface I. Other methods in P are neither overridden, nor hidden. The dynamic semantics in this case (that is, if there is a method m in P not mentioned in I which has the same name of a method in M) is rather complex: invocations in either M or P always refer to the corresponding definition in M and P, respectively, while invocations in clients are ambiguous and must be disambiguated by the programmer by an explicit casting.

Finally, we mention another proposal, [11], which tackles the interference problem at the level of objects, rather than classes, that is, in a delegation context.

6   Conclusion

We have presented JAVAMOD, a true module language constructed on top of Java-like classes, which allows to express, without enriching the syntax of the core level (that is, keeping pure Java as core language), a variety of constructs, including generic types, mixin classes and mutually recursive class definitions split in independent modules.

As already stated, the work presented in this paper solves one important part of the problem of integrating a rich module system with the Java language that is, the design of a typed module system which safely fits in the Java type system. Much remains to be investigated on the side of implementation/and or getting a realistic extension of Java. The simple reduction semantics we have provided for JAVAMOD [5] allows to obtain, starting from an arbitrary module expression, a basic module where classes are written in an enriched Java language (allowing class type annotations for the superclass in `extends` clauses) for which we have defined a simple model of execution. This theoretical result could directly lead to a direction for implementation. A much more difficult and interesting problem is that of providing an implementation actually constructed on top of Java. This last topic has not been properly investigated yet, however we have already discovered interesting implementation directions. For instance, the use of symbolic links (as supported in Unix, for instance) seems to be a promising (even though platform dependent) approach for implementing the merge operator; by modifying the system class loader this technics should work in principle also for the renaming operator. On the contrary, a correct implementation of the show operator seems to be more challenging, as correctly highlighted by the model defined in [5]. Finally, an extension of Java should also deal with many features which have not been considered here for simplicity, like abstract classes and interfaces, exceptions, overloading, static methods and fields and access modifiers. However, most of these features seem to be orthogonal to the main issues in designing the module type system tackled in this paper, hence should just imply more complexity, but no significant new problems; the most delicate point are those features which would be in a sense totally or partly redundant in presence of a true module system, like interfaces, visibility levels and packages, hence could be eliminated in JAVAMOD but still considered in order to get full compatibility with pure Java code.

On the more theoretical side, as extensively explained in Sect.3 and Sect.5, in this paper we have developed one of the two main solutions we have in mind for the problem of imported superclasses, that is, requiring exact matching and allowing the user to hide some components of an exported class in order to achieve this exact matching. As already stated, this solution has the advantage of keeping the type system simpler, but has the drawback that extra-components of the superclass are not part of the subclass type even when these extra-components do not interfere. We plan to fully investigate the second main solution, that is, the definition of a more complex type system allowing to specify in class types for imported classes also non interference requirements, as we have already done in Jam [1] in the easier case in which the non interference requirements involve only one class at time.

References

[1] D. Ancona, G. Lagorio, and E. Zucca. Jam: A smooth extension of Java with mixins. In E. Bertino, editor, *ECOOP'00 - European Conference on Object-Oriented*

Programming, number 1850 in Lecture Notes in Computer Science, pages 154–178, Berlin, 2000. Springer Verlag.

[2] D. Ancona and E. Zucca. A theory of mixin modules: Basic and derived operators. *Mathematical Structures in Computer Science*, 8(4):401–446, August 1998.

[3] D. Ancona and E. Zucca. A calculus of module systems. Technical Report DISI-TR-99-09, Dipartimento di Informatica e Scienze dell'Informazione, Università di Genova, 1999. Submitted for journal publication. Extended version of [4].

[4] D. Ancona and E. Zucca. A primitive calculus for module systems. In G. Nadathur, editor, *PPDP'99 - Principles and Practice of Declarative Programming*, number 1702 in Lecture Notes in Computer Science, pages 62–79, Berlin, 1999. Springer Verlag.

[5] D. Ancona and E. Zucca. True modules for Java-like languages: Design and foundations. Technical Report DISI-TR-00-12, Dipartimento di Informatica e Scienze dell'Informazione, Università di Genova, August 2000.

[6] L. Bauer, A.W. Appel, and E.W. Felten. Mechanisms for secure modular programming in Java. Technical Report CS-TR-603-99, Department of Computer Science, Princeton University, July 1999.

[7] V. Bono, A. Patel, and V. Shmatikov. A core calculus of classes and mixins. In R. Guerraoui, editor, *ECOOP'00 - European Conference on Object-Oriented Programming*, number 1628 in Lecture Notes in Computer Science, pages 43–66, Berlin, 1999. Springer Verlag.

[8] G. Bracha and W. Cook. Mixin-based inheritance. In *ACM Symp. on Object-Oriented Programming: Systems, Languages and Applications 1990*, pages 303–311. ACM Press, October 1990. SIGPLAN Notices, volume 25, number 10.

[9] G. Bracha and G. Lindstrom. Modularity meets inheritance. In *Proc. International Conference on Computer Languages*, pages 282–290, San Francisco, April 1992. IEEE Computer Society.

[10] G. Bracha, M. Odersky, D. Stoutmire, and P. Wadler. Making the future safe for the past: Adding genericity to the Java programming language. In *ACM Symp. on Object-Oriented Programming: Systems, Languages and Applications 1998*, October 1998. Home page: `http://www.cs.bell-labs.com/who/wadler/pizza/gj/`.

[11] M. Büchi and W. Weck. Generic wrapping. In E. Bertino, editor, *ECOOP'00 - European Conference on Object-Oriented Programming*, number 1850 in Lecture Notes in Computer Science, pages 201–225. Springer Verlag, 2000.

[12] K. Crary, R. Harper, and S. Puri. What is a recursive module? In *PLDI'99 - ACM Conf. on Programming Language Design and Implementation*, 1999.

[13] S. Drossopoulou and S. Eisenbach. Describing the semantics of Java and proving type soundness. In J. Alves-Foss, editor, *Formal Syntax and Semantics of Java*, number 1523 in Lecture Notes in Computer Science, pages 41–82. Springer Verlag, Berlin, 1999.

[14] D. Duggan. A mixin-based, semantics-based approach to reusing domain-specific programming languages. In E. Bertino, editor, *ECOOP'00 - European Conference on Object-Oriented Programming*, number 1850 in Lecture Notes in Computer Science, pages 179–200. Springer Verlag, 2000.

[15] D. Duggan and C. Sourelis. Mixin modules. In *Intl. Conf. on Functional Programming*, pages 262–273, Philadelphia, June 1996. ACM Press.

[16] R.B. Findler and M. Flatt. Modular object-oriented programming with units and mixins. In *Intl. Conf. on Functional Programming 1998*, September 1998.

[17] K. Fisher and J. Reppy. The design of a class mechanism for MOBY. In *PLDI'99 - ACM Conf. on Programming Language Design and Implementation*, pages 37–49, May 1999.

[18] K. Fisher and J. Reppy. Extending MOBY with inheritance-based subtyping. In *European Symposium on Programming 2000*, Lecture Notes in Computer Science, Berlin, 2000. Springer Verlag. To appear.

[19] M. Flatt and M. Felleisen. Units: Cool modules for HOT languages. In *PLDI'98 - ACM Conf. on Programming Language Design and Implementation*, pages 236–248, 1998.

[20] M. Flatt, S. Krishnamurthi, and M. Felleisen. Classes and mixins. In *ACM Symp. on Principles of Programming Languages 1998*, pages 171–183, January 1998.

[21] J. Gosling, B. Joy, and G. Steele. *The Java™ Language Specification*. Addison-Wesley, 1996.

[22] R. Harper and M. Lillibridge. A type theoretic approach to higher-order modules with sharing. In *ACM Symp. on Principles of Programming Languages 1994*, pages 127–137. ACM Press, 1994.

[23] A. Igarashi, B. Pierce, and P. Wadler. Featherweight Java: A minimal core calculus for Java and GJ. In *ACM Symp. on Object-Oriented Programming: Systems, Languages and Applications 1999*, pages 132–146, November 1999.

[24] X. Leroy. Manifest types, modules and separate compilation. In *ACM Symp. on Principles of Programming Languages 1994*, pages 109–122. ACM Press, 1994.

[25] X. Leroy. A modular module system. *Journal of Functional Programming*, 10(3):269–303, May 2000.

[26] B. Meyer. *Eiffel: The language*. Prentice Hall, 1992.

[27] R. Milner, M. Tofte, and R. Harper. *The Definition of Standard ML*. The MIT Press, Cambridge, Massachussetts, 1990.

[28] M. Odersky and P. Wadler. Pizza into Java: Translating theory into practice. In *ACM Symp. on Principles of Programming Languages 1997*. ACM Press, January 1997.

[29] D. Remy and J. Vouillon. Objective ML: An effective object-oriented extension to ML. *Theory and Practice of Object Systems*, 4(1): 27–50, 1998.

[30] C. Szyperski. Import is not inheritance. why we need both: Modules and classes. In O. Lehrmann Madsen, editor, *ECOOP'92 - European Conference on Object-Oriented Programming*, number 615 in Lecture Notes in Computer Science, pages 19–32, Berlin, 1992. Springer Verlag.

Selecting an Efficient OO Integration Testing Strategy: An Experimental Comparison of Actual Strategies

Vu Le Hanh [1], Kamel Akif [2], Yves Le Traon [1], Jean-Marc Jézéquel [1]

[1]: IRISA, Campus Universitaire de Beaulieu, 35042 Rennes Cedex, France.
{Hanh.Vu_Le, Yves.Le_Traon, Jean-Marc.Jezequel}@ irisa.fr
[2]: LAN/DTL/FT R&D Lannion, 2 av. Pierre Marzin, 22307 Lannion Cedex, France.

Abstract: The normalization of semi-formal modeling methods, such as the UML, leads to re-visit the problem of early OO integration test planning. Integration is often conducted under some incremental steps. Integration test planning aims at ordering the components to be integrated and tested in relationships with the already tested part of the system. This paper presents a modeling of the test integration problem from a UML design, then details existing integration strategies and proposes two integration strategies: a deterministic one called Triskell and an original semi-random one, based on genetic algorithms called Genetic. Strategies are compared in detail (algorithmic cost and optimization choices) and a large part of the paper is dedicated to an experimental comparison of each strategy on 6 real-world case studies of various complexities (from a "small" telecommunication software to the Swing Java library). Results show that a good modeling of this optimization problem associated with well-chosen algorithms induce a significant gain in terms of testing effort and duration.

Key word: Software Testing, Object-Oriented Modeling, UML, Test Economics, Test Cost, Integration Testing, Graph Algorithms, Stub Minimization.

1 Introduction

Design-for-testability aims at integrating design and testing in the same process, and includes the problem of test planning from early design stages. In the case of object-orientation, due to inheritance and dynamic binding, the control is no more centralized in the main encapsulation unit, namely the class. However, the testing task remains unchanged but must deal with the whole architecture to determine subtle errors. The particular problem tackled to testers by OO architectures (class and package diagrams) is the strong connectivity between their components. While integration testing is performed to find errors in component interfaces when they communicate with each others, the complexity of these architectures makes the classical integration strategies useless.

To efficiently pinpoint the errors, it is preferable to avoid the "big-bang" integration methods [1, 2]. Instead, an incremental strategy is appropriate: the more classical integration strategies are "bottom-up" and "top-down" ones. They are based on a graph representation of the system under integration that is assumed to be acyclic.

J. Lindskov Knudsen (Ed.): ECOOP 2001, LNCS 2072, pp. 381-401, 2001.

Bottom-up methods begin by testing leafs of the graph and then tests the upper levels step by step, while top-down methods begin by the top level and descends in the graph hierarchy step by step   [2]. In the first case, only test drivers have to be implemented, while the top-down also needs "stubs" for simulating the lower non-integrated components. These strategies are meaningless for most OO systems, where cycles of dependencies between components often exist, as it will be shown in the case studies. The integration problem must be re-thought for OO systems. A model must be defined and strategies proposed to take into account the highly connected structure of most OO designs.

This paper focuses firstly on the problem of bridging this gap between the actual design architecture, expressed by UML class and package diagrams, and an abstract modeling of the integration test problem (in terms of test dependence graph). Then, we concentrate on the algorithmic problem of producing the best integration test plan for delay-driven projects. The main difficulties for a cost/duration-efficient integration is the minimization of the number of "stubs" to be written (cost) and the number of steps needed to achieve the integration (duration). A stub is a dummy simulator used to simulate the behavior of a real component not yet integrated. In the paper, the performance of a strategy is thus related to the number of generated stubs and the number of integration steps.

Among the many existing proposals [4, 6, 9, 10, 11, 13] that deal with this problem, we concentrate on those of David C. Kung and al. [10] and Kuo Chung Tai & Fonda J. Daniels [4] since they both detail effective and feasible algorithms. A large part of the paper is thus devoted to an experimental comparison between the performances of these approaches with respect to two original strategies (one deterministic and one genetic based algorithm). This comparison is based on the complexity of the algorithm, the number of stubs needed as well as the number of integration steps. Six real-world case studies of various scales serve as the comparison benchmark. Since the theoretical problem is NP-complete, no optimal feasible solution is existing. However, for the chosen comparison criteria, the results reveal that the various approaches are not equivalent and that the proposed algorithms are very promising.

This paper is organized as follows. In Section 2, the two-dimensional (effort/duration) problem of integration testing is detailed. Section 3 opens with some definitions about structural test dependencies and outlines the mapping from UML to a test dependence graph (with a more complete set of modeling rules than the one presented in [12]). Then, four algorithms to compute an integration test plan by minimization of the number of stubs are outlined (Section 4): the Triskell and Genetic ones correspond to the main contributions of this paper with the experimental results presented in Section 5. One of the difficulties for such comparison is to exhibit significant criteria of cost/duration performances: our assumptions and their limitations are detailed. The experimental comparison between the performances of each strategy is presented at the end of the fifth section.

2   Stub Minimization and Testing Resource Allocation

Integration testing is defined here as the way in which testing is conducted to integrate components into the system. A "component" is a stable part of the software with a well-defined interface described wit e.g. a UML model: for sake of clarity, a component will be restricted either to a class or to its specific method in the detailed design. One of the main difficulties for a cost-efficient integration is to minimize the number of stubs to be written. Integration testing duration also depends on the number of testing resources available for performing the integration.

The problem of integration planning is a two dimensional one. One dimension of the problem is the allocation of the available testing resources (or testers) to the integration tasks, the second dimension concerns the minimization of the effort to create the stubs. For sake of clarity, we consider in this paper that the number of stubs to be created is a good indicator of the testing effort: we just mention that the nature of the stub and its complexity could be taken into account by *ad-hoc* adaptations of the presented algorithms. To deal with this two-dimensional problem, each strategy focus on one of these aspects first (both dimensions are NP-complete). Depending on the analysis of the problem, the integration strategies may either be allocation-first or stub-minimization-first guided.

2.1 Stub Minimization

Let us to define what is a stub: if a component C_1 uses one or more service(s) of another component C_2, we say C_1 *"depends"* on C_2. During the incremental integration process, when C_1 is integrated, if C_2 has not already been integrated, we have to simulate the services of C2. Such a simulator is usually called a *"stub"*.

In this paper, we model two types of stubs: specific stubs and realistic ones (see Figure 1).

- A *specific stub* simulates the services for the use of a given client only. This kind of stub forces the caller component to used a predefined calling sequences since the stub provides "canned" outcomes for its processing. In that case, the stub is specific to a particular caller component, and as many specific stubs have to be created as they are caller components.
- A *realistic stub* simulates all services that the original class can provide. In that case, the stub works whatever the caller component is using it.

Note that realistic stubs can be obsolete (but reliable) implementations of stubbed components (see Figure 1) as well as an available library that would be replaced by a dedicated component later.

A stub is not a real component and will not be used in the final product. Thus, we have to minimize the effort to create stubs. In particular, if we assume that every stub requires the same effort to be created, then the minimization of stub creation effort is synonymous with the minimization of the stub number. This assumption could be easily relaxed by associating complexity values to stubs, corresponding to their creation effort. No stub is needed when the dependencies between components in the system generate no cycles: integration strategies will thus differ mainly by the way they detect cycles and the criterion used to break them.

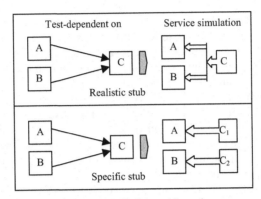

Figure 1. Realistic/specific stubs

2.2 Testing Resource Allocation

Let us define a *"tester"* as a testing team of a given fixed size. It represents a given unit of testing effort that can be allocated to a testing task. Let us make the following assumption to help presenting the test repartition strategy: a "tester" needs one time unit or *"step"* to integrate a component to the system and test it. This notion of step can easily be adapted by giving a weight to each component corresponding to its estimated testability. In terms of time measurement, the integration is a discrete process and not a continuous one: that is the reason why step notion is close to the real integration activity. However, the mapping of a "step" into a real-time measurement is not studied here since we only try to capture the following information: being given a system, which strategy requires the less time for achieving integration?

By another way, the question of testing resources allocation is: being given n testers, what is the best way to allocate integration testing tasks to minimize the number of steps of the integration?

Both problems, testing resource allocation and stub minimization, always go together. When we allocate a component to a "tester", the tester may have to create a stub, especially in the object-oriented paradigm where components can depend, directly or indirectly, on each other and vice-versa. Depending on the analysis of the problem, the integration strategies may either be allocation-first guided or stub-minimization-first guided. In the literature, David C. Kung and al. [10], Kuo Chung Tai and Fonda J. Daniels [4] proposed strategies to allocate the testing resources first but they did not explicitly deal with the dimension of stub minimization.

The third (Triskell [12]) and fourth (Genetic) ones correspond to our propositions. We argue that the best way to deal with this two-dimensional problem (both dimensions are NP-complete) is to first guide integration by minimizing stubs and then allocating resources.

3   From UML to Test Dependence Graph (TDG)

In this section, we recall the notion of test dependencies and its associated model called Test Dependence Graph (TDG). This model has been introduced in [7, 12] but the part of model concerning regression testing is simplified here. Indeed, implementation parts from specification/contractual ones are not distinguished in the context of integration testing. The presented model has also been extended to capture the polymorphic dependencies (through transitive relationships) as well as the nature of the dependence (Aggregation, Association, Inheritance or Implementation). We then obtain a general model on which all the published integration strategies can be implemented: Kung's ORD model (that is also the underlying model used by Tai & Daniels) is a particular case of the TDG. This common basis for modeling makes comparison possible.

Definitions

-   *Test Dependence Graph (TDG):* It is a directed graph whose vertices represent components (classes and/or included methods, depending on the detail level of the design) and directed edges represent test dependencies. In a TDG, loops may occur because components may be directly or indirectly test dependent from each other.
-   *Test dependence levels:* Depending on the level of detail in the design, we may define test dependencies between classes or between methods of classes (in case of high detail level). We distinguish three levels of test dependencies:
    1. *Class-to-class*: It is the dependence level that can be induced from a design model, as soon as a stable class diagram is available. A vertex in a TDG models a class. An edge of TDG links these vertices.
    2. *Method-to-class*: If a method m has an object of a class C declared in its signature, a method-to-class dependence exists between this method and this class. In TDG, we model this method and class by vertices. These vertices are linked with an edge.
    3. *Method-to-method:* This dependence can be inferred only by analyzing the implementation body of a method. If method m_1 calls method m_2, a method-to-method dependence exists between these methods. In the TDG, we model these methods by two vertices and directed edges connecting m_1 to m_2 and all redefinitions of m_2 in subclasses of class containing m_2 (dynamic binding).

From a UML class diagram, only class-to-class and method-to-class test dependencies can be inferred to build a TDG. Using information available in the UML dynamic diagrams, some method-to-method test dependencies can be inferred. If source code is available, then all test dependencies can easily be extracted to build a TDG.

Concerning only the most general class-to-class test dependencies, the TDG can be extracted from a design model such as a UML description of an OO system. The way the TDG is build is a (safe) over-estimation of the actual dependencies. In the TDG, an arrow from B to A means that "B is test dependent on A". If it is possible, A should be tested before B. When more detailed information is available on a system (through a detailed model or extracted from the code) we can produce a more accurate

TDG at the granularity of methods as explained in [12]. Since the actual strategies – except for Triskell one – do not take into account this level of detail, this part of the model is not used for comparison

Three main rules are used to map the UML model into a TDG as presented in Figure 2. Being given two components: A and B:

–   If B inherits (derives from) A, A is test-dependent on B by an inheritance dependence. The edge that connects vertex A to vertex B is labeled "I" in the TDG.

–   If A is a composite (an aggregate) of B, A is test-dependent on B by an aggregation dependence. The A to B edge is labeled "Ag" in the TDG.

–   If A is associated or depends on B, A is test-dependent on B by an association dependence. The A to B edge is labeled "As" in the TDG.

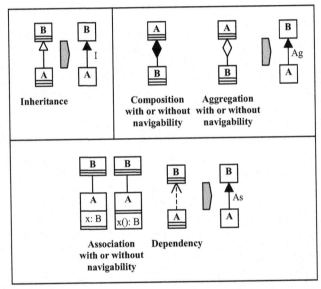

Figure 2. UML to TDG: Class-to-class edges: Main transformations

To deal with polymorphism dependencies (the rules (a) and (b) in the left part of Figure 3), we choose to add extra edges to the TDG. If a component A is test-dependent on a component B by an aggregation dependence or by an association dependence, A is test-dependent by an aggregation dependence or by an association dependence (respectively) on all components derived from B.

In the right part of Figure 3, we take into account abstract components and interface ones that cannot be instantiated. In the figure, rules (c) and (d) must be applied first, and then the third rule (e) for deleting the vertex corresponding to the abstract class B.

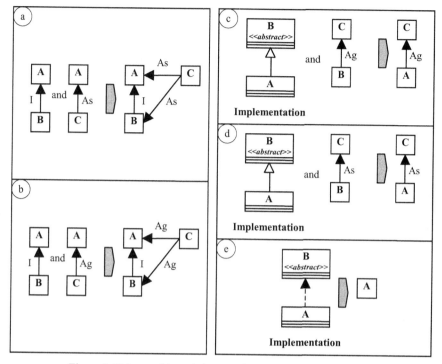

Figure 3. Polymorphic and abstract classes transformations rules

4 Integration Strategies

In this section, we present three deterministic strategies (Kung's, Tai-Daniels' and Triskell) and one semi-random strategy based on genetic algorithms (Genetic by Akif Kamel). All solutions presented here are based on a TDG. If a set of components is included into a cycle of dependencies, we say these components belong to the same **Strongly Connected Component** or **SCC**. The main difference between the various strategies lies in the way that cycles are detected and then broken.

To illustrate these strategies, we use a small example of TDG (see Figure 4). The outcome of each strategy will be presented step by step. Even if some algorithms may appear complex and not intuitive, we choose to detail the application of each strategy precisely on this small example to make the experiments repeatable and the paper self-contained.

Several points have to be noticed:

– Each strategy is presented in three parts, (i) a stub choice step, (ii) a resource allocation step and (iii) its illustration with the TDG of Figure 4.

– Since a stub is a dummy component, when a component A needs a stub for a component B during its integration, the integration will not be achieved until the component A has been tested with the real component B. In the result of our example, we underline this step of testing with the real component B by putting it in (parenthesis).

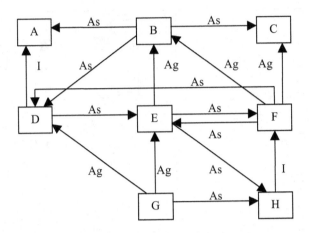

Figure 4. An example of TDG

- The result of an integration test strategy is a partial order tree, each vertex representing a component. For sake of conciseness, this partial order tree has been flattened as follows: when a choice between equivalent vertices is done, we use the ASCII code order of the vertex labels. For example, between vertices C and E, we will firstly choose C (topological sort).
- Stubs are needed because of the existing SCCs. Each strategy applies a proper criterion to remove some edges and break the SCC. Any successor from a removed edge is stubbed. Dotted arrows represent such edges and gray background boxes represent stubs

4.1 Kung and al.'s Strategy [10]

To choose a stub, Kung argues that an association relationship always exists inside a cycle and this kind of relationship is the weakest of three kinds: Inheritance, Aggregation and Association. To break a cycle, one of its association relationships is removed. The testing resource allocation procedure is based on the "*height*" of vertices in the TDG, i.e. the maximum number of vertices included in paths from the considered vertex to a leaf vertex. Then a leaf vertex has a height value of 1.

Although Kung gives a way to choose a stub, the problem of stub minimization is not explicitly taken into account since the strategy is first allocation-guided. This algorithm is illustrated in Figure 5.

(i) Stub choice:
- Search all SCCs using transitive closure.
- Assign a height for each SCC. This height is called *"major level"*.
- For each SCC, recursively remove association edges until there are no more cycles.
- Successors of removed association edges are stubbed. They are specific stubs.

(ii) Resource allocation:

- Without taking into account the edges removed in step 1, a height value called *"minor level"* is assigned to each vertex of each SCC. This value allows defining a partial order into a SCC.
- The vertices allocation is based on the *"pair (major level, minor level)"* that defines a partial order:

  smaller: $(x_1, y_1) < (x_2, y_2) \Leftrightarrow (x_1 < x_2) \lor (x_1 = x_2 \land y_1 < y_2)$
- The vertex with smaller pair (major level, minor level) will be allocated earlier. If two vertices have a same pair (major level, minor level), choose any one to stub.

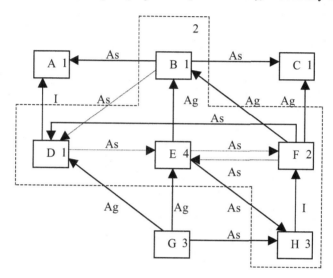

Figure 5. Kung and al.'s strategy

(iii) Illustration:

Table 1 and 2 present the application of Kung and al.'s strategy on the TDG of Figure 4. Table 1 underlines the SCC order and corresponding stub choice: the strategy requires 4 specific stubs (dotted arrows) and 3 realistic stubs (gray background boxes).

Table 1. The SCC and the edges to remove

SCC	Major Level	Edge to remove
{A}	1	∅
{B D E F H}	2	{BD, DE, EF, FE}
{C}	1	∅
{G}	3	∅

Table 2 shows the pairs (major level, minor level) of all vertices in Figure 4 and their integration order. The order in parenthesis concerns the re-allocation step: stub replacement by the real component for final integration and testing. The number of integration steps is 11 (the maximum order).

Table 2. Major level, minor level and integration order

Vertex	Major level	Minor Level	Integration order	Vertex	Major Level	Minor level	Integration order
A	1	1	1	E	2	4	8
B	2	1	3, (5)	F	2	2	6, (10)
C	1	1	2	G	3	1	11
D	2	1	4, (9)	H	2	3	7

4.2 Tai-Daniels' Strategy [4]

To choose a stub, Tai and Daniels adapt their strategy from Kung's argument concerning association priority in the allocation step. To break a given cycle, some association relationships are removed. For the resource allocation procedure height of vertices in the TDG is used to define an order. This algorithm is illustrated in Figure 6.

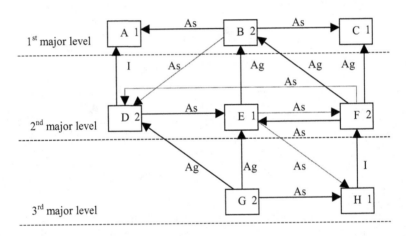

Figure 6. Tai-Daniels' strategy

(i) Stub choice:
- Assign a height for each vertex, using a depth-first algorithm, without taking into account the association relationships. This height is called *"major level"*.
- All successors of association edges from smaller major level to greater major level are stubbed.
- Successors of removed association edges are stubbed. They are specific stubs.
- In each major level, association edges are removed if they are in a cycle and their successor is a stub.
- If there is still a cycle, a weight is assigned to each edge of this cycle. The weight of edge "e" is calculated:
  weight (e) = (number of existing edges, incoming to predecessor of e, from other vertices in the same major level with predecessor of e) +

(number of existing edges, outgoing from successor of e, to other vertices in the same major level with successor of e).

–   Remove successively edges with respect to their priority weights until there are no more cycles.

(ii) Resource allocation:

–   Do not take into account the edges removed in the first part, assign a local height for each component in each major level using a depth-first algorithm. This number is called *"minor level"*.

–   Allocate vertices according to the order given by pairs (major level, minor level). The vertex with smaller pair (major level, minor level) will be firstly allocated. If two vertices have same priority, choose any one to allocate first.

(iii) Illustration:

Table 3 and Table 4 present the result of Tai-Daniels's strategy applied to Figure 4.

Table 3.   Major level and inter-level edges removed

Major Level	Vertices	Edge to remove
1	A, B, C	BD
2	D, E, F	EH
3	G, H	

Tai-Daniels' strategy requires 2 specific stubs (dotted arrows) and 2 realistic stubs (gray background boxes) for inter-level dependencies. The number of integration steps is 11 (the maximum order).

Remarks:
The edge FD in 2nd major level participates in the cycle (D E F) and D is a stub for upper major level (1st major level). So, to break this cycle, we remove this edge (3rd specific stubs). In 2nd major level, there is still a cycle (E F) and no E, neither F is ready a stub. Hence, to break this cycle, we have to use the edge weight.
The weight (EF) = 2 + 1 = 3, weight (FE) = 1 + 1 = 2. Between two edges, EF and FE, weight (EF) > weight (FE) and we choose to remove the edge EF (4th specific stubs). The successor of this edge is stubbed. F is the 3rd realistic stub.

Table 4.   Major level, minor level and integration order

Vertex	Major level	Minor level	Integration order	Vertex	Major level	Minor level	Integration order
A	1	1	1	E	2	1	4, (8), (10)
B	1	2	3, (6)	F	2	2	7
C	1	1	2	G	3	2	11
D	2	2	5	H	3	1	9

4.3 Triskell Strategy

Triskell strategy is a two-part strategy: the first part corresponds to the stub minimization problem while the second focus on testing resource allocation. The method does not take into account the type of relationship between components as a priority. To break a cycle, the vertex that participates in as many cycles as possible is stubbed. The underlying argument is that the nature of the relationship is less important than the effort to stub any relationship. So the algorithm is first stub-minimization guided. The nature of the relationship (association, inheritance, aggregation) is also taken into account only as a second priority, using Kung's argument (association first). The testing resource allocation procedure is based on the depth of vertices in TDG, i.e. the maximum number of vertices included in paths from the considered vertex to a root vertex. Then a root vertex has a depth value of 1. This algorithm is illustrated in Figure 7.

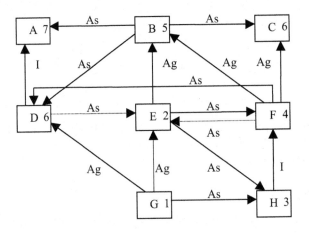

Figure 7. Triskell strategy

(i) Stub choice:
- Progressively stub the vertices, which participate in as many cycles as possible, using Tarjan's algorithm [15, 12]. Let *vertex_2_cycles (vertex)* be the function that results in the set of cycles to which the vertex belongs. When a vertex *v* is stubbed, each cycle of the *vertex_2_cycles (v)* set is broken and the incoming edge of v in this cycle is removed to create a specific stub. For a given vertex, there are as many specific stubs as the number of independent cycles traversing this vertex.
- When two vertices belong to the same number of cycles, according to Kung's argument, we stub the vertex which its incoming association edges belong to more cycles than the other. In case of equality, the next criterion consists of selecting the vertex with the lower incoming degree in the SCC. This criterion minimizes the number of specific stubs. Finally, if needed, an arbitrary order is taken, e.g. the vertex identifier ASCII code order

(ii) Resource allocation:

- Do not take into account the removed edges in the first part, assign a depth for each vertex
- Allocate vertices with priority of maximum vertex depth: bigger depth, earlier allocation. If two vertices have the same depth, we choose the vertex with smaller identification.

(iii) Illustration:

Table 5 shows all cycles to which each vertex belongs. The vertex E is traversed by the maximum number of cycles. This vertex is chosen to be stubbed (1st realistic stub). The incoming edges of E in these cycles are DE and FE. They are broken to create 2 specific stubs. Table 6 presents the depth of each vertex and its integration order. The number of integration step is 10.

Table 5.   vertex_2_cycles results

Vertex	vertex_2_cycles (vertex)	|vertex_2_cycles (vertex)|
A	-	0
B	(B D E), (B D E F), (B D E H F)	3
C	-	0
D	(B D E), (B D E F), (B D E H F), (D E F)	4
E	(B D E), (B D E F), (B D E H F), (D E F), (D E H F), (E F), (E H F)	7
F	(B D E F), (B D E H F), (D E F), (D E H F), (E F), (E H F)	6
G	-	0
H	(B D E H F), (D E H F), (E H F)	3

Table 6.   Depth and Test Order

Vertex	Depth	Test Order	Vertex	Depth	Test Order
A	7	1	E	2	7
B	5	4	F	4	5, (8)
C	6	2	G	1	10
D	6	3, (7)	H	3	6

4.4 Using Genetic Algorithms for Stub Minimization

Since the question of integration planning is a two-dimensional NP-complete problem, semi-random optimization algorithms have been studied. We present here an original application of genetic algorithms to this problem. On one hand, genetic algorithms (GAs) [5, 14] are applied to reduce the search space and direct it to reach a good solution. On the other hand, they allow escaping routes out of local optimization. They are widely used in many areas for problem optimization and are efficient for solving NP-complete problems. In our study we use them to search the first dimension of integration problem, the minimization of stub number.

GAs are iterative non-deterministic algorithms, one important characteristic of these algorithms is their generality and the ease of implementation. They require a fitness function, a mechanism to traverse the search space (via crossover and mutation operations) and a suitable solution representation (by individual and population).

In our strategy, the fitness function is the number of stubs, each individual is an integration order and the population is a set of integration orders. Our strategy consists of:

(i) Stub Choice:

Choose a maximum number of iterations.

For each SCC:

- Randomly generate some initial individuals (i.e. integration order) for the initial population P (0).
- Compute the fitness function (stub number) for each individual in the current population P (t).
- Choose two individuals with the best result of the fitness function.
- Generate P (t+1) from two chosen individuals via genetic operators: crossover and mutation.
- Repeat from the 2nd step to the end until the maximum number of iterations is reached.

(ii) Resource allocation:

Similar to Triskell algorithm.

(iii) Illustration:

We use two genetic operators:

- The mutation operator *MU (x, y, individual)*: it exchanges the *x-th* element and the *y-th* element of *individual*.

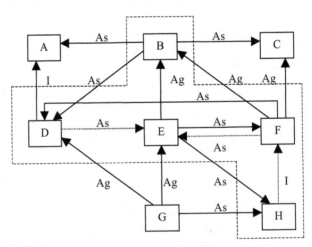

Figure 8. The SCC

- The crossover operator **CR (x, individual1, individual2)**: we use the partially mapped crossover PMX [14]. The new generated individual I_1 contains ordering information partially determined from its parents *individual1* and *2*. A random cut point *x* is chosen in both parents, the entire right part of *individual2* is copied in the new individual I_1. If an element of the left part of *individual1* is not present in I_1 then it is added to I_1. If this element exists in I_1, then its position in I_1 is determined and the element from *individual1* corresponding to this position is copied in I_1.

Both operators use one random function to define the position cut point. The number of iterations and the order for executing the genetic operations is also randomly chosen. Another operation **STOP (Population)** chooses the best individual in *Population* and stops the procedure. In case of equality, the individual which i-th element has smaller ASCII code.

Table 7 shows a manipulation of the SCC {B D E F H} with the initial integration orders are I_0 = {F E H D B} and I_1 = {E B D F H}. After 3 steps, we obtain the integration order (D, B, H, F, E). We stop and the integration order for whole TDG in Figure 4 is {A, C, D, B, H, F, (H), E, (D), (F), G}. The number of step is 11. The number of realistic stubs is 2 (E and F) and of specific stubs is 3 (DE, HF and EF).

Table 7.   Apply of Genetic Algorithm with Figure 4

Iteration	Population	Stub number (fitness function)	Genetic operation	Result
0	I_0 = {F E H D B} I_1 = {E B D F H}	4 4	MU (1, 5, I_1)	I_2 = {H B D F E}
1	I_0, I_2	4, 2	CR (3, I_0, I_2)	I_3 = {D B H F E} I_4 = {H E F D B}
2	I_2, I_3	2, 2	STOP (P_2)	I_3 = {D B H F E}

5   Case Studies

We choose to present six real-world case studies. One is from the telecommunication field and five others are in the domain of software technology ([1]).

1. A Telecommunication Switching System: Switched Multimegabits Data Service (SMDS) is a connectionless, packet-switched data transport service running on top of connected networks such as the Broadband Integrated Service Digital Network (B-ISDN), which is based on the Asynchronous Transfer Mode (ATM). A detailed description of an SMDS server design and implementation (totaling 22KLOC) can be found in [12]. The class-diagram studied here is composed of 37 classes implementing the core of the switch, with 72 connects.

2. Part of an Object-Oriented Compiler: The GNU Eiffel Compiler is a free open-source Eiffel compiler distributed under the terms of the GNU General Public

---

[1] All the benchmark input TDGs can be downloaded from http://www.irisa.fr/testobjets/testbenchmark

License as published by the Free Software Foundation. It is available for a wide range of platforms. The current distribution (available from http://SmallEiffel.loria.fr) includes an Eiffel to C compiler, an Eiffel to Java bytecode compiler, a documentation tool, a pretty printer and various other tools, with their sources (all in all, around 70KLOC). Its UML class diagram is available in MDL, PDF or Postcript format at http://www.irisa.fr/pampa/UMLAUT/smalleiffel.[mdl|pdf|ps]). The total size of this compiler is more than 300 classes but we dealt with its core only, totaling 104 classes with 140 connects.

3. InterViews graphic library: This case study is from Kung's article [10]. Its size is 146 classes and 419 connects.
4. Pylon library (http://www.eiffel-forum.org/archive/arnaud/pylon.htm). It is an Eiffel library for data structures and other basic features that can be used as a foundation library by more ambitious or specialized Eiffel libraries. Its size is 50 classes with 133 connects.
5. Base classes of Java 2 Platform Standard Edition Version 1.3 (http://java.sun.com/j2se/1.3/docs/api/index.html). Its size is 588 connected classes by 1935 connects.
6. Package "Swing" of Java 2 Platform Standard Edition Version 1.3 (http://java.sun.com/j2se/1.3/docs/api/index.html). Its size is 694 classes with 3819 connects.

Difficulties of the Study and Experimental Environment

Several remarks must be done to understand the scope and limitations of the study, and provide a stable basis for replication. The validity of the experiments depends mainly on the approximation of the cost of stubs construction. Ideally, the strategies should be compared not only in terms of stub number, but also in terms of stub complexity. Kung's classical approach argues that the complexity of the stubs depends on the nature of the stubbed relationship, since "association relation represents the weakest coupling between the two related classes" while "the other two relations, namely, inheritance and aggregation, involve not only control coupling, but also code dependence and data coupling" (see [10], p. 34). However, the complexity of the integration also depends on the complexity of the functionality to be simulated, e.g. number and complexity of methods of the stubbed class. Stubbing an inherited "empty" class (e.g. containing only attributes) may be much more easier than stubbing a provider class involving many possible complex method calls. In contradiction with Kung's argument, the practice show that cycles may occur with only inheritance and aggregation relationships. In conclusion, since there is no consensual basis, we choose to consider that nothing can be decided at class level. In the case studies, Triskell strategy mainly select association edges: 1 aggregation is stubbed for Pylon case study, 4 aggregations for java library and 2 aggregations and one inheritance for Swing. For the others, only association edges are selected.

Building the TDG for SMDS, Pylon and Small Eiffel cases studies was not automated, while we have implemented a builder program to extract from the Java and Swing libraries the dependencies. This little tool uses the introspection Java mechanism.

Results

We only display the detailed results for two case studies (InterViews and Swing) in Table 8 and Table 9. The first columns of the tables list the number of testers (from 1 to 10). The other columns list the number of steps needed to integrate all the components for each strategy. A gray background marks the best value. In addition, the last line of the tables gives the number of stubs we have to create to break cycles in the TDG. This number of stubs is not dependent on the number of testers for the presented strategies.

Based on the table results, we display in Figure 9 the relative efficiency (in terms of percentage) in comparison with the result of Triskell strategy. In these figures, the "% of step number" values correspond to the ratio of the number of steps required for the strategy under consideration and the result of Triskell strategy.

Table 8. Results with InterViews graphic library case study

testers number	Kung	Tai-Daniels	Genetic Algorithm	Triskell
1	155	204	157	152
2	84	105	79	76
3	61	72	53	51
4	49	55	40	38
5	44	46	32	31
6	39	41	27	26
7	37	36	23	24
8	35	31	21	22
9	35	28	20	21
10	32	27	19	21
stub number	13	22	8	6

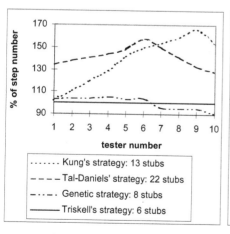

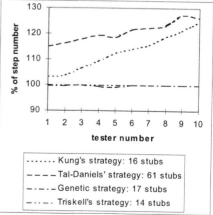

Figure 9. Relative results with InterViews (left) and Java Swing (right)

Table 9. Results with Java Swing library case study

testers number	Kung	Tai-Daniels	Genetic Algorithm	Triskell
1	740	826	715	717
2	373	418	358	359
3	255	282	239	239
4	197	215	179	180
5	162	171	143	144
6	137	146	120	120
7	119	126	103	103
8	107	111	90	90
9	97	102	80	80
10	90	91	72	72
stub number	16	61	17	14

The algorithms perform quite differently over the various case studies but main trends appear that will be discussed. Table 10 and Table 11 summarize the whole set of results obtained with five testers. The first table lists the number of stubs for each case study that was found by each strategy. The second table lists the number of steps for five testers, depending on strategy and case study. A gray background marks the best result in each line of the table.

Comparison of Algorithms and Comments

In [10], Kung et al. wrote that, according to their strategy, 8 stubs are required for the InterViews graphic library. Here, we get 13 stubs since Kung's algorithm does not specify the order of removed association relationships in the SCC. Here, we took the ASCII code order of the vertices. With another order we get 7 stubs, that is a better result than Kung with the same algorithm: due to this unspecified part, the algorithm results are not stable (in that case between 7 and 13 stubs). This remark reveals that the chosen order is very important and highly modifies the stub minimization efficiency.

Table 10. Stub number for each case study

Case studies	Kung	Tai-Daniels	Genetic	Triskell
SMDS, 37 classes, 72 connects	11	14	13	9
SmallEiffel, 104 classes, 140 connects	4	10	6	1
InterViews, 146 classes, 419 connects	13	22	8	6
Pylon, 50 classes, 133 connects	6	9	3	3
Java, 588 classes, 1935 connects	9	55	8	7
Swing, 694 classes, 3819 connects	16	61	17	14

Table 11. Step number for each case study (allocate for five testers)

Case studies	Kung	Tai-Daniels	Genetic	Triskell
SMDS, 37 classes, 72 connects	17	17	13	13
SmallEiffel, 104 classes, 140 connects	29	28	23	22
InterViews, 146 classes, 419 connects	44	46	32	31
Pylon, 50 classes, 133 connects	17	23	12	12
Java, 588 classes, 1935 connects	152	199	124	123
Swing, 694 classes, 3819 connects	162	171	143	144

Kung used a transitive closure to compute the SCCs. The complexity of this algorithm is $O(n^3)$ with n is the number of components. It requires much more time in comparison to other strategies that are based on depth-first algorithms: it can neither be used in a realistic large industry project nor for small systems at a detailed level of analysis (method level). On the contrary, Triskell is based on an adaptation of Bourdoncle's algorithm [3]. This algorithm itself is based on Tarjan's algorithm [15] (linear with the number of vertices). Then, the global algorithmic complexity is close to $O(n)$ – the pathological unrealistic graph where there are as many SCCs as they are vertices may lead to a $O(n^2)$ complexity.

Clearly, Tai-Daniels' strategy is the less efficient one both for stub minimization and integration duration. The reason of this disappointing behavior can be illustrated with the simple example given in Figure 10: the test order is (A, B, C, D, A) with one stub (D). In Kung's strategy and in our approaches, no stub is needed and the best order (B, D, A, C) is obtained. The difference between Kung and Triskell strategies is mainly due to the fact that Kung's strategy criterion is local (association first) while Triskell algorithm globally aims at reducing the number of stubs. We already discussed the reason we cannot compare the complexity of stubs at a class level of detail: all algorithms can be adapted to take into account this inherent complexity, but no objective comparison basis would have been available in that last case.

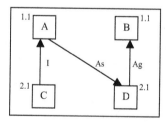

Figure 10.   With Tai and Daniels' strategy, D is stubbed to test A

The behavior of the genetic algorithm is promising, but seems to be less efficient than the deterministic optimized Triskell algorithm. Detailed results in annex show that it obtains sometimes a better result than Triskell. The main advantage of the Genetic strategy is that it can more easily be adapted to take into account the complexity of components, without extra computational cost. To conclude, Kung strategy behaves well but the computational cost is prohibitive for real projects. Tai-Daniels analysis of the problem is really pertinent but the strategy results are disappointing. Triskell is close to Kung but doesn't make any difference between stub types for determining a better result and Genetic fitness function should maybe be improved to be more efficient.

As qualitative result, we may say that integration strategies are mature enough to be really applied to large-scale projects for saving time and cost. An interesting viable, alternative to stub minimization, consist of performing big-bang integration only on the SCCs in all the cases in which their cardinality is small. The argument is that a little SCC identifies a coherent set of classes that can be tested in one time (big bang). Ideally, such a solution would let the decision of breaking a SCC to the tester. In the best case, no stub would be needed.

The assertion that cycles very rarely occur in an OO design is an opinion that is contradicted by all of ours experiments: most OO systems are highly connected and even well-written ones[1] include some of hard-to-test cycles. For instance, the Java library generates about 8.000 cycles that are broken with 7 stubs. A correlated consequence of our studies would be to pinpoint large cycles of dependencies global to several packages (since cycles into a package are acceptable).

6   Conclusion

The paper has dealt with an important issue in testing of object-oriented systems: the definition of a cost-effective integration testing process. The two-dimensional aspect of the problem of integration planning has been presented (stub minimization and testing resource allocation) as well as a model adapted to a comparison of four possible strategies. The rules for building this model from the UML have been given and the algorithms explained in detail. We have presented an empirical comparison of the performance of these algorithms to compute an integration test plan. This comparison was conducted on six real-world case studies. Both theoretical considerations (on algorithmic complexity and stub selection criteria) and experimental results allow us to differentiate these strategies. A lesson learnt from this comparison is that Triskell and Kung's strategies (the latter using Tarjan's algorithm to determine SCCs) are directly applicable on real industrial projects. The next qualitative step for improving integration testing would concern criteria to distinguish the cost of a stub. Other future work concerns on interactive strategies that combine big-bang and incremental integration. The creation of stubs could be reduced when the set of strongly connected classes corresponds to a well-defined subset of system functionality that can be reasonably tested in one block.

Acknowledgments

The authors would like to thank the anonymous reviewers for their helpful and constructive comments.

---

[1] Java Swing is often highly pointed for its very elegant OO designs

References

1. B. Beizer, "Software testing techniques," Van Norstrand Reinhold, 1990. ISBN 0-442-20672-0.
2. Robert V. Binder, "Testing Object-Oriented Systems, Models, Parterns and Tools", Addison Wesley, First printing, October, 1999, ISBN 0-201-80938-9
3. F. Bourdoncle, "Efficient Chaotic Iteration Strategies with Widenings", Proc. of the International Conference on Formal Methods in Programming and their Applications, Lecture Notes in Computer Science 735, Springer-Verlag (1993), 128-141, ISSN 0302-9743.
4. Kuo Chung Tai and Fonda J. Daniels, "Interclass Test Order for Object-Oriented Software," Journal of Object-Oriented Programming (JOOP), v 12, n 4, July-August 1999, 18-35, ISSN: 0896-8438.
5. D. E. Goldberg, " Genetic Algorithms in Search, Optimization and Machine Learning", Addison Wesley, 1989. ISBN: 0-201-15767-5
6. Mary Jean Harrold, John D. McGregor, and Kevin J. Fitzpatrick, "Incremental Testing of Object-oriented Class Structures," Proceedings, 14th International Conference on Software Engineering, May 1992. IEEE Computer Society Press, Los Alamitos, California. 68-80. ISBN 0-7695-0915-0.
7. Thierry Jéron, Jean-Marc Jézéquel, Yves Le Traon and Pierre Morel, "Efficient Strategies for Integration and Regression Testing of OO Systems", In proc. of the 10th International Symposium on Software Reliability Engineering (ISSRE'99), November 1999, Boca raton (Florida), 260-269, ISBN 0-7695-0807-3.
8. Jean-Marc Jézéquel, "Object Oriented Software Engineering with Eiffel," Addison-Wesley, mar 1996. ISBN 1-201-63381-7.
9. Paul C. Jorgensen and Carl Erickson, "Object-Oriented Integration Testing" Communications of the ACM, v 37, n 9, September 1994, 30-38, ISSN: 0001-0782.
10. David C. Kung, Gao, Jerry, Chen, Cris., "On Regression Testing of Object-Oriented Programs," The Journal of Systems and Software. v 32 n 1, Jan 1996, ISSN: 0164-1212.
11. Y. Labiche, P. Thévenod-Fosse, H Waeselynck and M.H. Durand, "Testing Levels for Object-Oriented Software". In proc of ICSE' 2000, June 2000, Limerick (Ireland) 138-145, ISBN 1-5811-3074-0.
12. Yves Le Traon, Thierry Jéron, Jean-Marc Jézéquel and Pierre Morel, "Efficient OO Integration and Regression Testing", IEEE Transactions on Reliability, v.49, n 1, March 2000, 12-25. ISSN 0018-9529.
13. John D. McGregor and Tim Korson, "Integrating Object-Oriented Testing and Development Processes," Communications of the ACM, v 37, n 9, September 1994, 59-77, ISSN: 0001-0782.
14. S.M. Sait, H.Youssef, "Iterative Computer Algorithms with Applications in Engineering Solving Combinatorial Optimization Problems", IEEE COMPUTER SOCIETY 1999.
15. R. Tarjan, "Depth-first search and linear graph algorithms", SIAM J. Comput., v.1, n 2, June 1972, 146-160, ISSN 1064-8275.
16. James Rumbaugh and Ivar Jacobson and Grady Booch,"The Unified Modeling Language Reference Guide",Addison-Wesley, 1998, ISBN 0-201-3099-8.

Quality and Understandability of Use Case Models

Bente Anda[1], Dag Sjøberg[1,2], and Magne Jørgensen[1]

[1]Department of Informatics
University of Oslo
P.O. Box 1080 Blindern
0316 Oslo
NORWAY
{bentea,dagsj,magnej}@ifi.uio.no

[2]Simula Research Laboratory
P.O. Box 1080 Blindern
N-0316 Oslo
NORWAY

Abstract. Use case models are used in object-oriented analysis for capturing and describing the functional requirements of a system. Use case models are also used in communication between stakeholders in development projects. It is therefore important that the use case models are constructed in such a way that they support the development process and promote a good understanding of the requirements among the stakeholders. Despite this, there are few guidelines on how to construct use case models.

This paper describes an explorative study where three different sets of guidelines were used for constructing and documenting use case models. An experiment with 139 undergraduate students divided into 31 groups was conducted. Each group used one out of the three sets of guidelines when constructing a use case model from an informal requirements specification. After completing the use case model, each student answered a questionnaire.

The results of the experiment indicate that guidelines based on templates support the construction of use case models that are easier to understand for the readers, than guidelines without specific details on how to document each use case. The guidelines based on templates were also considered as the most useful when constructing use cases. In addition to better understandability, our experiment indicates that the guidelines based on templates result in better use case models regarding also other quality attributes. Our results further indicate that it may be beneficial to combine the template guidelines with another set of guidelines that focus on the documentation of the flow of events of each use case.

Keywords. Object-oriented analysis, Requirements specification, Use Cases, UML, Understandability, Experiment

J. Lindskov Knudsen (Ed.): ECOOP 2001, LNCS 2072, pp. 402–428, 2001.

1 Introduction

The concept of use case modelling was introduced by Jacobson in 1992 [1]. He also introduced a use case driven approach to software development. Since then, use case modelling has become a popular and widely used technique for capturing and describing the functional requirements of a software system. It is also used as a technique for bridging the gap between descriptions that are meaningful to software users and descriptions that contain sufficient details for modelling and constructing a software system. A use case model has two parts, the use case diagram and the use case descriptions. The diagram provides an overview of actors and use cases, and their interactions. The use cases' text details the requirements. An actor represents a role that the user can play with regard to the system, and a use case represents an interaction between an actor and the system.

In a use case driven software development process, the use case model is recommended as a primary artefact and is, for example, input to design and a basis for planning, estimation, testing and documentation. In addition, a use case model will often be part of a contract between the development organization and the customer regarding the functional requirements of the system to be developed. Therefore, the quality of the use case model may have a large impact on the quality of the resulting software system. Nevertheless, there is no commonly agreed theory on how to construct use cases, and there are different opinions about what constitutes quality in use case models.

UML adopts use cases but offers little advice on how to apply them. The support for use case modelling in most UML CASE-tools is also limited. For example, they do not support traceability from use cases to other diagrams even though it is recommended in use case driven development.

Quality attributes of use case models and advice on how to construct them have been proposed in the literature [1-14]. These recommendations are mostly based on extensive experience from software projects. However, to our knowledge only the guidelines for use case authoring developed in the CREWS project [14] have been subject to empirical evaluation.

Use case models are frequently claimed to be easy to understand for the stakeholders involved in a development project [1-3], and a good understanding of the use case model is important if the use case model is to contribute successfully to the development project. In our opinion, understandability is therefore an important quality in use case models. Moreover, the large number of, sometimes contradictory, guidelines for use case modelling to choose from motivate the overall objective of this study: To empirically investigate the effect of different guidelines on the quality, in particular understandability, of a use case model.

We conducted an experiment with 139 students divided into 31 groups. The groups were organized in pairs; one group was the customer for a system to be developed, while the other group was the development team. The development teams used one out of three different sets of guidelines in the construction of a use case model for the system. The use case models were evaluated by the authors of this paper according to a set of quality attributes. To evaluate understandability, the students answered questions about the functionality in the use case models. The students were also asked about how useful they found the guidelines.

The remainder of this paper is organized as follows. Section 2 gives an overview of different guidelines and recommendations on use case modelling together with suggestions for properties of quality. Section 3 describes our experiment in details. Our results are presented in Section 4 and discussed in Section 5. Section 6 discusses threats to the validity of the results. Ethical considerations relevant to this experiment are discussed in Section 7. Section 8 concludes and describes future work.

2 Use Case Modelling

Use cases can be described in many ways ranging from an informal, unstructured style to a more formal style approaching pseudocode [16]. Different organizations construct and apply use case models differently [13]. Independently of the format and notation, deciding a suitable level of detail is a challenge. A too fine granularity makes the use case model difficult to grasp, while a too coarse granularity hides the complexity [2].

Cockburn [5] recommends that the format should be chosen for each project, and that the choice should be driven by both characteristics of the development team and the main purpose of the use case model. The level of experience in the team, both regarding application domain and regarding use case modelling, is a relevant factor because little experience may require more support from the use case format. Another relevant factor is the cohesiveness of the team since a team working closely together can write more casual use cases than a larger, perhaps geographically dispersed team.

The future use of a use case model in a development project should also be an important issue when determining the appropriate format. An example is applying use case models in estimating effort for software development projects [6,17,18]. We have conducted a case study that indicates that the format of the use case model impacts the estimates [18].

Different formats may also support other activities differently, for example, the ability to identify classes during design or the ability to validate and verify an architectural decision.

There are, in our opinion, challenges at three levels when constructing a use case model. All three levels may be improved by appropriate guidelines. In our experiment, we test one guideline at each of the three levels, which are respectively described in Sections 2.1, 2.2 and 2.3. Section 2.4 describes some quality attributes of use case models.

2.1 Minor Guidelines

Actors are identified by considering who will receive information from a system and who will provide it with information. Use cases are identified by asking what are the main tasks of each actor. The first set of guidelines used in our experiment, called Minor guidelines (alternative 1 in Appendix A), are based on those found in [1,6]. They describe how to identify actors and use cases, but give little direction on how to construct them.

We included this alternative in our experiment primarily because we wanted to investigate how the students documented their use case models when they were not given specific guidelines on how to do it. Another purpose was to study how a more elaborate description of how to identify actors and use cases affected the resulting use case models.

2.2 Template Guidelines

A template is often recommended for documenting use cases because the predefined structure of a template forces the developer to identify and include important elements in each use case [2]. Examples of templates can be found in [2,5,6,10,11,12]; their most typical content is shown in Table 1. Our second set of guidelines is thus based on templates. The Template guidelines (alternative 2 in Appendix A) include a template for describing actors and a template for describing for use cases. These templates are based on the templates used in [2,5,6].

Table 1. Content of templates

Property	[2]	[5]	[6]	[10]	[11]	[12]
Title	x	x	x	x	x	x
Actor(s)		x	x	x	x	x
Trigger	x	x				
Scope		x				
Summary	x		x	x	x	x
Preconditions	x	x	x	x	x	x
Basic flow of events	x	x	x	x	x	x
Extension points	x	x	x	x	x	
Alternate courses	x	x	x	x	x	x
Post-condition	x	x	x		x	x

2.3 Style Guidelines

There are different recommendations on how to structure the description of the flow of events. In [1] and [8], narrative text with alternatives and extensions is recommended. Cockburn [5] recommends that users should warm up with narratives, but that the final use cases should follow a predefined template, as narrative use cases are often ambiguous and lack structure.

The guidelines described in [14] focus on the individual events in the flow of events. The aim is to give each description of events a standard structure and thereby make them easier to read. There seems to be an agreement on the following advice on how to describe the flow of events and each single event:

- Each event should be numbered in order to show how the process moves forward.
- Each event should clearly show which agent is active.
- Each event should be described with a present tense verb phrase in active voice.

- The user's vocabulary should be used.
- Repetition in the flow of events should be handled with a *while, for* or *repeat..until* construction.

However, there is some disagreement on the following:

- Whether the flow of events should be described in one section with narrative text, as a numbered list of events or as a list of event-response pairs.
- The handling of alternatives. In [6] and [14] an *if..then* construction is recommended, while such a construct is warned against in [2].
- The use of pseudocode in the description of each event. The structure recommended by Ben Achour *et al.* [14] strongly resembles pseudocode, while Kulak and Guiney [2] claim that pseudocode is too different from the user's language.

We have used a modified version of the guidelines described in [14], which we call Style guidelines[1] (alternative 3 in Appendix A) as the third set of guidelines in our experiment. We have modified the guidelines slightly based on the results from the experiment described in [15]. That experiment indicated that some of the original guidelines were difficult to use since they were implemented by few of the participants, and some were superfluous since all the participants, including those who did not receive the guidelines, implemented them. We decided to use these guidelines because they had been subject to evaluation in two former controlled experiments and could thus be evaluated in a different context in our experiment.

2.4 Recommendations for Use Case Models

It is believed that the quality of use case models has an impact on the quality of other documents subsequently produced in the development process. Hence, it seems sensible to investigate which properties of a use case model contribute to its quality. Many recommendations exist, for example, the following found in [2,8,12-14]:

- The use case should be easy to read.
- The descriptions should not include any assumptions of design or implementation.
- The descriptions should not include interface details.
- Events that are not related to the overall goal of the use case should not be described.
- The action descriptions should be complete.
- The flow structure should be correct and unambiguous.
- The terminology should be consistent.

We have used these recommendations as a basis for the attributes against which the use case models in our experiment are evaluated.

---

[1] The original proposers of the guidelines called them guidelines for style and content. For simplicity reasons we will denote them just Style guidelines.

3 The Experiment

This section describes the participants in our experiment, how they were trained, the detailed procedure of this experiment and the marking scheme. Finally, the hypotheses are presented.

3.1 Experiment Participants

The experiment was conducted as part of a compulsory project in an undergraduate course in software engineering with 139 students divided into 31 groups. We conducted a survey to identify the students' background.

The students were mostly aged between 20 and 30. Out of the 139 students, 43 had some experience from professional software development, while 9 had a lot of experience. There were 20 students who had professional experience with requirements engineering, 4 of them had done use case modelling. None of the students were familiar with any of the guidelines used in this experiment.

The students with experience in either project management or the languages used in the course (UML and Java) were *evenly* distributed among the groups. The other students were *randomly* assigned to the groups. Making the groups as similar as possible was important to study the effects of the guidelines.

The groups were organized in pairs with one group having the role of customer for the system to be developed, while the other group had the role of development team. Each group participated in two pairs, in one pair as customer for either system A or B (see appendix B) and in the other pair as development team for the other system. There was one exception; one group was both customer and developer for system A because of the odd number of groups.

3.2 Training

The software engineering course consisted of lectures and seminars. The students were divided into six seminar groups led by graduate students. Requirements engineering was taught in a one-hour lecture; basic use case modelling was taught in another one-hour lecture and in a one-hour seminar. The students were taught the concepts of actors and use cases, and they were given two examples (the same two for all groups) on how to describe use cases and their flow of events. In another one-hour seminar, the students were taught the guidelines and examples of how to use them.

3.3 Procedure of Experiment

The first activity in the student project consisted in creating an informal requirements specification based on the description of the system for which they were customers. This requirements specification was then handed on to their development team. The development teams made a detailed requirements specification including a use case model. The groups had two weeks available for this task, and they had the opportunity to ask lecturers, seminar leaders and fellow students for help. It was recommended that they should talk to their customer in order to clarify their requirements.

When the requirements specification was completed, it was made available to the customer group. Some groups received use case models written using the same guidelines as they had used themselves, while others received use case models written using different guidelines.

The students then individually answered a questionnaire (shown in appendix C) with questions about the functionality in the use case model they had made themselves and about the functionality in the use case model they received from their development team. The questions were constructed based on the original system description. The questionnaire also included a question about how useful they found the guidelines, which was answered by ticking one of the following alternatives: *Very useful, quite useful, quite useless* or *very useless*. There were also questions about how much time they had spent working on both the informal and the formal specification, on communication with their development team and on reading through the use case model from the development team. The students had previously been asked to record effort so it should be possible for them to recapture the time used. It was compulsory to answer the questionnaire, and it was done at times normally scheduled for seminars. The students were given directions on how to answer the questions, and one of the authors was available for questions when they answered the questionnaires.

Answers to questions about functionality were used in another experiment to evaluate differences in understandability between requirements expressed in natural language and requirements expressed in an activity diagram [19]. In that experiment the participants were asked to tick the correct answer to a question from a list of possible an answers. In our experiment it was infeasible to give the participant a predefined list of alternative answers because we did not know the actual use cases beforehand. Instead the participants answered using free text. The questionnaire included two blank lines after each question to give the participants an indication of the length expected for their answers.

When answering the questionnaire, all the students had available a copy of their own requirements specification and the one made by their development team. On average they spent 40 minutes on these questions.

3.4 Marking Scheme

The resulting use case models were evaluated according to a list of different properties inspired both by the recommendations on how to write use cases described in Section 2 and by the marking schemes for flow of events suggested in [14,15]. Ben Achour *et al.* [14] used the following marking scheme in their experiment for evaluating the CREWS guidelines:

- Completeness for each event, determined by counting the amount of events that included agents, objects, communication sources and destination
- Completeness of the whole flow of events, determined by counting irrelevant action descriptions compared with a use case made by an expert on the application domain (a low count gave a high score)

- Number of correctly placed variations
- Number of homonyms and synonyms (a low count gave a high score)

In our experiment there were very few missing elements in the descriptions, so we decided not to include this aspect. Since our use case models were constructed from different informal specifications, we did not have the opportunity to compare the individual use cases with ideal solutions, but in our opinion there were very few irrelevant descriptions of events. We did, however, find missing or unrealistic descriptions, so the realism of the description of the flow of events was also considered in our evaluation. There were significant differences in how the students handled variations in the use cases. We have therefore counted both the number of variations for each use case model and the number of correct placements in the flow of events. The students used inconsistent terminology in the use case models. We therefore also included this aspect in our evaluation.

Cox & Phalp [15] describe a replication of the experiment conducted by Ben Achour *et al.* [14]. They found the original marking scheme difficult to use because it was too detailed to give a good overall assessment of the individual use cases. In addition to the marking scheme above, they therefore also evaluated the use cases more subjectively according to:

- Plausibility – the realism of the use case
- Readability – the flow of the use case
- Consistent structure – consistent terminology and use of present simple tense
- Alternative flow – consideration of variations

We found all these aspects relevant and therefore included them in our evaluation. In the two experiments described above, only single use cases were evaluated. In our experiment, complete use case models were constructed, each containing several use cases. Since we considered also aspects of the overall model, and because of the large number of use cases in our experiment, we used a slightly different marking scheme, which is based on a more overall evaluation of the use cases:

- Single diagram – the use case model should include one single diagram showing all the actors and use cases.
- Actors – the correct actors were identified. Correctness was determined relative to the informal requirements specification.
- Use cases – the correct use cases were identified. Correctness was determined relative to the informal requirements specification as above.
- Content – the description of each use case contained the information required by all the sets of guidelines: actor, assumptions that must be valid before the use case starts, flow of events, variations and post-conditions.
- Level of detail – the descriptions of each event were at an appropriate level of detail. There should be no unnecessary details about user interface or internal design. Each event should be atomic, that is, sentences with more than two clauses should be avoided.
- Realism – the flow of events was realistic, that is, the events follow a logical and complete sequence, and it is clearly stated where variations can occur.
- Consistency – the use of terminology was consistent.

Table 2. Properties supported by guidelines

Type of guideline	Single diagram	Actors	Use cases	Con-tent	Level of detail	Rea-lism	Con-sistency
Minor guidelines	X	X	X				
Template guidelines	X			X			
Style guidelines	X				X	X	X

Table 3. Marking scheme

Property	Mark	Comment
Single diagram	0-1	1 = correct, 0 = wrong
Actors	0-3	3 = all correct, 0 = all wrong
Use cases	0-3	3 = all correct, 0 = all wrong
Content	0-3	3 = all correct, 0 = all wrong
Level of detail	0-3	3 = all correct, 0 = all wrong
Realism	0-3	3 = all correct, 0 = all wrong
Consistency	0-2	2 = all correct, 0 = all wrong

The guidelines gave different support for these properties. Table 2 shows which guidelines support which properties. Each use case model was given a mark for each of these properties based on an overall assessment according to the marking scheme in Table 3.

The size of the use case models is also measured. Size is measured as a vector:

> < *Number of actors,*
> *number of use cases,*
> *median number of actions in the flow of events,*
> *median number of variations >*

We believe that the number of identified actors and use cases, together with the number of events and variations, indicate quality of the guidelines – the higher number, the better quality.

3.5 Hypotheses

This section presents the hypotheses tested in this experiment. Our first hypothesis ($H1_1$) is that different guidelines for constructing use case models have different effect on how well the use case models are understood by their readers.

$H1_0$: There *is no* difference in understanding when reading use case models constructed with different guidelines.

$H1_1$: There *is* a difference in understanding when reading use case models constructed with different guidelines.

Our second hypothesis ($H2_1$) is that the different guidelines have different effect on the understanding of the requirements from the point of view of those who use the guidelines to construct use case models.

H2₀: There *is no* difference in the understanding of the requirements when using different guidelines in the construction of use case models.

H2₁: There *is* a difference in the understanding of the requirements when using different guidelines in the construction of use case models.

Our third hypothesis (H3₁) is that the different guidelines are of different usefulness to those who construct the use case models.

H3₀: There *is no* difference in the usefulness of the different guidelines when constructing use case models.

H3₁: There *is* a difference in the usefulness of the different guidelines when constructing use case models.

4 Results

This section describes the results from the testing of the hypotheses. We used the non-parametric Kruskal-Wallis test since our data sets were not normally distributed. Results of the effect of the guidelines on other quality attributes are also presented.

4.1 Assessment of Understandability

After reading the completed questionnaires, we found that many of the questions about the functionality were irrelevant for the use case models describing system A. The reason was that many of them included other functionality than we had expected from the original description (Appendix B). We therefore consider only system B in the analysis of the answers about functionality.

The answers to the questions about functionality were compared with the functionality actually described in the use case models in order to determine their correctness. Each answer was given a mark of 0 (wrong answer or no answer), 1 (correct answer to a simple question or partially correct answer to a complicated question) or 2 (correct answer to a difficult question). Questions 1, 2 and 7 for system B (Appendix C) were classified as simple. The answers for system B could obtain a maximum of 13 points.

An example of a partially correct answer is when question B.2, "How is the roster made and updated, and who is responsible for it," has the answer "unit nursing officer." This answers the second part of the question but not the first part. The guidelines were compared regarding the score on correct answers for each individual customer and individual developer.

Table 4 shows the number of students who read the use case models for system B, distributed by the guidelines used in the construction of these models; similarly for the use case model construction. This table also shows the minimum, median, maximum and standard deviation of the scores on correct answers given by the readers and constructors, respectively.

Table 4 Descriptive statistics on the data used in the assessment of understandability

Type of guideline	Reading	Scores on reading				Constructing	Scores on constructing			
		Min	Median	Max	Std		Min	Median	Max	Std
Minor guidelines	14	2	6	11	2,6	13	5	8	12	2,4
Template guidelines	26	5	9	12	2,1	25	4	9	12	2,5
Style guidelines	27	1	8,5	13	2,9	28	2	9	13	2,7
Total	68					66				

Reading Use Case Models – Hypothesis H1. There was a significant difference in the score on correct answers between the customers who had read use case models constructed by developers who had used either the Template or Style guidelines compared with those who had used the Minor guidelines (Figure 1). There was no significant difference between the Template and Style guidelines, although the Template guidelines were slightly better.

The level of significance (alpha-level) chosen for this test was 0.05. The p-value of 0,021 obtained from the test signifies that we can reject $H1_0$ and that we can assume with a 95% probability that there is a difference between the guidelines.

```
Guidelines      N      Median     Ave Rank        Z
Minor          14      6,000        22,2        -2,61
Template       26      9,000        40,1         1,85
Style          28      8,500        35,4         0,32
Overall     68                      34,5

H = 7,58   DF = 2   P = 0,023
H = 7,70   DF = 2   P = 0,021  (adjusted for ties)
```

Fig. 1. Kruskal-Wallis test on correct answers for customers who had read use case models for system B

Half of the customers read use case models constructed using the same guidelines as they had used themselves in the role of developers. The other half read use case models constructed with guidelines with which they were unfamiliar. We investigated whether there was a difference in understanding related to whether the guidelines were familiar.

When the guidelines were familiar, there was a significant difference in favour of the Template guidelines (Figure 2). However, the number of subjects for the Style guidelines was much higher than for Minor or Template guidelines (24 vs. 5 and 6). This may explain why the Style guidelines did worse than when all the customers for System B were considered.

```
Guidelines     N     Median    Ave Rank          Z
Minor          5      9,000       15,3        -0,64
Template       6     11,000       28,8         2,84
Style         24      8,000       15,9        -1,83
Overall       35                  18,0
```

H = 8,11   DF = 2   P = 0,017
H = 8,49   DF = 2   **P = 0,014** (adjusted for ties)

Fig. 2. Kruskal-Wallis test on correct answers for customers who had read use case models for system B constructed with the same guidelines as they had used themselves

When the guidelines were unfamiliar, the Style guidelines apparently did well (Figure 3). However, this sample is very small (4), which means that we should not draw any conclusions on the effect of the Style guidelines from this test. We repeated the test with only the Minor and Template guidelines, and found a significant difference (p = 0,004) in favour of the Template guidelines.

```
Guidelines     N     Median    Ave Rank          Z
Minor          9      6,000        8,2        -3,19
Template      20      8,000       18,7         1,25
Style          4     11,000       28,3         2,48
Overall       33                  17,0
```

H = 13,45   DF = 2   P = 0,001
H = 13,73   DF = 2   **P = 0,001** (adjusted for ties)

* NOTE * One or more small samples

Fig. 3. Kruskal-Wallis test on correct answers for customers who had read use case models for system B constructed with different guidelines than they had used themselves

Understanding Requirements – Hypothesis H2. There were no significant differences between the guidelines when we compared the scores of the developers on the questions about functionality in the use case models they had constructed themselves (Figure 4). This indicates that the understanding of the requirements among those who had developed a use case model, depends primarily on other factors than the guidelines used when they constructed the use case model. The p-value of 0,835 obtained from the test indicates that we cannot reject $H2_0$.

Bente Anda, Dag Sjøberg, and Magne Jørgensen

```
Guidelines      N    Median    Ave Rank         Z
Minor          13    8,000       31,0         -0,53
Template       25    9,000       33,4         -0.04
Style          28    9,000       34,8          0,47
Overall     66                   18,0

H = 0,35   DF = 2   P = 0,838
H = 0,36   DF = 2   P = 0,835 (adjusted for ties)
```

Fig. 4. Kruskal-Wallis test on correct answers for developers who had constructed use case models for System B

4.2 Assessment of Usefulness – Hypothesis H3

The questionnaire given to the students also included a question about how useful they found the guidelines. This question was answered by ticking one of four alternatives and each alternative was given a mark: *very useful* = 3, *quite useful* =2, *quite useless* =1 and *very useless* = 0. This question was equally relevant to both system A and B. All the questionnaires were therefore included in this analysis. This gave a total of 138 subjects (one of the students did not answered this question).

The p-value of 0,113 obtained from this test gives a weak indication that the Template guidelines were found most useful. We repeated the test with only the Minor and Template guidelines, and found a significant difference in favour of the Template guidelines (p=0,039). This indicates that we can reject $H3_0$.

```
Guidelines      N    Median    Ave Rank         Z
Minor          33    2,000       61,7         -1,29
Template       44    2,000       77,8          1,68
Style          61    2,000       67,7         -0,46
Overall    138                   69,5

H = 3,31   DF = 2   P = 0,191
H = 4,37   DF = 2   P = 0,113 (adjusted for ties)
```

Fig. 5. Kruskal-Wallis test for developers on how useful they found the guidelines they had used

4.3 Assessment of Quality

The use case models constructed by the students in our experiment were evaluated according to the marking scheme described in Table 3, Section 3.4. Table 5 shows that use case models constructed using the Template guidelines obtained the highest overall score on the quality attributes. The developers using the Minor guidelines were best at understanding that they should make one single diagram, and they did better than those using the Style guidelines on identifying the correct actors and use cases. The use case models constructed using the Style guidelines obtained the highest score on consistency, that is, consistent use of terminology, and they did quite well on level of detail and realism.

Table 5. Average score on the properties of quality

Type of guideline	Single diagram	Actors	Use cases	Content	Level of det.	Real ism	Consist ency	Sum
Minor guidelines	Best (0,9)	Mid (2,3)	Mid (2,1)	Worst (1,1)	Worst (1,7)	Worst (1,7)	Mid (1,7)	Worst (11,3)
Template guidelines	Mid (0,8)	Best (2,6)	Best 2,5	Best (2,5)	Best (2,2)	Best (2,4)	Mid (1,7)	Best (14,6)
Style guidelines	Worst (0,6)	Worst (2,2)	Worst (1,8)	Mid (1,7)	Mid (1,9)	Mid (2,0)	Best (1,8)	Mid (12,0)

Table 6 shows the size of the use case models constructed using the different guidelines. The fields of the size vector contain the median value (see Section 3.4). The use case models constructed using the Minor guidelines included on average the largest number of actors and use cases, but the lowest number of events in each use case. Only one of the use case models constructed with these guidelines included variations. The use of the Template and Style guidelines resulted in use case models of approximately equal size. However, the use case models constructed with the Style guidelines had slightly more use cases, while those constructed with the Template guidelines included more variations.

Table 7 shows some typical mistakes committed by the subjects in this experiment related to each of the quality attributes.

Table 6. Median size for the use case models

Type of guideline	Size
Minor guidelines	<3,8,2,0>
Template guidelines	<2,5,5,2>
Style guidelines	<2,6,5,1>

Table 7. Typical mistakes in the use case models

Property	Typical mistake(s)
Single diagram	– Splitting the use case model into several diagrams, one diagram for each single use case.
Actors	– Omitting external systems. – Including several actors who have exactly the same goals when using the system and who should therefore have been a single actor.
Use cases	– Including auxiliary functions that were not part of the requirements, overlooking use cases. – Splitting events relating to the same goal on several use cases.
Content	– Omitting assumptions or result.
Level of detail	– Describing what happens inside the system or the user interface. – Giving a brief and too incomplete description.
Realism	– Including common functionality in several use cases when it should have been separated out as a use case on its own. – Omitting variation or neglecting to state where in the flow of events they can occur.
Consistency	– Using different words for the same entity.

5 Discussion

This section discusses how the different guidelines affected the understandability and quality in our experiment.

5.1 Minor Guidelines

The Minor guidelines contained the most elaborate description of how to identify actors and use cases. The use case models constructed using these guidelines included, on average, the largest number of actors and use cases. However, they did not receive the highest score on correct actors and use cases, which indicates that some of their actors and use cases were superfluous. These guidelines also received the lowest overall score on the quality attributes. In our opinion, this indicates that these guidelines gave insufficient support on how to document actors and use cases, because good support for documenting use cases would have helped remove the superfluous actors and use cases.

The groups who used the Minor guidelines seemed to have more problems following the guidelines than the other groups. The use case models constructed using these guidelines did significantly worse on understandability than the use case models constructed with the other guidelines. We believe the reason was that these use cases lacked a coherent structure. The students participating in this experiment also found these guidelines the least useful.

5.2 Template Guidelines

The results in Section 4.1 indicate that use case models constructed using the Template or Style guidelines are easier to understand than use case models constructed using the Minor guidelines. The tests on the scores on correct answers from the customers also give a weak indication that the Template guidelines are better than the Style guidelines. We believe that the structure imposed by the Template guidelines makes it easier to find information in these use case models.

The Template guidelines also did better than the other guidelines regarding different quality attributes of the use case models. In our opinion, this may indicate a relationship between those attributes and the understandability. For example, the groups that followed the Template guidelines handled variations better than the other groups. This is an important aspect since the basic flow of events is often well known, but the alternatives to the basic flow are often not thought of.

These groups followed the guidelines most closely, which indicates that the guidelines are easy to use. The Template guidelines were also considered significantly more useful than the Minor guidelines and slightly more useful than the Style guidelines. We believe that these differences may be due to the templates being easier to understand and apply because it is made explicit what information should be inserted. In our opinion, the support from a template may be particularly important in an environment where the developers have little experience with the application domain and therefore need to work a lot on the requirements to develop a good understanding. We also believe that the template is particularly useful for developers who have little experience with use case modelling.

5.3 Style Guidelines

Two experiments have previously been conducted to evaluate the Style guidelines regarding how they contribute to completeness, correctness and consistency in the use cases [14,15]. The results from the first experiment showed that the guidelines were usable and helpful in improving the use cases regarding those properties. (These guidelines were proposed by the same research group that conducted the experiment.) However, these results were not confirmed when the experiment was replicated [15], but both agree that the guidelines should be considered when authoring use cases.

In our experiment, the Style guidelines did almost as well as the Template guidelines when the understanding of the readers was compared, and they did better than the Minor guidelines on both quality attributes and usefulness. Hence, it appears that the Style guidelines did better in our experiment than in the experiment reported in [15]. This may be due to a different marking scheme or because the participants in our experiment had more time to thoroughly understand and apply the guidelines. We do not believe that the modifications we made to the original Style guidelines invalidate a comparison, because the changes we made consisted in removing parts of the guidelines that were not applied by the subjects in that experiment. In our opinion, this indicates that Style guidelines may successfully supplement Template guidelines.

6 Threats to Validity

This study is exploratory in the sense that we do not know any other studies where different guidelines on use case modelling have been compared. We would call it a semi-controlled experiment because it was done as part of a course, and thus we had not full control over all parts of the study. For example, we could not control the informal specifications from which the groups constructed the use case models. Moreover, we do not know in details how the students worked when constructing the use case models.

Determining how to analyze the results was a challenge, in particular regarding correctness of the answers to the questionnaires and the different attributes of the use case models. On the other hand, we believe that the organization in customer and developer groups contributed to a realistic setting. The next sections describe factors that we believe may have influenced our results.

6.1 Students as Subjects

Our experiment was conducted with students as subjects. It is therefore uncertain to what extent our results can be generalized to an industrial setting. However, many of the students in this experiment were experienced software developers who work part-time or previously worked in industry. Out of 139 students, 43 answered that they had *some* relevant experience, 9 answered that they had *a lot of* experience. In our opinion, a large percentage of the students may therefore be comparable to professional software developers with up to two years experience.

Use case modelling is a relatively new technique; many organizations are currently starting to use it. Hence, it is not uncommon that developers have none or only a little experience with use case modelling. So, typical professionals may not have much more experience with use case modelling *per se* than our students, but on the other hand, our students are less experienced with requirements and with modelling in general than are professionals.

Høst *et al.* [20] compared the results from students and professional software developers in a study on factors affecting the lead-time of software development projects. They did not find significant differences between the answers from the students and the professionals, even though knowledge of factors affecting lead-time appears to depend on experience from software development projects.

To overcome the difficulties of using students as subjects, we plan to carry out a similar experiment with 20 professionals as subjects in a four-hour experiment. The explorative nature of this study was an important reason why we chose to conduct an experiment with students as subjects even though they may not be fully compatible with professional developers. Therefore, we found it necessary to test our experimental design on students and perhaps eliminate some hypotheses before conducting an experiment with professionals, as recommended by Tichy [21].

6.2 Complexity of the Task

The use case models constructed in our experiment were smaller than most use case models describing real systems. Therefore, we do not know if our results are applicable when the use case models are considerably larger. We conducted a case study in industry on how to apply use case models in estimation [18]. One of the two software development projects used in that case study was characterized as medium sized. That project lasted 7 months, and the use case model consisted of 7 actors and 9 use cases, which is not substantially more than the number of actors and use cases in the use case models in the experiment reported in this paper. However, the number of events and variations was considerably higher than in our experiment. We therefore believe the use case models in our experiment may be comparable to use case models in small industrial projects.

Our guidelines did not handle secondary actors nor included and extending use cases, and alternative flows of events were handled superficially. This may also mean that the use case models in our experiment are not comparable to use case models for real systems on all aspects. We used quite simple guidelines because we wanted to limit the number of attributes of the use case models that we would have to consider. Again, the reason for this decision was the exploratory nature of our research. Nevertheless, we plan to conduct further studies using extended guidelines.

The differences in size among the use case models in our experiment may have influenced the correctness of the answers about functionality. A small use case model consisting of a small number of use cases described with few details may have made it easy to answer the questionnaire correctly despite low quality of the use model. Correspondingly, very detailed use case models may be time consuming to read, which in turn may lead to wrong answers even though they are of high quality. Another aspect of this, is that a high quality use case model may have appeared very convincing to the customer group, and thereby led them to believe that all their requirements were included even if they were not.

6.3 Participants Both as Customers and Developers

The organization into customer and developers meant that the readers of the use case models all had experience with writing use cases. This will not always be the case for all the stakeholders in a real project. Therefore, we cannot be sure that the result indicating that the use case models constructed using Template guidelines are the easiest to understand, is applicable to customers who are unfamiliar with use case modelling.

However, it is recommended that use case models should be constructed together with their future users. To enable the future users to participate in the use case modelling process, it is common to train them in basic use case modelling. Many customers therefore have some knowledge of use case modelling.

6.4 Motivation

In a large course like our software engineering course, there will inevitably be differences in motivation among the students. We observed differences in motivation regarding answering the questionnaires since the seminars where this was done were compulsory. The students were not used to attendance being compulsory, so some were quite negative about that.

6.5 Dependence on Informal Specifications

The use case models were constructed from informal specifications made by the customer groups. The informal specifications had varying quality, and there were differences in how closely they were followed by the development team. In the cases where the informal specification covers all the information in the use case model, the students may have been able to answer the questionnaire correctly without having understood the use case models. Moreover, although the students were given an explanation of how to answer the questionnaire, some may not have understood exactly on what they should base their answers.

6.6 Experience

Experience with use case modelling may lead to higher quality of the use case models independently of the guidelines. Experience with the application domain might in our experiment have affected the answers to the questionnaires as it may lead to expectations regarding the functionality [22]. However, there were few subjects with application domain experience. We believe that differences in experience did not affect the results since the students were randomly assigned to the groups.

6.7 Questionnaires

Some of the groups made specifications with functionality that was very different from what we expected to be the outcome when we wrote the system descriptions. This lead to some of the questions being irrelevant for some of the use case models. The questions generally seem to have been better suited for system B than for system A. Questions made specifically for each use case model would probably have made it easier to determine how well the use case model was understood. This was infeasible due to the large number of groups and that we wanted the students to fill in the questionnaires shortly after the use case models were completed.

The correctness of the answers was determined subjectively. This may represent a source of error, as it was not always obvious what the correct answer should be. However, the use case models were simple and the answers given were a maximum of two lines of text, so in most cases determining whether an answer was correct was relatively easy.

7 Ethical Considerations

Due to the project being compulsory, the workload on the groups should be approximately even. This meant that all the groups had to use some kind of guidelines, and that learning and implementing them should be equally work consuming. It should also be ensured that all the students had the opportunity to learn equally much.

In our experiment, we attempted to achieve not too large differences between the groups of students by not making the guidelines too different. Of course, this concern made it more difficult to observe the different effects of the various guidelines.

The results from the experiment were presented to the students in a one-hour lecture to give all the students a flavour of all the guidelines. As an afterthought, we realize that this was probably insufficient to ensure that all the students learned equally much. If such an experiment is to be repeated, we would recommend that all the students are given exercises including all the guidelines.

The students were in the questionnaire encouraged to give feedback on how they felt about the experiment. Most of the students were positive, for example, they reported that they through this experiment learned more about use case modelling than they would have done otherwise.

8 Conclusions and Future Work

We have identified three categories of guidelines for use case modelling, and we have conducted an experiment with the aim of detecting the effects of using them. The results from the experiment indicate that guidelines based on templates support the construction of use case models that are easier to understand for the readers than guidelines without specific details on how to document use cases. The guidelines based on templates were also considered by the participants as the most useful when constructing use cases. Our experiment further indicates that the guidelines based on templates result in better use case models regarding also other quality attributes.

Style guidelines focus on the documentation of the flow of events of each use case. They appear to have contributed to some of the quality attributes. Therefore, it may be beneficial to combine the template guidelines with style guidelines.

This study was exploratory. We will use the results as a basis for further studies both on how to improve the ease of understanding use case models and on how they should be used in subsequent phases of a development project. The following research activities are planned:

- A replication of this experiment using modified versions of the guidelines presented in this paper. The modifications will be based on the results from this experiment and on the extensions suggested in Section 6.2. We also intend to investigate the effects of the different guidelines on the understanding of the groups as a whole, by letting the groups answer the questionnaires instead of the individual participants.
- A follow-up controlled experiment similar to the one reported in this paper, but this time in industry with professional software developers.
- A case study on the application of use case models in software development projects in industry, in particular on how use case models can be used in estimating software development effort.
- A field experiment on how different stakeholders in a project understand use case models and how a reading technique may improve it [22].

Acknowledgements

We thank Lars Bratthall for useful comments on earlier versions of this paper and Erik Arisholm for guidance on the statistics. We also thank all the students who participated in the experiment. This research is funded by The Research Council of Norway through the industry-project PROFIT (PROcess improvement For the IT industry).

References

1. Jacobson, I. *et al.* Object-Oriented Software Engineering. A Use Case Driven Approach. Addison-Wesley, 1992.
2. Kulak, D. & Guiney, E. Use Cases: Requirements in Context. Addison-Wesley, 2000.
3. Booch, G., Rumbaugh, J. & Jacobson, I. The Unified Modeling Language User Guide. Addison-Wesley, 1999.
4. Cockburn, A. Structuring Use Cases with Goals. Technical report. Human and Technology, 7691 Dell Rd, Salt Lake City, UT 84121, Ha.T.TR.95.1, http://members.aol.com/acockburn/papers/usecases.htm, 1995.

5. Cockburn, A. Writing Effective Use Cases. Addison-Wesley, 2000.
6. Schneider, G. & Winters, J. Applying Use Cases – A Practical Guide. Addison-Wesley, 1998.
7. Constantine, L. L. & Lockwood, L. A. D. Software for Use. A Practical Guide to the Models and Methods for Usage-Centered Design. Addison-Wesley, 1999.
8. Rosenberg, D. & Scott, K. Use Case Driven Object Modelling with UML. Addison-Wesley, 1999.
9. Regnell, B., Andersson, M. & Bergstrand, J. A Hierarchical Use Case Model with Graphical Representation. Proceedings of Second IEEE International Symposium on Requirements Engineering (RE'95), York, UK, 1995.
10. Harwood, R. J. Use case formats: Requirements, analysis, and design. Journal of Object-Oriented Programming, Vol. 9, No. 8, pp. 54-57, January 1997.
11. Mattingly, L. & Rao, H. Writing Effective Use Cases and Introducing Collaboration Cases. Journal of Object-Oriented Programming, Vol. 11, No. 6, pp. 77-79, 81-84, 87, October 1998.
12. Jaaksi, A. Our Cases with Use Cases. Journal of Object-Oriented Programming, Vol. 10, No. 9, pp. 58-64, February 1998.
13. Firesmith, D.G. Use Case Modeling Guidelines. Proceedings of Technology of Object-Oriented Languages and Systems – TOOLS 30. IEEE Comput. Soc, Los Alamitos, CA, USA, 1999.
14. Ben Achour, C., Rolland, C., Maiden, N.A.M. & Souveyet, C. Guiding Use Case Authoring: Results of an Empirical Study. Proceedings IEEE Symposium on Requirements Engineering, IEEE Comput. Soc, Los Alamitos, CA, USA, 1999.
15. Cox, K. & Phalp, K. Replicating the CREWS Use Case Authoring Guidelines. Empirical Software Engineering Journal, Vol. 5, No. 3, pp. 245-268, 2000.
16. Hurlbut, R.R. A Survey of Approaches for Describing and Formalizing Use Cases. Technical Report: XPT-TR-97-03, Expertech, Ltd., 1997.
17. Martinsen, S.A. & Groven, A-K. Improving Estimation and Requirements Management Experiences from a very small Norwegian Enterprise. SPI 98 Improvement in Practice: Reviewing Experience, Previewing Future Trends. The European Conference on Software Improvement. Meeting Management, Farnham, UK, 1998.
18. Anda, B., Dreiem, H., Sjøberg, D. & Jørgensen, M. Estimating Software Development Effort Based on Use Cases – Experiences from industry. Submitted to UML'2001 (Fourth International Conference on th Unified Modeling Language).
19. Cioch, F.A. Measuring Software Misinterpretation. Journal of Systems and Software, Vol. 14, No. 2, pp. 85-95, February 1991.
20. Høst, M., Regnell, B. & Wohlin, C. Using Students as Subjects – A Comparative Study of Students and Professionals in Lead-Time Impact Assessment. Empirical Software Engineering, Vol. 5, No. 3, pp. 210-214, November 2000.
21. Tichy, W.F. Hints for Reviewing Empirical Work in Software Engineering. Empirical Software Engineering, Vol. 5, No. 4, pp. 309-312, December 2000.
22. Anda, B. & Jørgensen, M. Understanding Use Case Models. Proceedings of Beg, Borrow, or Steal Workshop, International Conference on Software Engineering, June 5, 2000, Limerick, Ireland.

Appendix A

This appendix contains the three sets of guidelines used in this experiment.

Alternative 1 – Minor guidelines

The Use Case Model should include:

1. A use case diagram that shows actors and use cases
2. A description of each actor
3. A description of each use case

Below is a description of the process that you should follow when constructing the use case model.

1. Start by identifying the actors
An actor is an entity that interacts with the system. Actors can be:
- A human user
- Another system which receives services from this one
- Another system which offers services to this one
- Actors are external to the system

The first step in identifying actors consists in finding users, but remember that users =/= actors:
⇒ Identify the most important users of the system
  - For whom will the system be constructed?
  - Who receives information from the system?
  - Who supplies the system with information?
  - Who removes information from the system?

⇒ Identify other users
  - Which interactions will de done with other systems?
  - What external hardware is necessary?
  - Who performs administration and maintenance?

The second step consists in finding roles:
⇒ Find out what roles the users have (roles encapsulate the way the system is used, but remember that roles are not equivalent to users nor to job-descriptions)
⇒ An actor constitutes a single role

2. Identify use cases and draw a use case diagram

⇒ The use cases describes what the actors wishes to do with the system, that is the actors goals

⇒ Each goal is represented by a use case

⇒ Identify use cases by looking at

- What are the main tasks of each actor?
- Will the actor read/write or change some of the information in the system?
- Should the actor inform the system about changes happening outside the system?
- Does the actor wish to be informed about unexpected changes?

3. Describe each actor

⇒ Give a brief description of each actor with name and most important goals when using the system.

4. Describe each use case in detail

⇒ Describe the flow of events in the use case, that is, all the steps in the interaction between actor and system that are necessary for the actor to reach his goal.

⇒ The description should show:

- The actors input
- Objects (including actors) that are involved
- Assumptions that are made about the objects
- The result of the use case

Alternative 2 – Template guidelines

The Use Case Model should include:

1. A use case diagram that shows actors and use cases.
2. A description of each actor according to the first template below.
3. A description of each use case according to the second template below.

Template for describing an actor:

Actor *<name>*	
Description *<A short text that describes the actor>*	
Examples	

Template for describing a use case:

Use Case *<name>*	
Actors *<name>*	
Trigger *<The event which starts the use case>*	
Prerequisites *<Constraints that must be met for the use case to be executed>*	
Post-conditions *<Conditions which are met when the use case terminates>*	
Normal flow of events *<A simple, brief description of the series of events of the most likely outcome>*	
Variations *<Variations on the normal flow of events, why it is followed, and outcome>*	
Use Case associations *<A list of other use cases that this use case is extended by or is used by>*	

Alternative 3 – Style guidelines

The Use Case Model should include:

1. A use case diagram that shows actors and use cases.
2. A description of each actor with name and most important goals when using the system.
3. A description of each use case which shows
   - The actors input
   - Objects (including actors) that are involved
   - Assumptions that are made about the objects
   - The result of the use case

In addition to this each use case should show the flow of events in the use case. The flow of events consists of a number of actions, and each action should be described so that it satisfies the guidelines below.

Style guidelines-
SG1: Write the UC normal course as a list of discrete actions in the form: <action#><action description>. Each action description should start on a new line. Since each action is atomic, avoid sentences with more than two clauses.
SG2: Use the sequential ordering of action descriptions to indicate strict sequence between actions. Variations should be written in a separate section.
SG3: Iterations and concurrent actions can be expressed in the same section of the UC, whereas alternative actions should be written in a different section.
SG4: Be consistent in your use of terminology, that is, use consistent names on actors, objects and actions in all action descriptions. Avoid use of synonyms and homonyms.
SG5: Use present tense and active voice when describing actions.
SG6: Avoid use of negations, adverbs and modal verbs in the description of an action.

Guidelines for content-
CG1: <agent ><action><agent>
CG2: <agent><action><object> <prepositional phrase>
CG3: 'If' <alternative assumption> 'then' <list of action descriptions>
CG4: 'Repeat until' <repetition condition> <list of action descriptions>
CG5: <action 1> 'while' <action 2>

Appendix B

This appendix includes the descriptions of the two systems for which the students should specify a use case model.

Description – System A

An opinion poll institute want a system with questionnaires on the Internet. The system should make it easy to publish questionnaires, as well as to fill in questionnaires on the Web. The answers to the questionnaires should be saved so that they can be exported to other tools (an example is "structured text" which can be imported into a spreadsheet). For some of the questions it will be necessary for the system to read a significant amount of text. The opinion poll institute want an easy overview of the answers received, for example, they want to know how many have answered the different questions. Notice that you shall not make a simple questionnaire on the Web, but a "questionnaire generator" for the Web.

Description – System B

A hospital ward needs a system for swapping duties between nurses. There will be a PC in the ward where the nurses can log in. The user interface should make it possible to register who swaps duties and for what period of time. First the swap is registered with status *inquiry*. When the head of the ward has accepted the swap, the status should be changed to *accepted*. Swaps that are not accepted should be registered with status *not accepted*. If the head of the ward has not responded to the inquiry within 24 hours, status should automatically be set to *accepted*. The nurses must be able to log on to the system to see if the swap of duties is accepted. All accepted duties should be saved so that they can be transferred to other systems.

Appendix C

This appendix shows the questions about functionality in the use case models that were included in the questionnaires given to the students.

Questions for System A:

1. How many questions can there be in a questionnaire? If there is a limit to the number, on what is this limit based?
2. Which different alternatives are allowed for the answers?
3. Is it possible to insert comments either to questions or to answers in questionnaires?
4. Is there any validation of questionnaires that have been completed? If the answer is "yes", how is the validation done?
5. Who has access to the answers from a survey?
6. What possibilities are there in the system for analyzing answers and who has access to these possibilities?
7. To which tool can answers from questionnaires be exported and how is this done?
8. What possibilities exist for changing questionnaires that have already been saved, and who has access to these possibilities?
9. What possibilities exist for changing answers or continue to answer a questionnaire that has already been completed, and who has access to these possibilities?
10. Who has access to publishing questionnaires?

Questions for System B:

1. Who has access to the system and how do they log on?
2. How is the roster made and updated, and who is responsible for it?
3. What possibilities are there in the system to look at rosters and who has access to the different rosters?
4. How is the second nurse (the one who does not initiate the swap) informed that another nurse wishes to swap duties?
5. How is the head of the ward informed about requested swaps?
6. How are the nurses (both the one who initiated the swap and the other) informed about whether a swap has been accepted?
7. Are there possibilities to delete a swap, that is, to return to the original roster?
8. What functionality exists in the system for transferring duties to other systems (for example, the system for paying out wages)?

Author Index

Lecture Notes in Computer Science

For information about Vols. 1–1976
please contact your bookseller or Springer-Verlag

Vol. 2020: D. Naccache (Ed.). Topics in Cryptology – CT-RSA 2001. Proceedings, 2001. XII, 473 pages. 2001

Vol. 2021: J. N. Oliveira, P. Zave (Eds.). FME 2001 Formal Methods for Increasing Software Productivity. Proceedings, 2001. XIII, 629 pages. 2001.

Vol. 2022: A. Romanovsky, C. Dony, J. Lindskov Knudsen, A. Tripathi (Eds.), Advances in Exception Handling Techniques. XII, 289 pages. 2001

Vol. 2024: H. Kuchen, K. Ueda (Eds.). Functional and Logic Programming. Proceedings, 2001. X, 391 pages. 2001.

Vol. 2025: M. Kaufmann, D. Wagner (Eds.), Drawing Graphs. XIV, 312 pages. 2001.

Vol. 2026: F. Müller (Ed.), High-Level Parallel Programming Models and Supportive Environments. Proceedings, 2001. IX, 137 pages. 2001.

Vol. 2027: R. Wilhelm (Ed.), Compiler Construction. Proceedings, 2001. XI, 371 pages. 2001.

Vol. 2028: D. Sands (Ed.). Programming Languages and Systems. Proceedings, 2001. XIII, 433 pages. 2001.

Vol. 2029: H. Hussmann (Ed.), Fundamental Approaches to Software Engineering. Proceedings, 2001. XIII, 349 pages. 2001.

Vol. 2030: F. Honsell, M. Miculan (Eds.), Foundations of Software Science and Computation Structures. Proceedings, 2001. XII, 413 pages. 2001.

Vol. 2031: T. Margaria, W. Yi (Eds.), Tools and Algorithms for the Construction and Analysis of Systems. Proceedings, 2001. XIV, 588 pages. 2001.

Vol. 2032: R. Klette, T. Huang, G. Gimel'farb (Eds.), Multi-Image Analysis. Proceedings, 2000. VIII, 289 pages. 2001.

Vol. 2033: J. Liu. Y. Ye (Eds.), E-Commerce Agents. VI, 347 pages. 2001. (Subseries LNAI).

Vol. 2034: M.D. Di Benedetto, A. Sangiovanni-Vincentelli (Eds.), Hybrid Systems: Computation and Control. Proceedings, 2001. XIV, 516 pages. 2001.

Vol. 2035: D. Cheung, G.J. Williams, Q. Li (Eds.), Advances in Knowledge Discovery and Data Mining – PAKDD 2001. Proceedings, 2001. XVIII, 596 pages. 2001. (Subseries LNAI).

Vol. 2037: E.J.W. Boers et al. (Eds.), Applications of Evolutionary Computing. Proceedings, 2001. XIII, 516 pages. 2001.

Vol. 2038: J. Miller, M. Tomassini, P.L. Lanzi, C. Ryan, A.G.B. Tettamanzi, W.B. Langdon (Eds.), Genetic Programming. Proceedings, 2001. XI, 384 pages. 2001.

Vol. 2039: M. Schumacher, Objective Coordination in Multi-Agent System Engineering. XIV, 149 pages. 2001. (Subseries LNAI).

Vol. 2040: W. Kou. Y. Yesha, C.J. Tan (Eds.), Electronic Commerce Technologies. Proceedings, 2001. X, 187 pages. 2001.

Vol. 2041: I. Attali, T. Jensen (Eds.), Java on Smart Cards: Programming and Security. Proceedings, 2000. X, 163 pages. 2001.

Vol. 2042: K.-K. Lau (Ed.), Logic Based Program Synthesis and Transformation. Proceedings, 2000. VIII, 183 pages. 2001.

Vol. 2043: D. Craeynest, A. Strohmeier (Eds.), Reliable Software Technologies – Ada-Europe 2001. Proceedings, 2001. XV. 405 pages. 2001.

Vol. 2044: S. Abramsky (Ed.), Typed Lambda Calculi and Applications. Proceedings, 2001. XI, 431 pages. 2001.

Vol. 2045: B. Pfitzmann (Ed.), Advances in Cryptology – EUROCRYPT 2001. Proceedings, 2001. XII, 545 pages. 2001.

Vol. 2047: R. Dumke, C. Rautenstrauch, A. Schmietendorf, A. Scholz (Eds.), Performance Engineering. XIV. 349 pages. 2001.

Vol. 2048: J. Pauli, Learning Based Robot Vision. IX. 288 pages. 2001.

Vol. 2051: A. Middeldorp (Ed.), Rewriting Techniques and Applications. Proceedings, 2001. XII, 363 pages. 2001.

Vol. 2052: V.I. Gorodetski, V.A. Skormin, L.J. Popyack (Eds.), Information Assurance in Computer Networks. Proceedings, 2001. XIII, 313 pages. 2001.

Vol. 2053: O. Danvy, A. Filinski (Eds.), Programs as Data Objects. Proceedings, 2001. VIII, 279 pages. 2001.

Vol. 2054: A. Condon, G. Rozenberg (Eds.), DNA Computing. Proceedings, 2000. X, 271 pages. 2001.

Vol. 2055: M. Margenstern, Y. Rogozhin (Eds.), Machines, Computations, and Universality. Proceedings, 2001. VIII, 321 pages. 2001.

Vol. 2056: E. Stroulia. S. Matwin (Eds.), Advances in Artificial Intelligence. Proceedings, 2001. XII, 366 pages. 2001. (Subseries LNAI).

Vol. 2057: M. Dwyer (Ed.), Model Checking Software. Proceedings, 2001. X, 313 pages. 2001.

Vol. 2059: C. Arcelli, L.P. Cordella, G. Sanniti di Baja (Eds.), Visual Form 2001. Proceedings, 2001. XIV, 799 pages. 2001.

Vol. 2064: J. Blanck, V. Brattka, P. Hertling (Eds.). Computability and Complexity in Analysis. Proceedings, 2000. VIII, 395 pages. 2001.

Vol. 2068: K.R. Dittrich, A. Geppert, M.C. Norrie (Eds.), Advanced Information Systems Engineering. Proceedings, 2001. XII, 484 pages. 2001.

Vol. 2072: J. Lindskov Knudsen (Ed.), ECOOP 2001 – Object-Oriented Programming. Proceedings, 2001. XIII, 429 pages. 2001.

Vol. 2073: V.N. Alexandrov, J.J. Dongarra, B.A. Juliano, R.S. Renner, C.J.K. Tan (Eds.), Computational Science – ICCS 2001. Part I. Proceedings, 2001. XXVIII, 1306 pages. 2001.

Vol. 2074: V.N. Alexandrov, J.J. Dongarra, B.A. Juliano, R.S. Renner, C.J.K. Tan (Eds.), Computational Science – ICCS 2001. Part II. Proceedings, 2001. XXVIII, 1076 pages. 2001.

Vol. 2091: J. Bigun, F. Smeraldi (Eds.), Audio- and Video-Based Biometric Person Authentication. Proceedings, 2001. XIII, 374 pages. 2001.

Vol. 2092: L. Wolf, D. Hutchison, R. Steinmetz (Eds.). Quality of Service – IWQoS 2001. Proceedings, 2001. XII, 435 pages. 2001.